European Communi

CW01424487

Andrew Charlesworth and Holly Cullen

Lecturers in Law at the University of Hull

PITMAN
PUBLISHING

PITMAN PUBLISHING
128 Long Acre, London WC2E 9AN

A Division of Longman Group Limited

First published in Great Britain 1994

© A Charlesworth and H Cullen 1994

A CIP catalogue record for this book can be obtained from the British Library.

ISBN 0–273–60305–1

10 9 8 7 6 5 4 3 2 1

Typeset by Land & Unwin (Data Sciences) Ltd
Printed and bound in Great Britain by Page Bros.

The Publishers' policy is to use paper manufactured from sustainable forests.

CONTENTS

For Karen and Dylan

PREFACE

Writing a book on European Community Law has often seemed as difficult as writing one's name on water, so quickly have developments occurred which affected Community law. Not least of these was the issue of whether the word 'Community' was still appropriate, with the establishment of The European Union. The uncertainty surrounding the Treaty on European Union was only resolved on 1 November 1993. The Uruguay round of the GATT negotiations was only successfully concluded in December 1993, and towards the end of that year failure and a resulting trade war seemed, at times, inevitable. As authors we could have lived with a trade war and the resulting decline of Western civilisation, but an inconclusive end to the chapter on the CAP would have been intolerable.

All these factors made our task more difficult, but a number of people have helped to make it somewhat easier, or at least less daunting. First, we would like to thank Patrick Bond of Pitman Publishing, who first encouraged, and then endured, this project. Our thanks also go to Elizabeth Tarrant, our editor.

At the University of Hull Law School it seems that the majority of our colleagues have been coerced into assisting in the completion of this book in some way or another. Professors Ferdinand von Prondzynski and David Freestone read and commented on the majority of the chapters. However, we must take full responsibility for the final result. The Law School Research Committee provided funding for research assistance during the summers of 1992 and 1993. Our research assistants, Stephen Vousden and Teresa Loftus, acted as excellent bloodhounds for elusive references and cross-references. Their contributions were positively sanity-saving. Last-minute research assistance from Dipti Hunter made 'absolutely final' deadlines manageable. Finally, to our colleagues Mike Feintuck, Dino Kritisiotis and Diane Ryland, who failed to flee with the necessary fleetness of foot and thus found themselves agreeing to proofread chapters, we must offer a thank you for preserving what remains of our fading eyesight.

Our families and friends listened to our problems with all the sympathy they could muster. To them and, in particular, Marion and Brian Charlesworth and Laurette and William Cullen, we say thanks and we promise that it's over now, at least until the next edition. Thanks must also go to Holly's husband, Dylan Griffiths, who endured with grace both the competition for the home personal computer, as deadlines for this book and his PhD dissertation converged, and the fact that his wife spent most of the first year of their married life in the company of another man.

We have attempted to state the law as at 1 January 1994. Certain major developments after that date, such as the conclusion of the GATT negotiations, have nonetheless been taken into account.

HC
AC

TABLE OF CASES
EUROPEAN COURT OF JUSTICE

TABLE OF CASES
EUROPEAN COURT OF JUSTICE

TABLE OF CASES
EUROPEAN COURT OF FIRST INSTANCE

TABLE OF COMMISSION DECISIONS

TABLE OF CASES
BEFORE NATIONAL COURTS

TABLE OF COMMUNITY TREATIES AND CONVENTIONS

TABLE OF COMMUNITY REGULATIONS

Regulation	Reference	
2496/89/EEC	OJ 1989 L240	*448*
3013/89/EEC	OJ 1989 L289	*417*
3312/89/EEC	OJ 1989 L321, Repealed	*222*
3427/89/EEC	OJ 1989 L331	*260*
4045/89/EEC	OJ 1989 L388	*430*
4046/89/EEC	OJ 1989 L388, Repealed	*222*
4064/89/EEC	OJ 1989 L395	*304*
354/90/EEC	OJ 1990 L38	*430*
386/90/EEC	OJ 1990 L42	*430*
1210/90/EEC	OJ 1990 L120	*446*
1715/90/EEC	OJ 1990 L160, Repealed	*222*
1863/90/EEC	OJ 1991 L170	*430*
2726/90/EEC	OJ 1990 L262, Repealed	*222*
307/91/EEC	OJ 1991 L37	*430*
563/91/EEC	OJ 1991 L63	*448*
594/91/EEC	OJ 1991 L67	*444, 456*
595/91/EEC	OJ 1991 L67	*430*
717/91/EEC	OJ 1991 L78, Repealed	*222*
719/91/EEC	OJ 1991 L78, Repealed	*222*
967/91/EEC	OJ 1991 L100	*430*
1534/91/EEC	OJ 1991 L143	*285*
1740/91/EEC	OJ 1991 L163	*417*
3908/91/EEC	OJ 1991 L370	*448*
356/92/EEC	OJ 1992 L39	*417*
880/92/EEC	OJ 1992 L99	*457*
1248/92/EEC	OJ 1992 L136	*260*
1249/92/EEC	OJ 1992 L136	*260*
1568/92/EEC	OJ 1992 L166	*417*
1738/92/EEC	OJ 1992 L180	*420*
1765/92/EEC	OJ 1992 L181	*420*
1766/92/EEC	OJ 1992 L181	*420*
2071/92/EEC	OJ 1992 L215	*417*
2075/92/EEC	OJ 1992 L215	*417*
2434/92/EEC	OJ 1992 L245	*246*
2455/92/EEC	OJ 1992 L251	*450*
2913/92/EEC	OJ 1992 L302	*208, 221*
3124/92/EEC	OJ 1992 L313	*417*
3411/92/EEC	OJ 1992	*285*
3508/92/EEC	OJ 1992 L355	*430*
3714/92/EEC	OJ 1992 L378	*417*
3887/92/EEC	OJ 1992 L391	*430*
3911/92/EEC	OJ 1992 L395	*234*
3952/92/EEC	OJ 1992 L405	*456*
125/93/EEC	OJ 1993 L18	*417*
259/93/EEC	OJ 1993 L30	*452*
363/93/EEC	OJ 1993 L42	*417*
404/93/EEC	OJ 1993 L47	*417*
638/93/EEC	OJ 1993 L69	*417*
1544/93/EEC	OJ 1993 L154	*417*
1548/93/EEC	OJ 1993 L154	*417*
1557/93/EEC	OJ 1993 L154	*417*

TABLE OF COMMUNITY DIRECTIVES

Directive	Reference
64/221/EEC	OJ 1964 L56, OJ Sp.Ed. 1963–64 117 *83, 246, 253–6, 262, 268*
64/222/EEC	OJ 1964 L56, OJ Sp.Ed. 1963–64 120 *266*
64/427/EEC	OJ 1964 L117, OJ Sp.Ed. 1963–64 148 *266*
67/548/EEC	OJ 1967 L196, OJ Sp.Ed. 1967 234 *436, 450*
68/151/EEC	OJ 1968 L65, OJ Sp.Ed. 1968 (I) 41 *91*
68/360/EEC	OJ 1968 L257, OJ Sp.Ed. 1968 (II) 485 *245, 252, 253*
68/364/EEC	OJ 1968 L260, OJ Sp.Ed. 1968 (II) 493 *266*
68/366/EEC	OJ 1968 L260, OJ Sp.Ed. 1968 (II) 509 *266*
68/368/EEC	OJ 1968 L260, OJ Sp.Ed. 1968 (II) 517 *266*
68/369/EEC	OJ 1968 L260, OJ Sp.Ed. 1968 (II) 520 *266*
70/50/EEC	OJ 1970 L13, OJ Sp.Ed. 1970 (I) 10 *225, 226, 228*
70/220/EEC	OJ 1970 L76, OJ Sp.Ed. 1970 (I) 171 *436, 449, 450*
70/523/EEC	OJ 1970 L267, OJ Sp.Ed. 1970 (III) 740 *266*
70/524/EEC	OJ 1970 840 *220*
71/304/EEC	OJ 1971 L185, OJ Sp.Ed 1971 (II) 678 *200*
71/305/EEC	OJ 1971 L185, OJ Sp.Ed. 1971 (II) 682 *200, 240*
72/159/EEC	OJ 1972 L96, OJ Sp.Ed. 1972 (II) 324 *124*
73/148/EEC	OJ 1973 L172 *262, 268*
73/183/EEC	OJ 1973 L124 *220*
74/556/EEC	OJ 1974 L307 *266*
75/34/EEC	OJ 1975 L114 *262*
75/117/EEC	OJ 1975 L45 *44, 361, 365, 370–2*
75/129/EEC	OJ 1975 L48 *399–401*
75/362/EEC	OJ 1975 L167 *266*
75/440/EEC	OJ 1975 L194 *44, 453*
75/442/EEC	OJ 1975 L194 *451*
76/160/EEC	OJ 1976 L31 *453*
76/207/EEC	OJ 1976 L39 *85, 88, 89, 361, 373–8, 381, 382*
76/464/EEC	OJ 1976 L129 *445, 453*
76/769/EEC	OJ 1976 L262 *450*
77/62/EEC	OJ 1977 L13 *240*
77/92/EEC	OJ 1977 L26 *266*
77/187/EEC	OJ 1977 L61 *401–3, 405*
77/249/EEC	OJ 1977 L78 *266*
77/311/EEC	OJ 1977 L105 *450*
77/435/EEC	OJ 1977 L172 *430*
77/452/EEC	OJ 1977 L176 *266*
78/319/EEC	OJ 1978 L84 *451*
78/659/EEC	OJ 1978 L222 *438, 453*
78/686/EEC	OJ 1978 L233 *266*
78/1015/EEC	OJ 1978 L349 *450*
78/1026/EEC	OJ 1978 L362 *266*
79/7/EEC	OJ 1979 L6 *361, 363, 364, 374, 375, 378–81*

Draft Directives

TABLE OF COUNCIL DECISIONS

Decision	Reference
2/54/HA	OJ 1954 1, OJ Sp.Ed. 1952–58 15 *152*
66/532/EEC	OJ 1966 2971 *209*
70/243/EEC	OJ 1970 L94, OJ Sp.Ed. 1970 (I) 224 *33*
76/787/EEC	OJ 1976 L278 *21*
85/257/EEC	OJ 1985 L128 *33*
85/338/EEC	OJ 1985 L176, OJ 1990 L81 *446*
85/368/EEC	OJ 1985 L199 *266, 267*
87/95/EEC	OJ 1987 L36 *345*
87/373/EEC	OJ 1987 L197 *16, 138, 427*
88/376/EEC	OJ 1988 L185 *33*
88/540/EEC	OJ 1988 L297 *456*
88/591/EEC	OJ 1989 L319 *30, 31*
89/286/EEC	OJ 1989 L112 *339*
91/352/EEC	OJ 1991 L192 *339*
91/353/EEC	OJ 1991 L192 *341*
91/385/EEC	OJ 1991 L208 *339*
91/394/EEC	OJ 1991 L218 *341*
91/396/EEC	OJ 1991 L217 *347*
91/423/EEC	OJ 1991 L235 *260*
91/424/EEC	OJ 1991 L235 *260*
91/425/EEC	OJ 1991 L235 *260*
91/690/EEC	OJ 1990 L377 *456*
91/691/EEC	OJ 1991 L377 *340*
92/242/EEC	OJ 1992 L123 *354*
92/264/EEC	OJ 1992 L137 *347*
93/350/ECSC, EEC, Euratom	OJ 1993 L144 *31*
93/389/EEC	OJ 1993 L167 *450*
94/5/EC	OJ 1994 L6 *339*

TABLE OF EC RULES OF PROCEDURE AND STATUTES

OTHER COMMUNITY INSTRUMENTS

Recommendation	Reference
84/549/EEC	OJ 1984 L298 *345*
89/349/EEC	OJ 1989 L144 *456*
92/131/EEC	OJ 1992 L49 *383*
92/241/EEC	OJ 1992 L123 *383*
94/441/EEC	OJ 1992 L245 *258*

Opinions	Reference
Equal Pay	OJ 1993 C248 *372*

Communication
Conciliation procedure, OJ 1975 C89 *23*
Draft EU Treaty, OJ 1984 C77 *5, 13*
Internal market/national treasures, COM (89) 594 *234*
Protection of personal data, COM (90) 314 *349*
Competition rules in the telecommunications sector, OJ 1991 C233 *342*
Telecommunications' tariffs, SEC (92) 1050 *346*
Subsidiarity, SEC (92) final *50, 51*
European Standardisation, OJ 1992 C96 *241*
Harmonised standards under Directive 89/336/EEC, OJ 1994 C49 *346*
Developing universal services for telecommunications services in a competitive environment, OJ 1994 C48 *348*

Notice
Agreements of Minor Importance, OJ 1986 C235 *282*
Interpretation of Art. 48, OJ 1988 C72 *258*
Ancillary Restraints, OJ 1990 C203 *304, 308*
Beer Agreements, OJ 1992 C121 *283*

Resolutions
Worker consultation, OJ 1986 C203 *406*
International telephone charges, OJ 1988 C257 *346*
Standardisation in the field of IT and telecommunications, OJ 1989 C117 *346*
Global warming, OJ 1989 C183 *450*
The comparability of vocational training qualifications, OJ 1991 C109 *267*
The protection of the dignity of women and men at work, OJ 1990 C157 *382*
Diplomas and certificates from third countries, OJ 1992 C187 *267*
Promotion of the Europe-wide numbering of telecoms services, OJ 1992 C318 *347*
Transparency of vocational qualifications and certification in the EC, OJ 1993 C49 *267*
Pricing structures and telecommunications tariffs, OJ 1993 C2 *347*

Miscellaneous
Community Patent Convention, OJ 1976 L17, OJ 1990 L401 *319*
Proposed Community Trademark Regulation, OJ 1980 C351, OJ 1984 C230, COM (92) 443 *320, 321*
Proposal re term of copyright, OJ 1992 C92, OJ 1993 C27 *328–30*
Community Charter on the Fundamental Social Rights of Workers *388–370*

ABBREVIATIONS

AC	Appeal Cases	EAGGF	European Agricultural Guidance and Guarantee Fund (often referred to as FEOGA – *Fonds européen d'orientation et de garantie agricole*)
ACP	African Caribbean Pacific states		
AJCL	American Journal of Comparative Law		
AJIL	American Journal of International Law	EC	European Community
All ER	All England Law Reports	ECB	European Central Bank
Anglo-Am LRev	Anglo-American Law Review	ECSC	European Coal and Steel Community
BDMA	British Direct Mailing Association	ECU	European Currency Unit
		ECJ	European Court of Justice
Bull EC	Bulletin of the European Communities	ECLR	European Competition Law Review
BYIL	British Yearbook of International Law	ECR	European Court Reports
		EEA	European Economic Area
CAP	Common Agricultural Policy	EEC	European Economic Community
CFI	Court of First Instance	EELR	European Environmental Law Review
CFSP	Common Foreign and Security Policy	EFTA	European Free Trade Association
CJHA	Co-operation in Justice and Home Affairs	EHRR	European Human Rights Reports Review
CLJ	Cambridge Law Journal		
CLP	Current Legal Problems	EIPL	European Intellectual Property Law
COM	Common Organisation of the Market or Commission Document	ELRev	European Law Review
		EP	European Parliament
COREPER	Committee of Permanent Representatives (*Comité des Représentants Permanents*)	EPC	European Political Co-operation
		ESCB	European System of Central Banks
CMLR	Common Market Law Reports	EU	European Union
		Euratom	European Atomic Energy Community
CMLRev	Common Market Law Review	FamLaw	Family Law
DG	Directorate General	FSR	Fleet Street Reports

GATT	General Agreement on Tariffs and Trade	LIEI	Legal Issues of European Integration
HarvLR or Harvard LR	Harvard Law Review	LQR	Law Quarterly Review
HRLJ	Human Rights Law Journal	OJ	Official Journal of the European Communities
IAT	Immigration Appeals Tribunal	MCA	Monetary Compensatory Amount
IBL	International Business Lawyer	MGQ	Maximum Guaranteed Quantities
ICLQ	International and Comparative Law Quarterly	MLR	Modern Law Review
		NILQ	Northern Ireland Legal Quarterly
Ind LJ	Industrial Law Journal	NLJ	New Law Journal
Int Lawyer	International Lawyer	OJLS	Oxford Journal of Legal Studies
IRLR	Industrial Relations Law Reports	PA	Public Administration
JBL	Journal of Business Law	PL	Public Law
JCMS	Journal of Common Market Studies	PPLR	Public Procurement Law Review
JESP	Journal of European Social Policy	SCA	Special Committee on Agriculture
JLIS	Journal of Law and Information Science	SEA	Single European Act
		SJ	Solicitors' Journal
JLS	Journal of Law and Society	TEU	Treaty on European Union
JPL	Journal of Planning and Environmental Law	WLR	Weekly Law Reports
		Yale LJ	Yale Law Journal
JSWL	Journal of Social Welfare Law (now JSWFL – Journal of Social Welfare and Family Law)	YEL	Yearbook of European Law

CHAPTER 1

Introduction

THE GOAL OF INTEGRATION IN POST-WAR EUROPE

The goal of integration in post-war Europe has been described by former President of the European Commission Roy Jenkins in the following terms:

> . . . the paradox that the European Community is and always has been from its earliest days, a body which has sought political ends through largely economic means. The political ends have obviously not been narrow party-political ends; they have been no less than the regeneration of Europe and the restoration of Europe's position and influence in the world which we so wantonly threw away in two European civil wars.[1]

As Holland comments, 'it would be myopic to regard the past four decades of European integration as a technocratic exercise principally devoted to capital expansion'.[2]

THE IMPETUS FOR INTEGRATION IN POST-WAR EUROPE

The history of the European Community is particularly a post-war phenomenon. Unlike the United Nations, there is no interwar predecessor to the EC. However, the idea of a unified Europe has much longer historical roots.[3] Both military conquest and utopian ideas, however, were unsuccessful in imposing or persuading an idea of Europe into existence. Military efforts only exacerbated the divisions in Europe. Intellectuals, being outside of mainstream politics, had little opportunity to develop their ideas into workable models of integration. In the nineteenth century, economic integration or freer trade between European states became accepted within mainstream politics. It is therefore understandable that, when Hitler's attempt to unify Europe by force of arms failed, economic integration would appear the most viable option.

As Jenkins stated, the idea of European integration as practised by the Community emerged in the context of rebuilding Europe after World War II. This goal united people of divergent political persuasions as well as across borders.[4] However, radical federalist ideas of European union gave way with the return of pre-war politicians and with them pre-war attitudes and divisions.[5] The first post-war European regional organisation was to prove a weak force for integration, although it has functioned excellently as a think tank for Western Europe and recently for almost the entire continent. The Council of Europe began with the

---

[1] Jenkins, 'Thatcher: A Satisfactory Alternative to Delors?' (1990) 4 *European Affairs* 57.
[2] Holland, *European Community Integration* (1993), at 7.
[3] As Urwin, *The Community of Europe* (1991), at 1

succinctly describes: 'Across the centuries, intellectuals and political leaders alike had dreamed of overcoming the unique historical characteristic of Europe: its extreme political fragmentation.'
[4] *Ibid.*, at 7–8.

Treaty of Westminster of 1949. It was designed to be a purely intergovernmental organisation, functioning along the lines of traditional international law. It has, nonetheless, produced numerous conventions which have set common standards for Europe, most notably the European Convention on Human Rights of 1950 and the European Social Charter of 1961.[6] It has been a broader organisation: currently, the Council of Europe has more than double the membership of the European Union. It has, therefore, provided a way into European integration for more reluctant States, and for the still somewhat unstable States of Eastern Europe. The Council of Europe was, in particular, more acceptable to the UK than ideas of European union.

From 1950, continental integrationists abandoned the attempt to include the UK in efforts to unite Europe in a more federal model. The Schumann Plan of 1950 proposed the pooling of coal and steel resources to be administered by a supranational High Authority. Both Robert Schumann, the French foreign minister, and the plan's drafter, Jean Monnet, saw this as an initial step on a progress towards full economic and political integration.[7] The Plan obtained support from European States so readily because, in addition to being a strictly limited form of integration, it served a practical purpose. The implementation of the Plan would free (then West) Germany from internationally-imposed regulation of its industry, but would enable European States, still anxious about German intentions, to monitor its activities. In addition, integrationists were in positions of power in many European States.[8] The resulting agreement, the Treaty of Paris establishing the European Coal and Steel Community (ECSC), was signed by Belgium, France, West Germany, Italy, Luxembourg and The Netherlands on 18 April 1951. Jean Monnet became the first President of the ECSC High Authority, resigning in 1955.

From coal and steel to the Common Market

Throughout the 1950s, attempts were made to advance European integration from its basis in the ECSC. Notable failures of this period are the European Defence Community[9] and the European Political Community. Both foundered on the rocks of nationalism – these were powers which governments were simply unwilling and, possibly, unable, to surrender. The European Political Community suffered from being too federal for nationalists and too nationalist for European integrationists. Instead of the European Defence Community, the Western European Union was established, its purely intergovernmental form allowing the UK to participate. It was, therefore, like the Council of Europe, a means of communication and some co-operation, but not of integration.

Economic integration was to prove the only way forward. Competing approaches were the increase of sectoral integration, favoured by Monnet, and the establishment of a Common Market, favoured by Paul-Henri Spaak.[10] Ultimately, both approaches were successful. From

---

6 Students beginning the study of Community law often confuse the Council and the Community, and wrongly categorise the European Convention on Human Rights (ECHR) as part of Community law. While the Court of Justice of the European Communities has referred to the ECHR as a source of general principles of Community law, it is a convention under the auspices of the Council of Europe, and not part of Community law. On the use of the ECHR by the Court of Justice, see Chapter 6.

7 Urwin, *op. cit.* note 3, at 44.

8 *Ibid.*, at 46.

9 See Fursdon, *The European Defence Community: A History* (1980).

10 Urwin, *op. cit.* note 3, at 73.

the 1955 meeting of foreign ministers at Messina, progress was made towards both the integration of nuclear energy and the establishment of a Customs Union and Common Market. The Spaak Committee reported in 1956 and was subsequently transformed into a Treaty-drafting conference. The result was two Treaties: the European Economic Community (EEC) Treaty and the European Atomic Energy Community (Euratom) Treaty. The Euratom Treaty operated as a sectoral Treaty, as had the ECSC. The EEC Treaty was a more ambitious document and one of an entirely different order. It set out to remove barriers, both State and private, to trade between the Member States, and to harmonise certain policy-making areas by creating common policies. The only common policy to come to fruition is the now infamous Common Agricultural Policy.[11] It operated as a *traité-cadre*, or framework Treaty, which establishes a set of principles and processes by which further decisions can be taken which will be binding on the signatories to the Treaty. A framework Treaty operates in a similar way to a constitution, by setting up institutions to pass binding measures and setting out the areas of competence of different authorities. The EEC Treaty established institutions similar to those under the ECSC Treaty and in the 1965 Merger Treaty the institutions of the three Communities were converged into one. Also, because the Treaty itself does not set out exactly the measures to be taken, but rather the general parameters of the policies to be adopted under its auspices, Member State interests were protected by the use of unanimous or qualified majority voting (which requires more than a simple majority of Member States). The latter procedure[12] is intended to recognise the relative power of the Member States by granting larger Member States more votes and protecting smaller Member States from consistently being outvoted by the larger Member States by requiring more than a bare majority of votes, but preventing one Member State from having an effective veto over certain matters (as would be the case under unanimous voting).

The issue of voting, and the fact that qualified majority voting was to become the norm after the transitional period which ended in 1962, brought the Community to its first crisis in the 1960s. As the UK was to become in the 1980s and 1990s, so France became isolated in its staunch opposition to Community control of policy in the 1960s. Under qualified majority voting, France's objections could be overridden by the other five Member States if they voted together. As a result France, under de Gaulle, was against moving to greater use of qualified majority voting without protection for national interests. First, an attempt was made to divert the direction of integration through the establishment of a committee to draft a Political Union Treaty with a more intergovernmental orientation, under Christian Fouchet, the French ambassador to Denmark. However, these proposals failed to attract the support of the other Member States. By 1965, French opposition to further integration hardened into a boycott of meetings of the Council of Ministers – the so-called 'empty chair' policy. This crisis was only resolved through the Luxembourg Accords, sometimes called the Luxembourg Compromise, which were thereafter relied upon by Member States to veto any measure which affected their 'very important interests'. The legal status of these Accords is questionable, but the principles contained therein were observed at least until the Single European Act (SEA).

---

[11] See Chapter 18. [12] Explained in Chapter 2.

Expanding the Community

The opposition of de Gaulle to Community plans was not restricted to substantive matters. During his presidency, he consistently opposed the admission of the UK to membership of the Community. While the UK had changed its attitude towards the Community early in the 1960s, it was made to wait over a decade between its first overtures and its accession to the EEC Treaty. Before joining the EEC, the UK was a member of the European Free Trade Association (EFTA). Fellow EFTA members Denmark and Norway applied soon after the UK for EEC membership, as did Ireland, which was not an EFTA member. Other EFTA members requested association agreements with the EEC. In 1963, de Gaulle announced France's opposition to the UK's application and the applications for enlargement were effectively dead.[13] A second set of negotiations between the UK and the Community began in 1967, only to end again with a public announcement by de Gaulle of his opposition to British membership. Progress on expansion, therefore, became possible only once de Gaulle resigned the French presidency. Denmark,[14] Ireland and the UK joined the EEC with effect from 1973. Norway was deeply divided on the issue of accession and after a narrow vote against accession in a national referendum withdrew from negotiations for membership of the Community until the late 1980s.[15]

In the 1980s, the enlargement of the Community has embraced southern Europe: Greece in 1981 and Spain and Portugal in 1986. All three States had only recently moved from authoritarian rule to democracy. As a result, membership of the Community was looked upon as a badge of achievement, a recognition of their having moved into the first ranks of Europe. These countries have also seen the Community as a means of providing the stability which prevents them from sliding back into dictatorship. Greece had signed an association agreement in 1962, which was suspended during the period of military government but was quickly revived after the re-instatement of democracy. The Community was initially somewhat more cautious about the idea of Greece's membership application. Greece (and later Spain and Portugal) was much weaker and less stable economically than the other Member States. A more complicated transition would be necessary. Spain began its negotiations from a weaker point, having had preferential trading arrangements with the EEC but not a full association agreement, while Portugal had been a member of EFTA. Internal financial conflicts within the Community prevented resolution of the enlargement issue for a number of years. It is probably not a coincidence that Spain's and Portugal's accession was accomplished at about the same time as the SEA.

Expansion is still a current issue for the European Union. While the question of allowing former Communist Eastern European States into the Union is still open, it appears that many of the remaining EFTA States will soon become members. A first step is the Agreement to create a European Economic Area (EEA), signed in 1992. This Agreement extends many of

13 de Gaulle was not opposed to the membership of the other applicants, but these States were not prepared to proceed without the UK.

14 Greenland, for which Denmark was then responsible in foreign policy matters, left the Community in 1985.

15 The difficulties experienced by Norway in reconciling itself to membership of the Community (now the Union) are still very much in evidence. In the current negotia- tions for enlargement Norway has proved the most diffi- cult applicant in terms of settlement, particularly over fishing rights. The scars of the 1972 referendum are still present in the Norwegian political psyche. This is par- ticularly remarkable considering the fact that the appar- ent success of the Union in accommodating Sweden and Finland means that Norway could be left economically isolated in the Scandinavian region.

the advantages of the Single Market to EEA countries, who in return will apply Community law within their jurisdictions.[16] It appears that the intention of this Agreement is to create a transitional phase for entry into full Union membership. This transitional phase may be quite short, as Austria, Finland, Norway and Sweden are currently in negotiations for membership.

The Single Market alternative

The SEA, like the Fouchet Plan, was intended as a distraction from plans for greater political integration. Unlike the Fouchet Plan, it was successful, although only for a relatively short period, after which pressures for political integration resurfaced. Even after the failure of the proposed European Political Community, the idea of some form of political union between the members of the Community persisted. The Luxembourg Accords contributed to a general disinterest of the Member States in further large-scale projects of integration during the late 1960s and the 1970s. Proposals for political union were advanced but no progress, other than enlargement, was made during this period. The Tindemans report of 1976 proposed an ambitious expansion of policy competence for the Community in areas such as defence, economic and monetary policy and industrial, social and regional policy. He also proposed strengthening the Commission and replacing the European Parliament with a more powerful two-chamber legislature. However, Tindemans also introduced the idea of a multi-speed Community, whereby integration would proceed at a variable pace from Member State to Member State. The report, being too federalist and not sufficiently consistent in its federalism, was never acted upon. A subsequent report on further integration by a committee termed the 'Three Wise Men'[17] in 1979. This report, like Tindemans recommending the strengthening of the Commission along with greater use of majority voting in the Council of Ministers, was also ignored. Tindemans' ideas on the expansion of the policy competence of the Community were picked up in the Genscher-Colombo Plan of 1981. The Genscher-Colombo Plan also recommended making the role of the European Council (the summit of heads of State or government of the Member States) more explicit. This point at least was responded to in the SEA which, while not defining the role of the European Council, gave it legal recognition for the first time, and in the Treaty on European Union (TEU) which gave the European Council a central role in the non-Community areas of Union policy.

The European Parliament's contribution to this explosion of models for the further integration was a complete draft Treaty on European Union in 1984.[18] The leader of the MEPs presenting the draft Treaty was Altiero Spinelli, an integrationist from the earliest days of the Community. The draft Treaty propounded the early federalist ideal of the Commission as an executive for the Community, and a reduction of the role of the Council of Ministers and the Member State governments. The Council of Ministers was envisaged under the draft Treaty as a second chamber of the legislative branch of the Community, the primary legislative body being the European Parliament. The draft Treaty was accepted by the European Parliament, but went no further. MEPs themselves were unable to make it an issue of the 1984 European Parliament election.

The draft Treaty at least caused the issue of European Union to be put on the agenda of

---

16 Some of the difficulties arising out of this Treaty are discussed in Chapter 4. Switzerland, in a national referendum in 1993, voted against ratifying the Agreement.

17 Barend Biesheuvel, Edmund Dell and Robert Marjolin.
18 See Caportorti et al., *The European Union Treaty* (1986).

the European Council in June 1984. This led to the establishment of yet another committee to discuss political reform within the Community, under the leadership of James Dooge, former Irish foreign minister. This committee, however, was intended to examine what common ground might exist between the governments of the Member States, rather than to construct an ideal model of political union. However, in its final report, the Dooge Committee asserted that in order for the Community to become a political entity institutional reforms strengthening the Commission and the European Parliament, limiting the use of unanimous voting in the Council of Ministers and limiting the European Council to a strategic role would be necessary.

It is at this stage that the possibility of an alternative emerges. Some Member States, particularly the UK, which were not prepared to move towards political union began to emphasise the need for greater *economic* union. The result of the proposal and counter-proposal situation was the establishment at the Milan European Council meeting in 1985 of an intergovernmental conference to examine the question of reform. While the mandate given to the working parties looking at the questions of reform emphasised the institutional questions, the outcome was oriented more to substantive issues. The SEA revived the goal of establishing the Community as a Single Market which, under the original EEC Treaty, was to have been achieved by 1970 but which, in the opinion of many, including Lord Cockfield, one of the British commissioners, was not yet in place. Many obstacles to free trade between the Member States still existed, and many Community measures would need to be adopted before the Community could truly be a Single Market. However, in order to accomplish the necessary measures needed to complete the Single Market, institutional reforms were necessary. The SEA reduced the use of unanimous voting by the Council and gave the European Parliament greater influence over the content of Community legislation. It also strengthened the Commission by reinforcing its power to initiate legislation, a power which was particularly important in measures aimed at harmonising national legislation in order to complete the Single Market. The Single Market was to be achieved by the end of 1992.[19]

Towards European Union

The aim of many of the protagonists within the Community to move to deeper integration was not satisfied by the SEA.

With the downfall of several communist governments in Eastern Europe, the debate within the Community was not only over the shape of the future, but of its scope. This has often been presented as a choice between widening the Community by expanding its membership, or deepening it through institutional reforms which would further integration, especially on the political level. The main demands of those who argued for deepening the Community were some form of political union, economic and monetary union and development of a 'social Europe' which would provide minimum standards for workers. Economic and monetary union was the first target.

The European Monetary System (EMS) was established in the early 1980s, under the Commission presidency of Roy Jenkins.[20] A later President, Jacques Delors, took up the issue

---

19 While many in politics and the media used '1992' as the shorthand for the Single Market project, the SEA actually sets out 1 January 1993 as the beginning of the Single Market.

20 Now Lord Jenkins of Hillhead.

of economic and monetary union as a missing element from the SEA package and made it the starting point for further integration. It was argued that the logic of the Single Market demanded a single currency for the Community as soon as possible, regulated by a Community central bank. In 1988–89 the Delors Committee examined the issue of economic and monetary union and proposed a three-stage plan for achieving a single currency for the Community. Some elements were already in place, such as the guarantee of free movement of capital. However, exchange rates of all the Member States needed to be integrated under the Exchange Rate Mechanism of the EMS. Furthermore, far greater economic convergence would be necessary in order to support a single currency. This would require Community policies on matters such as national budget deficits. The Delors Committee's report led to an agreement, not supported by the UK, to enter the second phase of economic and monetary union in January 1994 and to establish an intergovernmental conference on economic and monetary union in December 1990, which did receive UK support.

The logic of economic and monetary union led, for some Member States such as Germany, to political union. The Community, if it was to have power over such an important area of policy-making, had to ensure that its processes and institutions were properly democratic. Some also felt that reform of the institutions was a prerequisite to further enlargement; the Community had to get its own house in order before inviting in other States, some of which would only recently have become democratic themselves, particularly since a functioning democratic system was considered by the Member States to be a condition of entry for Eastern European States. As a result, a second intergovernmental conference, on political union, was convened. This conference concentrated on reform of the institutions and expanded areas of competence for the Community, particularly in foreign policy.

The Treaty which resulted, signed at Maastricht, The Netherlands in December 1991, was a series of compromises. Economic and monetary union was established, but the UK and Denmark were allowed to opt out of the third stage. Political union was established which did not replace the Community but existed as an overarching structure on top of it. The Treaty on European Union (TEU) is made up of three 'pillars'. The first is comprised of the three Communities, with the European Economic Community renamed the European Community. The second and third pillars exist outside the Community system and function on an intergovernmental basis, with the European Council having a primary role in setting the priorities of policy. These intergovernmental pillars are the Common Foreign and Security Policy[21] and Co-operation in Justice and Home Affairs.[22] The TEU also marked renewed failure of the Community to establish a more secure legal basis for the development of social policy, which the UK has consistently opposed. Originally, a new chapter on social policy was to be added to the EC Treaty but, instead, this framework exists as a protocol outside the Treaty and one in which the UK will not participate.

The principles of the TEU, set out in the first few Articles, display an ambivalence about further integration. While the idea of Union is proclaimed, it exists within the constraints of the protection of 'national identities' and the principle of subsidiarity, which is a principle of decentralisation. The advocacy of the principle of subsidiarity was one of the most prominent features of the UK bargaining position at the intergovernmental conferences. Subsidiarity, it was thought, would prevent the Community, and particularly the Commission, from taking on greater powers under the aegis of integration.

---

[21] See Chapter 4.　　　　　　　　　　[22] See Chapter 12.

Even the compromises granted to various Member States within the TEU and its many protocols did not guarantee a smooth passage from signature to ratification. In almost every Member State difficulties were experienced.[23] The most intractable of these were faced in Denmark where, on 2 June 1992, the population narrowly rejected the TEU in a referendum required under the Danish constitution in order to ratify the Treaty. The question then was how to give the Danish government the possibility of holding another referendum, and winning it, without reopening the Treaty for further negotiations. This latter possibility, it was thought, would lead to a totally new Treaty which might come about only after months or even years of renegotiation. The solution, reached at the Edinburgh summit of December 1992 under the UK Presidency of the Community, was to issue an interpretative decision of the European Council which aimed to meet the objections to the TEU amongst the Danish population without modifying the Treaty. The decision dealt with four areas: citizenship of the European Union; the third stage of economic and monetary union; defence aspects of the common foreign and security policy; and co-operation in justice and home affairs. The decision is followed by two declarations by the European Council: that the TEU does not prevent a Member State from providing more stringent measures of social, consumer and environmental protection than provided for under the Treaty and that Denmark will renounce its Presidency of the Union in any situation whereby defence implications arise. Finally, Denmark made three unilateral declarations: first, that citizenship of the European Union is separate from and does not undermine national citizenship; secondly, that Denmark must comply with its constitutional formalities in the event of the Union deciding to adopt a common policy on visa requirements for third-country nationals; and, thirdly, that the TEU must be understood in light of the decision and declarations. In May 1993 a second referendum was passed by the Danish population, with nearly 60 per cent voting in favour of the Treaty. The TEU came into force on 1 November 1993 after the final hurdle in the final Member State was cleared.[24]

DEFINING INTEGRATION

Early attempts to explain European integration as practised within the European Community tended to fall within neo-functionalist theory. Neo-functionalists explain international relations through examining the behaviour not only of States but of interest groups and bureaucracies. As a result, the Commission was a central focus of neo-functionalist writing on the Community.[25] Neo-functionalism explained integration through the idea, held by many of the originators of the Community, that integration in the economic sphere was inevitably expansionist and would move from economic union to monetary union. Further, according to this theory, economic integration would lead to political integration.[26] Neo-functionalism was largely abandoned from 1965, the year of France's 'empty chair' at the Council of Ministers, which led to the Luxembourg Accords and a shift of power from

---

[23] Morris and Lodge, 'Appendix: the referendums' in Lodge (ed), *The European Community and the Challenge of the Future*, 2nd edn (1993), at 386.
[24] The decision of the German Constitutional Court that the TEU was in conformity with the German Basic Law in October 1993 marked the end of the ratification process.
[25] George, *Politics and Policy in the European Community*, 2nd edn (1991), at 20–2.
[26] *Ibid.*, at 22–4.

the Commission to the Council. The approach was to some extent rediscovered with the events of the mid-1980s – the completion of the Single Market and the development of monetary union. The idea of spillover, that economic union would lead to political union, became attractive once again.[27] However, the failure of the Exchange Rate Mechanism in 1992 and the granting of national opt-outs in the TEU led to renewed disillusionment over the idea of 'inevitable' integration. Some critics have identified the move from low politics (economics and welfare) to high politics (foreign and defence policy; probably also monetary policy) as the stumbling block of neo-functionalism.[28] Certainly, these have been the areas in which the Commission has been least able to control the agenda. George concludes that neo-functionalism has little predictive value, but does assist in the analysis of how policies have been developed.[29]

Theories of federalism have more recently been used to describe European integration. Crudely, this meant that, progressively, policy-formulation in the Community will come to resemble that of a federal State such as Canada. Federalism may actually be truer to the roots of the post-war European ideal, as promoted by Jean Monnet.[30] The use of the language of federalism has provoked accusations that the goal of integrationists is to create a European super-State. Whether or not this is the case, such an end goal is little different from the political integration goal of the neo-functionalists. Neo-functionalism could be described as incremental federalism.[31] Nonetheless, federalism is not yet an adequate integration theory, since there is no agreement on its meaning outside the context of a nation-State.

STUDYING COMMUNITY LAW

This book is intended as an introduction to Community law. However, there is no substitute for reading primary materials. There are several parts to Community law cases, as reported in the *European Court Reports*, which are the official reports. In addition to the judgment of the Court, there is a summary of the facts and proceedings, including the arguments of the parties to the case, and the Advocate General's opinion. The judgments of the Court are often quite brief and refer to little authority. By reading the arguments of the parties and, particularly, the Advocate General's opinions, a better idea of how that area of the law has been developed and what theoretical and policy considerations underlie the judgment can be obtained.

In this book numerous areas of substantive law are covered, not just the usual Single Market law. This provides both students and teachers with the possibility of expanding the coverage of Community policy-making. Many of these areas, such as the environment, social policy and technology are the stuff of headlines in the daily newspapers as well as of academic study. At the end of each Chapter we have provided a list of selected further reading on the subject-matter of that Chapter. This is a selection of books and articles which go into greater detail than a textbook of this type is able to do. These reading lists can be

---

27 *Ibid.*, at 226–8. See also Ver Loren van Themaat, 'Some Preliminary Observations on the Intergovernmental Conferences: The Relation between the Concepts of a Common Market, a Monetary Union, an Economic Union, a Political Union and Sovereignty' (1991) 28 CML Rev 291.

28 George, *op. cit.*, note 25 at 32–3.

29 Ver Loren van Themaat, *op. cit.*, note 27 at 233–4.

30 Holland, *op. cit.*, note 2, at 5–6 and 8–9.

31 *Ibid.*, at 7.

used as a basis for research as well as for studying Community law in the context of a university or professional course. Some suggestions are from disciplines outside the legal field. The study of Community law benefits from the insights of economics and politics, as well as from legal analysis.

A NOTE ON TERMINOLOGY

While the European Community is now part of the European Union it is still possible to speak of Community law in the sense of the law arising from the European Community Treaty. Most of the material in this book relates to Community law, although there is some discussion of the TEU in general and of the other two pillars of European Union. The *Union* refers to the physical territory of the Member States as a whole and to the Member States acting other than under the EC Treaty. The *Community* either refers to the pre-TEU situation or to the Member States acting under the EC Treaty. Directives which predate the TEU will take the form of 12/90/*EEC* and after the TEU, 12/94/*EC*. The Commission has recently issued guidance concerning the names of the institutions now that the TEU is in force. The European Commission and European Parliament retain their current names, but the Council of Ministers is to be known as the Council of the European Union. In this book we have retained the old usage, since most of the legislation and case law which students will study will predate the TEU.

Cases from the Court of Justice are cited in the form of Case C-12/94, and from the Court of First Instance as Case T-12/94.

Further reading

Caportorti, F., et al., *The European Union Treaty* (Oxford: OUP, 1986).

Fursdon, E., *The European Defence Community: A History* (London: Macmillan, 1980).

George, S., *Politics and Policy in the European Community*, 2nd edn (Oxford: OUP, 1991).

Holland, M., *European Community Integration* (London: Pinter, 1993).

Urwin, D., *The Community of Europe* (London: Longman, 1991).

Ver Loren van Themaat, P., 'Some Preliminary Observations on the Intergovernmental Conferences: The Relation between the Concepts of a Common Market, a Monetary Union, a Political Union and Sovereignty' (1991) 28 CML Rev 291.

CHAPTER 2

Institutional framework

INTRODUCTION

Unlike many international organisations, the European Union, and the European Communities which form part of it, are capable of passing legislative acts which are binding on the Member States in their national law.[1] Consequently, there are constant tensions between the organisation itself and the Member States as to who will dominate these processes, and whether the outcomes of the legislative processes will be integrative or nationalist. This tension has been manifested within the institutions of the Community since its establishment. The Community institutions are the Commission, the Council of Ministers, the European Parliament, the Court of Justice (ECJ) and the European Central Bank, as set out in Article 4 EC.[2] The Commission and the Parliament have tended to promote the further integration of the Community, particularly through the harmonisation of Member State laws in order to facilitate the free movement of goods, services, persons and capital. The Council of Ministers, on the other hand, has expressed the Member State position, which has been sceptical about further integration and which has largely taken the view that where Member States cannot agree on a measure that the measure should not be passed. The original EC Treaty of Rome, in 1957, gave a dominant role to the Council of Ministers in the legislative processes. Later amendments have given the Commission and the Parliament an expanded role in influencing the content of legislation. However, the Council has always been able to use political means, such as agreements on the use of a Member State veto, to weight the balance in its favour.

This issue of institutional balance, therefore, is the theme running through the development of the Community institutions. Institutional balance rather than the separation of powers, executive, legislative and judicial, informs the Community constitutional structure.[3] The Commission, in particular, has argued that actions by the Council upset the institutional balance intended by the treaties. This debate is one which is frequently found in constitutional law: the constitution (or, in the case of the Community, the Treaties) sets out certain rules about how legislative institutions should behave, but in the process of acting on these rules, political practice changes the rules in the favour of the most powerful institution. The treaties themselves give predominance to the Council, and it has been able to maintain much of this power, despite amendments giving a wider role to the European Parliament.

The question of institutional balance has been complicated by the Treaty on European

---

1 Article 189 EC. This aspect of Community law is discussed in detail in Chapter 3 (supremacy) and in Chapter 5 (direct effect).

2 On the nature of an institution in the EC, see Freestone, 'Article 4 EEC' in Barav (ed). *Commentary on the EEC Treaty and the Single European Act* (1994).

3 The difficulty in tracking the executive, legislative and judicial functions within the Community is demonstrated by Lenaerts, 'Some Reflections on the Separation of Powers in the European Community' (1991) 28 CML Rev 11.

Union (TEU), which has created new structures which exist alongside the Community and which are linked together by the provisions on the Union itself. The TEU is equivocal. On the Community side it consolidates the increasing power of the Parliament by giving it, at last, a right of co-decision with the Council on some measures. However, outside the Community the Union's procedures are dominated by the Member States and the Council of Ministers. It is too early to say whether this will alter the institutional balance within the Community, but outside the Community the balance is firmly set against the integrative institutions.

In this Chapter, the role of each of the institutions will be examined in light of the issue of institutional balance. The development of the institutions since 1957 will be charted, particularly in light of the legislative procedures in Community law. There are also several bodies which are implicated in the legislative, financial and judicial processes of the Communities. The subsidiary bodies, such as the Economic and Social Committee, will be discussed in the context of the institutions with which they are most closely involved. Bodies such as the European Council, which have a great deal of influence on Community policy-making, will also be reviewed. The judicial institutions of the Community, the ECJ and the Court of First Instance, whose influence on the development of Community law will be seen throughout the book, will be examined here in a structural and institutional context.

The Union

The idea of Union has been used frequently in the history of the European Communities to express the ultimate goal of integration, mostly associated with the idea of the development of the EC from an economic bloc into a political entity. As a result, Union has, with few exceptions, been the property of the idealists and the federalists. Its integration into the Treaty on European Union (TEU), agreed by the governments of the Member States who are largely anti-federalist, has deprived it of its conceptual force, as it has been codified as an auxiliary structure rather than as a replacement for the Communities, and as a limited body without international legal personality.

The first serious attempt to put forward a project for political union was the draft European Political Community Treaty, presented in 1953.[4] This Community would have had a similar institutional structure to that adopted for the EC, but with an elected Parliament. However, the proposal succeeded in pleasing no one – federalists objected to the continuing active role of national ministers, but nationalists saw it as too integrationist. It collapsed without a single ratification.[5] The first use of the term 'Union' to describe political integration comes, however, from the Fouchet Committee's draft treaty of 1961, which essentially aimed at the co-ordination of foreign and defence policies at an intergovernmental level, rather like the Common Foreign and Security Policy in the TEU.[6] The next serious attempt at formulating a strategy for Union came with the Tindemans report of 1975, which again was never acted upon.[7] The recommendations of the report, however, were similar to the fields into which the EC has moved as a result of the TEU: foreign affairs, economic and monetary union, and social, regional and industrial policies. Institutionally, Tindemans was a

---

4 Urwin, *The Community of Europe* (1991), at 64–5.
5 *Ibid.*
6 *Ibid.*, at 105.

7 Everling, 'Reflections on the Structure of the European Union' (1992) 29 CML Rev 1053, at 1054.

federalist, favouring the strengthening of the Commission and the Parliament at the expense of the Council.[8] European Union, as a process rather than a structure, was revived in the Genscher-Colombo Plan in 1981, which recommended that the European Council, which was not yet formally recognised as a Community institution, report annually to the European Parliament on progress toward European Union.[9] In 1984, the European Parliament sponsored the drafting of a thorough treaty on European Union which had as its goal the conversion of the Communities into a single Union, which, among other changes, advocated a form of co-decision between the Council and the Parliament.[10] While the treaty itself never went beyond the Parliament, the idea of Union persisted in discussions about the future of the EC, even in the preamble to the Single European Act (SEA), which was seen by the British government as the alternative to European Union.

The Union which has resulted from the TEU bears little resemblance to the federalist projects described above. Originally, the intention was to transform the Community into a political and economic Union, to move the process of integration forward into less market-orientated areas such as foreign policy and home affairs. The result as seen in the TEU is a Union which does not replace the Community but structurally surrounds it. As the preamble states, 'The Union shall be founded on the European Communities, supplemented by the policies and forms of co-operation established by this Treaty'. Attempts have been made to provide an analogy in order to illustrate the concept of Union as set out in the Treaty. The most useful of these sees the Union as a process, relying in part on the preambular statement of 'a new stage in the process of creating an ever closer union among the peoples of Europe'.[11] Structurally, analysts have described the Union as resting on three pillars, which are the Communities (EC, ECSC and Euratom), supplemented by the Common Foreign and Security Policy and Co-operation in Justice and Home Affairs.[12] The Union is therefore around the Community, but not part of it. One author, who is highly critical of the TEU, sees the three Communities as one structure, with the Foreign and Home Affairs pillars distant and separate. The Union acts as the principal attachment between these 'pillars' and the Community, 'a loose tarpaulin-like structure . . . suspended artificially and tenuously above both the loose pillars and the Community as such'.[13]

Undeniably, the Union has a complex relationship with the Community, since it uses the Community institutions for its purposes, while accountability to those institutions is debatable. In fact, it can be seen as a regressive step in European integration, giving more power to the European Council and through it to the Member States, and eroding the power of the Parliament, the Commission and, perhaps most seriously, the ECJ. Article D of the TEU describes the European Council as providing 'the necessary impetus for [the Union's] development' and defining 'the general political guidelines thereof'. The roles of the other institutions are not defined by the TEU. It is simply stated, in Article E, that they will exercise their powers in accordance with the EC treaties and the provisions of the TEU. The extent of the powers of the European Council has never been defined by any of the EC

---

[8] Urwin, *op. cit.*, note 4, at 218–19. A similar silence met the federalist projects of the 'Three Wise Men' in 1978.

[9] *Ibid.*, at 221–2

[10] *Ibid.*, at 223.

[11] Everling, *op. cit.*, note 7 at 1059–60: 'It is only declared that integration has reached a stage of institu-tional independence and autonomy which in sum justifies it as being called a Union.'

[12] *Ibid.*

[13] Curtin, 'The Constitutional Structure of the Union: A Europe of Bits and Pieces' (1993) 30 CML Rev 17, at 23.

treaties, nor are its acts subject to review by the ECJ.[14] Unlike the Council of Ministers, it is not obliged to act on a proposal by the Commission, nor to seek the opinion of the Parliament or either of the consultative Committees (the Economic and Social Committee and the Committee of the Regions). It is equally unclear what would be the status of any guidelines for the Union passed by the European Council – it does not appear that they would have the status of Community legislation.[15] The tasks of the Union in the Common Foreign and Security Policy and in Co-operation in Justice and Home Affairs appear to be purely intergovernmental in nature, which raises further questions about the role of the EC institutions in the Union, although the Commission has a limited initiative role in the Home Affairs processes[16] and the Parliament a right to ask questions and make recommendations.[17] Where acts are to be adopted, it is the Council which does so, and it does not appear that the consultation of the Parliament is a requirement for the validity of any such acts as the right to be consulted as set out is a general rather than act-specific one.

The Union is now the overarching structure in European Community law. It has the potential to create profound changes in the institutional balance established in the EC treaties. However, the extent of such change will depend on how the other pillars of the Union (the Common Foreign and Security Policy and Co-operation in Justice and Home Affairs) are used by the Member States. If they are little used, or used in a way which is consistent with existing Community law, then there may be little or no impact on the institutional balance within the EC Treaty. If a large amount of policy-making is diverted into the non-Community pillars, two consequences could arise. Either there would be two streams to European legislative processes, one under Community law and one under the other two pillars, or the use of processes in which the European Council and the Council of Ministers are dominant could undermine the increased importance in the Community legislative processes achieved by the Commission, and particularly the European Parliament.

The Commission

The Commission has been the most controversial of the EC institutions, and probably the most misunderstood. Particularly in the United Kingdom, it is thought to have far greater legislative powers than it in fact possesses. Commissioners are purely servants of the EC, but act more in an executive capacity than a legislative one.

The Merger Treaty sets out the provisions relating to the composition of the Commission. Under Article 10 (Article 157 EC), the Commission is to consist of 17 members, 'chosen on the grounds of their general competence and whose independence is beyond doubt'. This requirement of independence is crucial. Article 10 prohibits Commissioners from seeking or taking instructions from Member State governments, or any other body, or from undertaking any action incompatible with the duties of Commissioner. Member States undertake not to seek to influence Commissioners. Commissioners may not engage in any other occupation while in office. Article 13 (Article 160 EC) enables the Council or Commission to request the

---

14 See Article 31 SEA and Article L TEU. However, Curtin, *op. cit.*, at 27 argues that by virtue of Article M TEU, which maintains the status of the existing Community treaties, except insofar as explicitly amended, the ECJ may annul any measure passed by the European Council which breaches an existing rule of Community

law. Similarly, see Everling, *op. cit.*, note 7, at 1063
15 Curtin, *op. cit.*, note 13, at 27.
16 Article K.4.
17 Articles J.7 and K.6. This is an obligation on the Presidency and the Commission, rather than the European Council.

ECJ to retire compulsorily a Commissioner who no longer fulfils the requirements of the post, or who has engaged in serious misconduct. Otherwise, the only disciplinary power over the Commission lies with the European Parliament, which may censure the Commission *as a whole* and thereby trigger the resignation of the entire Commission.[18]

A Commissioner must be a national of an EC Member State, and the Commission must include at least one national of each Member State.[19] Currently, France, Germany, Italy, the United Kingdom and Spain each have two nationals in the Commission. Commissioners are appointed by agreement of all Member States, for a renewable term of four years.[20] Any vacancy, whether by normal replacement, death, resignation or compulsory retirement, is filled for the remainder of the Commissioner's term of office.[21] Except for compulsory retirement, a Commissioner remains in office until replaced. The Commission has a President and six Vice-Presidents, appointed, after consultation with the Commission as a whole, from amongst its members, who serve renewable two-year terms.[22]

In addition to the strict requirements of independence on the part of individual Commissioners, the Commission as an institution is required to act collegially,[23] although it acts by majority.[24] The Commission does, however, delegate certain executive functions to its officials.[25] The Commission is thus divided into 22 Directorates-General (DGs), each of which deals with a particular sector of Community activity. Each DG is headed by a Commissioner, some of whom are responsible for more than one DG. DGs are divided into Directorates and subdivided into Divisions.

The European Community constitutional structure does not consist of a rigid separation of powers into executive, legislative and judicial.[26] The Commission provides an illustration of this fact, by having functions which can be classified into all three branches. Its basic functions are set out in Article 155 EC, although this is not exhaustive of its powers. In particular, the substantive provisions of the Treaty give the Commission investigative, quasi-judicial and legislative functions.

Executive powers

The Commission is in charge of the administration of Community policies, other than those which are administered by Member States on behalf of the Community. In particular, the Commission oversees the Customs Union and the Common Agricultural Policy. However, it is more visible to most people as the supervisor of Member State administration of Community policies. It is obliged, under Article 155, to 'ensure that the provisions of this Treaty and the measures taken by the institutions pursuant thereto are applied', and has

---

[18] Article 144 EC. This motion can only be passed by a two-thirds majority. As a result, although this motion has been attempted, it has never succeeded: see Freestone and Davidson, *The Institutional Framework of the European Communities* (1988), at 59.

[19] Article 10, Merger Treaty.

[20] Article 11, Merger Treaty.

[21] Article 12, Merger Treaty, which also provides that the Council may decide, unanimously, that a vacancy need not be filled.

[22] Article 14, Merger Treaty. However, the Council, acting unanimously, may amend the provisions relating to Vice-Presidents.

[23] This arises in part from the Commission's own rules of procedure, and in part from the ECJ interpreting Article 17, Merger Treaty as requiring collegiality through its requirement of decisions being taken by majority vote at meetings of the Commission rather than by individual Commissioners: see Toth, *The Oxford Encyclopaedia of European Community Law*, vol. 1 'Institutional Law' (1991), at 67.

[24] Article 17, Merger Treaty.

[25] See Toth, *op. cit.*, note 23, at 67–8.

[26] Lenearts, *op. cit.*, note 3.

therefore been described as the 'guardian of the treaties',[27] because of its powers to investigate and prosecute Member States' breaches of their obligations under Community law.[28] It is also responsible for drafting and implementing the Community budget[29] and for administering its four special funds:

- the European Social Fund,
- the European Development Fund,
- the European Agricultural Guidance and Guarantee Fund,
- the European Regional Development fund.[30]

Legislative powers

In the Community legislative processes, the main power of the Commission is that of proposal or initiative.[31] This power is particularly significant under the SEA, in matters of harmonising legislation leading to the establishment of the Single Market.[32] Many provisions of the EC Treaty which provide legislative competence require a proposal from the Commission, or make Commission-initiated legislation easier to pass than Council-initiated legislation. This is particularly the case in the harmonisation provisions, Articles 100 and 100A, which require a Commission proposal. Article 149(3) allows the Commission also to alter or withdraw its proposal if the Council has not yet acted.

The Commission does have some powers to enact legislation on its own. Primarily, this is in the area of delegated legislation, as allowed for by Article 155's provision for Council-delegated implementation powers, which is often used in agricultural matters. For example, the Council will pass a framework regulation, leaving to the Commission the task of setting prices on a weekly or monthly basis, through regulations or decisions. The Commission must act within the limits of the authority delegated to it by the Council, however.[33] While the Commission is often given quite wide discretion to enact implementing legislation, the Council has developed the practice of setting up committees of national experts to oversee the Commission's activities in this field.[34] The practice, concerning which the treaties were originally silent, is now recognised in the SEA-revised Article 145, which gives the Council the power to impose requirements on the Commission's implementing powers. The first legal act adopted under the SEA was the 'Comitology' decision, which sets out the ground rules for the use of these procedures.[35] There are three categories of committees: advisory, management, and regulatory. Advisory committees issue opinions

27 Toth, *op. cit.*, note 23, at 70–1.

28 This function is discussed in detail in Chapter 8.

29 Discussed in detail below.

30 See Toth, *op. cit.*, note 23, at 71.

31 Toth, *op. cit.*, note 23, at 72–3; Lenaerts, *op. cit.*, note 11, at 16 and 28.

32 For a critical view of this extended competence, see Edwards, 'The Impact of the Single Act on the Institutions' (1987) 24 CML Rev 19, at 26–7. A more positive view is taken by Bieber, 'Legislative Procedure for the Establishment of the Single Market' (1988) 25 CML Rev 711.

33 See Case 25/70, *EVGF* v *Koster* [1970] ECR 1161, which also approved the management committee system,

and Case 291/86 *Central-Import Munster* v *HZA Munster* [1988] ECR 3679.

34 This practice goes back to 1962, see Freestone and Davidson, *op. cit.*, note 18, at 113. Such Committees are mostly used for agriculture, but also for other areas of policy-making, such as regional development: *op. cit.* at 114. Lenearts, *op. cit.*, note 11, at 31, argues that the committee system can undermine the separation of legislative and executive power.

35 Decision 87/373/EEC. See Bradley, 'Comitology and the Law: Through a Glass, Darkly' (1992) 29 CML Rev 693, at 695.

which are not binding, although the Commission is obliged to take account of the committee's opinion.[36] The most common type of supervisory committee is the management committee,[37] which has the power to adopt, by qualified majority, measures which the Council may adopt, substituting them for the Commission's proposed implementing measures.[38] However, if the committee fails to adopt an opinion, the Commission measure stands. Regulatory committees are used mostly in harmonisation fields. Their powers are much stronger – if a regulatory committee fails to adopt an opinion on Commission measures, the result is referral to the Council for adoption of the measures. Only if the Council fails to act can the Commission measures stand as proposed. There are limits to the use of committees, however. In *Commission v Council*, the Court held that the rules in the Comitology decision were binding on the Council, and that the Council could only use that decision as a justification, or a similar decision subject to the rules in Article 190 EC which require the statement of a legal basis.[39] The committees are less intrusive in practice than the structure may lead one to believe, in that they very rarely issue unfavourable opinions.[40] However, it could be argued that the very presence of these committees exerts a chilling effect on the Commission, causing it to adopt conservative implementing measures in order to secure the favour of the committees.

The Commission is also active in adopting soft law, in other words, non-binding legislative acts such as recommendations or opinions,[41] which Article 155 gives it the power to do, 'if [the Treaty] expressly so provides or if the Commission considers it necessary'. These acts serve mostly advisory or consultative functions.[42]

Under the ECSC Treaty, unlike the EC and Euratom treaties, the Commission has law-making power as the rule, rather than the exception. It may adopt acts which are binding on Member States and affect undertakings and individuals.[43] Only in some cases is the Commission obliged to obtain the Council's approval.[44]

Judicial and quasi-judicial powers

The Commission investigates and issues binding decisions in competition matters under Articles 85 and 86 EC and the Merger Control Regulation.[45] It also issues regulations on anti-dumping proceedings. These can be seen as legislative or as quasi-judicial acts.[46]

The Council of Ministers

The Council of Ministers is comprised of national ministers from each of the Member States. Unlike most legislative bodies, its membership changes. It remains the Council of Ministers,

36 *Ibid.*, at 705.

37 These committees have their origin in Article 43(1) EC, on agricultural policy.

38 Toth, *op. cit.*, note 23, at 74.

39 Case 16/88, [1989] ECR 3457. Bradley, *op. cit.*, note 35, at 716–7, argues that the Comitology decision is not actually in conformity with the requirements of Article 145, in that it does not, *in itself*, impose requirements on the Commission, and is therefore not specific, as required by the ECJ in the above case.

40 Bradley, *ibid.*, at 721.

41 However, such acts may be used as guides in order to interpret national law as being in conformity with Community law, see Chapter 5.

42 Toth, *op. cit.*, note 23, at 71.

43 Article 14 ECSC.

44 For example, Article 58 ECSC, measures to deal with crisis resulting from decline in demand.

45 See Chapter 13.

46 See Chapter 7 for a discussion of *locus standi* to review of Commission quasi-judicial decisions.

and it will always have the same number of members as the number of Member States. However, the minister who attends the Council will depend on the issue under discussion. When the Council deals with agricultural issues, it is the national agriculture ministers who meet and vote on proposed legislation; when Economic and Monetary Union is discussed, it is the finance ministers who attend; when social policy is discussed, it is the national social affairs or employment ministers who attend.[47] However, the identity of the Council as an *institution* remains the same. As a result of the changing membership, the Council is essentially a part-time institution, although it is assisted by the Committee of Permanent Representatives, which supplies an element of continuity. Despite the fluidity of the Council, it has been and remains the most powerful of the Community institutions, and ensures the respect for Member State interests in the legislative processes. It nonetheless acts as a Community institution rather than as an intergovernmental body such as European Political Co-operation.

Article 146 EC provides that each Member State government shall delegate to the Council one of its members. Presidency of the Council is held by each Member State for a six-month period, by a rotation in absolute alphabetical order.[48] Meetings of the Council are convened by its President, either on its own initiative or at request of another member of the Council.[49] The Council's decision-making is done in closed meeting, and is therefore not subject to any form of scrutiny.[50] The result is that the ministers often engage in 'horse-trading', agreeing to support a measure in the interest of other Member States in exchange for reciprocal support for measures which they consider to be crucial for their interests.[51]

Council meetings are divided into two agenda. Agenda A items are those that are capable of being passed without discussion, and Agenda B contains the controversial items. This determination is only provisional. Agenda A items which prove to be problematic may be transferred to Agenda B.[52] Council Rules of Procedure provide for the possibility of a written vote in urgent cases, but only if all members agree.[53]

Under the EC Treaty, Article 145, the Council is responsible for the co-ordination of economic policies, has the power to take decisions and confers implementation powers on the Commission. Therefore, the Council is the main legislative body, although this has been mitigated somewhat by the co-decision procedure introduced under the TEU, which gives the European Parliament equal decision-making powers in certain fields. The EC Treaty has provided for three different forms of Council voting: simple majority, qualified majority, and unanimity. In practice, however, the overwhelming majority of decisions have been taken by unanimity.

Simple majority voting, which is used relatively rarely although being foreseen by Article 148(1) as the norm, means a majority of Member States. Qualified majority voting gives a

---

[47] The General Affairs Council is attended by the foreign ministers of the Member States: see Toth, *op. cit.*, note 23, at 135.
[48] This means an order based on the names of the States in their own languages, see Freestone and Davidson, *op. cit.*, note 18, at 67. Article 146 actually provides for two cycles of presidency, one beginning with Belgium and one with Denmark, the second rotation reversing the order of each pair of States, i.e. the first ends with Portugal then the UK, the second with the UK then Portugal. The second rotation was introduced in the Act of Accession of Spain and Portugal.

[49] Article 147 EC.
[50] However, in practice, the Commission is normally invited to attend, see Article 3 of the Council's Rules of Procedure.
[51] Freestone and Davidson, *op. cit.*, note 18, at 102–4. The Council is not obliged to produce official records of its votes.
[52] See Toth, *op. cit.*, note 23, at 136–7.
[53] Unanimous agreement to a written vote is a strict requirement: Case 68/86, *United Kingdom* v *Council* [1988] ECR 855.

'weight' to each Member State's vote. Seventy-six votes in total are distributed by Article 148(2) as follows:

Belgium	5
Denmark	3
Germany	10
Greece	5
Spain	8
France	10
Ireland	3
Italy	10
Luxembourg	2
The Netherlands	5
Portugal	5
United Kingdom	10

To create a qualified majority under this system of weighted votes, a total of 54 votes are needed. If the measure is based on a Commission proposal, any total of 54 is adequate, although this would require at least seven Member States' votes. If the measure originates from the Council itself, the 54 votes must come from at least eight States. This system protects the smaller Member States from being consistently outvoted by the larger ones.

Unanimity is required for many measures under the Treaty, including most harmonisation measures.[54] For example, the adoption, in May 1993, of the common position on the Directive on maximum working hours was opposed by the United Kingdom government. The stated legal basis of the Directive was Article 118a, which allows for the adoption of measures relating to health and safety of workers by qualified majority, following the co-operation procedure. The United Kingdom argued that the Directive could not be adequately justified as the regulation of health and safety, but rather as the harmonisation of social conditions, which could only be justified under Articles 100 and 235, which both require unanimity, and threatened to challenge the directive before the ECJ. Abstentions, however, do not prevent the adoption of unanimous measures.[55]

In practice, for most of the history of the EC, unanimous voting has been the rule in the Council. While unanimity was foreseen for the transitional period, Member States, particularly France, were reluctant to move to majority and qualified majority voting. As a result of a six-month campaign of non-participation by France in 1965, the Luxembourg Accords were passed. The Accords essentially record the agreement of the Member States on the issue of voting. The agreement grants special status to measures which a Member State considers involve its 'very important interests', and requires that the Council attempt to reach a unanimously accepted solution. Nonetheless, the Accords are problematic in two respects. One is that the text of the Accords is ambiguous – it records that there was a divergence of views amongst the six Member States as to the consequences of a failure to reach a mutually acceptable solution, although stating the opinion of France that discussion must continue until unanimous agreement is reached. A further ambiguity lies in the lack of an objective

---

[54] However, only a qualified majority is required for harmonisation to achieve the objectives of the Single Market, Article 100a EC, which *does* provide for greater participation of the European Parliament (see below, the co-operation procedure).
[55] Article 148(3) EC.

definition of 'very important interests'. One indication that there may be some objective element to this concept is the failure of the Council to accept the invocation of the Accords by the United Kingdom in 1982, on the basis that the measure which was sought to be blocked, farm price increases, was not the measure which involved the very important interests of the United Kingdom but another linked issue, the national contributions to the Community budget.[56]

The main problem with the Luxembourg Accords is their status. They do not fall into any category of legislative act under the Treaty, nor can they be seen as constituting an amendment to the Treaty, as they do not follow the required formalities. At most, due to the fact that Member States, including new accessions, consider themselves bound by the provisions of the Accords, they can be seen as equivalent to constitutional conventions. The status of the Accords was put into issue particularly with the adoption of the SEA, which introduced much more majority voting. Possibly, this could be seen as an implied repeal of the Accords. However, the practice of unanimity has not been substantially eroded. The significance of the introduction of more majority voting, particularly on harmonisation measures to achieve the Single Market, may be only in that it discourages Member States from abusing the blocking of measures in Council, because of the threatened use of the vote.[57]

The Council has no explicit supervision powers, but Article 152 EC allows it to request the Commission to initiate studies and to submit to it any appropriate proposals. It also fixes the remuneration of the Commissioners, Judges, Advocates General and Registrar of the ECJ,[58] and has the power to appoint the members of the Court of Auditors[59] and the Economic and Social Committee.[60] It also has the power to amend the statute of the ECJ and approve its Rules of Procedure,[61] and to establish the Court of First Instance.[62]

The Committee of Permanent Representatives (COREPER)

The legal basis for the existence of COREPER is found in Article 4 of the Merger Treaty, which provides that: 'A committee consisting of the Permanent Representatives of the Member States shall be responsible for preparing the work of the Council and for carrying out the tasks assigned to it by the Council'. However, a similar committee had existed since 1958, seven years before the Merger Treaty.[63] The members of COREPER are civil servants with ambassadorial rank. In carrying out its tasks, it is assisted by numerous working parties and committees. The Commission is normally represented at meetings of COREPER and its working parties/committees. These bodies are chaired by a representative of the Member State who holds the Community Presidency.[64] COREPER is divided into two bodies, one which discusses technical matters (COREPER I, composed of Deputy Permanent Representatives) and one which deals with more political issues (COREPER II, composed of the Permanent Representatives themselves).[65]

[56] Freestone and Davidson, *op. cit.*, note 18, at 69.
[57] Weiler, 'The Transformation of Europe' (1990) 100 Yale LJ 2403, at 2461–3.
[58] Article 6 Merger Treaty. It may also increase the number of Commissioners (Article 10 Merger Treaty), or Judges (Article 165 EC) and Advocates-General (Article 166 EC).
[59] Article 206.
[60] Article 194.
[61] Article 188 EC.
[62] Article 168A EC.
[63] Toth, *op. cit.*, note 23, at 76. It has been based on the Council's Rules of Procedure.
[64] *Ibid.*
[65] *Ibid.*

COREPER provides an element of continuity to the activities of the Council. It does all the preparatory work for Council meetings, by reviewing Commission proposals, and deciding whether it will be placed on Agenda A or Agenda B. This activity can be seen as a process of liaison between the Commission and the Council. While the need for continuity and permanence in Council working practice is undeniable, COREPER can be seen as an interference with the institutional balance intended by the original treaties, in that the power to set the Council agenda is in the hands of Member State nominees who are not subject to the same duties of loyalty to the EC as the Commission. Since it is a liaison, not only between the Commission and the Council, but also between the Member States and the Community institutions, it is not entirely a *Community* organ, and gives Member States greater influence over Community legislation than was originally intended.

The European Parliament

The European Parliament (EP), originally called the Assembly,[66] is the only institution whose members are elected by the people of the Community. Elections, which now take place every five years, began only in 1979,[67] before which its members were nominated by the Member States. As described above, the Council is the true legislature of the EC. As a result, the EP has much less extensive powers than national parliaments have. However, in the SEA and the TEU, it has been given greater powers to influence the content of legislation. These are its advisory powers. It also has a range of supervisory powers, which enable it to oversee the workings of the Commission and the Council.

There are currently 518 Members of the European Parliament (MEPs). National representation ranges from six (Luxembourg) to 81 (France, Germany, and the United Kingdom).[68] Article 138(3) EC provides that the elections should be governed by a uniform procedure, to be drawn up by the EP, and adopted by the Council, acting unanimously. The Council has been unable to adopt this code, largely due to the United Kingdom government's opposition to the use of proportional representation voting procedures, variants of which are used everywhere else in the Community.[69] MEPs are organised into transnational party groupings, but their work is mainly done in standing committees, which largely shadow the Commission's Directorates-General in terms of subject-matter. The EP's rules also provide for the election of a President and 12 Vice-Presidents from amongst its members, who organise the business of the EP.[70]

The issue of the seat of the EP has been a source of endless controversy within the EC. Article 216 requires the Member States to determine the seat of the institutions by common accord. They have been no more able to agree on this than on a common electoral system for the EP. It is evidence of the relative weakness of the EP within the institutional framework that it has been the main victim of this Member State wrangling, and has been unable to persuade the Member States to come to a final decision; this, despite the administrative and

---

[66] The SEA replaced 'Assembly' with 'European Parliament' in all the provisions which it amended. It did not, however, explicitly amend Article 4, except, perhaps, by implication of Article 3(1) SEA's statement that the institutions shall be designated as set out 'henceforth' – see Barav (ed.), *op. cit.*, note 2. The Assembly has termed itself the 'European Parliament' since 1962, see Freestone and Davidson, *op. cit.*, note 18, at 71.

[67] Council Decision 76/787, OJ 1976 L278/1, with annexed Act on direct elections.
[68] Article 138 EC.
[69] Freestone and Davidson, *op. cit.*, note 18, at 72.
[70] *Ibid.*, at 73.

time costs of the peripatetic nature of the EP as it exists now. The provisional arrangements made in 1958 still stand, confirmed by a Decision of 1965, which mean that the EP is based in Strasbourg, Brussels and Luxembourg, with its general secretariat located in Luxembourg. EP committees meet in Brussels, its plenary sessions are held in Strasbourg, and its secretariat and some part-sessions are in Luxembourg. The EP has called for a permanent determination on several occasions, but without any satisfactory response. The French government has protested whenever the EP has met outside Strasbourg, and Luxembourg took the EP to the ECJ over an EP resolution to hold all its plenaries in Strasbourg and to move its secretariat to Brussels.[71] The Court found that the EP had the right to determine its place of work insofar as not covered by the 1965 Decision. Luxembourg could not, therefore, complain about the loss of the plenaries, or the movement of *some* of the secretariat. However, those secretariat bodies such as the EP Bureau, which were explicitly placed in Luxembourg by the decision, could not be moved unilaterally by the EP, as the decision on the seat of the institutions is reserved to the Member States by Article 216 EC. Luxembourg challenged attempts at consolidation by the EP in a 1989 case,[72] with somewhat greater success, in that the proposed moves by the EP related to its General Secretariat, which was specifically located in Luxembourg in the 1965 Decision. France has also brought its concerns before the ECJ, in *France* v *European Parliament*,[73] when the EP passed a resolution calling for suitable facilities for plenary sessions to be constructed in Brussels. The Court again found in favour of the EP, stating that the provisional decision on the seat of institutions did not prohibit the holding of part-sessions away from Strasbourg, and that the Court was satisfied that the facilities were to be used for special or additional sessions only. The Court, in both these cases, has confirmed the institutional independence of the EP by interpreting the Member State's decision on the location of the institutions strictly. The EP is allowed the freedom to determine its places of work insofar as it does not breach the explicit terms of the decision. As a result, the EP could choose to have sessions on a rotating basis in each of the Member States, although this is unlikely as it appears that the intention of the EP is to consolidate its work in Brussels as much as possible.[74]

The EP's powers in relation to legislation take three forms. It may have the right to be consulted, the right to co-operate with the Council, or a right of co-decision with the Council. Some legislation can be passed without any involvement by the EP, but this is increasingly rare, particularly since many of the recent Community measures relate, directly or indirectly, to the harmonisation of laws of Member States, which has always required the opinion of the EP. Although only under the co-decision procedure does the EP share equal legislative powers with the Council, the right to participate in the legislative process is a prerogative of the EP, and an essential procedural requirement for the validity of Community legislation whose legal basis provides for such participation.[75] In particular, the Council may not choose the legal basis of a legislative measure so as to avoid or reduce the participation of the EP.[76]

---

71 Case 230/81, *Luxembourg* v *European Parliament*, [1983] ECR 255.
72 Joined Cases 213/88 and 39/89, *Luxembourg* v *European Parliament*, judgment of 28 November 1991.
73 Joined Cases 358/85 and 51/86, [1990] 1 CMLR 309.
74 The issue of the seat of the Parliament is discussed in greater detail in Freestone, 'Article 216' in Barav (ed.), *op. cit.*, note 2.

75 See Chapter 7.
76 Case 70/88, *Parliament* v *Council* [1990] ECR I-2041. A general discussion of the issue of legal basis and institutional balance can be found in Bieber, *op. cit.*, note 32, at 713–6.

Table 2.1 sets out the three possibilities for participation by the EP in the legislative process. Only in the co-decision process under the TEU can failure by the EP to adopt an act result in the measure's defeat. Under the co-operation procedure, the Council can always override the EP by acting unanimously. Although the use of conciliation is only *required* under co-decision, a conciliation procedure has been in existence since 1975.[77] The co-decision procedure is not called by that name in the TEU, which uses 'the procedure referred to in Article 189b'. However, earlier drafts of the TEU did use 'co-decision', and since under this procedure a measure cannot be adopted if it is not approved by both the Council and the EP, 'co-decision' as a term seems both convenient and accurate.

Under Articles 237 (on admission of new Member States) and 238 (conclusion of association agreements with non-Member States), as amended by the SEA, there also exists another category of co-decision, where the Council obtains the assent of the EP.

One criticism which can be made of all of the procedures in which the EP is involved, is the potential for extensive delay. Even where it only has the right to be consulted, because its opinion is essential for the validity of a measure, it has been suggested that the EP could engage in delaying tactics, by sending the proposed opinion back and forth between committee and plenary.[78] In the other two procedures, time limits are set. There remain, nonetheless, two problems. The first is that no time limit is set on the EP providing its opinion, or on the Council reaching the common position.[79] The second problem is that, particularly under the co-decision procedure, the aggregate of the time allowances for the various stages of the legislative process could lead to excessive delay and legislative backlog. However, it is undeniable that even the co-operation procedure gives the EP a more significant role. It has more than one opportunity to influence the content of the legislation, and can engage in more of a dialogue with the Council, rather than operating on the fringes of the process.[80] With such power naturally comes responsibility. The EP now must bear some of the blame for the cumbersome nature of Community legislative processes. It also must use its delaying tactics, whether controlled by explicit time limits or not, with care. The EP has choices as to whether or not it compromises with the Council and Commission. If it does not, under the co-decision procedure no act is adopted. A total legislative paralysis could be the result, if the EP and the Council choose to stand by their strict positions. Even under the co-operation procedure, the failure of the EP to accept the common position slows down the adoption of an act for up to four months. A consistent practice of unnecessary delaying tactics could undermine the reputation of the EP after a long period of establishing itself as a credible legislative body. The EP has, however, complained of the actions of the Council under the co-operation procedure. It has accused the Council of failure to inform fully of the reasons why it has reached a common position, which creates difficulties for the EP when deciding whether or not to accept the common position.[81]

The EP, as the only elected institution of the EC, has been the focus of much of the debate over the so-called 'democratic deficit'. The debate emerged as the Community began exercising more extensive legislative powers. The origin of the argument is the idea that the

---

[77] OJ 1975, C89/1. This applies to general acts which have financial implications.
[78] Freestone and Davidson, *op. cit.*, note 18, at 77–8.
[79] On the lack of constraint on the Council with respect to the common position, see Edward, *op. cit.*, note 32, at 24.

[80] *Ibid.* at 25.
[81] Bradley, 'Legal Developments in the European Parliament' (1990) 9 YEL 235, at 243; Bradley, 'Legal Developments in the European Parliament' (1991) 10 YEL 367, at 379.

Table 2.1: Consultation, Co-operation and Co-decision compared

Event	Consultation (EC treaty, various articles)	Co-operation Procedure (Art. 149(2) SEA, replaced by Art. 189c TEU)	Co-decision Procedure (Art. 189b TEU)
Commission proposal	yes	yes – sent to Council	yes – sent simultaneously to Council and EP
Opinion of EP (note that opinion of Economic and Social Committee or Committee of the Regions may also be necessary)	yes	yes	yes
Common position (CP) of EP and Council	no – Council can adopt measure by qualified majority or unanimously, depending on legal basis of measure; Council must act unanimously if amending Commission proposal	yes – Council adopts CP by qualified majority; Council must act unanimously if amending Commission proposal	yes – Council adopts CP by qualified majority; Council must act unanimously if amending Commission proposal
EP's action, within three months*	N/A	(a) approves CP, or (b) does nothing, Council may adopt measure in accordance with CP (c) amends by absolute majority, returns to Commission (d) rejects by absolute majority, Council may adopt in accordance with CP by unanimity within **three months***	(a) approves CP, or (b) does nothing, Council may adopt measure in accordance with CP (c) amends by absolute majority, returns to Commission (for opinion) and Council (d) rejects by absolute majority, Council may refer to Conciliation Committee; if EP confirms rejection, measure not adopted; EP may amend at this stage (time limit automatically extended by **two months** in this event)
Subsequent Commission and Council action	N/A	Commission, within **one month**, re-examines proposal; it then forwards re-examined proposal and EP amendments to Council, which may adopt measure within **three months***: (a) by qualified majority if in accordance with re-examined proposal; but (b) may adopt EP's amendments not accepted by Commission only by unanimity; or (c) by unanimity if amending re-examined position, even if going back to CP. If no action by Council, Commission proposal deemed NOT adopted	Within **three months***, Council may adopt measure by approving EP amendments by qualified majority, but must be unanimous on EP amendments to which Commission has given a negative opinion; if no Council approval, Conciliation Committee is convened
Conciliation Committee's action (Committee convened by Presidents of EP and Council, equal membership from both institutions; Commission participates with a view to reconciliation) and subsequent EP and Council action	N/A	N/A	(a) within **six weeks***, approves a joint text, which must be approved by qualified majority of Council and absolute majority of EP, within **six weeks***; if not adopted by both institutions, measure not adopted (b) does not approve a joint text within **six weeks***, measure NOT adopted unless within **six weeks***, Council confirms CP by qualified majority (possibly with EP amendments), and within a further **six weeks***, EP does NOT reject by absolute majority

* These periods may be extended by one month (co-operation, or where period is three months, co-decision) or two weeks (where period is six weeks, co-decision), by common accord between the Council and the EP.

lack of transparency in the decision-making processes by which Community legislation is enacted, and the lack of control over the unelected institutions were undemocratic and therefore undesirable.[82] Often it is thought that the fact that the EP is directly elected by the peoples of Europe is sufficient to vest in it the legitimacy that it is felt that Community legislative processes lack. This argument has been powerful, and has been influential in the expansion of the EP's legislative powers over the last decade. Weiler, however, is sceptical about the search for democratic legitimacy solely in the EP. He notes that integration inevitably causes the loss of at least some national democratic control, but that simply enhancing the power of the EP will not ensure legitimacy.[83] He argues that the Luxembourg Accords can be seen as a legitimating instrument, by ensuring that national polities are protected from arbitrary legislative action by the EC.[84] This, however, ignores the fact that Council decision-making is non-public, and that there is no way of requiring individual members of the Council to account to the citizens of the Member States which they represent over how they voted and why. The 'packages' of measures arranged by the Commission and COREPER may lead to ministers voting for measures which they have opposed, in order to secure the passage of measures which they support. Until the EP enjoys the support and loyalty from citizens which they accord to their national legislatures, it may not be the repository of legitimacy within the EC, but it is doubtful whether the Council of Ministers could ever play that role. Being the defender of national interest is not the same as being the defender of legitimacy.

The EP exercises supervision over the Commission in a number of ways. The most extreme is the power to censure the Commission, under Article 144 EC, which will result in the dismissal of the entire Commission. Such a motion must be carried by a two-thirds majority of MEPs. While motions of censure have been proposed before the EP, none has ever been carried. A motion of censure has only been considered once since the EP has been directly elected, proposed in 1990 by Jean-Marie Le Pen.[85]

The Commission also reports on an annual basis to the EP, as required by Article 143 EC. The EP discusses the annual general report of the Commission in open session. The Commission and the President of the Council also report to the EP during the year, such reports being debated by the EP.[86] Article 140 gives the Council and Commission the right to be heard before the EP, and imposes on the Commission an obligation to reply to questions put to it by the EP. The Council has agreed to answer questions despite the fact that it is not obliged to do so, but has not been as forthcoming as the Commission in its replies. Questions from MEPs are put during a formal question time.

The EP also has a role as a watchdog for the interest of individuals within the Community. Individual citizens of the EC have the right to petition the EP, a power which the EP has been formally exercising since 1989 and which is established as a right of European Union citizenship under Articles 8d and 138d TEU.[87] Of indirect interest to individuals, pressure groups have developed a system of lobbying the EP which has proved particularly effective

---

82 The main points of this argument are set out in Weiler, *op. cit.*, note 57, at 2466. A criticism of the EP's pre-SEA status is provided by Lodge, 'The European Parliament – from 'Assembly' to Co-legislature: Changing the Institutional Dynamics' in Lodge (ed.), *The European Community and the Challenge of the Future* (1989), at 58.

83 Weiler, *op. cit.*, at 2472.
84 *Ibid.*, at 2473.
85 Bradley (1991), *op. cit.*, note 81, at 381. The vote was 16 in favour of censure, 243 against and 5 abstentions.
86 Freestone and Davidson, *op. cit.*, note 18, at 80.
87 Bradley (1990), *op. cit.*, note 81, at 251.

for environmental groups, for example.[88] The EP has also undertaken studies on controversial issues, some of which are outside the normal range of activities of the EC, such as racism and xenophobia.[89]

The Economic and Social Committee

The Economic and Social Committee is an organ of the EC but is involved in the Community decision-making processes in many fields. It is a purely advisory body, having no role other than providing opinions on proposed legislation. It is established by Article 193 EC, which provides that it shall consist of representatives of various economic and social activity, including representatives of the general public. The drafting of Article 193, and in particular the provision that the Committee shall include members of the general public, tends to indicate that the Committee is intended to be a microcosm of public opinion rather than a committee of experts, such as are frequently constituted under international human rights treaties. Article 194 fixes the number of members of the Committee to be nominated by the Council, acting unanimously, from each Member State.[90] Members of the Committee act in their personal capacities, and, like Commissioners, are not to be bound by mandatory instructions and are to act 'in the general interest of the Community'.[91] Meetings of the Committee are convened by its chairman, at the request of the Council or Commission.[92] Article 197 EC states that the Committee shall include specialised sections for each area of activity covered by the Treaty, and in particular, agriculture and transport. The Committee may establish subcommittees, but opinions must be adopted by the Committee itself.

Article 198 EC reiterates that consultation of the Committee is mandatory if required by any article of the Treaty, but that the Committee may also be consulted in other circumstances, and the TEU confirms the power, exercised by the Committee since 1974,[93] to issue opinions on its own initiative. It would therefore appear that the status of the Committee is the same as that of the EP under Treaty articles which require only consultation of the EP. To a certain extent this is true, and the absence of a Committee opinion where one is required may likewise constitute the infringement of an essential procedural requirement (Article 173 EC) which would make the resulting legislation invalid.[94] However, Article 198 allows the Council or the Commission to set a deadline of at least 10 days (extended to one month under the TEU) on the Committee, after which failure to deliver the opinion 'shall not prevent further action', which would indicate that the opinion of the Committee is of a lesser status than that of the EP.[95] The areas in which a Committee

[88] Harlow, 'A community of Interests? Making the Most of European Law' (1992) 55 MLR 331, at 342–4.
[89] Report by the Committee on Inquiry into Racism and Xenophobia, Rapporteur, Mr Glyn Ford, Brussels, European Parliament Session Documents, 1989.
[90] Article 195 provides that each Member State is to submit a list of nominees which contains twice the number of places allotted to that Member State, and that the Council shall consult the Commission on the appointments, which should 'ensure adequate representation of the various categories of economic and social activity'.
[91] The latter phrase added by amendment of Article 194 by the TEU.
[92] Article 196 EC. As amended by the TEU, the article now allows the Committee to meet on its own initiative.
[93] Freestone and Davidson, op. cit., note 18, at 85–6.
[94] The Committee has never attempted to take the Council or the Commission before the ECJ in order to invalidate legislation where its opinion has not been supplied, and the 10-day limit has not been imposed. As it is not an institution, it is not certain whether it would be granted the same rights as the EP to protect its prerogatives, or whether it would be considered a non-privileged applicant.
[95] This is corroborated by the fact that the Council sets the Committee's rules of procedure.

opinion is required include agriculture, free movement of persons, competition, environment, and health and safety.

The Committee of the Regions

The TEU, at Articles 198a through 198c, establishes a new advisory Committee equivalent in status and working practices to the Economic and Social Committee. The purpose of the Committee of the Regions is to provide opinions on issues which might have particular effect on regions of the EC. This Committee is to be composed of representatives of local and regional bodies of the Member States. Since the word 'bodies' is used rather than 'governments', members of organisations other than local authorities or regional governments could be appointed. This will depend on the national legislation implementing the TEU in each Member State. Unlike the Economic and Social Committee, the Committee of the Regions must contain an equal number of alternate members.[96]

The Committee of the Regions functions in a similar way to the Economic and Social Committee, except that it is not empowered to set up specialised sections or subcommittees. In addition to its rights of consultation and the right to initiate opinions, it has the right to be informed when the Economic and Social Committee is consulted. If it considers that significant regional interests are at stake, it may issue its own opinion. The TEU provides that the Committee of the Regions must be consulted for the following matters: education, vocational training and youth (Article 126), culture (Article 128), public health (Article 129), trans-European networks (Article 129d), and economic and social cohesion (Article 130b, 130d and 130e).

The European Council

The European Council is defined as 'the Heads of State or Government of the Member States and the President of the Commission of the European Communities' by Article 2 SEA.[97] Nonetheless, the European Council has existed for over two decades, having been established in the Paris Communiqué of 1972, as a regular series of summits of the Heads of State or Government.[98] Until the recognition of the existence of the European Council in the SEA, it was entirely outside the EC framework, although it would be possible for the Heads of State or Government to meet as the Council of Ministers. Unless it is so constituted, it would be unable to pass legislation, and in fact, it has been used more as an intergovernmental summit than as a legislative body. Documents which have been adopted by the European Council, such as the Community Charter of the Fundamental Social Rights of Workers (the Social Charter) do not have binding status in Community law. The meetings of the European Council are usually directed to an overview of EC activities and the setting of general policy objectives. The meetings are chaired by the Head of State or Government of the Member State holding the Presidency of the EC, with three meetings each year. It has, since 1981, reported to the EP annually.[99]

Although the European Council is recognised under the SEA, it is not constituted as an EC

[96] Article 198a.
[97] The European Council is assisted by the Ministers for Foreign Affairs and a Member of the Commission.
[98] Freestone and Davidson, *op. cit.*, note 18, at 56.

These meetings were previously held on an *ad hoc* basis. On the history of EC summitry, see Urwin, *op. cit.*, note 4, at 172–5.
[99] Urwin, *ibid.*, at 168.

institution. Furthermore, nowhere in any EC treaty are its powers defined. Its acts are not reviewable by the ECJ, nor, despite the annual report, is the EP entitled to influence its deliberations. Until the TEU, its functions were of a general nature, related to deciding the political direction of the Communities. Therefore, until recently, there was no reason to subject it to review. Being outside the institutional framework could be seen as a way of giving the Member States freedom to take a broad view of the Communities and their possible future direction. The European Council has therefore been able to discuss matters not covered by the Community treaties, in particular monetary policy which has been developed only recently. The European Council has also been used as a forum for the resolution of inter-State disputes which could block further legislative developments.[100] It has also been in the European Council that proposals for further integration have been discussed and negotiated. More negatively, the existence, and the importance, of the European Council could be seen as a disruption of the institutional balance and as an undermining of the supranational character of the EC.[101]

The Court of Justice

The Court of Justice of the European Communities (ECJ) shares with the Commission, Council of Ministers and the European Parliament the status of Community institution. Its functions are purely judicial, although its activities have had a profound effect on the development of Community law, particularly in the development of its constitutional aspects.[102] Its task, according to Article 164 EC, is to 'ensure that in the interpretation and application of this Treaty the law is observed'. Since 1957, it has been the single judicial organ of the Communities, although it is now assisted in this role by the Court of First Instance.

The ECJ consists of 13 judges and six Advocates General.[103] It sits in plenary session, but may form chambers of three to five judges,[104] a practice which it has used with greater frequency in recent years. Judges and Advocates General are appointed by common accord of the Member States from 'persons whose independence is beyond doubt and who possess the qualifications required for appointment to the highest judicial offices in their respective countries or who are jurisconsults of recognised competence'.[105] The 'jurisconsults' clause allows solicitors, or academic or civil service lawyers without a professional qualification, to be appointed, even where they would not be eligible in their home jurisdictions. The term of office is six years, although re-appointment is possible. Every three years, either six or seven Judges, and three Advocates General, are replaced or re-appointed. The Judges themselves elect the President of the Court, who has a renewable term of three years, and the Court appoints its Registrar. Unlike the Commission, the Court's appointment procedures as set out in the Treaty make no provision for national balance. However, in practice there is one

---

100 For example, the dispute over British contributions to the Community budget, see Urwin, *op. cit.*, note 4, at 188 and 200–3.

101 Urwin, *ibid.*, note, at 175.

102 Subsequent chapters will deal with the jurisdiction and activities of the ECJ, particularly Chapters 5 (legal effect of Community acts), 6 (general principles of law), and 7 through 10 (jurisdiction of the Court).

103 Articles 165 and 166 EC.

104 Article 165 EC. However, cases brought by a Mem-

ber State or a Community institution must be heard by the full Court. The TEU amends this to require a plenary Court when a Member State or institution is a party to a case and *requests* that the case be heard by plenary Court. Types of cases which may be heard by chambers of the Court are listed in Article 95 of the Rules of the Court. Where, in such a case, a Member State or a Community institution is involved, it may insist on a plenary hearing.

105 Article 167 EC.

Judge from each Member State, plus an extra one from one of the five largest Member States (France, Germany, Italy, Spain and the United Kingdom) on a rotating basis.[106] One Advocate General comes from each of France, Germany, Italy and the United Kingdom, the other two from the smaller States on a rotating basis.[107] Each Judge or Advocate General has a cabinet, or personal staff.[108]

Advocates General, despite not being judges, are considered also to be members of the Court. Their function is similar to that of the *commissaire du gouvernement* in the Conseil d'Etat.[109] Article 166 EC provides that the Advocates General shall assist the Court in performing its duties under Article 164. Specifically, their role is 'with complete impartiality and independence . . . to make in open court, reasoned submissions on cases brought before the Court of Justice'. This is accomplished by the delivery of opinions as to the correct interpretation of the law in each case. While the Advocate General is required to be neutral as between the applicant and defendant, he or she *is* required to come to a conclusion, not simply to give a review of the relevant law. The opinion concludes with a recommendation of how the Court should decide the case. The Advocate General will often introduce new legal approaches which, even if not adopted by the Court in that case, may indicate the direction in which Community law will proceed. The opinions of Advocates General therefore are very detailed.

Article 29 of the Court's rules provides for language use. All EC official languages, plus Irish,[110] are possible for the conduct of a case, at the option of the applicant. However, where the defendant is a Member State, or a natural or legal person having the nationality of a Member State, the language of the proceedings will be the official language of that Member State. In preliminary rulings, the language of the referring court is used. The Court may allow another language to be used for all or part of the proceedings, except on preliminary rulings. Intervening Member States may use their own official language. The Registrar of the Court arranges for translations. The working language of the Court is French, including the deliberations of the Judges. However, Judges may put questions at the hearing in any of the Court's procedural languages. Advocates General may use their own language for opinions. Judgments are issued in the language of the case, and are then translated into the other Community languages. However, because French is the language of the Court's deliberations, even the decision in the language of the case, except where that language is French, is a translation. The translation of the judgment into all of the Community official languages usually takes several months.

Article 37 of the Statute of the Court provides for a right of intervention in proceedings before the Court. Member States and Community institutions have the right to intervene in any case. Other persons must establish an interest in the result of the proceedings in order to intervene, and may not intervene if the only parties to the case are Member States or Community institutions, or in cases between Member States and any of the institutions. Intervenors may only plead in support of one of the parties to the case.

The President of the Court will appoint a Judge Rapporteur for each case. The Judge Rapporteur prepares the preliminary report for the Court's use once the pleadings have

---

106 Neville Brown, *The Court of Justice of the European Communities*, 3rd edn (1989), at 15.
107 *Ibid.*,
108 *Ibid.*, at 16 and 17–18.
109 For similarities and differences between Advocates

General and *commissaires du gouvernement*, see Nevill Brown, *ibid.*, at 53.
110 Irish has never been used as the language of the case before the ECJ: see Neville Brown, *ibid.*, at 23–4.

closed. It is on the basis of this report that the Court will decide whether a case which could be heard by a Chamber of the Court should instead be heard by a plenary Court, or if related cases should be joined.[111]

The Court issues a single judgment which is the judgment of the Court, with no separate concurring or dissenting opinions. However, the decision itself may be made on a majority vote rather than by consensus.[112] The collegiality rule has two benefits. Primarily, it gives greater authority to the judgments of the Court that they are reached without dissent, usually by consensus. Secondly, it protects individual judges from domestic political pressures, in that no single judge can be held responsible for a judgment, which means that the possibility of not being re-appointed due to taking unpopular decisions does not arise. Judgments of the Court tend to be relatively brief, and refer to little case law. They follow the French practice of giving the disposition of the judgment preceded by numerous paragraphs setting out the facts, the pleadings of the parties, and the legal reasons on which the decision is based.[113] As a collegiate judgment, it has little of the personal judicial style which the common lawyer expects, and which reached its zenith in the judgments of Lord Denning. Often it is difficult to contextualise the judgment without also reading the opinion of the Advocate General, which tends to take an historical view and to supply far more detailed reference to previous case law.

The Court of First Instance

The workload of the ECJ has inexorably increased since its establishment, as Community law itself has proliferated.[114] Article 168a, added by the SEA, gave the Council the power to create the Court of First Instance, attached to the ECJ. Suggestions for reform of the Community judicial institutions go back to the 1970s,[115] but it is not surprising that it is in the SEA, which constitutes the most extensive re-think of the Community institutions, that the impetus for change finally met with results. Article 168a requires a request from the ECJ and the consultation of the Commission and the European Parliament. The Court of First Instance was ultimately established by a decision of the Council of Ministers of 24 October 1988.[116]

The jurisdiction of the Court of First Instance lies mostly in cases which involve primarily determinations of fact rather than law. It is concerned with cases which are brought by natural or legal persons rather than Member States or Community institutions. In particular, it deals with:

- staff cases,
- actions relating to Articles 50 and 57–66 ECSC (production quotas),
- actions relating to Articles 85 and 86 EC (competition),
- damages cases related to the above.[117]

111 *Ibid.*, at 226–7. There are two types of plenary court: the Petit Plenum of nine judges and the Grand Plenum of 13 Judges.

112 Article 27, Rules of the Court.

113 Neville Brown, *op. cit.*, note 106, at 43.

114 See Weatherill and Beaumont, *EC Law* (1993), at 134.

115 da Cruz Vilaca, 'The Court of First Instance of the European Communities: A Significant Step towards the Consolidation of the European Community as a Community Governed by the Rule of Law' (1990) 9 YEL 1, at 4–7 and 15–17.

116 Decision 88/591, as amended by OJ 1989 C215/1.

117 The ECJ was reluctant to recommend the transfer of jurisdiction in all damages cases intitially, due to the close relationship with declarations of invalidity of legislation: da Cruz Vilaca, *op. cit.*, note 115, at 28. On damages claims against the Community, see Chapter 9.

Staff cases and competition cases had consumed the time of the ECJ to a great degree, meaning that cases referred from national courts were subject to significant delay.[118] However, the ECJ continues to deal with a large number of cases, almost as many as before the establishment of the Court of First Instance.[119] The Council retained the power under Article 168a EC to expand the jurisdiction of the Court of First Instance, which it did by a decision of 8 June 1993, which gave the Court the jurisdiction to hear at first instance all cases brought by natural or legal persons, with the exception of anti-dumping proceedings.[120] Appeals from decisions of the Court of First Instance are made to the ECJ on points of law only.[121] This includes lack of competence, breach of procedure and infringement of Community law.[122]

The Court of First Instance consists of 12 Judges, appointed on the same criteria as the Judges of the ECJ, but it has no Advocates General specifically appointed to it. Like the ECJ, the Court of First Instance may sit in chambers of three or five judges, or in plenary session.[123] The Court of First Instance has its own rules of procedure, which although similar to those of the ECJ differ in some ways. In particular, it is not necessary for an Advocate General to be assigned to each case before the Court, since the Court of First Instance is not expected to play the same role of judicial law-maker that the ECJ plays, and the intention is to have a more streamlined procedure.[124] Articles 17 to 19 inclusive of the Court's Rules of Procedure set out the criteria by which the decision whether or not to appoint an Advocate General shall be made, largely based on whether the case presents legal or factual complexities which make the assistance of an Advocate General desirable. The only compulsory use of an Advocate General is when the Court sits in plenary session.[125] When an Advocate General is required, one of the Judges of the Court of First Instance fills that role.[126]

The Court of First Instance, being a trial court, provides in its Rules of Procedure for the amicable settlement of proceedings. Settlement has never been prohibited in cases before the ECJ, but no mechanism for its occurrence has been established in that forum. Article 64 of the Rules of Procedure explicitly gives the Court of First Instance the power to seek amicable settlement. This is done by means of meetings between the parties before the chamber or the Judge Rapporteur, where the Judge Rapporteur will review the case and suggest a possible fair settlement.[127]

---

118 On the expanding number of cases dealt with by the ECJ, and the attendant delays, before the establishment of the Court of First Instance, see Millett, 'The New European Court of First Instance' (1989) 38 ICLQ 811, and Kennedy, 'The Essential Minimum: The Establishment of the Court of First Instance' (1989) 14 EL Rev 7. On the docket of the Court of First Instance from 1989–92, see Vesterdorf, 'The Court of First Instance of the European Communities After Two Full Years in Operation' (1992) 29 CML Rev 897, at 903–4.

119 *Ibid.*, at 904.

120 Council Decision 93/350/ECSC, EEC, Euratom, of 8 June 1993, to come into force two months after publication, including the transfer of all pending cases in that category. Anti-dumping proceedings have not been transferred to the Court of First Instance due to opposition by the Commission and France: Millett, *op. cit.*, note 118, at 820–1.

121 Article 168a EC. Appeals to the ECJ are dealt with in Articles 49–54, Statute of the ECJ and Articles 110–123, Rules of Procedure, ECJ.

122 Article 51, Statute of the ECJ.

123 Decision 88/591, Article 2(4), supplemented by Articles 10, 12 and 14 of the Rules of Procedure of the Court. By a decision of 4 October 1989, OJ 1989, C/281/2, the Court established five chambers.

124 Vesterdorf, *op. cit.*, note 118, at 900, and da Cruz Vilaca, *op. cit.*, note 115, at 38.

125 Article 17, Rules of Procedure of the Court of First Instance.

126 Article 19, Rules of Procedure of the Court of First Instance. An Advocate General is rarely appointed, see Vesterdorf, *op. cit.*, note 118, at 905.

127 Vesterdorf, *ibid.*, at 914–15.

While the Court of First Instance has to a certain extent rationalised the judicial activities of the EC, it has not achieved its original aim of reducing the workload of the ECJ. This is not due to any failure on the part of the Court of First Instance, but rather to the increase in significance of Community law within Member States. Even if the ECJ dealt only with preliminary references from national courts, its workload is likely to increase, particularly as Community social policy, which would influence the law of every worker throughout the EC, becomes increasingly important. Furthermore, as Community law expands into the fields of intellectual property and technology, there may be a case for specialised tribunals in those areas.[128]

The Court of Auditors

One example of such a specialised court, already in existence, is the Court of Auditors, which deals with issues relating to the Community budget. Although not originally an institution, it has been included in the list in Article 4 EC by an amendment in the TEU.[129] It was established in 1977, under the 1975 Treaty Amending Certain Financial Provisions, and replaced the previous Audit Board. As a specialised tribunal, as opposed to a court with a more general jurisdiction, the nature of its membership differs somewhat from that of the two Courts. Its members are appointed by the Council, acting unanimously after consulting the European Parliament, rather than by the common accord of Member States, and are to be drawn from 'among persons who belong or have belonged in their respective countries to external audit bodies or who are especially qualified for this office.'[130]

The function of the Court of Auditors is described in Article 206a EC:

> The Court of Auditors shall examine whether all revenue has been received and all expenditure incurred in a lawful and regular manner and whether the financial management has been sound.

Its functions can be described as administrative rather than judicial, despite the use of the term 'Court' in its title. Its report enables the European Parliament to give a discharge to the Commission on the budget each year. The Court performs its functions on the spot, which means that, although located in Luxembourg, its members must travel to Brussels in order to audit Commission activities, and to Member States in order to monitor Member State implementation of Community policies.[131] In particular, the Court looks for fraud, or 'irregularities' as it prefers to call such activities.[132] Such irregularities occur, in the opinion of the Court, largely because of the decentralised implementation of Community policy and the resulting inconsistency in Member State verification procedures.[133]

In addition to audit functions, it many deliver opinions, by means of special reports, at the request of any of the institutions of the Community.[134] It adopts acts by majority of its members.

---

128 Suggested by da Cruz Vilaca, *op. cit.*, note 115, at 55.

129 This may indicate that the Court of Auditors was intended to have prestige which, interestingly, is not given to the Court of First Instance. The ECJ confirmed that the Court of Auditors is not to be regarded as an institution in Case 257/83, *Williams* v *Court of Auditors* [1984] ECR 3547. For an argument that the Court of Auditors should be considered an institution, see Kok, 'The Court of Auditors of the European Communities: "The Other European Court in Luxembourg" ' (1989) 26 CML Rev 345, at 347–8.

130 Article 206(3) EC.

131 Kok, *op. cit.*, note 129, at 349.

132 *Ibid.*, at 360–1.

133 *Ibid.*, at 360–3. Article 209a TEU obliges Member States to counter fraud against the financial interests of the Community.

134 Article 206a(4) EC.

The Community budget

The budget is an area in which the question of institutional balance is clearly in issue. However, unlike the adoption of legislation, the balance is more equally placed between the Parliament and the Council. The role of the Commission in the budgetary process is less significant than in legislation, where the power of initiative is an important factor.

The Community budget, although unifying the budgets previously governed by the three Community treaties, is not, however, comprehensive.[135] It does not include the income and expenditure relating to the ECSC operating budget, the European Investment Bank, EC and Euratom borrowing and lending, European Development Bank operations, European Schools, entities set up by Community law which have separate legal personality such as the European Foundation for the Improvement of Living and Working Conditions and the Euratom Supply Agency.[136]

Prior to 1970, the EC was funded by block grants from the Member States.[137] Article 201 EC[138] required the Commission to examine possibilities for funding from the Community's own resources, and to make a proposal on that matter to the Council for adoption by unanimity after consulting the EP. The Member States were also required to adopt the new budgetary provisions by their own constitutional methods. This was accomplished by a 1970 Decision.[139] Primarily, the 'own resources' come from a percentage of VAT collected by Member States, but also from payments made under Community law, such as agricultural levies.[140] A further change to the definition of own resources was made in 1988 as a consequence of the Interinstitutional Agreement on Budgetary Discipline:[141] a financial contribution based on GNP, instead of VAT.[142]

Toth[143] identifies five major principles governing the content and structure of the Community budget, arising from the relevant Treaty provisions, and the interpretation of those provisions by the institutions:

1. *The principle of 'complete and authentic budgetisation'*[144] – Article 199 EC, which provides that 'All items of revenue and expenditure of the Community, including those relating to the European Social Fund, shall be included in estimates to be drawn up for each financial year and shall be shown in the budget'. The TEU adds reference to the Common Foreign and Security Policy and Co-operation in Justice and Home Affairs.
2. *The principle of universality* – Article 3(1) of the Financial Regulations. This means

135 Article 20, Merger Treaty, as ameneded.
136 Toth, *op. cit.*, note 23, at 82–3.
137 Set out in Article 200 EC. Since the basis of funding changed before the expansion of the EC, only the original six Member States are mentioned. Article 200 EC was finally repealed by the TEU.
138 This Article is slightly amended by the TEU, but the substance remains unchanged., It simply takes into account the fact that the EC is already funded from its own resources.
139 Council Decision of 21 April 1970 on the Replacement of Financial Contributions from Member States by the Communities' Own Resources, 70/243, OJ (Special edition) 1970 L94/19, as amended by Council Decision of 7 May 1985 on the Communities' system of Own Resources, 85/257, OJ 1985 L128/5.

140 A complete list is given in Toth, *op. cit.*, note 23, at 86.
141 On the legal status of the Agreement, see Zangl, 'The Interinstitutional Agreement on Budgetary Discipline and Improvement of the Budgetary Procedure' (1989) 26 CML Rev 675, at 678.
142 Council Decision 88/376 of 24 June 1988 on the system of the Community's own resources. On the background to the decision to introduce a GNP-based payment, see Kolte, 'The Community Budget: New Principles for Finance, Expenditure Planning and Budget Discipline' (1988) 25 CML Rev 487, at 489–93.
143 *Ibid.*, at 83–6.
144 This phrase comes from Case 34/86, *Council v Parliament* [1986] ECR 2155, at 2209.

that no item of revenue can be designated specifically for a particular item of expenditure.

3. *The principle of annuality* – Article 202 EC, which requires that a budget be authorised for only one year's expenditure. Article 203(1) provides that the Community's financial year is the calendar year. However, Article 6(2) of the Financial Regulations allows for *commitment appropriations*, which are for legal obligations implemented over more than one financial year, to be continued into the next financial year.

4. *The principle of specification* – Article 202 EC provides that 'Appropriations shall be classified under different chapters grouping items of expenditure according to their nature or purpose'.

5. *The principle of equilibrium between revenue and expenditure* – Article 199 requires that the Community budget be in balance.

The Council and the EP are, together, the Budgetary Authority. However, the Council has the final say on compulsory expenditure, and the EP on non-compulsory expenditure. As a result, the distinction between these two categories is essential to the budgetary process. Article 203 defines compulsory expenditure as 'necessarily resulting from this Treaty or from acts adopted in accordance therewith'. However, the definition has not entirely resolved the controversy, in that the EP takes a much stricter view on what constitutes an act necessarily resulting from Community law than does the Council. The EP considers that the definition in Article 203 includes only expenditure resulting from the Community's legal obligations towards third parties.[145] As a result, the EP considered that compensation to the United Kingdom because of its overcontribution to the Community's own resources, since it was the result of an agreement between the Member States rather than a Community legal act, should be classified as non-compulsory expenditure, whereas the Council had classified it as compulsory.[146] This classification is relevant only to the setting of the budget, and becomes redundant in its implementation.

The other important distinction between compulsory and non-compulsory expenditure is that non-compulsory expenditure may only be increased annually on the basis of a fixed formula applied by the Commission. Article 203(9) requires the Commission to set the maximum rate of increase based on the GNP trend within the Community, the average variation of budgets within Member States and the trend of the cost of living during the preceding financial year. The Commission must communicate the maximum rate to the other institutions by 1 May of each year. The EP may, exercising its powers of amendment, increase the maximum rate of increase by half again, if the Council has set the increase at more than half the maximum rate, as determined by the Commission.[147] If, however, the Commission, Council or EP considers that the maximum rate is too low to enable the Community to perform its activities, then the Council, acting by qualified majority, and the EP, by a majority of its members and three-fifths of the votes cast, may agree to increase it. If there is no agreement between the Council and the EP on whether or not to increase beyond the maximum rate and the margin of manoeuvre, then the budget cannot validly be passed. This was confirmed in *Council* v *Parliament*,[148] where the EP attempted to pass the Community budget for 1986, with a rate of increase of non-compulsory expenditure greater

145 Dankert, 'The Joint Declaration by the Community Institutions of 30 June 1982 on the Community Budgetary Procedure' (1983) 20 CML Rev 701, at 707.

146 *Ibid.*, at 708.

147 This is referred to as the EP's margin of manoeuvre.

148 *Op. cit.*, note 144.

than its margin of manoeuvre, without the agreement of the Council. All the institutions involved in the budget process had agreed that an increase over the maximum rate calculated by the Commission would be necessary, but the EP and the Council disagreed as to the amount of increase. The EP attempted to pass the budget without securing the agreement of the Council on the rate of increase, and the Council sought annulment of the budget before the ECJ. The court agreed that the EP could not set the rate of increase alone when exceeding its margin for manoeuvre, despite the fact that it is entitled to amend the budget on non-compulsory expenditure. As a result, it is conceivable that the budget process could be stalled indefinitely over an inability of the EP and the Council to agree a rate of increase on non-compulsory expenditure.

Article 204 provides for interim financing of the Community if the budget is not adopted in time for the beginning of the financial year. This interim funding is allocated on a monthly basis, calculated as one-twelfth of the previous year's budget, and the Council may, by qualified majority, increase that amount. However, such funding may not be more than one-twelfth of the budget in preparation. This provision for interim funding has been used when the EP has exercised its power to reject the entire draft budget, which it has done in 1979 and 1984,[149] and when the budget has not been adopted before the beginning of the relevant financial year.[150]

As set out in Table 2.2 (*see* page 36), the procedure for adopting the budget is highly complex, involving as it does different rules for compulsory expenditure (CE) and non-compulsory expenditure (NCE). A further distinction is that between modifications and amendments. Amendments have the legal effect of changing the provisions of the draft budget. Modifications are merely proposals, which must be adopted by both institutions of the Budgetary Authority in order to effect change to the draft budget.

Implementation of the Budget is the responsibility of the Commission, acting in accordance with the Financial Regulations. It may also be subject to a management committee.[151] In addition, Articles 18 and 19 of the Financial Regulations require that each institution appoint a financial controller to monitor revenue and expenditure. Each year, under Article 205a EC, the Commission submits to the Council and the EP the previous year's accounts and a financial statement. The Court of Auditors audits all the Community accounts, and assists the Council and the EP in monitoring implementation of the budget. The Council and EP then examine the report of the Court of Auditors, and related documentation, and the EP, upon recommendation made by qualified majority of the Council, gives a discharge to the Commission in respect of the budget.[152]

In recent years, the issue of budget discipline has become a concern of the Member States. The Interinstitutional Agreement of 1988 was directed to the achievement of this goal, the Member States being of the opinion that Community expenditure was growing at an unacceptable rate.[153] The Commission accepted the budgetary discipline provisions in return for the amendment to the definition of own resources.[154] The Agreement imposes discipline by dividing non-compulsory expenditure into six categories and imposing absolute ceilings on

149 Freestone and Davidson, *op. cit.*, note 18, at 124.
150 Toth, *op. cit.*, note 23, at 97.
151 As discussed above under 'Commission'.
152 Article 206b EC, now Article 206(1), as amended by TEU.
153 Zangl, *op. cit.*, note 141, at 675. See also Kolte, *op. cit.*, note 142.
154 Zangl, *op. cit.*

Table 2.2   Adopting the Community Budget (Article 203 EC)

Event	Institution	Date/Delay	Action
Maximum rate of increase fixed	Commission	1 May	Consultation with Economic Policy Committee, then fixing of rate with reference to criteria in Article 203(9); must communicate maximum rate to all institutions
Expense estimates	All institutions	1 July	Submission of estimates to Commission
Preliminary Draft Budget	Commission	1 September (however, often submitted by 15 June)[155]	Consolidation of institutional estimates, with opinion; preliminary draft budget must contain estimate of revenue and expenditure
Draft Budget	Council	5 October	Adopted by qualified majority; must consult Commission, and where departing from preliminary draft budget, other institutions concerned
Amendment or Modification to draft budget (Budget may be adopted at this stage)	Parliament	45 days	– If approves draft budget OR takes no action, budget adopted – May amend NCE by majority of MEPs – May propose modifications to CE by absolute majority of votes cast

Finalising CE and modification of amendments to NCE	Council	15 days	– If no modification to EP amendments, and if EP modifications accepted, Budget adopted
			– With respect to CE:
			  • If modification does not increase total expenditure of an institution, modification accepted unless vote by qualified majority to reject
			  • If modification increases total expenditure of an institution, modification rejected unless vote by qualified majority to accept
			  • If rejecting a modification, may use Draft Budget figure or fix another amount
			– With respect to NCE:
			  • May propose modifications to EP amendments by qualified majority

Finalising NCE or rejection of entire draft budget	Parliament	15 days	– Is notified of action taken on its proposed modifications – If no action, budget adopted – May amend or reject Council modifications to its amendments by a majority of MEPs and three-fifths of votes cast – May reject entire draft budget and ask for a new draft, by a majority of MEPs and two-thirds of votes cast
Declaration of Adoption	President of Parliament	When budget adopted	This is the event that gives the Budget legal effect[156]

[155] Toth, *op. cit.*, note 23 at 119.   [156] *Council v Parliament, op. cit.*, note 144.

each, which must be observed at each stage of budgetary procedure.[157] The effect is to prevent money being moved around from one sector to another, and from one year to another. Budget discipline has now been elevated to a treaty principle by Article 201a TEU:

> With a view to maintaining budgetary discipline, the Commission shall not make any proposal for a Community act, or alter its proposals, or adopt any implementing measure which is likely to have appreciable implications for the budget without providing the assurance that that proposal or that measure is capable of being financed within the limit of the Community's own resources arising under the provisions laid down by the Council pursuant to Article 201.

European Central Bank[158]

Monetary policy is not a new concern within Europe. The TEU's provisions on Economic and Monetary Union (EMU) constitute the fourth attempt to achieve monetary integration amongst the Member States, the most recent being the European Monetary System established in 1979.[159] Monetary union has been viewed by many in the Community as a necessary complement to the Single Market.[160] The move towards EMU was begun by the Delors Report of 1989, arguing for a three-stage move towards monetary integration, which when complete would see monetary policy-making move from the Member States to a European System of Central Banks (ESCB).[161] The proposal was conditionally accepted by the European Council in 1990 and EMU became a subject for negotiations at the Intergovernmental Conferences leading up to the adoption of the TEU at Maastricht in December 1991. Unlike other new structures set up under the TEU, the ESCB and European Central Bank (ECB) are highly integrationist bodies, which have the explicit goal under EMU of supplanting national monetary policy-making,

The ECB is established by a protocol to the TEU.[162] Although not an institution, its acts are reviewable like those of the Commission, Council and EP. It is the centrepiece of the European System of Central Banks, of which all the central banks of the Member States are members, along with the ECB. The ESCB does not have separate legal personality from its constituent central banks. All action of the ESCB therefore must be taken via the national central banks and the ECB. The ESCB, composed as it is of the national central banks plus the ECB, has a federal structure. However, in this case, federalism cannot equal diversity or the goal of monetary integration would fail. Monetary sovereignty must be indivisible.[163] The ESCB is responsible for Community monetary policy, with a primary objective of maintaining price stability.[164] The ECB has the exclusive right to authorise the issue of bank notes under

---

157 Zangl, *op. cit.*, at 679–80. The six items are: EAGGF Guarantee; Structural operations; policies with multiannual allocations; other policies; repayments and administration; and monetary reserve.

158 The United Kingdom and Denmark have derogated from this part of the TEU.

159 Hahn, 'The European Central Bank: Key to European Monetary Union or Target?' (1991) 28 CML Rev 783, at 785–6.

160 *Ibid.*, at 789.

161 *Ibid.*, at 790.

162 Protocol on the Statute of the European System of

Central Banks and of the European Central Bank, and Title VI of the EC Treaty, as replaced by the TEU. In Article 109c EC, a Monetary Committee and, for the third stage of monetary union, an Economic and Financial Committee are also established.

163 Hahn, *op. cit.*, note 159, at 799.

164 Article 105 EC, as amended by TEU. However, the ESCB is also to 'support the general economic policies of the Community with a view to contributing to the achievement of the objectives of the Community as laid down in Article 2'.

the TEU's new chapter on monetary policy. The Statute of the ESCB and the ECB requires that both act with complete independence.[165]

For the ECB, independence is reinforced by the eight-year term of office of the President, Vice-President and the other members of the Executive Board, which is twice the term of office of a Commissioner.[166] The ECB has legal personality, which the Statute requires Member States to guarantee within their own legal systems.[167] The ECB also has legislative powers with respect to the ESCB. It has the power to take decisions necessary for accomplishing the tasks of the ESCB, to make recommendations and to deliver opinions.[168] In limited circumstances, it may also pass regulations.[169]

The Governing Council of the ECB is its main decision-making body. It consists of the members of its Executive Board and the Governors of the national central banks of the Member States.[170] Members of the Executive Board are appointed by common accord of the Member States from 'among persons of recognised standing and professional experience in monetary or banking matters', and include a President, Vice-President and four other members.[171] The President of the Council and a Commissioner may participate, without voting rights, in meetings of the ECB Governing Board, and, reciprocally, the President of the ECB shall be invited to attend Council meetings on monetary policy.[172] The ECB presents an annual report to the Commission, Council, EP and European Council.[173]

The ECB has extensive legislative powers, with the power to pass regulations on monetary policy, take decisions necessary to its functioning and that of the ESCB, and to make recommendations and deliver opinions.[174] It does not require a Commission proposal in order to make regulations within the fields permitted by Article 108a, and may impose fines or penalty payments on undertakings which fail to fulfil obligations under its regulations or decisions. It also has the right to be consulted on any Community act within its field of competence, and may submit opinions to the Community institutions or national authorities on such matters.[175]

The importance of the ECB as an institution will depend on the significance which monetary policy has for the Community in the future. The withdrawal of several Member States from the Exchange Rate Mechanism in 1992 and 1993 tends to indicate that monetary policy will play less of a role in the Community's future than was intended in December 1991 at Maastricht.

CONCLUSION

The European Community treaties have established a complex and sophisticated system of

---

[165] Article 7 of the Statute, and Article 107 EC.
[166] Article 109a(2)(b) EC. Hahn, *op. cit.* note 159, at 806–8, sets out some of the factors which may in practice threaten the independence of the Executive Board.
[167] Article 9 of the Statute, and Article 106 EC.
[168] Article 108a(1) EC.
[169] *Ibid.* Regulations may be made under Article 3.1, first indent (defining and implementing monetary policy), Article 19.1 (minimum reserves to be held by credit institutions in the Member States), Article 22 (clearing and payment systems) or Article 25.2 (prudential supervision of credit institutions and other financial institutions) of the Statute of the ESCB, and in circumstances laid down in acts of the Council under Article 106(6) EC (which refer to various articles of the Statute of the ESCB).
[170] Article 109a EC.
[171] Article 109a(2) EC.
[172] Article 109b EC.
[173] Article 109b(3) EC.
[174] Article 108a EC.
[175] Article 105(4) EC.

institutions for the setting of Community policy, as well as its implementation. There is a clear tension in those institutions between integrative, or *Communautaire*, pressures, and anti-integrative, or nationalist, pressures. The history of the Community treaties, until the TEU, was for integration gradually to increase, and for institutions such as the EP, which represent the Community interest, to acquire more power. There has been a counter-trend, however, outside the treaties, for the Member State interest to retrench, such as through the extensive use of unanimous voting in the Council. The TEU itself is ambivalent. While finally according the EP a power of co-decision with the Council on some legislation, it increases the power and influence of the European Council. Further, the sites of conflict over the pace of integration have multiplied under the TEU, with the Common Foreign and Security Policy, Co-operation in Justice and Home Affairs, and EMU each having separate means of functioning, each of which will seek its own institutional balance, and each of which interacts with the Community in diverse ways.

The battles for the soul of the Community have taken place in many areas. Whether the current situation constitutes the triumph of politics over constitutionalism is likely to become evident by the time of the next Intergovernmental Conferences, due to take place in 1996.

Further reading

Bieber, R., 'Legislative Procedure for the Establishment of the Single Market' (1988) 25 CML Rev 711.

Bradley, K. St. C., 'Comitology and the Law: Through a Glass, Darkly' (1992) 29 CML Rev 693.

Curtin, D., 'The Constitutional Structure of the Union: A Europe of Bits and Pieces' (1993) 30 CML Rev 17.

da Cruz Vilaca, J.L., 'The Court of First Instance of the European Communities: A Significant Step towards the Consolidation of the European Community as a Community Governed by the Rule of Law' (1990) 9 YEL 1.

Edwards, D., 'The Impact of the Single Act on the Institutions' (1987) 24 CML Rev 19.

Everling, U., 'Reflections on the Structure of the European Union' (1992) 29 CML Rev 1053.

Freestone, D. and Davidson, J.S., *The Institutional Framework of the European Communities* (London: Croom Helm, 1988).

Hahn, H., 'The European Central Bank: Key to European Monetary Union or Target?' (1991) 28 CML Rev 783.

Kok, C., 'The Court of Auditors of the European Communities: "The Other European Court in Luxembourg" ' (1989) 26 CML Rev 345.

Lenaerts, K., 'Some Reflections on the Separation of Powers in the European Community' (1991) 28 CML Rev 11.

Neville Brown, L. and Jacobs, F., *The Court of Justice of the European Communities*, 3rd edn by Neville Brown (London: Sweet and Maxwell, 1989).

Toth, A.G., *The Oxford Encyclopaedia of European Community Law,* vol. 1 'Institutional Law' (Oxford: Clarendon Press, 1991).

Urwin, D., *The Community of Europe* (London: Longman, 1991).

CHAPTER 3

Constitutional principles

INTRODUCTION

In the previous chapter, the evolution of the Community institutions was examined. Over time, the balance of power amongst the institutions and organs of the Community has shifted back and forth. In particular, it is important to note the shift of power to the Council of Ministers and its related bodies such as COREPER. While the treaties established a legislative process weighted in favour of the Community-orientated Commission because of its power to initiate legislation through proposals, the increased use of unanimous voting by the Council of Ministers shifted the balance in favour of Member State control for most of the Community's history. Legally, Community decision-making was centralised; in practice, it was decentralised. This decentralisation has persisted even in the face of greater participation of the EP in the legislative process. Despite the treaties, the Member States have often acted as if the Community was an instrument for the furtherance of national policies rather than an independent legal and political system.[1]

The tension which has caused these changes in the balance of power is one between two visions of the Community. One vision of the Community emphasises the existence of independent policy-making structures and the idea of the Community as a separate legal order. This has been described as supranationalism. The other vision emphasises the presence of national representatives in the policy-making process and the continued sovereignty of Member States. This has been described as intergovernmentalism.

Intergovernmentalism is the traditional view of international law. States are the only recognised subjects of international law, and international decision-making is effected only by the consent of all the States involved, such as by Treaty.[2] Intergovernmentalism is the view that international organisations are nothing more than the sum of their parts, which are States and only States. Supranationalism is directly opposed to this, and describes a state of affairs whereby an international organisation leads an independent existence from the States which created it. In particular, an organisation may be seen as supranational when its decisions are binding on its component States. It is thereby something more than the sum of its parts.

These two categories are not mutually exclusive. Organisations may have elements of both. This is particularly the case in the Community, where its very framework includes strong elements of both approaches. The Commission, as guardian of the treaties, and the Parliament, now that it is directly elected, present strong elements of supranationalism. The Council of Ministers, as primary legislative body, preserves a fundamental State involvement and, therefore, intergovernmental element. The balance of power has, over time, appeared to

---

1 Weiler, 'The Transformation of Europe' (1991) 100 Yale LJ 2403, at 2449.
2 For a critique of the statist view of international law, see Allott, *International Law and International Revolution: Reconceiving the World*, Josephine Onoh Memorial Lecture (1989).

move towards greater supranationalism. The EP has increased its power in the legislative and budgetary areas, and the Commission has become more influential as the Community has entered into an increasing number of fields in harmonisation of laws. States have nonetheless been able to maintain an overriding influence on decision-making due to the failure to use majority voting, the establishment of the European Council and the use of COREPER and supervisory committees. The TEU, which increases the powers of the Parliament, but takes certain policy areas out of the hands of the Community institutions altogether, demonstrates the continuing ambivalence of the direction of European integration. The question therefore is not whether or not the Community is supranational, but to what extent it is.

The ability of States to create blocking mechanisms like the Luxembourg Accords has led commentators to assert the triumph of the intergovernmental elements of the Community over its supranational elements.[3] One author, however, sees in the European Community a more complex form of supranationalism, part of which has been quite successful. Unlike some political commentators, who have focused solely on the structures and procedures of decision-making within the Community, Weiler has looked also at the substance of European Community law. According to Weiler, the supremacy of Community law, and its penetration into national legal systems, results in a high degree of normative (legal) supranationalism, even though decisional (political/institutional) supranationalism has been largely eroded.[4] Normative supranationalism relates to substantive rules and policies which are the result of decisional supranationalism, and also to the foundational rules which give direction to the system. An example of the latter is the doctrine of supremacy of Community law. While Member States are still able to determine the content of Community law through the Council of Ministers, their ability to ignore the results of the legislative process has been almost entirely cut off. Individuals have the capacity to invoke Community law before national courts in an ever-expanding range of circumstances.[5] The Commission, a supranational body, has the power to obtain judgment against Member States for failure to implement Community law.[6] Decisional intergovernmentalism, where Member States have a great deal of power to protect their national interests, is balanced by normative supranationalism, whereby they are obliged to respect Community law as an independent legal order.[7]

The tension between supranationalism and intergovernmentalism is evident in all of the following principles. The emergence of federal elements in the Community framework, and the constitutionalisation of the treaties, has led to an identification of the Community as a supranational organisation. The calls for the implementation of the principle of subsidiarity arise from an attempt to curb the growth of supranationalism and to re-assert the primary

---

3 For example, Heathcote, 'The Crisis of European Supranationality' (1966) 5 *Journal of Common Market Studies* 140 and Urwin, *The Community of Europe* (1991), at 115.

4 Weiler, 'The Community System: The Dual Character of Supranationalism' (1981) 1 YEL 267.

5 See Chapter 5.

6 See Chapter 8.

7 Weiler, *op. cit.* at 292–6, 304–6. Weiler, in his later article, 'The Transformation of Europe', *see* note 1, describes this balance as one between 'Exit' (the ability of a State to withdraw from an international organisation if it does not agree with its outcomes) and 'Voice' (the ability of a State to influence the outcomes of an international

organisation). In the case of the European Community, as Exit was closed off (the consequences of withdrawal were too risky and the possibility of a non-application of Community law reduced drastically), Voice was increased (the Council of Ministers has protected its key legislative role, and unanimity rather than majority voting has been the rule so that each Member State can protect its national interests). Insofar as the SEA and the Treaty on European Union have eroded Voice, 'Loyalty' may have emerged which dispenses with the need for a finely-tuned balance. The result of the Danish referendum on the Treaty on European Union may be evidence that a sufficient degree of Loyalty has not yet emerged, and that the balance of Voice may still be necessary.

role of Member States in key policy areas. However, it will be argued that subsidiarity only has meaning within systems which are substantially federalised. Supremacy of Community law is an important part of Weiler's concept of normative supranationalism, as is the *acquis communautaire*. Lastly, the idea of European citizenship is a concrete recognition of the Community as a supranational organisation.

Federalism – the 'ever closer union'

Acknowledging the existence of federal elements in the Community constitution is not equivalent to seeing the Community as a State or super-State. Federalism takes many forms, not all of which are inherently centralising.[8] While States have, in the past, formed the only known federations, most writers concede at least that the Community has federal characteristics.[9] The fundamental requirement for the existence of a federal system is that there should be a division of powers between different levels of government. While other elements have been listed as essential, they are, for the most part, implied by the first.[10] The classic definition of federalism requires that the central and regional governments are co-ordinate, in that neither is subordinate to the other, and that they each are independent within their own sphere of jurisdiction.[11] However, this is a somewhat awkward model to apply to the Community, where there are many shared areas of jurisdiction and the development of the federal nature of the Community has occurred incrementally over time, and not always through explicit constitutional development. However, the levels of government within the Community are certainly co-ordinate, as neither can be abolished by the other without amendment of the constitution itself.[12] They are also independent, as is confirmed by *Van Gend en Loos* v *Nederlandse Administratie der Belastingen*:

> . . . the Community constitutes a new legal order of international law for the benefit of which the States have limited their sovereign rights, albeit within limited fields . . . . Independently of the legislation of Member States, Community law therefore not only imposes obligations on individuals but is also intended to confer upon them rights which become part of their legal heritage.[13]

In addition, recent analyses of federalism have noted a shift from hierarchy to co-operation between levels, which is more in keeping with the Community's method of functioning.[14]

The main issue in the analysis of the Community as a federation is the division of powers between the Member States and the Community itself. The treaties, unlike most national federal constitutions, do not contain a list of central and regional powers which purports to be exhaustive. Some powers are clearly conferred exclusively on the Community. Some powers are acquired by the Community by the operation of pre-emption. Many areas, however, are not specifically assigned, and may be regulated on an internal level by the Member States, and on an inter-State level by the Community. As a result, most areas of

---

8 Lenaerts, 'Constitutionalism and the Many Faces of Federalism' (1990) 38 AJCL 205, at 206–7.

9 See Lenaerts, *ibid.*, who includes the Community in his study of federalisms, and Hartley, *infra*, who acknowledges federal elements in the Community, but denies that it is a federation as yet.

10 For example, see Hartley, 'Federalism, Courts and Legal Systems: The Emerging Constitution of the European Community ' (1986) 34 AJCL 229, at 231.

11 Wheare, *Federal Government*, 4th edn (1963).

12 This situation can be contrasted with the position of local governments, or the status of Northern Ireland, within the United Kingdom.

13 Case 26/62, [1963] ECR 1, at paragraph 4 of the decision.

14 Ladeur, 'European Institutional Reforms: Extra-National Management as an Alternative to Federalism?' [1990] LIEI 1, at 5.

legislative competence are concurrent. The 'federalisation' of the treaties has been accomplished by the ECJ, in part by demarcating jurisdictional boundaries, but mostly by authorising the expanding jurisdictional competence of the Community.

The Community has relatively few specifically assigned areas of legislative competence.[15] These powers may be exercised through legislation passed by the Council of Ministers acting by majority or qualified majority vote.[16] The Community's enumerated powers generally involve the development of policy areas specifically set out in the treaties, such as free movement, the common agricultural policy, transport, competition, state aid, the completion of the internal market, balance of payments, commercial policy, health and safety, the structural funds such as the Regional Development Fund, technology, environment, and day-to-day institutional matters.[17] There are also specific regulatory powers conferred by the ECSC and Euratom treaties. In matters which are not purely trade-related, the Community's specific powers are often narrowly defined. In social policy, the powers even to set health and safety standards are limited to 'minimum requirements for gradual implementation, having regard to the conditions and technical rules obtaining in each of the Member States'.[18] Community initiatives in technology are likewise restricted to framework programmes and promotional and information activities.[19] However, the restrictive nature of some of the Community's enumerated powers does not prevent further action by the Community in these fields. The Community's use of its harmonisation powers has extended its capacity to regulate many sectors which were originally seen as largely or exclusively within Member State jurisdiction.

The Community also has several implied powers resulting from the powers set out in the Treaty. The most important of these is the extension of an external relations power parallel to its internal jurisdiction.[20] The articles in Part I of the Treaty, while not granting new powers to the Community, have been used as justification for the expanded use of the harmonisation articles, and have most certainly extended the effect of Community law within Member States.[21] The *Casagrande* case[22] provides an example of how an explicit grant of jurisdiction, here the power to ensure free movement of workers throughout the Community, may be expanded to include the power to require that education grants be made on a non-discriminatory basis to children of such workers, even though, the Court acknowledged, the Community had no jurisdiction over education policy itself.[23] Also in the field of education, the power to set up a common vocational training policy under Article 128 EC was held to justify the creation of student-mobility schemes.[24] In the social field, the Court

15 There is some disagreement concerning which powers are exclusive to the Communities. Contrast Temple Lang, 'What Powers Should the European Community Have?', Institute of European Public Law Lecture (1992) at 1, footnote 1, and Toth, 'The Principle of Subsidiarity in the Maastricht Treaty' (1992) 29 CML Rev 1079, at 1080.

16 Lenaerts, *op. cit.*, note 8, at 214–15.

17 *Ibid.*

18 Article 118a EC, added by Article 21 of the SEA.

19 Title VI of Part III of the Treaty, added by Article 24 of the SEA.

20 See Chapter 4.

21 Sasse and Yourow, 'The Growth of Legislative Power of the European Communities' in Sandalow and Stein (eds), *Courts and Free Markets*, vol. 1 (1982) 92, at 93–4.

22 Case 9/74, *Casagrande* v *Landeshaupstadt* [1974] ECR 773.

23 Sasse and Yourow, *op. cit.*, note 21, at 94.

24 Case 242/87, *Commission* v *Council* [1989] ECR 1425. This case involved the Council decision on the ERASMUS programme. The Council changed the legal basis proposed by the Commission from Article 128 alone to Articles 128 and 235. The court found for the Council, but only on the basis that the scheme included certain research elements which could not be justified as part of vocational education. The student-mobility mechanism itself was found to be justified by Article 128. The conflict between the two institutions resulted from the fact that the inclusion of Article 235 transformed the decision from one requiring only a simple majority vote to one requiring unanimity.

has authorised the use of Article 118 EC, which does not mention any legislative power other than opinions, to pass a decision obliging Member States to consult the Commission and to inform it of draft measures concerning migrant workers from non-EC States.[25]

Arguably, the implied powers discussed in the preceding paragraph do not cause problems, in that they are theoretically contained within the enumerated powers.[26] The use of harmonisation powers, however, has led the Community into new fields of activity, although most of these innovations have subsequently been acknowledged by the SEA and the TEU. Jurisdiction over matters through harmonisation derives from Articles 100–100b EC.[27] Similarly, Article 235 provides for Community action 'to attain . . . one of the objectives of the Community' where 'this Treaty has not provided the necessary powers'. Through the use of these articles, the Community has regulated fields where its specific powers were limited under the Treaty, and has moved into certain fields such as environment, before the treaties provided explicit authorisation for Community action. These powers, it should be noted, are subject to stricter procedural controls than most of the enumerated powers, including consultation or co-operation with the Parliament and unanimous voting.

Harmonisation, or approximation, of laws, has been developed largely due to the identification by the ECJ of areas where, in the absence of Community standards, Member States could justify the use of differing national standards. This is particularly relevant in free movement of goods, where the Court, in the *Cassis de Dijon* case,[28] justified national regulation which could otherwise constitute measures equivalent to quantitative restrictions, if such measures did not amount to disguised discrimination and were related to areas of legitimate State regulation such as consumer protection. Article 36 similarly allows States to regulate in certain areas, including intellectual property, which would otherwise violate free movement of goods principles. As a result, significant obstacles to the creation of a Single Market exist and are justified by the Treaty rules themselves. The response of the Commission has been to attempt to harmonise many of these rules. Article 100 allows for the enactment of directives harmonising national rules which affect the establishment of the common market. It requires a unanimous vote of the Council. Although the word 'approximation' is used rather than harmonisation, the latter term describes the practice of the Council more accurately, since the resulting standards are not always a levelling up or down but may also take the form of an entirely new standard.[29] The utility of Article 100 is wide-ranging, although not unlimited. It appears not to be limited to the four freedoms of movement, since Article 100 was used as the basis for the Equal Pay Directive 75/117.[30] However, as legislation under Article 100 must be justified by reference to the common market, some directives which are only indirectly related to it have been justified under Articles 100 and 235 jointly.[31] One concrete limit to action under Article 100 is that the resulting harmonised rule must itself be in conformity with the Treaty.[32]

[25] Joined Cases 281 & 283–283/85, *Germany v Commission* [1987] ECR 3203.

[26] See Weller, 'Transformation', *op. cit.*, note 1, at 2442.

[27] Articles 101 and 102 provide for the harmonisation of national laws relating to competition, but these appear to be infrequently used.

[28] Case 120/78, *Rewe-Zentrale v Bundesmonopolverwaltung fur Branntwein* [1979] ECR 649.

[29] Currall, 'Some aspects of the Relation between Articles 30–36 and Article 100 of the EC Treaty, with a Closer Look at Optional Harmonisation' (1984) 4 YEL 169, at 176.

[30] *Ibid.*

[31] *Ibid.*, at 174–5, where the example of the Drinking Water Directive 75/440 is cited. Drinking water is 'a stage away from the use of water to manufacture food-stuffs, the first point, in reality at which the question of free trade arises'.

[32] *Ibid.*, at 182, 191–3.

Under the SEA, new jurisdiction to harmonise national law was created by Articles 100a and 100b. Article 100a provides, by derogation from Article 100, for a process of harmonisation of national law in preparation for the Single Market which took effect from 31 December 1992, as set out in the objectives in Article 8a. By virtue of paragraph 2, measures relating to fiscal provisions, free movement of persons and the rights and interests of employed persons are exempted from the purview of Article 100a. The limitations of paragraph 2, and the fact that Article 100a can only be used to achieve the objectives of Article 8a, has led at least one commentator to argue that the field of application of Article 100a is limited, and many of the measures adopted under it may be invalid.[33] This argument can only be accepted if a narrow view of Article 8a is valid. If, as argued above with respect to Article 100 and the 'common market', the notion of the 'Single Market' is wider than the four freedoms,[34] then Article 100a's limitations are only those explicitly stated. If the Single Market was limited to the four freedoms, then it would have been a more felicitous drafting to limit Article 100a to the free movement of goods, persons and capital. The open-ended drafting of Article 100a tends towards an expansive interpretation of the concept of the Single Market. The decision of the ECJ in the *Titanium Dioxide* case[35] supports the wider view of Article 100a. The Court decided that the Council had erred in choosing Article 130s instead of Article 100a as the legal basis of the contested directive, indicating that the latter article can be used as the basis for environmental protection legislation even when not related to free movement of goods.[36]

The use of Article 235 is even less fettered by substantive conditions. Its use must be related to one of the objectives of the Community. The objectives of the Community are set out in Articles 2 and 3 EC, in very broad language, but since there is no direct reference to these articles in Article 235, there appears to be no bar to use of other sources for the derivation of Community objectives.[37] There are two 'necessaries': first, that Community action is necessary to attain the objective in question, and second, that the Treaty has not provided the necessary powers. The former has never been discussed by the Court, but the latter was considered in the *Massey-Ferguson* case, where the Court took the view that Article 235 EC could be used even where the matter was explicitly covered by other EC provisions, where the Council considered that the use of Article 235 ensured the legal validity of the measure.[38] However, since the *Titanium Dioxide* case, it is now clear that the Council may not choose the legal basis of a measure in order to avoid the right of Parliament to co-operation or co-decision. In addition, the use of 'appropriate' to describe the permitted Community action under Article 235 may be said to imply a condition of proportionality.[39]

Article 235, even more than the harmonisation powers, has been used to expand the Community's legislative jurisdiction. Originally, it was used in a restrictive way, to justify action which was directly related to the establishment of the common market, such as

[33] Crosby, 'The Single Market and the Rule of Law' (1991) 16 EL Rev 451.
[34] Free movement of goods, free movement of workers, freedom of establishment/freedom to provide services, and free movement of capital.
[35] Case C-300/89, *Commission* v *Council* [1991] ECR 2851.
[36] See commentary by Somsen, (1992) 29 CML Rev (1992) 140.
[37] Hartley, *The Foundations of European Community*

Law, 2nd edn (1988), at 105–6; Weiler, 'Transformation', *op. cit.* note 1, at 2444.
[38] Case 8/73, *Hauptzollamt Bremerhaven* v *Massey-Ferguson* [1973] ECR 897, at paragraph 4 of the decision, where the Court stated that 'there is no reason why the Council could not legitimately consider that recourse to the procedure of Article 235 was justified in the interest of legal certainty.'
[39] Sasse and Yourow, *op. cit.*, note 21, at 95.

uniform customs legislation.[40] However, from the early 1970s it has been used, often in conjunction with Article 100 EC, to legislate on social and cultural matters.[41] Some of the initiatives which resulted from the expanded use of Article 235 EC are the European Regional Development Fund and the beginnings of environmental and monetary policy.[42]

Insofar as there are limits to the use of Article 235 EC, they must be similar to those mentioned for Article 100 EC. First, Article 235 cannot be used to violate the Treaty itself. For example, it could not be used to enact measures which would infringe upon the principle of free movement of goods. Secondly, as mentioned above, it could not be used as a way of avoiding the legislative prerogatives of the Parliament. Lastly, it could not be used to make Article 236 EC, concerning amendment of the EC Treaty, redundant, particularly with respect to institutional changes.[43]

When the Community moves into a field of regulation, the general rule is that it will be concurrently regulated. In some cases, however, Community jurisdiction is exclusive, preventing all Member State legislation, even where the Community had not yet acted.[44] This is notably the case with the Common Customs Policy.[45] In others, once the Community had begun to regulate an area, its action has a pre-emptive effect, prohibiting future national legislation even when not in actual conflict. The best example of this type of pre-emption occurs in the Common Agricultural Policy. Once the Community has set up a common organisation of the market for a given product, Member States may no longer regulate that market at all.[46] The possibility of pre-emption of concurrent jurisdiction leads to a difficult determination of how to interpret the silence of the Community legislator. It may leave jurisdiction for national legislation, or it may be a deliberate measure not to regulate the matter.[47]

A related problem with pre-emption is identifying where and how it operates. Most commentators see it as a consequence of the supremacy of Community law.[48] However, this approach would mean that pre-emption could operate only if the Community had actually legislated on an area. This would not be consistent with decisions of the ECJ on agricultural products, as mentioned above, which do not allow Member States to supplement Community regulation of markets, even if there is no actual conflict. Although the Court uses the language of supremacy and pre-emption interchangeably, there appear to be two situations in addition to direct conflict where pre-emption will operate: occupied field, and interference with the functioning of the Single Market.[49] This involves an interpretation of the relevant Community legislation to discover its intended relationship with Member State law. Sometimes the legislation will explicitly preserve an area of Member State competence or expressly remove it. In such cases the task of the Court is straightforward.[50] In the more

---

40 *Ibid.*, at 96.

41 *Ibid.*, at 96–7; Weiler, 'Transformation', *op. cit.*, note 1, at 2445–7.

42 *Ibid.*, at 97.

43 Weiler, 'Transformation', *op. cit.*, note 1, at 2450–1.

44 For a list of the powers which the ECJ has recognised as exclusive to the Community, see Temple Lang, 'The Development of European Community Constitutional Law' (1991) 25 *International Lawyer* 455, at 460.

45 Lenaerts, *op. cit.*, note 8, at 228–9.

46 See, for example, Case 83/78, *Pigs Marketing Board* v *Redmond* [1978] ECR 2347.

47 Lenaerts, *op. cit.*, note 8, at 225–7, contrasting the judgments of the Court in Case 50/76, *Amsterdam Bulb BV* v *Producktschap voor siergewassen* [1977] ECR 137, and Case 111/76, *Officier van Justitie* v *Van den Hazel* [1977] ECR 901.

48 A review of attempts to define pre-emption can be found in Cross, 'Pre-emption of Member State Law in the European Economic Community: A Framework for Analysis' (1992) 29 CML Rev 447, at 451–3.

49 Cross, *ibid.*, at 454, generalising from the Court's decision in Case 218/85, *CERAFEL* v *Le Campion* [1986] ECR 3513.

50 *Ibid.*, at 456–9.

complex area of the occupied field, the Court interprets the legislation to see whether the Community intended to create a complete system of regulation in that field. If so, the Court will consider that pre-emption operates.[51] Conflicts between national and Community law are dealt with as an issue of supremacy of Community law.

Recently, the ECJ has found it increasingly necessary to create boundaries between the areas of application of Community and national law. While the ECJ has never annulled a Community act for impinging on Member States' exclusive jurisdiction, it has been willing to declare legislation invalid due to incompatibility with the Treaty[52] or use of inappropriate procedure.[53] In addition, the Court has recently developed a willingness to identify areas in which Community law does not apply where there is concurrent jurisdiction between the Community and Member States. In two recent cases, the court refused to review national legislation for compatibility with Community human rights principles because the legislation was found to be wholly within the jurisdiction of Member States, in other words, that there was no Community dimension.[54] In a 1992 immigration case, there was a similar effort to determine whether there was a Community dimension for the purpose of deciding which law, national or Community, was applicable.[55]

One of the most important questions in any federation is where residual powers lie. Residual powers are those which are not explicitly assigned to either level of government by the constitution. In most federal States, the residual powers lie with the local or regional governments. In Canada, the power to make laws for the 'peace, order and good government of Canada' has been identified as granting residual powers to the federal government.[56] In the Community it appears that the Member States hold the residual powers, in that any power not conferred to the Community by the treaties remains with national governments. However, the capacity of the Community to acquire jurisdiction over a matter through harmonisation of laws or by use of Article 235 EC renders the value of the residual legislative power of little use.[57] Further, Treaty provisions which appear to reserve certain areas of legislative competence for the Member States do not in fact do so. Article 36 EC, which provides for exceptions to the prohibition on quantitative restrictions and measures having equivalent effect, is a permissive rule rather than a grant or reservation of power.[58] To the extent that there is an explicit grant of residual power within the Community legal system, it would likely be found in Article 235 EC, as described above, which has been likened to the 'necessary and proper' clause of the American constitution,[59] and which appears to have a virtually unlimited field of application.

51 *Ibid.*, at 459.
52 For example, in Cases 80 and 81/77, *Ramel v Receveur des Douanes* [1978] ECR 927, the Court held a regulation under the Common Agricultural Policy invalid for incompatibility with Articles 13 and 38–46 EC.
53 *Titanium dioxide* case, *op. cit.*, note 35.
54 Cases 60 and 61/84, *Cinéthèque v Fédération Nationale des Cinémas Françaises*, [1985] ECR 2605, Case C-159/90, *Society for the Protection of Unborn Children v Grogan* [1991] 3 CMLR 849.
55 Case C-370/90, *R v Immigration Appeal Tribunal and Surinder Singh, ex parte Secretary of State for the Home Department* [1993] 3 CMLR 358.
56 *Citizens' Insurance Company v Parsons* (1881) 7 App Cas 96. The description of the peace, order and good

government powers as residual is, however, controversial. A review of the arguments is set out in Hogg, *Constitutional Law of Canada* (1977), at 241–4.
57 Weiler, 'Transformation', *op. cit.*, note 1, at 2446; Lenaerts, *op. cit.*, note 8, at 220, where he notes that the residual powers held by the Member States are not reserved powers.
58 See for example, Case 153/78, *Commission v Germany* [1979] ECR 2555, at paragraph 5 of the decision: ' . . . the purpose of Article 36 EC is not to reserve certain matters to the exclusive jurisdiction of the Member States; it merely allows national legislation to derogate from the principle of the free movement of goods to the extent to which this is and remains justified'.
59 Weiler, 'Transformation', *op. cit.*, note 1, at 2443.

Subsidiarity

The lack of clarity and predictability in the division of competences between the Community and the national legislatures, and the expansion of Community jurisdiction, have led some Member States to advocate the wider application of the principle of subsidiarity to the legislative structure of the Community. A note of caution is necessary here. The term 'subsidiarity' is understood in different ways by different participants in the Community legislative processes. The enshrinement of the principle in Article 3b EC, as amended by the TEU, as well as in Articles A(2) and B TEU, has led to its greater acceptance as a governing principle, but not to any greater consensus as to its meaning. Article 3b EC does not provide a complete definition of subsidiarity, although it gives some indications of its implications:

> The Community shall act within the limits of the powers conferred upon it by this Treaty and of the objectives assigned to it therein.
>
> In areas which do not fall within its exclusive competence, the Community shall take action, in accordance with the principle of subsidiarity, only if and in so far as the objectives of the proposed action cannot be sufficiently achieved by the Member States and can therefore, by reason of the scale or effects of the proposed action, be better achieved by the Community . . .

The only common ground is that subsidiarity concerns the relationship of differing levels of authority within society. However, there is no agreement, when the principle is applied to the Community, as to its scope of application, and to what extent it ties the hands of the Community institutions.[60] The origins of subsidiarity derive from Roman Catholic social doctrine of the 1930s. The principle was set out in Pope Pius XI's Encyclical Letter of 1931, which addressed reconstruction of the social order.[61] The State, according to the analysis contained in the Encyclical, was taking to itself functions which had previously been performed by smaller social units, such as local communities and families, and was performing them less efficiently. The emphasis was on social organisation between individual conscience, communities such as the family and the State.[62] Barrington used this idea to articulate his opposition to big government, in his studies advocating decentralisation.[63] However, it is much more frequently found in more corporatist approaches to politics. An example of this may be found in the approach of the Dutch Christian Democrats, whose notion of the responsible society requires the strong to provide for the needs of the weak.[64] This does not necessarily call for State action, but for the encouragement of solidarity through private, para-public and public organisations, including local government.

Subsidiarity has been closely associated with the idea of European Union, beginning in the 1970s with the McDougal Report on public finance in the Community, which argued that integration required a more rational distribution of authority between different levels of government.[65] The 1975 Report on European Union and the draft European Union Treaty of

[60] Emiliou, 'Subsidiarity: An Effective Barrier against "the Enterprises of Ambition"?' (1992) 17 EL Rev 383, at 384, notes two general approaches, one centralising and another decentralising. He does, however, believe that subsidiarity establishes a presumption in favour of decentralised authorities.
[61] Wilke and Wallace, *Subsidiarity: Approaches to Power-sharing in the European Community*, RIIA Discussion Paper 27 (1990), at 12.

[62] *Ibid.*, at 13. Deriving from natural law, the individual and the family are seen as the primary bearers of rights, and therefore the State may not interfere with these protected spheres. However, individual participation in social institutions is seen as both a right and a duty.
[63] Wilke and Wallace, *op. cit.*, note 61, at 11 and 15–16.
[64] *Ibid.*, at 19.
[65] Emiliou, *op. cit.*, note 60, at 391.

1984 developed the principle of subsidiarity in the context of a greater definition of the powers of the Union and the Member States.[66] These documents foresaw the Union as a development of the Community, rather than the overarching creation it became in the TEU.[67] The 1975 Report used subsidiarity as a guiding principle for the allocation of powers between different levels of government. In 1984, however, it was also used as a guideline for decision-making on individual matters.[68] The latter provision on subsidiarity has informed its ultimate codification.[69]

Following the accession of Spain and Portugal, a Commission study group headed by Tommasso Padoa-Schioppa examined the challenges facing the Community in integrating economic policy. The study group used the principle of subsidiarity in formulating its guidelines. However, the conditions it set for the legitimacy of Community intervention were cross-border spill over effects, which was contained in the 1984 draft Treaty provision on subsidiarity, and treating unemployment as a priority.[70] It took the efficiency argument associated with subsidiarity as a two-way street – for some purposes, efficiency demanded supranational regulation.[71]

Article 130r(4) of the SEA applied the principle of subsidiarity explicitly, the first treaty provision to do so[72]:

> The Community shall take action relating to the environment to the extent to which the objectives referred to in paragraph 1 can be attained better at Community level than at the level of the Member States.

In the *Titanium Dioxide* case, the issue of the subsidiarity provision in Article 130r(4) was not discussed, but the Court, by expanding the possibility of environmental legislation under Article 100a EC and not explicitly limiting the scope of Article 130s EC, has not taken a strict view of the requirements of subsidiarity in environmental matters.[73] In the TEU, the explicit reference to subsidiarity in environmental policy has been removed, presumably because of the general statement in Article 3b EC.

With Article 3b, subsidiarity in Community law moves from academic discussion to constitutional principle. However, applying the principle will be more difficult. It applies only when powers are shared concurrently by the Community and the Member States.[74] It therefore applies to specific exercises of power, rather than to which powers may be exercised by the Community as opposed to by the Member States. Article 3b sets out two criteria for deciding whether Community action is appropriate: effectiveness and scale. For the criterion of effectiveness to be fulfilled, the proposed act must not be capable of being

---

[66] Toth, *op. cit.*, note 15, at 1088–9.
[67] See Chapter 2.
[68] Toth, *op. cit.*, note 15, at 1089–90.
[69] *Ibid.*: ' . . . the Union shall only act to carry out those tasks which may be undertaken more effectively in common than by the Member States acting separately, in particular those whose execution requires action by the Union because their dimension or effects extend beyond national frontiers.'
[70] Wilke and Wallace, *op. cit.*, note 61, at 29. Unemployment was perceived as a potential problem arising from Spain and Portugal's accession to the Community.
[71] *Ibid.*
[72] However, Giscard d'Estaing is of the opinion that the foundation of the principle of subsidiarity may be found in Article 4 EC, requiring that the institutions shall act within the limits of the powers conferred in the Treaty: *The Principle of Subsidiarity*, EP Committee on Institutional Affairs (European Parliament, 1990), at 4.
[73] Case C-300/89, *op. cit.*, note 35; Somsen, *op. cit.*, note 36.
[74] Toth, *op. cit.*, note 15, at 1085–6, argues that, in fact, there are no concurrent powers in the EC Treaty framework. Emiliou, *op. cit.* note 60, at 392, says that concurrent powers are those whose 'exercise is suspended and made subject to compliance with certain procedural and substantive conditions'.

achieved sufficiently by the Member States. Scale involves cross-boundary effects. There is no indication of how these two criteria should be applied, nor how they should be balanced in the event that they produce conflicting results.[75] The question of scale is somewhat easier to grasp, in that the cross-border effects of an issue may be an arguable point, but it is at least a focused argument. Effectiveness, the idea that an objective cannot be *sufficiently* achieved by the Member States, and that it can be achieved *better* by Community action, raises several alternative approaches.[76] A presumption in favour of Member State competence may make the exercise easier, but this is a controversial interpretation. The Commission has developed a very different interpretation:

> Far from putting Community action in a straitjacket, it allows it to be expanded where circumstances so require, and conversely, to be restricted or abandoned where it is no longer justified.[77]

The British government sees the dynamic of subsidiarity as having only two points, the Community and the Member States.[78] Accordingly, the utility of subsidiarity for the British government is as a method for reclaiming jurisdiction over matters, particularly social policy, which have gradually come to be regulated by the Community. One minister's rephrasing of the principle makes this eminently clear – ' . . . things should not be done at the Community level unless they cannot be done at national level'[79] – and the British presidency of the Community in 1992 called it the 'principle of minimum interference'.[80] This would not only constitute a major reversal of the constitutional direction of the Community, but would also contradict the idea of an organic society which underpins most formulations of the principle.

The Commission has taken a much narrower view of the requirements of subsidiarity. Commissioners have made statements accepting the need for decentralisation and limiting their own powers,[81] but the practice does not always match the rhetoric. While the increased significance attached to the principle by Member States has led the Commission to alter somewhat its strategy on the implementation of the Social Charter,[82] in some cases the Commission considers it sufficient that Member States implement policies formulated at Community level.[83] The Commission sees subsidiarity as requiring a lesser intensity of action, such as the use of non-binding measures or framework directives, which leaves Member States greater room for discretion in implementation, but it sees the Community continuing to have a major policy role.[84] The Commission has therefore proposed an interinstitutional

---

[75] Toth, *op. cit.*, note 15, at 1097.

[76] Temple Lang, *op. cit.*, note 15, at 16. Emiliou, *op. cit.*, note 60, at 393, thinks that this criterion could actually have a centralising effect, and sees the scale test as an application of the effectiveness test.

[77] *The Principle of Subsidiarity*, Communication of the Commission to the Council and the European Parliament SEC (92) 1990 final, Brussels 27 October 1992. The Commission also argues that its right of initiative cannot be registered by applying the principle of subsidiarity.

[78] The fact that the logic of subsidiarity could equally apply to Scotland, Wales, Northern Ireland or local government generally in Britain, is ignored in this approach; see Lord Mackenzie-Stuart, *The European Community: Catchwords and Reality*, Josephine Onoh Memorial Lecture 1991 (1991), at 11.

[79] Francis Maude, quoted in Wilke and Wallace, *op. cit.*, note 61, at 21.

[80] Cited in Toth, *op. cit.*, note 15, at 1105. This interpretation does not appear to be consistent with subsidiarity as it is set out in Article 3b EC, which sets a standard of sufficiency, not necessity.

[81] Spicker, 'The Principle of Subsidiarity and the Social Policy of the European Community' (1991) 1 JESP 3, at 3 (Bruce Millan), 3–4 (Jacques Delors), and 11 (Sir Leon Brittan).

[82] *Ibid.*, at 11 (leaving some steps entirely to Member States, and using non-binding acts such as opinions and recommendations for others). See Chapter 17.

[83] *Ibid.*, at 12.

[84] *The Principle of Subsidiarity*, *op. cit.*, note 77.

agreement which would provide a framework in which subsidiarity could be applied in the legislative process.[85] The essential requirement, for the Commission, is that subsidiarity be integrated with the legislative processes, such as determining whether there is a sufficient legal basis for the proposed act, and not become a pre-condition for legislation.

Subsidiarity is an element of federalism, not a substitute for it. Commentators with differing views on the definition of subsidiarity have agreed that it can only be understood within the context of an explicitly federal system.[86] While the term 'subsidiarity' is of recent origin, principles similar to it can be found in all federal constitutions.[87] The irony of the current British position on subsidiarity is that it implicitly acknowledges the constitutionalisation and federalisation of the Community. What subsidiarity requires for its operation is a more rigid codification of Community and Member State powers. This is evident from the 1975 Report, the 1984 draft Treaty and from comments on a draft of the TEU in 1991, where Valery Giscard d'Estaing MEP advocated an approach to subsidiarity which would involve an explicit reconsideration of the division of powers within the Community, with Community powers based on the criteria of effectiveness and cross-boundary impact.[88] Such a move would only make the federalisation of the Community concrete rather than implicit.

While subsidiarity, once a consensus is reached, may assist in the political understanding of how power should be exercised within the Community, it cannot, in itself, enable courts or politicians to say whether any particular exercise of jurisdiction belongs with the Community, the Member States or with local or regional governments within the Member States. It is not an oracle from which answers to questions of power-sharing are automatically produced. In the absence of a new division of powers informed by subsidiarity, the principle is difficult to apply in a litigious setting. Issues of effectiveness, efficiency and appropriateness are not really legal concepts.[89] The fact that the preamble and Title I of the TEU are excluded from the Court's jurisdiction could possibly restrict the ability of the Court to interpret subsidiarity in specific cases.[90] If the courts, however, are not to determine whether the principle of subsidiarity leads to Member State or Community competence, then who should make such a determination? The result could simply be continued conflict between the Community institutions and Member States.[91] While subsidiarity, like supremacy, can assist in our understanding of the relationship between Community and national law, it cannot define it alone. At best it can create a presumption of jurisdiction in favour of the Member States. However, given the complexity of the jurisdictional divide, such a presumption may have little utility.

85 *Ibid.*
86 Emiliou, *op. cit.*, note 60, at 386, and Toth, *op. cit.*, note 15.
87 In the American Constitution: 'The powers not delegated to the United States by the Constitution or prohibited by it to the States, are reserved to the States respectively, or to the people.' German Constitution: 'The exercise of governmental powers and the discharge of governmental functions shall be incumbent on the Lander in so far as this Basic Law does not otherwise prescribe or permit.' (See Wilke and Wallace, *op. cit.*, note 61, at 2, 4, 8; Emiliou, *op. cit.*, note 60, at 388–9.) Canadian Constitution: 'In each Province the Legislature may exclusively make Laws in relation to Matters coming within the Classes of Subject next hereinafter enumerated . . . Generally all Matters of a merely local or private Nature in the Province.'
88 *Op. cit.*, note 72, at 6.
89 On the difficulties facing the ECJ in applying subsidiarity, see Lord Mackenzie-Stuart, *op. cit.* note 78; Wilke and Wallace, *op. cit.*, note 61, at 5–7.
90 Toth, *op. cit.*, note 15, at 1102.
91 Temple Lang, 'Powers', *op. cit.*, note 15, at 10, warns of how subsidiarity could be used in a way which paralyses the Community.

Supremacy of Community law

Due to the range of concurrent powers between the Community and the Member States, it is essential to establish which law will be paramount over the other in the event of conflict.[92] This is a requirement of any federation – where the valid laws of the central and regional authorities conflict, one must prevail over the other. While it is not immediately apparent from the Treaty that Community law should be supreme, the ECJ has derived the principle from the obligation to ensure the application of Community law contained in Article 5 EC. Supremacy obtains not only for legislation enacted before the Community provision was passed but for later legislation as well.[93]

The *Van Gend en Loos* case, quoted above, established the Community as an independent legal order from the Member States. However, it was *Costa* v *ENEL*,[94] which introduced the doctrine of supremacy. After reaffirming the independence of Community law, the Court went on:

> The integration into the laws of each Member State of provisions which derive from the Community, and more generally the terms and the spirit of the Treaty, make it impossible for the States, as a corollary, to accord precedence to a unilateral and subsequent measure over a legal system accepted by them on a basis of reciprocity. Such a measure cannot therefore be inconsistent with that legal system. The executive force of Community law cannot vary from one State to another in deference to subsequent domestic laws, without jeopardising the attainment of the objectives of the Treaty set out in Article 5(2) and giving rise to the discrimination prohibited by Article 7.
>
> . . .
>
> The precedence of Community law is confirmed by Article 189, whereby a regulation 'shall be binding' and 'directly applicable in all Member States'. This provision, which is subject to no reservation, would be quite meaningless if a State could unilaterally nullify its effects by means of a legislative measure which could prevail over Community law.

The Court added that to allow Community law to be overridden by national law would 'deprive it of its character as Community law', indicating that supremacy was an integral part of the Community legal system, not an addition.

The implications of supremacy were more clearly spelled out in the *Simmenthal* case.[95] First, the ECJ emphasised that supremacy affected both prior and future legislation:

> in accordance with the principle of the precedence of Community law, the relationship between provisions of the Treaty and directly applicable measures of the institutions on the one hand and the national law of the Member States on the other is such that those provisions and measures not only by their entry into force render automatically inapplicable any conflicting provision of current national law but – in so far as they are an integral part of, and take precedence in, the legal order applicable in the territory of the Member States – also preclude the valid adoption of new national measures to the extent to which they would be incompatible with Community provisions.[96]

92 Temple Lang, *op. cit.*, note 44, at 460.

93 This demonstrates the supranational nature of the Community legal system. With international law, for some States, subsequent law supersedes previous international obligations for the purpose of internal law: see Weiler, 'Transformation', *op. cit.*, note 1, at 2415.

94 Case 6/64, [1964] ECR 585.

95 Case 106/77, *Amministrazione delle Finanze dello Stato* v *Simmenthal* [1978] ECR 629.

96 *Ibid*, at paragraph 17 of the decision.

In this case, the Court added a new legal basis to the foundations of supremacy. Supremacy was linked to the reference procedure in Article 177 EC. In order for this procedure to be effective, the Court reasoned, the answer given in a reference must be capable of being applied by the national court. If Community law was not supreme over national law, this would be impossible. Concluding, the Court asserted the obligation of national courts to apply Community law in its entirety, and in particular, to ignore any rule of national law which might prevent it from enforcing the Community rights of individuals.[97]

The obligation to ignore conflicting national law was demonstrated more pointedly in the *Factortame* case.[98] Once again the importance of ensuring the effectiveness both of Community law generally, as required by Article 5 EC, and the Article 177 EC reference procedure in particular, was set out by the Court as a basis for its decision. As a consequence, Member States must disapply any rule which prevents the reference procedure from being effective. In *Factortame*, the applicants challenged British legislation which limited the possibility of registering a ship as British to persons and companies with a genuine connection with the country. The applicants, Spanish companies, were refused registration of their ships under the new registration system. The inability of the applicants to obtain an injunction against the Secretary of State for Transport, due to Crown privilege, was found to be an impediment to an effective reference. Without interim measures, the ultimate result in the case would be useless to the applicants because of the losses suffered due to the passage of time during which they could not operate their ships. The Court cited *Simmenthal*, and extended the scope of the rule in that case to cover interim measures:

> It must be added that the full effectiveness of Community law would be just as much impaired if a rule of national law could prevent a court seised of a dispute governed by Community law from granting interim relief in order to ensure the full effectiveness of the judgment to be given on the existence of the rights claimed under Community law. It follows that a court which in those circumstances would grant interim relief, if it were not for a rule of national law, is obliged to set aside that rule.
>
> That interpretation is reinforced by the system established by Art. 177 of the EC Treaty.[99]

While *Factortame* considered the temporary disapplication of a rule of national law, supremacy of Community law may, in some circumstances, require that Member States repeal conflicting legislation, not just disapply it.[100] As a matter of legal certainty, the existence of conflicting national law creates a situation of ambiguity which should not exist. There should be no question as to whether to rely on Community law or national law or both.

Community law is supreme even over provisions of national constitutions. *Internationale Handelsgesellschaft*[101] involved a possible conflict between a Community system of export licences for agricultural products, and human rights provisions of the German Constitution. The applicant argued that the Community regulation should be invalidated due to its conflict with the Constitution. The ECJ rejected any possibility of Community law being judged against national standards, even constitutional ones. The Court ultimately applied its own

---

97 *Ibid.*, at paragraphs 21 through 24 of the decision.
98 Case C-213/89 *R* v *Secretary of State for Transport ex parte Factortame Ltd* [1990] ECR I–2433.
99 *Ibid.*, at paragraphs 21 and 22 of the decision.

100 Case 167/73, *Commission* v *France* [1974] ECR 359.
101 Case 11/70, [1970] ECR 1125. The facts and decision of this case are set out in greater detail in Chapter 6.

human rights standards to the case, but refused to use national standards as anything but a possible source of Community law.

Accommodating supremacy in national law

While the development of the doctrine of supremacy of Community law by the ECJ has been straightforward, not so the accommodation of this principle by national legal and judicial systems. Some States, such as Belgium,[102] have managed the accommodation with relative ease. For others, whether monist (considering national and international law as a single system) or dualist (seeing international law as a separate system, which must be explicitly incorporated into domestic law), more complex strategies have been followed, sometimes to avoid the issue, sometimes to make supremacy palatable to the national system. The development of human rights principles by the ECJ was the Community reaction to the German courts' challenge to the supremacy of Community law. Three other States, the United Kingdom, France and Italy have accepted supremacy gradually, after a long process.

For the UK, the stumbling block has been the sovereignty of Parliament. As a result, for most of the period of British membership of the Community, the courts have derived the right to apply Community law from the European Communities Act rather than from Community law itself.[103] The courts have treated the Act as a permission by Parliament to apply Community law. However, under the usual rules of statutory interpretation, legislation which is subsequent to the European Communities Act would prevail over it. The courts nonetheless have been able largely to avoid the problem of absolute conflict of Community and British law.[104]

Finally, in *Factortame*,[105] the issue of conflict was addressed, with the response from the ECJ that a rule of English law must be disapplied, despite argument by the British government that this was a new remedy which the Court had no power to create. The ECJ, however, was of the view that the necessary remedy existed in English law, and that the matter involved the removal of a barrier, not the creation of a remedy. Supremacy of Community law required that the barriers to effective enforcement of Community law rights, created by national law, must be disapplied.

When the case returned to the House of Lords, Lord Bridge explicitly recognised that supremacy of Community law derived from the Community itself:

> If the supremacy within the European Community of Community law over the national law of Member States was not always inherent in the EC Treaty it was certainly well established in the jurisprudence of the Court of Justice long before the United Kingdom joined the Community. . . . Under the terms of the 1972 Act it has always been clear that it was the duty of a United Kingdom court, when delivering final judgment, to override any rule of national law found to be in conflict with any directly enforceable rule of Community law.[106]

102 See *Minister for Economic Affairs* v *Fromagerie Franco-Suisse 'Le Ski'*, Cour de Cassation, Belgium, 21 May 1971, [1972] CMLR 330.
103 *Macarthys Ltd* v *Smith* [1980] ICR 672 (CA) (per Cumming-Bruce and Lawton LJJ).
104 This was accomplished partly through construction, as in *Garland* v *British Rail Engineering Ltd* [1983] 2 AC 751, and partly through not referring certain types

of controversial cases: see Arnull, 'Article 177 and the Retreat from Van Duyn' (1983) 8 EL Rev 365.
105 *Op. cit.*, note 98. For the history of the passage of this case through the British courts, see Szyszczak, 'Sovereignty: Crisis, Compliance, Confusion, Complacency?' (1991) 16 EL Rev 480.
106 *Factortame* v *Secretary of State for Transport (No 2)* [1991] All ER 106 at 108 (HL).

However, it appears still open to question whether British courts would apply Community law as supreme if Parliament explicitly derogated from Community rules.[107] For the ECJ there is no question – Community law must be made effective. For the British courts, a more complex calculation may be necessary. Furthermore, the use by the House of Lords of the phrase 'directly enforceable rule of Community law' appears to leave intact its earlier ruling in *Duke* v *GEC Reliance Ltd.*[108] In that case, the House of Lords refused to interpret a provision of the Sex Discrimination Act 1975 in the light of the Community Equal Treatment Directive, due to the fact that the British legislation pre-dated the Directive and therefore the Act could not be seen as implementing legislation.[109] *Factortame*, if it applies only to directly enforceable Community law, does not oblige British courts to interpret legislation in accordance with Community law which is neither directly applicable nor directly effective.

France has experienced great difficulties in accommodating the supremacy principle, which have only recently been resolved. Article 55 of the French Constitution provides that ratified treaties have a legal authority superior to that of statutes. However, the principle contained in the article has not always been applied strictly. The approach used by the courts is known as the 'matter' doctrine, originally developed by the Cour de Cassation, the highest civil law court.[110] A court, faced with the possible incompatibility of a statute and a Treaty provision, will first attempt to interpret the two so that no incompatibility exists. If, however, this is not possible, the court will apply the Treaty over the statute only if the Treaty is subsequent to the statute. The problem, therefore, lies in applying the supremacy doctrine to statutes which post-date the EC Treaty.

The traditional case law of the Conseil d'Etat, the highest administrative court, was not very receptive to the application of European Community law. In *Syndicat Général de Fabricants de Semoules de France*,[111] the Conseil d'Etat decided that the ordannance in question had the force of statute. Since the ordannance was subsequent to the regulation, the Conseil decided that it could not apply the levy imposed by a Community agricultural regulation. Similarly, the Conseil refused to apply the direct effect of directives in the *Cohn-Bendit* case.[112] Despite the clear case law on direct effect, the Conseil concentrated on the fact that directives are only binding as to result, and that the Member State can choose the means of achieving that result. The Conseil seemed to consider the possibility of relying directly on the Directive as an interference with the Member State's freedom to implement directives by its own chosen method. Cohn-Bendit, according to the Conseil, should have contested the illegality of the *décret* implementing the Directive, rather than relying directly on the Directive itself.[113]

The means by which the problem of accommodating supremacy might be resolved was revealed in a 1975 decision of the Conseil Constitutionnel on the issue of whether abortion

107 Oliver, 'Fishing on the Incoming Tide' 54 Modern L Rev (1991) 442, at 445–6.
108 [1988] AC 618.
109 Where legislation post-dates Community directives, the courts have been willing to interpret in accordance with Community law: *Pickstone* v *Freemans plc* [1989] AC 66; *Litster* v *Forth Dry Dock and Engineering Co. Ltd* [1989] 1 All ER 1134.
110 Manin, 'The *Nicolo* Case of the *Conseil d'Etat*: French Constitutional Law and the Supreme Administrative Court's Acceptance of the Primacy of Community Law over Subsequent National Statute Law' (1991) 28 CML Rev 499 at 501.
111 [1970] CMLR 395.
112 *Ministre de l'Intérieur* v *Cohn-Bendit* [1980] 1 CMLR 543.
113 Tatham, 'Effect of European Community Directives in France: The Development of the *Cohn-Bendit* Jurisprudence' (1991) 40 ICLQ 907, at 910. Tatham goes on to demonstrate how the Conseil has eroded the practical effect of this decision, by allowing indirect reliance on the content of Directives.

violated the right to life as contained in the European Convention on Human Rights. The Conseil Constitutionnel clearly stated that review under Article 55 of the Constitution for conformity with treaty law, was distinct from its role in constitutional review of statute law under Article 61.[114] As was to become clear in later cases, this would enable civil and administrative law courts to deal with the issue of conformity with Community law. If Article 55 review had been subsumed under Article 61 constitutional review, only the Conseil Constitutionnel would have been able to undertake such review. The invitation offered by the abortion decision was taken up by the Cour de Cassation later that year in the case of *Administration des Douanes* v *Société Cafés Jacques Vabre*,[115] where the defendant argued that Article 95 EC, prohibiting discriminatory internal taxation, prevented France from charging higher tax on coffee processed in The Netherlands than on coffee processed in France. The Advocate General of the Cour de Cassation demonstrated to the court that, following the abortion decision, it could use Article 55 of the Constitution to apply Community law to the case, but suggested that the court should rely on the Community principle of supremacy rather than on domestic constitutional law. The Cour de Cassation did not follow this suggestion and used Article 55, but in doing so killed off the matter doctrine definitively. On the civil side, therefore, review of legislation for compatibility with Community law was established.

However, the separate system of administrative law courts continued to refuse to apply Community law as a standard in domestic French law until 1989. In fact, the Conseil d'Etat further distanced itself from the application of Community law through the development of the concept of '*loi-écran*', which stated that a statute ('*loi*') enacted subsequent to a Treaty provision acted as a screen ('*écran*'), preventing the administrative courts from applying the Treaty provision to administrative acts made under the authority of the subsequent statute.[116] In 1989, the anomaly between civil and administrative courts was finally resolved. Again the Conseil Constitutionnel paved the way. In 1988, acting as an electoral court, the Conseil Constitutionnel evaluated the French Electoral Code in light of the European Convention on Human Rights, using Article 55 as justification.[117] In the *Nicolo* case of 1989,[118] the Conseil d'Etat was acting as an electoral court for the elections to the European Parliament. Nicolo challenged the validity of the French elections to the European Parliament on the basis that citizens of French overseas territories could not legally have participated in the elections, whether as voters or as candidates. In particular, he argued that the relevant provisions of the electoral statute were contrary to the EC Treaty. The Commissaire du Gouvernement, who functions in a manner similar to an Advocate General in the ECJ, advised the Conseil to use Article 55 in order to examine the compatibility of the statute with the Treaty. The Conseil did so, and agreed that the statute was not in fact incompatible with Article 227 EC (which defines the territory of the European Community). With the finding that the statute was in conformity with the Treaty, the Conseil moved away from the *Semoules* decision, and towards accepting Community law as supreme. However, because the Conseil appeared to justify the overriding nature of Community law on the basis of Article 55, rather than on the

114 15 January 1975, discussed in Manin, *op. cit.*, note 110, at 503.
115 [1975] 2 CMLR 336.
116 Judgment of 13 May 1983, *SA Rene Moline*, Rec. Lebon, 191. For discussion of this concept and its later rejection by the French administrative courts, see Tou-chard, 'A propos de l'arrêt *Nicolo*' (1990) 106 *Revue de Droit Public et de la Science Politique* 801.
117 See Pollard, casenote on *Nicolo*, (1991) 16 EL Rev 267, at 272.
118 *Application of Raoul Georges Nicolo* [1990] 1 CMLR 17.

supremacy principle, the status of secondary Community legislation such as directives, and of decisions of the ECJ, remained unclear.[119] This ambiguity was largely resolved throughout the case of *Boisdet* in 1991, where the Conseil d'Etat justified a decision applying Community law on the basis of Community law itself, specifically the case law of the ECJ, rather than on Article 55.[120]

The Italian constitutional court (*Corte Costituzionale*) has been the setting for many conflicts over the supremacy issue. The early cases in which the ECJ established the principle of supremacy, *Costa* and *Simmenthal*, were both references from the Italian courts. Even after these pronouncements of the ECJ, the constitutional court remained reluctant to enforce Community law which conflicted with national law. Like the German constitutional court, it was initially reluctant to override the Constitution, particularly guarantees of fundamental rights, but eventually accepted Community rights as a substitute.[121] The specific acceptance of supremacy began in 1984 with the *Granital* case. In this case, concerning a conflict between a Community regulation and national legislation, the constitutional court decided that in such cases of conflict, the courts should disapply national law.[122] Unlike the French courts, the Italian constitutional court relied solely on Community law to justify the overriding of national law. It took an approach which used the concept of pre-emption, stating that once a Community regulation existed on a matter, the Italian State was no longer competent to legislate, meaning that only the Community provision should apply. However, doubts remained as to the scope of recognition of supremacy. Since, under Article 189 EC, Community regulations automatically become part of national law, but Treaty provisions and directives do not, the *Granital* decision created confusion as to how far the constitutional court would apply supremacy.

Later cases have further established the supremacy of Community law in the Italian legal system. In 1985, in *Spa Beca* v *Amministrazione delle Finanze*,[123] the constitutional court decided that Italian courts must also disapply national legislation which conflicts with judgments of the ECJ. This ruling was strengthened by the later decision in *Provincial di Bolzano* v *Presidente Consiglio Minstri*.[124] Here the constitutional court dealt with a conflict between national law and Treaty articles concerning equality of treatment of self-employed persons. The court moved away from the pre-emption approach adopted in *Granital*, and justified its decision by reference to supremacy as used by the ECJ. Specifically, it stated that Article 164 EC required the courts and administrative authorities of Member States to follow the judgments of the ECJ on provisions of Community law having direct effect. The court thereby explicitly recognised the supremacy of directly effective Community law.

119 See Manin, *op. cit.*, note 110, at 511–17, for a criticism of the use of French constitutional law to justify the supremacy of Community law.
120 *Boisdet* [1991] 1 CMLR 3.
121 See Chapter 6, and Hervouet, 'Politique jurisprudentielle de la Cour de Justice et des juridictions nationales: Reception du droit communautaire par le droit interne des Etats' (1992) 108 *Revue de Droit Publique et de la Science Politique*' 1257, at 1263–4.
122 *Societe Granital* v *Ministero delle Finanze*, 20 June 1984, (1984) 21 CML Rev 756; discussed in Hervouet, *op. cit.*, at 1273–5, and in Gaja, 'New Developments in a Continuing Story: The Relationship between EEC Law and Italian Law' (1990) 27 CML Rev 83.
123 See Gaja, *op. cit.*, at 83–4.
124 1989, I, 1076.

Acquis communautaire

The literal translation of this phrase is Community patrimony.[125] However, it does not refer to patrimony in a commercial sense, but rather to a body of legal 'assets': the entire body of Community law, including the treaties, all secondary legislation and judicial and quasi-judicial decisions made by Community institutions, as well as the non-binding acts such as opinions and resolutions of institutions.[126] The emergence of this concept can be traced to the enlargement of the Communities, and is contained in Articles 2 through 4 of each of the Acts of Accession marking an enlargement of the Community. Normally, when a State accedes to a treaty already in existence, it becomes bound only by the treaty itself, not by any acts done under the treaty before its accession. When new Member States joined the European Communities, however, it was necessary that they be bound by all the acts done by virtue of the treaties, not just the treaties themselves. It is essential for the operation of the Communities that all Member States be in the same position legally in terms of obligations under Community law and policy.[127]

The concept of *acquis communautaire* has also been significant within the context of European Union. The 1984 draft Treaty foresaw the Union taking over the *acquis communautaire*.[128] The TEU signed in 1991 for the first time brings the concept into a mainstream Community Treaty, with the idea that the *acquis* is something to be both maintained and developed further. This Treaty is very much a forward-looking document, and the *acquis* is acknowledged as the base to build on:

Article B
The Union shall set itself the following objectives:

. . .

- to maintain in full the *acquis communautaire* and build upon it with a view to considering, through the procedure referred to in Article N(2), to what extent the policies and forms of co-operation introduced by this Treaty may need to be revised with the aim of ensuring the effectiveness of the mechanisms and institutions of the Community. . . .

Article C
The Union shall be served by a single institutional framework which shall ensure the consistency and the continuity of the activities carried out in order to attain its objectives while respecting and building on the *acquis communautaire*.

. . .

In the Protocol on Social Policy, known as the 'Social Chapter', the 11 Member States who were parties agreed to develop further the *acquis communautaire* in this specific area, stating:

125 See Opinion of Advocate General Ver Loren Van Themaat, in Joined Cases 39, 43, 85 and 88/81, *Halyvourgiki Inc. and Helleniki Halyvourgi SA v Commission* [1982] ECR 593, at 619.
126 Toth, *The Oxford Encyclopaedia of European Community Law*, volume 1: *Institutional Law* (1991), at 9. The fullest definition contained in the case law comes from the Opinion of Advocate General Reischl, in Case 161/78, *P. Conradsen A/S v Ministeriet for Skatter og Afgiter* [1979] ECR 2221, at 2248: ' . . . all the regu-

lations, decisions, directives, etc. adopted by under the Treaties, and all decisions since the Communities were established'.
127 By virtue of the concept of *acquis communautaire*, Member States also commit themselves to the goals of the Community as well as to its binding law, see Article 3(3) of the Acts of Accession. Article 3 of the Accession Treaty relating to Britain is applied in Case 44/84, *Hurd v Jones* [1986] ECR 29.
128 OJ 1984 C77/83.

. . . that this Protocol and the said Agreement are without prejudice to the provisions of this Treaty, particularly those which relate to social policy which constitute an integral part of the 'acquis communautaire'. . . .

Nonetheless, it has been argued that the TEU is equivocal concerning the *acquis communautaire*. It may pledge to maintain and build upon the existing body of Community law, but may also undermine it by allowing opt-outs contained in Protocols, such as the exemption for Danish legislation governing second homes, the Protocol guaranteeing the application of the Irish constitutional provision outlawing abortion and the United Kingdom opt-outs from the third stage of Economic and Monetary Union and the Social Chapter.[129] Such derogations erode the uniformity of application of Community law. This could affect the integrity of the concept of the *acquis communautaire*, which, in enlargement situations, requires that Member States take Community law as they find it, not on a pick and choose basis. The danger of the current precedent is in the endorsement within the Treaty itself of such a 'menu' attitude to the obligation to apply Community law. The conflict between the old and new approaches to the *acquis communautaire* can be best demonstrated in the Social Chapter opt-out. The Chapter itself pledges the 11 participating Member States to build on the existing *acquis communautaire*, whereas the permission for the United Kingdom to remain outside the process means that there will be two types of *acquis* within the Community.[130]

European citizenship

European citizenship is key to the idea of the European Community as a supranational organisation. However, the original EC treaties left the issue of citizenship to the Member States, although theoretically this matter could always have been the subject of harmonising legislation under Article 100 or Article 235 EC. Citizenship is formally established by the TEU, requiring that a Member State treat nationals of other Community States in the same way as its own in certain matters relating to the traditional privileges attached to citizenship, such as voting and diplomatic representation. Initially, citizenship was not on the agenda in the negotiations on European Union. However, the concern of some Member States to improve the democratic elements of the Community led to the inclusion of this issue in the discussions of the Intergovernmental Conferences which led up to the TEU.[131]

European citizenship grew out of free movement of persons under the EC Treaty. Free movement of workers and freedom of establishment are primarily economic freedoms. Even before European citizenship became a concrete legal category, however, some writers saw in the right to freedom of movement within the Community, along with its ancillary rights such as equality of access to social security, an emerging citizenship.[132] This citizenship, if it could truly be so termed, was very limited in comparison with national citizenship rights. It could be more aptly described as 'passport rights'.

129 Curtin, 'The Constitutional Structure of the Union: A Europe of Bits and Pieces' (1993) 30 CML Rev 17, at 44–66.
130 On the equivocal status of the Social Chapter Protocol, see Curtin, *ibid.*, at 53–9.
131 Closa, 'The Concept of Citizenship in the Treaty on European Union' (1992) 29 CML Rev 1137, at 1153–7.

132 See, for example, Evans, 'European Citizenship: A Novel Concept in EEC Law' (1984) 32 AJCL 678, and 'Nationality Law and European Integration' (1991) 16 EL Rev 190; also Plender, 'An Incipient Form of European Citizenship' in Jacobs (ed.), *European Law and the Individual* (1976) 39.

Citizenship involves the extension of political rights to these persons who have moved to another Community Member State, and demonstrates the main difference between the concepts of the Single Market and the Union. The intention of the Single Market was to perfect the economic freedoms on which the Community was based. The Union involves much more co-operation on political and cultural levels, and thus citizenship is a necessary underpinning to its achievement. It is significant that citizenship is set out as part of the political union rather than the European Community. Matters pertaining to the Union are not subject to the jurisdiction of the Court. Ironically, one of the most supranational elements of the Treaty is governed by a primarily intergovernmental structure.

European citizenship is not equivalent to national citizenship. It can be most easily understood as a supplement to nationality of a Member State. In fact, the definition of European citizenship set out in Article 8 of the TEU makes the citizenship of a Member State a requirement of European citizenship. European citizenship is therefore a limited concept, providing limited rights. Member States are free to discriminate against non-nationals in those areas not protected by Community law.[133] Nonetheless, Articles 8 through 8e provide for considerable political rights, although conditional on further legislation being passed by the Council. This is a significant advance over prior Community law, which never foresaw a direct political relationship between citizens and the Community – even the elected representatives of the peoples of Europe were not the ultimate lawmakers within the Community until the 1991 Treaty.

Article 8a makes the right of free movement an incident of citizenship. The primary political right established is the right to vote, contained in Article 8b. This comprises two elements: the right to vote in municipal elections, and the right to vote in elections to the EP. These two types of elections are considered to be exempt from the concern over infringements of sovereignty. European Parliament elections involve the Community rather than national interest. Municipal elections do not directly influence State policy, and furthermore involve the exercise of delegated rather than original legislative authority.[134] These voting rights, however, do not come into effect with the Treaty. The Council must unanimously pass legislation providing for detailed arrangements, on proposal from the Commission, and after consulting the EP, by 31 December 1994. In addition to the right to vote for the EP regardless of where they live in the Community, citizens will have the right to petition the Parliament and to apply to the Ombudsman, as provided for in Article 8d.

The other main right is the right to external protection by the diplomatic and consular authorities of other Member States, set out in Article 8c. Citizens are entitled to such protection when in non-EU States where their own State does not have diplomatic representation. This right is to be secured by 31 December 1993, with rules established by agreement between the Member States and international negotiation, not by Community legislation.

Article 8e provides for the future development of citizenship. The Commission must report to the EP, the Council and the Economic and Social Committee before 31 December 1993 and every three years thereafter on the application of the provisions on citizenship. On this basis, the Council may, acting unanimously on a proposal of the Commission and after consulting the Parliament, adopt provisions to strengthen or add to citizenship rights, 'which

---

133 Closa, *op. cit.*, note 131, at 1139–41.　　　　134 *Ibid.*, at 1147–8.

it shall recommend to the Member States for adoption in accordance with their respective constitutional requirements'.

The value of these rights has yet to be seen. However, it is significant that there is now a specific part of the Treaty which consolidates all the rights of citizenship.[135] In addition, the term 'citizen' has been explicitly recognised within Community law. It is no longer a catch-all term for a collection of largely unrelated rights, nor an aspiration, but rather a legal reality.

CONCLUSION

Federalism was very much a feature of the debates leading up to the adoption of the TEU. Some Member States were concerned to establish with greater clarity the respective roles of national and Community policy-making. The emergence of supranational elements within Community law has given rise to this debate over federalism. Federalism is not a situation which may obtain in the future, but has a grounding in the present state of Community law. As in all federal systems, there is a tension between centralising and decentralising tendencies. Controversies over the use of harmonising legislation are examples of this. The debate over the principle of subsidiarity also reflects this tension. The infinite flexibility of the principle, however, seems to lead to a situation whereby everyone agrees on the need for the principle, but there are several different agendas on how it should be applied.

The TEU contains substantial evidence of the federalisation of the Community treaties. In addition to the principle of subsidiarity, it also gives to all Member State nationals certain additional citizenship rights as citizens of the European Union. Even as an addition to Member State citizenship rather than a replacement for it, this innovation was not accepted wholeheartedly by States. Citizenship was the subject of one of the declarations made at the Edinburgh Summit in order to enable Denmark to hold a second referendum on the TEU. Denmark was guaranteed that Union citizenship did not prevent Member States from deciding who would qualify as their citizens.

The ECJ has also contributed to the federalisation of the Community. It has largely done this through its enhancement of the status of Community law, through the enforcement of the supremacy of Community law over conflicting Member State law. This constitutes one of the centralising tendencies in Community institutional law.

The debate over how far the Community should resemble a federal State will doubtless continue for the foreseeable future, with new issues being raised by the prospect of enlargement of the Community to include European Free Trade Association States such as Austria, as well as Eastern European States. However, one option is no longer open – for the Community not to contain any federal elements at all.

Further reading

Closa, C., 'The Concept of Citizenship in the Treaty on European Union' (1992) 29 CML Rev 1137.

Cross, E.D., 'Pre-emption of Member State Law in the European Economic Community: A Framework for Analysis' (1992) 29 CML Rev 44.

---

[135] *Ibid.*, at 1157.

Curtin, D., 'The Constitutional Structure of the Union: A Europe of Bits and Pieces' (1993) 30 CML Rev 17.

Emiliou, N., 'Subsidiarity: An Effective Barrier against "the Enterprises of Ambition"?' (1992) 17 EL Rev 383.

Gaja, G., 'New Developments in a Continuing Story: The Relationship between EC Law and Italian Law' (1990) 27 CML Rev 83.

Hartley, T.C., 'Federalism, Courts and Legal Systems: The Emerging Constitution of the European Community' (1986) 34 AJCL 229.

Jacobs, F. (ed.), *European Law and the Individual* (Amsterdam: North-Holland, 1976).

Lenaerts, K., 'Constitutionalism and the Many Faces of Federalism' (1990) 38 AJCL 205.

Manin, P., 'The *Nicolo* Case of the *Conseil d'Etat*: French Constitutional Law and the Supreme Administrative Court's Acceptance of the Primacy of Community Law over Subsequent National Statute Law' (1991) 28 CML Rev 499.

Temple Lang, J., 'The Development of European Community Constitutional Law' (1991) 25 *International Lawyer* 455.

Toth, A.G., *The Oxford Encyclopaedia of European Community Law, volume 1: Institutional Law* (Oxford: Clarendon Press, 1991).

Toth, A.G., 'The Principle of Subsidiarity in the Maastricht Treaty' (1992) 29 CML Rev 1079.

Weiler, J., 'The Transformation of Europe' (1991) 100 Yale LJ 2403.

Weiler, J., 'The Community System: The Dual Character of Supranationalism' (1981) 1 YEL 267.

CHAPTER 4

External relations

INTRODUCTION

As the Community, and now the Union, has developed legislative competence in numerous policy areas, the issue of who should represent these interests in the international sphere has become more important. The power to negotiate and sign treaties on matters over which the Union has legislative competence has presented some problems, but these have largely been resolved by the ECJ. The question of the status of the Union as an international actor has created greater problems. The Member States have considered that there may be advantages to collective action in international relations matters. However, they have been reluctant to allow the Community institutions to acquire power over such matters, particularly as they pertain to defence and security issues. As a result, international action has largely taken place at an intergovernmental level. European Political Co-operation (EPC) enabled the Member States to make collective foreign policy statements. Under the Common Foreign and Security Policy (CFSP) established by the TEU, more concrete action could result, but this will depend on the will of the Member States.

The Union's main presence on the international stage, particularly in recent years, has been in the Uruguay round of negotiations on the General Agreement on Tariffs and Trade (GATT). The conflicts between the Union and the United States of America over the need for reform in the Common Agricultural Policy have been key events in the round, and at times threatened to prevent the conclusion of a new GATT treaty.

The Union has also had a long-standing involvement with the African, Caribbean and Pacific (ACP) States through the Lomé Conventions. These treaties set out the trade relationships with the Union, and give producers in these States certain rights of access to the Single Market.

Treaty-making powers

Certain limited treaty-making powers are conferred by the EC Treaty. However, of greater importance are the implied powers developed by the ECJ. It could be said that the right to make treaties is a consequence of the granting of legal personality to the Community under Article 210 EC, or at least the extension of that legal personality from the internal legal sphere to the international legal sphere.[1]

Articles 111, 113 and 238 EC provide for the only express treaty-making powers granted to the Community under the EC Treaty. Article 111 provides for the negotiations of tariff agreements with non-EC States. Article 113 is broader, allowing for the negotiation of

---

[1] In Case 6/64, *Costa* v *ENEL* [1964] ECR 1141, at 1159, the Court referred to the Community's 'capacity of representation on the international plane'.

treaties relating to the common commercial policy of the Community.[2] Article 238 provides for the conclusion of association agreements with non-EC States or international organisations, 'establishing an association involving reciprocal rights and obligations, common action and special procedures'.

Article 228 EC provides for the procedure which is to be adopted by the Community when entering into a treaty, although there are certain specific procedures set out in the Treaty articles granting explicit treaty-making powers. This article provides that the Commission will negotiate any treaty which the Community has the power to conclude, but the Council has the power to conclude the treaty, with the EP having the right to be consulted. Articles 229–231 EC pledge the Community to the maintenance of relations with several international organisations: the United Nations, GATT, the Council of Europe and the Organisation for Economic Co-operation and Development.

Despite these explicit external relations powers of the Community, which might have led to a strict interpretation that the Treaty was intended to be exhaustive on the Community's international role, the ECJ has implied powers in other areas. The interpretative mechanism used by the Court is the doctrine of parallelism, which states that the Community's international relations power should be co-extensive with its internal legislative powers. This doctrine was developed in the *ERTA* case.[3] This case involved the efforts of the Community to establish a common transport policy. Specifically, the objective was the conclusion of a European Road Transport Agreement with several non-EC States, and the issue was whether the Member States or the Community were competent in this area.[4] The Council had adopted a Resolution committing the Member States to the co-ordination of their approaches in developing the Agreement, and nominating the President of the Council to act as spokesman. The Commission challenged the validity of the Resolution on the grounds that under the procedure set out in Article 228 EC, it alone had the power of negotiation of the Agreement. The Court said that in the absence of a specific attribution of external relations competence in this area, the general system of external relations in the Treaty should be examined. The attribution of legal personality to the Community under Article 210 EC, according to the Court, meant that 'in external relations, the Community enjoys the capacity to establish contractual links with third countries over the whole field of objectives defined in Part One of the Treaty'.[5] Therefore, the treaty-making power may arise not only from specific attributions in Part One such as Article 113 EC, but may also 'flow from other provisions of the Treaty and from measures adopted, within the framework of those provisions, by the Community institutions'.[6] This is particularly the case, according to the Court, in the implementation of common policies such as the common transport policy, which had been legislated on by means of Regulation 543/69. External relations competence in such matters could not be separated from internal legislative competence.

However, it was not clear from the *ERTA* case exactly where it was permissible to look

2 The scope of the treaty-making power under Article 113 EC has been interpreted by the Court in an expansive way: see Opinion 1/78, *International Agreement on Natural Rubber* [1978] ECR 2871, and Case 45/87, *Commission v Council* [1987] ECR 1493.

3 Case 22/70, *Commission v Council* [1971] ECR 263.

4 Hartley, in *The Foundations of European Community Law*, 2nd edn (1988), at 158–61, examines the background to the *ERTA* case.

5 *Ibid.*, at paragraph 14. This reasoning, as applied in the later *Kramer* case, is criticised by Burrows, 'The Effects of the Main Cases of the Court of Justice in the Field of the External Relations Competences on the Conduct of the Member States' in Timmermans and Volker (eds) *Division of Powers Between the European Communities and their Member States in the Field of External Relations* (1981) 111, at 113.

6 *Ibid.*, at paragraph 16.

when attempting to derive a Community external relations power, since the Court referred both to the Treaty and to acts of the institutions. The question to be answered was whether the Treaty alone could ground an implicit external relations power, or whether the existence of some more explicit legislation on a matter was necessary. This was clarified to some extent in the *Kramer* case five years later, which dealt with power to conclude treaties within the scope of the Common Agricultural Policy, specifically a treaty on conservation of biological marine resources.[7] Here the Court decided that external relations power 'arises not only from an express conferment by the Treaty, but may equally flow implicitly from other provisions of the Treaty, from the Act of Accession and from measures adopted within the framework of those provisions, by the Community institutions'.[8] A final clarification was added in the *Inland Waterway Vessels* opinion,[9] where the Court stated that 'the authority to enter into international commitments may not only arise from an express attribution by the treaty, but equally may flow implicitly from its provisions'.[10] Such external relations power would arise 'by implication from the provisions of the Treaty creating the internal power and in so far as the participation of the Community in the international agreement is, as here, necessary for the attainment of one of the objectives of the Community'.[11] Therefore, the existence of Community legislation on a given policy area is not necessary for the external relations power to exist. The key element is the necessity of treaty-making to the attainment of a Community objective. This even goes beyond the idea of necessity of a common policy under the Treaty, as there are many objectives of the Treaty, such as ensuring the four freedoms, which are not strictly speaking common policies of the Community.[12]

The definition of necessity is, under the approach taken by the Court, crucial. The court has analysed this as a question of whether the exercise of external relations power by the Member States could amount to an interference with the exercise of Community jurisdiction over a matter.[13] It has also looked at necessity as a question of whether the implementation of an international agreement entered into by the Member States would necessarily involve the Community.[14] These views of the necessity issue explain the insistence of the Court that the acquisition of external relations competence by the Community operates to pre-empt Member State competence.[15] However, in many cases involving Community treaty-making, whether under express or implied powers, a mixed procedure has been used, whereby Member States and the Community are all involved in the negotiation of the treaty and are all parties to the treaty. This may, more than anything else, reflect the uncertainty of implied international relations powers in parallel to internal legislative powers, the extent of which is frequently a matter of dispute. In the *Natural Rubber Agreement* case, the Commission requested an opinion as to whether the draft agreement, as a mixed agreement, was compatible with the EC Treaty. The Court gave a rather equivocal opinion, holding that

7 Joined Cases 3, 4 and 6/76, [1976] ECR 1279.
8 *Ibid.*, at paragraphs 19–20.
9 Opinion 1/76, *Draft Agreement Establishing a European Laying-up Fund for Inland Waterway Vessels* [1977] ECR 741.
10 *Ibid.*, at paragraph 3. Barav, 'The Division of External Relations Power between the European Economic Community and the Member States in the Case-law of the Court of Justice' in Timmermans and Volker (eds) *op. cit.*, at 35, points out that unlike earlier cases, the Court does not refer here to acts of the institutions.

11 *Ibid.*, at paragraph 4.
12 See Barav, *op. cit.*, note 10, at 36.
13 Ruling 1/78, *Draft Convention of the International Atomic Energy Agency on the Physical Protection of Nuclear Materials, Facilities and Transports* [1978] ECR 2151 (ruling under Article 103 of the Euratom Treaty).
14 *Ibid.*, at paragraph 32.
15 *ERTA* case, *op. cit.*, note 3, at paragraph 31. The general concept of pre-emption is explained in Chapter 3.

Member States could be parties if they were financing the scheme. Since that question had not yet been resolved, the Member States could continue to participate in the negotiations for the agreement.

Article 228 EC grants the Court the power to give opinions on any draft treaty. Any such opinion is limited to the extent to which the proposed treaty is incompatible with the EC treaties. The Commission, the Council or a Member State may request the Court's opinion. The opinion may extend to the implications of the draft treaty for the institutions of the Community.[16] It is likely that the opinion should be sought before the treaty is concluded. This is indicated by the wording of Article 228 itself, and by the case law of the Court.[17] However, the ECJ, *obiter* in an early opinion, stated that the exercise of the treaty-making power could be reviewed under Articles 169, 173 or 177 EC.[18] The procedure for opinions under Article 228 EC is similar to that for other Court proceedings, except that the Court sits in private session, and the opinions of the Advocate Generals, all of whom participate, are not published.[19]

The most striking example of the Court's exercise of its power of review is in the two recent opinions on the treaty establishing the European Economic Area (EEA). This is a mixed agreement, negotiated by the Community and its Member States with the Member States of EFTA. The initial opinion was requested by the Commission while the EEA Treaty was still under negotiation.[20] The questions submitted by the Commission all related to the position of the ECJ under the draft EEA Treaty. The problem was that the Community was anxious to preserve the *acquis communautaire*,[21] and therefore to ensure homogeneity of interpretation of the rules which would be shared across the EEA. As a result, the judicial systems of the Community and EFTA were to be integrated to a large extent. The Commission requested the opinion of the Court on the following questions:

1 The question of the compatibility of the presence of judges of the Court of Justice on the EEA Court with the Court's Opinion 1/76 (on the draft agreement on the European laying-up fund for inland waterway vessels);
2 The question of the compatibility with the EEC Treaty of extending to the EFTA countries the right to intervene in Community cases pending before the Court of Justice;
3 The question whether it is possible, without amending the EEC Treaty, to allow courts from EFTA countries to submit to the Court of Justice questions on the interpretation of the agreement;
4 The question whether the system of courts provided for in the agreement is permissible under Article 238 of the EEC Treaty.[22]

The Court first found that the stated goal of homogeneity was not in fact achieved by the draft EEA Treaty, in that the goal of that treaty differed from that of the Community treaties. While the goal of the Community was economic integration of the Member States,

---

16 Opinion 1/75, [1975] ECR 1360; this is confirmed the Rules of Procedure of the Court, Article 107. See also ECJ opinions 1/91 and 1/92, on the setting up of the European Economic Area, *infra*.
17 *Ibid*. See Barav, *op. cit.* note 10, at 31.
18 *Ibid*., at 1361.
19 Article 108, Statute of the ECJ.

20 O'Keeffe, 'The Agreement on the European Economic Area' [1992] LIEI 1, at 12.
21 The totality of Community law, including not only the treaties, but also all legislation and the case law of the ECJ and the Court of First Instance. The concept of *aquis communautaire* is discussed in detail in Chapter 3.
22 Opinion 1/91, *Re the Draft Treaty on a European Economic Area* [1992] 1 CMLR 245, at 260.

the draft EEA Treaty, according to the Court, had the more limited goal of 'the application of rules on free trade and competition in economic and commercial relations'.[23] These differing goals operate despite the fact that identical language is used in the EC and draft EEA Treaties. It was the existence of these differing objectives that created dangers for the autonomy of the Community judicial system. Since the EEA Court would not be bound by the interpretations given by the ECJ on similarly-worded rules, but the ECJ would be bound by the EEA Treaty, which would become part of the Community legal order, the judicial system established by the draft Treaty conflicted with Article 164 EC in particular, but generally with the fundamental rules of the Community legal order. The fact that judges from the ECJ were to sit on the EEA Court would not necessarily prevent this undermining of the *acquis communautaire*. The Court did accept the idea that the courts of EFTA States could avail themselves of the system of references to the ECJ, but not that the decisions on such references would be non-binding. This situation could give rise to uncertainty concerning the status of rulings given by the Court under Article 177 EC. The Court then found that an amendment to the Statute of the Court would be sufficient to give EFTA States the right to intervene in cases before the ECJ. Lastly, Article 238 EC could not give the power to set up a judicial system which conflicted with Article 164 EC.

This decision demonstrates the far-reaching review which the Court is prepared to undertake in order to preserve the integrity and autonomy of the Community legal system. The Court was willing to stall, or perhaps even prevent, the achievement of the EEA Treaty in order to ensure that the judicial structure of the EEA did not undermine the *acquis communautaire*. Article 228 EC provides that if the ECJ decides that a draft treaty is incompatible with the EC Treaty, then it can be brought into force by using the procedure under Article N TEU,[24] which provides for the adoption of treaties amending the Union treaties by adoption in accordance with the constitutional procedures of each Member State. However, the decision of the Court that the EEA judicial arrangements are in conflict with the very foundations of the EC Treaty may exclude this possibility.[25]

The Council then requested that the Commission renegotiate the treaty. While this was a highly controversial move,[26] it did confirm the importance of the ECJ in the Community legal system, and specifically in external relations. In the renegotiated treaty, the idea of EEA courts was eliminated entirely. The language of the treaty articles concerning references by the courts of the EFTA States to the ECJ now indicates that the decision of the Court would be binding, although this is not explicitly set out.[27] Disputes over interpretations of the EEA Treaty are to be referred to a Joint Committee, and if no agreement is reached, the parties may request a ruling from the ECJ.[28]

The renegotiated treaty was then referred to the ECJ.[29] This second opinion is much shorter, as the Court accepted the renegotiated treaty as compatible with Community law. The fact that the EFTA Court would 'have jurisdiction only within the framework of EFTA and will have no personal or functional links with the ECJ',[30] and would be established by a separate agreement between the EFTA States, meant that the autonomy of the Community

---

[23] *Ibid.*, at paragraphs 15–18 of the opinion.
[24] Pre-TEU, the procedure to be followed was that set out in Article 236 EC (now repealed).
[25] See O'Keeffe, *op. cit.*, note 20, at 16.
[26] *Ibid.*, at 18, especially footnote 94.
[27] Article 107 of the EEA Treaty. The full text of the re-

vised treaty may be found at [1992] 1 CMLR 921.
[28] Article 111 of the EEA Treaty.
[29] Opinion 1/92, *Re the Draft Treaty on a European Economic Area (No 2)* [1992] 2 CMLR 217.
[30] *Ibid.*, paragraph 13.

legal system would be maintained. The *acquis communautaire* would not be undermined because the EFTA Court would not be part of the Community legal order in any way. The obligation of the Joint Committee[31] to review the development of the law by the ECJ and the EFTA Court, and to act to preserve the homogeneity of the law supported the integrity of Community law, despite the divergence of objectives of the EC and EEA regimes, but only insofar as the Committee was obliged to observe the binding nature of decisions of the ECJ.[32] The Court was also satisfied that the revised provisions on references from the courts of EFTA States guaranteed that the rulings of the ECJ would be binding.[33]

The power of the ECJ to give opinions on the validity of draft treaties, and to determine whether the Community has the power to enter into such treaties, has been crucial to the development of the Community's treaty-making power. By developing the doctrine of parallelism, it has expanded the international legal capacity of the Community. This capacity has been further expanded by the use of the concept of pre-emption to exclude the possibility of Member States making treaties which could undermine Community policies. Lastly, through the use of its power to give opinions on draft treaties under Article 228 EC, it has ensured that treaties entered into by the Community are compatible with existing Community law, and do not undermine the Community legal order.

European Political Co-operation and the Common Foreign and Security Policy

Security policy has been a continual problem for Europe throughout the life of the Community, a constant factor of post-war Europe. The division of Europe into East and West, as well as the question of what would be the role of Germany in the aftermath of Nazism, made security questions in particular, and foreign policy in general, unattractive to an organisation interested in integration.[34]

Until the TEU, European Political Co-operation (EPC) was the major means by which co-ordinated action could be taken by the Community Member States in foreign affairs questions. EPC operated outside the Community institutional framework, usually through the European Council summits. In the 1950s, two unsuccessful attempts were made to involve the Community in foreign affairs, through the proposed European Defence Community and European Political Community. However, throughout the 1950s and 1960s, the Community was inward-looking, and developed primarily in the economic sphere. By 1969, the Community felt less able to ignore world events, and at the Hague Summit of the Heads of State and Government, EPC was initiated.[35] The goals of EPC have been defined as: 'to ensure greater mutual understanding with respect to major issues of international politics, by exchanging information and consulting regularly; to increase their solidarity by working for a harmonisation of views, concertation of attitudes and joint action when it appears feasible and desirable'.[36] The function of EPC has always been the facilitation of common positions

---

31 Article 105 of the EEA Treaty.
32 Opinion 1/92, *op. cit.*, note 29, paragraphs 21–3. O'Keeffe, *op. cit.*, note 20, at 22–3, expresses doubts over whether the revised judicial system will in fact guarantee homogeneity.
33 *Ibid.*, paragraph 37.
34 An overview of the problems of regional security in Europe can be found in Salmon, 'The Union, the CFSP

and the European Security Debate' in Lodge (ed.) *The European Community and the Challenge of the Future*, 2nd edn (1993) 252.
35 Holland, *European Community Integration* (1993), at 118, discusses the emergence of EPC.
36 *Report by the Foreign Ministers of the Member States on the Problems of Political Unification*, 1970 *Bulletin of the European Communities*, vol. 1, 9, at 11.

and common action rather than the agreement of binding policies. The essence of EPC has always been consensus. Unlike Community legislative procedures, there is no possibility of agreeing to a position by majority vote. There is unanimity or there is nothing. Further, the operation of EPC through the European Council has effectively excluded the participation both of the Commission and the EP. EPC has been conducted by the Foreign Ministers of the Member States, assisted by a Political Committee and *ad hoc* working groups.[37]

Reform of EPC had been suggested as early as 1975, but this proposal integrated foreign policy into the Community to an extent which was unacceptable to most Member States. It was accepted that EPC had reached a plateau, where few advances in common action in international relations could be undertaken within the existing framework.[38] Like the European Council, EPC was legally recognised for the first time in the SEA. Article 30 SEA contains the definition of EPC, and sets out how it will function. A fuller definition of EPC than that of the 1970 Ministerial Report is provided by Article 30(2):

> (a) The High Contracting Parties undertake to inform and consult each other on any foreign policy matters of general interest so as to ensure that their combined influence is exercised as effectively as possible through co-ordination, the convergence of their positions and the implementation of joint action.
> (b) Consultations shall take place before the High Contracting Parties decide on their final position.
> (c) In adopting its positions and in its national measures each High Contracting Party shall take full account of the positions of the other partners and shall give due consideration to the desirability of adopting and implementing common European positions.
>
> In order to increase their capacity for joint action in the foreign policy field, the High Contracting Parties shall ensure that common principles and objectives are gradually developed and defined.
>
> The determination of common positions shall constitute a point of reference for the policies of the High Contracting Parties.
> (d) The High Contracting Parties shall endeavour to avoid any action or position which impairs their effectiveness as a cohesive force in international relations or within international organisations.

The Commission is given status within EPC for the first time, under Article 30(3), and, to a lesser extent, the EP under Article 30(4). The beginnings of a concern with security issues can be found in Article 30(6)(a):

> The High Contracting Parties consider that closer co-operation on questions of European security would contribute in an essential way to the development of a European identity in external policy matters. They are ready to co-ordinate their positions more closely on the political and economic aspects of security.

These amendments did not significantly change the practice of EPC, but laid the foundation for the move to a common foreign and security policy. The divergence between the aspirations of Article 30 and the requirement of consensus led to delayed action or inaction, particularly in sensitive areas such as the Gulf War and the former Yugoslavia.[39] Another factor which challenged the consensus rule was the prospect of enlargement of the

---

37 Holland, *op. cit.*, note 35, at 119–21. In 1973, further procedural developments were made in the Copenhagen Report, and in the 1981 London Report the EPC's procedures began to be codified.

38 Salmon, *op. cit.*, note 34, at 257.

39 Holland, *op. cit.*, note 35, at 134–9.

Community. Not only would the sheer numbers in an enlarged Community make consensus difficult, but several prospective Member States maintain a state of permanent neutrality, which would cause severe problems if only unanimous action was possible.[40]

The limited success of EPC in co-ordinating European action in the international sphere was sufficient, nonetheless, to inspire the effort in the 1991 Intergovernmental Conference on Political Union to extend EPC.[41] The failures of EPC led to something of a crisis, in that the choice seemed to be between the abandonment of EPC altogether, or the development of a better foreign policy system. The *status quo* did not appear to be an option. Eventually, as part of the move toward Political Union, the proposal to create new foreign policy structures seemed to prevail. However, the controversy moved on from whether or not there should be common foreign policy structures to their scope, and the procedures which would be followed, particularly with respect to voting procedures.[42] The result, as set out in the TEU, is the Common Foreign and Security Policy (CFSP). Article J declares that 'A common foreign and security policy is hereby established', but the policy is just an empty shell until defined by the Union and the Member States.

The CFSP is not a common policy in the way that the Common Agricultural Policy is. It exists outside the Community institutional framework as a separate pillar of the TEU.[43] It also exists alongside national foreign policies – the CFSP is not intended to replace national external relations. Security policy is now a Union concern, by virtue of Article J.4(2), leading possibly to a common defence policy. The definition of the objectives of the CFSP is set out in Article J.1(2):

- to safeguard the common values, fundamental interests and independence of the Union;
- to strengthen the security of the Union and its Member States in all ways;
- to preserve peace and strengthen international security, in accordance with the principles of the United Nations Charter as well as the principles of the Helsinki Final Act and the objectives of the Paris Charter;
- to promote international co-operation;
- to develop and consolidate democracy and the rule of law, and respect for human rights and fundamental freedoms.

The objectives are far more specific, far broader and far more security-orientated than EPC, even under the SEA. The main actors in the CFSP are the Council and the European Council. The European Council sets the guidelines as to which areas could be the subject of joint action, and the Council is empowered to make the decision that a matter should be the subject of joint action.[44] The Council also determines whether or not qualified majority voting should be used.[45] Review by the ECJ of acts done under the CFSP is specifically excluded under Article L TEU.

The CFSP brings together every possible permutation of action within the framework of the Union. The Member States have specific rights and obligations with respect to information, consultation and co-ordination of policy, under Article J.2. The Member States

---

40 The problems faced by neutral States in joining the community are canvassed by Subedi, 'Neutrality in a Changing World: European Neutral States and the European Community' (1993) 42 ICLQ 238.

41 Holland, *op. cit.*, note 35, at 119.

42 *Ibid.*, at 124.

43 See Chapter 2. The CFSP can use the Community institutions for its purposes, however, particularly the Council.

44 Article J.3(1) TEU.

45 Article J.3(2) TEU.

collectively, acting as the European Council, have the overarching power to setting guidelines on what will be discussed under the CFSP. The Community institutions also have roles, with the Council acting as main legislator, while the Commission is to be fully associated with all activities under the CFSP. The Commission, along with the Member States, may refer questions under the CFSP to the Council. A Political Committee, established under Article J.8(5), has the function of delivering opinions on the international situation, either at the request of the Council or on its own initiative. The Presidency of the Union represents the Union in matters relating to the CFSP.

The CFSP is potentially limited in scope. The European Council's guidelines may leave little room for devising common action. Further, it falls to the Council to decided whether common action or a common position is necessary. It is never obliged to act under the CFSP. Any decisions on common positions or common action will be made unanimously unless the Council itself has defined the question as a matter on which decisions will be made by qualified majority voting. This is likely to lead to the same kind of 'lowest common denominator' decisions which characterised EPC.[46] Lastly, the existence of a common position does not entirely restrict Member States from independent action, as long as such action is in conformity with the common position.

The EP is all but excluded from the CFSP process. Article J.7 requires only that the Presidency of the Union consults the EP on 'the main aspects and the basic choices' of the CFSP, and ensures that the EP's views are taken into consideration. The Presidency and the Commission have the further obligation to ensure that the EP is kept informed about the CFSP. Nothing prevents the EP from discussing foreign policy questions, however, and it takes very seriously its role in the democratic review of Union foreign policy.[47] Under EPC, the Parliament had obtained the agreement of the Member States to be allowed to put questions to the Foreign Ministers.[48]

A slight accommodation has been made for Member State neutrality within the TEU. Although all 12 Member States participate in the CFSP, Greece, Denmark and Ireland are not parties to a Declaration annexed to the Treaty on the Western European Union (WEU). The nine declaring States agree, under this Declaration, that the WEU forms part of the development process of the Union.[49]

Relations with GATT[50]

As stated above, Article 229 EC confers on the Commission the responsibility of maintaining relations with GATT. This is the most important international relations issue for the Union in the economic sphere. During a seven-year period ending on 15 December 1993, multilateral negotiations, called the Uruguay round, took place on a new world trade agreement. During most of that time the crucial conflict was between the United States of America and the Union.[51] The Union and the USA have extensive trading relations, and are

[46] Lodge, 'From Civilian Power to Speaking with a Common Voice: The Transition to a CFSP' in Lodge (ed), *The European Community and the Challenge of the Future*, 2nd edn (1993) 227, at 246.
[47] Bieber, 'Democratic Control of European Foreign Policy' (1990) 1 EJIL 148.
[48] *Ibid.*, at 168.
[49] The potential role of the WEU is discussed in Lodge, *op. cit.*, note 46, at 235.
[50] The 'Final Act Embodying the Results of the Uruguay Round of Multilateral Trade Negotiations' abolishes the GATT *per se* and replaces it with the new World Trade Organisation.
[51] 'The gavel descends and GATT becomes history', *Independent*, 16 December 1993.

now the most powerful trading blocs in the world. Consequently, it is not surprising that there has been an increase in trade disputes between the Union and the USA since the early 1980s, largely fought through GATT dispute-settlement mechanisms.[52] In the last days of the Uruguay round, smaller States complained that the Union and the USA had re-opened issues which had been presumed resolved, considering this practice an abuse of power in the context of multilateral negotiations.[53]

The problems which the Union has experienced in the GATT negotiations arise from the very nature of the system set up under the Treaty of Rome and the SEA. These treaties establish a common, and then a Single, Market. Goods and services move freely within the boundaries of the Single Market, but goods from outside may be subject to the full creativity of the national legislator to create boundaries to trade. Nowhere is this more prevalent than under the special regime created by the Common Agricultural Policy, which not only facilitates the exclusion of outside goods, but also subsidises European producers. It is the issue of agricultural subsidies, and the possibility of reform of the Common Agricultural Policy, which has exercised the minds of Union negotiators during the Uruguay round.[54] However, this is not a new problem. The commercial and agricultural policies established under Community law have been in issue in GATT negotiations since 1960.[55]

In the negotiations, the Commission negotiates for the entire Union, but each Member State retains its separate vote, although this is only a formality.[56] The Commission exercises the rights of the Member States on their behalf, and is a participant in all GATT bodies except the Budget Committee, the latter being excluded since the Member States pay the GATT contributions.[57] GATT has accepted the dual membership system adopted by the Union, making only the formal distinction between the Union and States by providing that its agreements are open for signature by 'contracting parties to the GATT and by the EEC [now the Union]'.[58] In fact, all customs territories are admissible as parties to GATT, under Article XXXIII.[59] However, the Union has been treated as a member with full rights in a way that other customs territories have not.

Relations with the developing world: the Lomé Conventions

The Union has concluded a series of association agreements with a group of African, Caribbean and Pacific (ACP) States on trade and development matters. The trade aspect of the agreements creates a quasi-common market between the Union and the ACP States, eliminating customs duties and non-tariff barriers to ACP goods coming into the Union, and granting Union-produced goods most-favoured-nation status in the ACP countries. Notably, however, this regime does not apply fully to agricultural products.[60] On the development

---

[52] Featherstone, 'The EC and the US: Managing Interdependence' in Lodge, (ed), *The European Community and the Challenge of the Future*, 2nd edn, (1993) 271, at 273.
[53] 'The gavel descends . . . ', *op. cit.*, note 51.
[54] This issue is discussed in greater detail in Chapter 18.
[55] Petersmann, 'The EEC as GATT Member – Legal Conflicts Between GATT Law and European Community Law' in Hilf, Jacobs and Petersmann, (eds), *The European Community and Gatt* (1989) 23, at 35.
[56] Everling, 'The Law of the External Economic Rela-

tions of the European Community' in Hilf, Jacobs and Petersmann, 85 *op. cit.*, at 93. Petersmann, *ibid.*, at 37, points out that consensus is the rule in GATT, so the retention of the vote is of little use to the Member States.
[57] Petersmann, *ibid.*, at 36.
[58] *Ibid.*, at 37.
[59] *Ibid.*, at 39.
[60] Lasok and Bridge, *The Law and Institutions of the European Communities*, 4th edn (1987), at 60.

side, the Conventions provide, from the European Development Fund, grants to small or medium-size industries, the provision of industrial expertise and stabilisation of export earnings (the Stabex system).

The Lomé Conventions were preceded by the Yaoundé Conventions of 1964 and 1969, which involved former colonies of the Member States. These Conventions were related to the desire of States such as France to maintain trading relationships with former colonies after decolonisation.[61] The first Lomé Convention was signed in 1975, in order to accommodate some of the former colonies of Britain after the 1972 enlargement.[62] The second, third and fourth Conventions were signed in 1979, 1984 and 1989, the last to cover a period ending in 1999. The third Lomé Convention integrated a food aid policy into the development aspects of the Treaty. It provided for the interests of the ACP States to be taken into account to a greater extent in food aid, particularly the export of agricultural surpluses.[63] It also provided guidelines which the Community agreed to follow in all provision of such aid, which require consistency of food aid with other development policies, and the prevention of undermining prices for domestically-produced goods. In the fourth Lomé Convention, only the trade provisions are to last for 10 years. The European Development Fund will need to be replenished after five years. The development provisions of the fourth Lomé Convention have moved into structural adjustment policies, which makes aid conditional on the adoption of acceptable macroeconomic policies by the recipient State.[64]

There is a fear that, given the restructuring problems facing Eastern Europe, the Union will redirect its energies and funds in the development field away from the ACP States towards the European region.[65] Furthermore, enlargement of the Union to include the remaining Scandinavian States, who have a more global approach to development, may encourage the Union to favour States with a good human rights record and to move away from a generalised regime such as Lomé.[66] Lastly, the completion of the Single Market, with its elimination of all trade barriers between Member States, could make the Union more inward-looking again, particularly in light of the economic difficulties experienced by all Member States in the early 1990s. All these factors call into question the future of the Lomé Convention regime.

CONCLUSION

The Community, and now the Union, has been characterised as 'an economic giant but a political dwarf'.[67] This can be demonstrated by the relative significance of the Union in the recent GATT negotiations, as opposed to its relative impotence in the face of the break-up of Yugoslavia. The responsibility for this state of affairs lies with the Member States, who have jealously guarded their national sovereignty in all fields of foreign relations, unless, such as in acting as a counter-weight to the United States of America in the GATT negotiations, the pooling of sovereignty makes the Union stronger than the sum of its parts.

[61] Hewitt, 'Development Assistance Policy and the ACP' in Lodge (ed.), *The European Community and the Challenge of the Future*, 2nd edn (1993) 300, at 305.

[62] *Ibid.*, at 300.

[63] Snyder, 'The European Community's New Food Aid Legislation: Toward a Development Policy?' in Snyder and Slinn (eds), *International Law of Development: Comparative Perspectives* (1987) 271, at 279.

[64] Hewitt, *op. cit.*, note 61, at 307–8.

[65] *Ibid.*, at 301–2.

[66] *Ibid.*, at 301, 303–4.

[67] Lodge, *op. cit.*, note 46, at 229.

The Union is still searching for a foreign policy identity outside trade negotiations. However, the structures and procedures as they exist at present are probably incapable of permitting that development. As a result, Union foreign policy will continue to be inconsistent and often incoherent. The need for unanimity will prevent the reaching of a common position in many cases. In cases where common positions are reached, this will often be driven, as was the issue of recognition of Croatia, Slovenia and Bosnia-Herzegovina, by the national considerations of the dominant Member States.

As for the position of the Union on development issues, the 1990s appear to have brought an increase in challenges with a concurrent reduction in the economic resources with which to address them. The Union will have to make difficult choices before the end of the decade as to its development priorities. Further, it will have to consider whether its current methods of structuring development aid continue to be appropriate, in the light of the possibility of changed values and goals for its development policy.

Further reading

Hartley, T.C., *The Foundations of European Community Law,* 2nd edn, (Oxford: Clarendon Press, 1988), Chapter 6.

Hewitt, A., 'Development Assistance Policy and the ACP' in J. Lodge (ed.), *The European Community and the Challenge of the Future*, 2nd edn (London: Pinter, 1993), at 300.

Holland, M., *European Community Integration* (London: Pinter, 1993), Chapter 5.

Lodge, J., 'From Civilian Power to Speaking with a Common Voice: The Transition to a CFSP' in J. Lodge (ed.), *The European Community and the Challenge of the Future*, 2nd edn (London: Pinter, 1993), at 227.

O'Keeffe, D., 'The Agreement on the European Economic Area' [1992] LIEI 1.

Petersmann, E.-U., 'The EEC as GATT Member – Legal Conflicts between GATT Law and European Community Law' in M. Hilf, F. Jacobs and E.-U. Petersmann (eds), *The European Community and GATT* (Deventer: Kluwer, 1989), at 23.

Subedi, S.P., 'Neutrality in a Changing World: European Neutral States and the European Community' (1993) 42 ICLQ 238.

Timmermans, C. and Volker, E., *Division of Powers between the European Communities and their Member States in the Field of External Relations* (Deventer: Kluwer, 1981).

CHAPTER 5

Legal effect of Community acts

INTRODUCTION

The EC Treaties contain no provision establishing the legal status of the Treaties themselves in the national law of the Member States. With respect to Community secondary legislation, Article 189 EC provides only the basic principles governing the legal force of regulations, directives and decisions. More importantly, the provisions of Article 189 EC have been interpreted and expanded by the ECJ so that Community law has a much stronger legal force in national legal systems than was originally thought possible. The Court has used several concepts to give effect to Community law so that individuals can rely upon it before their national courts. Three main concepts have been developed: (i) direct effect, which enables individuals to rely on Community law before national courts; (ii) the duty of interpretation; and (iii) State liability for improper implementation. The first of these, direct effect, requires Community rights to be clearly granted by a treaty or directive provision. Interpretation enables national courts to use Community law, even non-binding acts such as recommendations, to interpret rights granted less clearly by Community legislation, into national law. Lastly, the ECJ has established that there should be a right of action against States who do not properly implement Community law, even where the Community legislation in question does not give rise to direct effects.

The conceptual legal basis for many of these developments lies in Articles 5 and 189 EC.[1] Article 5 provides that:

> Member States shall take all appropriate measures, whether general or particular, to ensure fulfilment of the obligations arising out of this Treaty or resulting from action taken by the institutions of the Community. They shall facilitate the achievement of the Community's tasks.
>
> They shall abstain from any measure which could jeopardise the attainment of the objectives of this Treaty.[2]

Article 189 EC sets out the nature of the different forms of Community secondary legislation:

> . . .
>
> A regulation shall have general application. It shall be binding in its entirety and directly applicable in all Member States.
>
> A directive shall be binding, as to the result to be achieved, upon each Member State to whom it is addressed, but shall leave to the national authorities the choice of form and methods.
>
> A decision shall be binding in its entirety upon those to whom it is addressed.
>
> Recommendations and opinions shall have no binding force.

---

[1] Curtin, 'Directives: The Effectiveness of Judicial Protection of Individual Rights' (1990) 27 CML Rev 709, at 714–15.

[2] Temple Lang, 'Community Constitutional Law: Article 5 EEC Treaty' (1990) 27 CML Rev 645.

These two articles have also been the basis of supremacy of Community law.[3] The ECJ has also used Article 5 EC extensively as an interpretative principle in many areas of Community law. As such, it has become the legal justification for the doctrine of effectiveness of Community law. Effectiveness should not be confused with direct effect.[4] The former is a general interpretative principle, which enables the ECJ to determine the content of particular provisions of Community law.[5] Direct effect is the means by which individuals may rely on Community law rights within their domestic legal systems. It can be seen as an aspect of effectiveness, but it is a separate concept.

It is also important to recognise that direct applicability is a distinct concept from direct effect.[6] Unfortunately, in early cases the ECJ used the two phrases interchangeably.[7] As will be demonstrated below, direct applicability has an entirely different role in Community law. Certainly, it was the only way in which the Treaty foresaw that Community legislation could penetrate national legal systems. The Court has never explicitly made the distinction, but it is quite clear that direct applicability, as defined by the Treaty, has markedly different implications from direct effect as developed by the ECJ.

The possibility of individuals invoking Community rights has been crucial in the implementation of Community law. The enforcement procedures applied by the Commission are limited and time-consuming.[8] In addition, it is always possible that inadequate implementation only becomes evident through the experience of the law by individuals. The ECJ, in developing direct effect and related concepts, has facilitated the enforcement of Community law, by making every citizen of the Community a potential enforcement official.

Direct applicability

The only form of Community law which is expressly described as having legal force in the systems of the Member States is the regulation. By virtue of Article 189 EC, 'A regulation shall have general application. It shall be binding in its entirety and directly applicable in all Member States'. This eliminates the need for Member States to pass legislation incorporating the regulation.[9] In fact, Member States *must* not attempt to implement regulations. The crucial point arising from the concept of direct applicability is that regulations become part of the national legal systems as *Community* law, and are applied as such.[10] Any attempt by a Member State to transform a regulation into national law through adopting it as a law by ordinary legislative procedures will be void.

The 1973 enforcement action against Italy gave the Court the opportunity to expound in detail the idea of direct applicability, and the prohibition on the implementation of regulations.[11] Italy had adopted a decree implementing a regulation providing premiums for

---

3 See Chapter 3.

4 On the relationship between direct effect, the doctrine of effectiveness and supremacy of Community law, see Case 106/77, *Amministrazione delle Finanze dello Stato v Simmenthal* [1978] ECR 629.

5 Temple Lang, *op. cit.*, note 2, at 664.

6 Winter, 'Direct Applicability and Direct Effect: Two Distinct and Different Concepts in Community Law' (1972) 9 CML Rev 425, especially at 431–7. He explains how direct applicability in Article 189 EC differs from the concept of direct applicability in international law.

7 For a rare attempt to correct this, see the opinion of Advocate General Reischl in Case 148/78, *Pubblico Ministero v Ratti* [1979] ECR 1629.

8 See Chapter 8.

9 Winter, *op. cit.*, note 6, at 436.

10 The independence of regulations is affirmed by the Court in, for example, Case 31/78, *Bussone v Minister for Agriculture and Forestry* [1978] ECR 2429, at paragraph 30.

11 Case 39/72, *Commission v Italy* [1973] ECR 101. See also Case 55/77, *Maris v Rijksdienst voor Werkenemerspensioenen* [1977] ECR 2327, at paragraph 17.

the slaughtering of surplus dairy cattle. The Court agreed with the Commission that this was a serious breach of fundamental Community law. The Court objected not only to the fact that Italy had 'distorted' the provisions of the regulation in enacting them,[12] but also to the mere fact of attempting to enact the regulation:

> By following this procedure, the Italian Government has brought into doubt both the legal nature of the applicable provisions and the date of their coming into force. . . . all methods of implementation are contrary to the Treaty which would have the result of creating an obstacle to the direct effect of Community Regulations and of jeopardising their simultaneous and uniform application in the whole of the community.[13]

After quoting Article 189 EC's definition of the legal status of regulations, the Court continued:

> In consequence, it cannot be accepted that a Member State should apply in an incomplete or selective manner provisions of a Community Regulation so as to render abortive certain aspects of Community legislation which it has opposed or which it considers contrary to its national interests.[14]

There are two important points in the Court's reasoning highlighted in the paragraphs above. First, we see the Court re-affirming the nature of regulations. They are intended to apply simultaneously and uniformly throughout the Community and, in particular, they must apply notwithstanding any objection a Member State may have had when the Council adopted the measure. Secondly, the fact of implementation creates a doubt in the mind of the public as to the status of the law, whereas the law should be unambiguously Community law. The Court concluded its decision by adding that the attempt to prevent the full and complete application of the regulation amounted to a 'failure in the duty of solidarity'.[15] Although Article 5 EC is not referred to in this decision, solidarity is one of the duties which arise out of that article.[16]

The independence of Community regulations was reiterated in the *Variola* case.[17] This includes, for the ECJ, any measure which might interfere with the jurisdiction of the Court to interpret Community law, and any measure which conceals from the public the fact of the Community nature of the law. No internal law can be set up against a Community regulation.[18]

The only exception to the prohibition on national implementation measures with respect to regulations is where the regulation itself specifically authorises them.[19] These will usually be fairly limited, such as administrative and financial measures for the collecting or distributing of money, rather than the primary legislation which is usually required in order to achieve the result required by a directive. The ECJ has accepted that administrative or procedural rules may be necessary in order for the regulation to be fully effective.[20] The implementing

---

12 *Commission* v *Italy*, at paragraph 15.

13 *Ibid.*, at paragraph 17. Note the ambiguous use of the term 'direct effect'.

14 *Ibid.*, at paragraph 20.

15 *Ibid.*, at paragraph 25.

16 See Temple Lang, *op. cit.*, note 2, at 677.

17 Case 34/73, *Fratelli Variola* v *Amministrazione Italiana delle Finanze* [1973] ECR 981.

18 *Ibid.*, at paragraph 15.

19 *Bussone, op. cit.*, note 10.

20 Case 94/77, *Fratelli Zerbone Snc* v *Amministrazione delle Finanze dello Stato* [1978] ECR 99. In Case 272/83, *Commission* v *Italy* [1985] ECR 1057, the Court allowed that such administrative implementation may require the incorporation of some provisions of the regulation in question into the implementation measures. Incorporation is normally prohibited, as it conceals the nature of the act as a Community rather than a national measure.

powers include the adoption of interpretative measures, although these cannot be binding,[21] and the imposition of sanctions[22] for breach of the provisions of the regulation. This mitigation of the strict rule of independence of regulations seems to have been developed for reasons of efficiency of application, as a commonsense rule, rather than a conceptual development of the nature of regulations as set out in Article 189 EC.

Nonetheless, it could be argued that any regulation which provides for an element of discretion in its implementation is not a true regulation, and that the Court should be more careful in allowing for Member State discretion, however narrowly defined. Just as the idea of clear rights being created by directives has been objected to on the ground that it undermines the true nature of a directive (which is supposed to be binding only as to result), a regulation which provides for discretionary elements of implementation may not be truly a regulation, which is to be immediately binding in its entirety and is to have the status of Community law. At the very least, discretionary implementation undermines the distinction between regulations and directives. Importantly, national courts are required to ensure that the measures implementing the regulation do not undermine the content of the regulation.[23]

Direct applicability does not automatically imply that individuals may acquire rights from any particular regulation. Unlike direct effect, which *always* signifies that the legislation in question grants rights to individuals, direct applicability designates the legal status of the regulation, which may or may not create justiciable rights, according to the drafting of the regulation. Regulations are described as being capable of creating individual rights, not as creating them by the nature of the act.[24] It is essentially a matter of judicial interpretation. The Court must determine whether or not the regulation creates rights against the State, and the legislature must do nothing to frustrate such rights.[25] Nonetheless, most regulations do have direct effects. For example, the regulation may require certain national measures to be adopted.

Regulations may create pre-emption, meaning that the existence of Community legislation in an area may preclude further legislation by Member States.[26] This obligation not to legislate in such a way as to interfere with the exercise of Community jurisdiction is strict:

> From the moment that the Community adopts regulations under Article 40 of the Treaty establishing a common organisation of the market on a specific sector the Member States are under a duty not to take any measure which might create exemptions from them or affect them adversely.[27]

Regulations, therefore, become part of national law in their entirety. For individuals, they are exactly like any other national law. National courts must take account of them, whether or not they create rights for individuals. The status of regulations as *part* of national law is different from the duty of conform interpretation, where national courts use Community law

21 Fratelli Zerbone, *op. cit.*, at paragraph 27, and per Advocate General Warner at 126.
22 Case 50/76, *Amsterdam Bulb BV v Produktschap voor Siergewassen* [1977] ECR 137, at paragraph 33.
23 Case 230/78, *SpA Eridania-Zuccherifici v Ministry of Agriculture and Forestry* [1979] ECR 2749.
24 Case 43/71, *Politi v Ministry of Finance* [1971] ECR 1039. The effect of a regulation, according to the Court, by virtue of Article 189 EC, is to prevent the adoption of incompatible national measures (paragraph 9).

25 Case 93/71, *Leonisio v Minister for Agriculture and Forestry* [1972] ECR 287, paragraphs 19–22 and the opinion of Advocate General Roemer, at 300–1.
26 Case 74/69, *Hauptzollamt Bremen-Freihafen v Waren-Import-Gesellschaft Krohn and Co* [1970] ECR 451, at paragraph 4.
27 *Amsterdam Bulb, op. cit.*, note 22, at paragraph 8.

in order to *interpret* national law. National legislatures may not deal with regulations, nor, in some cases, with the subject matter of the regulation.

Direct effect

The status of the EC Treaty in the domestic legal systems of the Member States would normally depend on whether the national legal system was *monist* or *dualist* with respect to international law. Monist legal systems consider all law, national and international, to be one single system, and therefore treaties do have some automatic status within the legal system.[28] Dualist legal systems apply a separation between national and international law. In a dualist system, such as that in the UK, treaty law has to be enacted explicitly into national law in order to have effect in the domestic legal system. Otherwise, it has only interpretative value, in that the courts will presume that the legislature does not wish to violate international obligations undertaken by the executive.

The ECJ, however, has developed a new concept of legal penetration into the Member States' legal systems: direct effect. Direct effect means that Treaty provisions can create rights which individuals may rely on before their domestic courts. It is only by considering the usual relationship of national and international law, as set out above, that direct effect can be seen in context. In the case which established the concept of direct effect, *Van Gend en Loos*,[29] the Court declared that the Community could not be understood as just another international organisation, created by a treaty which was a contract between States. The Community instead is to be seen as a relationship between the Community, the Member States and individual persons and undertakings. It was nothing short of a revolution.

In *Van Gend en Loos*, the Commission argued that Article 12 EC, prohibiting customs duties and charges having equivalent effect, created rights which individuals could rely on against a Member State which had failed in its obligations under that Article. The Court accepted these arguments, rejecting the opinion of Advocate General Roemer that the Treaty created obligations on Member States which did not correlate to rights of individuals. It began by rejecting the argument that the EC Treaty was just another international agreement:

> the Community constitutes a new legal order of international law for the benefit of which States have limited their sovereign rights, albeit within limited fields, and the subjects of which comprise not only Member States but also their nationals.[30]

The consequence of this, for the Court, is that individuals have rights and obligations arising out of the Treaty which are enforceable at national law:

> Independently of the legislation of Member States, Community law therefore not only imposes obligations on individuals but is also intended to confer upon them rights which become part of their legal heritage. These rights arise not only where they are expressly granted by the Treaty, but also by reason of obligations which the Treaty imposes in a clearly defined way upon individuals as well as upon the Member States and upon the institutions of the Community.[31]

28 However, there is a great deal of variation in the application of this principle; see discussion of the supremacy of Community law in Chapter 3.
29 Case 26/62, *Van Gend en Loos* v *Nederlands Administratie de Belastingen* [1963] ECR 1. On the background to the case, see Pescatore, 'The Doctrine of "Direct Effect": An Infant Disease of Community Law' (1983) 8 EL Rev 155, at 156–7.
30 *Van Gend en Loos, op. cit.,* at 12.
31 *Ibid.*

Significantly, the Court rejected the argument that the existence of an enforcement procedure in Articles 169 and 170 EC precluded the direct reliance on Treaty rights by individuals before their national courts. Two reasons were given. First, the idea was put forward that the individual rights created by directly effective Treaty law were of a different character from the right of the Commission to ensure the effective functioning of the Community in a more general sense.[32] Secondly, the additional possibility of discovering and correcting failures to implement Community law would create fuller enforcement of the Treaty.[33]

Direct effect can be distinguished from direct applicability in that it relates to specific rights rather than entire legislative acts. Direct effect of a Community law provision does not mean that the provision becomes part of national law. Instead it means that the rights created by the provision are capable of being invoked in national law. The difference is slight in practice but important in terms of the special status of regulations under Article 189 EC.

Not every Treaty article is capable of creating direct effects. The Court set out in *Van Gend en Loos* criteria which have been followed since, although the language used by the Court to describe these criteria changes. In order to create direct effects, the right must be clear and precise, it must be unconditional or legally perfect, and it must not depend on further implementation by the Community institutions or the discretion of Member States.[34] The Court also indicated that the obligation on Member States should be negative rather than positive, but this factor seems to have been ignored by the Court subsequently, although most directly effective provisions of the Treaty do involve an absolute prohibition.

That a Treaty article is 'clear and precise' usually means a clear prohibition or statement of right. For example, any provision which declares that discrimination shall be eliminated would be sufficiently clear and precise for direct effect.[35] If a provision, on the other hand, gives Member States a discretion as to an element of the obligation, then direct effect will not apply.[36] Such discretion is seen as an interposition between Community law and the individual. The lack of clarity or precision in a Treaty article may be cured, to a certain extent, by the adoption of secondary legislation which supplements and explains the imprecise terms.[37] The criterion of unconditionality often relates to the expiry of a transitional period.[38] Until the expiry of such a transitional period, the obligation is not legally perfect and cannot be directly effective.[39] Another example of conditionality is contained in Article 48(3) EC which requires implementing regulations to be adopted. Transitional provisions may themselves create direct effects, such as Article 31 EC's prohibition on the introduction of new restrictions on the free movement of goods.[40] The necessity of further action by the Member States or the Community institutions, usually the Commission, will also prevent direct effect, again because of the interposition of further discretion between the legal rule and the individual.[41] The Court has become somewhat less

---

32 *Ibid.*, at 13. See also Case 28/67, *Molkerei-Zentrale Wastfalen/Lippe GmbH v Hauptzollamt Paderborn* [1968] ECR 143, at 153.
33 *Ibid.*
34 *Ibid.* See also Case 57/65, *Lutticke v Hauptzollamt Saarlouis* [1966] ECR 205.
35 *Molkerei-Zentrale, op. cit.*, note 32, at 152–3.
36 *Ibid.*, at 156.
37 Case 41/74, *Van Duyn v Home Office* [1974] ECR 1337.
38 For directives, this will be the period, usually two or three years, during which Member States are to enact all

necessary implementation measures.
39 *Lutticke, op. cit.*, note 34; Case 33/70, *SACE v Italian Ministry of Finance* [1970] ECR 1213, at paragraphs 9–10; Case 18/71, *Eunomia v Italy* [1971] ECR 811, at paragraph 7.
40 Case 13/68, *Salgoil v Italy* [1968] ECR 453, at 460. Once the condition of supplying lists of product areas liberalised had been supplied, Article 31 EC was no longer subject to a condition, and could be directly effective.
41 Case 6/64, *Costa v ENEL* [1964] ECR 585.

strict in its application of this criterion. The fact that a Treaty article provides for the enactment of directives in order to implement fully its objects does not preclude the article itself creating directly effective rights.[42] In directives, the fact that a Member State may choose between a number of ways of implementing the objectives of the directive does not prevent direct effect from being created,[43] particularly if the provision in question defines the scope of Member State discretion.[44] However, it would appear that where the creation of institutions is involved, the Member State's discretion on that matter will preclude direct effects.[45]

The three criteria for finding that a provision of Community law creates direct effects are interrelated. In fact, the Court has decided that a Treaty article was conditional when it could be argued that it was more a matter of whether or not it was drafted in sufficiently precise terms.[46] Sometimes the line between conditionality and discretion of Member States is fine as well. The condition may be the adoption of measures by a State, which could also be seen as the retention of residual discretion. The only possible distinction is that conditionality implies that at some stage the Member State's discretion may be exhausted, such as when a certain measure is adopted, whereas residual discretion implies that the discretion is retained in perpetuity. However, such a distinction does not clearly arise from the case law.[47]

Originally, direct effect was considered only in the context of actions by individuals against Member States. It was inevitable that individuals should also seek to rely on Community law rights against other individuals. Direct effect acting between an individual and a Member State is termed vertical direct effect. When the direct effect of Community law rights is raised in an action between individuals, it is called horizontal direct effect.

The recognition of direct effect of Treaty provisions as between individuals began in *BRT* v *SABAM*, where the Court acknowledged that the main competition provisions, Articles 85 and 86, create direct effects between individuals.[48] Later that year, in *Walrave and Koch* v *Union Cycliste Internationale*, dealing with discrimination in free movement of persons and freedom to provide services, the Court made the following statement:

> Prohibition of such discrimination [Articles 7, 48 and 59] does not only apply to the action of public authorities but extends likewise to rules of any other nature aimed at regulating in a collective manner gainful employment and the provision of services. The abolition as between Member States of obstacles to freedom of movement for persons and to freedom to provide services, which are fundamental objectives of the Community as contained in Article 3(c) of the Treaty, would be compromised if the abolition of barriers of national origin could be neutralised by obstacles resulting from the exercise of their legal autonomy by associations or organisations which do not come under public law.[49]

One case which is regarded as confirming horizontal direct effect in Community law is *Defrenne* v *SABENA*,[50] concerning Article 119 EC, which guarantees equal pay between men

---

[42] Case 2/74, *Reyners v Belgium* [1974] ECR 631, at paragraph 26.

[43] Case 286/85, *McDermott and Cotter v Minister for Social Welfare* [1987] ECR 1453, at paragraph 15.

[44] Case 126/82, *Smit v Commissie Grensoverschrijdend Beroepsgoedernvervoer* [1983] ECR 73, at paragraph 12.

[45] Joined Cases C-6 and C-9/90, *Francovich v Italy* [1992] IRLR 85.

[46] Case 203/80, *Casati* [1981] ECR 2595.

[47] Implicitly, however, the distinction may be seen in Case 8/81, *Becker v Finansamt Munster-Innenstadt* [1982] ECR 53.

[48] Case 127/73, *Belgische Radio en Televisie v Société Belge des Auteurs, Compositeurs, et Editeurs* [1974] ECR 51, at paragraph 16.

[49] Case 36/74, [1974] ECR 1405, at paragraphs 17–18.

[50] Case 43/75, [1976] ECR 455. The substantive issues of this case are discussed in detail in Chapter 16.

and women for equal work. Advocate General Trabucchi argued in his opinion that 'fundamental objectives' of the Treaty referred to in the decision in *Walrave and Koch* must be interpreted liberally, and that direct effect should be extended to Article 119. Further, he argued, the crucial factor was not to whom a provision of Community law is addressed, but the nature of the provision itself.[51] The ECJ accepted these arguments, emphasising the importance of the social objectives of the Community and reiterating the irrelevance of the addressee of a measure for the purposes of direct effect.[52] In dismissing arguments relating to the scope of direct effects of Article 119, the Court stated:

> In fact since Article 119 is mandatory in nature, the prohibition on discrimination between men and women applies not only to the action of public authorities, but also extends to all agreements which are intended to regulate paid labour collectively, as well as to contracts between individuals.[53]

The breadth of the language used by the Court effectively closed the issue of whether or not Treaty articles created direct effects between individuals.

Direct effect of secondary legislation

Article 189 EC makes a clear distinction between the nature of regulations and directives. Regulations, as seen above, are binding in national law in their entirety. Directives are binding 'as to the result to be achieved', and are stated to be binding on *Member States*. It would therefore appear that the implementation and enforcement of directives is a matter between the Member States and the Community, in which individuals have no role. Individuals, it would appear, benefit from directives only when and insofar as they are implemented[54] in domestic law. From Article 189, it would appear that individuals rely on regulations as Community law, but on directives as national law.[55] However, from the moment that the ECJ found that Treaty articles could create direct effects, the possibility of the same concept being applied to directives arose. It was, nonetheless, over a decade later that the issue was clarified.

The possibility of extending direct effect beyond Treaty articles first happened in *Grad* v *Finanzamt Traunstein*.[56] In *Grad*, the Court was perhaps on safe ground, in that it was dealing with decisions:

> although it is true that by virtue of Article 189, regulations are directly applicable and therefore by virtue of their nature capable of producing direct effects, it does not follow from this that other categories of legal measures mentioned in that article can never produce similar effects. In particular, the provision according to which decisions are binding in their entirety on those to whom they are addressed enables the question to be put whether the obligation created by the decision can only be invoked by the Community institutions against the addressee or whether such a right may possibly be exercised by all

---

51 *Ibid.*, at 483.
52 *Ibid.*, at paragraphs 11 and 31.
53 *Ibid.*, at paragraph 39.
54 The transposition of directives into national law is termed 'implementation' rather than 'incorporation' since the directive itself is not enacted into national law, either automatically or by national legislation, but rather its provisions are used as a guide to legislation. Theoreti-

cally, if a Member State's law is in compliance with the directive's goals, no action is required for that Member State to have fully implemented the directive.
55 Case 102/79, *Commission* v *Belgium* [1980] ECR 1473; *Becker, op. cit.*, note 47; Case 270/81, *Felicitas* v *Finanzamt für Verkehrsteuern* [1982] ECR 2771, at paragraphs 24 and 26.
56 Case 9/70, [1970] ECR 825.

those who have an interest in the fulfilment of this obligation. It would be incompatible with the binding effect attributed to decisions by Article 189 to exclude in principle the possibility that persons affected may invoke the obligation imposed by a decision. Particularly in cases where, for example, the Community authorities by means of a decision have imposed an obligation on a Member State or all the Member States to act in a certain way, the effectiveness ('*l'effet utile*') of such a measure would be weakened if the nationals of that State could not invoke it in the courts and the national courts could not take it into consideration as part of Community law.[57]

The leap of logic from a decision addressed to Member States, which is binding in its entirety but only on Member States, and which does not become part of national law, to a directive, which is also binding only on Member States but only as to result, is not a great one. In addition, *Grad* concerned a decision the effective date of which was determined by a directive, so the element of the nature of directives was raised in that case, although all the Court said about the directive was that the decision could not become directly effective until the expiry of the time limit set by the directive. A further step was taken towards the recognition of direct effect of directives in *SACE v Italian Ministry of Finance*,[58] where a directive was found to create direct effects in conjunction with a Treaty article. However, the Court had not yet stated that directives could create direct effects on their own.

The Court took the final step in 1974, with the *Van Duyn* case.[59] This case put in issue the direct effect of Article 48 EC, on free movement of workers, and of Directive 64/221, which defines 'public policy' for the purpose of applying the Treaty's free movement of persons rules. The Court repeated its ruling in *Grad* that Article 189 did not exclude direct effects of measures other than regulations, and that the binding nature of directives required the possibility of those concerned invoking it. The Court continued:

In particular, where the Community authorities have, by directive, imposed on Member States the obligation to pursue a particular course of conduct, the useful effect of such an act would be weakened if individuals were prevented from relying on it before their national courts and if the latter were prevented from taking it into consideration as an element of Community law.[60]

The original basis for finding that directives could product direct effects is therefore the doctrine of effectiveness in general. Finding that directives could produce direct effects has always been controversial. The United Kingdom government, however, unsuccessfully argued that direct effect of directives undermines the distinction between regulations and directives created in Article 189 EC.[61]

Related to effectiveness is the idea of legal certainty. The Court has also represented the uncertainty of unimplemented or improperly implemented directives as a reason for creating directly effective rights from directives:

So long as a directive has not been properly transposed into national law, individuals are unable to ascertain the full extent of their rights. That state of uncertainty for individuals subsists even after the Court has delivered a judgment finding that the Member State in question has not fulfilled its obligations under the directive and even if the Court has held

---

[57] *Ibid.*, at paragraph 5.
[58] *Op. cit.*, note 39.
[59] *Op. cit.*, note 37. However, the first case where the direct effect of a directive was held to exist where *no*

Treaty article was in issue was Case 51/76, *Verbond* [1977] ECR 113.
[60] *Van Duyn, op. cit.*, note 37, at paragraph 12.
[61] *Ibid.*, at paragraph 11.

that a particular provision or provisions of the directive are sufficiently precise and unconditional to be relied upon before a national court. Only the proper transposition of the directive will bring that state of uncertainty to an end and it is only upon that transposition that the legal certainty which must exist if individuals are to be required to assert their rights is created.[62]

Legal certainty is, in this situation, however, an argument that works both ways. Since not all directives are directly effective, and since it is not always obvious from reading a directive whether any of its provisions are directly effective, the question of direct effect itself creates uncertainty.

The Court has developed another justification, which has been relied on more extensively. In *Ratti* [63] the illegitimacy of pleading one's own default as defence was developed almost as an extension of the effectiveness principle:

Particularly in cases in which Community authorities have, by means of directive, placed Member States under a duty to adopt a certain course of action, the effectiveness of such an act would be weakened if persons were prevented from relying on it in legal proceedings and national courts prevented from taking it into consideration as an element of Community law.

Consequently a Member State which has not adopted the implementing measures required by the directive in the prescribed periods may not rely, as against individuals, on its own failure to perform the obligations which the directive entails.

However, soon after the direct effect of directives was established, horizontal direct effect of some Treaty articles was developed. The prospect of individuals and corporations being responsible for the obligations imposed in hundreds of directives had profound implications for legal certainty within the Community.[64] Arguments against horizontal direct effect focus on the nature of directives themselves: that they are addressed to Member States only, that only Member States are responsible for the non-implementation of directives, that directives are not directly applicable (although neither are Treaty articles) and that directives need not be published.[65] The arguments in favour of horizontal direct effect are based primarily on considerations of fairness and equity: that the conditions for direct effect are the same for directives as for Treaty articles and therefore should be applied in the same way, that the ECJ has always looked to the content rather than the form of a measure so the classification of an act as a directive is not determinative of its effects, that the principle of effectiveness requires that directly effective directives should be binding on individuals as well as Member States, that arbitrary discrimination would occur between public and private sector employees in some cases, and that the distinction between the State and the private sector would be difficult to draw.[66]

The Court, as a result, has dealt with the issue cautiously. To a large extent, it has created other methods of penetrating legal systems, such as duty of interpretation, rather than

[62] Case C-208/90, *Emmott* [1991] 3 CMLR 894.
[63] *Op. cit.*, note 7.
[64] Easson, 'Can Directives Impose Obligations on Individuals?' (1979) 4 EL Rev 67, at 75 et seq.
[65] *Ibid.*, at 70–3.
[66] *Ibid.* at 73–5, and 76–7. In fact directives are published in the Official Journal in the same way as regula-

tions. Easson also reviews some early opinions of Advocates General indicating that direct effect may be invoked against parties other than Member States, but it is more useful to look at the general considerations since the case law of the ECJ has since resolved itself, at least temporarily, against horizontal direct effect.

enforcing any horizontal direct effect of directives. However, this does not mean that direct effect of directives has not been expanded. It has been done, however, by expanding the concept of 'the State' which can be held responsible for the failure of implementation.

Marshall v *Southampton and South West Hampshire Area Health Authority (Teaching)*[67] appeared to resolve two issues: the extent of vertical direct effect and whether or not directives could produce horizontal direct effects. Marshall relied on the prohibition of sex discrimination in Directive 76/207 to justify her claim that her enforced retirement at 62, when men only had to retire at 65, violated Equal Treatment Directive 76/207. For Advocate General Slynn, the fact that directives are addressed to Member States, and not individuals, was sufficient to justify limiting direct effects to the State, as individuals cannot be held responsible for the failure of the State to implement a directive properly. Direct effect does not make conflicting legislation void. It only gives individuals rights that they may claim in the event of improper or incomplete implementation. The fact that direct effect operates only in cases of non-implementation, individuals otherwise relying on the national implementation measures, reinforces the idea of limited direct effect. The Advocate General was of the opinion that the definition of 'the State' was a matter for the national courts, but that, as a matter of Community law, the concept should be construed broadly, including the State as employer, not only in its functions of legislator or administrator of policy.[68] He considered that the State functions of legislation and administration were always in the background, and that this distinguished the State as employer from private employers. The Court accepted the argument for excluding horizontal direct effect but using a broad definition of vertical direct effect:

> With regard to the argument that a directive may not be relied upon against an individual, it must be emphasised that according to Article 189 of the EEC Treaty the binding nature of a directive, which constitutes the basis for the possibility of relying on the directive before a national court, exists only in relation to 'each Member State to which it is addressed'. It follows that a directive may not of itself impose obligations on an individual and that a provision of a directive may not be relied upon as such against a person. . . .
>
> It must be pointed out that where a person involved in legal proceedings is able to rely on a directive as against the State he may do so regardless of the capacity in which the latter is acting, whether as employer or public authority. In either case it is necessary to prevent the State from taking advantage of its own failure to comply with Community law.[69]

One consequence of the lack of horizontal direct effect of directives, particularly given the basis of direct effect in the principle that a Member State may not plead its own fault, is that Member States may not rely on unimplemented directives against individuals.[70]

The main consequence of the *Marshall* decision is that the Court has extended the range of public authorities which can be held responsible for non-implementation of Community law. It would follow logically from that holding, that aspects of the State which may have less responsibility for implementing Community law, or none at all, will nonetheless be subject to claims of directly effective rights. In *Fratelli Constanzo* v *Comune di Milano*, the Court stated

---

[67] Case 152/84, [1986] ECR 723. The substantive issues in this case are discussed in Chapter 16.

[68] This has been a controversial decision, but it is not without precedent. State responsibility for its actions as an employer was earlier applied by the European Court of Human Rights in *Young, James and Webster* v *United Kingdom* (1981) 3 EHRR 20.

[69] *Marshall, op. cit.*, note 67, at paragraphs 48–9.

[70] Case 80/86, *Officier Van Justitie* v *Kolponhuis Nijmegen* [1987] ECR 3969.

that directly effective directives are binding on all the authorities of a Member State, defined as 'all organs of the administration, including decentralised authorities such as municipalities'.[71] While this definition indicated a wide concept of the State, and included all levels of State authority, the question of public sector bodies with no legislative or administrative responsibility for Community directives remained open until the *Foster* case of 1990.[72] A first, relatively uncontroversial step was taken in *Johnston* v *Chief Constable of the Royal Ulster Constabulary*, where the Court found that the police would be part of the State:

> Whatever its relations may be with other organs of the State, such a public authority, charged by the State with the maintenance of public order and safety, does not act as a private individual. It may not take advantage of the failure of the State, of which it is an emanation, to comply with Community law.[73]

The Court, in *Foster*, finally made the attempt to define the outer limits of the State.[74] The defendant in this case was British Gas plc, which highlights the difficulty of definition of the State in the contemporary political system. British Gas had been a State-owned utility, which was privatised by means of a sale of its shares to the public. At the time when the facts underlying the applicant's complaint of sex discrimination arose it was still publicly-owned, but by the time the ECJ heard the case it had been privatised. The Court could have provided a definition which would have excluded British Gas no matter what its form, or one which included British Gas no matter what its form or one which made private ownership incompatible with being an element of the State. This last possibility would have been the most controversial, in that there is a wide discrepancy within the Community as to which utilities or public services are owned or operated directly by the State. Serious anomalies would be created, not only between public sector and private sector workers, but also between workers in the same job but in different Member States.

Once again, the opinion of the Advocate General unravels the conceptual difficulties underlying the problem facing the Court. Advocate General Van Gerven began with the justification for direct effect of directives: the fact that a Member State must not be allowed to plead its own failure to implement a directive. This leads to vertical direct effect only. He then proceeded from the point of the *Marshall* decision, which indicated that the concept of State should be interpreted broadly. Since, in *Marshall*, the organ of the State, namely the health service, which had been found to be an appropriate body against which the direct effect of directives could be invoked, was not one which was responsible for the implementation of Community law, then the concept of the State must be one which goes beyond the legislative and administrative authorities. This is further supported, argued the Advocate General, by the use of language such as 'emanation of the State', 'organ of the State', 'public authority' and 'State authority'. The important distinction was therefore 'the State' and 'the individual'. In doing so, uniformity of application between the Member States must be taken into consideration. This would therefore exclude relying on the form of a possible organ of the State. As a preliminary conclusion the Advocate General proposed that 'a Member State, and any public body charged with functions by the State, regardless of the

---

71 Case 103/88, [1989] ECR 1839, at paragraph 32.
72 For a critique of the approach of the ECJ to the concept of the State, see Curtin, 'The Province of Government: Delimiting the Direct Effect of Directives in the Common Law Context' (1990) 15 EL Rev 195.

73 Case 222/84, [1986] ECR 1651, at paragraph 56.
74 Case C-188/89 [1990] ECR 3313; Curtin, *op. cit.*, note 72, at 208–10, discusses the national court decisions in this case.

capacity in which it acts or its relations with other public bodies, may in no event derive advantage from the failure of the Member State to comply with Community law'.[75] In refining this proposed definition, the Advocate General discussed the concept of the State as applied in other areas of Community law, such as State aids. He stressed the importance of not relying on the criterion of public control alone, as argued by the appellants, since this would include potentially every regulated activity. Likewise, he rejected the argument of the defendant that only 'the classic duties of the State' should be covered. This would include only the legislative, executive and judicial functions, and is also difficult to apply. The scope of the executive function is particularly problematic, and raised questions of the effect of privatisation. The two elements finally isolated by the Advocate General were the 'exercise of a public function' and that there is 'real control' by the State.[76] This element of control would be consistent with the justification of the State being denied the right to rely on its failure to implement – such control would mean that the State was present in the entity in question, rather than a regulator in the background.

The Court of Justice condensed the formula proposed in the Opinion to:

> a body, whatever its legal form, which has been made responsible, pursuant to a measure adopted by the State, for providing a public service under the control of the State and has for that purpose special powers beyond those which result from the normal rules applicable in relations between individuals.[77]

In terms of 'special powers', this would include, arguably, any public utility which retained its monopoly, whether national or regional, after privatisation. The degree of State control necessary, outside the issue of special powers, is very much an open question. The concept of public service is likewise a matter of great debate. As a result, while *Foster* does provide a framework in which the State can be defined, it has not eliminated the uncertainty which *Marshall* created. The fact that the Court has left to national courts the application of this definition also undermines the attempt to establish a definition which could be applied with a high degree of uniformity throughout the Community.

This continuing uncertainty has led to the revival of the issue of horizontal direct effect of directives. In a second *Marshall* case, Advocate General Van Gerven argued for the inclusion of horizontal direct effect, although this was not necessary for the disposition of the case and was not referred to in the Court's judgment.[78] Another case before the Court raises the issue more clearly, and could in effect overturn the first *Marshall* decision.[79]

Direct effect has also been applied to international agreements to which the Community is a party.[80] This has largely been applied to Association agreements with non-Community States.[81] The General Agreement on Trade and Tariffs (GATT) has been found to create direct effects in part.[82]

---

[75] *Ibid.*

[76] *Ibid.*

[77] *Ibid.*, at paragraph 20.

[78] Case C-271/91, *Marshall v Southampton and South West Hampshire Area Health Authority (No. 2)*, opinion of 26 January 1993, decision of 2 August 1993.

[79] Case C-91/92, *Paola Faccini Dori* discussed in Van Gerven, 'The Horizontal Effect of Directive Provisions Revisited: The Reality of Catchwords', Institute of European Public Law Lecture (1993). The case involves a woman wishing to cancel a contract for language lessons. Present Italian law does not allow her to do so, but an unimplemented directive, 85/577, would give her that right. The defendant is a private company, with no element of State participation.

[80] Case 104/81, *Kupferberg* [1982] ECR 3641.

[81] For example, *Kupferberg*, ibid.

[82] Joined Cases 21–24/72, *International Fruit Company* [1972] ECR 1219.

Duty of interpretation

Direct effect itself is an exercise in interpretation. The ECJ must analyse the provisions of the directive to decide whether or not it fulfils the conditions for direct effect. The Court also interprets national law in the light of Community law as part of its task. It considers whether or not a Member State has adequately implemented Community law in the course of enforcement proceedings initiated by the Commission. In any reference procedure, of two possible interpretations of national law, the ECJ will recommend that a national court follows that which is in conformity with Community law.[83] The question has become, in recent years, which national law could be subject to such an interpretation, and to what extent should courts go beyond their national interpretative rules in applying Community law in this way. In other words, to what extent can interpretation be used as a method of Community law penetration into national legal systems?

Interpretation of national law in accordance with obligations arising under Community law became an important issue after the ECJ decided in *Marshall* that directives could not be horizontally directly effective. Litigants seeking to rely on directives against private sector parties could not invoke the directives as of right. Instead, attempts were made to require national courts to read Community law rights into the relevant legislation.

However, the foundations of the duty of interpretation were laid in a case which predates *Marshall*, and which was decided while the question of horizontal direct effect was still open. *Von Colson v Land Nordrhein-Westfalen*, and related case *Harz v Deutsche Tradex GmbH*,[84] exemplified the problem of the anomalies created by lack of horizontal direct effect, since in the former case the defendant was a regional authority of a State and in the latter, a private company. The plaintiffs had both initiated proceedings under German sex discrimination law, arguing the defendants had refused to engage them because of their sex. The problem arose because the German legislation, as interpreted by the German courts, only allowed for damages based on out-of-pocket expenses. The plaintiffs argued that this limitation on remedies infringed the obligations put on Member States by the Equal Treatment Directive 76/207.

Direct effect, it was agreed by the parties, could not be applied because the provision of the directive did not fulfil the criteria. Advocate General Rozes proceeded from that point. Because the remedies provision of Directive 76/207 was not sufficiently precise and unconditional to create direct effects, the plaintiffs could not require the adoption of any sanction in particular, such as an obligation to conclude a contract of employment with the victim of discrimination. This, according to the Advocate General, did not, however, lead to an unfettered Member State discretion, due to the Member State's obligation to achieve the result required by the directive. This obligation, in Article 189 EC, is reinforced by the obligations arising out of Article 5 EC to make Community law effective. The principle of effectiveness means that Member States must not only establish procedures for remedies, but must create sanctions as well. Implementing measures must serve to achieve the result foreseen by the directive, and the ECJ, using Article 5 and the principle of equal treatment,

---

[83] See, for example, Case 32/74, *Haaga* [1974] ECR 1201, at paragraph 6; see also Case 111/75, *Impresa Construzione Comm Quirino Mazzalai v Ferrovia del Renon* [1976] ECR 657 and Case 270/81, *Felicitas Rickmers-Linie v Finanzamt Hamburg* [1982] ECR 2771.

[84] Case 14/83 [1984] ECR 1891 and case 79/83 [1984] ECR 1921.

may define the scope of Member State obligations more precisely. The principles governing effective sanctions should therefore, argued the Advocate General, be:

1 Comparable to sanctions applied to offences of the same gravity;
2 Proportionate to the seriousness of the offence, which is a breach of a fundamental principle of the Treaty;
3 The deterrent effect of the sanctions provided for by at particular national law or regulation must be assessed on the basis of those requirements.[85]

Applied to the national law in question, the interpretation of the damages clause leading to the reimbursement only of out-of-pocket expenses did not result in an effective remedy, because it would not deter employers from engaging in discrimination and was not proportionate to the seriousness of the breach.

The ECJ agreed that Member States must be free to choose the ways and means of implementing the directive, but that the obligation to adopt 'all the measures necessary to ensure that the directive is fully effective, in accordance with the objective which it pursues' places limits on Member State discretion.[86] The Court emphasised the necessity of sanctions which would act as a deterrent to behaviour in contravention of the directive. The Court then established this obligation of effectiveness of national implementing measures as a duty of interpretation:

> It follows that, in applying the national law specifically introduced in order to implement Directive 76/207, national courts are required to interpret their national law in the light of the wording and purpose of the directive in order to achieve the result referred to in Article 189(3).[87]
>
> It is for the national court to interpret and apply the legislation adopted for the implementation of the directive in conformity with the requirements of Community law, in so far as it is given the discretion to do so by national law.[88]

The duty of interpretation in *Von Colson* is limited, as set out above, in two ways. It is restricted to legislation specifically designed to implement Community law, and therefore previous legislation would be excluded. Further, national courts may only act within the discretion given to them within their domestic legal systems. At this stage, the ECJ did not appear to consider it necessary to create Community rules of interpretation for national courts to use in comparing national law with Community obligations.

Some uncertainty about the extent of the duty of interpretation remained. The Court decided, in *Pretore de Salo*,[89] that a directive could not, of itself and independently of a national law adopted by a Member State for its implementation, have the effect of determining or aggravating the liability in criminal law of persons who act in contravention

---

[85] *Ibid.* These three criteria were applied in Case 68/88, *Commission* v *Greece* [1989] ECR 2965, at paragraph 24. In Case C-177/88, *Dekker* v *Stichting Vormingscentrum voor Jong Volwassen* [1990] ECR I-3941, the obligation to provide effective remedies was extended to mean that the national legislation must be capable of grounding the complete liability of those responsible. See also *Marshall (No 2), op. cit.*, note 78.

[86] *Von Colson, op. cit.*, note 84, at paragraph 15.
[87] *Ibid.*, at paragraph 27.
[88] *Ibid.*, at paragraph 28. These principles were specifically applied in *Johnston, op. cit.*, note 73, and in *Kolpinghuis Nijmegen, op. cit.*, note 70.
[89] Case 14/86, *Pretore de Salo* v *X* [1989] 1 CMLR 71.

of the provisions of the directive. This statement is possibly still justified despite the Court's expansion of the duty of interpretation in later cases, since criminal liability raises particular questions of fairness and legal certainty.

The duty of interpretation arising out of *Von Colson* has been described by some commentators as 'indirect effect' in that individuals do not rely on rights in the directive itself, but rather seek the application of principles of Community law into national law by means of the interpretation of domestic legislation.[90] While this phrase illustrates the fact that the enforcement of Community principles is through the medium of national law, the duty of interpretation is not a mirror image of direct effect. It has been developed to a stage where it is broader than direct effect, and applies to measures which could never create direct effects. However, the phrase indirect effect does emphasise the fact that the duty of interpretation arises out of Community law and not national law.[91]

Kolpinghuis Nijmegen confirmed the duty of interpretation, but was cautious about extending it. Advocate General Mischo was willing to extend the duty to legislation which was not specifically for the purpose of implementing Community law, if the Member State had taken the view that no measures of implementation were necessary to bring national law into compliance with its Community obligations. The Court decided the case on the ground that a Member State could not rely on an unimplemented directive against individuals. However, it also reiterated the *Von Colson* and *Pretore de Salo* decisions and added that the duty of interpretation arises irrespective of whether or not the implementation period for a directive has expired.[92] It would therefore appear that the duty of interpretation is not entirely based on the principle that a Member State cannot plead its own fault, since Member States cannot be held responsible for failure to implement Community law until any delay for implementation has expired. Instead the duty appears to be a spur to implementation, enabling the national courts to identify how far national law is currently in conformity with Community obligations. The ECJ also suggested weakening the restriction of the duty of interpretation to implementing legislation, by stating that the duty applied to 'national law, and in particular the provisions of a national law specifically introduced in order to implement the directive'.[93]

The duty of interpretation has been expanded to cover a wider scope of Community measures. Direct effect has been justified based on the fact that Treaty provisions, regulations, directives and decisions are all characterised by some form of binding effect under Article 189 EC. The status of Community 'soft law', recommendations and opinions, in national law was assumed to be negligible until *Grimaldi*.[94] Here the Court recognised the distinction between direct effect and the duty to interpret, which it saw as a different form of legal effect. The Court also used wider language in describing the content of the duty of interpretation. Grimaldi sought to have the condition he suffered from recognised by a

---

[90] Notably, Fitzpatrick, 'The Significance of EEC Directives in UK Sex Discimination Law' (1989) 9 OJLS 336. However, he has somewhat reformulated his approach: Docksey and Fitzpatrick, 'The Duty of National Courts to Interpret Provisions of National Law in Accordance with Community Law' (1992) 21 Ind LJ 113.

[91] Fitzpatrick, *op. cit.*, note 90, at 344–5.

[92] On the possible problems for national courts applying this ruling, see da Burca, 'Giving Effect to European Community Directives' (1992) 55 MLR 215, at 218.

[93] *Op. cit.*, note 70. Steiner, in 'Coming to Terms with EEC Directives' (1990) 106 LQR 144, at 157–8, argues that in the United Kingdom, the duty of interpretation arises from the European Communities Act. However, this does not seem to be consistent with the statements of the ECJ, that the duty arises from the EC Treaty itself, specifically Article 5.

[94] Case C-322/88, *Grimaldi* v *Fonds de Maladies Professionnelles, Brussels* [1989] ECR 4407.

Belgian tribunal. The condition was listed on the European Schedule of Industrial Diseases, annexed to Commission Recommendation of 23 July 1962 concerning the adoption of a European schedule of occupational diseases.[95] Advocate General Mischo dismissed the possibility of the recommendation, which was undeniably a true recommendation, being capable of producing direct effects. The fact that Article 189 EC does not assign binding character to recommendations makes such a finding impossible. The Court went further, as it had done in *Von Colson*, by considering the duty of interpretation. After rejecting the possibility of direct effects, the Court continued:

> However, in order to give a comprehensive reply to the question asked by the national court, it must be stressed that the measures in question cannot therefore be regarded as having no legal effect. The national courts are bound to take recommendations into consideration in order to decide disputes submitted to them, in particular where they cast light on the interpretation of national measures adopted in order to implement them or where they are designed to supplement binding Community provisions.[96]

In addition to extending the duty of interpretation to recommendations, the Court weakened the insistence it made in *Von Colson* on the national legislation being for the purpose of implementing Community law. The Court states that the duty exists *in particular* when interpreting implementing or supplementary legislation, but no longer restricts it to these instances. This could possibly be explained by the fact that the recommendation in question was over two decades old at the time – determining whether the Belgian legislation purported to implement the recommendation might have been impossible.

The final step in establishing the duty of interpretation as a key aspect of the legal effect of Community law in national systems came in *Marleasing*.[97] The plaintiff argued that the formation of the defendant company was illegal because of the lack of cause.[98] The defendant argued that this ground of nullity could not be raised against it as the causes of nullity of companies were exhaustively determined by the First Company Law Directive 68/151. Here there could be no argument that the national legislation in question was an implementation of Directive 68/151. The Spanish Civil Code provisions on the validity and nullity of contracts, which had been in the past applied to the formation of companies, predate Spain's accession to the Community. Relying on the direct effect of the First Company Law Directive appeared to be out of the question since the defendant was a private sector company, although Advocate General Van Gerven was of the opinion that the Directive fulfilled the criteria for vertical direct effect. The Court confirmed its *Marshall* ruling in *Marleasing*, rejecting the possibility of horizontal direct effect of directives. The Advocate General, and subsequently the Court, went on to build on the foundations of *Von Colson* and *Grimaldi*. The requirement that the law should be intended as an implementation of Community law was discarded. Since Article 5 EC is the basis for the duty, and that article places a duty on all national authorities to do everything in their power to achieve the goals of Community law, a restrictive approach cannot be justified. The language used by the Court is broadly inclusive:

---

[95] OJ/1962/2188.
[96] *Grimaldi, op. cit.*, note 94, at paragraph 18.
[97] Case C-106/89, *Marleasing SA* v *La Comercial Internacional de Alimentación SA* [1992] 1 CMLR 305.

[98] The civil law concept of cause is similar to the common law concept of consideration, but is broader.

in applying national law, whether the provisions in question were adopted before or after the directive, the national court called upon to interpret it is required to do so, so far as possible, in the light of the wording and purpose of the directive in order to achieve the result pursued by the latter and thereby comply with the third paragraph of Article 189 EEC.[99]

Although the latter part of the paragraph quoted above is similar to the language used in *Von Colson*, it is more explicit that the national court is required to construct an interpretation of national law which achieves the goals of the directive. Courts are required to do everything possible to achieve the conformity of national law with Community law.[100] It has been argued that the 'everything possible' formulation could undermine legal certainty, which in *Kolpinghuis Nijmegen* was identified as a limitation on the duty of interpretation.[101]

All that seems to be excluded now is a *contra legem* interpretation – that a national court should interpret domestic legislation in contradiction of its clear language in order to implement Community law. Although *Marleasing* does not specifically exclude this, it is probably impossible to require national courts to overrule their own laws as a matter of interpretation rather than on the supremacy principle.[102] Advocate General Van Gerven was clear, however, that the duty to interpret should arise when 'the provision in question is to any extent open to interpretation' and that legal certainty and non-retroactivity must be protected.[103] A further remaining question is the extent to which the duty of interpretation could be applied to the common law. For example, if an equivalent case to *Marleasing* arose in the United Kingdom or Ireland, would the duty of interpretation require national judges to make exceptions to their usual interpretation of consideration in common law contracts?

The real achievement of *Marleasing*, however, is to reduce substantially the impact of the lack of horizontal direct effect of directives.[104] Although interpretation of Community obligations into national law is a less certain method than the direct reliance on rights as drafted in Community legislation,[105] it does provide an opportunity for national courts to avoid the discrimination against individuals suing private sector defendants.

Given the early arguments that attributing direct effect to directives undermines the distinction between regulations and directives, it could be argued that the duty of interpretation is more appropriate to the nature of directives, given the fact that the directive is result-orientated rather than a literal transposition of rights into the national legal system. While this justification is weaker in the case of soft law such as recommendations, at this stage the national judiciary has sufficient discretion to take into consideration the difference in the level of obligations imposed on Member States by different forms of Community law.

State liability for failure to implement Community law

Until recently, the ECJ was of the opinion that while Member States were *responsible* for the non-implementation of Community law, but the potential *liability* of Member States for

---

[99] *Marleasing, op. cit.*, note 97, at paragraph 8.
[100] Docksey and Fitzpatrick, *op. cit.*, note 90, at 119.
[101] da Burca, *op. cit.* note 92, at 229–31.
[102] *Ibid.*, at 228–9. On the resistance of some courts to the implications of the supremacy principle, see Chapter 3.

[103] *Marleasing, op. cit.*, note 97.
[104] Docksey and Fitzpatrick, *op. cit.*, note 90, at 117–20.
[105] Snyder, 'The Effectiveness of European Community Law: Institutions, Processes, Tools and Techniques' (1993) 56 MLR 19, at 43, discusses the difficulties facing national courts attempting to apply *Marleasing*.

non-implementation was a matter for national law.[106] Generally, the only condition was that procedural guarantees for actions based on Community law must be no less favourable than for similar actions under national law,[107] although national courts are obliged to disapply national procedural rules which violate Community law principles.[108]

A first step was taken in *Johnston*, where the ECJ stated that there must be an effective judicial remedy for persons who considered themselves wronged by a failure of implementation of Community law.[109] In 1989, the Court was presented with an explicit question as to whether, as a matter of Community law, a Member State could be held liable to damages for infringement of Community law rights.[110] However, the question was phrased in terms of liability for directly effective Community law. Since the ECJ found that the directive in question did not create direct effects, it decided that it was not necessary to answer the question on liability for damages.

In late 1991, however, the ECJ accepted the principle of Member State liability for breach of Community law, and did not tie liability to direct effects. *Francovich* v *Italy*,[111] raised two issues: whether Directive 80/987 on the protection of workers upon insolvency of their employer created direct effects, and whether a Member State could be held liable for damages for non-implementation of Community law. The Court decided, after a careful analysis of the Directive, that it could not produce direct effects because it was not sufficiently precise concerning the identity of the institution which was to guarantee compensation to beneficiaries of the Directive.[112]

The fact that Italy was in default in its implementation of the Directive was not contested, since the ECJ had decided that point in an enforcement action by the Commission over two years previously.[113] However, since State liability in damages for non-implementation was a new development, the Court went into detail in explaining the justification for the principle of liability. The Court recalled the development of supremacy of Community law, direct effect and the duty of interpretation. Advocate General Mischo had argued that, as a consequence of existing Community law, including *Factortame*,[114] an appropriate legal remedy must be created if one does not already exist. As with other developments in the legal effect of Community law in national legal systems, the basis was derived from Article 5 EC and its doctrine of effectiveness. Effectiveness requires, according to the Court, that individuals must be able to obtain compensation for a breach of Community law attributable to a Member State, especially where the full effect of Community law is conditional on

---

106 See for example, *Emmott, op. cit.*, note 62; Case 60/75, *Russo* v *AIMA* [1976] ECR 45; under the ECSC Treaty, Case 6/60, *Humblet* v *Belgium* [1960] ECR 559.

107 Case 45/76, *Comet* v *Produktschap voor Siergewassen* [1976] ECR 2043.

108 Case 39/70, *Fleischkontor* v *Hauptzollamt Hamburg* [1971] ECR 49, where the ECJ found that national procedural rules allowed importers fraudulently to infringe a Community Regulation on quality of meat, because those rules required German courts too much discretion on whether or not to trust the statement of an importer.

109 *Op. cit.*, note 73, at paragraph 59.

110 Case 380/87, *Enichem Base* v *Commune de Cinisello Balsamo* [1989] ECR 3491; at paragraph 3, the question was put as follows: 'Is the administration required under Community law to pay compensation where an unlawful administration measure taken by it infringes a right

under Community law . . . which upon its incorporation in the Italian legal system, whilst retaining its Community character, takes the form of a protected interest?'

111 *Op. cit.*, note 45.

112 For criticisms of the Court's approach to direct effect in this case, see Curtin, 'State Liability Under Community Law: a New Remedy for Private Parties' (1992) 21 ILJ 74, and Szyszczak. 'European Community Law: New Remedies, New Directions?' (1992) 55 MLR 690.

113 Case 22/87, *Commission* v *Italy* [1989] ECR 163.

114 Case C-213/89, *R* v *Secretary of State for Transport, ex parte Factortame* [1990] ECR I-2433, in which the ECJ decided that effectiveness of Community law required that national courts disapply a national rule of law which prevents the granting of interim relief pending a reference to the ECJ.

Member State action. The principle of liability in damages for breach of Community law by a Member State, the Court concluded, is inherent in the scheme of the Treaty.

The Court went on to lay down the conditions for Member State liability. The first condition is that the result required by the directive includes the conferring of rights for the benefit of individuals. The second is that the content of the rights must be determinable from the directive. Lastly, there must be a causal link between the damage suffered and the breach of obligation. Procedural conditions are to be left to national courts, but must not be less favourable than conditions applying to similar actions under national law, and must not make recovery excessively difficult or impossible.

Although the first two conditions are similar to the concept of direct effect, the fact that the Court found Italy liable in damages despite finding that the Directive did not create direct effects, means that these conditions are broader than direct effect. However, the extent to which a directive does not create direct effects yet still fulfils the conditions of creating rights which are determinable by reference to the directive is as yet uncertain. Where conditions are placed on a right which is otherwise precise, or further Member State action is required, then liability may be possible despite lack of direct effects. It is possible that a Member State might also be liable for failure to implement directives which do create direct effects, but where the damage suffered is the result of the action of a private individual. A question which the Court did not address is whether a previous judgment of breach under Article 169 would be necessary before a *Francovich* action could be taken.[115] The judgment deals only with liability for breach of directives, but since this liability is said to be inherent in the scheme of the Treaty, it is probable that liability would result from other forms of Community law. However, this would be restricted to binding forms of Community law, as recommendations and opinions do not place any obligations on Member States. It has even been suggested that *Francovich* could lead to a cause of action arising from the general duty of solidarity in Article 5 EC, even where no specific breach of Community obligations has occurred,[116] although this would seem inconsistent with the conditions of liability set out by the Court, which require that the content of the right be derivable from the legislation in question.

The fact that so many background conditions, including, for now, the definition of the causal link between damage and breach of obligation, are left to national courts could lead to significant variation in the application of this form of liability in the different Member States. Until the ECJ further defines the conditions of liability, an action based on the *Francovich* ruling will be a hybrid action. Although arising from Community law, many conditions will be defined by national rules on State responsibility. The result may be, over time, a harmonisation of rules on State responsibility.[117]

Francovich does represent an advance in the protection of individuals' Community law rights. Since it applies to rights which may not be sufficiently precise and unconditional to attract direct effect, it covers situations that direct effect will miss. It may even provide assistance in situations where *Marleasing* cannot, since liability will exist even in the absence

---

115 However, in issues of Community liability, the Court has rejected the need for annulment of a measure as a prior condition to an action for damages. See Chapter 9.
116 Ross, 'Beyond *Francovich*' (1993) 56 MLR 55, at 66–8.

117 Curtin, 'Directives', *op. cit.*, note 1, at 727, is of the opinion that national procedural rules have undermined the effectiveness of Community law.

of any relevant national legislation.[118] Although it is, in some respects, a radical departure from the attempt to enforce Community law rights through the creation of rights or through interpretative strategies, it can still be traced to the idea that a Member State cannot take advantage of its own failure to comply with Community obligations.[119] It is perhaps a bridge between direct effect and Commission enforcement, in that it remains in the hands of individuals but focuses on Member State responsibility rather than individual rights. A successful *Francovich* action may give the aggrieved individual only compensation, not the right he or she would have had if the Community measure had been properly implemented.[120] It therefore supplements other methods of ensuring legal effect of Community acts in national legal systems, but cannot supplant them.

CONCLUSION

The issue of direct effect of Community law has been controversial since its development by the ECJ in *Van Gend en Loos*. Certainly, the concept of direct effect moves Community law into a whole new category of international organisation, because it integrates international law passed by the Community into national legal systems. The Community, as an international organisation, has been as much legally-driven in its development as it has politically. This means that the ECJ has a role and status which other international courts do not have. Without direct effect, it is arguable that the development of the Community would have been much slower. It is likely that without individuals having the ability to enforce Community law against their Member States, many Community initiatives would have been meaningless. This is exemplified by the *Defrenne* case, where the impetus for the enforcement of Article 119 EC was not the Commission, but an individual woman worker. Before that case, despite the fact that Article 119 is a Treaty obligation, Member States believed that they could take their time in implementing it.[121] Direct effect therefore makes the individual a motor of integration.

The continuing issue of horizontal direct effect brings forward again questions over the methods used by the ECJ, and whether it can justify its actions from the EC treaties. The developments by the ECJ have given particular importance to Article 5 EC, and the principle of effectiveness which has been found to reside within it. This principle that Community law must be effective has not only justified the recent developments in *Marleasing* and *Francovich*, but has become a framework for discussing Community law in general. Horizontal direct effect of directives would appear to be the next logical step in ensuring that Community law is not just words on paper but can have effects on the lives of individuals within the Community.

Further reading

Curtin, D., 'Directives: The Effectiveness of Judicial Protection of Individual Rights' (1990) 27 CML Rev 709.

---

118 Snyder, *op. cit.*, note 105, at 44.

119 Ross, *op. cit.*, note 116, at 60, argues that other remedies may also be available, given the constant case law of the ECJ insisting on effective remedies.

120 *Ibid.*, at 61.

121 This issue is discussed in detail in Chapter 16.

Curtin, D., 'The Province of Government: Delimiting the Direct Effect of Directives in the Common Law Context' (1990) 15 EL Rev 195.

da Burca, G., 'Giving Effect to European Community Directives' (1992) 55 MLR 215.

Docksey, C. and Fitzpatrick, B., 'The Duty of National Courts to Interpret Provisions of National Law in Accordance with Community Law' (1992) 21 Ind LJ 113.

Fitzpatrick, B., 'The Significance of EEC Directives in UK Sex Discrimination Law' (1989) OJLS 336.

Pescatore, P., 'The Doctrine of "Direct Effect": An Infant Disease of Community Law' (1983) 8 EL Rev 155.

Ross, 'Beyond *Francovich*' (1993) 56 MLR 55.

Snyder, F., 'The Effectiveness of European Community Law: Institutions, Processes, Tools and Techniques' (1993) 56 MLR 19.

Temple Lang, J., 'Community Constitutional Law: Article 5 EEC Treaty' (1990) 27 CML Rev 645.

Winter, J.A., 'Direct Applicability and Direct Effect: Two Distinct and Different Concepts in Community Law' (1972) 9 CML Rev 425.

CHAPTER 6

General principles of law

INTRODUCTION

The constitutional nature of adjudication before the ECJ is nowhere more apparent than in the creation and development by the Court of the general principles of European Community law. Only the development of the doctrine of direct effect is a possible rival to the general principles as the most significant contribution of the Court to the maturing of the Community legal system. These principles have grown to become an important source of European Community law.

The emergence of the general principles can be examined on two levels. The first is the need for such guidance in order that the Community legal order may function more efficiently and more justly. The second is the justification for such judicial creativity within the treaties. As to the first level, it is a truism that constitutions cannot be exhaustive, and a hard political fact that they are exceedingly difficult to amend. There will be inevitable gaps in the rules. Judges, faced with cases where no explicit rule applies, must choose between deciding that a party has no remedy, or deriving a principle which would justify a remedy. It has often been argued that the absence of a black-letter rule in constitutional cases does not deprive a party of a 'right to win'.[1] The creation of significant law by the courts is therefore often more acceptable in this field than in more rule-bound ones, such as taxation.[2] There are various ways in which judges deal with the issue of gaps. The common law is a system designed to deal with the need for flexibility and creativity in law and judging. Likewise, in discussing constitutional legal reasoning, writers on the American and Canadian constitutions have emphasised the creative aspects of the task of judging.[3] A system which cannot deal with the gaps and find solutions to problems raised by the gaps, runs the risk of grinding to a halt.

In the Community, the limitations of the codified law are acute. It was apparent at a very early stage that the ECSC Treaty was not comprehensive enough to deal with the cases that were coming before the ECJ, in as much as specific provisions were not always capable of providing adequate solutions to the problems to be addressed by the Court. Thus the Court was faced with a situation where it was compelled either to formulate its own general principles or adopt certain of those general principles used by the Member States. In *Netherlands* v *High Authority*[4] the Advocate General stated that in order to interpret Community law the Court would have to take notice of the law of the Member States. This

---

1 Notably, Dworkin, *Taking Rights Seriously*, (1978).
2 See, for example, Gibson 'Interpretation of the Canadian Charter of Rights and Freedoms: Some General Considerations' in Tarnopolsky and Beaudoin, *Canadian Charter of Rights and Freedoms: Commentary* (1982) 25.

3 See Dworkin and Gibson, *op. cit.*, notes 1 and 2, and Tribe, *American Constitutional Law*, 2nd edn (1988).
4 Case 6/54, [1955] ECR 103.

was especially true where the Treaty used terms which had a technical legal meaning in Member States, as in *Assider* v *High Authority*,[5] where the term *detournement de pouvoir* was in dispute. This was reinforced by the Advocate General in *Fédération Charbonnière de Belgique* v *High Authority*,[6] where he stated that the Court could not refuse to give a judgment simply because there was a lacuna in Community law. The significance of these opinions was widened with the decision in *Algera and others* v *Assembly*,[7] which involved the revocation of administrative acts which the Court accepted were a normal part of the legal systems of all the Member States but about which nothing was stated in the Treaty. The Court not only implicitly accepted those opinions but went on to outline those principles which were to be found in the law of the Member States which were in its opinion applicable to the circumstances of the case.[8]

In terms of justification, the Court has found several anchors within the treaties for its development of general principles. Some principles, such as non-discrimination, are extrapolated from specific provisions within the EC Treaty. For those principles which have not even a shadowy presence within the Treaty, three provisions have justified the actions of the European Court.[9] The first two are contained within Section 4 of the EC Treaty, 'The Court of Justice'. Article 164 obliges the Court to ensure that 'the law is observed', and Article 173 empowers the Court to annul Community legislation for 'infringement of this Treaty, or any rule of law relating to its application'.

These two statements allow the Court to go outside the treaties for Community law. The third relevant provision provides some direction for the Court as to where it should look for these non-codified rules of Community law. Article 215 orders the Community to make good any damage it has caused, 'in accordance with the general principles common to the laws of the Member States'. While Article 215 purports to deal only with liability of the Community, the Court has clearly used this statement as its basic guideline in developing a considerable judge-made element in Community law. That having been said, some principles have been developed primarily with reference to international law. Some are principles not recognised in the national legal systems of all 12 Member States. Even when such principles are present throughout the Community, the form in which they are adopted by the ECJ is usually based primarily on the concept as it exists in one Member State in particular. Regardless of the source of its derivation, once a general principle is adopted by the ECJ, it becomes an independent rule of Community law and leads a separate existence from that of the same principle in the legal system or systems which spawned it.

General principles are an important source of law within the Community. This will be amply demonstrated in the four chapters to follow. A brief outline of the utility of the general principles is as follows. They are key interpretive concepts, used to clarify ambiguous parts of EC legislation. In judicial review cases under Article 173 EC, an act of the Community institutions can be annulled due to the failure to observe any rule of law related to the application of the Treaty, which includes the general principles of law. Article 173 also permits annulment for failure to observe an essential procedural requirement, which has been

---

5 Case 3/54, [1954–6] ECR 63, at 74.
6 Case 8/55, [1956] ECR 245, at 292.
7 Joined Cases 7/56 and 3–7/57, [1957] ECR 39.
8 Notably the principle of revocability of an administrative measure vitiated by illegality, *ibid.*, at 55–6.

9 See Hartley, *The Foundations of European Community Law*, 2nd edn (1988), at 130–1.

held to include the right to a hearing. The grounds of review listed in Article 173 also apply to review of failure to act (Article 175), indirect challenge (Article 184) and references to the ECJ from national courts (Article 177). Therefore, the general principles are a crucial part of the judicial review process in Community law. In addition, it is possible to invoke the violation of a general principle as the basis for an action for damages against the Community under Article 215 EC.[10] The general principles are therefore of great practical, as well as constitutional, importance.

Human rights

Given the preoccupation of the original Community treaties with trade and other economic matters, it is perhaps not surprising that concern for human rights came somewhat late to the EC. The Community's initial conception of itself was far narrower than it is today, and there was perhaps a division of labour between the Community and the Council of Europe, which was responsible for the regional efforts in the human rights field. Nonetheless, it was to become apparent that a legal system without human rights would create constitutional difficulties for several Member States.

Whilst the Court was willing to accept certain principles, these did not appear to include the fundamental rights that all six of the original Member States were committed to protect, either explicitly in their constitutions or, in the case of France, implicitly in the preamble to the Constitution. The treaties which established the three European Communities did not contain any provisions pertaining to the protection of fundamental rights. This may have been as a result of arguments over Article 3 of the proposed Treaty to establish the European Defence Community, which stated:

> The Community takes measures only to the extent which is necessary for the fulfilment of its task; it preserves the political rights of the citizens and the fundamental rights of the individuals.[11]

Certainly when the German delegation to the discussions on the Rome Treaties wanted a similar provision, which would have been in line with their own Constitution, the other delegations rejected their arguments because it was felt that it would be impossible for the organs of the Communities to take into account the Constitutions of all the Member States, which would in turn allow Member States an unfortunate loophole by which to avoid restrictions or duties placed on them by the Community.[12]

However, the matter was made more complex by the Court's decision in *Costa* v *ENEL*[13] because it also stated clearly that Community law had absolute supremacy over national law. Thus if there was a conflict between the two, fundamental rights, even if enshrined in a Member State's Constitution, would be disregarded. This in addition to the fact that the Court was unwilling to accept that fundamental rights were part of the basic principles of Community law meant that, in effect, fundamental rights could not be argued for or protected in front of the Court. This was reiterated in a number of other cases[14] and was

---

10 Case 74/74, *CNTA v Commission* [1975] ECR 533.
11 (1954) BGB1, Part II, 343, 346; translated by Zuleeg, 'Fundamental rights and the Law of the European Communities' [1971] CML Rev 446.
12 Zuleeg, *ibid.*
13 Case 6/64, [1964] ECR 585.

14 Case 14/68, *Walt Wilhelm v Bundeskartellampt* [1969] CMLR 100; Case 28/67, *Molkereizentrale v Hauptzollampt Paderborn* [1968] CMLR 187; Case 16/65, *Scharwze v Einfur- und Vorratsstelle für Getreide und Futtermittel* [1965] ECR 877.

regarded with dismay by both Germany and Italy, as articles in their Constitutions provided explicitly for the protection of fundamental rights[15] and it was feared that these might be overruled by EC law.

It was not until *Stauder* v *City of Ulm*[16] that the ECJ was prepared expressly to accept that the fundamental rights of the individual should be part of the basic principles of Community law. The case, a reference by the *Verwaltungsgericht* of Stuttgart, followed a decision by the Commission to allow the Member States to distribute cheap butter to citizens who were receiving State assistance and who would not be able to afford butter at normal prices. Article 4 of this decision stated that butter could only be made available to such people in exchange for a coupon. The Federal Republic of Germany duly issued coupon cards for the butter which were attached to a counterfoil on which the beneficiary's name and address were written, which the German translation of the decision appeared to require. The coupons were only be valid if presented to a retailer while still attached to the counterfoil. The plaintiff in the proceedings before the *Verwaltungsgericht* was entitled to butter coupons by dint of having been a war victim, but felt that it was discriminatory that he and other such victims should be obliged to show their names and addresses to retailers and that this was a violation of his fundamental rights under Articles 1 and 3 of the *Grundgesetz*. The Court held that on examination of the drafting history, the relevant passage of the Commission decision had been mistranslated in the German and Dutch texts as these provided for a more onerous test than the French and Italian texts, which did not require the coupon to be personalised but merely individualised. However, the Court went further and, agreeing with the opinion of the Advocate General, stated that it was its duty to make sure that the fundamental rights of the individual were protected, as these were part of the general principles of Community law derived from the common tradition of the Member States.

Sources

While *Stauder* opened the door by recognising that the Community should be bound by human rights principles, the derivation of such principles remained an open question. Originally, the Court had refused to examine national constitutions for principles of Community law. In *Stork* v *High Authority*,[17] the Court rejected a claim based on human rights provisions of the German Constitution, declaring such to be outside its authority. It saw its jurisdiction as deriving solely from the explicit words of the treaties. After *Stauder* declared their existence, the source of human rights in the Community was clarified in two cases: *Internationale Handelsgesellschaft* and *Nold*.

Internationale Handelsgesellschaft GmbH v *EVST*[18] was primarily a case about the relationship between Community law and national constitutional law. However, it is also the foundation for most of the ECJ's work in developing human rights as general principles of EC law. This case concerned the question whether a system of 'agricultural guarantees' or deposits, which had been established by the Commission in the form of regulations for the purpose of controlling the functioning of the common market in cereals, was contrary to

---

15 Possibly because of the totalitarian regimes they had both endured.

16 Case 29/69, [1969] ECR 419.

17 Case 1/58, [1959] ECR 17. Similarly, see Cases 36–8 and 40/59, *Prasident Ruhrkolen-Verkaufsgesellschaft mbH* v *High Authority* [1960] ECR 423, and Case 40/64, *Sgarlata* v *Commission* [1965] ECR 215.

18 Case 11/70, [1970] ECR 1125.

Articles 2 and 14 of the *Grundgesetz*. It was referred to the ECJ by the Frankfurt am Main Administrative Court under Article 177 of the EC Treaty. The Court began by restating that law stemming from the Treaty could not be overridden by, or made to conform to, national law without damage to the Community legal order, and thus fundamental rights as enshrined in Member States' Constitutions or general principles of their constitutional structure could not be argued before it. The Court nonetheless stated that it was necessary to examine Community law for equivalent principles. It was now of the opinion that:

> Respect for fundamental rights forms an integral part of the general principles of law protected by the Court of Justice. The protection of such rights, whilst inspired by the constitutional traditions common to the Member States, must be ensured within the framework of the structures and objectives of the Community.[19]

and that it should examine:

> in the light of the doubts expressed by the *Verwaltungsgericht*, whether the system of deposits has infringed rights of a fundamental nature, respect for which must be ensured in the Community legal system.[20]

However, this did not fully resolve the issue from the point of view of the German Constitutional Court when the case returned to it after the ECJ reference. The Constitutional Court held that as matters stood within the Community, it was not possible to state that Community law adequately protected fundamental rights, and indeed that,

> As long as the integration process has not progressed so far that Community law also receives a catalogue of fundamental rights decided on by a parliament and of settled validity, which is adequate in comparison with the catalogue of fundamental rights contained in the Constitution, a reference by a court in the Federal Republic of Germany to the *Bundesverfassungsgericht* in judicial review proceedings following the obtaining of a ruling of the European Court under Article 177 of the Treaty is admissible and necessary if the German court regards the rule of Community law which is relevant to its decision as inapplicable in the interpretation given by the European Court, because and in so far as it conflicts with one of the fundamental rights in the Constitution.[21]

This led to the Constitutional Court holding that it did have jurisdiction.[22] However, on the merits of the case the Constitutional Court held that disputed regulations did not breach the fundamental rights guaranteed by the *Grundgesetz*.

The German Constitutional Court continued to lay claim to the ability to examine Community measures, with a view to deciding their compatibility with the basic rights provisions of the *Grundgesetz*, although it never actually found any measure to be

19 *Ibid.*, at 1134.
20 *Ibid.*
21 IHT [1974] 2 CMLR 540, at 554.
22 The Court was however split on this point, and three of the eight judges presented a dissenting opinion in which they claimed that fundamental rights were already protected by the system of law in the European Community. To illustrate their point they referred to Case 8/55, *Fédération Charbonnière de Belgique* v *High Authority* [1954–56] ECR 245; Case 15/57, *Compagnie des Hauts Fourneaux de Chasse* v *High Authority* [1958] ECR 211; Joined Cases 17 and 20/61, *Klöckner* v *High Authority* [1962] ECR 325; Case 11/70, *Internationale Handelsgesellschaft GmbH* v *EVST* [1970] ECR 1125; and Case 5/73, *Balkan-Import-Export* v *Hauptzollamt Berlin-Packhof* [1973] ECR 1091. This they claimed showed that the Community had recognised the principle of proportionality from the beginning of its case law as the criterion for the legality of actions of the Community organs. *Ibid.*, at 559.

incompatible. However by 1979, it appeared to be moving towards a more conciliatory attitude in the case of *Steinike & Weinlig*,[23] where it was stated:

> The Court leaves open whether, and if so, to what extent – for instance, in view of political and legal developments in the European sphere occurring in the meantime – the principles contained in its decision of 29 May 1974 can continue to claim validity without limitation in respect of future references of norms of derived Community law. Principles of law which the European Court of Justice in interpreting the Treaty, declares to be the content of the Treaty in the framework of a preliminary ruling under Article 177(1)(a) EEC do not in principle without prejudice to the binding effect of a preliminary ruling, stand at the level of derived Community law but are to be included in primary Community law.[24]

The matter appears to have been finally settled in the case of *Re Wünsche Handelsgesellschaft*,[25] where the German Federal Constitutional Court stated that all the main Community institutions had clearly recognised that they had a legal duty to observe fundamental rights (including proportionality) when exercising their powers and pursuing Community objectives, and that this acceptance of the role of fundamental rights had reached the stage where they could be considered to be firmly rooted in Community law, and not easily by-passed or swept away. Thus the German Federal Constitutional Court felt that it was no longer necessary to decide on the applicability of secondary Community legislation cited as the legal basis for any acts of German courts or authorities, and that it would no longer review such legislation by the standard of the fundamental rights contained in the Constitution. However, as in the similar Italian case *Frontini* v *Ministero delle Finanze*,[26] the Constitutional Court left itself a fall back position, in as much as it did not rule out the possibility of it reviewing future legislation, should it appear that the Community's protection of fundamental rights had fallen below the standard of rights necessary to achieve compatibility with the Constitution.[27]

The *Nold* case[28] expanded the permissible sources of Community human rights. Here, the challenge was to the withdrawal of the applicant's status as a wholesaler of coal, the applicant arguing that his right to pursue his trade was being infringed. The Court recognised that a question of human rights was raised. It reiterated its use of constitutional human rights declarations as a source, but added:

> Similarly, international treaties for the protection of human rights on which the Member States have collaborated or of which they are signatories, can supply guidelines which should be followed within the framework of Community law.[29]

This formula allows the Court a wide range of sources. It does not require that all Member States have ratified a treaty, or even that they are all signatories to it. A treaty to whose drafting Member States have contributed, but which some have refused to sign, could be used as a source of human rights principles within the EC, because it is evidence of a State's

23 25 July 1979, [1980] CMLR 531.
24 *Ibid.*, at 537.
25 [1987] 3 CMLR 225.
26 [1974] CMLR 372, at 389, where the Italian Constitutional Court held that, 'If ever Art 189 EEC had to be interpreted as giving the EEC organs an unacceptable power to violate the fundamental principles of the Italian

Constitution or the inalienable rights of man, the Italian Constitutional Court reserves the right to control the continuing compatibility of the Treaty as a whole with such fundamental principles.'
27 [1987] 3 CMLR 225, at 265.
28 Case 4/73, *Nold* v *Commission* [1974] ECR 491.
29 *Ibid.*, at paragraph 13.

opinion on human rights matters.[30] The *Nold* formula – constitutions plus relevant international treaties – has since been uniformly used by the Court as the parameters for human rights developments. A variation has been used in the Treaty on European Union:

> **Article F**
>
> . . .
>
> 2. The Union shall respect fundamental rights, as guaranteed by the European Convention for the Protection of Human Rights and Fundamental Freedoms signed in Rome on 4 November 1950 and as they result from the constitutional traditions common to the Member States, as general principles of Community Law.

The Court has extensively used the European Convention on Human Rights (ECHR) in its discussions of human rights. This Convention has, not surprisingly, been the source of most of the Court's human rights determinations, particularly in recent years. The degree of protection afforded to human rights by the Member States varies widely. The ECHR constitutes the only standard which is common to all Member States of the Community. The turning point appears to have been the ratification of the Convention by France in 1974. Equally unsurprisingly, the Court has also used the limitation formulas contained in the Convention in order to explain the scope of human rights. Notably, in the *Rutili* case,[31] the Court used the principles of limitation contained in the second paragraphs of several articles of the ECHR, in order to expand on the idea of 'limitations justified on grounds of public policy' in Article 48(3) EC:

> Taken as a whole, these limitations placed on the powers of Member States in respect of control of aliens are a specific manifestation of the more general principles, enshrined in Articles 8, 9, 10 and 11 of the Convention . . . and in Article 2 of Protocol 4 of the same Convention . . . which provide, in identical terms, that no restrictions in the interests of national security or public safety shall be placed on the rights secured by the above-quoted Articles other than such as are necessary for the protection of those interests in a democratic society.[32]

In addition to the ECHR, the case law of the Court has recognised rights deriving from International Labour Organisation treaties, the Council of Europe's European Social Charter,[33] and has referred to the International Covenant on Civil and Political Rights and the International Covenant on Economic, Social and Cultural Rights.[34]

The Court has recognised a number of specific human rights as constituting general principles of law. The tendency has been to recognise rights on a case by case basis, rather than adopting entire bills of rights from national constitutions or international treaties as general principles. This cautious approach has led to a curious 'Community Bill of Rights':

- right to a fair hearing[35] (Articles 6 and 13 ECHR)

30 Mendelson, 'The European Court of Justice and Human Rights' (1982) 1 YEL 125, at 151.
31 Case 36/75, *Rutili* v *Ministre de l'Intérieur* [1975] ECR 1219.
32 *Ibid.*, at paragraph 32.
33 See Case 149/77, *Defrenne* v *SABENA* [1978] ECR 1365.
34 Case C-262/88, *Barber* v *Guardian Royal Exchange Insurance Company* [1990] 2 CMLR 513, at 547 (opinion of Advocate-General Van Gerven).
35 Case 98/79, *Pescataing* v *Belgium* [1980] ECR 691; Case 222/84, *Johnston* v *Royal Ulster Constabulary* [1986] ECR 1651.

- the right to privacy[36] (Article 8 ECHR)
- the right to family life[37] (Articles 8 and 12 ECHR)
- freedom of religion[38] (Article 9 ECHR)
- freedom of expression[39] (Article 10 ECHR)
- trade union rights[40] (Article 11 ECHR)
- the right to own property or to pursue a trade[41] (Protocol 1, Article 1, ECHR).

Not all of these rights have been discussed in the context of the ECHR. In particular, the right to property and the right to pursue a trade have largely been discussed within the context of their recognition in the German Constitution. However, as all these rights exist in the ECHR, which is the common standard of human rights within the Community, it is essential to examine the relationship between these two systems of supranational law in Europe.

The European Convention on Human Rights

As is evident from the preceding sections, the ECHR has been the main source for the ECJ in expounding human rights as a general principle of EC law. This Convention has been referred to in the preamble of the SEA and in Article F of the TEU, although the latter provision, it should be noted, by virtue of Article L, is not justiciable by the ECJ. However, the relationship between the EC and the ECHR has never been precisely defined, and, to a certain extent, is the subject of controversy.

There are inevitable problems arising from the fact that although all EC Member States are parties to the ECHR, the EC itself is not. This creates certain anomalies. If human rights are violated by an EC Member State, the victim will have the right to bring an application before the European Commission on Human Rights.[42] If, however, a similar violation is committed by the EC, the victim has no such access, and can only attempt redress through the EC's own remedies.

This has been made clear by the European Commission on Human Rights. It has rejected applications against the EC because the Community is not a party to the ECHR.[43] Furthermore, the Commission on Human Rights has also rejected an application where the allegations were made against a Member State which was implementing EC law, because Community law, however implemented, is outside the jurisdiction of the ECHR institutions.[44]

There has been some controversy as to the exact status of the ECHR within the Community legal system. Until recently, the Court had given no indication of its opinion on

---

36 *Stauder, op. cit.,* note 16; Case 136/79, *National Panasonic (UK) Ltd v Commission* [1980] ECR 2033.

37 Case 12/86, *Demirel v Stadt Schwabisch Gmund* [1987] ECR 3719; Case 249/86, *Commission v Germany* [1989] ECR 1263.

38 Case 130/75, *Prais v Council* [1975] ECR 1589.

39 Case C-260/89, *Elliniki Radiofonia Tileorassi Anonimi Etairia v Dimotiki Etairia Pliroforissis and Sotirios Kouvelas* [1991] ECR 2925; Case C-159/90, *Society for the Protection of Unborn Children v Grogan* [1991] 2 CMLR 849.

40 Case 175/73, *Union Syndicale v Council* [1974] ECR 917.

41 *Internationale Handesgesellschaft, op. cit.,* note 18; Case 44/79, *Hauer v Land Rheinland-Pfalz* [1979] ECR 3727.

42 For a recent detailed discussion of the procedure before the European Commission on Human Rights, see Van Dijk and Van Hoof, *Theory and Practice of the European Convention on Human Rights,* 2nd edn (1991).

43 See, for example, *Confédération Française Démocratique du Travail v European Communities,* Application no. 8030/77, 13 DR 231; *Dufay v European Communities,* Application no. 13539/88.

44 *C.M. and Co. v Federal Republic of Germany,* Application no. 13258/87.

the matter, but there was disagreement amongst the Advocates General. Advocate General Trabucchi in Case 118/75 *Watson and Belmann*[45] stated that the ECHR cannot be regarded as having been incorporated into the Community legal order, but could only be used as a source to establish principles common to the Member States. Advocate General Capotorti, in *Defrenne (No. 3)*,[46] referred to the principle of non-discrimination as a principle also contained in the ECHR, and that the ECHR formed part of Community law which the ECJ had a duty to protect. He appears, at the very least, to consider the ECHR as a special source of law, and perhaps sees it as incorporated into Community law. The Court itself has, in recent years, since the explicit reference to the ECHR in the preamble to the SEA, accorded a special significance to the Convention in its recognition of human rights as general principles, without going as far as stating that it is, as a whole, an integral part of Community law.[47] A further problem is that even when the Court has referred to ECHR rights, it has only rarely examined any case law on the rights. This is, however, consistent with the general approach taken by the Court – that law from other systems which is adopted as a general principle of Community law takes on an autonomous existence from the same principle in its original system.

Authors have also been divided on the issue of the binding nature of the ECHR. Drzemczewski has taken the position that the ECHR in itself is not binding on the Community.[48] It is only binding insofar as specific provisions of the Convention have been recognised by the ECJ as general principles of EC law. Schermers, on the other hand, has argued that, despite not being a party to the ECHR, the Community is nonetheless bound by its guarantees. Since, at the time of ratification of the ECHR in 1950, the EC was not a separate legal entity, and since no State can transfer more powers than it possesses, then the Member States could only have transferred powers to the EC in 1957 subject to their obligations under the human rights treaty.[49] This argument would also apply to later accessions, as the practice of the Community has been that States who wish to become members, and who have not already ratified the ECHR, demonstrate their democratic credentials by doing so before admission to the EC.

However, even if the ECHR was binding on the Community, that fact alone would not provide a means of access to the ECHR mechanisms in Strasbourg. Only by becoming a party to the ECHR could the Community enable those under its jurisdiction to redress their human rights grievances through the European Commission and Court of Human Rights. The proposals which have been made for ratification involve the drafting of a special protocol to the ECHR, since the view of the EC Commission is that some provisions of the ECHR are not appropriate for implementation by a supranational organisation.[50] Community

---

[45] Case 118/75, [1976] ECR 1185, at 1207.

[46] *Op. cit.*, note 33, at 1384–5.

[47] Case C-260/89, *Elliniki Radiofonia Tileorassi Anonimi Etairia* v *Dimotiki Etairia Pliroforissis and Sotirios Kouvelas, op. cit.*, note 39, paragraph 41.

[48] Drzemczewski, 'The Domestic Application of the European Human Rights Convention as European Community Law' (1981) ICLQ 118.

[49] Schermers, 'The European Communities Bound by Fundamental Human Rights' (1990) 27 CML Rev 249, at 251–2. A similar argument was made by Advocate General Warner in Case 7/76, *IRCA* [1976] ECR 1213,

at 1237, with respect to constitutional guarantees of rights, although this argument, if it had been followed, could lead to assertions that human rights should be applied to a Community citizen only to the extent that such rights are recognised by the Member State of which that person is a citizen.

[50] Commission Communication on Community Accession to the European Convention for the Protection of Human Rights and Fundamental Freedoms and Some of its Protocols, Annex II, paragraph 6. The Communication does not specify which provisions it considers inappropriate for Community implementation.

ratification of the ECHR has been raised seriously by the Commission twice – in 1979[51] and in 1990.[52] The more recent proposal contains a thorough discussion of the merits of the move, as well as an attempt to refute objections. The most significant objection, particularly for the United Kingdom and Eire, is the potential effect of the ECHR on the national law of Member States, via the Community doctrine of direct effectiveness. While the UK and Eire have ratified the ECHR, unlike most other Member States they have not incorporated it into their domestic law.[53] It can therefore not be relied upon directly before national courts. However, as will be argued below, there has been some impact on national legal systems, in that national authorities implementing EC law must respect human rights which, whatever the status of the ECHR as a whole, include several specific ECHR rights.

Degree of protection afforded

Without a doubt, the ECJ has been generous in its recognition of human rights as general principles of Community law. However, it is highly questionable whether the record of the Court is so commendable in the enforcement of human rights. In case after case, it has recognised that a particular right is relevant to the proceedings but has justified a limitation on that right, or has interpreted it narrowly, when an important Community goal was at stake. The most significant examples can be found in the cases alleging infringements of the right to property and the right to pursue a trade or business. No such cases have been successful. Privacy rights have fared somewhat better, having been enforced in the *Stauder* case. However, when the implementation of competition policy is involved, the Court has been less generous in its interpretation, as in *National Panasonic (UK) Ltd* v *Commission*.[54]

While the Court has referred to the ECHR in numerous cases, the first case where a violation was found of a right contained in that Convention was *Kirk* in 1984.[55] In *Kirk*, the Court applied Article 7 ECHR (the prohibition on retroactive penal law), explicitly accepting it as a new general principle of Community law, despite the fact that the issue had not been raised either by the applicant or by the Advocate General.[56] More recently, the Court has directly applied Article 10 (freedom of expression), stating it to be a general principle, in the *ERT* case.

The view which the Court appears to have adopted in applying human rights principles has been best expressed by Advocate General Van Gerven in a recent Opinion:

> A feature of this case law is that it does not confer direct effect in the Community legal order on the provisions of the above-mentioned international treaties but regards those treaties, together with the constitutional traditions common to the Member States, as helping to determine the content of the general principles of Community law. This stance enables the Court, in establishing general principles in the particular (socio-economic) context of Community law, also to take into account the imperatives of the fundamental freedoms and of the Community market organisations, which are intended to bring about the integration of the market.[57]

[51] *Op. cit.*, note 49, at 256.
[52] *Op. cit.*, note 50.
[53] Denmark is in the same situation but is considering the incorporation of the ECHR into domestic law. No such moves have been contemplated by the British or Irish governments.
[54] Case 136/79, [1980] ECR 2033.

[55] See Foster, 'The European Court of Justice and the European Convention for the Protection of Human Rights' (1987) 8 HRLJ 245.
[56] Case 63/83, R v *Kirk* [1984] CMLR 522. See also comment by Foster at (1985) 10 EL Rev 276.
[57] Case C-159/90, *Society for the Protection of Unborn Children* v *Grogan, op. cit.*, note 39, at 876.

This attitude treats human rights as an integral part of Community law, but not as having automatic supremacy in the way that constitutional guarantees of human rights do. The Court appears to put Community freedoms of movement and the implementation of competition policy ahead of fundamental rights.

Effect on national law[58]

As was demonstrated in Chapter 5, the impact of Community law on Member States increased markedly during the 1970s and 1980s. It is interesting to note that a similar development has occurred with respect to human rights, the ECJ extending the effect of human rights as general principles of law to the acts of Member States in implementing EC law.[59]

The beginnings of this extension go back to cases decided in 1985 and 1987. The first stage was defining where EC general principles could not operate. In *Cinéthèque SA* v *Fédération Nationale des Cinémas Françaises*,[60] a case involving French legislation limiting the availability of video recording of films, Article 10 ECHR was raised by the applicant. Advocate General Slynn reiterated that the ECHR did not form part of Community law, and that no general principle guaranteeing freedom of expression had been established.[61] The Court left open the question of the existence of the right in the Community legal order, but asserted that it was outside the Court's jurisdiction to examine the conformity of national legislation with human rights principles, when such legislation was entirely within the jurisdiction of the national authorities.[62] In *Demirel* v *Stadt Schwabisch Gmund*,[63] where the applicant was relying on the right to respect for family life as contained in Article 8 ECHR, the Court repeated the *Cinéthèque* dictum in a slightly looser format. The only national law which the Court cannot examine, under this formulation, is that which lies outside the scope of Community law. Finding that the relevant national law was not an implementation measure of the Turkish Association Agreement on which the applicant relied, because it was beyond the scope of that Agreement, the Court rejected the applicant's claim.

The Court's approach changed markedly with *Wachauf* v *Bundesamt fur Ernahrung und Forstwirtschaft*.[64] Here the Court had to examine the legality of national implementing rules which deprived the plaintiff of his leasehold, without compensation, as a result of a quota Regulation under the Common Agricultural Policy. The source of the plaintiff's grievance was unquestionably a national law, although it was a measure of implementation of Community law. Advocate General Jacobs explicitly stated in his opinion that human rights, here property rights, must be observed by States when implementing Community legislation. The Court did not find a violation of property rights because it was of the view that the relevant regulations were capable of being applied in such a way as to avoid infringement of such rights. However, it did state that national authorities implementing Community rules are bound by human rights as general principles of Community law, and that implementing

---

[58] For a general discussion of this issue, see Coppel and O'Neill, 'The European Court of Justice: Taking Rights Seriously?' (1992) 12 *Legal Studies* 227, at 230–44.
[59] The argument that the development of human rights by the ECJ parallels the development of the doctrines of supremacy and direct effectiveness is made by Dallen, 'An Overview of European Community Protection of Human Rights, With Some Special References to the UK' (1990) 27 CML Rev 761.
[60] Joined Cases 60 & 61/84, [1985] ECR 2605.
[61] *Ibid.*
[62] *Ibid.*, at paragraph 26.
[63] Case 12/86, [1987] ECR 3719.
[64] Case 5/88, [1989] ECR 2609.

authorities should apply rules in accordance with the requirements of the general principles.[65] When comparing this statement to those in the *Cinéthèque* and *Demirel* judgments, it may appear to be a matter of saying the glass is half-full rather than half-empty, but it does demonstrate a change of attitude by the Court.

This is borne out by the next relevant case, *Elliniki Radiofonia Tileorassi Anonimi Etairia v Dimotiki Etairia Pliroforissis and Sotirios Kouvelas.*[66] While *Wachauf* allowed the Court to look at national legislation implementing Community law, this case goes further. As in *Cinéthèque*, freedom of expression was at issue. However, the Court paid a great deal more attention to the claim. The Court referred to *Cinéthèque* and *Demirel* as authority for the proposition that the Court may not examine national legislation which is not within the framework of Community law.[67] However, the Court continued, once national legislation is within the Community framework, the Court is obliged to supply all the elements of interpretation which are necessary to the national court's determination of whether that legislation is in conformity with human rights recognised by the Court. In particular, since the State relied on Articles 56 and 66 to justify the legislation in question, such justification must be examined in light of general principles of Community law, especially human rights. As a result, national courts must evaluate such national law in the light of all relevant rules of Community law, including freedom of expression.

This approach was confirmed in the *Grogan* case, although it was not applied, the Court finding that there was no Community dimension.[68] Advocate General Van Gerven devoted a substantial portion of his opinion to the discussion of the permissibility of the Court's examination of national law in light of human rights norms, and to the application of Article 10 to the facts of the case. The Court cited the *ERT* judgment with approval, but distinguished it on the grounds that the legislation under review was outside the scope of Community law.

As a result, the extent to which human rights, as general principles of Community law, are binding upon States, depends on whether the legislation or other State action is within the framework of Community law. Therefore, a party before a British court could request that a statute be reviewed for its compatibility with human rights if the law has a Community dimension, in particular if it is an implementing measure. This creates anomalies within British law, as there is no means to make such a challenge if the law has nothing to do with the Community.[69]

Proportionality

The principle of proportionality has been one of the most important of the general principles in shaping the actions of both the Community and the Member States. It has been widely acknowledged that the origins of the principle of proportionality are to be found in German administrative law, and that it was outlined and refined by both the German legislature and the German administrative courts.[70] However, defining the principle of proportionality is no

[65] *Ibid.*, at paragraph 19.
[66] *Op. cit.*, note 39.
[67] *Ibid.*, at paragraph 42.
[68] *Op. cit.*, note 39.
[69] See the judgment of the House of Lords in *Brind* v *Secretary of State for the Home Department* [1991] 1 All ER 720.
[70] For example, see Jowell and Lester, 'Proportionality: Neither Novel nor Dangerous' in Jowell and Oliver (eds), *New Directions in Judicial Review*, Current Legal Problems (1988).

precise matter. When its use by the German courts, the French courts and the ECJ is examined, it will be seen that the principle of proportionality can have subtly different meanings, and be used to differing ends, and it is thus useful to consider briefly both these differences, the reasons for them, and how the Community has come to use the principle of proportionality in its own particular way.

French and German law

As far as French law is concerned, the arrival of a recognised, as opposed to an implicit, doctrine of proportionality, that is a doctrine explicitly outlined by the Conseil d'Etat, occurred relatively recently in French legal history, with the leading case of *Ville Nouveau L'Est*.[71] In the *Ville Nouveau L'Est* case there was a planning decision to build a new town near Lille, integrating both new faculties for the University and accommodation for the students. In order to prepare a site for the new town, it was proposed to purchase compulsorily an area of land and demolish the 88 relatively new houses which had been built on it. This was not well received by the local people who, on appeal, challenged the decision of the Minister to continue with the compulsory purchase on that grounds that it was an issue of public interest (*d'utilité publique*). The Lille administrative tribunal upheld that challenge and the Minister appealed to the Conseil d'Etat. The Conseil d'Etat reversed the decision of the administrative tribunal but stated that:

> an operation cannot be legally declared *d'utilité publique* unless the interference with private property, the financial cost, and, where they arise, the attendant inconveniences on the social plane are not excessive having regard to the interest of the operation.[72]

This analysis of the administrator's decision, with the measuring or balancing of the costs and advantages defined as *le bilan coût-avantage*, certainly appeared to be a bold and controversial[73] move by the judiciary into an area traditionally forbidden to them by the separation of powers doctrine. As a result of this, the Conseil d'Etat was at pains to explain that it would be inaccurate to assume that it had simply plucked the concept out of the air. Guy Braibant, a member of the Conseil d'Etat, stated in a later report[74] that while the lead in recognising that such a doctrine had a valid place in administrative law had been taken by the Germans, Swiss and the International Labour Organisation, nonetheless the French judiciary had already been applying the basic principle.[75]

In German administrative law, the principle of proportionality is to be found as part of a principle called *Verhältnismäßigkeit*.[76] The legal thinking behind the principle of main

71 *Ministre de L'Equipement et du Logement v Fédération de Défense des Personnes Concernées par le Projet Actuellement Dénommé Ville Nouveau Est*, CE 28 May 1971.

72 Translation, Brown and Garner, *French Administrative Law*, 3rd edn (1983), at 60. Guy Braibant, as if to prove that the UK judiciary do not have the monopoly on colourful expression, refers to the doctrine as not to 'shoot a swallow with a cannon' or to 'crush a fly with a sledgehammer'. Quoted in Jowell and Lester, 'Proportionality: Neither Novel not Dangerous', *op. cit.*, note 70, at 54.

73 Kahn, 'Discretionary Power and the Administrative Judge' (1980) 29 ICLQ 521, and Laubadere, 'Le contrôle juridictionnel du pouvoir discrétionnaire dans la

jurisprudence récente du Conseil d'Etat français' *Mélanges M Waline*, vol. II, 531.

74 Braibant, 'Le Principe de Proportionnalité', *Mélanges Walines* (1974), vol. 2, 280.

75 Jowell and Lester, 'Proportionality: Neither Novel nor Dangerous', *op. cit.*, note 70, at 54.

76 The principle of *Verhältnismäßigkeit*, which appears to equate roughly to what an English court would call reasonableness, contains as one of its three heads the principle of proportionality which is also called somewhat confusingly, *Verhältnismäßigkeit*. In order to avoid confusion they will be referred to as the main and lesser principles of *Verhältnismäßigkeit* respectively.

Verhältnismäßigkeit bears some resemblance to the French doctrine of *le bilan coût-avantage* in as much as it requires the judiciary to engage in a balancing process, between the ends that the administrative body intends and the means by which it is attempting to achieve them. There is also a degree of resemblance to the English doctrine of *Wednesbury* unreasonableness, in that in order for an administrative act to stand it must not infringe against any of the heads of that principle. The three heads are suitability, necessity and proportionality (lesser *Verhältnismäßigkeit*).[77] Proportionality requires the administrative body to weigh up the benefit to the community of an action as opposed to the damage caused to individual rights. If the damage to the rights of the individual is significantly greater than the gain by the community the administrative act will be quashed. This, however, has to be viewed in the light of the fact that the administrative courts are loathe to interfere unless there is an obvious disproportion.[78] It should be noted that the German Federal Constitutional Court (*Bundesverfassungsgericht*) has stated that this principle is derived from the status of the FRG as a 'Rechtsstaat,' and thus it should have constitutional force.[79]

The role of the Conseil d'Etat is very much as an overseer of the French administrative system, ensuring that it remains within the law. The German administrative courts are not concerned with the wider policy issues but rather solely with protecting the rights of the individual against administrative excesses.[80] Thus while the Conseil d'Etat is effectively part of the French administrative hierarchy, the German administrative courts are in essence supervisory bodies. With that proviso, however, it should be noted that both French and German administrative law contain principles which have been derived by the courts from areas other than those legislative documents which lay down the duties and responsibilities of the administrative courts. The French *principes généraux du droit* of which doctrines such as *erreur manifeste* and *le bilan coût-avantage* are but two, and various German doctrines such as equality of treatment and indeed *Verhältnismäßigkeit* in its broader sense, have been derived in order to deal with certain situations, almost always concerning individual rights, not covered by legislation, that the courts have felt it necessary to deal with. This, despite the extreme bias against judicial inventiveness in the field of administrative discretion in French administrative law and the clear outlines given to the German administrative courts by legislation. Thus in the French courts proportionality appears as a controversial judge-made doctrine to enable the courts to step outside the confines of their usual role as determined by the doctrine of separation of powers, whilst in the German courts it has been elevated to a considerably higher constitutional level.[81]

---

[77] Singh, *German Administrative Law: In Common Law Perspective* (1985), at 89.

[78] *Ibid.*, at 90.

[79] Nedjatigil, 'Judicial Control of Administrative Discretion: A Comparative Study' (1985) 14 *Anglo-American L Rev* 97, at 113.

[80] *Ibid.*

[81] The judgement of the House of Lords in the case of *Brind and others* v *Secretary of State for the Home Department, op. cit.*, note 69, would appear to have, for the moment at least, created a formidable barrier against the acceptance of the doctrine of proportionality as any-

thing other than another category of *Wednesbury* unreasonableness, and a very vague category at that. Their Lordships were at pains to emphasise that they felt the doctrine of proportionality as they understood it being advanced by counsel for the applicants was a test that went further than that of Wednesbury unreasonableness and that they were not at all happy with this interpretation.

Community law

It was not until *Internationale Handelsgesellschaft GmbH v EVST*[82] that the issue of fundamental rights was explicitly addressed and the principle of proportionality recognised (*see* the human rights section *supra*). However, the principle of proportionality had already found its way into the language of the Court, even if it was not prepared at that time to admit it was a fundamental principle. It appears to have first appeared in Community law in *Fédération Charbonnière de Belgique v High Authority*.[83] Here it was held that the High Authority, when reacting to illegal conduct under the ECSC Treaty, must do so in proportion to the breach. The case, which dealt with coal pricing, revolved around the action that the High Authority could legitimately take to deal with undertakings which failed to reduce their prices to the required level.

This was then followed in *Compagnie des Hauts Fourneaux de Chasse v High Authority*,[84] where it was held that in regulating the market in ferrous scrap, the High Authority had no 'obligation to use its power to make regulations only on the condition that no interest is adversely affected' but that,

> This does not mean that the High Authority may ignore the special interests of those concerned and act so harshly that those interests are compromised very much more than can be reasonably expected. On the contrary the High Authority is bound to act with all the circumspection and care required to balance and assess the various, often conflicting, interests involved and to avoid harmful consequences insofar as, within reason, the nature of the decision to be taken permits.[85]

Nold v High Authority (No 1)[86] demonstrated that the doctrine outlined by the Court was not going to be used to allow the High Authority to ride roughshod over the newly developing concept of 'good administration' in Community law. The High Authority using powers granted under Article 65 of the ECSC Treaty was able to authorise joint selling agreements, if it decided that such agreements were essential in order to achieve a substantial improvement in production or distribution and were not more restrictive than was necessary for that purpose. In this case the Court held the High Authority had failed in four decisions to give sufficient and proper statements of the factual and legal considerations behind those decisions. This in turn meant that the Court was unable to review the decisions, notably with regard to whether the High Authority had paid due regard to Article 65(2). This, the Court held, was equivalent to an absence of reasons, and thus three of the decisions were annulled and the fourth partially so. So while the case itself turned on the absence or otherwise of reasons, reasons were required in effect in order that the Court could decide if there had been a breach of proportionality. It is noticeable that the Court went against the recommendations of the Advocate General, who felt that the High Authority's duty to give reasons should be interpreted much less rigorously.

In *Klöckner v High Authority*[87] the Court made it quite clear that the High Authority was bound to take account of the principle of proportionality, but also noted that in doing so it also had to ensure that the principle of proportionality was reconciled with the principle of

---

82 *Op. cit.*, note 18.
83 Case 8/55, [1954–56] ECR 245.
84 Case 15/57, [1958] ECR 211.
85 *Ibid.*, at 228.

86 Case 18/57, [1957] ECR 121.
87 Joined Cases 17 and 20/61, [1962] ECR 325. This judgment was repeated almost word for word in Case 19/61, *Mannesmann v High Authority* [1962] ECR 371.

legal certainty. Thus the High Authority was in a situation where it needed to use certain broad, clear and objective criteria to establish and maintain the financial arrangements for ensuring the continuing stability of the Common Market. The very nature of this made it impossible for the High Authority to take into account every variation of economic unit that would be subject to its action, or the High Authority would be unduly fettered and thus probably ineffective.[88]

The role of the doctrine was extended to the EC institutions' own relations with their staff with *Wollast* v *EEC*[89] where the applicant, a temporary nurse on a rollover contract with the staff of the Commission, was turned down for a full-time post on the grounds of her alleged poor conduct at an accident. The Advocate General's recommendation, accepted by the Court, echoes the attitude later adopted by the French Conseil d'Etat towards disproportionate penalties in disciplinary cases involving civil servants:[90]

> I do not think that taking account of all the circumstances of the case, the applicant's conduct and according to her file she was an excellent nurse, justified a penalty equivalent to dismissal by reason of this single incident.

In *Internationale Handelsgesellschaft GmbH* v *EVST*[91] the Advocate General, Alain Dutheilleit de Lamothe, submitted that the principle of proportionality was a general principle of Community law following the cases of *Fédération Charbonnière de Belgique* v *High Authority*[92] and *Compagnie des Hauts Fourneaux de Chasse* v *High Authority*[93] and that it was also guaranteed by an express provision of the Treaty in that Article 40(3) allows only those measures necessary for the attainment of the objectives set out in Article 39.

This was followed in *Einfuhr und Vorratsstelle für Getreide und Futtermittel* v *Köster*[94] and *Einfuhr und Vorratsstelle für Getreide und Futtermittel* v *Gunther Henck*.[95] These decisions laid the way open for the use of the doctrine of proportionality in *Wilhelm Werhann Hansamuhle & Others* v *Council*.[96] These cases were concerned with the common organisation of the market in cereals, specifically durum wheat. The German applicants were seeking compensation for damage caused to them due to the way in which the common market in cereals was organised and managed, as the system of aids for production of durum wheat was not accompanied by measures that would guarantee to mills of Member States not producing that cereal the availability of imported wheat from third countries at the same price level as that paid by their French and Italian competitors. The breach of proportionality was supposed to have resulted from the threshold price for the wheat having been set higher than was necessary to protect the Community market, contrary to Article 40(3) of the Treaty. This claim was rejected by the Court without a clear indication of why the Council's actions were not disproportionate. Indeed, a full statement of the reasoning behind the ECJ's use of the doctrine of proportionality was not outlined until *Balkan-Import-Export* v *Hauptzollamt Berlin-Packhof*[97] and *Schlüter* v *Hauptzollamt Lörrach*.[98] Both cases dealt with the question of whether Regulation 974/71/EEC[99] was in conflict with the principle of

---

[88] *Ibid.*, at 340.
[89] Also known as the *Schmitz* case, Case 18/63, [1964] ECR 96–7.
[90] See Brown and Garner, *op. cit.*, note 72, at 158.
[91] *Op. cit.*, note 18.
[92] *Op. cit.*, note 83.
[93] *Op. cit.*, note 84.

[94] Case 25/70, [1970] ECR 1125, at 1147.
[95] Case 26/70, [1970] ECR 1161.
[96] Joined Cases 63–69/72, [1970] ECR 1229.
[97] Case 5/73, [1973] ECR 1091.
[98] Cases 9/73, [1973] ECR 1135.
[99] OJ 1971 L106.

proportionality, as it attempted to deal with the effect of the floating DM and guilder upon the agricultural trade and Community intervention system by authorising a system of compensatory amounts which the relevant Member States could charge on imports and grant on exports in their trade with both Member States and third countries. This in turn meant that the compensatory amounts were not based on any profit made by an importer on the rate of exchange but, rather, solely on the relationship between the official parity of the DM compared with the dollar, and its true parity. The court held in both cases that alternative suggestions were unworkable in practice, and in a passage identical in both cases stated that:

> In exercising their powers, the Institutions must ensure that the amounts which commercial operators are charged are no greater than is required to achieve the aim which the authorities are to accomplish: however, it does not necessarily follow that that obligation must be measured in relation to the individual situation of any one particular group of operators . . . . The court is not satisfied then that in weighing up the advantages and disadvantages of the system . . . the Council imposed burdens on traders which were manifestly out of proportion to the object in view.[100]

The principle of proportionality has played a large part in the development of both the Common Agricultural Policy and great freedoms of the Community, such as the freedom of movement of goods and the freedom of movement of persons, and it is within these areas that it is possible to see how it has developed and changed as a Community principle.

The Common Agricultural Policy

It is hardly surprising, given the potential number of administrative decisions at both Community and Member State levels, that the doctrine of proportionality has played a significant role in developing the administration of the CAP, not least in ensuring that the Member State administrations in pursuing nationalistic aims and policies did not disrupt its smooth functioning. *Schlüter & Maak* v *Hauptzollamt Hamburg*[101] provides one of the initial examples of this. The case concerned export refunds under the provisions of Regulation No. 1041/67/EEC,[102] notably whether the production by the exporter of an exit certificate referred to in Article 5 of that Regulation constituted a sufficient statement for the purposes of Article 17(2) of Regulation No. 1009/67/EEC[103] of the exporter's intention to qualify for the refund and fulfil the requirements of the provision, as the German authorities required the exporters also to make an application on a separate form. The Court held that, while in order to ensure the smooth functioning of the complicated system of export refunds any application for refunds must be made in writing and the Member State might also for reasons of administrative organisation require exporters to make an application in the form required by national law, they could not punish failure to so do by forfeiture of the right to a refund. The judgment stated that 'a formalism which would go further than is necessary for the effective supervision of these operations should be avoided'.[104] In other words, a formalism that was out of proportion to the aim to be achieved would not be accepted; also, effectively

---

100 [1973] ECR 1091, at 1111–12 and [1973] ECR 1135, at 1155–6.
101 Case 94/71, [1972] 1 ECR 307.
102 Detailed rules for the application of export refunds on products subject to a single price refund.
103 Which established the common organisation of the market in sugar.
104 *Op. cit.*, note 101.

to penalise the exporter the whole of the monetary refund was out of proportion to the purported offence and could not be allowed.[105] This decision was followed in *Firma Robert Unkel* v *Hauptzollamt Hamburg-Jonas*,[106] where the Court reaffirmed the decision in precisely the same words.[107]

The Court has also used the principle of proportionality to regulate the way in which the Commission uses deposits and securities to ensure the smooth running of the CAP. In *Beste Boter*,[108] a processing deposit lodged by an undertaking for intervention butter purchased at a reduced price was declared forfeit by the competent national intervention agency for non-compliance with Community rules on butter processing. This was held by the Court not to be disproportionate to achieve the objective desired, which was to dispose of surplus butter to the food industry even though the purchaser had sold the butter to another party who intended to process it. This was followed by *SA Buitoni* v *FORMA*.[109] Here Article 3 of Regulation 499/76/EEC amending Regulation 193/75/EEC laying down common detailed rules for the application of the system of import and export licences and advance fixing certificates for agricultural products, required the forfeiture of a security in the event of delay in furnishing proof of importation, which was the same penalty as for non-compliance with the import licence itself. The Court held that this was too severe a penalty for a lesser offence and was therefore disproportionate.[110]

Following these cases the Court began to develop the concept of principal and secondary obligations in terms of proportionality with regard to deposits and securities. In the case of principal obligations, their observance is held to be of fundamental importance to the proper functioning of a Community system and their infringement may be punished by a total forfeiture of the security, without there being any breach of proportionality. In the case of secondary obligations, their infringement should not be punished with the same rigour as is applied to the failure to fulfil a principal obligation.[111]

This is demonstrated by *Société RU-MI* v *FORMA*,[112] where failure to denature skimmed milk intended for animals other than young calves as laid down by regulation, and for which the special aid granted was significantly higher, led to both the withholding of aid and forfeiture of security. The Court held that the Commission was not obliged to vary the severity of the measure in question according to the gravity of the failure to comply with the obligation, in view of the risk that it might be used for other unauthorised purposes where

---

105 It should be noted, however, in Case 57/72, *West-zucker GmbH* v *Einfuhr- und Vorratsstelle für Zucker* [1973] ECR 321, the Court was at pains to emphasise that 'the Commission enjoys a significant freedom of evaluation, which must be exercised in the light of the objectives of the economic policy laid down by Regulation 1009/67/EEC within the framework of the CAP' and that 'When examining the lawfulness of the exercise of such freedom the courts cannot substitute their own evaluation of the matter for that of the competent authority, but must restrict themselves to examining whether the evaluation of the competent authority contains a patent error or constitutes a misuse of power,' suggesting some judicial qualms about the role that principles such as proportionality allowed the Court to play in determining Community policies.

106 Case 55/74, [1975] ECR 9.

107 See more recently Case 46/82, *Germany* v *Commission*, [1983] ECR 3549, where a Member State successfully challenged the Commission on the grounds of excessive formality.

108 Case 99-100/76, [1977] ECR 861, at 870–4.

109 Case 122/78, [1979] ECR 677, at 682–5.

110 See also Case 240/78, *Atalanta Amsterdam BV* [1979] ECR 2137, at 2148–57 (forfeiture of deposits and storage aids due to failure to send documentation in the time period laid down).

111 For a more detailed if dated look at the area of deposits, see Barents, 'The System of Deposits in Community Agricultural law: Efficiency v Proportionality' [1985] EL Rev 329.

112 Case 272/81, [1982] ECR 4167, at 4176–81.

the denaturing departed even slightly from the method required. Thus the breach was of a principal obligation.[113] In *Maas v BALM*[114] Maas had successfully tendered for a contract to transport 5000 tonnes of food aid to Ethiopia and carried out that contract successfully. However, its security was declared forfeit on the grounds that the goods had not been shipped within the correct period and that the ships were older than the 15 years specified in the applicable regulation. The Court held that given that the food aid had arrived safely and on time, and that the ships used were well maintained and of top class in recognised shipping classification registers, neither breach was of a principal obligation.

The nature and position of deposits within the legal framework are precisely summed up in *Maizena Gesellschaft mbH v Bundesanstalt für Landwirtschaftliche Marktordnung*,[115] following the clear guidelines given in *Société pour l'Exportation des Sucres v OBEA*.[116] The principle of proportionality has also been used as a check on the manner in which the Commission carries out the general organisation of the Common Market, such as in the early case of *Effem v Hauptzollamt Lüneberg*[117] concerning export levies on cattle fodder. Here the Court held that an across-the-board standard levy was inappropriate on the grounds that it was disproportionate:

> For the fixing of the export levy on the said products, account is taken *inter alia* of the quantity of cereals necessary for the manufacture of the products under consideration, and of the opportunities for and conditions of sale of the products in question on the world market. Consequentially the fixing of a standard levy which is applicable irrespective of the quantity, whether negligible or considerable, of cereals included in the products concerned cannot comply with these provisions.[118]

In the *Skimmed milk* cases[119] the Commission attempted to deal with a large surplus of skimmed milk powder by making manufacturers of animal feedstuffs purchase skimmed milk rather than soyameal or fishmeal to use as the protein component of their food stuffs. The problem with this solution was that the cost of the skimmed milk was about three times that of soyameal. The Court held, in a classic definition of proportionality, that 'The obligation to purchase at such a disproportionate price constituted a discriminatory distribution of the burden of costs between the various agricultural sectors. Nor . . . was such an obligation necessary in order to achieve the objective in view . . . the disposal of stocks of skimmed

---

113 See also Case 273/81, *Société Laitiere de Gace v FORMA* [1982] ECR 4193, at 4200–5 (skimmed milk – failure to comply with requirement as to maximum water content) and Case 66/82, *Fromancais SA v FORMA* [1983] 1 ECR 395, at 402–7 (prevention of speculation in reduced price butter), Case 9/85, *Nordbutter v Germany* (1986) ECR 2831 (failure to submit required information within a 10-day period), Case 199/87, *Mads Peder Jensen v Landbrugsministeriet* [1988] ECR 5045 and Case 358/87, *Kurt Drewes v Bezirksregierung Lüneberg* [1989] ECR 911 (non-marketing of milk and milk products – failure to fulfil obligations under a premiums scheme).
114 Case 21/85, [1986] ECR 3537.
115 Case 137/85, [1987] ECR 4587, in which the Advocate General Mischo referred explicitly and with approval to the article by Barents, *op. cit.*, note 111.

116 Case 56/86, [1987] ECR 1423.
117 Case 95/75, [1976] 1 ECR 361.
118 Note that in Schmitthoff, 'The Doctrines of Proportionality & Nondiscrimination' [1977] EL Rev 329, one of the early pieces recognising the importance of proportionality, this quote is made a nonsense of by the omission of the words 'irrespective of the quantity, whether negligible'.
119 Case 114/76, *Bela-Mühle Josef Bergmann KG v Grows-Farm GmbH & Co KG* [1977] ECR 1211, at 1219–21, Case 116/76, *Granaria BV v Hoofdproduktschap voor Akkerbouwprodukten (No 1)* [1977] ECR 1247 at 1262–6, Cases 119–120/76, *Olmühle Hamburg AG v Hauptzollamt Hamburg Waltershof* [1977] ECR 1269, at 1286–7.

milk powder'. It should be noted, however, that while breach of the principle of proportionality is frequently argued in front of the Court in matters concerning the general organisation of the Common Market, the occasions when the Court holds the Commission to be in breach are rare.[120]

Free movement of goods

This area of Community law (see Chapter 11) has seen extensive use of the principle of proportionality. The following two cases demonstrate how the Court applies the principle. In *Officier van Justitie* v *De Peijper (Centrafarm BV)*, [121] Advocate General Mayras examined the case law up to that point and emphasised that Member States' powers under Article 36 'are limited by the fact that the measures adopted for the purpose of the objective which it is sought to attain must be adequate and also that these measures must be proportionate to the aim it is sought to achieve',[122] and that the Dutch regulations in question were not just a 'superfluous formality'. Those regulations sought to ensure that an importer of pharmaceutical goods must produce certain documents, including some from the manufacturer, of the product relating to their composition and manufacture before being able to place a product on the Dutch market. However, the regulations made it virtually impossible for a parallel importer to fulfil these criteria, if the manufacturer and his duly appointed representatives in Holland refused to provide the said documents. The Court acknowledged that 'health and the life of humans rank first among the property or interests protected by Article 36' and also that 'it is for the Member States, within the limits imposed by the Treaty, to decide what degree of protection they intend to assure and in particular how strict the checks carried out are to be'. Despite this, the Court was adamant that such national rules and practices could only be covered by Article 36 if there were not other less restrictive procedures and practices which could be used to achieve similar ends. This was especially true if the procedures used were designed primarily to save public money or administrative time, unless there would be an unreasonably large burden upon these if the procedures were not used.

The *De Peijper* case was referred to in *Heinz Schumacher* v *Hauptzollamt Frankfurt am Main*,[123] which also involved the importation of pharmaceuticals. Here an individual purchased a product in France and posted it to his address in Germany. The product in question cost some four times the price in Germany that it did in France. However, the product was intercepted and impounded by German customs officials. The product, which consisted of an extract of artichoke, was available in both Member States without a prescription. Advocate General Tesauro was of the opinion that, as shown in *De Peijper*, it was clear that pharmaceutical preparations were included in the product to which the principle of free movement of goods applied, and that while certain exceptions could still be made under Article 36 as the harmonisation of the national laws on medicinal preparations was not yet complete, such exceptions were to be kept to a minimum, basically on the

---

120 See for example Case 59/83, *SA Biovilac NV* v *EEC* [1984] 5 ECR 4057, where the Commission was held to be adequately reconciling the aim of ensuring a fair standard of living for the agricultural community with the aim of stabilising markets despite the loss suffered by Biovilac; also Case 68/86, *UK* v *Council* [1988] 1 ECR 855 and Case 84/87, *Erpelding* v *Secretaire d'Etat à l'Agriculture et à la Viticulture* [1988] ECR 2647.
121 Case 104/75, [1976] ECR 613.
122 *Ibid.*, at 648.
123 Case 215/87, [1989] ECR 617.

grounds of protection of health. In this case he felt the principle of proportionality was in effect superfluous given that the product was available in both countries without a prescription and there was no evidence of the purported impounding being on health grounds.

In essence, the doctrine of proportionality as applied by the ECJ to cases concerning the free movement of goods has evolved into a two-stage test. This involves what one might term the balancing of costs and advantages as a first stage, and the German doctrine of the least restrictive procedure to achieve the aim required as a second stage. Thus the first stage in evaluating national rules which have potential to affect the free movement of goods, is to establish whether the administration has correctly decided whether a product should come under either the derogations provided for in Article 36 and/or the 'mandatory requirements' outlined in the *Cassis de Dijon* case.[124] That is, on balance, there is enough of a risk for it to be proportionate to take action which might affect the free movement of goods. Therefore in the *Schumacher* case, when the Advocate General stated that he did not feel that there was a need for the use of the principle of proportionality he was not wholly correct, as both he and the Court had, in rejecting the submission by the German authorities that the ban on the product in question was on public health grounds, already applied the first leg of the test, which was that in applying a law to a product which did not require it, the aim of the German authorities had not been legitimate and was thus disproportionate. If the national law passes the first part of the test, it then faces the second part which asks whether the action taken to achieve a legitimate aim is the least restrictive method readily available to the authorities. In *De Peijper*, by contrast, the Court held that there was a legitimate aim in requiring the composition and manufacture information about drugs being imported into Holland, and the legislation thus passed the first test. However, the Court held that a procedure which effectively prevented parallel importing and allowed a manufacturer a monopoly of the importing and marketing of the product was almost certainly unnecessarily restrictive, unless the authorities could clearly prove that other rules and practices would clearly be beyond the means of a normal administration. Thus it was likely that the Dutch legislation would fail the second part of the test.

An example of the way in which the ECJ has used the principle of proportionality in a series of related cases in order to ensure the ongoing application of the free movement of goods in a particular area can be examined in the field of imports of meat and meat products. In *Simmenthal Spa v Italian Minister for Finance*,[125] it was held that systematic veterinary and public health inspections at the frontier by the importing State would be disproportionate, in as much as they would involve unnecessary expense and delay, without any great benefit, as they would merely duplicate the veterinary and public health inspections made before the produce left the exporting State. In *W J G Bauhuis v The Netherlands State*[126] it was held that veterinary and public health inspections within the exporting Member State, for purposes other than those of the directive, including those to meet the requirements of another Member State which were no longer justified, were incompatible with Community law, being charges having an effect equivalent to customs duties. In *Commission v Germany*[127] the Court held that the German government's concern about the

124 Case 120/78 *Rewe-Zentral AG v Bundesmonopolver-waltung für Branntwein* [1979] ECR 649.
125 Case 35/76, [1976] ECR 1871; see also Case 70/77, *Simmenthal Spa v Amministrazione delle Finanze dello* *Stato*, [1978] ECR 1453.
126 Case 46/76, [1977] ECR 5.
127 Case 153/78, [1979] ECR 2555.

presence of trichinae in pig meat did not justify a ban on the whole range of meat products as there was no reason to suppose that the crossing of a border in between slaughter and processing increased the risk of the presence of trichinae or made it any harder to detect. Thus the ban was disproportionate to the aim to be achieved, which could in any case be achieved by methods involving much less restriction upon the free movement of goods.[128]

The principle of proportionality has also been used to address some of the more modern concerns of both individual Member States and the Community as a whole, such as the question of whether Member States could ban drink and food products containing additives and how Member States should protect the environment. As far as the first issue is concerned, following the cases of *Sandoz BV*,[129] *Motte*[130] and *Ministère Public* v *Claude Muller & Others*[131] it was clear that Community law allowed Member States to adopt legislation which would subject the use of additives to prior authorisation, as this legislation would genuinely be protecting human health, by restricting the unlimited use of food additives. However, in the above cases the Court had made it plain that any prohibition on the marketing of products containing additives which were authorised in the Member State of production but which were banned in the Member State of importation, would be subject to the proportionality test as to its necessity and effectiveness in protecting public health. This conclusion was borne out by *Commission* v *Germany*[132] concerning the German laws on beer purity which were held to be in breach of Article 30 and unjustified on the grounds of public health under Article 36, as the public could be protected by other less restrictive means such as proper product labelling.[133]

The issue of the environment was tackled in *Commission* v *Kingdom of Denmark,*[134] where the Court considered whether a law which was adopted by the Danish government to protect the environment, by restricting the quantity of beer and soft drinks which might be marketed by a single producer in non-approved containers to 3000 hectolitres per annum (and provided that a deposit and return system was established), in order to enable more efficient recycling, was in fact proportionate to the aim pursued. The Danish government had originally required that producers and importers should only use approved containers, but the producers complained that such a law would force them to manufacture or purchase containers approved by the Danish government at a substantial extra cost. The Danish government was aware that either system involved 'trading rules which are capable of hindering, directly or indirectly, actually or potentially, intra-Community trade' and could thus be considered as measures having an effect equivalent to quantitative restrictions,'[135] and that the Court in a number of cases had ruled that requirements as to the type of packaging for goods which may be used are national measures capable of affecting trade between Member States.[136] However, in *Procureur de la Republique* v *Association de Defense des*

128 See also Case 30/79, *Land of Berlin* v *Wild-Geflügel-Eier-Import GmbH & Co KG (Wigei)* [1980] ECR 151.
129 Case 174/82, *Officier van Justitie* v *Sandoz BV* [1983] ECR 2445.
130 Case 247/84, *The State* v *Leon Motte* [1985] ECR 3887.
131 Case 304/84, [1986] ECR 1511.
132 Case 178/84, [1987] ECR 1227.
133 See also Case 261/81, *Walter Rau Lebensmittelwerke* v *De Smedt PVBA* [1982] ECR 3961, paragraph 12; Case 407/85, *Drei Glocken GmbH & Gertraud Krit-* zinger v *USL Centro-Sud & Provincia Autonomia di Bolzano* [1988] ECR 4233.
134 Case 302/86, [1988] ECR 4607.
135 Case 8/74, *Procureur du Roi* v *Dassonville* [1974] ECR 837, at 852.
136 Case 261/81, *Walter Rau Lebensmittelwerke* v *De Smedt PVBA* [1982] ECR 3961; Case 104/75, *Officier van Justitie* v *De Peijper (Centrafarm BV)* [1976] ECR 613 and Case 16/83, *Prantl* [1984] ECR 1299.

Bruleurs d'Huiles Usagées[137] the Court had held that the protection of the environment is 'one of the Community's essential objectives' and that it might therefore justify certain limitations upon the principle of the free movement of goods. This view appears to have been confirmed by the SEA which inserted into Part Three of the EC Treaty a new Title VII, which by Article 130 R included the preservation, protection and improvement of the quality of the environment as one of the objectives of action to be taken by the Community. It therefore appeared that national measures taken for the protection of the environment were capable of constituting the type of mandatory requirements which were recognised in the *Cassis de Dijon* case as limiting the application of Article 30 of the Treaty in the absence of Community rules. However, the Advocate General in the *Kingdom of Denmark* case stated that the judgment in the *Cassis de Dijon* case could not be taken to mean that the Member States had free rein in their choice of measures, as the level of protection required to fall within those mandatory requirements cannot be excessive or unreasonable and the measures taken to achieve a particular requirement have to be necessary and proportional.[138] The Court held that protection of the environment was an important objective, but that the measures taken by the Danish government were disproportionate to the objective pursued as, given the small percentage of imported beverages sold in Denmark, the risk to the environment from their containers was limited and thus did not justify a quantitative restriction upon their import. Thus the Danish government in applying such a system was failing to fulfil its obligations under Article 30 of the EC Treaty.

Free movement of persons

The two-stage test that appears to be applied in cases concerning the free movement of goods, can also be seen at work in cases concerning the free movement of persons. From the earliest cases such as *Rutili* v *Minister for the Interior*[139] there is a clear balancing carried out by the Court in assessing whether the Member State was correct in deciding that an individual should be restricted in his or her movement within the Community on one of the grounds permitted to Member States by Article 48(3), in as much as allowing that person free movement would have effects upon public decency, morality or other grounds that were out of proportion to his or her continued right of free movement.[140] The second stage of the test is less clear at that point, although in *Rutili* it could be argued that the French government's failure to prove that its restriction on Rutili's right to free movement was the least restrictive method that could be found was, at least in part, a contributory factor to the failure of its case. The two-stage test can be seen more clearly in *Van Binsbergen*[141] and

137 Case 240/83, [1985] ECR 531.
138 Per Advocate General Sir Gordon Slynn [1988] ECR 4607, at 4622.
139 *Op. cit.*, note 31 (for the facts of the case see Chapter 12).
140 Although this seens to have failed in Case 41/74, *Van Duyn* [1974] ECR 1337, where Ms Van Duyn was refused entry to the UK on the grounds that she was a Scientologist, even though Scientology was not subject to any form of prohibition in the UK and British citizens were free to take part in Scientologist activities. This apparent misunderstanding was taken up in Cases 115 and 116/81, *Adoui and Cornuaille* v *Belgium* [1982] ECR 1665, where the Court stated that a Member State would have to actively and repressively prevent its own citizens from such activities before it could use them as grounds to bar other Community nationals – Arnull, *The General Principles of EEC Law and the Individual* (1990) at 277.
141 Case 33/74, *Van Binsbergen* v *Bestuur van de Bedrijfsvereniging voor de Metaalnijverheid* [1974] ECR 1299.

following cases[142] concerning the public interest exemption, and cases such as *Royer*[143] and *Watson and Belmann*[144] concerning the ability of Member States, first, to impose conditions upon nationals of other Member States for the purposes of monitoring their whereabouts and, secondly, to impose penalties for failing to comply with those conditions.[145]

Equality

The principle of equality means in essence that there should be an absence of discrimination in the treatment of comparable cases. The concept of equality or non-discrimination can be seen in Article 7 of the EC Treaty (prohibition of discrimination on the grounds of nationality), Article 119 (equal pay for men and women for equal work) and Article 40(3) (prevention of discrimination between producers and consumers within the Community). However, above and beyond those specific expressions of equality contained in the EC Treaty, the ECJ has also developed a much wider general principle of equality.

The Court began to develop that principle in *Hauts Fourneaux et Aciéries Belges* v *High Authority*,[146] where it held that under Article 3 (b) of the ECSC Treaty the

> institutions of the Community are required . . . to ensure . . . that all comparably placed consumers in the common market have equal access to the sources of production . . . . Failure to observe the principle of equality of treatment of consumers in the matter of economic rules . . . may constitute misuse of powers affecting the persons or classes of persons deliberately sacrificed.[147]

This meant that, in making policy, the institutions had to avoid making distinctions between different groups in the Community who were likely to be affected by that policy.

The statement of the principle of equality in *Aciéries Belges* was reformulated somewhat in *Société des Fonderies de Pont-à-Mousson* v *High Authority*, where the Court described discrimination as 'dissimilar treatment of comparable situations',[148] and in *Barbara Erzbergbau* v *High Authority*, where the view was that discrimination existed where 'unequal conditions are laid down for comparable cases'.[149] The principle was then further broadened in nature in *Italy* v *Commission*, where it was stated that discrimination might occur not only where similar situations were treated differently but also where different situations were treated identically.[150] However, the mere fact that similar situations were treated differently or different situations were treated identically leading to distinctions between different groups in the Community did not of itself mean that discrimination prohibited by the Treaty had occurred.[151] In order for discrimination of an illegal nature to be proved, the decision under attack had to be shown to be arbitrary and unjustified.[152]

Such arbitrary and unjustified decision-making has been claimed in a number of cases

---

142 Such as Case 39/75, *Coenen* v *Sociaal-Economische Raad* [1975] ECR 1547.
143 Case 48/75, *Procurer du Roi* v *Royer* [1976] ECR 497.
144 *Op. cit.*, note 45, at 1199–1200. See also Case 157/79, *R* v *Pieck* [1980] ECR 2171.
145 See Arnull, *op. cit.*, note 140, Chapters 1 and 4, for a detailed discussion of the use of the principle of proportionality in the area of the free movement of persons.
146 Case 8/57, [1958] ECR 245.

147 *Ibid.*, at 256.
148 Case 14/59, [1959] ECR 215, at 230.
149 Joined Cases 3–18, 25 and 26/58, [1960] ECR 173, at 192.
150 Case 13/63, [1963] ECR 165, at 177.
151 Case 283/83, *Firma A. Racke* v *Hauptzollamt Mainz* [1984] ECR 3791, at 3800.
152 Case 11/74, *Union des Minotiers de la Champagne* v *France* [1974] ECR 877, at 886.

concerning Community officials, such as *Airola* v *Commission*[153] (successfully) and *Van den Broeck* v *Commission*[154] (unsuccessfully), both of which concerned sex discrimination outside the scope of Article 119 by the Commission under the Staff Regulations of Officials.

Community officials have also been involved in more recent actions which demonstrate the principle. In *W Christianos* v *Court of Justice*,[155] there was an application for annulment of a decision of the ECJ complaints committee on family allowances for children paid direct to the person with custody of the children. It was argued that the system of weighting of family allowances according to the place of residence of the person with custody of the children, which meant that a Greek wife living in Greece and having custody of a child received less than a Greek wife living in Luxembourg in the same situation, breached the principle of equality. The Court rejected this on the grounds that the weighting was in fact to achieve equality in the purchasing power of such remuneration, given the differences in the cost of living between the various Member States. In *François Retter* v *Caisse de Pensions des Employés Privés*,[156] a preliminary ruling dealt with the issue of a Luxembourg law which purported to exclude an official of the High Authority of the ECSC from obtaining pension rights from the Luxembourg pension fund for private employees that officials of the EC and EAEC could claim, due to the uncertain nature of the status of the Staff Regulations of Officials of the ECSC. Here it was held that if the Staff Regulations of Officials of the ECSC were to be held to be of lesser consequence than those of the EC and EAEC, the staff of the ECSC would be deprived of rights and opportunities granted to EC and EAEC staff which would be a breach of the principle of equality in that there would then be an arbitrary and unjustified distinction between different groups of European officials.

The established place of the principle of equality as a general principle of Community law was clearly stated in *Firma Albert Ruckdeschel & Co* v *Hauptzollamt Hamburg-St Annen*.[157] In the same case the Court laid out what has become essentially the standard rule for equality, 'That similar situations shall not be treated differently unless differentiation is objectively justified'.[158]

This wider general principle has now been applied back to the cases stemming from the articles of the Treaty that were mentioned above, thus in cases concerning Article 40(3) such as *Frico* v *Voedselvoorzienings In- en Verkoopbureau*[159] and *AGPB* v *ONIC*[160] the Court could state that

> as a specific enunciation of the general principle of equality the prohibition of discrimination expressed in the second subparagraph of Article 40(3) of the Treaty does not prevent like situations from being treated differently where such treatment is objectively justified.[161]

The idea that the principle of equality should prevent arbitrary and unjustified distinctions between different groups in the Community has been further developed by *Klensch* v

---

153 Case 21/74, [1975] ECR 221. See also Case 20/71, *Sabbatini* v *European Parliament* [1972] ECR 345. In Cases 75 and 117/82, *Razzouk and Bedoun* v *Commission* [1984] ECR 1509, there was a successful application on the ground of sex discrimination by a man.
154 Case 37/74, [1975] ECR 235, followed in Case 257/78, *Devred* v *Commission* [1979] ECR 3767.
155 Case 33/87, [1988] ECR 2995.
156 Case 130/87, [1989] ECR 865.

157 Case 117/76, [1977] ECR 1753, at 1769; see also Cases 124/76 and 20/77 *Moulins et Huileries de Pont-à-Mousson SA* v *Office National Interprofessionel des Céréales* [1977] ECR 1795.
158 *Ibid.*
159 Joined Cases 424–425/85, [1987] ECR 2755.
160 Case 167/88, [1989] ECR 1653.
161 *Ibid.*, at 1684.

Secrétaire d'Etat à l'Agriculture et à la Viticulture[162] and *APESCO v Commission*,[163] where it was held under Article 40(3) that Member States must comply with the principle of equality when adopting measures concerning only their own nationals, when formulating measures purporting to implement Community regulations relating to the organisation of the agricultural markets.

It is interesting to note that there appears to have been a degree of confusion in the case law of the ECJ, between the principle of equality and that of proportionality, a situation examined in detail by Herdegen.[164] He claims that this similarity appears to stem from the decisions in the *Skimmed milk* cases,[165] where despite a clear outlining of the differences between the two principles by Advocate General Capotorti, the Court appeared to overlap them to a large degree. This, in his opinion, was further complicated by the decisions in the *Isoglucose* cases,[166] in which the Court effectively combined the two principles, a piece of judicial reasoning not at all justified by a comparative examination of the Member States' legal systems where the two rules are almost entirely exclusive.[167] While both principles have a common element in that under both, decisions must pass a test of reasonableness,[168] it is certainly difficult to follow the logic of the Court in these cases in combining the two principles, and recent case law does not appear to support a clear and logical relationship between them beyond that common element.

Legal certainty

Although some concept of legal certainty, and its attendant sub-concepts of legitimate expectation, non-retroactivity and vested interests, seems to be recognised by most legal systems including those of the EC Member States,[169] as with the doctrine of proportionality (*see* above), both the principles of legal certainty (*Rechtssicherheit*) and legitimate expectation (*Vertrauensschutz*) as used by the ECJ appear, in their basic formulations, to have been obtained from German law.[170] It was claimed by Akehurst that this was due to the fact that the majority of cases coming before the ECJ up to and at the time he was writing (1981–82) were cases referred by German courts and tribunals, and the Court was attempting to use concepts in its decisions that would be comprehensible[171] to the German judiciary.[172]

Legal certainty can be defined in very wide terms as being that wherever possible the law should be both readily ascertainable by those to whom it applies and should be predictable in terms of its application and existence. However, such a broad generalisation is considerably

---

162 Joined Cases 201–202/85, [1986] ECR 3477.
163 Case 207/86, [1989] 3 CMLR 687. See also Case C–370/88, *Procurator Fiscal, Stranraer v Andrew Marshall* [1991] 1 CMLR 419.
164 Herdegen, 'The Relation Between the Principles of Equity and Proportionality' (1985) 22 CML Rev 683.
165 *Op. cit.*, note 119.
166 Cases 103 and 145/77, *Royal Scholten-Honig Holdings Ltd v Intervention Board for Agricultural Produce* [1978] ECR 2037.
167 Herdegen, *op. cit.*, note 164, at 687.
168 *Ibid.*, at 691.
169 See, for examples in UK law, Hadfield 'Judicial Review and the Concept of Legitimate Expectation' [1988] NILQ 103.

170 See Usher, 'The Influence of National Concepts on Decisions of the European Court' (1976) 1 EL Rev 359, at 363 and 366, and Akehurst, 'The Application of General Principles of Law by the Court of Justice of the European Communities' [1981] BYIL 29, at 38. It should be noted that in German law both the principle of non-retroactivity and *Vertrauensschutz* actually fall under the wider principle of *Rechtssicherheit*, and that as with proportionality (*Verhältnismäßigkeit*), *Rechtssicherheit* is considered to have constitutional status.
171 And it is suspected, acceptable to them as well, given the attitude of the German courts towards ECJ rulings for much of its early history.
172 Akehurst, *op. cit.*, note 170, at 39.

inferior to an examination of the way in which legal certainty has been applied in Community law, which is primarily by way of use of its sub-concepts, of which legitimate expectation and non-retroactivity will be examined.[173]

Legitimate expectation

The principle of legitimate expectation can be explained thus: Community measures, including the actions of Member States in implementing such measures, must not violate the reasonably held belief of a party affected by those measures that he would be treated in a certain way by a Community institution,[174] unless such a violation is unavoidable in protecting the public interest. The definition of reasonable belief or expectation for this purpose, is that any knowledgeable and experienced party dealing in the area affected, who was acting in a sensible and prudent manner, would be likely to have relied upon that expectation. In *Van den Bergh en Jurgens BV and Van Dijk Food Products (Lopik) BV v Commission*[175] the Court gave a clear definition when it stated that,

> . . . any trader in regard to whom an institution has given rise to justified hopes may rely on the principle of the protection of legitimate expectations. On the other hand, if a prudent and discriminating trader could have foreseen the adoption of a Community measure likely to affect his interests, he cannot plead that principle if the measure is adopted.

Given that the Court has on many occasions emphasised that it is unwilling to undertake more than a very limited review of Council and Commission decisions in the economic sphere,[176] it is obvious that if the reasonableness of the trader's belief is not clear cut, any claim for breach of legitimate expectations will almost certainly fail.

However, the ECJ has not allowed this concept of limited review to prevent it from occasionally forcing Community institutions to rethink regulations, as was demonstrated in *J Mulder v Minister Van Landbouw en Visserij*[177] and the related *Georg Von Deetzen v Hauptzollamt Hamburg-Jonas*.[178] But, when these cases are contrasted with a related case, *Cornée and others v COPALL and others,*[179] a clear example of the limits placed on the principle emerges. The actions arose out of the imposition of a charge or superlevy imposed by the Commission on milk production. This superlevy was designed to penalise overproduction by dairy farmers which was creating excessive structural surpluses. If farmers exceeded their reference quantities which were based on milk production in a given reference year, the excess production became subject to the superlevy. Mulder and Von Deetzen had previously given a five-year non-marketing undertaking under Regulation 1078/77/EEC. This Regulation had been designed to cut milk production, by giving farmers who offered a five-year non-marketing undertaking a non-marketing premium. This undertaking happened to cover the reference year, thus both Mulder and Von Deetzen, having a nil reference

---

173 The concept of vested interests has a very limited part to play in EC law, and even that role can be subsumed into the concept of non-retroactivity.

174 Or a national administration applying Community regulations.

175 Case 265/85, [1987] ECR 1155 (concerning the use by the Commission of Christmas butter schemes as a way of reducing intervention butter stocks).

176 *Op. cit.*, note 101. See also Case 98/78, *Firma A.*

Racke v Hauptzollamt Mainz [1979] ECR 69; Case 138/79, *Roquette Frères v Council* [1980] ECR 3333, at paragraph 25; Case C-331/88, *Regina v Minister of Agriculture, Fisheries and Food and Another, ex parte Fédération Européenne de la Santé Animale (Fedesa) and Others* [1991] 1 CMLR 507, at paragraph 8.

177 Case 120/86, [1988] ECR 2321.

178 Case 170/86, [1988] ECR 2355.

179 Case 196/88, (Transcript), Decision of 11 July 1989.

quantity during that period, were cut out of the dairy market. The Court held that while producers who voluntarily left the market could not have a legitimate expectation to resume production on the same terms as before, they did have a legitimate expectation of not being entirely cut out of the market because they had taken advantage of a temporary scheme, encouraged by the Commission, to stop production in the short term. This was not something that the producers could have legitimately foreseen when taking advantage of Regulation 1078/77/EEC, which itself offered no clue as to such an outcome. Thus the Court held the superlevy regulation to be partially invalid.

In the case of *Cornée and others*, farmers in France who had, following Directive 72/159/EEC, executed approved development plans, argued that the national rules implementing the superlevy, in taking no account of their plans, were in breach of the principle of legitimate expectation. Here the Court held that, despite the prior approval of the plans by the national authorities, there was no breach. The farmers had no right to continue production according to their plans if the global market restrictions changed and further national restrictions were imposed. Being in possession of that knowledge, and presumably aware of the conditions within the Community market in milk production and marketing, they could have foreseen that their reference quantity might fall and therefore had no legitimate expectation that they would be able to continue as they had planned.[180]

Thus it can be seen that the applicant who raises the principle by way of founding an action for damages for non-contractual liability or a ruling invalidating a Community measure, must pass a three point test. First, he must prove that his alleged reasonable expectation was legitimately raised by the actions and/or activities of the administration challenged. Secondly, some reliance was placed on that expectation and, thirdly, a loss was suffered by him as a result of that reasonable expectation not being realised.[181] If the applicant can successfully prove his case, following the *CNTA* case[182] he may claim damages under Article 215(2) of the EC Treaty or similar provisions in the other treaties.

The need to prove reasonable belief in order successfully to raise the principle appears to rule out expectations of undue profit from exploiting a Community system, for instance by speculation,[183] as it would appear to be a logical conclusion that upon notice of that weakness, the Community institutions would take immediate action to remove it. In *Hauptzollamt Hamburg-Jonas* v *P Krucken*,[184] following the decisions in *Thyssen AG* v *Commission*[185] and *Hauptzollamt Krefeld* v *Maizena*,[186] the Court also ruled out claims of legitimate expectations by parties who were benefiting from situations which came about because of mistaken or wrongful acts on the part of the Commission or its officials, or practices of Member States which did not conform to Community rules, on the grounds that

> . . . the principle of the protection of legitimate expectations cannot be relied upon against a precise provision of Community law and that the conduct of a national authority responsible for applying Community law, which acts in breach of that law, cannot give rise

---

180 For these and further examples, see Sharpston, 'Legitimate Expectations and Economic Reality' [1990] EL Rev 103, which contains a fairly exhaustive list of the case law of the ECJ relating to both the principle of legitimate expectations and the principle of non-retroactivity.
181 Case 112/77, *August Töpfer & Co. GmbH* v *Commission* [1978] ECR 1019.
182 Case 74/74, *CNTA* v *Commission* [1975] ECR 533.
183 See Case 2/75, *EVGF* v *Mackprang* (1975) ECR 607

(speculation by a trader in the intervention system for grain). Speculation by traders is extremely damaging to the stability of Community intervention systems and thus the Commission will take measures to prevent it wherever possible, with the full support of the Court.
184 Case 316/86, [1988] ECR 2213.
185 Case 188/82, [1983] ECR 3721.
186 Case 5/82, [1982] ECR 4601.

to legitimate expectations on the part of the economic operator that he will benefit from treatment which is contrary to Community law.[187]

The Court appears to use the principle of legitimate expectations both as a ground for holding Community measures invalid[188] and as a method of interpreting Community law.[189] It is most often raised, however, by way of an action for damages for non-contractual liability or a ruling that a Community measure is invalid, usually against Community institutions.

Non-retroactivity and vested rights

The theory of non-retroactivity in its simplest form is that expounded by the Court in *Firma A. Racke* v *Hauptzollamt Mainz*:

> a measure adopted by the public authorities shall not be applicable to those concerned before they have the opportunity to make themselves acquainted with it.[190]

However, the Court then proceeded in that case to construct a two-part test for occasions when retroactive measures would be allowed. Retroactive measures were permissible where, first, the aim of the Community institution making the measure could not be achieved in any other way and, secondly, the legitimate expectations of those concerned were adequately considered.[191] Thus it cannot be said that retroactive Community measures will never be valid, but rather that the Court will hold them to be valid only in very exceptional circumstances.

The concept of vested rights means that a party has obtained by his actions, or those of the Community, certain rights which the Court will be reluctant to allow to be destroyed without good reason, and is effectively only important as a method of determining whether Community measures are in fact purporting to act retroactively.

However, retroactivity of Community measures can, it is argued, be further divided into true retroactivity and quasi-retroactivity.[192] True retroactivity occurs where a Community measure is applied to situations which have already occurred; quasi-retroactivity occurs where a Community measure is applied to ongoing situations. It seems that in the former case, unless there are clear and compelling reasons for the retroactive measure, it will be held invalid by the Court. However, in the latter case it appears that quasi-retroactivity is something which parties are likely to have to accept, and if they wish to avoid its effects they should ensure that their contracts contain provision for adaptation in the event of changes due to quasi-retroactive Community measures.[193] In *Rewe-Zentrale GmbH* v *Hauptzollamt Emmerich*[194] the Advocate General assessed the position as follows:

187 But see below for discussion of the retroactive withdrawal of unlawful or mistaken Community measures.
188 *August Töpfer & Co. GmbH* v *Commission, op. cit.,* note 181.
189 See Usher, *op. cit.,* note 170. See also Case 78/74, *Deuka* v *EVGF* [1975] ECR 421; Case 5/75, *Deuka* v *EVGF* [1975] ECR 759 and Case 88/76, *Société pour l'Exportation des Sucres* v *Commission* [1977] ECR 709.
190 Case 98/78, [1979] ECR 69.
191 See opinion of Advocate General Tesauro in Case C-337/88, *Società Agricola Fattoria Alimentare SpA* v *Amministrazione delle Finanze dello Stato* [1991] 1 CMLR

872, at 881, and the decisions in Case 224/82, *Meiko-Konservenfabrik* v *Federal Republic of Germany* [1983] ECR 2539 and Case 114/81, *Tunnel Refineries Limited* v *Council* [1982] ECR 3189.
192 See Hartley, *op. cit.,* note 9, at 140.
193 Case 246/87, *Continentale Produkten-Gesellschaft Erhardt-Renken GmbH & Co* v *Hauptzollamt München-West* [1989] ECR 1151, at 1174, paragraph 17 (retroactive imposition of anti-dumping duty).
194 Case 37/70, [1971] ECR 23, opinion of Advocate General Lamothe, at 45.

> . . . although in general the principle of legal certainty militates against a Community act's taking effect from a point in time before its publication, the application of this principle must be tempered by the requirements of economic law. This in fact implies that, going beyond an overstrict notion of the principle of non-retroactivity, a distinction must be made between retroactivity *stricto sensu* and a new situation termed by various contemporary experts in public law 'the immediate application of new provisions to pre-existing situations' which is frequently encountered in economic affairs.[195]

In the case of retroactive withdrawal of mistaken or unlawful Community measures, or national provisions implementing Community measures, the Court has held that:

> withdrawal . . . is permissible providing that the withdrawal occurs within a reasonable time and provided that the [Commission] has sufficient regard to how far the application might have been led to rely on the lawfulness of the decision.[196]

The Court has been unwilling to accept retroactive penal measures, and in *R* v *Kirk*[197] the use of such measures was ruled invalid.

Summary

As can be seen from the above, the principle of legal certainty is a complex one. The sub-principles of legitimate expectation and non-retroactivity overlap to a large degree, and it can be difficult to separate the different strands within the case law. The Court, in reaching decisions in cases concerning legitimate expectations and non-retroactivity, has generally done so by, first, greatly restricting the scope of its review of decisions on such grounds and, secondly, when examining cases where these principles have been raised, by using quite pragmatic economically based criteria. The Court is well aware of the economic consequences of its decisions,[198] and where possible, unless a significant injustice has been done, will avoid rulings which would cause undue strain upon the Community institutions. This has a consequence that few cases brought on the grounds of breach of legitimate expectation and non-retroactivity are successful. Sharpston[199] argues that at the end of the day, 'economic sense' tends to win out. It is debatable, given the shifting nature of both modern economics and Community policy, whether 'economic sense' is in fact a fair or indeed a particularly certain criterion upon which to decide cases which may result in the financial devastation of the applicants.

Right to a hearing

The right to a hearing is one of the main contributions of English administrative law to the development of Community institutional law. While the right to a hearing is a principle which can be found, in one form or another, in the administrative law systems of most

---

[195] Quoted in Sharpston, 'Legitimate Expectations and Economic Reality' *op. cit.*, note 180.

[196] Case 14/81, *Alpha Steel Ltd* v *Commission* [1982] ECR 749; Case 15/85, *Consozio Cooperative d'Abruzzo* [1987] ECR 1005. See also Case 111/63, *Lemmerz-Werke GmbH* v *High Authority* [1965] ECR 677.

[197] Case 63/83, [1984] ECR 2689, [1984] 3 CMLR 522.

[198] For instance, the *Mulder* and *Von Deetzen* decisions

left the Council with the problem of attempting to find extra milk quotas where it was clear that no room for extra existed, and have led to further prolonged actions before the Court: *op. cit.*, notes 177, 178. See Sharpston, 'Legitimate Expectations and Economic Reality', *op. cit.*, note 180, at 111.

[199] Sharpston, *ibid.*, at 160.

Community Member States, the form which has been adopted by the ECJ has closely followed that of English law.

Sources

The case which established the right to a hearing as a general principle of Community law is *Transocean Marine Paint Association* v *Commission*.[200] The Association was a group of manufacturers which had made an agreement concerning the composition of their products, trade marks, quality control and division of sales territory. The agreement had been granted an exemption from EC competition rules under Article 85(3) EC. When the Association applied for a renewal of the exemption, the Commission subjected it to new conditions. The Association argued that it had not been allowed to make its objections to these new conditions known to the Commission, and that, as a result, the Commission's decision was vitiated by procedural defect. The Association relied on Article 2 of Regulation 99/63/EEC and Article 19 of Regulation 17/62/EEC, both of which obliged the Commission to notify concerned undertakings of its decisions, and to allow such undertakings to make known their views. The Court saw these Regulations as simply applications of 'the general rule that a person whose interests are perceptibly affected by a decision taken by a public authority must be given the opportunity to make his point of view known'.[201] It therefore annulled the Commission decision. It is, however, in the opinion of Advocate General Warner that we see the origins of the right to a hearing. He went through the various administrative law systems of the Member States, beginning with the English rules of natural justice, and demonstrated the existence of the right to a hearing in most of them.[202] He concluded that the right to be heard forms part of the law which Article 164 obliges the Court to observe.

Previously, the right to be heard had been applied to specific circumstances provided for by Community legislation. As mentioned above, the regulations governing the Commission's procedures for investigating breaches of the Community's competition policy provided for certain rights to be heard. Equally, the Staff Regulations governing the rights of Community employees granted such rights in disciplinary and dismissal cases. In *Alvis*,[203] concerning unfair dismissal, the applicant complained of not having been given the opportunity to defend himself and of not having been informed of the reasons for his dismissal. The Court recognised a generally accepted principle that an employee is entitled to respond to allegations before disciplinary action is taken. Nonetheless, it found that the infringement of this principle was not sufficiently serious to justify annulling the decision to dismiss. It is unlikely, since the expansion of the right to a hearing as a general principle, that such a decision would be reached again. The Court has been rigorous in its application of this principle, which could be regarded as one of the most successful of the general principles in actually protecting the rights of individuals.[204]

[200] Case 17/74, [1974] ECR 1063.
[201] *Ibid.*, at paragraph 15.
[202] *Ibid.*, at 1088–9.
[203] Case 32/62, *Alvis* v *Council* [1963] ECR 55.
[204] In Case C-49/88, *Al-Jubail Fertilizer Co* v *Council* [1991] 3 CMLR 377, paragraph 16 of the decision, the Court pointed out that: 'with regard to the right to a fair hearing, any action taken by the Community institutions must be all the more scrupulous in view of the fact that, as they stand at present, the rules in question do not provide all the procedural guarantees for the protection of the individual which may exist in certain national legal systems.'

When does the right arise?

The ECJ has not been consistent in the language it has used to describe the circumstances under which the right to a hearing would arise. In *Transocean*, the right was said to apply to anyone 'whose interests are perceptibly affected'.[205] An apparently stricter test was used in *Mollet* v *Commission*, where the principle was that 'when any administrative body adopts a measure which is liable gravely to prejudice the interests of an individual it is bound to put him in a position to express his point of view'.[206]

The situation has been clarified since *Hoffmann-La Roche* v *Commission*.[207] In that case, involving competition policy, the Court formulated the rule that the right to a hearing, as a general principle, arose 'in all proceedings in which sanctions, in particular fines or penalty payments, may be imposed'.[208] This is the case even in purely administrative proceedings. This formula is certainly more restrictive than that in *Transocean*, although it is probably wider than *Mollet*. The Court, moreover, has expanded the range of cases where the right to a hearing can be claimed to include investigative proceedings prior to the adoption of anti-dumping regulations.[209] The judicial development of the right as a general principle is, of course, in addition to any right to a hearing which arises purely from Community legislation.

The Court has also clarified the circumstances in which the right to a hearing cannot be claimed. In *Nicolet Instrument GmbH* v *Hauptzollamt Frankfurt am Main-Flughafen*,[210] the plaintiff was unsuccessful in its claim that it should have been consulted before the Commission took a decision concerning the imposition of a duty on the equipment which it wished to import, because the decision had been taken in the context of importation by another party into another Community Member State, and that as a result, the plaintiff was not directly concerned by that decision. A similar conclusion was reached by the Court in *Bureau Européen des Unions des Consommateurs (BEUC)* v *Commission*,[211] which related to an anti-dumping proceeding. In such a proceeding, no measures could be adopted which would adversely affect BEUC or the consumers it represents. Therefore, BEUC had no right to be heard.

What does the right to a hearing include?

The right to information

The first of the two elements of the right to a hearing identified in the *Transocean* case is the right to be 'clearly informed, in good time, of the essence'[212] of the matter under consideration. It is clearly the core of the right. In the *Ozlizlok* case, the right to be informed of the nature of the proceedings was considered to be part of the minimum which the Community is to observe.[213] However, beyond information as to the existence and nature of proceedings, the Court has been equivocal as to the right of parties to information held by Community institutions. There is clearly no right to full disclosure of all documents and information which a party may claim to be relevant to the hearing in question. The purpose

205 *Op. cit.*, note 200, at paragraph 15.
206 Case 75/77, [1978] ECR 897, paragraph 21.
207 Case 85/76, [1979] ECR 461.
208 *Ibid.*, at paragraph 9.
209 See, most recently, *Al-Jubail Fertilizer Co* v *Council*, *op. cit.*, note 204, paragraph 15.

210 Case 203/85, [1986] ECR 2049.
211 Case C-170/89, [1992] 1 CMLR 820.
212 *Op. cit.*, note 200, at paragraph 15.
213 Case 34/77, *Ozlizlok* v *Commission* [1978] ECR 1099.

of the right to information, according to the Court, is to ensure that the second part of the right to a hearing, the right to make representations, is not illusory.[214] Therefore, the facts on which the Commission is relying must be made known, but the entire contents of the file need not be communicated. It would nonetheless appear, given the seriousness with which the Court treats the right to a hearing, that if, at the hearing itself, it became clear that the party was not aware of all the salient facts, the hearing may be annulled. This is due to the apparent objective nature of the minimum information requirement. The Court does not see it as a matter of Commission discretion, except insofar as the Commission decides to communicate more information than is absolutely required. In fact, the Court has on occasion been sceptical of Commission arguments. In the *Quinine Cartel* cases,[215] the Commission refused to communicate certain information on the ground that it must protect the business secrets of other undertakings. The Court rejected this argument for two reasons:

1 the Commission was itself alleging that these undertakings were exchanging information in a way that violated EC competition rules; and
2 the Commission could have requested permission from these undertakings to disclose the information to the applicant, but did not do so.[216]

At least in competition matters, the burden on the Commission is now heavier. In its Twelfth Report on Competition Policy, the Commission established a procedure for allowing access to the whole file for all undertakings concerned. The Court of First Instance has acknowledged that this procedure does go beyond the requirements of the right to a hearing as a general principle, but has stated that the Commission has bound itself by this new standard, which the courts will enforce.[217] There are certain categories of information, however, which are not susceptible of disclosure, even under the new procedure in competition cases: business secrets of another undertaking, Commission internal documents and confidential information.[218]

Where the Commission does have some discretion is in the *manner* of communication of information. It may choose the most appropriate means of providing information to the party concerned.[219] Nonetheless, the Court places a significant duty of diligence on the Commission in its communication of relevant information.[220] If, for example, the Commission fulfils its duty of disclosure orally, it may be obliged to prove that the disclosure actually took place.[221]

The right to make representations

The second main strand of the right to a hearing in Community law is the right to make observations or representations to the Community institution which is making the relevant

---

214 Cases 56 and 58/64, *Consten and Grundig v Commission* [1966] ECR 299, at 338.
215 Case 41, 44 and 45/69, *ACF Chemiefarma NV v Commission* [1970] ECR 661.
216 *Ibid.*, at paragraphs 37–40. The applicant did not succeed in having the decision annulled, because, since it admitted that a concerted practice existed, it could not have been prejudiced by not having this information which went solely to the existence of a concerted practice.

217 Case T-7/89, *SA Hercules Chemicals NV v Commission* [1992] 4 CMLR 84.
218 *Ibid.*
219 *Al-Jubail Fertilizer Co, op. cit.*, note 204, at paragraphs 17 and 20 of the decision.
220 Case 264/82, *Timex v Council and Commission* [1989] ECR 3137.
221 *Al-Jubail Fertilizer Co, op. cit.*, note 204, paragraph 20.

decision.[222] It is part of the essential minimum that a person be given the opportunity to defend his or her interests.[223]

It is clear from the *Transocean* case that failure to allow a party to submit comments on a case before a decision is taken is a violation of the right to a hearing. However, there are many less blatant actions which could impair the ability to make an adequate defence to allegations, while not eliminating altogether the possibility of representations. Such was the argument made by the applicant in *Eisen und Metall Aktiengesellschaft* v *Commission*.[224] The applicant in that case alleged that its rights of defence had not been respected because the Commission had not made any inquiry into the defence evidence, and had failed to inform the applicant that it had no intention of doing so. The position of the Commission was that once it had given the applicant the opportunity to submit its comments, it had discharged its obligations under Article 36 ECSC, on which the applicant relied. The Court agreed with the Commission that it would not be required to go further if it was satisfied that its preliminary investigation had been sufficient.[225] This ruling appears to give the Commission a wide discretion to refuse to follow up possible defences raised by the party concerned. Possibly, the Court may in future limit this discretion to a reasonable refusal to make further investigations.

It is also clear that the Court has extended the rights of defence beyond the pure right to make comments on the case file before a decision is made. Adequate time to prepare a defence has been considered by the Court to be crucial to the observance of the right to a hearing, as was demonstrated in the *Almini* case. Almini was a Commission employee who had been served with a notice of retirement. He was sent a letter dated 20 January which required him to submit his views by 26 January. The Court was of the opinion that this was insufficient time to allow the applicant his full rights of defence.[226] From this decision, it is apparent that the Court is willing to take a purposive view of the right to make representations. It speaks of a failure to respect 'elementary safeguards' in procedure.[227] An applicant could therefore claim that an insufficient opportunity to make a defence had been provided and that, as a result, the right to a fair hearing had been denied. If the *Eisen* case is taken into account, the view of the Court may be considered to be the following: a party will be provided the best possible opportunity to make a defence in any situation where the right to a hearing arises, but the Community institutions need not take any action as a consequence of matters raised in that defence.

The issue of the right to call witnesses was raised in *Van Eick*.[228] This case must be understood within the context of the Staff Regulations, which specifically provide that an official charged with a disciplinary offence has the right to call witnesses. It is, however, in the view of the Court, for the Disciplinary Board to decide whether an application to call a witness has been sufficiently justified. The Board was entitled to take the view that only some of the named witnesses need be called. In another staff case, the Court analysed the issue in terms of the general principle of the right to a hearing.[229] The rule of *audi alteram partem*

222 *Transocean, op. cit.*, note 200, at paragraph 15 of the decision.
223 *Ozlizlok, op. cit.*, note 213. See also, Joined Cases 100–103/80, *Musique Diffusion Française* v *Commission* [1983] ECR 1825.
224 Case 9/83, [1984] ECR 2071.

225 *Ibid.*, at paragraph 32 of the decision.
226 Case 19/70, [1971] ECR 623.
227 *Ibid.*, at paragraph 17 of the decision.
228 Case 35/67, [1968] ECR 342.
229 Case 141/84, *De Compte* v *European Parliament* [1985] ECR 1951, at paragraph 17.

requires that both parties have equal opportunities to be present during the examination of witnesses and to put any relevant questions to them. To do otherwise would lead to a serious inequality between the parties to a hearing.

On the question of the right to counsel, the Court has considered it only within the context of the Staff Regulations. In interpreting these Regulations, it rejected a Commission argument that the right to counsel only arises when specifically provided for in the Staff Regulations, and extended this right to all staff cases.[230] Further, the Court stated, this would include the right for the applicant's counsel to have access to the disciplinary file. It is conceivable that, should the case arise, the Court would be willing to extend the right further to all cases where the right to a hearing applies.

The right to reasons

The right to reasons for a decision can perhaps be related to the right to information, but has been developed by the Court partly as an extrapolation from Article 190 EC, and therefore is a somewhat separate issue. Article 190 obliges the Council and Commission to state the reasons on which their decisions are based. The extent of the obligation under Article 190 was discussed in the *Quinine Cartel* cases. It does not oblige the Commission to discuss all issues of fact and law raised by the parties.[231] All that is required is that the parties and the Court are aware of the essential factors leading to the decision.[232]

The duty to give reasons has also been recognised independently of Article 190. In *Almini*, the Court found that the letter notifying the applicant of his retirement was misleading, in that it referred to grounds which were not those on which the Commission was in fact making its decision. That this was identified as a separate ground of violation of the applicant's right to a hearing demonstrates that the Court regards the duty to provide reasons as an integral part of the right. Similarly, a failure to provide sufficient information concerning a decision not to employ a person has been treated by the Court as a breach of the duty to give reasons.[233]

Legal professional privilege

Regulation 17/62/EEC, concerning the procedure in competition cases, grants the Commission wide investigatory powers. It obtains much of its documentation from on-site investigations at the premises of the undertakings concerned. Nothing in the Regulation limits the Commission's powers of search and seizure. While, as stated above, the Commission does not disclose to other undertakings any documents which contain business secrets, until *A M & S v Commission*[234] there were no restrictions on the documents which the Commission itself could examine. *A M & S* raised the issue of whether an undertaking being investigated could claim lawyer-client privilege on documents which the Commission wished to seize. The claim of privilege can be seen as the inversion of the right to information – it is the right to control the information which the Commission may use against a party in a hearing.

Advocate General Slynn examined the use of legal professional privilege throughout the Community. Two main approaches exist: the UK rule, where it is the relationship of

---

[230] Case 115/80, *Demont v Commission* [1981] ECR 3147.
[231] *Op. cit.*, note 215, at paragraphs 76–7 of the decision.
[232] *Ibid.*, at paragraph 78 of the decision.
[233] *Mollet, op. cit.*, note 206.
[234] Case 155/79, [1982] ECR 1575.

confidentiality between the lawyer and client which gives rise to the privilege; and the civil law rule that it is only those documents which are prepared in the context of a court case which are considered confidential (sometimes called the 'litigation privilege'). The Court followed the Advocate General's recommendation that the more restrictive approach be followed. Privilege is therefore subject to two conditions. First, the documents must have been made for the purposes and in the interests of the client's right of defence. Secondly, the documents must emanate from independent lawyers who are not bound to the client by a relationship of employment. The latter condition is related to the idea of the lawyer as an officer of the court, although it undeniably creates anomalies. The restrictive view taken by the Court can be justified by the fact that it is the rule common to all the Member States, whereas the wider view of privilege would go further than most national legal systems. In addition, it is more closely related to the right to a fair hearing than is the more general privilege, and therefore fits in better with the overall scheme of the general principles.[235]

CONCLUSION

It has frequently been averred that the ECJ in adopting the wide range of general principles that now exist, has gone rather further than the powers granted to it in the Treaty allow. A notable debate on the issue was that between Cappelletti and Rasmussen in the *European Law Review* over the issue of whether the ECJ was (in Rasmussen's words) 'running wild'.[236] The question is whether developing general principles of law which can be used to interpret or even to annul properly adopted legislation is a usurpation of the legislator's task. In essence, those who favour judicial restraint argue that if there are defects or gaps in either the enacted law or the Community treaties, it is the job of the legislature, not the judiciary, to correct or complete the law. The Community legislative process is characterised by delay and compromise. Further, as was pointed out in the Introduction to this chapter, constitutions, or fundamental treaties such as the EC Treaty, are not easily amended, a fact which has been amply exemplified by the difficulties experienced by Member States in ratifying the TEU. Should litigants have to wait years for the law to be corrected, and find themselves without a remedy in the interim? Those who favour judicial activism of the type which has created the general principles argue that the Community legal order would be brought into disrepute if it was incapable of delivering justice to individuals.

The general principles are by no means a system of perfect justice. They have been developed unevenly, even idiosyncratically, in as much as the principles that the ECJ uses frequently bear little relationship to the national rules on which they purportedly are based. The ECJ has often put fundamental Community policies such as the maintenance of competition ahead of principles of human rights or legitimate expectations. Often the most effective general principles are those which enable the ECJ to interpret Community law in accordance with individuals' rights rather to annul measures adopted by the institutions. In this way, the ECJ appears to recognise that it must show some deference to the legislative branch.

---

235 For commentary on this case, see Forrester, (1983) 20 CML Rev 75 and Faull, (1985) 10 EL Rev 119.
236 Cappelletti, 'Is the European Court of Justice "Run-

ning Wild"?' (1987) El Rev 3; Rasmussen, 'Between Self-Restraint and Activism: a Judicial Policy for the European Court' (1988) El Rev 28.

Further reading

Akehurst, M., 'The Application of General Principles of Law by the Court of Justice of the European Communities' [1981] BYIL 29.

Arnull, A., *The General Principles of EEC Law and the Individual* (Leicester: Leicester University Press, 1990).

Barents, R., 'The System of Deposits in Community Agricultural law: Efficiency v Proportionality' [1985] EL Rev 329.

Brown, L.N. and Garner, J.F., *French Administrative Law*, 4th edn (Oxford: OUP, 1993).

Coppel, J. and O'Neill, A., 'The European Court of Justice: Taking Rights Seriously?' (1992) 12 *Legal Studies* 227.

Cummins, R.J., 'The General Principles of Law, Separation of Powers and Theories of Judicial Decision in France' (1986) 35 ICLQ 594.

Dallen, R.M., 'An Overview of European Community Protection of Human Rights, with some special references to the UK' (1990) 27 CML Rev 761.

Dauses, M.A., 'The Protection of Fundamental Rights in the Community Legal Order' (1985) 10 EL Rev 398.

Foster, N., 'The European Court of Justice and the European Convention for the Protection of Human Rights' (1987) 8 HRLJ 245.

Green, N., 'Directives, Equity and the Protection of Individual Rights' [1984] EL Rev 295.

Hailbronner, K., 'The Principle of Proportionality', General reports to the 10th International Congress on Comparative Law (Budapest 1981) Section IV.D.2 at 831.

Herdegen, M., 'The relation between principles of Equity and Proportionality' [1985] 22 CML Rev 6.

Hilf, M., 'The Application of Rules of National Administrative Law in the Implementation of Community Law' [1983] 3 YEL 79.

Jowell, J.L. and Oliver, D., (eds.) 'New Directions in Judicial Review' [1988] Current Legal Problems.

Korah, V., 'The Rights of the Defence in Administrative Proceedings under Community Law' [1980] Current Legal Problems 73.

MacBride, J. and Neville Brown, L., 'The United Kingdom, the European Community and the European Convention on Human Rights' (1981) 1 YEL 167.

Mackenzie Stuart, 'Control of power within the European Communities' [1986] 11 HL Rev 1.

Mendelson, M.H., 'The European Court of Justice and Human Rights' (1982) 1 YEL 125.

Merrills, J.G., *The Development of International Law by the European Court of Human Rights* (Manchester: Manchester University Press, 1988).

Schermers, H.G., *Judicial Protection in the European Communities,* 4th edn (Deventer: Kluwer, 1987).

Schermers, H.G., 'The European Communities bound by Fundamental Human Rights' (1990) 27 CML Rev 249.

Schmitthoff, C.M., 'The Doctrines of Proportionality and Nondiscrimination' [1977] EL Rev 329.

Schwarze, J., 'The Administrative law of the Community and the Protection of Human Rights' [1986] CML Rev 401.

Sharpston E. 'Legitimate Expectations and Economic Reality' [1990] EL Rev 103.

CHAPTER 7

Judicial review of Community acts

INTRODUCTION

This chapter deals with the role and nature of judicial review by the ECJ in determining the legality of Community acts. It examines which acts are susceptible to review, who can lodge an application for review, and permissible grounds of review. It will also consider the issues of review for failure to act, and pleas or exceptions of illegality. In particular, this chapter will focus on a number of important issues which point up the difficulties faced by the ECJ when attempting to construct a framework for judicial review of Community acts which is legally certain and conforms to the ECJ's perception of the rule of law, while remaining within the broad guidelines of the EC Treaty. Such issues include the developments concerning the standing of the European Parliament, and the complex issue of the methods of ascertaining the standing of other non-privileged applicants under Article 173 and Article 175. These issues have been the subject of much academic debate, and the reasoning by which the ECJ has reached decisions in each has been both praised and criticised. As will be seen below, the issue of the standing of the European Parliament under both articles, as well as the standing of other bodies such as the European Central Bank, may finally be decided with the coming into force of the TEU, but it appears that there is still considerable doubt as to the efficacy, desirability and certainty of the present methods of ascertaining the standing of other non-privileged individuals.

Review of Community acts under Article 173

Acts susceptible to review

In the first paragraph of Article 173, the ECJ is given the power to review the legality of acts of the Council and Commission other than recommendations or opinions.[1] If this were to be interpreted strictly, it would mean that, in effect, only the first three acts mentioned in Article 189, that is, regulations, directives and decisions, would be susceptible to review. However, it is clear that the ECJ has not been minded to interpret the paragraph so narrowly. The issue of measures taken by Commission and Council which, while having binding effect, do not

---

1 Article 173, paragraphs 1 and 2, as amended by Article G(53) TEU:

    The Court of Justice shall review the legality of acts adopted jointly by the European Parliament and the Council, of acts of the Council, of the Commission and of the ECB, other than recommendations and opinions, and of acts of the European Parliament in-

tended to produce legal effects *vis-à-vis* third parties.

    It shall for this purpose have jurisdiction in actions brought by a Member State, the Council or the Commission on grounds of lack of competence, infringement of an essential procedural requirement, infringement of this Treaty or of any rule of law relating to its application, or misuse of powers.

take the form of any of the recognised categories in the Treaty was examined by the ECJ in *Netherlands VHA* v *Commission*,[2] where the ECJ decided that a letter sent by an employee of the Commission stating its viewpoint to an applicant was not merely an opinion, as the Commission claimed, but had the effect of a decision. This was followed by the *ERTA* case,[3] where the Council argued that the proceedings under challenge did not constitute an act for the purposes of Article 173 as they were 'no more than a co-ordination of policies amongst Member States within the framework of the Council and . . . created no rights, imposed no obligations and did not modify any legal position'.[4] The ECJ, however, held that the proceedings in question did have legal effects and that in order to ensure observance of the law in the interpretation and application of the Treaty as required by Article 164, it would be wrong to restrict reviewable acts to those mentioned in Article 189.[5]

The effect of this is to subject to review by the ECJ any act that will have binding effect (or put another way, legal force) on the applicant. In order to determine whether such a binding effect exists, the ECJ will examine the nature or substance of the act rather than the form which it takes or the designation given to it by its originator.[6] It has yet to be determined whether oral decisions can be subject generally to action for annulment.[7]

It should be noted that with regard to Council decisions, a Member State may, if it wishes, apply for the nullification of an act for which it had earlier voted in favour at Council, as the use of that right under Article 173 is not conditional upon the voting positions when the regulation was adopted.[8]

Where the applicant is not a Member State, the Council or the Commission, the ECJ's power to review is more limited in scope. The fourth paragraph[9] of Article 173 states that:

> Any natural or legal person may, under the same conditions, institute proceedings against a decision addressed to that person or against a decision which, although in the form of a regulation or a decision addressed to another person, is of direct and individual concern to the former.

The interpretation which the ECJ has placed on this wording will be examined in more detail below.

---

2 Joined Cases 8–11/66, *First Cement-Convention Case* [1967] ECR 75. Indeed, the Court had already accepted, under the ECSC Treaty, in both Cases 53–4/63, *Lemmerz-werke* [1963] ECR 239 and Cases 1 and 14/57, *Société des Usines à Tubes de la Saar* v *High Authority* [1957–8] ECR 105, at 114, that it could and should examine an act which, although it was framed as an opinion or other non-binding act, was claimed by the applicants to be a disguised decision: An act of the High Authority constitutes a decision when it lays down a rule capable of being applied, in other words, when by the said act the High Authority unequivocally determines the position which it decides to adopt if certain conditions are fulfilled.

3 Case 22/70, *Commission* v *Council* [1971] ECR 263. This ruling was followed in Case 60/81, *IBM* v *Commission* [1981] ECR 2639, at 2651. Similar reasoning was also used in the *Les Verts* case (*see* below) to extend

Article 173 review to the EP, and in Joined Cases 193 and 194/87, *Maurissen and others* v *Court of Auditors* [1989] ECR 1045, to extend it to the Court of Auditors, neither of which are mentioned in Article 173.

4 Case 22/70, *Commission* v *Council*, at note 3, *op. cit* at 276, paragraph. 36.

5 *Ibid*, at 276–7.

6 Case 60/81, *IBM* v *Commission*, at note 3, *op. cit.* at 2651.

7 See Schermers and Walbroeck, *Judicial Protection in the European Communities*, 4th edn, (1987), at 301 where it is noted that in a staff case, Case 316/82 and 40/83, *Kohler* [1984] ECR 641, at 656, the Court accepted that an oral decision could be subject to action for annulment.

8 Case 166/78, *Italy* v *Council* [1979] ECR 2575, at 2596.

9 Previously the second paragraph prior to the TEU.

The ability to lodge a review

Privileged applicants

The Member States, the Council and the Commission are considered to be privileged applicants in Article 173 actions. This means that those institutions are automatically accorded *locus standi* when bringing an action.[10] It is of value to consider the possible reasoning behind this automatic grant of *locus standi*, especially when it is clear that it grants a significant amount of power to those institutions, power which has not been equally granted to other Community institutions.

Weiler[11] explores the argument that one could justify any such perceived imbalance in *locus standi* powers on the premise that the institutions which have been granted privileged status are those which represent a general interest. He claims that this argument may well apply to the role assigned to the Commission by the EC Treaty under Article 155, of '. . . ensuring that the provisions of [the] Treaty . . . are applied'. The Commission has to have the necessary powers to ensure that the other institutions and organs of the Community operate within the powers allotted by the Treaty and do not implement illegal measures in breach of Article 173, and might thus be seen as the 'principal repository of the general interest in the Community'.[12] However, the position of the Council and Member States is somewhat different. While there are reasons which might justify privileged status, these could apply equally well to the Parliament, which has not until recently been granted any degree of privileged status.[13] For instance, Weiler notes that both Council and Member States are in a position where they 'represent different constituencies, with different interests . . . different shades of the general interest'.[14] Also, as both Council and Member States take part in the creation and implementation of Community law,[15] the fact that they have automatic *locus standi* enables the process of Community decision making to proceed smoothly, as they can attack the legality of a measure after it has been adopted without unduly disrupting the decision-making process by concerted opposition at that stage.[16] However, the Parliament has now reached a state in its development where it clearly represents yet another aspect of the general interest, and it now has a clear part to play in Community decision-making, not least in the budgetary sphere. It is arguments such as these that underlie much of the controversy and resulting case law surrounding the issue of the standing of the Parliament.

The European Parliament and European Central Bank

As stated above, the EP was not granted privileged status under Article 173 when the Treaty was drafted, probably because during the early development of the Community the Parliament's participation in the formal decision-making process was minimal. As such, the

---

10 A Member State may thus bring an action against a Community act even where that act is aimed at another Member State. See Case 6/54, *Netherlands* v *High Authority* [1954–6] ECR 103, regarding a decision of the High Authority relating to coal companies in Germany, and Case 41/83, *Italy* v *Commission* [1985] ECR 873, concerning a Commission decision directed at British Telecom.
11 Weiler, 'Pride and Prejudice – *Parliament* v *Council*' (1989) 14 EL Rev 334.
12 *Ibid.*, at 338.
13 *Ibid.*

14 *Ibid.*, at 339.
15 It should be understood that Member States will play a role above and beyond that carried out by their representatives at Council, notably where there is a change of government or radical shift of policy in a Member State while Community legislation is being considered. Council decisions, for example, may thus perhaps be considered a 'snapshot' of Member States' opinions at a particular point in time.
16 Weiler, *op. cit*, note 11, following Case 166/78, *Italy* v *Council, op. cit.*, note 8.

need for it to protect its prerogatives and the ability of other applicants to bring Article 173 actions against it were necessarily limited. This lack of privileged status was noted during proceedings leading to the drafting of the SEA, and indeed the Commission made a formal proposal at the intergovernmental conference that preceded the drafting that the Parliament be given the right to bring proceedings under Article 173. That proposal was not accepted and the SEA did not in the event change the status of the Parliament under Article 173.[17] Thus the only way that the Parliament could become involved in Article 173 actions was by way of an intervention under Article 37 EC Statute of the Court, as it had in the *Isoglucose cases*.[18] Even this limited power was challenged by the Council, which argued that only parties with the right to bring an action should be allowed to intervene. The ECJ ruled that the right to intervene was not in any way linked to the right to bring an action, and that to prevent the Parliament from intervening under Article 37 EC Statute of the Court would affect 'its institutional position as intended by the Treaty and in particular Article 4(1)'.[19]

However, the role of the Parliament has undergone considerable change since the drafting of the Treaty, indeed the entire balance between the institutions of the Community has changed,[20] and in *Les Verts – Parti Ecologiste* v *European Parliament*[21] the effect of this change on the ability of other applicants to bring Article 173 actions against it became clear. In that case[22] the French Ecology Party brought an action under Article 173 for the purpose of reviewing the Parliamentary Bureau's decision to allocate funding to various bodies supposedly to pay for an information campaign prior to the 1984 Parliamentary elections. The applicants were primarily concerned to challenge this on the grounds that such an allocation was in effect repayment of those bodies' campaign costs, something that, under the Act of 20 September 1976, remained in the province of national law.[23] The ECJ held that Article 173 was designed to allow for the judicial review of any act or measure of a Community institution that could have binding effect:

17 *Ibid.*, at 344. The proposal may be found in the *Bulletin of the European Parliament*, PE 100.805/Add.2 of 10.10.85, at 25.
18 Case 138/79, *Roquette Frères* v *Council* [1980] ECR 3333, and Case 139/79, *Maizena* v *Council* [1980] ECR 3393. In these cases, the Parliament sought to intervene on behalf of private parties who had challenged the adoption of a Council regulation on the grounds that its adoption had occurred without Parliament having given its opinion, a mandatory part of the procedure.
19 [1980] ECR 3333, at 3357. See Bebr, 'The Standing of the European Parliament in the Community System of Legal Remedies: A Thorny Jurisprudential Development' (1990) CML Rev 170, at 172; and Arnull, 'Does the Court of Justice have Inherent Jurisdiction?' (1990) 27 CML Rev 683, at 692.
20 See Chapter 2.
21 Case 294/83, [1986] ECR 1339. Annulment proceedings against acts of the Parliament had been brought before, in Case 230/81, *Luxembourg* v *European Parliament* [1983] ECR 255, and Case 108/83, *Luxembourg* v *European Parliament* [1984] ECR 1945, both of which concerned the long-standing argument over where the places of work of the European Parliament should be sited. However, in these cases, as all three Communities

were affected, the admissibility of these proceedings was decided under Article 38 ECSC which gives the ECJ the power to annul an act of the Assembly or the Council, where the application is made by the High Authority or by a Member State. It is interesting to note that in the former case the Court stated 'there is no express provision in those Articles [Article 173 EEC, Article 146 Euratom] for active or passive participation of the Parliament in proceedings before this Court' [1983] ECR 255, at 282. See Dashwood, 'The European Parliament and Article 173 EEC: The Limits of Interpretation' in White and Smythe (eds), *Current Issues in European And International Law* (1990), at 75–6, and Bradley, 'The Variable Evolution of the Standing of the European Parliament in Proceedings Before the Court of Justice' [1989] YEL 27.
22 Which followed two unsuccessful attempts to challenge Parliamentary proceedings regarding the draft budget for 1984, Case 295/83 and Case 296/83, both of which failed, not on the grounds that acts of Parliament could not be challenged, but rather that the applicants were not directly affected. See Bradley, *ibid.*, at 36.
23 *Op. cit.*, at 1361. See also 'The Greens scale the barrier of Article 173 EEC' (1986) 11 EL Rev 189.

The European Economic Community is a Community based on the rule of law, inasmuch as neither its Member States nor its institutions can avoid a review of the question whether measures adopted by them are in conformity with the basic constitutional charter, the Treaty. In particular, in Articles 173 and 184, on the one hand, and Article 177 on the other, the Treaty established a complete system of legal remedies and procedures designed to permit the Court of Justice to review the legality of measures adopted by the institutions.[24]

It stated that when the Treaty was drafted, the Parliament was given no such power and thus there was no need for Article 173 to deal with the issue. However, with the expansion of the Parliament's powers, and the consequent ability to engage in legally binding acts, notably in the budgetary sphere,[25] it would be anomalous if the Parliament alone were exempt from judicial review proceedings under Article 173 to challenge those acts. Thus the ECJ came to the conclusion that:

An interpretation of Article 173 of the Treaty which excluded measures adopted by the European Parliament from those which could be contested would lead to a result contrary both to the spirit of the Treaty as expressed in Article 164 and to its system. . . . It must therefore be concluded that an action for annulment may lie against measures adopted by the European Parliament intended to have legal effects *vis-à-vis* third parties.[26]

In adopting this position, the ECJ appears to have been following the line of reasoning that it set out in its decision in the *ERTA* case.[27]

The *Les Verts* case meant that while the Parliament was now subject to certain of its acts being capable of challenge under Article 173, it had as yet failed to gain privileged status for itself. That, Parliament argued, would leave it at a considerable disadvantage compared to the other Community institutions, and thus the logical extension of the ECJ's reasoning in *Les Verts* was that Parliament must have privileged status in order to create 'the necessary balance in relations between the institutions'.[28] However, this viewpoint received a major setback in *Parliament v Council (Comitology)*.[29] Here the Parliament sought to establish finally in proceedings against the Council, for annulment of Decision 87/373/EEC, that it had privileged status under Article 173, something which the Council was implacably opposed to. In his Opinion, Advocate General Darmon attempted to set out a middle ground between the parties, which in granting a limited status to the Parliament to defend its own prerogatives, fell between the total equality with the other institutions required by the Parliament and the Council's desire for Parliament to remain without any standing.[30] The ECJ in its judgment, however, was to reject the proposed middle ground. Its ruling began by ending the growing, if poorly grounded, debate regarding whether the Parliament could gain standing as a legal person under the second paragraph[31] of Article 173, stating that the Parliament, being a Community institution, was clearly not a legal person.[32] It then went on to dismiss the

24 *Op. cit.*, at 1365.
25 Following the Budgetary Treaties of 1970 and 1975.
26 *Op. cit.*, at 1366, and followed in Case 34/86, *Council v European Parliament* (Budget case) [1986] ECR 2155.
27 Case 22/70, *Commission v Council, op. cit.*, at note 3.
28 Note the Resolution of the European Parliament of 9 October 1986, OJ 1986 C 283/85 to this effect.
29 Case 302/87, [1988] ECR 5615.

30 *Op. cit.*, at 5631–6. Academic writings of the time accurately forecasted that the Advocate General's solution was difficult to reconcile with Article 173, first paragraph and would effectively create a sub-class of privileged applicants, with less than full status. See Dashwood, *op. cit.*, note 21, at 82.
31 Now the fourth paragraph, following the amendments made by the TEU.
32 *Op. cit.*, at note 29, at 5643.

Parliament's claim for privileged status, rejecting the argument of the requirement of equality between the institutions based on the *Les Verts* case on the grounds that the decision in that case was designed only to ensure the Treaty aim to 'establish a complete system of judicial protection against acts of Community institutions which are capable of having legal effects' and that there was no *prima facie* connection between the liability to suit and the right to bring an action, under Article 173.[33] It then examined the issue of whether Parliament might be granted standing to defend its own prerogatives, as suggested by the Advocate General. It noted in passing that the SEA had not given Parliament that right and pointed out that where the defence of the Parliament's prerogatives was at issue, 'Article 155 of the Treaty confers . . . on the Commission the responsibility for ensuring that Parliament's prerogatives are respected and for bringing for that purpose such actions for annulment as might prove to be necessary'.[34] Thus the ECJ, without examining the merits of the case, stated that 'the applicable provisions, as they stand, do not enable the ECJ to recognise the capacity of the European Parliament to bring an action for annulment'.[35]

Despite the distinctly unfavourable ruling in the *Comitology* case, and in the face of academic misgivings[36] about the chances of obtaining a more favourable decision from the ECJ so soon after that inauspicious defeat, the Parliament pressed ahead with another annulment action, against Regulation 3954/87/Euratom in *Parliament v Council (Chernobyl)*.[37] This regulation followed the disaster at the Chernobyl nuclear plant, and was concerned with maximum radiation levels in foodstuffs and feedstuffs. The Council felt this was best carried out under Article 31 Euratom under which Parliament need only be consulted. Parliament, however, felt that it should be carried out under Article 100a of the EC Treaty which required co-operation procedures to be utilised. When its opinion was rejected, Parliament initiated annulment proceedings against the resulting regulation.

The Council, in this case, essentially relied upon the same line of argument that had brought success in the *Comitology* case. The Commission, on the other hand, while in this instance agreeing with the Council on the merits of the case, was still of the opinion that the Parliament 'in common with the other institutions, has the right to bring an action for annulment'.[38] It argued that, in situations such as this, the Commission would not be in a position to protect the Parliament's prerogative, either because the Commission had originated the disputed act, or had proposed it to Council, and in such situations it was wholly illogical that the Commission should then be the body asked to bring an action to annul the act on behalf of the Parliament. Parliament sought to distinguish the case from *Comitology* by examining the causes of action left to it by the ECJ in that case to protect its prerogative, and concluding that none was suitable, argued that there was thus an area where some legally binding actions of the institutions were not subject to review.

In his Opinion, Advocate General Van Gerven was of the view that the ECJ had been correct not to allow the Parliament privileged standing solely on the argument that there had to be a connection between the liability to suit and the right to bring an action under Article 173. That would have signally affected the political balance between the institutions in the Parliament's favour, contrary to the aims of the Treaty. However, following the reasoning in

33 *Ibid.*, at 5642.
34 *Ibid.*, at 5644.
35 For wider discussion of this case see Weiler, *op. cit*, note 11, and Bradley, *op.cit.*, note 21.
36 E.g., Weiler, *ibid.*

37 Case C-70/88 [1990] ECR I-2041; see also Bradley, 'Sense and Sensibility: *Parliament v Council* continued' (1991) 16 EL Rev 245.
38 Debates of the European Parliament, Annex to OJ No. 2-370/156, *op.cit.*, quoted in Bradley, at 248.

the *Les Verts* case, he felt that allowing an institution the right to protect its prerogatives would not disturb the political balance and was in fact essential to prevent just such disturbance by ensuring that disputes between the institutions over the extent of their powers could be judicially resolved.

The ECJ ruled that it was clear in this case that,

> the circumstances and the arguments . . . showed . . . the existence of those various legal remedies provided for by the Euratom Treaty and by the EEC Treaty, however effective and varied they may be, were not sufficient to guarantee in all circumstances, that an act of the Council or the Commission which disregarded the Parliament's prerogatives would be censured.[39]

Thus, while it was still not prepared to accord the Parliament privileged status, it was prepared to accept that there should be a restricted right of action in those cases where Parliament was able to show a legitimate interest in the annulment of an act, that is where the Council or Commission infringed upon its prerogatives. In contrast to the ruling in *Comitology*, the ECJ held that:

> . . . the absence in the Treaties of a provision giving the Parliament the right to bring an action for annulment might constitute a procedural gap, but it could not prevail over the fundamental interest which attached to the maintenance of and compliance with the institutional balance of the Treaties.[40]

There are several points to note about this apparent change of heart by the ECJ. It appears that the direction the ECJ took in its ruling in *Comitology* can be considered a dead end, especially as the ECJ was not minded to distinguish it in the *Chernobyl* case and thus allow it to retain any precedental force.[41] The ECJ, by stating that there was a failure adequately to protect the Parliament's prerogatives, was obviously of the opinion that that decision could no longer stand.[42] Certainly in the two cases which have followed the *Chernobyl* case, *European Parliament* v *Council* (*Student's Rights*),[43] and *European Parliament* v *Council*,[44] the ECJ has been quick to defend the position it has adopted. In the *Student's Rights* case, the UK attempted to have the Parliament's action declared inadmissible on the grounds that the ECJ's case law required that there be a 'disagreement between the Commission and the Parliament's legal viewpoint concerning its own powers in order for the Parliament to have standing to bring an action'.[45] The ECJ rejected this view and restated the two-point test in the *Chernobyl* case that 'an action for annulment brought by the Parliament is admissible providing that the action seeks only to safeguard its prerogatives and that it is founded only on submissions alleging their infringement'.[46]

The *Chernobyl* case, and those following it, show a clear determination on the part of the ECJ to ensure that the Community should adhere to the principle of the rule of law rather than attempting to preserve legal certainty at all costs. Thus, even if the treaties did not explicitly grant rights to the institutions which would ensure that a balance and a division of roles is maintained between them, it seems that the ECJ will be willing to fill any such 'procedural gaps' or lacunae that develop as the Community matures. A sign that the ECJ's

---

[39] Case C-70/88, *op. cit.*, at note 37, at 2072.
[40] *Ibid.*, at 2073.
[41] See Bebr, *op. cit.*, note 19.
[42] Note the slightly different conclusion reached in Arnull, 'Owning Up to Fallibility: Precedent and the Court

[of] Justice' (1993) 30 CML Rev 247, at 258.
[43] Case C-295/90, [1992] 3 CMLR 281.
[44] Case C-65/90, not yet reported.
[45] *Op. cit.*, note 43, at 292.
[46] *Ibid.*, at 300.

attitude both to its own role and to the importance of the rule of law may reflect attitudes elsewhere in the Community can be seen in that both the Parliament and ECB were formally given the limited right to protect their prerogatives via actions under Article 173 by Article G(53) of the TEU.[47]

Non-privileged applicants

While the issue of the standing of the Parliament under Article 173(1) has clearly caused the ECJ difficulties, its main problem has always been with those applicants who fall under the heading of 'natural and legal persons' in what is now Article 173(4)[48]. Here the case law would seem to bear out the conclusion that the ECJ has decided to err on the side of caution by interpreting the paragraph very strictly. This appears to be on the grounds that to do otherwise would result in the ECJ being inundated with annulment proceedings.[49] Thus applicants are faced with a very rigorous two-stage test to determine whether they have the requisite *locus standi* to bring an action. The first part of the test defines the limited range of actions that may be challenged.

(a) *A decision that is addressed to the applicant*. This head poses the least problems for the ECJ. If the applicant can prove that the disputed act addressed to him has consequences that affect his legal position, that act will, whatever its form, effectively constitute a decision. If, however, the act in dispute is a non-binding act, it cannot be a decision and thus may not be challenged.[50] This can be seen most clearly in the competition law sphere where applicants have challenged Commission decisions addressed to them declaring them to be in breach of Community competition law or imposing fines.[51]

(b) *A decision that is addressed to another person*. Here the applicant must not only prove that the act in dispute is a decision, but also that it is of direct and individual concern to him. Decisions addressed to Member States can fall under this heading, as stated by the ECJ in *Plaumann & Co v Commission*:[52]

> The contested decision was addressed to the government of the Federal Republic of Germany and refuses to grant it authorisation for the partial suspension of customs duties on certain products imported from third countries. Therefore the contested measures must be regarded as a decision referring to a particular person and binding that person alone.

(c) *A decision that takes the form of a regulation*. The ECJ, in interpreting this in *Confédération Nationale des Producteurs de Fruits et Légumes v Council*,[53] noted that

---

47 Article 173, paragraph 3:
  The Court shall have jurisdiction under the same conditions in actions brought by the European Parliament and by the ECB for the purpose of protecting their prerogatives . . .
48 Previously the second paragraph, prior to the TEU.
49 This is familiar judicial argument in UK law where the stated concern is to avoid unnecessary and vexatious litigation, although in actions before the ECJ it should perhaps be considered less plausible in the light of the cost/time factors involved in bringing cases.
50 Case 53–4/63, *Lemmerz-werke v High Authority* [1963] ECR 239.
51 Cases 56 and 58/64, *Consten and Grundig v Com-mission* [1966] ECR 299; Case 17/74, *Transocean Marine Paint v Commission* [1974] ECR 1063; Case T-51/89, *Tetra Pak Rausing SA v Commission* [1994] 4 CMLR 334.
52 Case 25/62, [1963] ECR 95, at 107.
53 Cases 16–17/62, [1962] ECR 471, at 478, followed in Cases 19/62 and 22/62, *Fédération Nationale de la Boucherie en Gros et du Commerce en Gros des Viandes*; *Stichting voor Nederlandse zelfstandige Handel en Industrie*; *Syndicat de la boucherie en gros de Paris*; and *Zentralverband des Deutschen Getreide-, Futter- und Dungemittelhandels ev. v Council* [1962] ECR 491, at 498.

Article 189 EC Treaty made a clear distinction between decisions[54] and regulations[55], and concluded that except where on examination by the ECJ the nature of a purported regulation was such that it was clearly of individual concern to specific individuals and thus of the nature of a decision, natural and legal persons could not apply to have regulations annulled. This distinction was examined by the Advocate General in *Extramet Industrie* v *Council* [56] where he drew upon the judgments in *Zuckerfabrik Watenstedt* v *Council* [57] and *Plaumann & Co* v *Commission*[58] to arrive at the following definitions 'the fundamental characteristic of a regulation is that it is "applicable to objectively determined situations" and involves "legal consequences for categories of persons viewed in a general and abstract manner" (Zuckerfabrick). . . . Decisions, on the other hand, are characterised by the limited number of persons affected by them (*Plaumann*).'

The reasoning behind the ECJ's stance is both clear and pragmatic. Regulations are used primarily as legislative measures, being designed to create Community law which is directly applicable in all Member States. They will thus, by their very nature, affect individuals throughout the Community. The ECJ is therefore faced with a situation where, if all regulations could be easily challenged by individuals, the legislative process in the Community would almost certainly be dramatically disrupted, and individuals and companies would not be able to approach the implementation of procedures to conform with regulations with any certainty. It is in order to prevent such disruption that Article 173(2) is so rigidly interpreted and true regulations may not be challenged.[59] Unfortunately this has the effect of making the case law in this area complex and confusing, as the ECJ attempts to tread a path which conforms to this reasoning while endeavouring to uphold the rights of individuals in those situations where the rationale of particular regulations is in question.

Direct and individual concern[60]

If the applicant is not directly addressed by the contested act, but can show that the act falls within one of the other two headings above, he has to prove that the act which he is requesting be annulled is of direct and individual concern to him.[61] There is thus no right under Article 173 to challenge acts of general application, a fact that has played a major part in the case law surrounding this area.[62] This area of law has, however, been made more complex by the ECJ's decisions in a number of discrete areas of case law which will be examined below.

Individual concern

Individual concern has proved to be the largest stumbling block for applicants. In *Plaumann & Co* v *Commission*[63] the ECJ put forward the following test to be satisfied:

[54] Article 189, paragraph 4: A decision shall be binding in its entirety upon those to whom it is addressed.
[55] Article 189, paragraph 2: A regulation shall have general application. It shall be binding in its entirety and directly applicable in all Member States.
[56] Case C-358/89, [1991] ECR I-2501.
[57] Case 6/68 [1968] ECR 409.
[58] Case 25/62, *op. cit.*, at note 52.
[59] Case 789/79, *Calpak SpA* v *Commission* [1980] ECR 1949.

[60] See Barav, 'Direct and Individual Concern: An Almost Insurmountable Barrier to the Admissibility of Individual Appeal to the EEC Court.' (1974) 11 CML Rev 191, and Rasmussen, 'Why is Article 173 Interpreted against Private Plaintiffs' (1980) 5 EL Rev 112.
[61] Case 222/83, *Differdange* v *Commission* [1984] ECR 2889.
[62] Greaves, '*Locus Standi* under Article 173 EEC When Seeking Annulment of a Regulation' (1986) 11 EL Rev 119.
[63] *Op. cit.*, at note 52.

Persons other than those to whom a decision is addressed may only claim to be individually concerned if that decision affects them by reason of certain attributes which are peculiar to them or by reason of circumstances in which they are differentiated from all other persons and by virtue of these factors distinguishes them individually just as in the case of the person addressed.

This test was followed in *Alfred Toepfer KG* v *Commission*,[64] one of the rare instances (apart from the anti-dumping cases) where the ECJ held that the applicant had direct and individual concern. Here, the applicant was one of a number of maize importers who, following a decision of the Commission to reduce the levy on maize to nil, applied for an import licence to import a large amount of maize into Germany. At this point, the German government rejected those applications and announced that it was requesting a Commission decision as to whether it could take safeguard measures allowing it to reject applications for import licences. That decision was forthcoming and the Commission retroactively authorised the German government to take the relevant safeguard measures. Toepfer thereupon brought an action to have that decision annulled. As was the case in *Bock* v *Commission*,[65] the ECJ held that as the act was retroactive in nature, it was clearly possible to differentiate the applicants from all others, which meant that they were clearly individually concerned.

While those cases involved a decision addressed to a Member State, in *International Fruit Company* v *Commission*[66] the ECJ was called upon to examine whether a disputed regulation was in fact a decision and, if it was, whether that decision was of direct and individual concern to the applicants. The applicants were fruit importers who had applied for import licences for apples. The number of licences available in a given period was laid down in a Commission regulation, and the Commission then decided how many licences were to be issued by referring to information supplied by Member States as to the number of applications made the previous week. The ECJ held that by using this system the Commission, despite its use of the form of regulations, was in fact really making decisions which were affecting the legal position of the applicants, because by reaching a decision with reference to the previous week's applications, the Commission was creating a closed group of applicants which no other importer was capable of joining.

This approach was followed in *CAM* v *Commission*[67] where importers had entered into contracts before the Commission passed a regulation increasing the threshold price for cereals. Again the ECJ held that they were distinguishable as a closed group by the retroactive nature of the regulation.

The ECJ has, in more recent cases, adopted the position that where the act in dispute is of a regulatory nature, for instance, an act designed to affect the activities of an open class of importers as in *Spijker*[68] or *Binderer*[69] the very fact that it is regulatory means that it cannot be deemed to be of direct and individual concern to any applicant. Even where those individuals affected can be determined by number or identity, if the act can be seen as regulatory, it cannot be challenged. In *Koninklijke Scholten Honig* v *Council & Commission (No 1)*[70] the ECJ stated:

64 Case 106–7/63, [1965] ECR 405.
65 Case 62/70, *Chinese Mushrooms case* [1971] ECR 897.
66 Cases 41–4/70, [1971] ECR 411.
67 Case 100/74, [1975] ECR 1393.
68 Case 231/82, *Spijker Kwasten BV* v *Commission* [1983] ECR 2559 (concerning a decision addressed to another person).
69 Case 147/83, *Binderer* v *Commission* [1985] ECR 271 (concerning a regulation).
70 Case 101/76, [1977] ECR 797 and Case 789/79, *Calpak SpA* v *Commission* [1980] ECR 1949.

> A regulation is a measure which applies to objectively determined situations and produces legal effects with regard to categories of persons regarded generally and in the abstract. The nature of a measure as a regulation is not called in question by the possibility of determining more or less precisely the number or the identity of the persons to whom it applies at a given moment, so long as it is applied by virtue of an objective factual or legal situation defined by the measure in relation to its objective . . .[71]

The ECJ determines general application by reference to the nature of the contested measure and especially the legal effects which it was intended to produce or did in fact produce.[72]

The ECJ's rather complex reasoning is part of the source of the confusion surrounding Article 173 actions, for it might be reasonable for an applicant to feel that, where it was possible to determine that he and a precise number of others were affected by an act, he would be individually and directly concerned. Indeed, if the act in dispute is specifically aimed at that group as it exists at that point in time, this would result in the creation of a closed group because no other individual could join later and be affected by the act. In such circumstances the act would not be regulatory in nature because it would have no future effect, and it would thus be a decision which would individually and directly concern the members of that group. However, if the act is designed to cover both existing and possible future members of that group (even where it is unlikely that others will in fact join due to the high costs), the group cannot be a closed group and the act would clearly be generally applicable and thus regulatory in nature.

There appear to have been two distinct areas where the ECJ has been prepared to relax this rather rigid attitude. The first area is related to the balance in powers and accountability of the Community institutions, and the second concerns Community competition law and the related issues of anti-dumping proceedings and State aids.[73]

The first set of cases began with *Les Verts – Partie Ecologiste* v *European Parliament*, in which the ECJ considered[74] the issue of the standing of the French Ecology Party in challenging an act of the European Parliament (*see* above for details).[75] In terms of satisfying the test of direct concern, the French Ecology Party obviously had a concern in the manner in which the funding in question was administered and allocated, and the procedure for that allocation was automatic, thus excluding the use of discretion on the part of the allocators. On the issue of individual concern, however, the ECJ ignored the established case law which, if followed, would clearly have resulted in the application being ruled inadmissible. The French Ecology Party was not part of a closed group, rather it was part of a potentially very wide group as the decision taken could affect other political groupings who had not yet declared an interest in standing in the elections. Indeed the French Ecology Party was itself in a position where it might or might not be affected by the decision depending on whether it decided to field candidates in the election. The ECJ ruled that

> . . . groupings which were represented and which were therefore identifiable at the date of the adoption of the contested measure are individually concerned by it. . . . it must be

---

71 *Op. cit*, at 797.
72 Case 253/86, *Sociedade Agro Pecuaria Vincente Nobre Lda* v *Council* [1988] ECR 2725; also Case 26/86, *Deutz and Geldermann* v *Council* [1987] ECR 941 and Cases 233–5/86, *Champlor* v *Commission* [1987] ECR 2251.
73 For a detailed examination of anti-dumping adminis-

trative procedure see below; also Didier, 'EEC Anti Dumping Rules and Practices' [1980] 17 CML Rev 349.
74 Case 294/83. It should be noted that this was despite the fact that the Parliament did not raise the issue of admissibility.
75 Under 'European Parliament and European Central Bank'.

concluded that the applicant association, which was in existence at the time when the 1982 Decision was adopted and which was able to present candidates at the 1984 elections, is individually concerned.[76]

and that the French Ecology Party thus had standing. However, as with the *Chernobyl* case, the ECJ appears to have been minded to allow standing on policy grounds connected with the development of a rule of law based framework of judicial review, rather than to expand the availability of judicial review under Article 173(2).[77]

The second set of cases involves those decisions that Hartley[78] terms quasi-judicial determinations. He defines quasi-judicial determinations as being where

> . . . the determination is to a large extent made on the basis of objective considerations and is the culmination of a procedure which has judicial features. Such determinations are predominantly decisions of fact and law rather than discretionary decisions.

In such cases, there is often some form of participation in the pre-decision proceedings by the party wishing to challenge the decision, and it is this participation which has been used to explain the ECJ's willingness to accept that the party should have *locus standi* in any consequent annulment proceedings brought under Article 173(2); however, more recent cases have sometimes cast doubt upon this interpretation. As stated above, the three main areas where such cases have arisen, are competition law, cases involving State aids, and anti-dumping legislation. Of these it is the area of anti-dumping which has been most problematic.

In competition cases[79] it is accepted that firms which are investigated by the Commission under Articles 85 and 86 EC and who are found to be in breach of Community law are entitled to challenge the decision as an applicant to whom a decision is addressed. In the case of a complainant who has lodged a complaint with the Commission and who under Community competition law may participate in the administrative proceedings, including the hearing, following *Metro-SB-Grossmärkte v Commission (No 1)*[80] that complainant will be regarded as individually concerned, even if the effect of the decision is such as to affect other members of an open category.

In State aid cases (*see* below[81]), while complainants are not granted the same level of recognition that they have in both competition and anti-dumping administrative proceedings, they have been allowed to participate in investigatory proceedings under Article 93. In *COFAZ v Commission*[82] the applicants wanted a decision of the Commission not to proceed with the investigation in which they were involved annulled. The ECJ held that their application would be admissible as individuals with the status of complainants, if their market position was significantly affected by the alleged aid, this despite the argument from the Commission that the applicants were in fact part of an open category of fertiliser producers.

76 *Op. cit.*, at 1369.
77 The *Les Verts* case has been followed by the Court in Case 78/85, *Group of the European Right v Parliament* [1986] ECR 1753 (application held inadmissible) and Case 34/86, *Council v European Parliament (First Budget)* [1986] ECR 2155 (application held admissible).
78 Hartley, *The Foundations of European Community Law*, 2nd edn (1988), at 354.
79 Dinnage, '*Locus Standi* and Article 173 EEC: The effect of *Metro Grossmärkte v Commission*' (1979) 4 EL Rev 15.

80 Case 26/76, [1977] ECR 1875; also Case 210/81, *Demostudio Schmidt v Commission* [1983] ECR 3045 and Case 75/84, *Metro v Commission* [1986] ECR 3021.
81 See Chapter 8.
82 Case 169/84, *Compagnie Française de l'Azote v Commission* [1986] ECR. 391; also Joined Cases 67, 68 and 70/85, *Van der Kooy v Commission* [1988] ECR 219. See Hartley, *op. cit.*, note 78, at 358 and Arnull, 'Owning up to Fallibility: Precedent and the Court of Justice', *op. cit.*, note 42, at 257.

In anti-dumping cases[83] proceedings are brought under the rules contained in Council Regulation 2176/84/EEC[84] and, where necessary, duties are imposed upon producers and importers by Commission regulation in the case of provisional duties and by Council regulation in the case of definitive duties.[85] This means that if producers or importers wish to challenge the imposition of duties they have to satisfy the test of Article 173(2). This issue was first raised in the *Japanese Ball Bearing* cases.[86] Here, the applicants were producers and importers. The producers were explicitly named in the Regulation and the importers were the exclusive importers of the producers' products. The ECJ thus had no difficulty in accepting the admissibility of the action by the producers – 'The contested measure therefore constitutes a decision which affects only the major producers and their subsidiaries and must therefore be considered to be a decision concerning them adopted in the guise of a regulation'[87] – or the importers – '. . . the special feature of Article 3 which sets it apart is it does not concern all importers but only those who have imported [products] manufactured by the four major Japanese producers named in the article'.[88]

However, while clarifying the debate over the status of producers (and exporters),[89] this case provided a misleading picture of the admissibility of action by importers. In a number of cases following it importers' applications were held inadmissible.[90] In *Alusuisse*, the ECJ first distinguished the *Japanese Ball Bearing* cases because they were brought by European-based producers and exporters[91] and both producers and exporters were expressly named in the relevant Regulation.[92] It then rejected the argument that because the various parties had participated in the anti-dumping administrative procedure the resulting measure was in fact a number of decisions capable of being challenged by those parties. It did so on the grounds that the method of identifying an act as either a regulation or a decision was not to be found in the proceedings leading to its adoption, but rather in the nature and effects of the measure itself.[93] In *Allied Corporation*, where a provisional anti-dumping duty was at issue, an action by an importer of chemical fertiliser failed as the importer in question was just one of many importers who could have imported the fertiliser.

However, the ECJ did accept as admissible actions brought by importers against anti-dumping measures in *Sermes* v *Commission*[94] where the existence of the dumping was established by reference to the importer's resale price, and in *Neotype Techmashexport* v *Commission and Council*[95] where the level of duty was determined by reference to those

83 Arnull, 'Challenging EC Anti-Dumping Regulations: the Problem of Admissibility' [1992] ECLR 73, and Greaves, 'Judicial Review of Anti-Dumping Cases by the European Court of Justice' [1985] ECLR 135.

84 Which replaced Regulation 3017/79/EEC.

85 Article 13, Regulation 17/79/EEC.

86 Case 113/77, *NTN Toyo Bearing Company Ltd & Others* v *Council* [1979] ECR 1185; also Case 118/77, *ISO* v *Council*, Case 119/77, *NSK & Others* v *Council and Commission*, Case 120/77, *Koyo Seikjo Co Ltd* v *Council and Commission* and Case 121/77, *Nachi Fujhikoski Corporation* v *Council*.

87 *Ibid.*, at 1325.

88 *Ibid.*, at 1327.

89 The *Japanese Ball Bearing* cases were followed in Case 236/81, *Celanese Chemical Co* [1982] ECR 1183 (where the producer was held to have been expressly named in

the regulation) and Joined Cases 239/82 and 275/82, *Allied Corporation* v *Council* [1984] ECR 1005 (where exporters were held to have been expressly named in the regulation).

90 Case 307/81, *Alusuisse Italia* v *Council and Commission* [1982] ECR 3463 and Joined Cases 239/82 and 275/82, *Allied Corporation* v *Council*, *op. cit.*, note 89.

91 *Op. cit.*, at 3471.

92 *Ibid.*, at 3472.

93 *Ibid.*, at 3473.

94 Case 279/86, [1987] ECR 3109, also Case 301/86 *Frimodt Pedersen* v *Commission* [1987] ECR 3123 and Case 205/87, *Nuova Ceam* v *Commission* [1987] ECR 4427.

95 Joined Cases C-305/86 & C-160/87, [1990] ECR 1-2945.

prices.[96] More recently, in *Extramet Industrie* v *Council* [97] the ECJ shifted position in allowing as admissible the action of an importer who, according to previous case law, did not have an admissible case but who would have suffered great damage to its business if the proposed duty on its imports was imposed. The grounds the ECJ gave were short and not particularly convincing, in that it sought to explain the applicant's admissibility on the grounds that the applicant's position was different to those of other undertakings and thus it was individually concerned. In doing so the ECJ did not refer to previous case law which quite explicitly said that such grounds were not enough to establish individual concern.[98] This shift of position has left the case law of anti-dumping even further removed from the general rules on admissibility and thus even less certain as an indicator of ECJ policy.

The status of complainants with regard to Article 173(2) actions has also been considered in *Fediol* v *Commission*[99] and *Timex* v *Council and Commission*.[100] In *Fediol* the applicant was a trade association which lodged a complaint with the Commission in which it requested that anti-subsidy proceedings be brought against imports of soya bean cake from Brazil. The Commission after due consideration and consultation with the Brazilian government decided not to begin proceedings, and sent this decision in the form of a letter to Fediol. Fediol then applied to have the decision annulled. The ECJ, in assessing admissibility, examined the Dumping Regulation and concluded that it granted the complainants specific rights against the Commission which had been ignored. The ECJ also held, in a judgment later to be echoed in cases such as *Les Verts* and *Chernobyl*, that in accordance with the principles embodied in Article 164 complainants should be able to seek review by the ECJ, under Article 173, of the exercise of those powers granted by the Dumping Regulation to Community institutions to conduct investigations and take protective measures.

In *Timex* the applicant lodged a complaint with the Commission regarding the import of Russian watches. An anti-dumping administrative procedure was duly held and a duty imposed on the imports. However, Timex was unhappy with the duty imposed and applied to the ECJ, claiming first that the duty that was imposed was negligible and also that no duty had been imposed on the movements of the watches. Both Council and Commission claimed that the application was inadmissible on the grounds that Timex was not mentioned in the Regulation's articles; that the Regulation was not addressed to Timex; and that Timex could not be directly and individually concerned. Following the ruling in *Fediol* the ECJ held that as the Regulation in question was based on a complaint initiated by Timex; Timex was virtually the only EC producer; and the procedure adopted was supposed to be based on the effect upon Timex of the imports, that Timex was individually and directly concerned and thus,

> the applicant is therefore entitled to put before the Court any matters which would facilitate a review as to whether the Commission has observed the procedural guarantees granted to complainants by Regulation No. 3017/79 . . . or . . . has committed

96 Arnull, *op. cit.*, note 42, at 255.

97 Case C-358/89, [1991] ECR I-2501. Note that the Advocate General's Opinion contains a useful examination of the case law to that point.

98 *Ibid.*, at 2531.

99 Case 191/82, [1983] ECR 2913. It should be noted that the successful application in this case has implications for the ruling in Cases 16–17/62, *Confédération Nationale des Producteurs de Fruits et Légumes* v *Council, op. cit.*, note 53; that trade organisations cannot be individually concerned with a measure such as a regulation affecting the general interests of the category of business which it represents. See further Greaves, 'Locus Standi under Article 173 EEC When Seeking Annulment of a Regulation', *loc. cit.*, note 62, at 129.

100 Case 264/82, [1985] ECR 849.

manifest errors in its assessment of the facts, has omitted to take any essential matters into consideration or has based the reasons for its decision on considerations amounting to misuse of powers.[101]

The ECJ thus side-stepped previous rulings which suggested that the distinction between a regulation and a decision, determined by the nature and effects of the measure itself and not in the proceedings leading to its adoption, was vital to an applicant's case.[102]

It is apparent from the case law that the ECJ has differentiated between producer, importer and complainant in its acceptance of various arguments relating to standing in anti-dumping cases, but that the differentiation does not appear to have settled into a clear pattern. It is also the case that criteria which have been successfully used in State aid and competition cases have so far failed in anti-dumping cases.[103] This does not aid the development of legal certainty in this already uncertain area.

It is debatable as to how much influence the cases in the areas of the accountability of the Community institutions and Community competition law will have upon the generally accepted position of the ECJ with regard to individual concern, and it seems probable that the ECJ will remain inclined to distinguish these lines of case law on their particular facts.

Direct concern

The above case law shows that the ECJ has generally been more concerned with the issue of individual concern than that of direct concern. Thus in many cases, if an applicant can show individual concern, direct concern may appear to be automatically assumed. However, the ECJ has not left direct concern undefined, and it has a role to play in the determination of standing.

Brown and Jacob[104] note that the ECJ has applied a similar approach to direct concern as it has to direct effect, that is, that the applicant must show that there is a clear link between himself and the application of the decision and that the person implementing the decision has no real discretion as to how it is implemented.[105] In *CAM v Commission*[106] Advocate General Warner defined the role of direct concern as follows:

> If the action to be taken by the Member State on the decision is automatic, or is, at all events, a foregone conclusion, then the decision is of direct concern to any person affected by that action. If on the other hand, the decision leaves it to the Member State whether to act or not to act, it is the action or inaction of the Member State that is of direct concern to the person affected, not the decision itself.

In the latter circumstance, the direct concern with the Member State's action or inaction is clearly insufficient to provide standing. This approach can be seen in *Alcan*,[107] where the ECJ

[101] *Ibid.*, at 850.
[102] See also Case C-135/90, *Gimelec and others v Commission*, not yet reported.
[103] Contrast Case 307/81, *Alusuisse Italia v Council and Commission, op. cit.*, at note 90, with Case 26/76, *Metro Grossmärkte v Commission (No 1), op. cit.*, note 80 and Case 169/84, *COFAZ v Commission, op. cit.*, note 82.
[104] Brown and Jacobs, *The Court of Justice of the European Communities*, 3rd edn (1989), at 113. However, Schermers and Walbroeck, *op. cit.*, note 7, at 217, argue that this analogy should not be taken too far.
[105] See Case 113/77, *NTN Toyo Bearing Company Ltd & Others v Council, op. cit.*, note 86, at 1205; also Case 294/83, *Les Verts – Partie Ecologiste v European Parliament, op. cit.*, note 21, at 1367; Case 55/86, *AR-PSOL v Council* [1988] ECR 13; Case C-152/88, *Sofrimport SARL v Commission* [1990] ECR I-2477.
[106] Case 100/74, [1975] ECR 1393, at 1410.
[107] Case 69/69, *SA Alcan Aluminium Raeren v Commission* [1970] ECR 385.

held that the applicant was not directly concerned, as Belgium, the Member State to whom the decision was addressed, was free to choose how it implemented the distribution of the aluminium allocation at issue, thus the fact of discretion was used to reject the claim.

The *Alcan* case can, however, be contrasted with *Bock* v *Commission*[108] and *Piraiki-Patraiki* v *Commission*.[109] In the *Bock* case, the German government had applied for authorisation to block imports of chinese mushrooms, which was granted by the Commission. Despite the fact that in theory the German government had a choice of whether or not to use the authorisation granted by the Commission, the ECJ held that the fact that the German authorities had communicated with the applicant that they intended to use the authorisation to reject his application, and indeed had applied for that authorisation with pending cases in mind, was sufficient for their apparent discretion not to be an issue and to cause the matter to be of direct concern to the applicant. More recently in *Piraiki-Patraiki,* where the applicants were seeking to annul a decision of the Commission to authorise the imposition of a quota system on the import of cotton yarn from Greece by the French government, the ECJ made it clear that it was not interested in discussing the theoretical aspects of the case. It stated that there was of course the theoretical possibility that the French government might not use the Commission's authorisation, but on the particular facts of the case the ECJ had no doubt that the French government would apply it in practice.

The ECJ is undoubtedly aware of the fact that in many instances the applicants are in a position to bring an action under Article 177 in their national courts.[110] When looking at the ECJ's decisions relating to Article 173(2) applications, it is difficult to disagree with Hartley's statement that 'it is hard to avoid feeling that the ECJ decides first whether it wants the application to be admissible and then applies whichever test will produce the desired result'.[111] It is certainly true that the ECJ has often paid scant regard to its own existing case law when reaching decisions in this area. Arnull[112] suggests that this is both inevitable and desirable, as the view that the ECJ should be accorded the status of law creator, rather than simply law interpreter, gains support.

Grounds of review

Applicants who successfully pass the barrier of admissibility have four main grounds on which they may apply for annulment of measures under Article 173. These grounds, originally derived from the French administrative law but increasingly influenced by the administrative law of the other Member States, notably that of Germany and the UK, are (i) lack of competence, (ii) infringement of an essential procedural requirement, (iii) infringement of the EC Treaty or of any rule of law relating to its application, and (iv) misuse of powers. The effect of the influence of other Member States' administrative law has been to blur the somewhat stricter demarcations between these headings to be found in French administrative law[113] to the point where 'the various grounds are drawn up in such wide terms that they

108 Case 62/70, *op. cit.*, note 65.
109 Case 11/82, [1985] ECR 207.
110 Cases 89/86 and 91/86, *L'Etoile Commerçiale* v *Commission* [1987] ECR 3005. Note Cases 103 and 145/77, *Royal Scholten-Honig (Holdings) Ltd* v *Intervention Board for Agricultural Produce* [1978] ECR 2037, where the applicant was successful with an Article

177 reference having failed at the admissibility stage under Article 173.
111 Hartley, *op. cit.*, note 78, at 345–6.
112 Arnull, 'Owning up to Fallibility: Precedent and the Court of Justice' *op. cit.*, note 42, at 264.
113 Brown and Garner, *French Administrative Law*, 4th edn (1993), at 152–7.

encompass amongst themselves almost all conceivable cases of illegality'.[114] However, for the use of one of these heads to be successful, the applicant must prove that the scale of the breach claimed is large enough to put the validity of the act under attack in doubt[115] and that generally the breach was such as to have an effect on the eventual nature of that act.[116]

Lack of competence

This ground has certain similarities to the UK administrative law ground of substantive *ultra vires*. It may be successfully invoked where a Community institution has attempted to carry out an act for which it has not been granted the requisite power by the Treaty or other Community legislation.[117] Thus the Commission or Council may not adopt measures in areas outside the Treaty, nor may either adopt measures in areas that lie solely within the competence of the other. As the institutions are not inclined deliberately to attempt to adopt measures in areas outside the Treaty, much of the limited case law on this ground relates to improper delegation of powers.[118]

Infringement of an essential procedural requirement

Acts of the Community institutions must be carried out in accordance with the correct procedures. Failure to observe the correct procedures may leave the measure susceptible to annulment, dependent upon whether the ECJ considers that the procedure ignored is essential, that is, that the measure under attack would have been substantially different if the procedure had in fact been followed.[119] Failure to provide adequate reasons for a decision will, in Article 173 actions, almost always be found to be a breach of an essential procedural requirement,[120] even where the resulting measure is not significantly affected.[121] The ECJ has also held that the requirement to consult is an essential procedural requirement.[122]

Infringement of the EC Treaty, or of any rule of law relating to its application

This heading is extremely wide in scope,[123] and indeed the other headings could, in theory, fit within in it. It is generally argued in cases where applicants are alleging breach of any of the general principles of law, such as proportionality and legitimate expectations (*see* above, Chapter 6) or breach of human rights. It is argued in nearly all annulment actions.

Misuse of powers

This heading covers the use by an institution of its powers for an unlawful purpose, or for a purpose which, while lawful, was not the purpose for which the power was originally

---

114 Toth, *The Oxford Encyclopaedia of European Community Law* (1990), vol. 1, at 282.

115 Case 156/79 and 51/80, *Gatreau v Commission* [1980] ECR 3955.

116 Case 209–15/78 and 218/78, *Van Landewijck v Commission* [1980] ECR 3125.

117 Joined Cases 281, 283–5 and 287/85, *Germany, France, Netherlands, Denmark and UK v Commission* [1987] ECR 3203; Case 264/86, *France v Commission* [1988] ECR 973.

118 Case 9/56, *Meroni v High Authority* [1958] ECR 133; Case 23/75, *Rey Soda v Cassa Conguaglio Zucchero* [1975] ECR 1279.

119 Case 30/78, *Distillers Company v Commission* [1980] ECR 2229.

120 Case 24/62, *Germany v Commission* [1963] ECR 63; Joined Cases 8–11/66, *Netherlands VHA v Commission (First Cement-Convention Case)* [1967] ECR 75.

121 Case 45/86, *Commission v Council* [1987] ECR 1493.

122 Case 138/79, *Roquette Frères v Council* [1980] ECR 3333 and Case 139/79, *Maizena v Council* [1980] ECR 3393.

123 And certainly wider than any ground of review to be found in UK law.

intended. Limited use of this heading has been made with regard to the EC Treaty, probably because of the difficulty in establishing a case.[124]

Procedure for application for review under Article 173

Paragraph three of Article 173 states that

> The proceedings provided for in this Article shall be instituted within two months of the publication of the measure, or of its notification to the plaintiff, or, in the absence thereof, on the day on which it came to the knowledge of the latter, as the case may be.

With regard to publication of measures brought by the institutions, Article 191 of the EC Treaty states that

> Regulations shall be published in the Official Journal of the Community. They shall enter into force on the date specified in them or, in the absence thereof, on the twentieth day following their publication.
> Directives and decisions shall be notified to those to whom they are addressed and shall take effect upon such notification.

Thus only regulations are required by Community law to be published, although directives and decisions are often published in the Official Journal as well. There has been no judicial determination as to whether the fact that directives and decisions are published, or that a person may know of a regulation before it is published, has any effect upon the point from which time begins to run. Further and more detailed provisions for the determination of time limits can be found in Articles 80 and 81(1) of the Rules of Procedure of the European Court.

Where a directive or decision is not published and the potential applicant is not the addressee, it appears that the time begins to run from the point where the applicant is made aware of the measure's existence.[125] In *Eridania v Commission*[126] Advocate General Roemer was of the opinion that where the applicants were aware that a decision which related to them had been published in the Official Journal, but had made no effort to obtain details of that decision, the point at which time began to run was the moment that they could have obtained the text should they have so wished.

In cases where a potential applicant is prevented by some mishap from bringing proceedings within the allotted time, Article 42(2) of the Statute of the ECJ states that 'No right shall be prejudiced in consequence of the expiry of a time limit, if the party concerned proves the existence of unforseeable circumstances or of *force majeure*'. However, the case law shows that the ECJ is not inclined to interpret this exception particularly leniently.[127]

The effects of annulment[128]

When an applicant is successful in obtaining an action for annulment, Article 174(1) states

124 Case 18 and 35/65, *Gutmann. v Commission* [1966] ECR 103 (staff case); Cases 59 and 129/80, *Turner v Commission* [1981] ECR 1920 (staff case).
125 See Advocate General Gand's Opinion in Case 69/69, *Alcan v Commission, op. cit.*, note 107, at 395.
126 Joined Cases 10 and 18/68, [1969] ECR 459, at 484.
127 Case 76/79, *Konecke* v *Commission* [1980] ECR

665; Case 152/85, *Misset v Council* [1987] ECR 223; Case 352/87, *Farzoo and Kortmann v Commission* [1988] ECR 2281; Case C-59/91, *France v Commission*, not yet reported.
128 Toth, 'The Authority of Judgments of the European Court of Justice: Binding Force and Legal Effects' (1984) 4 YEL 1.

that the ECJ shall declare the act in question void. This declaration means in effect that the act never existed.[129] Thus all previous and further actions based upon it are similarly void. However, in the case of a regulation the ECJ is able to state, under Article 174(2), that some of its effects may be considered as definitive. Such definitive effects may be required for reasons such as legal certainty or, as in the cases of *Commission* v *Council*[130] and *Commission* v *Council*,[131] where Council regulations on payment of Community staff had been held to be illegal by the ECJ, to ensure that staff were paid in the period between the annulment and the promulgation of legal Council regulations on the matter.[132] The ECJ has also extended the scope of Article 174(2) to acts other than regulations, as in *Simmenthal*,[133] where it annulled a decision addressed to the Member States, only with regard to Simmenthal.

Where the ECJ annuls only part of a measure, the remaining part will be regarded as have being confirmed by the ECJ and thus incapable of being contested in any future action for annulment. However, the rejection by the ECJ of an application for annulment of a measure does not preclude that measure being challenged by different parties in a separate action based on different grounds of illegality.[134]

When annulling a measure, the ECJ has no power to replace it with one of its own, or to require the institution at fault to replace it,[135] but, as Article 176 of the Treaty states that

> The institution whose act has been declared void or whose failure to act has been declared contrary to this Treaty shall be required to take the necessary measures to comply with the judgment of the Court of Justice. . . .

and such necessary measures will obviously involve the non-enforcement of the act by the Community institutions involved, there will obviously be pressure on the institution to replace it to some degree with a further measure.[136] This is especially true in cases where annulment may require other forms of positive action, such as repealing any subordinate acts as may have been carried out under the auspices of the annulled act. If the act in question was annulled on procedural grounds such as failure to give reasons or failure to consult, there is usually nothing to stop the institution starting the process again, carrying out those procedures correctly, and then repassing the act in identical form, and it appears that in certain circumstances, if legal certainty allows, as in *Amylum* v *Council*,[137] that act could be retroactive in nature.

---

129 See Case 1/54, *France* v *High Authority* [1954] ECR 1, where Article 1 of Decision 2/54 of the High Authority was annulled. This case was followed by Case 2/54, *Italy* v *High Authority* [1954] ECR 37, Case 3/54, *ASSIDER* v *High Authority* [1954] ECR 63 and Case 4/54, *ISA* v *High Authority* [1954] ECR 91, where the applicants sought to challenge the same provision. In the first of those cases the Court held (at 55) that the provision 'cannot be formally annulled since it has already been annulled prior to the present judgment' and in the other two cases held that no decision was called for on that issue.

130 Case 81/71, [1973] ECR 575.

131 Case 59/81, [1982] ECR 3329. See also Case 56 and 58/64, *Consten and Grundig, op. cit.,* note 51.

132 See also Case 34/86, *Council* v *Parliament (Budget case)* [1986] ECR 2155; Case 264/82, *Timex* v *Council, op. cit.,* note 100.

133 Case 92/78, [1979] ECR 777, at 811.

134 Case 3/54, *ASSIDER* v *High Authority, op. cit,* note 129, and also Case 84/78, *Tomadini* v *Amministrazione delle Finanze dello Stato* [1979] ECR 1801, at 1813, which was an action for annulment of a regulation that had already been examined by the Court in Case 12/78, *Italy* v *Commission* [1979] ECR 1731.

135 Cases 142 and 156/84, *BAT and R.J. Reynolds* v *Commission* [1987] ECR 4487.

136 In Case 266/82, *Turner* [1984] ECR 10, the Court has extended the express permission granted to the Commission in Article 34 ECSC, allowing it a 'reasonable time' to conform with the ruling of nullity, to the EC Treaty which does not contain such a provision.

137 Case 108/81, [1982] ECR 3107.

Review for failure to act[138]

While the EC Treaty recognises that measures taken by the institutions should be subject to review and a remedy available to those affected by illegal measures, it also recognises that failure of the institutions to act should be addressed. This is covered by Article 175 which states:

> Should the Council or the Commission, in infringement of this Treaty, fail to act, the Member States and the other institutions of the Community may bring an action before the Court of Justice to have the infringement established.
>
> The action shall be admissible only if the institution concerned has first been called upon to act. If, within two months of being so called upon, the institution concerned has not defined its position, the action may be brought within a further period of two months.
>
> Any natural or legal person may, under the conditions laid down in the preceding paragraphs, complain to the Court of Justice that an institution of the Community has failed to address to that person any act other than a recommendation or an opinion.

This action against failure to act has seen relatively limited use, possibly due to the fact that the ECJ has been inclined to treat admissibility of actions very strictly.[139]

Privileged applicants

As with Article 173, Article 175 differentiates between a class of applicants with privileged status and a class with non-privileged status, although both must show that the inaction complained of relates to 'the omission of an act which is obligatory on the institution'.[140] Although the wording of Article 175(1) is different from that Article 173 in that 'Member States and the other institutions of the Community may bring an action', which would, on the face of it, appear to include the EP, there was again some debate as to the standing of the EP,[141] notably on the ground that the Parliament was meant to have only a political role within the Community.[142] However, when the Parliament brought an action in *Parliament* v *Council*[143] protesting the failure of the Council to adopt a measure on Community transport policy, the ECJ held that Article 175(1) included the Parliament and thus gave it the same right of action as the other institutions. The reasoning used in that case was similar to that later used in the *Chernobyl* case regarding the Parliament's standing under Article 173, in that the ECJ stated that the Parliament had to be able to exercise the same rights in this area as the other institutions, or there would be an imbalance between them that would be contrary to Article 4 of the Treaty. With regard to the political argument the ECJ stated that

> . . . the fact that the European Parliament is at the same time the Community institution whose task it is to exercise a political review of the activities of the Commission, and to a

---

138 Toth, 'The Law as it Stands on the Appeal for Failure to Act' [1975] LIEI 65.

139 Due, 'Legal Remedies for Failure of European Community Institutions to Act in Conformity with EEC Treaty Provisions' (1990–1) *Fordham International Law Journal* 341.

140 Case 6/70, *Borromeo Arese* v *Commission* [1970] ECR 815.

141 See Toth., *op. cit*, note 138.

142 *Ibid.*, at 76.

143 Case 13/83, *Common Transport Policy case*. [1985] ECR 1513. See Fennel, 'The Transport Policy Case' (1985) EL Rev 264.

certain extent those of the Council, is not capable of affecting the interpretation of the provisions of the Treaty on the rights of actions of the institutions.[144]

Parliament has however made only limited use of this right since that ruling, commencing only one other action, with regard to the failure of the Council to submit the 1988 draft budget to the Parliament within the time limit laid down in the Treaty.[145]

In this respect, after the decision in the *Les Verts* case and those following it,[146] there appears to be a compelling argument for the Parliament also to be subject to judicial review on the ground of inaction.[147] While there has yet to be a ruling by the ECJ on this matter, the ruling in the Transport case, in recognising the ability of the Parliament to bring an action against the Council or Commission for failure to act, would leave the Parliament in a superior position *vis-à-vis* those institutions, if they were unable in turn to bring an action against it. It would also be anomalous if, as appears to be the case under Article 175(3), natural and legal persons could bring an action against the Parliament when the Commission and Council could not. Such an omission would also seem to run counter to the rule of law argument used by the ECJ in *Les Verts*.[148] The TEU addresses this by amending Article 175(1) so as to include the Parliament with the Council and Commission, in more definite terms than at present. The European Central Bank is also given privileged standing, but only in those areas which lie 'within its field of competence'.[149]

Non-privileged applicants

Under Article 175(3), natural or legal persons have the right to bring an action on the ground that an institution has failed to address to them any act other than a recommendation or an opinion. This right to bring an action is somewhat more limited than that available to parties bringing an action under Article 175(1). This limitation takes the form of two requirements that must be shown by the applicant. First, that the act attacked falls within the category of legally binding acts listed in the Article[150] and, secondly, that the non-adopted act which it is claimed that the defendant institution should have adopted in order to fulfil its Treaty obligations, would have been addressed to the applicant had it in fact been adopted.[151] This latter requirement is stricter then the direct and individual concern test for Article 173 and has the effect of excluding those potential applicants who wish to complain about inaction with regard to another individual,[152] such as in circumstances where the

---

144 *Ibid.*, at 1588.

145 Case 377/87, *Parliament v Council* [1988] ECR 4017. See Bradley, 'The Variable Evolution of the Standing of the European Parliament in Proceedings Before the Court of Justice', *op. cit.*, note 21, at 39, and Bebr, 'The Standing of the European Parliament in the Community System of Legal Remedies: A Thorny Jurisprudential Development', *op. cit.*, note 19, at 173.

146 See pp 137–41.

147 See Minor, 'Further Skirmishes on Election Spending' (1987) 12 EL Rev 191, at 194.

148 See Bebr, 'The Standing of the European Parliament in the Community System of Legal Remedies: A Thorny Jurisprudential Development', *op. cit.*, note 19, at 179.

149 Article G(54) TEU.

150 See Case 15/70, *Chevally v Commission* [1970] ECR 975; Case 6/70, *Borromeo Arese v Commission, op. cit.*, note 140, where the applicants were attempting to obtain an opinion from the Commission on the issue of compatibility of a national law with the Treaty; and Case 182/80, *Gauff v Commission* [1982] ECR 799, where the applicant was asking the Commission to state whether or not it was on a 'blacklist' for Community contracts.

151 Which would exclude regulations as these are not addressed to individuals. Case 60/79, *Producteurs de Vins de Table et Vins de Pays v Commission* [1979] ECR 2429.

152 Case 15/71, *Mackprang v Commission* [1971] ECR 797.

Commission is perceived to be failing to take action under EC competition rules.[153] It has been suggested that this restriction is inconsistent with the purpose of Article 175 and that the direct and individual concern test as used in Article 173 would be more appropriate.[154]

There is some apparent academic disagreement as to how, and how far, the ECJ has been inclined to broaden the scope of Article 175(3). Schermers suggests that it should be seen in the same light as Article 173(3), as being an issue of direct and individual concern.[155] Others, however, see it not in terms of the ECJ applying a test of direct and individual concern but rather as granting standing in those circumstances where the applicant can show that he has a legal right to claim the adoption of an act.[156] Arnull, by contrast, holds to the strict interpretation.[157] Given the relatively consistent application by the ECJ of the 'unity principle'[158] which purports to link Articles 173 and 175 in order to create a complete system of Community judicial remedies, it would appear that Schermers's contention may well be the closest to the true attitude of the ECJ.

Procedure

In order for an applicant to bring proceedings under Article 175, he or she must first call upon the institution to act; once this has been done, the institution called upon to act must either do so, or define its position within two months.[159] The 'call', or 'invitation to act', must fulfil two criteria in that it must request the institution to act and make clear that this request is being made with possible Article 175 action in mind.[160]

Definition of position by an institution may simply take the form of deciding not to take an act and informing the applicant of that decision. In *Alfons Lütticke GmbH* v *Commission*[161] the ECJ held that the applicants, who had applied under both Article 175 and Article 173 in an attempt to get the Commission to bring an Article 169 action against the Federal Republic of Germany for breach of Community obligations, would be unsuccessful on both grounds. This was because the Commission had defined its position in the letter notifying the applicants that no action was to be taken, and that the decision in the letter, as it had no binding force upon the applicants, could not be annulled under Article 173.[162] The ECJ could also have held the action inadmissible as the Commission is granted a discretion whether to act under Article 169 and thus is under no obligation to begin proceedings.[163] The

153 Case 246/81, *Lord Bethell* v *Commission* [1982] ECR 2277.
154 Advocate General Dutheillet de Lamothe in Case 15/71, *Mackprang* v *Commission, op. cit.*, note 152, at 806 Brown and Jacobs, *The Court of Justice of the European Communities, op. cit.*, note 104, at 124.
155 Schermers and Waelbroeck, *op. cit.*, note 7, at 449.
156 Steiner, *Textbook on EEC Law*, 3rd edn, (1992), at 335.
157 Arnull, in Wyatt D. and Dashwood A., *European Community Law*, 3rd edn (1993), Chapter 5.
158 With The Exception Of The *Comitology* case where the Court held that the two articles should not necessarily be so linked.
159 Although Schermers and Waelbroeck, *op. cit.*, note 7, at 227 note that because the purpose of the action is to obtain an act, not censure the Council or Commission in

any way, failure to adopt that act or define a position within two months will be irrelevant if the institution does eventually act or define a position. See Case 75/69, *Hake Case* [1970] ECR 541, where the Court decided that the Commission, in acting after the time limit expired, had still negated the need for a ruling, but did however place all costs upon the Commission. See also Case 377/87, *Parliament* v *Council* [1988] ECR 4017.
160 Case 10 & 18/68, *Eridania* [1969] ECR 459; Case 84/82, *Germany* v *Commission* [1982] ECR 1451; Case 13/83, *Parliament* v *Council, op. cit.*, note 143.
161 Case 48/65, [1966] ECR 19.
162 See also Case 125/78, *GEMA* v *Commission* [1979] ECR 3173.
163 Case 247/87, *Star Fruit Company SA* v *Commission* [1989] ECR 291; Case C-87/89, *Sonito and others* v *Commission* [1990] ECR I-1981, at 2009.

ruling in *Lütticke* may, however, be contrasted with the position in *Fediol*,[164] where following the serving of notice upon the Commission under Article 175 by Fediol requesting the initiation of anti-dumping proceedings against Brazil, the Commission sent a letter to Fediol stating that no proceedings would be held. The ECJ allowed Fediol to challenge that decision under Article 173 in order to protect its procedural rights.

If the institution does decide to act, it is under no obligation to do so in the manner which the applicant has requested. In *Irish Cement Ltd* v *Commission*[165] the ECJ held that

> Article 175 refers to failure to act in the sense of failure to take a decision or to define a position, and not the adoption of a measure different from that desired or considered necessary by the persons concerned.

Norgetreide v *Commission*[166] appears to show that where an institution refuses to adopt an act requested, this will in effect be a definition of position acceptable to the ECJ for the purposes of Article 175. In this case the applicants sought to challenge the act of the Commission defining its position using Article 173. However, because the applicants were requesting an amendment of a regulation which could only be achieved by a legal act, which itself would be a regulation and thus of a general nature, they could not show the direct and individual concern required for Article 173 and were thus unable to overturn that act of definition of position.

It has been pointed out by Toth[167] that an institution's ability to overcome an Article 175 action by defining its position can create a situation where the institution is immune from judicial review on that issue. The other possible outcomes of a request to act – a positive response of adopting the act requested; a negative response of formal rejection of the act; and the adoption of an act different to that requested – are potentially open to challenge under Article 173. Where however, the institution defines its position, it generally cannot be challenged under either Article 173 or Article 175. This may be mitigated to some extent by the ECJ's requirements for a satisfactory definition of position. In the *Transport Policy* case the ECJ noted that the Council, in its reply to the letter from the EP calling upon it to act, had only stated what action it had already taken and failed to address the issue of whether it considered it had in fact failed to act. The reply also made no mention of the Council's viewpoint as to the measures that the Parliament alleged remained to be taken. This, the ECJ held, was not a satisfactory definition of position.

The consequences of a successful action

If the ECJ finds that an institution has failed to act, it will declare that failure to act to be contrary to the Treaty. It cannot carry out that act itself, nor can it require that the institution in default, when acting on the ECJ's decision as provided by Article 176, carry it out in a particular manner or to achieve a particular result. In the event of an institution still failing to take action, there is no sanction available, other than the possibility of another Article 175 action.

---

164 Case 191/82, *op. cit*, note 99.
165 Cases 166 and 220/86, [1988] ECR 6473, at 6503. See also Gravell, 'Article 173 and 175 in the Context of State Aid' (1989) 14 EL Rev 228 (note that the conclu-sion is somewhat scrambled); Case 8/71, *Deutsche Komponistenverband* v *Commission* [1971] ECR 705.
166 Case 42/71, [1972] ECR 105.
167 Toth, *op. cit.*, note 138, at 82.

Plea or exception of illegality

Failure to bring proceedings under Article 173 within the stipulated two-month time limit does not render a measure immune from attack. Article 184 EC states that:

> Notwithstanding the expiry of the period laid down in the third paragraph of Article 173, any party may, in proceedings in which a regulation of the Council or of the Commission is in issue, plead the grounds specified in the first paragraph of Article 173, in order to invoke before the Court of Justice the inapplicability of that regulation.

Thus while a measure may be immune from an action for nullification, any decision based on that measure may be attacked by a person affected by it on the grounds of illegality. The plea can, however, only be used indirectly. Thus, an individual bringing proceedings to question the validity of a decision may endeavour to do so by disputing the legality of the regulation under which it was made. The plea may not, however, be used directly to attack a regulation and thus cannot be used to ground an independent cause of action.[168] Article 184 proceedings, in effect, allow parties to challenge regulations indirectly at the time of their execution where they would not be able to challenge them directly when first promulgated.

In *Simmenthal* v *Commission*[169] the ECJ, in line with its position on Article 173, deviated from the literal text of the Treaty in holding that the plea of illegality, which according to Article 184 may only be invoked against regulations, was also applicable to other acts of the institutions which, although they were not in the form of a regulation, produced similar effects. It went on to state that natural and legal persons should thus be able to challenge these acts under Article 184 as they would be unable to do so under Article 173.

The ECJ's stance has led to a continuing debate over whether Member States may use Article 184 to attack a measure. In *Italy* v *Council and Commission*,[170] Advocate General Roemer, in his opinion, felt that the wide nature of the wording of the Article did not preclude the right of Member States to use it; and that Member States should be allowed that right because 'the defects by which a regulation may be vitiated frequently only appear in their full force when they are applied to particular cases'.[171] However, the ECJ was disinclined to explore the issue commenting only that 'under that Article, any party may, in the case of proceedings against a regulation, resort to the means provided in Article 173(1) to invoke the inapplicability of that regulation'.[172]

This apparent ability of Member States to invoke Article 184 was criticised by Bebr[173] on a number of grounds, the most convincing of which were that Member States were in a much stronger position than private individuals to have measures annulled under Article 173, and use of Article 184 would allow the avoidance of the time limits of Article 173. Barav,[174] on the other hand, was inclined to side with Advocate General Roemer. In later proceedings, *Commission* v *Belgium*,[175] the ECJ held that

---

168 Cases 31 and 33/62, *Wöhrmann* v *Commission* [1962] ECR 501, Case 33/80, *Albini* v *Council and Commission* [1981] ECR 2157. It has been suggested that UK lawyers might thus regard the use of Article 184 as being broadly similar to collateral challenge proceedings. This is a potentially misleading argument, given that collateral challenge proceedings may only be used as a defence to an action, which is not the case with Article 184 proceedings.
169 Case 92/78, [1979] ECR 777, at 800.

170 Case 32/65, [1966] ECR 389.
171 *Ibid.*, at 414.
172 *Ibid.*, at 409.
173 Bebr, 'Judicial Remedy of Private Parties against Normative Acts of the European Communities: The Role of the Exception of Illegality' (1966) 4 CML Rev 7.
174 Barav, 'The Exception of Illegality in Community Law: A Critical Analysis' (1974) 11 CML Rev 366.
175 Case 156/77, [1978] ECR 1881.

it is impossible for a Member State which has allowed the strict time limit laid down . . . in Article 173 to expire without contesting by the means available under that article, the legality of the Commission decision addressed to it, to be able to call into question that decision by means of Article 184 of the Treaty.

However, it is clear that the ruling in this case is by no means definitive, as it is capable of being interpreted in two very different ways. Lasok and Bridge,[176] for instance, are of the opinion that the impossibility of the use of Article 184 would be applicable to any act which a Member State could have attacked under Article 173; while Steiner,[177] on the other hand, is equally adamant that the case turns solely on its facts and does not therefore preclude Member States from using Article 184. Arnull[178] goes still further than Steiner and suggests that there is no reason why both the Member States and the institutions should not be able to use Article 184. To sum up the debate, there is some evidence that a Member State might be able to invoke the plea against a regulation, but it can clearly not invoke it against an individual decision addressed to it, and on the issue of directives Arnull suggests that following *Commission v Greece*[179] once the time limit for an Article 173 action has elapsed, these too cannot be challenged.[180] As yet the ECJ has either not been inclined, or not been asked, to give definitive rulings on these points.

However, in *BASF AG and Others v Commission*,[181] the Court of First Instance extended the ability to challenge where the time limits had expired, on the grounds that the measure in question in that case contained particularly serious and manifest defects and should therefore be held non-existent. In its judgment the Court of First Instance was of the opinion that where the issue of such defective measures is raised, it is in the public interest of the Community that they be examined by the Court, even if the Court has to raise the issue of its own accord.

The consequences of a successful plea

If the ECJ does accept the plea of illegality the regulation is not, as with Article 173, annulled. Instead the ECJ will declare it to be inapplicable with reference to the case before it. It is the decision which the parties are contesting based on that regulation that will be annulled. The regulation itself remains in force, as do all other decisions taken under it. That having been said, the fact that a decision taken under the regulation has been successfully challenged on the ground of illegality generally results in the Council or Commission replacing the regulation.

CONCLUSION

It is clear from the above discussion that the provisions for judicial review contained in the Treaty were by themselves inadequate, leaving, as they did, important gaps in the ability of

---

176 Lasok and Bridge, *Law and Institutions of the European Communities*, 4th edn (1987), at 280.
177 Steiner, *op. cit.*, note 156, at 345.
178 Arnull, *op. cit.*, note 157, at 155.
179 Case 226/87, [1988] ECR 3611.

180 Arnull, *op. cit.*, note 157, at 155.
181 Cases T-79/89, T-84–86/89, T-89/89, T-91-2/89, T-94/89, T-96/89, T-98/89, T-102/89, T-104/89, [1992] 4 CMLR 357. See Weatherill and Beaumont, *EC Law* (1993), at 232.

the ECJ to apply judicial review to certain proceedings of the institutions. It is equally clear, however, that the ECJ has been unwilling, primarily on the ground of ensuring the rule of law within the Communities, to allow those gaps to remain and that it has been capable of developing procedures to fill those gaps via its case law. The procedures chosen have not always met with unanimous support from academic writers, but nonetheless the necessity of adopting procedures of some kind appears to have been widely accepted. It is obvious from the more recent case law that judicial review of Community institution actions by the ECJ is still evolving, and that the ECJ has been willing to reconsider its decisions in earlier cases where following such decisions would impede the progress towards a coherent and seamless policy of judicial review.

It is to be hoped that the ECJ will either pull together the diverse strands of its case law regarding standing under Articles 173 and 175, so that developments in areas such as anti-dumping can be consistently applied and relied upon in all judicial review cases, or explicitly acknowledge that actions in those areas of Community activity are to be governed by different rules. If a distinction between those areas and a more general policy of judicial review is retained, it would be desirable if the areas in which those developments apply, and those where they do not, were to be defined in clearer terms than at present. As matters stand, in that there appear to be different tests for different areas of case law, the ability to obtain judicial review of the actions of the institutions will remain unclear, and thus unsatisfactory.

Further reading

Article 173

Arnull, A., 'Does the Court of Justice have Inherent Jurisdiction ?' (1990) 27 CML Rev 683.

Arnull, A., 'Challenging EC Anti-Dumping Regulations: the Problem of Admissibility' [1992] ECLR 73.

Arnull, A., 'Owning Up to Fallibility: Precedent and the Court of Justice' (1993) 30 CML Rev 247.

Bebr, G., 'The Standing of the European Parliament in the Community System of Legal Remedies: A Thorny Jurisprudential Development' (1990) 27 CML Rev 170.

Bradley, K., 'The Variable Evolution of the Standing of the European Parliament in Proceedings Before the Court of Justice' (1989) YEL 27.

Dashwood, A., 'The European Parliament and Article 173 EEC: The Limits of Interpretation' in White, R. and Smythe, B. (eds), *Current Issues in European and International Law* (London, 1990).

Greaves, R., 'Judicial Review of Anti-Dumping Cases by the European Court of Justice' [1985] ECLR 135.

Greaves, R., '*Locus Standi* under Article 173 EEC When Seeking Annulment of a Regulation' (1986) 11 EL Rev 119.

Mataraso, 'The Independent Importers Right of Review of Anti-dumping Regulations before the Court of Justice of the European Communities' (1989) 12 *Fordham International Law Journal* 682.

Rasmussen, H., 'Why is Article 173 Interpreted Against Private Plaintiffs' (1980) 5 EL Rev 122.

Toth, A.G., 'The Authority of Judgments of the European Court of Justice: Binding Force and Legal Effects' (1984) 4 YEL 1.

Article 175

Due, O., 'Legal Remedies for Failure of European Community Institutions to Act in Conformity With EEC Treaty Provisions' (1990–1) *Fordham International Law Journal* 341.

Toth, A.G., 'The Law as it Stands on the Appeal for Failure to Act' [1975] LIEI 65.

Article 184

Barav, A., 'The Exception of Illegality in Community Law: A Critical Analysis' (1974) 11 CML Rev 366.

Bebr, G., 'Judicial Remedy of Private Parties Against Normative Acts of the European Communities: The Role of the Exception of Illegality' (1966) 4 CML Rev 7.

CHAPTER 8

Enforcement of Community law

INTRODUCTION

The European Community could not function in its present form if Member States were allowed to infringe Community law with impunity, for instance, by refusing to implement a directive within the correct time period; or implementing national policy which contravenes a treaty obligation, such as imposing a limit on the free movement of persons. There are thus administrative and judicial procedures contained within the Treaty, designed to ensure that Member States heed their Community obligations. The procedures in question are to be found in Articles 169 and 170, Article 93(2), Article 100a(4), and Article 225.

Article 169 provides a three-stage procedure under which the Commission may press a Member State to comply with its obligations,[1] and Article 170 allows an action to be brought by another Member State, after the matter has been brought to the attention of the Commission, both parties have presented their arguments to the Commission, and the Commission has been given the opportunity to give a reasoned opinion.[2] Further to these provisions, the Commission or a Member State may derogate from the procedures provided in Article 169 and 170 in the following cases:

- where a Member State makes improper use of the ability to provide State aid – Article 93(2);
- where a Member State makes improper use of the powers provided in Article 223 concerning matters of national security and those in Article 224 concerning measures necessary in times of war, international tension and internal disturbance – Article 225; and
- where a Member State makes improper use of the derogation procedure provided by Article 100a(4), paragraph 1, concerning harmonisation of national laws – Article 100a(4), paragraph 3.

---

[1] Article 169:

If the Commission considers that a Member State has failed to fulfil an obligation under this Treaty, it shall deliver a reasoned opinion on the matter after giving the State concerned the opportunity to submit its observations.

If the State concerned does not comply with the opinion within the period laid down by the Commission, the latter may bring the matter before the Court of Justice.

[2] Article 170:

A Member State which considers that another Member State has failed to fulfil an obligation under this Treaty may bring the matter before the Court of Justice.

Before a Member State brings an action against another Member State for an alleged infringement of an obligation under this Treaty, it shall bring the matter before the Commission.

The Commission shall deliver a reasoned opinion after each of the States concerned has been given the opportunity to submit its own case and its observations on the other party's case both orally and in writing.

If the Commission has not delivered an opinion within three months of the date on which the matter was brought before it, the absence of such opinion shall not prevent the matter from being brought before the Court of Justice.

In practice, the Commission, pursuant to the role given to it under Article 155 as the primary guardian of the Treaty, has begun the majority of proceedings for breach of Community obligations, and brought all but one of the cases in this area, having taken over others initiated by Member States.[3]

As far as Articles 169 and 170 are concerned, the obligation that they refer to does not just mean a primary obligation under the Treaty, but also legislative acts adopted by the institutions, provisions in the Treaties of Accession, and provisions in treaties which the Community has concluded with third parties under Article 228, which states at paragraph (2) that 'Agreements . . . shall be binding on the institutions of the Community and on Member States'.[4] There is still some debate as to the status of both the general principles of law[5] and conventions agreed by the Member States under Article 220.[6]

It should be noted that the action is taken against the Member State and not against the national government. This in effect negates any defence that the matter is out of the hands of the government due to procedural provisions[7] or the actions of other national institutions such as the legislature, which was the defence raised by the Belgian government in *Commission* v *Belgium*.[8] The ECJ dismissed that argument, stating that

> . . . the liability of a Member State under Article 169 arises whatever the agency of the State whose action or inaction is the cause of the failure to fulfil its obligations, even in the case of a constitutionally independent institution.[9]

Procedure by the Commission under Article 169

The administrative or preliminary procedure

In practice, before initiating the formal Article 169 procedure, the Commission will first attempt an informal negotiated resolution to the problem. This informal procedure takes the form of the Commission notifying the Member State that it considers the Member State to be in breach of Community law and asking for its comments on the matter. This will normally be followed up by discussions between the Commission and representatives of the Member State. This informal warning is traditionally said to be effective in the majority of cases,

3 Case 141/78, *France* v *United Kingdom (Re Fishing Mesh)* [1979] ECR 2923 (discussed in detail below).
4 See Case 104/81, *Hauptzollampt Mainz* v *Kupferberg* [1982] ECR 3641, at 3662.
5 Dashwood and White, 'Enforcement actions under Articles 169 and 170' (1989) 14 EL Rev 388, propose at 390 that general principles of law have to be covered by Articles 169 and 170 as they 'are integral to the legal order established by the Communities'. See also Barav, 'Failure of Member States to fulfil their obligations under Community law' (1975) 12 CML Rev 369, and Mertens de Wilmars and Veroughstraete, 'Proceedings against Member States for failure to fulfil their obligations' (1970) 7 CML Rev 385. However, both Hartley, *The Foundations of European Community Law* (1988) and Schermers and Waelbrock *Judicial Protection in the*

European Communities, 4th edn (1987), remain unconvinced that a situation would arise where the matter would be at issue.
6 Hartley, *ibid.*, feels that they clearly do not fall within the scope of Article 169 action, while Dashwood and White, *op. cit.*, are more ambivalent. Both however quote the Community Patent Convention, which contains its own enforcement procedure and does not involve the Commission, as an example of a convention which is obviously outside the scope of Article 169 action.
7 Case 58/81, *Commission* v *Luxembourg* [1982] ECR 2175.
8 Case 77/69, [1970] ECR 237.
9 *Ibid.* at 243. Case 58/81, *Commission* v *Luxembourg*, *op cit*, note 7.

although there is some disagreement about this,[10] and in such cases it is not necessary to invoke the formal procedure. The length of time taken by the informal procedure may prove to be important in the later formal stages, should they be required. If the informal procedure has taken place over a lengthy period of time, short time periods in the formal proceedings may be more acceptable to the ECJ, as the Commission will have had the opportunity to make the Member State fully aware of the extent and implications of its breach.[11]

The formal procedure

If the Member State is not agreeable to a resolution of the issue at the informal stage, the Commission may begin the first of the three procedural stages contained in Article 169. This results in the Commission notifying the Member State, by letter of formal notice, that the Commission considers the Member State's position to be in breach of Community law and requesting that the Member State present its own observations regarding the matter. As this is only a request and not a demand, it has been held that the Member State is under no obligation to formally defend its position at this point in the proceedings.[12] However, the ECJ appears to be relatively strict with regard to the Commission's adherence to what the ECJ considers to be essential procedural requirements under Article 169;[13] certainly the formal notification has been held to be 'an essential formal requirement of the procedure under Article 169'.[14] This appears to be because the letter giving notice is 'intended to delimit the subject matter of the dispute and to indicate to the Member State which is invited to submit its observations the factors enabling it to prepare its defence'.[15] Thus, failure to give such notice or adequately to indicate the subject matter or extent of the breach alleged, means that the Member State will not be given a chance either to stop the infringing activity or to compose an adequate defence of the reasons why it is adopting such activity.

As far as the Commission is concerned, the letter also defines the scope of its case, as the ECJ will not allow it to include any further issues, either in its reasoned opinion[16] or in proceedings before the ECJ,[17] that were not originally contained in the letter sent to the

---

10 Brown and Jacobs, *The Court of Justice of the European Communities*, 3rd edn (1989), at 77, suggest that two out of three cases are settled in this manner. Audretsch, *Supervision in European Community Law*, 2nd edn (1986) suggests that the figure is up to 85 per cent. However, Weatherill and Beaumont, *EC Law* (1993) suggest that the figures from both the *Seventh Annual Report to the European Parliament on Commission Monitoring of the Application of Community Law 1989*, OJ 1990 C232/1 and the *Eighth Annual Report to the European Parliament on Commission Monitoring of the Application of Community Law 1990*, OJ 1991 C338/1 show a rather different picture, with a steadily increasing number of letters of formal notice being issued. In 1990, there were 1535 cases investigated by the Commission and 960 letters of formal notice. While the number of cases was comparable to the previous two years, the number of letters of formal notice had nearly doubled from 1988. It would therefore be probably fair to say that the number of cases settled at this stage is closer to 50 per cent than 85 per cent.
11 Contrast Case 85/85, *Commission v Belgium* [1986]

ECR 1149 with Case 293/85, *Commission v Belgium* [1988] ECR 305.
12 See Case 211/81, *Commission v Denmark* [1982] ECR 4547, at 4557.
13 For example, Case 7/69, *Commission v Italy* [1970] ECR 111, at 117 and Case 31/69, *Commission v Italy* [1970] ECR 25, where the Commission failed to allow the Member State to put forward its arguments on the complaints formulated.
14 Case 211/81, *Commission v Denmark, op. cit.*, note 12.
15 Audretsch, *op. cit.*, note 10, at 30
16 Case 51/83, *Commission v Italy* [1984] ECR 2793.
17 See Case 232/78, *Commission v France* [1979] ECR 2729, where the Commission amended its original conclusions during oral procedure at the Court, thus preventing the Member State from presenting its own conclusions during the earlier dialogue; Case 124/81, *Commission v UK* [1983] ECR 203, where the Commission extended its application during the written proceedings, again preventing the Member State from presenting its own conclusions at an earlier stage.

Member State. It is worth noting that while failure on the part of a Member State to avail itself of the opportunity to submit its observations is not of great importance, failure of the Member State to aid the Commission during an Article 169 investigation may leave that Member State open to a finding by the ECJ of breach of Article 5 of the Treaty.[18]

After the Member State has been given a reasonable period of time in which to reply to the Commission's formal letter[19] – a period of time in which there may well be further negotiations between the Member State and the Commission – the Commission will then decide whether to present a reasoned opinion on the matter. There has, in the past, been academic disagreement about whether the Commission was obliged to present a reasoned opinion in every circumstance, or whether the matter was left to its discretion. This argument was sparked by the potentially contradictory wording of the two paragraphs of Article 169. The first paragraph states that the Commission 'shall deliver a reasoned opinion', but the second paragraph states that the Commission 'may bring the matter before the Court of Justice'. It appears that contemporary thinking is that it would be illogical to force the Commission to produce a reasoned opinion if it does not, at the end of the procedure, intend to press ahead with an application to the ECJ.[20]

The reasoned opinion, if forthcoming, should provide: the legal grounds and submissions that the Commission will be seeking to rely upon should the case need to go before the ECJ; the measures the Commission feels should be taken to end the breach;[21] and a time limit for the Member State to comply. The legal grounds and submissions presented in the reasoned opinion may not afterwards be changed if the Commission decides to place an application before the ECJ with respect to that case.[22] As the name suggests, the reasoned opinion must be just that, and there has been some disagreement as to what the Commission must do to show reasoning.[23] In *Commission v Italy (The Pigmeat Case)*[24] the ECJ held that, 'the opinion referred to in Article 169 of the Treaty must be considered to contain a sufficient statement of reasons to satisfy the law when it contains – as it does in this case – a coherent statement of the reasons which led the Commission to believe that the State in question has failed to fulfil an obligation under the Treaty'.[25] This appears to be the line followed in contemporary case law.

18 Greece appears to be a particularly persistent offender in this regard. See Case 240/86, *Commission v Greece* [1988] ECR 1835; Case 272/86, *Commission v Greece* [1988] ECR 4875; Case C-35/88, *Commission v Greece* [1990] 1 ECR 3125. Weatherill and Beaumont, *op. cit.*, note 10, at 169, point out that in Case 240/86, Greece was found by the ECJ not to be in breach of its obligations in the main action, only in its continued non co-operation with the Commission.
19 There is no fixed time for reply, and what is considered 'reasonable' will vary with the circumstances of the case, i.e., where it is imperative to prevent a continuing serious breach the time will, of necessity, be fairly short. Audretsch, *op. cit.*, note 10, at 26, states that the standard period is 30 days, but that in urgent circumstances this may be reduced to a little as 3 to 10 days.
20 Contrast Evans, 'The Enforcement Procedure of Article 169: Commission Discretion' (1979) 4 EL Rev 442, at 444, with Wyatt and Dashwood, *European Community Law*, 3rd Edn (1993), at 112. Audretsch, *op. cit.* note 10, at 49, suggests that even should an individual or a Member State be inclined to press the Commission

for a reasoned opinion, there is no legal (as opposed to political) procedure by which this could be obtained. This is because, first, the measures adopted by the Commission in Article 169 proceedings do not constitute binding measures and, secondly, the Commission has a discretion as to whether to proceed in any given instance which means that no action under Article 175 can be taken against it. See the sections in Chapter 7 above on Article 173 and Article 175 procedure, especially Case 48/65, *Alfons Lütticke GmbH v Commission* [1966] ECR 19 and Case 247/87, *Star Fruit v Commission* [1989] ECR 291.
21 Case 7/61, *Commission v Italy* [1961] ECR 317, at 334.
22 Case 186/85, *Commission v Belgium* [1987] ECR 2029, at 2051; Case 290/87, *Commission v The Netherlands* [1989] ECR 3083, at 3103.
23 See Audretsch, *op. cit.*, note 10, at 46.
24 Case 7/61, [1961] ECR 317.
25 Ibid., at 327. See also Case 325/82, *Commission v Germany* [1984] ECR 777, at 793.

If the Member State acts upon the measures suggested by the Commission with regard to ending the breach, it must bear in mind that the Commission is not the final arbiter of the rights and duties of the Member State. Thus, the fact that the Member State has acted upon the measures that the Commission has proposed in a reasoned decision may not be used as a reason to prevent future parties from claiming that it is still in breach of Community law.[26]

As far as the time limits for the Member State to comply with the Commission's opinion are concerned, the time limit cannot be varied by the ECJ[27] but, as noted above, the ECJ will have regard both to the extent of the informal consultation and the time between the delivery of the letter of notification and the reasoned opinion itself in determining whether the Commission has allowed a reasonable period of time. Very short periods of time for compliance are generally frowned upon by the ECJ, and if found unreasonable may result in a following application to the ECJ being ruled as inadmissible.[28] Generally, if requested at an early stage, the Commission will extend time limits set under this procedure, notably where there are procedural limitations and delays in the Member State's legislature.

Time limits are also used by the ECJ to determine a cut off point for the purposes of proceedings before it. This will occur in those cases where the Member State has complied with the opinion, but after the time limit has expired, and the Commission has decided to proceed with the application. This may be important for a variety of reasons, not least in establishing a time frame for possible later proceedings including liability for damages on the part of the Member State.[29] A high proportion of cases which have entered the formal process end at this stage.

The judicial procedure

If the Member State is still unwilling to recognise and correct the breach of Community law, the next step is for the Commission to bring the matter before the ECJ. Thus, the final step in the full Article 169 procedure would normally be the judgment of the ECJ.[30] As already discussed, it appears that the Commission has a discretion at all stages of the Article 169 procedure as to whether or not to continue, and this is true of the judicial stage of proceedings. Even at this late stage it is not too late for the Member State to correct the breach, and cases are often brought by the Commission which are then settled during the proceedings, with the result that the ECJ is not obliged to pass judgment.[31] With regard to the application procedure, the ECJ has stated on a number of occasions that given the wide discretion granted to the Commission under Article 169 regarding the manner and speed with which breaches of the Treaty by the Member State are to be eliminated, there is effectively

---

26 Cases 142 & 143/80, *Amministrazioni delle Finanze dello Stato* v *Essevi and Salongo* [1981] ECR 1413, at 1433.

27 Case 28/81, *Commission* v *Italy* [1981] ECR 2577, at 2582; Case 29/81, *Commission* v *Italy* [1981], 2585, at 2591.

28 See, for example, Case 74/82, *Commission* v *Ireland* [1984] ECR 317, where a period of just five days was viewed with some disapproval by the Court, although it let the application stand.

29 Case 39/72, *Commission* v *Italy* [1973] ECR 101, at 117. Note also, Joined Cases C-6/90 and C-9/90, *Francovich and Bonifaci* v *Italian State* [1991] 1 ECR 5403.

30 Although as noted below, some States require more persuading than others.

31 See Weatherill and Beaumont, *op. cit.*, note 10, at 172 for statistics. However, as noted above, once the time limit in the reasoned opinion is passed the Commission may decide to press ahead with the case, regardless of a change of heart on the part of the Member State, e.g., Case 7/61, *Commission* v *Italy* [1961] ECR 317, where the Court held that the Commission was entitled to continue even where compliance by the Member State had been achieved. This is often seen as serving to clarify the law for the other Member States.

no time limit within which the Commission must bring its case before the ECJ.[32] Thus the only condition for bringing such an action is that the time limit set in the reasoned opinion must have expired.

When the Commission brings its action before the ECJ, it must ensure that its complaint remains within the scope set out in its letter of formal notice, and that the legal grounds raised are those set out within its reasoned opinion. Failure to observe these limits to the action will, as already seen, result in the ECJ rejecting the application.[33] On the other hand, the application must not be too sparse. An application which refers only to the letter of formal notice and reasoned opinion without the exact grounds for the application and further explanation of the surrounding circumstances will also probably fail.[34]

When an action is brought, the Member State and the other institutions may intervene to support or reject the submission or order of one of the parties before the ECJ under Article 37 of the Statute of the ECJ;[35] however, private parties may not.

Over the years, Member States have been increasingly imaginative in their attempts to construct successful defences to Article 169 actions. However, the ECJ has rarely looked favourably upon such defences.[36] A commonly argued defence is that the Member State concerned is hampered in its attempts to remedy the breach by constitutional, institutional or administrative difficulties. However, as noted in the Introduction to this chapter, in an Article 169 action the Commission and ECJ are concerned with the compliance of the Member State *in toto*, not just with the compliance of the national government.[37] Thus in *Commission v Belgium*,[38] when the Belgian government, faced with an action for Treaty violation on the grounds of breach of Article 95, argued that it had attempted to remedy the breach but that this had been delayed by the Belgian Parliament, a body which the government had no power to order to pass the necessary legislation, the ECJ held that this was no defence. Italy, with its turbulent post-war political scene has had particular problems in this respect.[39] A similar attitude has been taken to delays in implementing or enforcing Community law purportedly caused by problems with trade unions[40] and autonomous regional institutions.[41] It has been suggested that an Article 169 action could also be brought in the event that a Member State court fails to comply with its obligations under the Treaty, although reservations have been

32 Case 7/68, *Commission v Italy* [1968] ECR 423, at 428; Case 7/71, *Commission v France* [1971] ECR 1003, at 1016.

33 See above, at note 22.

34 Case C-347/88, *Commission v Greece* [1990] 1 ECR 4747.

35 See, for example, Case C-280/89, *Re British Fishing Boats: EC Commission (Spain intervening) v Ireland* [1993] 1 CMLR 273 (the Court granted Spain leave to intervene in support of the order sought by the Commission); Case C-246/89, *Re Nationality of Fishermen: EC Commission (Spain intervening) v United Kingdom (Ireland intervening)* [1991] 3 CMLR 706 (the Court granted leave to the Kingdom of Spain to intervene in support of the form of order sought by the Commission and to Ireland to intervene in support of the form of order sought by the United Kingdom).

36 Weatherill and Beaumont, *op. cit.*, note 10, at 172, note that fewer than one in ten cases brought before the Court result in a successful outcome for the Member

State concerned. Given the extensive pre-judicial procedure, this can hardly be surprising.

37 Case 77/69, *Commission v Belgium* [1970] ECR 237, at 243; although Case 16/69, *Commission v Government of the Italian Republic* [1969] ECR 377 is a lone exception to this rule. It is suggested by Hartley, *op. cit.*, note 5, at 289 and Schermers, *op. cit.*, note 5, that this is in fact a mistake, an assumption seemingly borne out by the fact that the Court in its judgment refers to the 'Italian Republic' and not the 'Italian Government'.

38 Case 77/69, [1970] ECR 237.

39 See, for example, Case 28/81, *Commission v Italy* [1981] ECR 2577; Case 91/79, *Commission v Italy* [1980] ECR 1099.

40 Case 128/78, *Commission v United Kingdom* [1979] ECR 419 (use of tachographs).

41 Case 1/86, *Commission v Belgium* [1987] ECR 2797 (water pollution measures); Cases 227–30/85, *Commission v Belgium* [1988] ECR 1 (environmental measures).

expressed about the desirability of such action.[42] It also appears that where national legislation is absent[43] or violates Community directives,[44] the fact that the local or regional authorities have the ability to implement the necessary local legislation is inadequate to meet the requirements of Community law.

An interesting defence was run by the French government in the *French Merchant Seamen* case.[45] Here certain provisions of the French Maritime Code were clearly in breach of Community law in as much as they discriminated between French workers and workers of other nationalities in certain jobs. However, before the ECJ, the French government argued that as, in practice, the code was not enforced by its officials, the national legislation did not require amendment, being clearly inapplicable.[46] The ECJ, noting that the position in French law was rendered confusing by this state of affairs, especially for foreign nationals, disagreed with that interpretation, stating that enforcement by administrative practices was not sufficient for compliance with Community law.

Force majeure has also been argued on a number of occasions.[47] Possibly the most unconvincing attempt was that used in *Commission v Italy*,[48] where the Italian government defended its non-implementation of a Community directive by pointing to the fact that the data processing centre that was to have provided for the implementation of the directive had been bombed. The ECJ felt that a bombing could be safely considered *force majeure* and thus might have been a usable defence in this case, but then went on to point out that the resulting delay of four and a half years was perhaps rather longer than reasonable, even in those circumstances. Thus the utility of such an event in raising a defence of *force majeure* obviously decreases over time.

Member States have also argued that the measures they had adopted which the Commission alleged breached their Treaty obligations were necessary because of a failure by the Community institutions to comply with their obligations, or a failure on the part of another Member State. In *Commission v Belgium and Luxembourg*[49] the two governments argued that the only reason that they were in breach of Community law was that the Commission had failed to adopt certain measures that it was entitled to so do. The ECJ answered this argument by stating that it was based on a false interpretation of Community law. It did not just create the type of reciprocal obligations which in

> international law allows a party, injured by the failure of another party to perform its obligations, to withhold performance of its own . . . this relationship between the obligations of the parties cannot be recognised under Community law . . . the Treaty is not limited to creating reciprocal obligations between the different natural and legal persons to whom it is applicable, but establishes a new legal order which governs the powers, rights and obligations of the said persons, as well as the necessary procedures for taking

42 See Weatherill and Beaumont, *op. cit.*, note 10, at 173; Wyatt and Dashwood, *op. cit.*, note 20, at 117; Dashwood and White, *op. cit.*, note 5, at 391; and the Opinion of Advocate General Warner in Case 9/75, *Meyer-Burckhardt v Commission* [1975] ECR 1171, at 1187.

43 Case 96/81, *Commission v The Netherlands* [1982] ECR 1791.

44 Case C-157/89, *Commission v Italy* [1991] 1 ECR 57.

45 Case 167/73, *Commission v France* [1974] ECR 359.

46 An argument apparently based on the concept of direct effect. See Steiner, *Textbook on EEC Law*, 3rd edn

(1992), at 312; also Case 102/79, *Commission v Belgium* [1980] ECR 1473; contrast these with Case 29/84, *Commission v Germany* [1986] 3 CMLR 579; but note the more recent decision in Case 168/85, *Commission v Italy* [1986] ECR 2945.

47 For a general discussion of the use of *force majeure* as a defence, see Magliveras, 'Force Majeure' in Community Law' (1990) 15 EL Rev 460.

48 Case 101/84, *The Traffic Statistics Case* [1986] 2 CMLR 352.

49 Joined Cases 90 and 91/63, [1964] ECR 625.

cognisance of and penalising any breach of it. Therefore, except where expressly provided, the basic concept of the Treaty requires that the Member State shall not take the law into their own hands. Therefore the fact that the Council failed to carry out its obligations cannot relieve the defendants from carrying out theirs.

Likewise, in *Commission v France*[50] the ECJ held that the fact that the belief that a Member State had failed to fulfil its obligations did not justify another Member State breaching Community law in order to correct the perceived effect of the first breach. The ECJ noted that the Treaty provides mechanisms, such as those contained in Article 169 and Article 170, for the very purpose of addressing those problems.

In enforcement actions under Article 169, the Commission bears the burden of proof and a Member State can successfully defend against an action for breach of Community obligations by showing that the Commission cannot actually prove that the alleged breach took place, or that the Member State was in fact to blame.[51]

Action against Member States by Member States under Article 170

As noted above, Member States have very rarely brought cases concerning failure to fulfil Community obligations under Article 170. They prefer instead, it seems, to allow the Commission to bring the cases, and then to intervene in the case when the matter comes before the ECJ. However, in *France v United Kingdom (Re Fishing Mesh)*[52] the French government brought a successful case against the United Kingdom with regard to an Order in Council which purported to set minimum sizes for the mesh in fishing nets.

The action arose after a French trawler master was convicted of using nets within UK fishery limits which were of a smaller size than the limits set. The French government claimed that the UK's Order in Council ignored the EC Council's Hague Resolution of 1976 which said that until the implementation of common Community measures Member States could adopt unilateral measures in the area of fishery, but only if they first consulted the Commission and sought its approval. In this the French government was supported by the Commission, which stated that the UK government had also disregarded Article 3 of Council Regulation 101/76/EEC which in laying down a common structural policy for the fishing industry required Member States to give prior notice of any alterations to fishery rules. The ECJ held that by not notifying both the other Member States and the Commission of the measure to be adopted, and in failing to seek the approval of the Commission, the UK had failed to fulfil its obligations under Article 5 EC, Annex VI of the Hague Treaty and Articles 2 and 3 of Regulation 101/76/EEC.

Article 93(2) actions concerning State aids[53]

Articles 92 to 94 of the Treaty are concerned with the provision of aid by Member States to 'certain undertakings' or 'certain goods'. The concern of the Community is to prevent such

50 Case 232/78, [1979] ECR 2729.
51 Case 290/87, *Commission v The Netherlands* [1989] ECR 3083.
52 Case 141/78, *op. cit.*, note 3.
53 See Audretsch, *op. cit.*, note 10, at 198–223; Dashwood, 'Control of State Aids in the EEC: Prevention and Cure under Article 93' (1975) CML Rev 43; Gilmour,

'The Enforcement of Community Law by the Commission in the Context of State Aids: The Relationship between Articles 93 and 169 and the Choice of Remedies' (1981) 18 CML Rev 63; Slot, 'Procedural Aspects of State Aids: The Guardian of Competition versus the Subsidy Villains' (1990) 27 CML Rev 741.

aid from distorting or threatening to distort Community markets with the resultant effect on intraCommunity trade.

The Article 93 procedure effectively distinguishes between two types of State aid: (i) new State aids and alterations to existing State aids that have been notified to the Commission; and (ii) new State aids and alterations to existing State aids that have not been notified to the Commission. However, the wording of the Article is far from precise, which can lead to procedural confusion.[54]

Article 93(1) outlines the responsibility of the Commission to ensure that such aids (including existing aids) are kept under review and to advise the Member State as to particular measures required. Article 93(2) is concerned with the enforcement of Community policy in this area, and the first part contains a derogation from the procedures laid down in Articles 169 and 170. It should be noted that the existence of this procedure does not render it compulsory for the Commission to use Article 93 instead of Article 169 in all circumstances where there may be evidence of State aid. Indeed, the ECJ stated in *Commission* v *Greece* that

> the appropriate procedure for obtaining a declaration that the rules of the common organisation of the markets have been infringed is the procedure for a declaration against Member States under Article 169 of the Treaty. Although, . . . Article 93(2) of the Treaty set up a procedure specifically adapted to the special problems created by State aid with regard to competition in the Common Market the existence of that procedure in no way prevents the compatibility of an aid scheme in relation to Community rules other than those contained in Article 92 from being assessed under the procedure provided for in Article 169.[55]

The derogation allows for a slimmed down procedure, whereby the Commission, after notifying the parties involved and requesting their comments,[56] may move directly to a decision that the relevant State aid should be abolished or altered within a set period of time.

Failure by the Commission to follow the correct procedure under Article 93(2), especially where it then requires the Member State to recover the aid given from the beneficiaries, will probably lead to the ECJ striking the Commission decision down. This occurred in *British Aerospace plc and Rover Group Holdings plc* v *Commission*,[57] where the Commission sought to compel the British government to recover from British Aerospace £44.4 million which the Commission deemed to be illegal aid. That decision was adopted without following the procedures laid down in Article 93(2), and without giving British Aerospace or Rover an opportunity to present their views. The ECJ held:

> Where the Commission has issued a decision authorising State aid, subject to conditions, and later concludes that certain governmental concessions to the same beneficiaries constitute State aids which were not authorised by and which breached the conditions laid down in the earlier decision, it has two remedies. In so far as there was a breach of the conditions and terms of the earlier decision, the Commission may refer the matter directly

---

54 See Flynn, 'State Aid and Self Help' [1983] EL Rev 297, at 299.
55 Case C-35/88, [1992] 1 CMLR 548. Here the Court also referred to the following cases: Case 72/79, *Commission* v *Italy* [1980] ECR 1411; Case 290/83, *Commission* v *France* [1985] ECR 439.

56 This involves not just the Member State but also the undertakings affected by the measure – see Case 59/79, *Producteurs de vins de table et vin de pays* v *Commission* [1979] ECR 2425.
57 Case C-292/90, [1992] 1 CMLR 853.

to the European Court under Article 93(2)(ii) EEC, by-passing the procedures for an Article 169 action. On the other hand, in so far as there was a new aid which had not been examined in the procedure leading up to the earlier decision, the Commission must issue a decision following the full procedure laid down in Article 93(2)(i) EEC, which includes a hearing of the interested parties. But it is not entitled merely to issue a decision to the Member State requiring it to recover money allegedly constituting State aid in breach of the earlier decision, without following the procedure of Article 93(2)(i) and without giving the beneficiaries an opportunity to be heard.[58]

If the Commission follows the correct procedure and the Member State does not carry out the required action within the time limit set, the Commission, or any other interested State, may refer the matter to the ECJ directly.

The second part of Article 93(2) concerns the procedure by which a Member State may apply to the Council to have the aid in question declared compatible with the common market, thereby derogating from Article 92 and legislation under Article 94. The Council's decision in this matter must be unanimous. In the event of a Member State applying for such a derogation, any Commission action already taking place under Article 93(2) will be suspended until the Council has reached a decision or until three months has passed without a Council decision.

Article 93(3) states that all new or substantially altered State aid plans must be submitted to the Commission for comments. Once notified, the Commission has two months to decide whether or not to begin the Article 93(2) procedure,[59] during which period the Member State may not implement its proposed measures (the stand-still clause). When that period is over,[60] if the Commission has not submitted comment or begun action under Article 93(2), the Member State may proceed with the implementation of the State aid. In the event that an Article 93(2) action is begun, the stand-still clause remains in effect. If the Member State proceeds with the State aid without waiting for either the Article 93(2) or the Article 93(3) procedure to conclude, the Commission may issue an interim order suspending its implementation. If the Member State fails to heed this interim order within the time limit set by the Commission, it may open proceedings before the ECJ.[61]

Non-notification does not mean that the State aid is automatically deemed to be incompatible with the common market.[62] However, Article 93(3) applies equally to non-notified aids as it does to notified aids, thus the Commission review and the stand-still procedure apply, but it seems that the two-month rule for a Commission comment or decision to implement Article 93(2) action will not.[63] Failure to notify the Commission of a State aid does not prevent the Commission beginning Article 93(2) proceedings, and the Commission need not fix a time limit for compliance by the Member State in such circumstances.[64] Interim orders may again be applied, here to make the Member State

---

[58] *Ibid.*, at 873.

[59] Case 120/73, *Lorenz v Germany* [1973] ECR 1471.

[60] It appears that there is a deal of controversy over when the two months begins to run. The Commission seems to proceed on the understanding that it begins to run from the point at which the Commission has received all the necessary information, see Case 84/82, *Commission v Germany* [1984] ECR 1451, and Slot, *op. cit.*, note 53, at 745.

[61] Case C-142/87, *Belgium v Commission* [1990] ECR 959.

[62] Case C-301/87, *France v Commission* [1990] 1 ECR 307.

[63] Slot, *op. cit.*, note 53, at 751.

[64] Case 173/73, *Italy v Commission* [1974] ECR 709, at 717, but in such cases there are no time limits and the stand-still clause operates until the Commission makes a decision (see below). See *Agence Europe* 5367 9 Nov. 1990, at p. 10 for Commission procedure in such cases, also Slot, *op. cit.*, note 53, at 745.

suspend the aid and supply the necessary information for the Commission to consider the legality of the aid.

Commission decisions under the Article 93(2) procedure must be made within a reasonable time. In *RSV* v *Commission*,[65] which involved a delay of 26 months, the court held that the delay 'could in the case in point establish a legitimate expectation on the applicant's part so as to prevent the Commission from requiring the Netherlands authorities to order the refund of the aid' and struck down the repayment requirement. This should, however, be contrasted with *Re Aid to Eni-Lanerossi: Italy (Spain intervening)* v *Commission*,[66] where a delay of 55 months was held not to establish a legitimate expectation because the Italian government failed to notify the Commission of its action in providing further State aid beyond that authorised, for the undertakings affected, and indeed had stated at an earlier date that it did not intend to provide them with further aid. It also constantly asked for further time to reply to the Commission's requests for information, and some relevant information only four days before the final decision. The ECJ held:

> When a Member State which grants aid contrary to the duty of notification laid down in Article 93(3) EEC subsequently displays reluctance to provide the appropriate information to the Commission, it is itself responsible for prolonging the examination procedure; it cannot therefore rely on the length of that procedure as a ground for a legitimate expectation regarding the compatibility of the aid in question with the Common Market.[67]

If the Commission decides that the State aid is compatible with the Treaty, that decision may be challenged under Article 173.[68] Individuals who can show that they are adversely affected by proposed or implemented aids, and who play a clear role in the Commission's Article 93(2) procedure, are likely to have standing,[69] as are those who would have benefited from a State aid which the Commission has decided against.[70] If the challenge is successful and the Commission decision annulled,[71] it seems likely that the stand-still clause will be replaced from the date of the ECJ's judgment.[72]

If the Commission decision under Article 93(2) is that the aid granted by a Member State should be abolished or amended, notification of this decision will be published in the L series of the Official Journal. Weatherill and Beaumont note that there is no such publication procedure for those decisions which permit State aids, and point out that this is an additional handicap for those adversely affected by the decision and who might want to challenge it under Article 173, as such a challenge must be begun within two months of the decision.[73]

As noted above, the Commission is able to force repayment of illegal aid. This can be achieved for both notified and non-notified aid. Such action may appear to have the effect of wiping out the unfair advantage granted to the undertaking concerned. However, whilst the ECJ has stated that with regard to such recovery the Commission must consider whether it is

65 Case 223/85, [1987] ECR 4617.

66 Case C-303/88, [1993] 2 CMLR 1.

67 *Ibid.*, at 56. This followed the judgment in Case C-5/89, *Commission* v *Germany* [1990] ECR I-3437, where the ECJ emphasised that national authorities could not be allowed to rely on their own unlawful conduct in order to deprive decisions taken by the Commission under Articles 92 and 93 of their effectiveness.

68 Cases 166/86 and 220/86, *Irish Cement Ltd* v *Commission* [1988] ECR 6473.

69 Case 169/84, *Compagnie Française de l'Azote SA* v *Commission (Cofaz I)* [1986] ECR 391, at 408.

70 Case 730/79, *Philip Morris Holland* v *Commission* [1980] ECR 2671.

71 See, for example, Case C-169/84, *Société CdF Chimie Azote et Fertilisants SA* v *Commission* (Cofaz II) [1992] 1 CMLR 177.

72 Slot, *op. cit.*, note 53, at 750.

73 Weatherill and Beaumont, *op. cit.*, note 10, at 184.

in fact possible for the Member State to recover the illegal aid,[74] issues such as whether repayment would drive the recipient of the aid into bankruptcy have been held not, in and of themselves, enough to prevent recovery,[75] and this suggests that the recovery procedure is designed more to be a procedural consequence of breach than any levelling mechanism between competitors.[76]

Article 225 actions

A further derogation from Articles 169 and 170 can be found in Article 225 EC, which is designed to limit the potential use of Articles 223 and 224 which are concerned with the related issues of national and international security.[77] Under Article 223, Member States may withhold information which may be detrimental to their security interests,[78] and may take such measures as they deem necessary for national security purposes, to protect the production of, and trade in, arms, munitions and war materials.[79] Under Article 224 Member States are required to consult each other in order that the common market is not unduly affected by any measures that Member States may have to take in the event of serious internal disturbances, war, threat of war, etc. The first paragraph of Article 225 requires the Commission to examine if measures taken under Articles 223 and 224 can be adjusted to conform with the Treaty. The second paragraph states that the Commission or any Member State may bring a case before the ECJ directly, where they consider that another Member State has made improper use of the powers granted under Articles 223 and 224. In such a case the hearing would be held *in camera*. So far there has been no information released as to whether consultation under Article 224 has ever occurred; the same is true of examinations by the Commission under Article 225(1). There have been no applications to the ECJ under Article 225(2).[80]

Article 100a(4) actions

The final derogation from Articles 169 and 170 is found in Article 100a(4) of the Treaty.[81] Under Article 100a, the Council may derogate from the unanimous vote required under Article 100, in those matters where measures are being taken to approximate provisions in the Member State regarding the establishment and functioning of the internal market, and may instead adopt measures by a qualified majority.[82] Member States are permitted to derogate from the harmonised position in certain circumstances, if the derogations are notified to the Commission[83] and have been verified by the Commission as not being

---

[74] Case 52/84, *Commission* v *Belgium* [1986] ECR 89.
[75] *Ibid.*; Case 63/87, *Commission* v *Greece* [1988] ECR 2875.
[76] See Wyatt and Dashwood, *op. cit.*, note 20, at 541; also Case C-142/87, *Re Tubemeuse: Belgium* v *Commission* [1990] ECR 1005.
[77] Flynn, 'How well will Article 100a(4) work? A comparison with Article 93' (1987) 24 CML Rev 689, at 692.
[78] Article 223(1)(a) EC.
[79] Article 223(1)(b) EC.
[80] References to it have been made in Case 6/64, *Costa* v *ENEL* [1964] ECR 585, at 594, and in the Advocate General's Opinion in Case 222/84, *Johnston* v *Chief*

Constable of the Royal Ulster Constabulary [1986] ECR 1651, at 1654.
[81] Article 100a was added by Article 18 of the SEA, and Article 100a (1) amended by Article G(22) TEU.
[82] Subject to the provisions in Article 189B.
[83] Article 100a(4), paragraph 1:
 If, after the adoption of a harmonisation measure by the Council acting by a qualified majority, a Member State deems it necessary to apply national provisions on grounds of major needs referred to in Article 36, or relating to protection of the environment or the working environment, it shall notify the Commission of these provisions.

arbitrary or a restriction on trade.[84] However, the Commission or any Member State may bring a case before the ECJ directly, where they consider that another Member State has made improper use of the derogations permitted in Article 100a(4). At the present time, as with Article 225, which it was clearly modelled on, Article 100a(4) has not led to any actions before the ECJ.[85]

Failure to fulfil Community obligations

In the event that the Commission's contentions are sustained by the ECJ in an Article 169 action, the Member State will be found to be in breach of its duties under the Treaty, and Article 171 of the Treaty will thus apply.[86] This judgment is declaratory in nature and there is no penalty, either for the initial breach or to ensure that the judgment is enforced. Nor can the ECJ order the Member State to engage or desist in a particular course of action. There has also been, as yet, no attempt by the ECJ to set a precise period of time for the Member States during which they must take the necessary steps to comply with a judgment, although very long periods of time have come in for judicial criticism in Article 171 actions.[87] Despite this, it is usual at this stage of proceedings for the recalcitrant Member State to be persuaded to take the necessary steps to remedy the breach. However, this is not always the case and there are a number of instances of Member States being repeatedly brought before the ECJ due to failure to take corrective action on a particular matter. An example of this is the Italian government's three visits to the ECJ regarding a tax on the export of art treasures, held three times by the ECJ to be in breach of Article 16 of the Treaty.[88]

Prior to the TEU, the limited utility of the Article 169 procedure in cases of concerted breach of the Treaty was shown up by the fact that in such circumstances the only remedy open to the Commission was to begin another round of infringement proceedings encompassing both the original breach of the Treaty and the failure to comply with the ECJ's ruling under Article 171. Towards the end of the 1980s, there was a significant rise in both the number of declaratory judgments that had not been complied with, and the number of secondary proceedings[89] that the Commission had had to initiate. This was partly due to the increasing number of initial actions taken by the Commission, which had become more aggressive in its pursuit of defaulting Member States and in so doing had begun to discover more of the issues over which Member States were unprepared to co-operate fully with the Community. This led to worries that the Article 169 procedure was simply not having the required effect of ensuring the conformity of Community law across all Member States. The result of this concern is that the TEU has amended Article 171 by adding a second

---

84 Article 100a(4), paragraph 2:
  The Commission shall confirm the provisions involved after having verified that they are not a means of arbitrary discrimination or a disguised restriction on trade between Member States.
85 See Flynn, *op. cit.*, note 77, at 692.
86 Article 171:
  If the Court of Justice finds that a Member State has failed to fulfil an obligation under this Treaty, the State shall be required to take the necessary measures to comply with the judgment of the Court of Justice.

87 See Case 69/86, *Commission v Italy* [1987] ECR 773.
88 Case 7/68, *Commission v Italy* [1968] ECR 423; Case 18/71, *Eunomia v Italian Ministry of Education* [1971] ECR 811; Case 48/71, *Commission v Italy* [1972] ECR 527.
89 And indeed tertiary proceedings.

paragraph.[90] While the judgment of the ECJ in an initial action by the Commission under Article 169 remains declaratory, subsequent proceedings under Article 171 following failure by the Member State adequately to rectify that breach allow for punitive measures.

Under Article 171(2), if the Commission is of the opinion that a Member State has not taken the necessary measures to rectify a previously declared breach, it must carry out a further procedure. It must first request that the State submit observations as to the Commission's opinion of its behaviour. The Commission, if not satisfied at this point, must then issue a reasoned opinion detailing the points on which the Member State has failed to comply with the ECJ's judgment. This reasoned opinion will contain a time limit for the Member State to take the requisite action to comply. If the Member State persists with its breach after the time limit expires, the Commission may bring the case back to the ECJ. On bringing the case, the Commission will be required to specify a lump sum or penalty payment to the ECJ that it considers appropriate to the breach. If the ECJ finds that the Member State has failed to comply with its previous judgment it can impose a lump sum or penalty payment upon it. This is likely to be the one proposed by the Commission, but the ECJ has the discretion to impose a larger or smaller sum, or indeed no penalty at all.

While this power is, in theory, a significant boost to the powers of the ECJ, at least one commentator[91] has already pointed out that if a Member State is disinclined to comply with the original judgment under Article 169, it is likely to be similarly disinclined to comply with the payment of any lump sum or penalty payment stemming from a further action based on that judgment. Others[92] are of the opinion that given the apparent unlimited discretion of the ECJ over the potential size and duration[93] of the penalties imposed in such cases, both Commission and ECJ will have to give a great deal of thought as to the circumstances in which the procedure is used and the penalties imposed. It remains to be seen, therefore, how effective these augmented powers will actually be in practice, and whether the desire of the Commission and ECJ not to alienate Member States through excessive use or excessive fines can be balanced with the need to more forcefully encourage Member States to honour their obligations under the Treaty.

Interim measures

While, as noted above, the ECJ cannot order a Member State in breach of Community law to engage or desist in a particular course of action in a judgment requested under Article 169, it can do so during the proceedings by way of an application for interim measures under

---

90 Article 171(2), as amended by Article G(52) TEU:

If the Commission considers that the Member State concerned has not taken such measures it shall, after giving that State the opportunity to submit its observations, issue a reasoned opinion specifying the points on which the Member State concerned has not complied with the judgment of the Court of Justice.

If the Member State concerned fails to take the necessary measures to comply with the Court's judgment within the time-limit laid down by the Commission, the latter may bring the case before the Court of Justice. In so doing it shall specify the amount of the lump sum or penalty payment to be paid by the Member State concerned which it considers appropriate in the circumstances.

If the Court of Justice finds that the Member State concerned has not complied with its judgment it may impose a lump sum or penalty payment on it.

This procedure shall be without prejudice to Article 170.

91 Weatherill and Beaumont, *op. cit.*, note 10, at 182.

92 Wyatt and Dashwood, *op. cit.*, note 20, at 120.

93 *Ibid.* In as much as it appears that the Court could, for instance, penalise a Member State a certain sum for every day that the Member State failed to comply with the original judgment.

Article 186 of the Treaty.[94] There were doubts prior to 1977 as to whether interim measures could be used in cases involving breach of Community obligations without implicitly prejudging the proceedings.[95] However, in *Commission v United Kingdom*,[96] an Article 93(2) proceeding, the Commission applied for interim measures to stop the UK government continuing to grant aids to UK pigmeat producers, in defiance of a Commission decision that these should end immediately, until the main action reached the ECJ, and this was granted. The ECJ held that the Commission's decision was binding upon a Member State unless the Member State successfully applied to the ECJ via Article 173 to have the decision annulled. It was not the place of the Member States to decide whether or not Community law was being properly applied by the Commission – they could not be allowed to be 'judges in their own cause,' that power was reserved to the ECJ alone. This case was shortly followed by *Commission v Ireland*,[97] which concerned the application of interim measures in Article 169 proceedings. Here the ECJ adjourned its decision twice to attempt to let the parties settle the issue amicably, but when this failed, the ECJ granted the Commission's request for interim measures. In these cases, the ECJ began to construct the four-stage test that it applies in such cases. Audretsch lists these as follows:

- Is the application not manifestly ill founded?
- Has an urgent need for such measures been proved?
- Is there threat of irreparable damage?
- Is it within the powers of the ECJ to take the measures which the Commission is asking for?[98]

Of these, the two most often at issue, and indeed very often linked, are the second and third questions. By way of example, in *Commission v Belgium*[99] the Commission applied for an order under Article 186 of the Treaty and Article 83 of the Rules of Procedure to require Belgium to accept university students from the other Member States on the same conditions as its own nationals. Up to that point Belgium had been charging students from other Member States an additional enrolment fee. The ECJ in considering the arguments, decided that the fact that students needed to know whether the fee would be charged, as term had already begun, and some students were being denied places on the ground that they had not paid the fee, meant that the matter was of urgency. Further, in missing classes that they should be attending, there was a risk of serious and irreparable damage to the interests of those students. The ECJ, however, conscious of the need to balance the interests of the parties in an action based on Article 186 of the Treaty, also required that those students undertake in writing to pay the fee should the main application be dismissed by the ECJ.[100] By contrast, in *Commission v Italy*,[101] which concerned a request for an order granting the

94 Article 186

    The Court of Justice may in any cases before it prescribe any necessary interim measures.

    See also Article 36 of the Statute of the European Court and Articles 83–90 of the Rules of Procedure of the Court of Justice.

95 Audretsch, *op. cit.*, note 10, at 128.

96 Joined Cases 31/77R and 53/77R, [1977] ECR 921.

97 Case 61/77R, [1977] ECR 937.

98 Audretsch, *op. cit.*, note 10, at 129.

99 Case 293/85R, [1985] ECR 3521.

100 Which it duly was, on the ground that Belgium had not been given enough time to respond to the Commission's complaints regarding the failure adequately to implement the decision in Case 293/83, *Gravier v City of Liège* [1985] ECR 593, at 606, either before or after its reasoned opinion.

101 Case 352/88R, [1989] ECR 267.

authorisation for an airline to operate a scheduled route from Manchester to Milan, the ECJ failed to find the likelihood of a serious and irreparable loss. It thus held that as a result there was no ground for finding the type of urgency which would warrant the granting of the order.

With the exception of the cases of *Commission* v *United Kingdom*[102] and *Commission* v *Ireland*[103] noted above, which were heard by the full Court, the standard procedure is that such cases are heard by the President of the Court, although the President has the discretion to refer the matter to the full Court.[104]

There is a slight academic difference of opinion as to the availability of interim measures under Article 171 actions. In *Commission* v *France*,[105] concerning the contentious issue of UK lamb and mutton exports to France, France was initially held in breach of its Community obligations in a judgment in Article 169 proceedings[106] but refused to comply with that judgment. The Commission proceeded to bring Case 24/80 under Article 171 for failure to comply. Then, shortly afterwards, it alleged a further breach of Article 171 after Case 232/78 had been decided and began Case 97/80R, applying at the same time for interim measures. In his Opinion, Advocate General Capotorti stated that he felt that the application should be rejected as neither urgency nor serious and irreparable harm was proved. The ECJ agreed that the application should be rejected, but on a different ground, i.e., that it was not necessary. It stated that France was already under a duty to comply with Community law and that in applying for interim measures the Commission was in fact asking the ECJ to grant an order restating its judgment in the original case. Audretsch holds that, in as much as the ECJ did not explicitly rule out the possibility of interim measures in an Article 171 action in its judgment, the matter remains open.[107] Weatherill and Beaumont, however, argue that, in practical terms the judgment rules out such a conclusion.[108] Of the two arguments it is respectfully submitted that the latter is considerably more convincing.

CONCLUSION

There has been a significant rise in the number of Article 169 proceedings over the last 12 years, with 335 letters of formal notice issued in 1982, rising to 960 in 1990.[109] This rise appears to be the result of a conscious decision by the Commission actively to pursue failure on the part of Member States. The Member States seem willing to let the Commission handle the judicial stage of enforcement proceedings, although they still play an important role in initiating such proceedings. The increase in numbers of proceedings has inevitably put some strain on the Commission, and it seems that as a result of this the Commission has increasingly adopted a position of encouraging individuals to pursue failures by the Member States[110] in the national courts using the Article 177 procedure. This may also be due to a suspicion on the part of the Commission that the ECJ may in fact be more sympathetic towards individual actions brought under Article 177[111]

---

102 Joined Cases 31/77R and 53/77R, *op. cit.*, note 96.
103 Case 61/77R, *op. cit.*, note 97.
104 Article 85, Rules of Procedure of the Court of Justice.
105 Joined Cases 24/80 and 97/80R, [1980] ECR 1319.
106 Case 232/78, [1979] ECR 2729.
107 Audretsch, *op. cit.*, note 10, at 134.

108 Weatherill and Beaumont, *op. cit.*, note 10, at 188.
109 *Ibid.*, at 168.
110 See Chapter 10.
111 Certainly it appears that the ECJ has, in recent years, rejected an increasing percentage of actions brought by the Commission under Article 169.

Actions under Article 93(2) have also seen an increase, and the Commission seems more inclined in the recent cases to request repayment of illegal aid. However, this area remains both complex and confusing. As Slot notes,[112] the Commission has contributed to this state of affairs; by failing to take a firm stance regarding notification and time limits, it has not provided clear directions for compliance by the Member State. The power under Article 94 to make regulations to simplify the whole Article 93 process, or at least to determine the conditions under which Article 93(3) will apply, remains unused. While the Commission has attempted to provide some guidance by way of notices, these cannot adequately substitute for a regulation based on Article 94.[113]

At present neither Article 225 nor Article 100a(4) proceedings have reached the ECJ. It would seem likely that of the two procedures, it is the Article 100a(4) procedure that will see the first action. Given the controversial nature of qualified majority voting under Article 189, it cannot be long before a Member State, in attempting to derogate from a harmonisation measure with which it disagrees that has been adopted by this procedure, falls foul of either the Commission or another Member State.

Further reading

Article 169, Article 170

Audretsch, H., *Supervision in European Community Law*, 2nd edn (1986).

Audretsch, H., 'Supervision in the EEC, OECD and Benelux – A Difference in Degree, But Also in Kind?' (1987) 36 ICLQ 838.

Barav, A., 'Failure of Member States to fulfil their obligations under Community law' (1975) 12 CML Rev 369.

Danielle, 'Italy and EEC law in 1990' (1991) 16 EL Rev 417.

Dashwood, A. and White, R., 'Enforcement actions under Articles 169 and 170' (1989) 14 EL Rev 388.

Evans, A., 'The Enforcement Procedure of Article 169: Commission Discretion' (1979) 4 EL Rev 442.

Everling, U., 'The Member States of the European Communities before their Court of Justice' (1984) 9 EL Rev 215.

Gaja, G., 'New Developments in a Continuing Story: The Relationship between EEC Law and Italian Law' (1990) 27 CML Rev 83.

Grey, C., 'Interim measures of protection in the European Court' (1979) 4 EL Rev 80.

Magliveras, K.D., '*Force Majeure* in Community Law' (1990) 15 EL Rev 460.

Merterns de Wilmars, J. and Veroughstraete, I.M., 'Proceedings against Member States for failure to fulfil their obligations' (1970) 7 CML Rev 385.

Article 93, Article 100a(4), Article 225

Dashwood, A., 'Control of State Aids in the EEC: Prevention and Cure under Art. 93' (1975) CML Rev 43.

Flynn, J., 'State Aid and Self Help' (1983) 8 EL Rev 297.

---

112 Slot, *op. cit.*, note 53, at 760.   113 *Ibid.*

Flynn, J., 'How well will Article 100a(4) work? A comparison with Article 93' (1987) 24 CML Rev 689.

Gilmour, D., 'The Enforcement of Community Law by the Commission in the Context of State Aids: The Relationship between Articles 93 and 169 and the Choice of Remedies' (1981) 18 CML Rev 63.

Slot, P.J., 'Procedural Aspects of State Aids: The Guardian of Competition versus the Subsidy Villains' (1990) 27 CML Rev 741.

CHAPTER 9

Community liability

INTRODUCTION

The EC Treaty creates no system of law relating to contract and tort or delict. Neither does it provide for which system of national law, if any, should apply to cases brought against the Community for breach of contract or other legal obligations. The ECJ is therefore in a position of having to develop an entire law of obligations for an economically sophisticated jurisdiction, which is made up of States following divergent systems of law.[1] The ECJ has chosen to be cautious in this field of law. In contractual matters, the practice of the Commission has helped to ensure that there are few issues of conflicts of law to be decided by the Community. The ECJ has used the wide range of legal expertise amongst its personnel to apply national law to all Community contracts. It has wisely not attempted to reinvent the wheel, since no one has ever argued that the Community needs an autonomous law of contract.

In cases of non-contractual liability, the Treaty provides slightly more guidance to the ECJ, directing it to general principles of law. The court has used the general framework of fault, causation and damage to create an autonomous law of non-contractual liability for the Community. This autonomous law has been of great benefit to the Community, in that the rules developed by the ECJ have placed severe obstacles before applicants seeking damages. In particular, the rules on liability for policy errors has almost never been successful. Even when applicants have been successful in establishing liability, the ECJ has frequently reduced the amount of damages payable to applicants by applying notions of duty to mitigate damages and contributory fault. Lastly, the ECJ has diverted many cases to Member State courts where issues of concurrent liability with a Member State arise.

Contractual liability

The first paragraph of Article 215 EC contains the only substantive rule of Community law relating to contractual liability: 'The contractual liability of the Community shall be governed by the law applicable to the contract in question.' Community law therefore simply provides a choice of law rule, rather than its own rules of contract, although there is nothing in Article 215, paragraph 1, which would prevent the ECJ from developing an independent Community law of contract. The rule in the Treaty means that the rules of private international law are to be applied by the ECJ to any contract before it. However, the Community does not have its own rules of conflicts of law.[2] The ECJ would therefore have to decide *how* to decide the applicable law of a contract to which the Community is party.

---

1 There are three categories of legal systems in the Community: common law (UK and Eire), Scandinavian law (Denmark), and Roman-derived civil law (the other nine Member States).

2 Hartley, *The Foundations of European Community Law*, 2nd edn (1988), at 447.

An applicant could possibly avoid the problem entirely by taking the Community to court in its own national courts, since the Community has legal personality in all Member States.[3] If a case of choice of law over a contract were to arise before the ECJ, however, it is likely that it would use the provision in the second paragraph of Article 215, which states that non-contractual liability will be determined according to the general principles of law common to the Member States. The use of general principles has permeated the entire practice of the ECJ,[4] so it would not be surprising to see the Court attempting to derive general principles for the determination of the applicable law of a Community contract.

In practice, however, this issue has not been placed before the ECJ, because the Commission practice is to insert a choice of law clause in all contracts that it concludes on behalf of the Community. In one case, a party to a contract argued that conflicts of law rules should be applied, but the ECJ found that the contract was clear on the applicable law and that therefore no recourse to the conflicts rules was necessary.[5] The ECJ clearly wishes to avoid the uncertainty of trying to determine general principles of conflicts of law, and will therefore even look to material incorporated by reference in order to find a choice of law agreed by the parties.[6] The question of how well the ECJ applies the contract law of the Member States in these cases does not appear to have been raised.

Article 181 EC[7] gives the ECJ jurisdiction over arbitration clauses in Community contracts:

> The Court of Justice shall have jurisdiction to give judgment pursuant to any arbitration clause contained in a contract concluded by or on behalf of the Community, whether that contract be governed by public or private law.[8]

The ECJ, under Article 38(6) of its Rules of Procedure, will require a copy of the arbitration clause. However, it will accept written proof of the terms of the arbitration clause from correspondence and other documentation relating to a contract which is essentially oral.[9] This leads to a somewhat ambiguous situation, whereby, although there is no rule requiring that arbitration clauses be in writing, the rules of procedure followed by the ECJ require written proof of any arbitration clause.

The general rule concerning jurisidiction, for contractual and non-contractual matters, is concurrent jurisdiction. Only where, as under Article 181, the ECJ is specifically granted jurisdiction, is the jurisdiction of national courts automatically excluded. Article 183 EC sets out the basic principles of the court's jurisdiction:

> Save where jurisdiction is conferred on the Court of Justice by this Treaty, disputes to which the Community is a party shall not on that ground be excluded from the jurisdiction of the courts or tribunals of the Member States.

3 Article 210 EC.
4 See Chapter 6.
5 Case 318/81, *Commission v CODEMI* [1985] ECR 3693.
6 *Ibid*. See also Case 23/76, *Luigi Pellegrini & C.S.a.s. v Commission* [1976] ECR 1807, where the ECJ derived the terms and choice of law of a contract from the oral agreement between the parties to govern their contract by a draft agreement created under a tender process, where the applicant was temporarily substituting for the successful tenderer who had repudiated the contract.
7 Article 35.4 of the Statute of the European System of Central Banks and the European Central Bank, and Article 19.4 of the Statute of the European Monetary Institute, provide an identical rule for contracts concluded by or on behalf of the European Central Bank.
8 In some Member States, general administrative law rather than civil law applies to contracts concluded by public authorities.
9 *Pellegrini, op. cit.*, note 6.

This rule is somewhat ambiguous. Clearly national courts, according to their own jurisdictional rules, will have jurisdiction where such has not been granted to the ECJ. However, the effect of ECJ jurisdiction is less clear: does it create exclusive or concurrent jurisdiction? Article 181 EC, for example, does not specifically exclude the jurisdiction of Member State courts. All such provisions simply state that the ECJ shall have jurisdiction, not that it shall have exclusive jurisdiction. While this ambiguity does not appear to have created problems for the Community legal system, it could potentially cause great uncertainty. The ECJ has, as will be discussed below, developed rules assigning jurisdiction to itself and national courts with respect to concurrent liability of the Community and a Member State, but has not made any statement of a general nature that its jurisdiction is exclusive.

The TEU establishes special jurisdictional rules for the European Central Bank and the European Monetary Institute. Article 35.2 of the Statute of the European System of Central Banks and the European Central Bank provides for a presumption in favour of the jurisdiction of the courts of the Member States:

> Disputes between the ECB, on the one hand, and its creditors, debtors or any other person, on the other, shall be decided by the competent national courts, save where jurisdiction has been conferred on the Court of justice.[10]

Unlike the EC Treaty provisions, the relationship between Member State and Community jurisdiction is clear – ECJ jurisdiction excludes the jurisdiction of the national courts. It would have been helpful, in fact, if the TEU had amended Article 183 EC in similar language in order to clarify its provisions.

Non-contractual liability

The second and third paragraphs of Article 215 EC set out the skeletal framework of non-contractual liability of the Community:

> In the case of non-contractual liability, the Community shall, in accordance with the general principles common to the laws of the Member States, make good any damage caused by its institutions or by its servants in the performance of their duties. The preceding paragraph shall apply under the same conditions to damage caused by the ECB or by its servants in the performance of their duties.[11]

Article 178 EC provides that the ECJ will have jurisdiction over actions arising under Article 215(2) EC. Article 43 of the Statute of the ECJ provides that there will be a five-year limitation period on the taking of actions relating to the non-contractual liability of the Community. Article 43 states that the limitation period runs from the occurrence of the event complained of. The ECJ has interpreted Article 43 to mean that the period begins to run from the moment when the damage suffered by the applicant actually materialises, rather than from the date of the relevant acts of the Community institutions.[12] A duty to compensate is not legally complete until that moment. However, the limitation period is

---

10 Article 19.2 of the Statute of the European Monetary Institute provides for the same rule with respect to the EMI.

11 As amended by Article G (78) TEU.

12 Joined Cases 256, 257 and 267/80 and 5/81, *Birra Wurhrer v Commission* [1982] ECR 85.

interrupted by any proceedings before the ECJ, or an application for review under Articles 173 or 175 EC, if such actions are brought within time.[13]

Liability actions are brought, not against the Community as a whole, but against the institution or institutions which are responsible for the actions which led to the damage suffered. This was established in the *Werhahn* case,[14] where the Commission and the Council both argued that they should be the sole defendant. The ECJ was of the opinion that:

> Under the Community legal system . . . it is in the interests of a good administration of justice that where Community liability is involved by reason of the act of one of its institutions, it should be represented before the Court by the institution or institutions against which the matter giving rise to liability is alleged.[15]

By virtue of Article 215, the Community is also liable for the acts of its servants in the performance of their duties. The key case on liability for acts of servants is *Sayag v Leduc*.[16] Leduc was an official employed by Euratom, who was driving a car in which Sayag and another were passengers, during his employment. Leduc drove them in his own car, but had a travel order from Euratom. The passengers were injured in a traffic accident during the trip, and sued in Belgian courts, where Leduc argued that he was acting in performance of his duties and therefore his employer was liable. The Belgian *Cour de Cassation* referred the matter to the ECJ under Article 177 EC. The ECJ took a restrictive view of the phrase 'in the performace of their duties', finding that it applied only when 'by virtue of an internal and direct relationship, [such acts] are the necessary extension of the tasks entrusted to the institutions.'[17] The ECJ has never dealt directly with the issue of whether the Community is liable for acts of its agents, but even if it would accept such liability, it is likely that it would be interpreted in a similarly restrictive fashion.[18]

Article 215 allows the ECJ to have recourse to the general principles of law common to the Member States. This does not mean that the ECJ will adopt such principles only to the extent that they are accepted by all the Member States. In the same way as it has dealt with general principles in judicial review cases, it has extracted general principles of fault, causation and damage which are common to all Member State systems of tort or delict, and has built up an autonomous law of liability for the purpose of Article 215 EC.[19] National systems are only a starting point, and Community liability contains elements not found in any national system.

The criteria for non-contractual liability for acts other than those of general application, can be seen from the case of *Compagnia Italiana Alcool v Commission*:[20]

> According to the established case law of the Court, those conditions [of non-contractual liability] are the incurring of damage, the existence of a causal link between the damage

13 Joined Cases 5, 7 and 13–24/66, *Kampffmeyer v Commission* [1967] ECR 245.
14 Joined Cases 63–9/72, *Werhahn v Council* [1973] ECR 1229.
15 *Ibid.*, at paragraph 7.
16 Case 9/69, *Sayag v Leduc* [1969] ECR 329.
17 *Ibid.*, at 335. Leduc had first attempted to rely on the immunity granted to the Community for official acts under the Protocol on the Privileges and Immunities of the European Communities, Article 12(a), also unsuccessfully: Case 5/68, *Sayag v Leduc* [1968] ECR 395.

18 Hartley, *op. cit.*, note 2, at 461–2, is of the opinion, based on Case 18/60, *Worms v High Authority* [1962] ECR 195, that the Community would be liable for the acts of its agents.
19 Advocate General Roemer in Case 5/71, *Zuckerfabrik Schoppenstedt v Council* [1971] ECR 975, at 989, and Advocate General Gand in *Sayag v Leduc, op. cit.*, note 16, at 340.
20 Case C-358/90, [1992] 2 CMLR 876, at paragraph 46.

relied on and the conduct alleged against the institutions, and the unlawful nature of that conduct.

In terms of grounds of liability, there are two different regimes under Community law. Article 40 ECSC limits liability to situations of fault. Under the EC Treaty, liability is not limited to fault, and the ECJ has found the Community liable for what could constitute maladministration. In a staff case,[21] EC officials had been given wrong information about pensions, and had acted upon this information. The Commission had made a wrong interpretation of the rules, and even after it discovered the possible error, according to the applicants, did not inform them until they had made irrevocable decisions to take early retirement, based on their supposed pension entitlements from the Community. The ECJ said that initial misinterpretation did not give rise to liability, but that failure to take steps to correct the situation after the Commission knew of the error did give rise to liability. This case could be interpreted as fault-based liability, since the it was the 'wrongful act'[22] of the Commission in not informing the applicants rather than its original good faith error which gave rise to liability. However, it does indicate the possibility of some form of strict or non-fault-based liability, which has never been explicitly rejected by the ECJ.

In another case on non-fault liability, the ECJ failed to answer a question concerning *'l'égalité devant les charges publiques'*.[23] Advocate General Mayras was of the opinion that the applicants had not met the requirements for the action under French law, but the ECJ ignored the question, asserting that the contested measures were intended to benefit the persons in the applicant's situation, and therefore the applicant had no cause for complaint.[24] More recently, in a similar case, the ECJ again left the quesion of liability without fault open, simply arguing that the necessity of an applicant proving damage beyond the normal risks of business, 'would have to be applied *a fortiori* if the concept of liability without fault were accepted in Community law.'[25]

For fault-based liability, it will be necessary to establish that the Community owed a duty towards the applicant. In *Adams* v *Commission*,[26] the ECJ found that the Commission owed the applicant a duty of confidentiality. Adams had supplied information to the Commission concerning the violation by his employers Hoffman-La Roche of Community competition law, on the condition that his identity would not be revealed. He later left his employment and moved from Switzerland to Italy. Through the carelessness of the Commission, Hoffman-La Roche discovered that Adams had been the source of the information used by the Commission. Adams was charged with economic espionage under Swiss law, and was arrested a year later, when he re-entered Switzerland. He was held in solitary confinement, and ultimately convicted of the charge, with the penalty imposed being a one-year suspended sentence. During the investigation before his trial, his wife was interrogated, and later committed suicide. Adams sued the Commission for damages, seeking compensation for

---

21 Case 19/69, *Richez-Parise* v *Commission* [1970] ECR 325.
22 *Ibid.*, at paragraph 31. The applicants failed in part, however, because they failed 'to adduce sufficient evidence to establish that their requests for termination of service were based on the wrong information supplied to them and not corrected in good time' – paragraph 43. The ECJ felt that the best remedy would be to give them extra time to benefit from the grant system set up by the Commission as an alternative to pension rights.
23 Case 9 and 11/71, *Compagnie d'Approvisionnement* v *Commission* [1972] ECR 391. This action under French law is intended to correct the unequal imposition of burdens by the act of a public authority.
24 *Ibid.* at paragraph 46.
25 Case 59/83, *SA Biovilac NV* v *EEC*, [1984] ECR 4057, at paragraph 28.
26 Case 145/83, [1985] ECR 3539.

material and emotional damages.[27] The ECJ found that the Commission owed Adams a continuing duty of confidentiality, even after he left the employment of Hoffman-La Roche, and a duty to warn him of the fact that his former employers had become aware of his involvement in the Commission investigation. In *Briantex* v *Commission*, the applicants unsuccessfully attempted to establish a duty to provide correct information concerning the EEC-China Business Week.[28] The applicants' complaint was based on the fact that they were unable to conclude contracts with any of the Chinese representatives because the Italian textile quota had been exhausted. They were unsuccessful in their claim because the circumstances were such, according to the ECJ, that no duty was owed specifically to the applicants to provide full and accurate information – the event was not intended to facilitate the concluding of contracts, but was instead a general contact meeting.

The applicant must further establish that, even where a duty is owed, it is owed by the Community. This emerges from the decision in *Francesconi* v *Commission*,[29] where the applicants blamed the Commission for its failure properly to supervise the wine market and thereby to prevent the marketing of adulterated wines which had caused the death of relatives of the applicants. The ECJ found in this case that the scheme of supervision of the Community wine market was such that the Member States rather than the Commission were responsible for ensuring the quality of wine intended for human consumption.

The Community will not be at fault if its actions can be seen to benefit the applicant. In *Emerald Meats Limited* v *Commission*,[30] the ECJ found that the interventions by the Commission actually gave the applicants more assistance than it was legally obliged to do. As a result, the ECJ found that the Commission could not be held to have acted unlawfully.

Once an unlawful act committed by the Community has been established, it is necessary to demonstrate that it actually caused the damage suffered by the applicant. This is often a very heavy burden on the applicant, since it will be difficult in the case of loss because of Community action in a given market, to isolate one cause of market fluctuations as being crucial. It will always be easier for the Community institutions to show that there were other factors which caused or could have caused the applicant's damage. This difficulty is demonstrated in *GAEC* v *Commission*,[31] where the applicants alleged that a Commission decision granting aid to German farmers caused greater exports from Germany to France and thus reduced the prices on the French market. The applicant failed on the causation point because the decreases in price did not precisely coincide with the application of the Commission decision. Further, there is no causal link in cases where, even if the illegality had not occurred, the applicant would still have suffered damage.[32] There may be an intervening cause, particularly due to changes in market prices, which means that the applicant's loss has more to do with international price movements than with Community action.[33]

---

[27] The case was ultimately settled for £200 000 in damages, including £100 000 for mental anguish, plus £176 000 in costs: see Hartley, *op. cit.*, note 2, at 468.

[28] Case 353/88, [1989] ECR 3623.

[29] Joined Cases 326/86 and 66/88, [1989] ECR 2087.

[30] Joined Cases 106 and 317/90 and 129/91, judgment of 20 January 1993.

[31] Case 253/84, [1987] ECR 123.

[32] *Compagnia Italiana Alcool, op. cit.*, note 20, at para-

graph 47.

[33] For example, see Case 169/73, *Compagnie Continentale* v *Council* [1975] ECR 117 and Case 26/81, *Oleifici Mediterranei* v *EEC* [1982] ECR 3057. In these cases, the ECJ found that the applicants, as prudent traders, should have been aware of the uncertainty and likelihood of a change in Community policy with respect to prices or monetary compensatory amounts.

Liability for acts having legal effects

As with State liability in national law, the establishment of liability for legislative acts by the Community is a particularly difficult area. Because it involves declaring that the Community acted illegally in adopting a measure, such liability is closely related to judicial review and creates the same questions about the judiciary second-guessing the legislature. The ECJ experienced some difficulty in establishing the borderline between judicial review and liability, and the relationship between the two forms of action. The only guidance provided in the Treaty is Article 176 EC:

> The institution or institutions whose act has been declared void or whose failure to act has been declared contrary to this Treaty shall be required to take the necessary measures to comply with the judgment of the Court of Justice.
>   This obligation shall not effect any obligation which may result from the application of the second paragraph of Article 215.
>   This Article shall also apply to the ECB.

It is because of these considerations that liability cases involving Community leglislation have been the most important and the most controversial. The close relationship between judicial review and liability actions can be seen from the fact that the ECJ will only admit actions arguing illegality of a Community action, where it is an act which has binding legal effect.[34]

Liability for choices of economic policy

Most Community legislation, being related to the establishment of the Common, and now the Single, Market or the development of the Common Agricultural Policy, involves choices of economic policy. The ECJ therefore has had to deal with the difficult problem of how much discretion should be allowed to the Community institutions, when individuals and businesses claim to have suffered damage.[35] In part the ECJ has used causation to prevent the Community from being liable, in the sense that where the Community has simply reacted to market changes, it is not liable for damage suffered by businesses. The ECJ will not find in favour of applicants who essentially argue that the Community should insulate them from fluctuations in prices. The formula which has been developed, as a result, requires more than mere illegality on the part of the Community institutions, but instead what could be called gross fault.

An early problem which the ECJ had to resolve is the relationship of liability for legislative acts embodying choices of economic policy to actions for the annulment of those acts. In particular, the question which arose was whether it was necessary to obtain a declaration of invalidity under Article 173 EC before taking a liability action under Article 215 EC. Article 176 EC simply guaranteed that a successful annulment action did not preclude a subsequent liability action. If it would be necessary to obtain a declaration of invalidity, applicants would be restricted, despite the five-year limitation period in Article 43 of the ECJ Rules of Procedure, to taking at least the initial annulment action within two months, as required by Article 173.

[34] Case C-50/90, *Sunzest (Europe)* v *Commission*, [1991] ECR I-2917, and Case C-117/91, *Bosman* v *Commission*, judgment of 4 October 1992.
[35] In Case 106/81, *Kind* v *EEC* [1982] ECR 2885, the ECJ explicitly recognised the need to allow the Community a wide measure of discretion, particularly with respect to the Common Agricultural Policy, which is the cause of many Article 215 actions.

The first case to deal directly with this issue decided that annulment of the measure which caused the damage was a prerequisite. The ECJ, in *Plaumann* v *Commission*,[36] found that: 'An administrative measure which has not been annulled cannot of itself constitute a wrongful act on the part of the administration inflicting damage upon those whom it affects.' This position was reversed in *Lutticke* v *Commission*,[37] where the ECJ emphasised that Article 215 was intended to be an independent form of action. It is possible, however, to bring simultaneous annulment and compensation actions.[38]

Once the ECJ had decided that an Article 215 action is independent from claims for annulment of the Community acts causing the damage, the next step was to develop a formula for determining liability for acts involving choices of economic policy. The formula was first set out in the *Schoppenstedt* case.[39] Although this is often referred to as the *Schoppenstedt* formula, it is usually cited by the ECJ in the form in which it was restated in *Bayerische HNL et al.* v *Council and Commission (Second Skimmed-milk Powder cases)*[40]: 'the Community does not incur liability on account of a legislative measure which involves choices of economic policy unless a sufficiently serious breach of a superior rule of law for the protection of the individual has occurred.' Each of the three requirements, the existence of a superior rule of law, the rule being intended for the protection of the individual and the breach being sufficiently serious, has been developed by the ECJ since the formula was first adopted.

The *Schoppenstedt* formula has been applied to a Community directive, but without the applicant succeeding in its claim.[41]

The concept of superior rule of law has been liberally interpreted. It includes not only rules contained in the treaties, but also at least some of the general principles of law. Legitimate expectation, in particular, has been accepted by the ECJ as a superior rule of law.[42] However, not every rule contained in the EC Treaty would appear to constitute a superior rule of law. In *Kind*[43] and the *Compagnia Italiana Alcool*[44] case, the ECJ found that Article 190 EC was not sufficiently important to be a superior rule of law. However, the ECJ seems to be unclear as to whether this provision does not result in liability because it is not a superior rule of law or because it is not for the protection of the individual. In *Kind*, the ECJ said that the right to reasons 'is designed to enable to Court to exercise its powers of review of the legality of such measures in the context of Article 173 for the benefit of individuals to whom that remedy is made available by the Treaty'.[45] It is difficult to determine from this statement whether the requirement of providing reasons is for the benefit of the ECJ alone, or whether, through Article 173, it is also for the benefit of the individual.

The distinguishing features of rules which are for the protection of the individual remain somewhat vague. The ECJ has rarely dealt with this question directly. *Kampffmeyer*[46] stated

36 Case 25/62, [1963] ECR 95, at 108.

37 Case 4/69, [1971] ECR 325, at paragraph 6: 'It would be contrary to the independent nature of this action as well as to the efficacy of the general system of forms of action created by the Treaty to regard as a ground of inadmissibility the fact that, in certain circumstances, an action for damages might lead to a result similar to that of an action for failure to act under Article 175.' This has more recently been confirmed in Case 175/84, *Krohn* v *Commission* [1986] ECR 753.

38 Case C-152/88, *Sofrimport* v *Commission* [1990] ECR I-2477, where the applicant succeeded in recovering damages and in achieving a partial annulment of the contested Regulations.

39 *Op. cit.*, note 19, at paragraph 11.

40 Case 83/76, [1978] ECR 1209, at paragraph 4.

41 Case C-63/89, *Les Assurances du Crédit SA* v *Council and Commission* [1991] 2 CMLR 737.

42 Case 74/74, *CNTA* v *Commission* [1975] ECR 533, and *Sofrimport, op. cit.*, note 38.

43 *Op. cit.*, note 35.

44 *Op. cit.*, note 20.

45 *Op. cit.*, note 35, at paragraph 14.

46 *Op. cit.*, note 13.

that rule of law may be for protection of individuals generally, not necessarily the plaintiff in particular. The ECJ explicitly distinguished the concept of 'for the benefit of the individual' under the *Schoppenstedt* formula, and the concept of 'direct and individual concern' under Article 173 EC. Nor does the breach of provisions relating to the powers of the institutions attract liability, because these rules are not for the protection of individuals.[47] Given that institutions have been permitted to use the review process to protect their prerogatives under the EC Treaty even where the Treaty itself did not grant this right, it is logical that those rules are considered to be primarily for the benefit of the institutions themselves, and only indirectly of benefit to individuals.

The main obstacle to a successful action under the *Schoppenstedt* formula has been the requirement that the breach of the superior rule of law intended for the protection of the individual must be sufficiently serious. It means more than the measure could be subject to annulment or a declaration of invalidity, more than mere illegality. In the *HNL* case the 'sufficiently serious' requirement was set out as the idea that the Community institution must have 'manifestly and gravely disregarded the limits of its powers'.[48] This has been further refined in later cases. Mostly the ECJ has looked to the extent of the damage suffered by the applicant, but has sometimes looked instead to the extent to which the law has been violated. In the *Quellmehl and Gritz* cases,[49] the applicants were successful in claiming damages because their loss went beyond the risks normally inherent in business. The ECJ also emphasised the fact that the damage was focused on a small group.[50] In the Isoglucose cases,[51] the ECJ acknowledged that the applicants had borne a manifestly unequal burden, but looked to the extent to which the law had been violated and ruled that the applicants needed to show that Community behaviour was verging on the arbitrary. A further element to the requirement of a sufficiently serious breach has been added by recent case law: the Community may still escape liability if it can invoke an overriding public interest.[52]

Concurrent liability with a Member State

Questions of concurrent liability frequently arise, since Member States are often responsible for implementation of Community policies, or at least aspects of it. National authorities may have a certain amount of discretion in how certain policies will affect individuals within their jurisdiction. They will sometimes collect levies in agricultural matters. While these levies are the Community's money, the ECJ tends to look more closely at who collected the money than who owns it after collection. Such situations leave potential applicants in a difficult situation. While the Community has legal personality in all Member States, it has not been possible for applicants to sue both the Community and a Member State in national courts. The ECJ has allowed certain concurrent liability cases to proceed before it, but has not made the Member State a party to the action. The separation of the Member State and Community

[47] Case C-282/90, *Vreugdenhil v Commission*, judgment of 13 March 1992, paragraphs 20–1.
[48] *Op. cit.*, note 40, at paragraph 6.
[49] Case 64/76, *Dumortier et al. v Council and Commission* [1979] ECR 3091.
[50] This may reflect a confusion with the closed group idea used to enable individuals to challenge decisions in the form of regulations under Article 173 EC. See Chapter 7.
[51] Joined Cases 116 and 124/77, *Amylum and Tunnel Refineries v Council and Commission* [1979] ECR 3497, at paragraph 19; also, Case 143/77, *KSH NV v Council and Commission* [1979] ECR 3593.
[52] *Sofrimport, op. cit.*, note 38, and Joined Cases C-104/89 and 37/90, *Mulder et al. v Commission and Council*, [1992] ECR I-3062.

judicial systems places additional burdens on applicants,[53] since it is not always obvious from the facts of a case whether the ECJ will consider itself to be the most appropriate forum for the dispute.

The ECJ recognised the problems inherent in this dual system to deal with concurrent liability in the first case to involve the issue. In *Kampffmeyer*,[54] the applicants took two concurrent actions: one against Germany before its courts, and one against the Community before the ECJ. The ECJ was concerned to avoid double compensation, and decided that the German courts should deal with the issue of the liability of the German authorities before the ECJ dealt with the liability of the Community. The ECJ appeared to consider that primary liability would lie with the national authorities and that the Community's liability would only be subsidiary, although it gave no reasons for this allocation.[55] The next case on concurrent liability, *Haegeman v Commission*,[56] like *Kampffmeyer*, involved the paying of levies. Whereas in *Kampffmeyer*, the money had been held by the Member State, in *Haegeman* it was paid to the Community after being collected by the Belgian authorities. This made no difference to the ECJ – it was still of the opinion that reimbursement should be sought from the national authorities. Since the claim for damages was related to the claim for repayment of the levy, both should be heard by the same court, in other words the national court.

The ECJ's approach to concurrent liability in situations where the applicant had paid an amount to a national authority was most clearly stated in *Société des Grands Moulins des Antilles v Commission*:[57]

> The refusal by a Community institution to pay a debt which may be owed by a Member State under Community law is not a matter involving the non-contractual liability of the Community.

The ECJ does not consider that amounts paid to national authorities under Community law constitute acts or omissions of the Community. Since this case it now seems clear that actions in restitution or quasi-contract involving the concurrent liability of the Community and a Member State, should be taken against the Member State before its courts.[58] Since most instances of concurrent liability will involve the payment of money to national authorities, the ECJ has succeeded in diverting most cases of concurrent liability away from itself.

Problems may arise, however, if the applicant has no remedy before the national courts. In *Kampffmeyer*, the applicants were told that they must exhaust national remedies before seeking compensation before the ECJ. In *Société Roquette Frères v Commission*,[59] the applicant took simultaneous actions before the French courts and the ECJ. It was successful before the French court in obtaining repayment of the levy, but was not awarded interest because the Community had held the money, not France. The ECJ again decided that this damages question was ancillary to the repayment issue, and therefore should be decided by the same court. The fact that the French court was clearly unwilling to give the applicant a remedy did not seem to matter, despite the statement by the ECJ in *Kampffmeyer* that it wished to avoid both overcompensation and undercompensation. The ECJ has not always required exhaustion of national remedies.[60] However, it has only dispensed with this

---

53 See Wils, 'Concurrent Liability of the Community and a Member State' (1992) 17 EL Rev 191.
54 *Op. cit.*, note 13.
55 Hartley, 'Concurrent Liability in EEC Law: A Critical Review of the Cases' (1977) 2 EL Rev 249, at 251.
56 Case 96/71, [1972] ECR 1005.
57 Case 99/74, [1975] ECR 1531.
58 Hartley, *op. cit.*, note 2, at 489.
59 Case 26/74, [1976] ECR 677.
60 Recently confirmed in Case 20/88, *Roquette Frères SA v Commission* [1989] ECR 1553.

requirement when it has found that the Community institution was the correct defendant in any event. In *Krohn*,[61] the issue was the refusal of national authorities to grant the applicant an import licence, where this refusal was based on Commission instructions. The ECJ held that the national authority was not the proper defendant because the Commission was responsible for the act complained of. It was not necessary to exhaust national remedies if they would not be effective. In this case, since the national authority had no discretion in taking the decision to refuse the import licence it would be unable to provide a remedy.

Where the fault is based in tort or delict rather than restitution, the ECJ is more likely to allow an applicant to proceed against the Community,[62] although it has not been entirely consistent on this point. In *Krohn*, the ECJ seems to have collapsed together the issue of where the case should be brought, and the need to exhaust national remedies where the case should be brought first before the national courts and then proceed before the ECJ. Since this case involved unliquidated damages (the loss of profits as a consequence of the wrongful denial of the licence) rather than a restitutionary claim, on the ECJ's own analysis it should be heard by the ECJ. However, in another case claiming compensation for damage caused by a national decision implementing Community policy, the ECJ did not deal with the issue of exhaustion of national remedies, but simply decided that, since the decision in question was not *required* by any Community measure, it was an act of the national authorities and should be pursued through the national courts.[63] In order for the Community to be the correct defendant, it must have produced an act capable of having binding legal effect.[64] If the action of the Community provides only non-binding guidance to the national authorities, the Community will not be liable.

It is unfortunate that the ECJ has not provided clearer guidance in this area. It is also unfortunate that it does not consistently follow approaches which initially appear to be clear. The only rule seems to be a presumption against ECJ jurisdiction, and the primacy of national remedies. Commentators on this area of Community law have frequently criticised the ECJ for failing both to clarify the law and to make access to justice easier to obtain.[65]

Damages

Even in the cases where the ECJ has found that the Community was liable towards an individual, it has been prepared to reduce the amount of damages payable to the applicant on a number of grounds, such as the speculative nature of the damage or contributory fault by the applicant. There are several examples of this practice of the ECJ. In *Kampffmeyer*,[66] loss of profit was allowed where contracts had already been concluded, but because of the speculative nature of the enterprise only 10 per cent of profits was compensated. In *CNTA*,[67] the applicant claimed for loss because the Commission's cancellation of monetary compensatory amounts caused the applicant to be exposed to the risk of currency

---

61 *Op. cit.*, note 37.

62 *Roquette Frères, op. cit.*, note 60. The applicants were unsuccessful, but on the basis that the illegality by the Commission was not sufficiently serious.

63 Joined Cases 89 and 91/86, *L'Etoile Commerciale v Commission* [1987] ECR 3005.

64 Case 133/79, *Sucrimex. v Commission* [1980] ECR 1299.

65 Hartley, *op. cit.*, note 55; Wils, *op. cit.*, note 53.

66 *Op. cit.*, note 13.

67 Case 74/74, *CNTA v Commission*, [1976] ECR 797 (hearing on the issue of damages only, the issue having been deferred by the ECJ in the first decision, pending a possible agreement by the parties as to the amount of compensation, see paragraphs 2–4).

fluctuations. The ECJ found, however, that the applicant was not in fact exposed to risk because its purchaser had the option under the contract to pay either in French or American currency. Since the purchaser in fact paid in French francs, and therefore the applicant did not have to worry about exchange rates, the ECJ decided that it had suffered no loss.[68] This approach to damages is consistent with the ECJ's approach to liability. The ECJ does not believe that traders should be able to rely on the Community to protect them against the risks of the market. As a result, applicants will not be compensated for speculative profits or profits lost because of badly-negotiated contracts. The damage must exceed inherent risks of the enterprise.[69]

The ECJ will also reduce the basic amount of damages if the applicant has contributed to its own loss. In *Adams*[70] the ECJ found contributory fault on the part of the applicant because he failed to inform the Commission of his location after leaving Hoffman-La Roche and by returning to Switzerland he exposed himself to criminal prosecution. Therefore, the damages were reduced by half. The ECJ has also recognised a duty of applicants to mitigate their damage. This will include, as in *Mulder*,[71] the duty to undertake alternative forms of commercial activity when Community action renders the applicant's original business uneconomic or impossible.

Damages will be the only remedy in cases of non-contractual liability. The ECJ has no power under Articles 178 and 215, second paragraph, to order specific performance.[72]

CONCLUSION

While the ECJ has been willing to be creative in developing concepts to deal with review and enforcement of Community law, it has been less so in the civil law areas of Community law. Perhaps this is because it is more difficult to find principles which are truly common to the Member States. It is also possible that the ECJ is reluctant to enlarge its jurisdiction over cases where extensive fact-finding is necessary, and prefers to deal with pure issues of law as it does under the Article 177 EC reference procedure.[73]

The restrictive interpretation of liability principles seems to date from the period in the 1970s of the Community's ill-advised attempts to regulate the surplus of milk production and the isoglucose saga. The potential for multi-million ECU damages in these cases seems to have moved the ECJ to insulate the Community from liability as much as possible. The ECJ does not appear to have reconsidered its approach at any time since then. However, this approach does have some systemic advantages. It helps to ensure the stability and legal certainty of Community policies by discouraging the taking of actions which, while not formally leading to annulment, would in practice require the withdrawal of Community measures long after the period for challenge had expired.

---

[68] *Ibid.* The applicant argued that in order to ensure that the purchaser paid in French francs, it had been required to waive interest on arrears, and that this *quid pro quo* constituted its loss. The ECJ found that the applicant had not proved that the waiver was consideration for payment being made in French francs only: paragraphs 12–16.

[69] See *Biovilac, op. cit.,* note 25: ' . . . an action for damages brought under Article 215 of the Treaty for un-

lawful legislative action cannot succeed unless the damage alleged by the applicant exceeds the limits of the economic risks inherent in operating in the sector concerned.'

[70] *Op. cit.,* note 26.

[71] *Op. cit.,* note 52.

[72] *Les Assurances du Crédit, op. cit.,* note 41.

[73] See Chapter 10.

Further reading

Hartley, T.C., *The Foundations of European Community Law*, 2nd edn (1988), Chapter 17.

Wils, W., 'Concurrent Liability of the Community and a Member State' (1992) 17 EL Rev 191.

CHAPTER 10

References to the European Court of Justice

INTRODUCTION

The Article 177 procedure is the primary method of ensuring the integration of the Community legal order. That is, it provides a means of harmonising the way in which Member States implement and administer Community law. Thus Community legislation should be interpreted the same way by an Italian court as it is by a German court, in similar proceedings. As the ECJ stated in *Rheinmühlen v Einfuhr- und Vorratsstelle Getreide*:[1] 'Article 177 is essential for the preservation of the Community character of the law established by the Treaty and has the object of ensuring that in all circumstances this law is the same in all States of the Community.'

In general the attitude of the Member States' courts towards this procedure is a positive one, as is reflected by this statement from the judgment in the UK case of *Customs and Excise Commissioners v ApS Samex*,[2] where the court held that the ECJ

> has a panoramic view of the Community and its institutions, a detailed knowledge of the Treaties and of much subordinate legislation made under them, and an intimate familiarity with the functioning of the Community which no national judge denied the collective experience of the Court of Justice could hope to achieve.[3]

The legal protection of individuals within the Community is also greatly strengthened by the Article 177 procedure. The ability to use Article 177, via Member State courts, to obtain preliminary rulings from the ECJ makes available to individuals remedies which might otherwise only be available via direct actions, with all the problems of standing and observation of time limits that such actions entail, or indeed might not be available at all.

The procedure under which references are made to the ECJ reads as follows:

> The Court of Justice shall have jurisdiction to give preliminary rulings concerning:
> (a) the interpretation of this Treaty;
> (b) the validity and interpretation of acts of the institutions of the Community and of the ECB;[4]
> (c) the interpretation of the statutes of bodies established by an act of the Council, where those statutes so provide.
> Where such a question is raised before any court or tribunal of a Member State, that court or tribunal may, if it considers that a decision on the question is necessary to enable it to give judgment, request the Court of Justice to give a ruling thereon.

---

1 Case 166/73, [1974] ECR 33, at 38.
2 [1983] 1 All ER 1042.

3 *Ibid.*, at 1055.
4 Amended to include the ECB by Article G(56) TEU.

Where any such question is raised in a case pending before a court or tribunal of a Member State against whose decisions there is no judicial remedy under national law, that court or tribunal shall bring the matter before the Court of Justice.

Use of Article 177 actions

Article 177 actions are concerned with both the validity and interpretation of Community law. An examination of the statistics shows that references regarding the interpretation of Community legislation are considerably more common than those concerned with validity. The ECJ is not entitled to go further than assessing the validity of, and interpreting, Community law. Therefore it cannot apply Community law to the given facts of the case,[5] nor may it rule on the validity of national law[6] as this would encroach upon the jurisdiction of the national courts. Thus Article 177 procedure is essentially non-hierarchical, in that the ECJ and the national courts are supposed to work in co-operation. The ECJ's attitude has certainly been to smooth the way for effective use of the procedure by, for instance, avoiding excessive insistence on formalities of form.[7] While the reference procedure is not an adversarial proceeding, Article 20 of the Statute of the Court grants the opportunity to make written and oral observations to both the parties to the action as well as to the Member States, the Commission and the Council, and requires that the ECJ notify those bodies upon receipt of a reference.

In terms of assessing validity, it has been made clear in *Foto-Frost* v *Hauptzollamt Lübeck Ost*[8] that the ECJ has exclusive jurisdiction in the matter of declaring Community legislation invalid; thus national courts only have the power to find a Community measure valid in circumstances where there are no grounds for doubt. However, in *Zuckerfabrik Süderithmarschen* v *Hauptzollamt Itzehoe*[9] it was held that a national court could make an interim order suspending an act of a national authority which was based on a Community measure, where the following criteria were fulfilled:

- The national court is persuaded that 'the factual and legal circumstances relied on by the applicants are such . . . that serious doubts exist as to the validity of the Community regulation on which the contested administrative measure is based'.
- The national court feels that there is urgency, that is, that it is necessary for interim measures to be adopted and to take effect before the decision on the substance of a case, in order to avoid serious and irreparable damage to the party seeking them. In such cases, following the ECJ's previous case law, purely financial damage is not likely to be regarded as irreparable.
- The suspension of enforcement must retain the character of an interim measure. That is, a national court may grant such a suspension only until such time as the Court has

[5] Joined Cases 91 and 127/83, *Heineken Brouwerijen v Inspecteurs der Vernootschapsbelasting* [1984] ECR 3435.

[6] Case 26/62, *Van Gend en Loos v Nederlandse Administratie der Belastingen* [1963] ECR 1.

[7] See, for instance, Case 16/65, *Firma C. Schwarze v Einfuhr- und Vorratsstelle fur Getreide und Futtermittel* [1965] ECR 877.

[8] Case 314/85, [1987] ECR 4199. See also Arnull, 'National Courts and the Validity of Community Acts' (1988) 13 EL Rev 125 and Bebr, 'The Reinforcement of the Constitutional Review of Community Acts under Article 177 EEC Treaty (Cases 314/85 and 133–6/85)' (1988) 25 CML Rev 667.

[9] Joined Cases C-143/88 and C-92/89, [1991] ECR I-415. See Schermers (1992) 29 CML Rev 133.

delivered its ruling on the question of validity. In such circumstances, it is incumbent upon the national court, should the question not yet have been referred to the Court of Justice, to refer that question itself; in doing so, setting out the reasons for which it believes that the regulation must be held to be invalid.

- The national court has an obligation to ensure that full effect is given to Community law and thus, where the validity of Community regulations is challenged, it must take account of the interest of the Community, which is that such regulations should not be set aside without proper guarantees. Thus a national court faced with an application for suspension must examine whether the Community measure in question would be without value if not immediately implemented. Also, if suspension of enforcement of a measure may involve financial risk for the Community, the national court should consider requiring the applicant to provide adequate guarantees, such as the deposit of money or other security.[10]

There are dangers to the line taken in *Zuckerfabrik*, the most obvious being that it could create a situation where the conditions under which national measures implementing Community legislation might be suspended are different in each Member State. It is clearly with this scenario in mind that the ECJ laid out such strict criteria:

> . . . uniform application is a fundamental requirement of the Community legal order. It therefore follows that the suspension of enforcement of administrative measures based on a Community regulation, whilst it is governed by national procedural law, in particular as regards the making and examination of the application, must in all the Member States be subject, at the very least, to conditions which are uniform so far as the granting of such relief is concerned.

With regard to national courts making interim orders suspending national legislation on the ground that it appears to be invalid due to conflict with a valid Community measure, the leading case is *R v Secretary of State for Transport, ex parte Factortame (No 1)*.[11] Here, the House of Lords requested a preliminary ruling on the question of whether a national court could be prevented by a rule of national law from temporarily disapplying national legislation to provide interim protection of putative Community law rights. The ECJ held that it could not, as Community law would not be fully effective if, 'a rule of national law could prevent a court seised of a dispute governed by Community law from granting interim relief in order to ensure the full effectiveness of the judgment to be given on the existence of the rights claimed under Community law'.[12]

Jurisdiction of the ECJ under Article 177, paragraph 1

Article 177, paragraph 1 outlines the jurisdiction of the ECJ with regard to the EC Treaty. The ECJ also has jurisdiction to give preliminary rulings under the ECSC,[13] Euratom,[14] Merger, Budgetary and Accession Treaties. In addition, the ECJ has jurisdiction regarding those treaties agreed between the Member States that expressly include provisions to that

---

10 See also Schermers, *ibid.*, at 134.

11 Case C-213/89, [1991] 1 AC 603; [1990] 3 CMLR 1. This was the first reference in this case, being followed by C-221/89, *R v Secretary of State for Transport, ex parte Factortame (No 2)* [1991] 3 CMLR 589. See also Gravells [1989] *Public Law* 568; Gravells [1991] *Public*

Law 180; Oliver (1991) 54 MLR 442.

12 Case C-213/89, *op. cit.*, note 11, at 29. See further Oliver, 'Interim Measures: Some Recent Developments' (1992) 29 CML Rev 7.

13 Article 150 ECSC.

14 Article 14 Euratom.

end, such as the Protocol to the Convention on the Mutual Recognition of Companies and Legal Persons 1968 and the Protocol to the Brussels Convention on Jurisdiction and the Enforcement of Judgments in Civil and Commercial Matters 1968.[15] The ECJ has jurisdiction regarding the acts of the Community institutions, and this is not limited to those acts which have binding force or which are directly applicable.[16] For this purpose it appears that 'the institutions' includes the EP[17] and possibly the ECJ itself.[18] The TEU also adds the European Central Bank to the institutions.

With regard to international law, it appears that the ECJ will have jurisdiction to give preliminary rulings only where the Community has, via an act of one of its institutions, become a party to the agreement.[19] The ECJ has further extended this to mean that it will have jurisdiction to give preliminary rulings on decisions made by such bodies as are created by those agreements.[20] Where Member States have entered into agreements outside the Community, even if all the Member States are in fact party to such an agreement, the ECJ will not have jurisdiction.[21] The case law in the area of international agreements has, however, been somewhat clouded by the ECJ's rulings with regard to its jurisdiction to interpret the General Agreement on Tariffs and Trade (GATT) to which the Community is not technically a party, although in practice it has taken up the obligations and duties of the Member States.[22]

The ECJ does not have jurisdiction to give preliminary rulings upon questions relating to national law.[23] In cases where this has been at issue, either the national courts have managed to word the questions in a manner that makes them questions of Community law, or the ECJ has interpreted inadmissible questions to make them questions of Community law.[24] In such cases the ECJ has then replied in terms such as:

> Although the Court when giving a ruling under Article 177, has no jurisdiction to apply the Community rule to a specific case, or, consequently, to pronounce upon a provision of national law, it may however provide the national court with the factors of interpretation depending on Community law which might be useful to it in evaluating the effects of such a provision.[25]

---

[15] The former Protocol is identical in scope to Article 177, but the latter contains a restriction as to which courts and tribunals may request a preliminary ruling.

[16] See Case 113/75, *Giordano Frecassetti v Amministrazione delle Finanze dello Stato* [1976] ECR 983 (recommendation); Case C-322/88, *Grimaldi v Fonds des Maladies Professionelles* [1989] ECR 4407 (recommendation).

[17] Case 208/80, *Lord Bruce of Donington v Aspden* [1981] ECR 2205.

[18] See Hartley, *The Foundations of European Community Law*, 2nd edn (1988), at 250 and Schermers and Waelbrock, *Judicial Protection in the European Communities*. 4th edn (1987), at 386.

[19] See Case 181/73, *Haegeman v Belgium* [1974] ECR 449 (agreement between Community and a non-Member State (in this case Greece) concluded by the Council); Case 12/86, *Demirel v Stadt Schwäbisch Gmünd* [1987] ECR 3719 (agreement between Community and Turkey).

[20] Case C-18/90, *ONEM v Bahia Kziber* [1991] ECR I-119. See Neuwahl, 'Social Security under the EEC-Morocco Co-operation Agreement' (1991) 16 EL Rev 326.

[21] Such as the European Convention on Human Rights (ECHR) (Case 149/77, *Defrenne v SABENA (No 3)* [1978] ECR 1365, at 1378) and the Statute of the European School (Case 44/84, *Hurd v Jones* [1986] ECR 29). It should be noted that with regard to the ECHR the Court has begun in its case law to adopt some parts of the Convention as fundamental principles.

[22] See Schermers and Walbroeck, *op. cit.*, note 18, at 389, Hartley, *op. cit.*, note 18, at 252 and Joined Cases 267–9/81, *Amministrazione delle Finanze dello Stato v SPI and SAMI* [1983] ECR 801.

[23] Case 24/64, *Dingemans v Bestuur der Sociale Verzekeringsbank* [1964] ECR 647; Case 59/75, *Pubblico Ministero v Manghera* [1976] ECR 91.

[24] Joined Cases 209–13/84, *Ministerie Publi v Asjes* [1986] ECR 1425.

[25] Case 112/75, *Directeur regional de la securité sociale de Nancy. v Auguste Hirardin and Caisse regionale d'assurance maladie du Nord-Est* [1976] ECR 553, at 560; Case 97/83, *Melkunie* [1984] ECR 2367, at 2382.

The preliminary ruling in such cases will usually leave the national court in no doubt as to the status of the national rule with regard to Community law.

In *Dzodzi v Belgium*[26] and also *Krystyna Gmurzynska-Bscher v Oberfinanzdirecktion Köln*[27] the ECJ held that it had jurisdiction to give a ruling under Article 177 where it was asked to interpret a Community ruling which, while it was not itself applicable, was referred to in national legislation with regard to determining a set of rules to be used in circumstances purely internal to the Member State. Its reasoning was based on the principle that it was of importance to the whole Community legal order that Community law should be interpreted uniformly, regardless of the circumstances in which it was to be applied. If the national court decides that the interpretation of Community law is at issue, even where the case concerns purely domestic matters, it was correct for it to ask the ECJ for a preliminary ruling. Inaccurate interpretation of Community law by a national court in a purely domestic case would be as damaging as inaccurate interpretation in a Community case, with regard to its effect on the harmonisation of that law throughout the Community.

Who can refer to the ECJ under Article 177, paragraph 2?

With regard to those bodies who can make a reference to the ECJ, Article 177, paragraph 2 refers rather generally to 'any court or tribunal'. This has left the ECJ with considerable discretion which it has exercised on a case-by-case basis.[28] The ECJ has ruled that the issue of whether or not a body is a 'court or tribunal' for the purposes of Article 177 is not a matter for national legislation but rather a Community matter[29] and has thus developed its own rules for this determination. These rules essentially involve the ECJ examining the role, composition and status of the body in question; the name the body bears appears to have no relevance in the assessment.[30] In *Vaasen*,[31] which concerned a request for a preliminary ruling from a Dutch social security arbitration tribunal (the *Scheidsgerecht van het Beamtenfonds voor het Mijenbedriff*), the ECJ looked at the nature of the tribunal and held that the following points meant that it should be considered a 'court or tribunal' for the purposes of Article 177:

- The Dutch Minister for Social Affairs and Public Health appointed its members, designated the Chairman and laid down its rules of procedure.
- It was a permanent body charged with the settlement of disputes under Article 89 of the RBFM,[32] and it was bound by the same sort of rules of adversary procedure as ordinary courts of law.
- Those persons referred to in the RBFM were automatically members of the

---

26 Joined Cases C-297/88 and 197/89, [1990] ECR I-3763. See Bravo-Ferrer Delgado and La Casta Munoa, (1991) 29 CML Rev 152.

27 Case C-231/89, [1990] ECR I-4003.

28 See Alexander and Grabandt, 'National Courts Entitled to Ask Preliminary Rulings under Article 177 of the EEC Treaty: The Case Law of the Court of Justice' (1982) 19 CML Rev 413 and Bebr, 'Arbitration Tribunals and Article 177' (1985) 22 CML Rev 489.

29 Case 61/65, *Vaasen v Beamtenfonds Mijenbedriff.* [1966] ECR 261; Case 246/80, *Broekmeulen v Huisarts Registratie Commissie* [1981] ECR 2311.

30 UK bodies from which the Court has accepted references include the National Insurance Commissioner (Case 99/80, *Galinsky v Insurance Officer* [1981] ECR 941), the Special Commissioners of Income Tax (Case 208/80, *Lord Bruce of Donington, op. cit.,* note 17) and the Employment Appeal Tribunal (Case 96/80, *Jenkins v Kingsgate Clothing Productions Ltd* [1981] ECR 911).

31 *Op. cit.,* note 29.

32 *Reglement van het Beamtenfonds voor het Mijenbedriff.* This governs the relationship between the *Beamtenfonds* and those insured by it.

Beamtenfonds. As such they were bound to take any disputes between themselves and their insurers to that tribunal as the proper judicial body.
- It was bound to apply rules of law and not equity.

Following *Vaasen*, in *Nederlandse Spoorwegen* v *Minister van Verkeer en Waterstaat*,[33] Advocate General Mayras considered in great detail the nature of the Litigation Section of the Dutch *Raad van State* to determine whether it was a court for the purposes of Article 177. He concluded that, as it had the following characteristics, it was such a court:

- It was set up by the Dutch Constitution and was entrusted by the legislature with certain judicial powers.
- Its composition was laid down by law.
- While it only presented reasoned advice to the Crown, which then had the option whether or not to give that advice the Royal Assent, it gave that advice in accordance with a procedure based on that applied in adversary proceedings.

The ECJ appears to have accepted this opinion as it did not examine the issue of jurisdiction in its judgment.

By contrast, in *Borker*[34] the ECJ held that the Paris *Conseil de l'Ordre des Avocats à la Cour* was not a 'court or tribunal' on the ground that the proceeding for which it was requesting a preliminary ruling was not 'a case which it is under a legal duty to try, but a request for a declaration relating to a dispute between a member of the Bar and the Courts or tribunals of another MS'. As a result, the *Conseil* was not exercising any judicial function, and the ECJ could not therefore have the necessary jurisdiction to give a ruling.

The ruling in *Vaasen* was both confirmed and expanded in *Broekmeulen* v *Huisarts Registratie Commissie*.[35] Here, the case concerned a reference from the *Commissie van Beroep Huisartsgeneeskunde* (Appeals Committee for General Medicine), a body set up by the Royal Netherlands Society for the Promotion of Medicine, which the Dutch government had stated was not a court or tribunal under Dutch law. In its judgment the ECJ referred to the criteria used in *Vaasen*,[36] but also added that given that a doctor intending to establish himself in The Netherlands would have to be recognised by the Society, an appeal from an unfavourable decision would automatically be heard by the Appeals Committee and that there appeared to be no right of appeal from the Appeals Committee, it must have the right to request preliminary rulings.

> If, under the legal system of a Member State, the task of implementing [Community] provisions is assigned to a professional body acting under a degree of governmental supervision, and if that body, in conjunction with the public authorities concerned, creates appeal procedures which may affect the exercise of rights granted by Community law, it is imperative, in order to ensure the proper functioning of Community law, that the Court should have an opportunity of ruling on issues of interpretation and validity arising out of such proceedings. . . . in the absence, in practice, of any right of appeal to the ordinary courts, the Appeals Committee, which operates with the consent of the public authorities

[33] Case 36/73, [1973] ECR 1299.
[34] Case 138/80, [1980] ECR 1975, at 1977.
[35] Case 246/80, [1981] ECR 2311.
[36] That the composition of the Appeals Committee in- volved a 'significant degree of involvement on the part of the Netherlands public authorities'; and it determined disputes on the adversarial principle.

and with their co-operation, and which, after an adversarial procedure, delivers decisions which are in fact recognised as final, must, in a matter involving the application of Community law, be considered as a court or tribunal of a Member State within the meaning of Article 177 of the Treaty.[37]

As far as arbitration tribunals are concerned, in *Handels-og Kontorfunktionaerernes Forbund: Danmark v Dansk Arbejdsgiverforening, ex parte Danfoss A/S*[38] the ECJ held that a Danish Industrial Arbitration Board governed in composition and procedure by Danish law, rather than by the parties involved, and whose decision was final was to be regarded as a court or tribunal for the purpose of Article 177.

The issue of private arbitration tribunals, with no input from public authorities, is somewhat different. This matter was considered in *Nordsee Deutsche Hochseefischerei GmbH v Reederei Mond*.[39] Here an arbitrator, in a dispute related to performance of a contract entered into by a number of German shipbuilders, attempted to refer a matter to the ECJ for a preliminary ruling. The contract at issue contained a clause stating that in the event of disagreement between the parties on any question arising from the contract a final decision was to be given by an arbitrator, all recourse to the ordinary courts being excluded. In accordance with that clause the arbitrator had been appointed by the Chamber of Commerce of Bremen after it had become apparent that the parties to the dispute could not agree on the appointment of an arbitrator.

The ECJ was not, however, willing to accept that the arbitrator fell within the scope of the definition of a 'court or tribunal' as enunciated in its previous case law. It noted that:

- when the contract was entered into the parties involved had a choice of whether to leave any disputes to be resolved by the ordinary courts, or to take the matter to arbitration by way of a clause inserted in the contract. Thus there had been no obligation to go to arbitration;
- the public authorities were not involved in that decision to opt for arbitration, nor where they automatically involved in the event that arbitration was required.

The ECJ then went on to state that while it would have no jurisdiction in private arbitration cases at first instance, where there was an appeal to the ordinary courts from a decision of an arbitrator, the ordinary courts could then make a valid reference.[40]

The above cases concerned administrative bodies which might be perceived as not performing sufficient judicial functions to qualify as a 'court or tribunal'. In *Pretore di Salò v Persons unknown*[41] the ECJ had to consider the issue of whether, if a court has other functions above and beyond those that would normally be expected of a court, this would affect its status as a court for the purposes of Article 177. The case involved a reference, asking for an interpretation of a directive, from an Italian *pretore*, a magistrate who combines the tasks of public prosecutor and investigating judge. The Italian government did not expressly argue a lack of jurisdiction on the part of the ECJ, but did suggest that the *pretore* was not carrying out a judicial function at the time that he made the reference. The Court replied that it had:

[37] Case 246/80, *op. cit.*, note 35, at 2328.
[38] Case 109/88, [1991] 1 CMLR 8.
[39] Case 102/81, [1982] ECR 1095.
[40] *Bulk Oil (Zug) AG v Sun International Ltd* [1984] 1 All ER 386 (QBD), referred as Case 174/84 [1986] ECR 559.
[41] Case 14/86, [1987] ECR 2545. See Arnull, 'The Scope of Article 177' (1988) 13 EL Rev 40.

jurisdiction to reply to a request for a preliminary ruling if that request emanates from a court or tribunal which has acted in the general framework of its task of judging, independently and in accordance with law, cases coming within the jurisdiction conferred on it by law, even though certain functions of that court or tribunal in the proceedings which give rise to the reference for a preliminary ruling are not, strictly speaking, of a judicial nature.[42]

Discretion of courts and tribunals to refer under Article 177, paragraph 2

The procedure for obtaining a preliminary ruling may only be undertaken by a domestic court or tribunal, a reference cannot be made by the parties to the domestic action. Article 177 makes a distinction between courts whose decisions can be appealed under national law (Article 177, paragraph 2) and those of final resort (Article 177, paragraph 3). For courts whose decisions can be appealed under national law, the power to make a reference is generally discretionary; for courts of final resort, it is compulsory.

With regard to the decision whether to refer, the national court has sole discretion as to whether a reference on a point of Community law is required in order for it to reach a judgment. In *Rheinmühlen*[43] the ECJ held that, in order to make this meaningful, it was clear that 'a rule of national law whereby a court is bound on points of law by the rulings of a superior court cannot deprive the inferior courts of their power to refer to the Court questions of interpretation of Community law involving such rulings'.[44] Thus, unless a superior court had already put substantially the same questions to the ECJ, an inferior court was unrestricted as to its discretion to refer.

It is left to the national court to decide when to request for a preliminary ruling in proceedings before it. While emphasising this discretion, based upon the points that the national court has the best knowledge of the case and has the responsibility for ensuring that it is decided correctly, the ECJ has attempted to give some guidelines to national courts as to when it might be most advantageous to request preliminary rulings. In *Irish Creamery Milk Suppliers Association* v *Government of Ireland*[45] the ECJ noted that at the time a reference is made, it would be useful for the facts of the case at issue to have been established and for all issues of purely national law to have been settled, in order that the ECJ could concentrate on those issues relevant to it. The national court also decides the nature and relevance of the questions forwarded to the ECJ for consideration. In *Costa* v *ENEL*[46] it was stated that 'Article 177 is based upon a clear separation of functions between national courts and the Court of Justice, it cannot empower the latter either to investigate the facts of the case or to criticise the grounds and purpose of the request for interpretation'.[47]

The national court may even refer a question to the ECJ when the parties to the action before it have not raised the issue, as was the case in *Salonia* v *Poidomani & Giglio*,[48] where

---

42 *Ibid.*, at 2567.
43 Joined Cases 146 and 166/73, *Rheinmühlen-Düsseldorf* v *Einführ- und Vorratsstelle für Getreide und Futtermittel* [1974] ECR 33.
44 *Ibid.*, at 38.
45 Joined Cases 36 and 71/80, [1981] ECR 735. See also Case 72/83, *Campus Oil* v *Minister for Industry and En-*

ergy [1984] ECR 2727; Case 14/86, *Pretore di Salò* v *Persons unknown, op. cit., note 41.*
46 Case 6/64, [1964] ECR 585.
47 Ibid., at 593. See also Case 13/68, *Salgoil SpA* v *Ministero per il Commercio con l'Estero* [1968] ECR 453.
48 Case 126/80, [1981] ECR 1563.

the Court held that:

> In providing that reference for a preliminary ruling may be submitted to the Court where 'a question is raised before any court or tribunal of a Member State', the second and third paragraphs of Article 177 of the Treaty do not intend to restrict this procedure exclusively to cases where one or other of the parties to the main action has taken the initiative of raising a point concerning the interpretation or the validity of Community law, but also extend to cases where a question of this kind is raised by the national court or tribunal itself which considers that a decision thereon by the Court of Justice is 'necessary to enable it to give judgment'.[49]

The ECJ will not generally look at the facts behind the reference, or question whether the reference is in fact necessary, but there are exceptions to this rule. In *Foglia* v *Novello (No 1)*[50] the ECJ refused to accept a reference from an Italian court, primarily on the ground that there was no genuine dispute between the parties in the domestic action, as that action was designed solely to gain condemnation of the legislation of another Member State as being contrary to the Treaty. The Italian court then made a second reference essentially requesting that the ECJ clarify its judgment in the first reference.[51] The ECJ restated its opinion in the first case regarding the lack of a genuine dispute, but then went on to say that if the Italian court could come up with new facts to support the need for the ECJ to examine the relevant Treaty provision, it should resubmit its reference. It also pointed out that national courts should make clear their reasoning as to why a preliminary ruling was necessary to reach a judgment in the action before them, if this was not obvious from the material provided to the ECJ. Despite the academic furore caused by the *Foglia* cases[52] they appear to have had limited impact upon the case law of the ECJ.[53] Indeed, in two cases decided between the judgments in *Foglia (No 1)* and *Foglia (No 2)*, in which the facts were broadly similar, the ECJ found no difficulty in accepting the references.[54] Hartley points out that this apparent anomaly may well be due to the fact that the ECJ was attempting to be politic in its approach towards France, which might not have been best pleased in having its taxes challenged in this manner rather than under an Article 169 procedure (*see* above, Chapter 8).[55]

In *Salonia* v *Poidomani & Giglio*[56] and *Falciola Angelo SpA* v *Comune di Pavia*[57] the ECJ also noted that it could reject references on the grounds that they were attempting to obtain a preliminary ruling on matters of interpretation or validity of Community law that were quite clearly not relevant to the actual case or subject matter of the main action. There is

---

[49] *Ibid.*, at 1577.

[50] Case 104/79, [1980] ECR 745.

[51] Case 244/80, *Foglia* v *Novello (No 2)* [1981] ECR 3045.

[52] See Barav (1980) 5 EL Rev 443, Bebr (1980) 7 CML Rev 525; Wyatt (1981) 6 EL Rev 449; Bebr, 'The possible implications of *Foglia* v *Novello II*' (1982) 19 CML Rev 421.

[53] For example, Case 261/81, *Walter Rau* v *de Smedt* [1982] ECR 3961; Case C-150/88, *Parfumerie-Fabrik* v *Provide* [1989] ECR 3891, but see Case C-83/91, *Meilicke* v *ADV/ORGA*, note 58 below.

[54] Case 140/79, *Chemical Faramaceutici* v *DAF* [1981] ECR 1 and Case 46/80, *Vinal* v *Orbat* [1981] ECR 77.

[55] Hartley, op. cit., note 18, at 259.

[56] Case 126/80, *op. cit.*, note 48. In this case the argument that there were no valid grounds for a preliminary ruling was rejected by the ECJ.

[57] Case C-286/88, [1990] ECR I-191. In this case, the argument was successful. The Italian court purported to require an interpretation of Council Directives 71/304/EEC and 71/305/EEC, but the court merely informed the ECJ that it would have to apply those directives in the dispute brought before it. The ECJ stated that it was clear from the actual wording of the order for reference that the court was in fact concerned with obtaining a ruling on the potential Community implications of the enactment of Italian Law No 117/88 of 13 April 1988 on compensation for damage caused in the exercise of judicial functions and the civil liability of the judiciary.

case law to suggest, however, that where a national court has failed to give clear, or indeed any, reasons for the need for a preliminary ruling, this will not necessarily result in the ECJ refusing to accept the reference.[58]

Where the ECJ has made a previous ruling, there is nothing to stop it changing its mind at a later date as it is not bound by its previous decisions. Also its rulings in Article 177 references declaring an act of an institution, in particular a Council or Commission regulation, to be void are directly addressed only to the national court which brought the matter before the Court. Thus, while it is sufficient reason for any other national court to regard that act as void for the purposes of a judgment which it has to give, it does not mean that national courts are deprived of the power given to them by Article 177 of the Treaty and they have the discretion to decide whether there is a need to raise once again a question which has already been settled by the Court where the Court has previously declared an act of a Community institution to be void. There may be such a need in particular if questions arise as to the grounds, the scope and possibly the consequences of the invalidity established earlier.[59] This may involve the ECJ being asked to rule on the same question for a different court with different parties,[60] or for the same court with the same parties[61] (both same). A national court may also make more than one reference in a case[62] but, as was noted in *Wünsche* v *Germany*,[63] it should not attempt to use the second reference to contest the validity of the first. If the ECJ is asked to make a ruling on a point it has already dealt with, it will generally do so. In such circumstances, unless it decides that the previous ruling was, for some reason, wrongly decided it will simply repeat the form and often the words of the earlier ruling.[64]

If the proceedings before the national court, for which the ruling is required, are terminated before the reference can be made, or the court making the reference withdraws it or the reference is set aside by a higher court, the ECJ will have no jurisdiction to hear it.[65] The issue of the legality of Member States allowing appeals against a decision to refer or not to refer was addressed by Advocate General Warner in the *Rheinmühlen* case,[66] where he was of the opinion that to allow an appeal from a decision to refer was an improper fetter on the court's discretion. The ECJ however rejected this viewpoint stating that an order for reference is 'subject to the remedies normally available under national law'.[67]

In the UK, under Order 114, rule 6 of the Rules of the Supreme Court, an Order making a

[58] Joined Cases 98, 162 and 258/85, *Bertini* v *Regione Lazio* [1986] ECR 1885. But contrast Case C-83/91, *Meilicke* v *ADV/ORGA*, not yet reported, decision of 16 July 1992, which suggests that the ECJ is of the opinion that it would exceed the limits of its function if it decided to give a ruling without having available the elements of fact and law necessary to give a useful reply to the questions referred to it.

[59] Case 66/80, *ICI* v *Amministrazione delle Finanze dello Stato* [1981] ECR 1191.

[60] Case 28/67, *Molkerei-Zentrale Westfalen* v *Hauptzollamt Paderborn* [1968] ECR 143, regarding the ECJ's interpretation of Article 95 EC in Case 57/65, *Lütticke* v *HZA Saarlouis* [1966] ECR 205.

[61] Case 8/78, *Milac* v *HZA Freiberg* [1978] ECR 1721, regarding the ECJ's ruling in Case 28/76, *Milac* v *HZA Freiberg* [1976] ECR 1639.

[62] See *Foglia* case, *op. cit.*

[63] Case 69/85, [1986] ECR 947. The ECJ noted that valid reasons for a re-reference included 'when the national court encounters difficulties in understanding or applying the judgment, when it refers a fresh question of law to the Court, or again when it submits new considerations which might lead the Court to give a different answer to a question submitted earlier' (at 953).

[64] As in Case C-350/89, *Sheptonhurst Ltd* v *Newham BC* [1991] ECR I-2387, repeating ruling in Case C-23/89, *Quietlynn Ltd* v *Southend BC* [1990] ECR I-3059, see Arnull, note 8, *op. cit.*, at 252.

[65] Case C-159/90, *Society for the Protection of the Unborn Child* v *Grogan* [1991] 3 CMLR 849; Case 338/85, *Pardini* v *Ministero del Commercio con L'Estero* [1988] ECR 2041.

[66] Joined Cases 146 and 166/73, *op. cit.*, note 43.

[67] *Ibid.*, at 147.

reference to the ECJ under Article 177 is held to be a final order. This means that an appeal lies to the Court of Appeal without leave. In the case *Procurator Fiscal, Elgin* v *Cowie*[68] the Scottish High Court of Justiciary was of the opinion that it should interfere with a lower court's decision to refer to the ECJ only where it felt that the decision was clearly unfounded.[69] Where a judge refuses to make a reference to the ECJ under Article 177, leave to appeal must be obtained from either the High Court or the Court of Appeal, as the decision is an interlocutory order.[70]

Compulsory references by national courts of last resort under Article 177, paragraph 3[71]

Article 177, paragraph 3 clearly states that where a court or tribunal of a Member State, against whose decisions there is no judicial remedy under national law (court of final resort), is faced with a question of Community law, that court or tribunal shall bring the matter before the ECJ. However, the ECJ has not been inclined to interpret this strictly, in terms of that in such circumstances a reference must *always* be made; rather the ECJ has been inclined to allow national courts a degree of discretion in the referral procedure. In *Da Costa en Schaake* v *Nederlandse Belastingadministratie*[72] the Court held that, while Article 177 clearly required national courts against whose decisions there are no remedies under national law to refer all questions of interpretation of Community law to the ECJ, where the ECJ had already made such an interpretation in an earlier case (especially where the question raised was essentially the same) such a reference was likely to be purposeless. The situation and question in *Da Costa* were essentially the same as those in *Van Gend en Loos*,[73] although the cases involved different parties, and the ECJ pointed the referring court to the *Van Gend en Loos* ruling.

As noted above, the fact that cases raise similar or identical questions to those already answered by the ECJ does not prevent national courts from raising them again; the importance of the ruling in *Da Costa* lies in the fact that the ECJ was prepared to state that national courts of final resort had some degree of discretion as to whether to refer or not. This was taken a stage further in *CILFIT* v *Ministro della Sanità*,[74] where the ECJ embraced the doctrine of *acte claire*, that is, where a point of law is clear and free from doubt, either on its face or because the ECJ has already ruled on it, the national court need not refer. However, the ECJ warned the national courts that

> Before it comes to the conclusion that such is the case, the national court or tribunal must be convinced that the matter is equally obvious to the courts of the other Member States and to the Court of Justice. Only if those conditions are satisfied may the national court or

[68] [1990] 3 CMLR 445.
[69] The case was eventually referred as Cases C-251–252/90, *Procurator Fiscal, Elgin* v *Kenneth Gordon Wood and James Cowie* [1992] 2 CMLR 493.
[70] *Bulmer* v *Bollinger* [1974] 2 All ER 1226, at 1233. See also Hartley, *op. cit.*, note 18, at 277; Dine, Douglas Scott and Persaud, *Procedure and the European Court* (1991), at 51.
[71] In the UK the procedures for making a reference under Article 177 may be found in the following places:

Court of Appeal and High Court – Order 114, rule 1 RSC; County Courts – rule 19 (II). See further Dine, Douglas-Scott, and Persaud, *op. cit.*, note 70 and Maclean, *European Community Law Textbook* (1992).
[72] Joined Cases 28, 29 and 30/62, [1963] ECR 31.
[73] Case 26/62, *op. cit.*, note 6.
[74] Case 283/81, [1982] ECR 3415.

tribunal refrain from submitting the question to the Court of Justice and take upon itself the responsibility for resolving it.[75]

The ruling in *CILFIT* and the doctrine of *acte claire* have been the subject of much discussion, both academic and judicial, not least in the UK.[76] In cases such as *Customs and Excise Commissioners v ApS Samex*,[77] *R v Pharmaceutical Society of Great Britain, ex parte The Association of Pharmaceutical Importers*[78] and *R v Secretary of State for Transport, ex parte Factortame Limited*,[79] arguments based on the ruling in *CILFIT* were cited as the reason for referring questions to the ECJ. By contrast, in *R v Secretary of State for Social Services, ex parte Bomore Medical Supplies Ltd and Eurochem Ltd*[80] and *R v ILEA, ex parte Hinde, Duverly and Phillips*,[81] the *CILFIT* ruling was used to justify, somewhat more controversially, failure to make a reference. In *Magnavision NV v General Optical Council*[82] in the Divisional Court, a major flaw in the *CILFIT* ruling was made evident. Here the defendant was convicted by magistrates for breach of section 21 of the Opticians Act 1958 which prohibited the sale of optical appliances except by or under the supervison of a registered medical practitioner or optician. On appeal to the Divisional Court the applicant requested a preliminary ruling as to whether section 21 of the Opticians Act 1958 breached Article 30 EC. The Divisional Court's ruling after examination of the ECJ's case law – that, first, there was no need to refer the question and, secondly, there was no breach of Article 30 EC by section 21 of the Opticians Act 1958 – appears to have been deeply questionable.[83] Following judgment the Divisional Court was asked to certify that there were points of law in the case that should be considered by the House of Lords. This it refused to do.[84] That decision left the applicant with no further remedy, as there is no appeal against such a refusal, and without the certificate requested no appeal could be made to the House of Lords. The Divisional Court was then asked to refer to the ECJ a question regarding the scope of Article 30. It again refused, this time on the grounds that a judgment had already been given in the case. This, in effect, made the Divisional Court the national court of final resort and left the applicant faced with a misinterpretaion of Community law about which he could do nothing.[85]

The above discussion raises the issue of what is to be considered a national court of final resort. In *Costa v ENEL*[86] the ECJ's ruling implies that any court or tribunal, in a given case, from which under national law there is no appeal from its decision falls within Article 177, paragraph 3, even if in other cases it would be possible to appeal against decisions of that court or tribunal. It is clear however, that at least in the UK, the nature of the judicial

[75] *Ibid.*, at 3430. Thus, after *CILFIT* there appear to be three basic exceptions to the strict rule that questions of interpretation of Community law raised before the national court against whose decisions there are no remedies under national law must be referred. These are: (i) Where the question raised is irrelevant to the outcome of the case. (ii) Where previous decisions of the ECJ have already dealt with the point of law in question. (iii) Where the correct application of Community law is so obvious that there is no scope for any reasonable doubt as to how to resolve the question.
[76] See, for example, Wyatt, 'Article 177(3) – the Court cautiously endorses the *acte claire* doctrine' (1983) 8 EL Rev 179; Rasmussen 'The European Courts' *Acte Claire*

Strategy in *CILFIT*' (1984) 9 EL Rev 242; Arnull, 'The uses and abuses of Article 177 EEC' (1989) MLR 622.
[77] [1983] 1 All ER 1042.
[78] [1987] 3 CMLR 951.
[79] [1990] 3 CMLR 375.
[80] [1986] 1 CMLR 228.
[81] [1985] 1 CMLR 716.
[82] [1987] 1 CMLR 887.
[83] See, for instance, Case 8/74, *Procureur de Roi v Dassonville* [1974] ECR 837.
[84] *Magnavision NV v General Optical Council (No 2)* [1987] 2 CMLR 262.
[85] See further, Arnull, *op. cit.*, note 76, at 632.
[86] Case 6/64, *op. cit.*, note 46.

proceedings may render the application of this rule problematical. As a final example of some of the uncertainities, Wyatt and Dashwood catagorically state that: 'It means any court, even if not the highest court, against whose decision there is no judicial remedy in the instant case. Accordingly the Court of Appeal is obliged to refer, if leave to appeal to the House of Lords is refused.'[87] Yet this interpretation may not fit squarely with the judgment in *Generics (UK) Ltd v Smith, Kline & French Laboratories Ltd*[88] (CA), where the Court of Appeal held: 'We are not, of course, the final appellate court for the purposes of Article 177 of the Treaty, even though an appeal to the House of Lords lies only with leave. . . . So we are not obliged to refer the question to the EEC Court of Justice. But we have discretion.'

Legal effects of preliminary rulings[89]

When assessing the legal effects of preliminary rulings, it is useful to distinguish between rulings on interpretation and rulings on validity. In terms of rulings on interpretation, the Court has held that such rulings are binding on the national courts as to the interpretation of the Community provisions and acts in question.[90] Further:

> The interpretation which, in the exercise of the jurisdiction conferred upon it by Article 177, the Court of Justice gives to a rule of Community law clarifies and defines where necessary the meaning and scope of that rule as it must be or ought to have been understood and applied from the time of its coming into force. It follows that the rule as thus interpreted may, and must, be applied by the courts even to legal relationships arising and established before the judgment ruling on the request for interpretation, provided that in other respects the conditions enabling an action relating to the application of that rule to be brought before the courts having jurisdiction are satisfied.

Therefore, in general, a ruling by the ECJ can be relied upon by third parties to support a claim based on facts occurring before the date of the ruling.[91] There are, however, exceptions to this rule, for instance as seen in *Defrenne v SABENA*.[92] The ECJ, anxious not to create undue reliance on such exceptions, set out in *Amministrazione delle Finanze dello Stato v Denkavit Italiana*,[93] two rules limiting their scope:

- it is for the Court of Justice alone to decide upon the temporal restrictions to be placed on the interpretation which it lays down; and
- such a restriction may be allowed only in the actual judgment ruling upon the interpretation sought.[94]

87 Wyatt and Dashwood, *European Community Law* (1993), at 149.
88 [1990] 1 CMLR 416.
89 See Toth, 'The Authority of Judgments of the European Court of Justice: Binding Force and Legal Effects' (1984) 4 YEL 1; Alexander, 'The Temporal Effects of Preliminary Rulings' (1988) 9 YEL 11.
90 Case 52/76, *Benedetti v Munari* [1977] ECR 163.
91 See Case 61/79, *Amministrazione delle Finanze dello Stato v Denkavit Italiana* [1980] ECR 1205; also Joined Cases 66, 127 and 128/79, *Amministrazione delle Fi-*

nanze dello Stato v Salumi [1980] ECR 1237, at 1260; Case 811/79, *Amministrazione delle Finanze dello Stato v Ariete* [1980] ECR 2545, at 2553; Case 826/79, *Amministrazione delle Finanze dello Stato v Mireco* [1980] ECR 2559, at 2573.
92 Case 43/75, [1976] ECR 455.
93 Case 61/79, *op. cit.*, note 91.
94 *Ibid.*, at 1223; see also Alexander, *op. cit.*, note 89, at 14; Case 69/80, *Worringham and Humphreys v Lloyds Bank Limited* [1981[ECR 767; Case 309/85, *Barra v Belgian State* [1988] ECR 355.

Regarding rulings on validity, the ECJ has stressed that its rulings under Article 177 should be consistent with judgments in actions for annulment under Article 173. Therefore, despite the fact that a ruling under Article 177 is technically addressed to (and binding upon) the national court which brought the matter before the ECJ, it provides sufficient reason for any other national court to regard that act as void in cases before them.[95] It also seems that where the ECJ has ruled that an institution's act is void under a Article 177 reference, that, as with Article 173, the insitution should move to take the necessary measures to ensure that its act is in line with the Court's judgment.[96]

CONCLUSION

Article 177 references have become increasingly important in ensuring the conformity of national laws with Community law. The use of Article 177 as the predominant means of seizing the ECJ of matters relating to conformity with Community law has confirmed the role of the ECJ as more like a constitutional court than a court of first instance. Like the German Constitutional Court, the ECJ is better adapted to dealing with questions of law rather than fact and it does not appear to be inclined to adopt or create a formal system of evidence. As noted elsewhere (*see* Chapter 8), Article 177 references are increasingly being used in preference to the Commission or Member States beginning actions under Article 169 or Article 170. In addition, the fact that Article 173 has been interpreted so restrictively with regard to *locus standi* (see Chapter 7) has diverted many complainants into the national courts and thus to Article 177 references. The ECJ appears to have collaborated in this movement towards increasing use of Article 177 by ensuring that there is easy access to the ECJ under this procedure via rulings such as *CILFIT* (although, as noted above, *CILFIT* has the potential to create as many problems as it solves). In creating guidelines in *CILFIT*, the Court made it clear that it was not enthusiastic about national courts interpreting Community law, but the manner in which it has attempted to prevent this from happening within the strictures of Article 177 has led to a situation where, as the *Magnavision* case shows, breaches of Community law may be approved by the national courts, with no further recourse to the ECJ.

Further reading

Arnull, A., 'The Scope of Article 177' (1988) 13 EL Rev 40.

Arnull, A., 'National Courts and the Validity of Community Acts' (1988) 13 EL Rev 125.

Arnull, A., 'The uses and abuses of Article 177 EEC' (1989) MLR 622.

Arnull, A., 'References to the European Court' (1990) 15 EL Rev 375.

Alexander, W., 'The Temporal Effects of Preliminary Rulings' (1988) 8 YEL 11.

Alexander, W. and Grabandt, E., 'National Courts Entitled to Ask Preliminary Rulings under Article 177 of the EEC Treaty: The Case Law of the Court of Justice' (1982) 19 CML Rev 413.

Beaumont, P.R., 'European Court and jurisdiction and enforcement of judgments in both civil and commercial matters' (1990) 39 ICLQ 700.

---

[95] Case 66/80, *ICI v Amministrazione delle Finanze dello Stato* [1981] ECR 1191.   [96] *Ibid.*

Bebr, G., 'Arbitration Tribunals and Article 177' (1985) 22 CML Rev 489.

Bebr, G., 'The Reinforcement of the Constitutional Review of Community Acts under Article 177 EEC Treaty (cases 314/85 and 133–6/85)' (1988) 25 CML Rev 667.

Dashwood, A. and Arnull, A., 'English Courts and Article 177 of the EEC Treaty' (1984) 4 YEL 255.

Gray, C., 'Advisory Opinions and the European Court of Justice' (1983) 8 EL Rev 24.

O'Keeffe, D., 'Appeals Against an Order to Refer under Article 177 of the EEC Treaty' (1984) 9 EL Rev 87.

Oliver, P., 'Interim Measures: Some Recent Developments' (1992) 29 CML Rev 7.

Rasmussen, H., 'The European Court's *Acte Clair* strategy in *CILFIT*' (1984) 9 EL Rev 242.

Rasmussen, H., 'Between Self-Restraint and Activism: a Judicial Policy for the European Court' (1988) 13 EL Rev 28.

Toth, A.G., 'The Authority of Judgments of the European Court of Justice: Binding Force and Legal Effects' (1984) 4 YEL 1.

Watson, J., 'Experience and Problems in Applying Article 177 EEC' (1986) 23 CML Rev 207.

CHAPTER 11

Free movement of goods

INTRODUCTION

The principle of the free movement of goods within the Community is an integral part of the establishment of the Common Market and, with free movement of persons, services and capital, is one of the four essential 'freedoms' regulated by the Treaty and guarded with great zeal by the ECJ. Indeed, it is such a vital tenet of the Community that it has acquired a force bettered at Community law level only by the veneration of the Common Agricultural Policy and at the UK national level only by the respect of the courts for the phrase 'national security'. Because of the importance of the principle to the Community, the volume of both case law and legislation relating to it is immense and a totally comprehensive survey is far beyond the scope of this textbook.[1]

As such, this Chapter will examine the role played by, and effect of, the Customs Union and the Common Commercial Policy. It will then move to an examination of how and why certain practices are prohibited and others are permitted under the headings of customs duties and charges having equivalent effect, and quantitative restrictions and measures having equivalent effect. The issue of tackling the barriers which still remain after the supposed completion of the internal market, including variations in national standards, both technical and fiscal, will also be considered.

The Chapter will thus examine the main themes relating to the principle of free movement of goods and, in particular, the often imaginative ways in which the Member States have endeavoured to resist its advance and so protect their national producers and their markets.

The origins of the principle of free movement of goods are to be found in the EC Treaty, Article 3(a) of which provides for 'the elimination, as between Member States, of customs duties and of quantitative restrictions on the import and export of goods, and of all other measures having equivalent effect'; and Article 7a[2] which states that 'The internal market shall comprise an area without internal frontiers in which the free movement of goods, persons, services and capital is ensured in accordance with the provisions of this Treaty'.

This is outlined in much greater detail in Part III, Title I, of the Treaty.[3] Here, Articles 12–29 deal with the elimination of customs duties between Member States and charges having an equivalent effect, and Articles 30–37 deal with the issue of elimination of quantitative restrictions and all measures having an equivalent effect. In particular Articles 30 and 34 prohibit the imposition by Member States of quantitative restrictions and all measures having equivalent effect, on imports and exports. Article 36 provides the exceptions to Articles 30–34.

---

1 See for a more detailed, if somewhat dated, analysis, Gormley, *Prohibiting Restrictions on Trade within the EEC* (1985); Oliver, *Free Movement of Goods in the EEC*, 2nd edn 1988.

2 Note Articles 7, 7a, 7b, 7c were former Articles 8, 8a, 8b, 8c and were changed by Article G(9) TEU.

3 Following the TEU, Part Three of the Treaty consists of former Parts Two and Three (Article G.D TEU).

REMOVAL OF FISCAL BARRIERS TO FREE MOVEMENT OF GOODS

The concept of a Customs Union

Article 9 (1) EC states that:

> The Community shall be based upon a customs union which shall cover all trade in goods and which shall involve the prohibition between Member States of customs duties on imports and exports and of all charges having equivalent effect, and the adoption of a common customs tariff in their relations with third countries.

The result of this is that the Customs Union is wider in scope than an organisation such as the EFTA, inasmuch as the Member States not only eliminate customs duties between themselves but they adopt a common position on tariffs charged to any other nation. Thus, goods from a third nation will face the same tariffs whether imported into the UK or Germany.

Article 9(2) further states that:

> The provisions of . . . [Articles 12–17 and 31–37] . . . shall apply to products originating in Member States and to products which are in free circulation in Member States.

This ensures that products which enter the Community market from third countries are as capable of enjoying free movement within it as goods which were produced within the Community, once the initial tariff at the Community's external border is paid and they enter into free circulation within a Member State.

In relation to third country imports there are two main considerations to be noted with regard to Article 9 (2). First, there is the issue of the place of origin of the goods in question and, secondly, there is the meaning of 'free circulation'.

The place of origin of goods is determined with reference to Regulation 2913/92/EEC.[4] This states that where goods are produced or wholly obtained within one country, that country is deemed to be the place of origin.[5] It is frequently the case, however, that goods will undergo a production process in more than one country. In such circumstances the Regulation provides that the place of origin is the country where the last economically justifiable process occurred, provided that that process resulted in a new product or was an important or essential phase of the manufacture of the good.[6] Thus, cosmetic changes to a product are unlikely to be considered sufficient to justify a change in its place of origin, as the ECJ has held that there must be a 'significant qualitative change' for this to occur.[7] The assembly of goods in a particular country may justify that country being listed as the place of origin but this will depend on the value added to the particular product as a result of the assembly.[8]

'Free circulation' of goods is dealt with in Article 10 EC which states that:

> Products coming from a third country shall be considered to be in free circulation in a Member State if the import formalities have been complied with and any customs duties or

---

[4] OJ 1992 L302.
[5] Ibid.
[6] Ibid.
[7] Case 49/76, *Uberseehandel* v *Handelskammer Hamburg* [1977] ECR 41; contrast with Cases 34/78 and

114/78, *Yoshida* [1979] 115 and 151.
[8] Case C-26/88, *Brother International* v *HZA Giessen* [1989] ECR 4253 where less than 10 per cent added value was held not to be enough for Community origin.

charges having equivalent effect which are payable have been levied in that Member State, and if they have benefited from a total or partial drawback of such duties or charges.

Definition of 'goods'

It should be noted that the Treaty makes no attempt to define 'goods' for the purpose of Article 9; instead we must look to judgments of the ECJ in order to ascertain the extent of the term. In *Commission v Italy*[9] the ECJ held that:

> . . . by goods, within the meaning of Article 9 of the EEC Treaty, there must be understood products which can be valued in money and which are capable, as such, of forming the subject of commercial transactions.

Further to this, in the cases of *Guiseppe Sacchi*,[10] *R v Thompson, Johnson and Woodiwiss*,[11] and *Commission v Ireland*[12] the ECJ has attempted to provide a clearer distinction between 'goods', 'services' and 'capital'. In the *Sacchi* case this was because the definition of 'goods' as laid out in the *Commission v Italy* case would, in theory, be capable of application to television signals, as they could be said to be an item provided for remuneration and thus be capable of being the subject of financial transactions. The ECJ held, somewhat opaquely, that:

> . . . although it is not ruled out that services normally provided for remuneration may come under the provisions relating to goods, such is however the case, as appears from Article 60, only in so far as they are governed by such provisions. It follows that the transmission of television signals, including those in the nature of advertisements, comes, as such, within the rules of the Treaty relating to services.[13]

Inasmuch as it is possible to attribute meaning to this, it appears that the ECJ considers that services are services unless the Community, via legislation, states that they are goods for a particular purpose.

In *R v Thompson, Johnson and Woodiwiss* the ECJ was faced with the issue of determining whether coins were goods or capital, and in its judgment stated that if the coins are legal tender in a Member State they are not goods, but rather a means of payment and as such they are not subject to the principle of the free movement of goods. In *Commission v Ireland* the ECJ decided that 'goods' for the purpose of free movement of goods included goods and materials supplied in the course of the provision of a service.

Customs duties, taxation and tariffs

An examination of the Articles concerned with elimination of customs duties between the Member States, Articles 12–17, shows that of these, the majority, Articles 13–17, are of mainly historical interest, except inasmuch as they may be relevant to the study of the conditions precedent upon the accession of new Member States to the Community.[14] Article 12, however, remains of importance in affirming the Community aim of preventing the application of new customs duties or the increase of existing ones by the Member States.

---

9 Case 7/68, [1968] ECR 423.
10 Case 155/73, [1974] ECR 409.
11 Case 7/78, [1978] ECR 2247.
12 Case 45/87, [1988] ECR 4929.
13 See also Case 52/79, *Procureur du Roi v Debauve*

[1980] ECR 881.
14 The transitional period for Member States to conform with the requirements of those Articles expired in June 1968, see Decision 66/532/EEC, OJ 1966, at 2971.

General prohibition on customs duties under Article 12

Article 12 states that:

> Member States shall refrain from introducing between themselves any new customs duties on imports or exports or any charges having equivalent effect, and from increasing those which they already apply in their trade with each other.

Given its clarity of purpose, its precision and its unconditional nature, the ECJ had no problem with declaring Article 12 to be directly effective in *Van Gend en Loos* v *Nederlandse Administratie der Belastingen*[15] where the Dutch authorities had attempted to charge a customs duty on imports of ureaformaldehyde. It is useful to note that the concept of crossing a frontier is an important one in terms of the operation of Article 12. If the levy complained of is imposed on identical goods produced in the relevant Member State, even where the national production is only a small percentage of the total of those goods sold within the Member State, Article 12 cannot be invoked.[16]

In *Commission* v *Italy*,[17] which concerned a tax on the export of art treasures, the ECJ, after dismissing the argument that the items at issue were not 'goods' for the purposes of Article 12, went on to dismiss the Italian government's second argument, which was that the tax was required in order to ensure that national art treasures remained in Italy. The ECJ took the attitude that this argument was irrelevant. In its view the tax was a tax on goods crossing an internal Community border which would have the effect of impeding intra-Community trade, and that this rendered it contrary to Article 12 and thus illegal, regardless of the laudability of its professed aim. This pragmatism was similarly displayed in *Sociaal Fonds etc* v *Brachfeld and Chougol Diamond Co.*[18] Here, the Belgian government sought to justify a levy on the value of imported diamonds, the funds from which were used to provide social security benefits for workers in the national diamond industry, which was being challenged by way of an Article 177 reference. Belgium argued that as the levy charged was not for the protection of national production, as Belgium was not a diamond producer, and it was not designed to raise money for the State, the funds going as they did to worker welfare, there could be no breach of Articles 9 and 12. As with the *Commission* v *Italy* case, the ECJ was not impressed by these arguments. It was pointed out that a levy placed on goods because they crossed a frontier, no matter how small the levy, was in breach of Article 12 because the system of reduction and removal of customs duties or charges having equivalent effect set up by Article 12 was not conditional, but absolute.

Charges having equivalent effect to customs duties

The *Sociaal Fonds* case also demonstrates the extent to which the ECJ has used the concept of 'a charge having equivalent effect to a customs duty' to widen the scope of Article 12 well beyond simple customs charges. Indeed, the rule used in that case, with slight semantic adjustments, is still used by the Court:

> . . . the justification for the prohibition of charges having an effect equivalent to customs duties lies in the fact that any pecuniary charge, however small, imposed on goods

---

15 Case 26/62, [1963] ECR 1.
16 Case 70/79, *Commission* v *France* [1981] ECR 283.

17 Case 7/68, *op. cit.*, note 9.
18 Cases 2 and 3/69, [1969] ECR 211.

by reason of the fact that they cross a frontier constitutes an obstacle to the movement of goods in that it artificially increases the price of imported or exported goods in relation to domestic goods. It follows that any pecuniary charge, whatever its designation and mode of application, which is imposed unilaterally on goods by reason of the fact that they cross a frontier constitutes a charge having an effect equivalent to a customs duty within the meaning of Articles 9, 12, 13 and 16 of the Treaty.[19]

The concept of 'a charge having equivalent effect to a customs duty', and its strict application, thus allows the ECJ to avoid difficulties with the interpretation of national legal rules; if the charge at issue has any economic effect the application of the Community rule will permit no semantic quibbling on the part of the Member States.

Charges for services

The application of Article 12 is rendered somewhat more problematic, however, by the fact that in certain cases the charges that the Member States are seeking to justify may not be clearly customs duties imposed by reason of the crossing of a frontier, nor charges having equivalent effect. In such cases the Member State involved will usually claim that the charge being levied is in fact a fee paid for a service rendered. While this type of claim offers a way around the rule in Article 12 the ECJ has only rarely been minded to accept them. Member States have attempted to justify a diverse range of 'services' by this means, including health and sanitary inspections,[20] the collection of data for a statistical survey which it was claimed would aid traders,[21] quality control inspections,[22] extended opening hours for customs posts beyond accepted national working hours,[23] and the issue of import licences by a national agricultural intervention agency.[24]

The ECJ has held that in such cases a charge imposed on goods by reason of the fact that they cross a frontier is not a charge having equivalent effect prohibited by the Treaty and is thus acceptable and not subject to Article 12 prohibition only if:

> . . . it constitutes consideration for a specific service actually and individually rendered to the trader, in an amount proportionate to that service. For that to be so there must be a specific or individual benefit provided to the trader.[25]

Thus, in *Commission v Italy*,[26] involving a levy to finance the gathering of statistics, the ECJ held that while the statistics gathered might be useful to the Italian government there was no

19 See for example, Case 340/87, *Commission v Italian Republic* [1989] ECR 1483; Case 18/87, *Commission v Federal Republic of Germany* [1988] ECR 5427.

20 Case 87/75, *Bresciani v Amministrazione Italiana delle Finanze* [1976] ECR 129 (veterinary and public health inspections carried out on the importation of raw cowhides); Case 35/76, *Simmenthal Spa v Italian Minister for Finance* [1976] ECR 1871 (veterinary inspection of a consignment of beef and veal intended for human consumption); Case 251/78, *Firma Denkavit Futtermittel GmbH v Minister of Food* [1979] ECR 3369; Case C-111/89, *The State (Netherlands) v P Bakker Hillegom BV* [1990] ECR I-1735; Case C-137/89, *Commission of the European Communities v Italian Republic* (Transcript) 14 March 1990.

21 Case 24/68, *Commission v Italy* [1969] ECR 193.

22 Case 63/74, *Cadsky v Instituto Nazionale per il Commercio Estero* [1975] ECR 281.

23 Case 340/87, *Commission v Italian Republic, op. cit.,* note 19.

24 Cases 52 and 55/65, *Germany v Commission* [1966] ECR 159.

25 Case 63/74, *Cadsky, op. cit.,* note 22; Case 132/82, *Commission v Belgium* [1983] ECR 1649; Case 340/87, *Commission v Italian Republic op. cit.* note 19.

26 Case 24/68, *op. cit.,* note 21.

obvious benefit which could be traced to individual traders, thus the levy was a charge equivalent to a customs duty and therefore prohibited by Article 12.

As the ECJ has held that the sum charged must be proportionate to the cost of its supply, it is clear that flat rate charges based on the value of the goods involved are unacceptable, even in circumstances where a service is provided which might be legitimately charged for.[27]

Thus, in principle, a charge can be said *not* to have equivalent effect to a customs duty in four main circumstances; first, if it forms part of a general system of internal charges systematically covering, according to the same criteria, national products and imported or exported products;[28] secondly, if it constitutes payment for a service actually rendered to a trader of an amount proportionate to such service;[29] thirdly, if, under certain circumstances, it relates to inspections carried out to fulfil obligations laid down by Community law;[30] and fourthly, if, under certain circumstances, it relates to inspections carried out to fulfil obligations laid down by instruments of general international law to which all Member States are party.[31]

The rule against internal taxation under Article 95 EC

Customs duties and charges having equivalent effect are only half of the problem when it comes to dealing with fiscal barriers to the free movement of goods within the Community. The second half of the problem relates to the issue of internal taxation being placed on imported goods by the Member States. Such internal taxation cannot constitute a customs duty or charge having equivalent effect because it does not come into effect as a result of goods crossing a frontier. It would, however, have the identical effect of protecting national production of the goods in question. It is obvious that if discriminatory measures could be imposed by tax measures once goods had crossed the national frontier, the removal of customs duties and charges having equivalent effect levied at the border would potentially be rendered meaningless. This problem was foreseen by those drafting the Treaty and duly addressed in Article 95 EC.[32] This states that:

27 Case 170/88, *Ford Espana v Spain* [1989] ECR 2305.
28 Case 132/78, *Denkavit* [1979] ECR 1923.
29 Case 158/82, *Commission v Denmark* [1983] ECR 3573.
30 Case 46/76, *WJG Bauhuis v The Netherlands State* [1977] ECR 5; Case 18/87, *Commission v Germany* [1988] ECR 5427. Although with regard to this area the Court has held that the following conditions must be satisfied:
  (a) the inspection for which the charge is being made must be required by Community law and not just permitted by it, Case 314/82, *Commission v Belgium* [1984] ECR 1543;
  (b) the charge must not exceed the actual cost of the inspection in connection with which it is charged;
  (c) the inspections in question are obligatory and uniform for all the products concerned in the Community;
  (d) they are prescribed by Community law in the general interest of the Community;
  (e) they promote the free movement of goods, in particular by neutralising obstacles which could arise from unilateral measures of inspection adopted in accordance with Article 36 of the Treaty.

31 Case 89/76, *Commission v Netherlands* [1977] ECR 1355; Case C-111/89, *The State (Netherlands) v Bakker Hillegom BV* [1990] ECR I-1735.
32 It has also been expressly noted by the ECJ in a number of cases including Cases 2 and 3/62, *Commission v Belgium and Luxembourg* [1962] ECR 425; and Case 262/86, *Gabriel Bergandi v Directeur General Des Impots, La Manche* [1988] ECR 1343 where it was stated that:

  As the court held in Case 168/78, *Commission v France* [1980] ECR 347; Case 169/78, *Commission v Italy* [1980] ECR 385; and Case 171/78, *Commission v Denmark* [1980] ECR 447, within the system of the EEC Treaty, Article 95 supplements the provisions on the abolition of customs duties and charges having equivalent effect. Its aim is to ensure free movement of goods between the member-States in normal conditions of competition by the elimination of all forms of protection which may result from the application of internal taxation that discriminates against products from other member-States. Thus Article 95 must guarantee the complete neutrality of internal taxation as regards competition between domestic products and imported products.

No Member State shall impose, directly or indirectly, on the products of other Member States any internal taxation of any kind in excess of that imposed directly or indirectly on similar domestic products.

Furthermore, no Member State shall impose on the products of other Member States any internal taxation of such a nature as to afford indirect protection to other products.

Member States shall, not later than at the beginning of the second stage, repeal or amend any provisions existing when this Treaty enters into force which conflict with the preceding rules.

Thus, Article 95(1) prevents Member States from imposing discriminatory taxation upon goods identical or similar to those produced by national producers, whilst Article 95(2) goes further in preventing indirect protection to national products by internal taxation of imported goods which, while not identical or indeed similar, are potentially in competition for the same national consumers.[33] Article 95 applies equally to goods produced in the Community, and to goods which have been produced by third countries and placed into free circulation within the Member States.[34] It can be seen that, as a result, Article 95 effectively complements Article 12, although the two provisions have been held by the ECJ to be mutually exclusive.[35]

True fiscal charges

The fact that Article 95 allows Member States to impose internal taxation provisions on the condition that they do not differentiate between similar domestic and imported products or do not afford indirect protection to national products does not mean that Member States are able to use it to justify the imposition of charges for purposes other than raising revenue for the State. In the related cases of *Hauptzollamt Flensburg v Hermann C Andresen GmbH and Co KG*[36] and *Pabst & Richarz KG v Hauptzollamt Oldenburg*[37] a charge was imposed on both domestic and imported products with the purpose of removing the burden of funding the Federal Spirits Monopoly from domestic products. The ECJ held that Article 95 could not be extended to allow any kind of compensation between a tax on imported products and a charge of a different nature imposed for economic purposes on the similar domestic product, except where the imported product and the similar domestic product were both subject equally to a government tax which was introduced and quantified by the public administration. Thus, for the purposes of Article 95 the term 'taxation' should be regarded as covering:

> . . . only that part of the price which the monopoly is required by law to remit to the State Treasury as a tax on spirits, determined as to amount, to the exclusion of all other elements or charges, economic or other, included in the calculation of the monopoly selling price.

[33] As we shall see, the treatment of the various types of alcoholic drink has seen particular use of Article 95(2) by the ECJ which, given that much of the case law revolves around complex topics such as VAT and excise duty, is perhaps an unfortunate juxtaposition for the concentration of both author and reader.

[34] Case 193/85, *Cooperativa Co-Frutta* [1987] ECR 2085, at 2110. There had been some doubt up to that point as to whether third country imports could benefit from Article 95 EC, as Article 95 was not in the sections of the Treaty named by Article 9(2) where it states that goods in free circulation are subject to the principle of free movement. It appears from Joined Cases C-223 and 224/90, *Simba* [1992] ECR I-3713 that barring specific Community legislation to the contrary it is not unlawful to discriminate against direct imports from third countries.

[35] Case 10/65, *Deutschmann v FRG* [1965] ECR 469.

[36] Case 4/81, [1981] ECR 2835.

[37] Case 17/81, [1982] ECR 1331.

Article 95(1)

Direct discrimination

As might be expected, given both its precise wording and its close relationship to Article 12, Article 95 has been held to be capable of direct effect[38] from the end of the transitional period.[39] This may well explain why there have been relatively few cases brought to the attention of the ECJ where direct discrimination has been alleged.

An example of such direct discrimination is *Lutticke v Hauptzollamt Saarlouis*.[40] Lutticke, an importer of powdered milk, requested customs clearance for a consignment of milk powder from Luxembourg. This clearance was granted, but subject to payment of turnover equalisation tax.[41] The ECJ held that as the same product supplied by a German producer would not have been subject to such a tax, there was a clear violation of Article 95.[42]

Further, in *Schottle & Sohne v Finanzamt Freudenstadt*[43] a German tax on the carriage of goods by road came under consideration. On its face, the tax appeared to have the legitimate aim of diverting long-distance traffic from road haulage towards the railways and inland waterways. However, under that tax the short-distance transport of goods which could not reasonably be diverted from the roads was exempted from charge. The ECJ held that, in this case, for the taxation of the imported product to be considered higher and thus directly discriminatory for the purpose of Article 95 it was sufficient that in certain circumstances, however limited, the national product might be transported without being subject to tax for the same distance within the Member State while the imported product was subject to the tax solely because the border was crossed. In such circumstances, the minor and incidental nature of the obstacle created by the national tax and the fact that it could only have been avoided in practice by abolishing the tax were not sufficient to prevent Article 95 from applying.

In *Bobie-Getrankevertrieb v Hauptzollampt Aachen-Nord*[44] the ECJ examined a German beer tax, which for domestic products operated on a sliding scale where the higher the output of a producer the higher the tax payable by them, but for imported products worked on a fixed rate. This meant that some large importers could benefit from the tax system but small importers paid more than their German equivalents. The ECJ stated that even though there was an advantage to some, or indeed most, importers, the fact that even a few importers suffered meant that Article 95 applied and Germany was in breach of Community law.[45]

It is clear therefore that where there is obvious discrimination the ECJ has taken a pragmatic

---

38 Case 57/65, *Lutticke v Hauptzollamt Saarlouis* [1966] ECR 205 (Article 95(1)); Case 27/67, *Fink-Frucht v Hauptzollamt Munchen-Landsbergstrasse* [1968] ECR 223; Case 28/67, *Mokerei-Zentrale v Hauptzollampt Paderborn* [1968] ECR 143 (Article 95(2)). Weatherill and Beaumont, *EC Law* (1993) at 358 note that the economic complexities of the two paragraphs might have justified a different outcome, but as the situation stands all the major free movement of goods provisions are directly effective and this has proved vital in overcoming Member States' obstructive tactics.

39 1 January 1962.

40 Case 57/65, *op. cit.*, note 38.

41 For a tax to be defined as a turnover tax it must have the effect of compromising the functioning of the common system of VAT by levying a charge on the move-

ment of goods and services and on commercial transactions in a way comparable to VAT. The essence of VAT consists in the application to commercial transactions of a general tax on consumption exactly proportional to the price of the goods and services, whatever the number of transactions which take place in the production and distribution process before the final stage at which tax is charged. Case 262/86, *Gabriel Bergandi v Directeur General Des Impots, La Manche, op. cit.*, note 32.

42 See also Case 27/67 *Fink-Frucht v Hauptzollamt Munchen-Landsbergstrasse, op. cit.*, note 38.

43 Case 20/76, [1977] ECR 247.

44 Case 127/75, [1976] ECR 1079.

45 See also Case C-47/88, *Commission v Denmark* [1990] ECR I-4509.

approach, by insisting that evidence of any discrimination is sufficient to breach Article 95. The fact that the discrimination may at times be to the advantage of importers has been ignored because to take such factors into account would result in the ECJ having constantly to evaluate differing national tax regimes to decide whether the advantages to importers outweighed the disadvantages. It is much simpler and swifter to outlaw discrimination of any type.

Member States' internal taxation systems

Article 95 does not automatically prevent Member States from establishing the type of national taxation system that they think appropriate, as long as those systems do not discriminate directly or indirectly against imported goods. This applies equally to the charging of higher or lower taxes on certain products to achieve some legitimate national aim[46] and the availability or otherwise of forms of tax relief to support certain types of business.[47] In all such cases, the difficulty of applying such regimes to imported goods is not an acceptable reason for discriminating against them.[48] Discrimination under Article 95(1) may be found in the rate of taxation, the way in which the goods are assessed for taxation or in the rules for the application of such taxation.[49]

Indirect discrimination

Member States rarely are careless enough to leave themselves open to a charge of direct discrimination under Article 95. Thus, rather than having a policy which discriminates against imported goods as such, they will tend instead to base taxation systems upon certain criteria which, while they appear neutral on their face, in fact have the effect of indirectly discriminating against imported products when actually applied. In *Humblot v Directeur des Services Fiscaux*[50] the French authorities set up a system which used two different mechanisms to levy an annual car tax. Cars which had a power rating of less than 16CV were taxed on a rising scale up to the 16CV point with a maximum tax of 1100 francs. Cars with a power rating higher than 16CV were taxed a flat rate of 5000 francs. There was no French produced car with a power rating of above 16CV, so only imported cars were subject to the higher level of tax. The ECJ held that:

> . . . as Community law stands at present the Member States are at liberty to subject products such as cars to a system of road tax which rises progressively in amount depending on an objective criterion . . . This is not true of a system like the one at issue . . . consumers seeking comparable cars . . . would naturally choose from cars above and below the critical power rating . . . However liability to the special tax entails a much larger increase in taxation than passing from one category of car to another in a system of progressive taxation . . . [and] is liable to cancel out the advantages which certain cars imported from other Member States might have in consumers' eyes over comparable cars of domestic manufacture.

46 Case 21/79, *Commission v Italy* [1980] ECR 1.
47 Case 148/77, *Hansen v Hauptzollampt Flensburg* [1978] ECR 1787; Case 196/85, *Commission v France* [1987] ECR 1597.
48 Case 21/79, *Commission v Italy op. cit.*, note 46.
49 Case 55/79, *Commission v Ireland* [1980] ECR 481; Case 17/81, *Pabst and Richarz v Hauptzollamt Oldenburg* [1982] ECR 1331.

50 Case 112/84, [1985] ECR 1367. See also Case 433/85, *Feldain v Directeur des Services Fiscaux* [1987] ECR 3521 concerning the revised French law which was also found to be in breach of Article 95 although, unfortunately, the ECJ failed to make clear whether there was a breach of the first or the second paragraph. See Lonbay (1989) 14 EL Rev 48.

This case may be compared with that of *Chemial Farmaceutici* v *DAF*[51] where the Italian authorities sought to tax denatured synthetic ethyl alcohol, of which little was produced in Italy, at a higher rate than denatured ethyl alcohol produced by fermentation, even though the two products could be used interchangeably. The ECJ refused to hold that the taxation was in breach of Article 95 as the Italian tax fell within a broader government policy of encouraging the use of agriculturally produced products over products derived from petroleum, which the ECJ felt was a valid economic aim which could be given effect by fiscal means. There was no discrimination as the tax hampered Italian production of denatured synthetic ethyl alcohol to the same extent as it did imports.[52] It should be noted that this type of justification may only be used where indirect discrimination is alleged, it is not a valid excuse for direct discrimination.

Discrimination by Member States against their own producers

While Member States may not discriminate against imported goods by means of internal taxation there is nothing in Article 95, or indeed elsewhere in the Treaty, to stop them discriminating against their own producers. While this may sound unusual, especially in the light of the general attitude taken by the Member States to the protection of their own producers, this issue has come before the ECJ on a couple of occasions. For instance, in *Grandes Distilleries Peureux* v *Directeur des Services Fisceaux*[53] the ECJ stated that neither Article 37 nor Article 95 were breached by France's rules on alcohol taxation, which actually discriminated against its national producers. Thus, Member States can levy a higher tax on home production and imports, although this may be subject to the restrictions on discriminatory taxation of exports.

Discriminatory refund of charges

It has been suggested that a discriminatory effect may be discovered if the means to which the proceeds of a tax are put is examined.[54] Whilst the payment of money to national producers will generally be covered by the provisions in Article 92 EC concerning State aids, where a clear link can be established between a particular tax nominally levied upon both national producers and importers of a particular good, and a benefit to those national producers, it would seem clear that there a discriminatory refund of taxation does occur. In such circumstances Article 95 would apply, unless the refund completely repaid the cost of the tax to the national producer, in which case Article 12 would apply as only the imported product would be being taxed. In its judgment in *Rewe-Zentrale etc.* v *Hauptzollampt Landau/Pfalz*[55] the ECJ did not seem minded to use Article 95 to deal with such circumstances. However, this stance changed in *Commission* v *Italy*[56] where it was stated that when an issue of internal taxation required examination in the light of Article 95, this included taking into account the purpose to which the money raised by that internal taxation

---

[51] Case 140/79, [1981] ECR 1, see also Case 46/80, *Vinal* v *Orbat* [1981] ECR 77 and Case C-132/88, *Re Taxation of Motor Cars: Commission* v *Greece* [1990] ECR I-1567.
[52] See also Case 196/85, *Commission* v *France* [1987] ECR 1597 (justifiable to confer tax concessions to protect economically weak regions of a Member State, even where these might constitute indirect discrimination).

[53] Case 86/78, [1979] ECR 897.
[54] Weatherill and Beaumont, *op. cit.*, note 38, at 348.
[55] Case 45/75, [1976] ECR 181.
[56] Case 73/79, [1980] ECR 1533; see also Joined Cases C-78–C-83/90, *Societe compagnie Commerciale de l'Ouest and others* v *Recevuer Principal des Douanes*, 11 March 1992.

was put. Thus, a clear link between the tax and support for the national producers would appear to be a breach of Article 95, and possibly also Article 92. It is useful to note that where the help to the national producer is the same as, or more than, the tax levied the sole effect of the levy is to place a duty on imported products and this would appear to fall within the scope of Article 12.[57]

Meaning of 'similar'

The issue of what constitutes a 'similar' product for the purpose of Article 95(1) is an important ingredient in deciding the Article's scope. Of course, if an imported product is not similar to a national product it may still be considered in the light of Article 95(2), but while a finding of a breach of Article 95(1) will require the Member State to equalise the taxation of the relevant imported and national products, a breach of Article 95(2) does not require equalisation, but rather that any protective element of the taxation is removed. This 'protective element' will, inevitably, be less easy to determine.

Similarity appears to be determined by an assessment of both the nature of the products in question and the uses to which they can be put. At earlier points in its jurisprudence the ECJ appears to have been of the opinion that such similarity might be suggested by the fact that the products in question were listed under the same headings in the Member State for the purposes of taxation, payment of tariffs or gathering of statistical information,[58] or that they were classified under the same heading in the Common Customs Tariff.[59] On the other hand, this method of determining similarity suffered from the fact that the ECJ seemed to be equally of the opinion that the fact that products were not classed under the same headings in those situations did not automatically mean that they were not similar.[60] In other cases of that period the ECJ seemed to take a rather wider and economic-based view of the test to be applied.[61] The product area which has most tested the ECJ's ability to determine whether products were similar or not is that of alcoholic beverages, which will be discussed in more detail below. It is interesting to note that where the Commission is of the opinion that products are similar for the purpose of competition law, this does not appear to be taken into account when they come to argue issues of similarity for the purposes of Article 95. The ECJ on the other hand is not so changeable in its stance.[62]

Article 95(2)

As outlined above, Article 95(2) EC only comes into play when it appears that there is discrimination against an imported product for which there is no identical or similar domestic product against which directly to compare the fairness of the taxation. In such circumstances, Article 95(2) is used to ensure that Member States do not indirectly protect

---

[57] Although the ECJ has stated that this will only be the case where the only purpose of the refund is to support the taxed national producers and both product taxed and product benefited must be the same, see Case 105/76, *Interzuccheri* v *Ditta Rezzano e Cavassa* [1977] ECR 1029.
[58] Case 27/67, *Fink-Frucht* v *Hauptzollamt Munchen Landsbergstrasse, op. cit.,* note 38.
[59] Case 45/75, *Rewe-Zentrale etc* v *Hauptzollampt Landau/Pfalz, op. cit.,* note 55.

[60] Case 168/78, *Commission* v *France* [1980] ECR 347; Case 169/78, *Commission* v *Italy* [1980] ECR 385.
[61] Case 216/81, *Cogis SpA* v *Italian Finance Ministry* [1982] ECR 2701.
[62] See, for example, the argument and decisions in Case 184/85, *Commission* v *Italy* [1987] ECR 2013 and Case 193/85, *Cooperativa Co-Frutta, op. cit.,* note 34 concerning the similarity of bananas to other fruit and the argument and decision in Case 27/76, *United Brands Company* v *Commission* [1978] ECR 207.

national products which, while not similar, are nonetheless in competition with the imported product because a consumer making a purchase in that product area is likely to be faced with a choice between the two. A product area which demonstrates both the potential for indirect protection and the difficulties of determining when a breach of Article 95(2) has occurred is that of alcoholic beverages.

The relationship of Article 95(1) and Article 95(2) – the alcohol cases

As noted above, a product area which has been widely used by the ECJ to refine its approach to concepts such as 'similarity' and which also demonstrates both the potential for indirect protection and the difficulties of determining when a breach of Article 95(2) has occurred, is that of alcoholic beverages.

It appears from the case law that similarity in terms of alcoholic beverages is capable of deduction from the method in which they are made, and attributes such as strength, taste and organoleptic qualities.[63] In *John Walker* v *Ministeriet for Skatter*[64] the issue was whether liqueur fruit wine was similar to Scotch whisky. The ECJ examined the method of production of each, distillation in the case of whisky, fermentation in the case of wine; and the relative percentages of alcohol that each contained, here, whisky, at 40 per cent alcohol, was found to be roughly twice as strong as the wine. As a result the ECJ held that there was clearly no similarity.

The problem faced by the Commission was that the Member States tended to have systems in place to tax alcoholic beverages and that these would have different rates of tax for different categories of product. What was apparent in most cases, however, was that these tax systems tended to have a bias built into them which favoured the products made in the particular Member State. As a result, the Commission began a series of actions against Member States alleging breach of Article 95. In the first three actions against France,[65] Italy[66] and Denmark[67] the ECJ accepted the Commission's claims without examining in great detail which of the two paragraphs of Article 95 were being breached.

In *Commission* v *Ireland*[68] a separate issue concerning Article 95(1) arose. In that case Irish law did not discriminate in terms of the rates of duty applicable to various forms of alcoholic beverage but provided for Irish producers of spirits, beer and made wine provisions for deferment of payment of between four and six weeks according to the product. In the case of the same products from other Member States, however, the duty was payable either at the date of importation or on delivery from the customs warehouse. The Commission argued that the fact that Irish products were granted deferral of payment beyond the date on which the products were put on the market conferred on national producers a financial benefit in comparison with importers who were obliged to pay the duty on the actual date on which the products were released to the market, and that this caused a disadvantage to imported products in competition with the corresponding Irish national production.

The ECJ held, in declaring Ireland to be in breach of its Community obligations, that:

63 Case 106/84, *Commission* v *Denmark* [1986] ECR 833 (wine made from grapes similar to wine made from other fruit) see also Case 277/83, *Commission* v *Italy* [1985] ECR 2049 (Marsala wines similar to other liqueur wines).
64 Case 243/84, [1986] ECR 875.

65 Case 168/78, *Commission* v *France* [1980] ECR 347.
66 Case 169/78, *Commission* v *Italy* [1980] ECR 385.
67 Case 171/78, *Commission* v *Denmark* [1980] ECR 447.
68 Case 55/79, [1980] ECR 481.

It is necessary, for the purposes of the application of the prohibition on discrimination laid down in Article 95 of the EEC Treaty, to take into consideration, not only the rate of tax, but also the provisions relating to the basis of assessment and the detailed rules for levying the various duties . . . the decisive criterion of comparison for the purposes of the application of Article 95 is the actual effect of each tax on national production on the one hand and on imported products on the other, since even where the rate of tax is equal the effect of that tax may vary according to the detailed rules for the basis of assessment and levying thereof applied to national production and imported products respectively.

However, in the case of *Commission* v *United Kingdom*[69] matters proved rather more difficult for the Commission. Here the two alcoholic beverages at issue were wine and beer and the ECJ was unprepared to accept, without considerably more analysis on the part of the Commission, that the levying of a heavier tax on wine was in any way a breach of Article 95. Thus, it was three years after the original set of cases before the Commission was in a position to attempt finally to persuade the ECJ that the UK was in breach.[70]

The problem lay in the fact that wine and beer are not, on any analysis, similar products, as they are produced by different methods and wine is generally two to three times as strong as most beers. Thus, Article 95(1) was not applicable to the situation. In order to bring the matter within the scope of Article 95(2) the Commission had to prove that the two products were in competition with each other and that the higher tax on wine indirectly benefited beer producers in the UK. After careful analysis the Commission, supported by Italy, produced evidence that convinced the ECJ that the two drinks were interchangeable, particularly at the cheaper end of the market and the UK was held to be in breach of Article 95(2). The ECJ also noted that the effect of the heavy UK tax on wine had almost certainly affected the issue of consumer substitutability (i.e. whether a consumer would choose wine or beer for consumption), inasmuch as it made wine a luxury item for most people. Thus, the UK in arguing that there was no real substitutability did so from a position where it had effectively ensured, consciously or not, that that would be the case by virtue of its own existing tax laws. The ECJ stated that:

. . . for the purpose of measuring the possible degree of substitution between beverages, it is impossible to restrict oneself to consumer habits in a member-State or in a given region. In fact, those habits, which are essentially variable in time and space, cannot be considered to be immutable; the tax policy of a member-State must not therefore serve to crystallise given consumer habits with a view to consolidating an advantage acquired by national industries concerned to comply with them.

The result of the judgment in this case was that the Chancellor of the Exchequer altered the duty on both products. The cost of beer in the UK was thus increased and the cost of wine decreased, to move the taxation levels of the two products closer together. It seems that the UK market for wine has markedly increased since that point, although no commentator has so far claimed that this case was the sole cause of the increase, and the ECJ's own comments about consumer habits, being naturally changeable, may very well apply.

[69] Case 170/78, [1980] ECR 417.

[70] Case 170/78, [1983] ECR 2265.

The relationship between Articles 9 and 12 and Article 95 EC

As noted above, Articles 12 and 95 EC are complementary, but the ECJ has ruled that they are mutually exclusive.[71] The consequence of this is that a fiscal measure put in place by a Member State will either be a customs duty or charge having equivalent effect and thus covered by Article 12 EC, or a measure forming part of the Member State's internal taxation system, in which case it will be covered by Article 95 EC. In the former case it will be an unlawful charge, while in the latter it will be deemed lawful unless it discriminates against goods on the ground of nationality. However, while there is no middle ground between the Articles it may be difficult to place a charge squarely within either category. The important consideration to be taken into account in determining which Article is relevant is that where the charge under examination is capable of being seen as part of the Member State's internal taxation system, being based on some general criteria concerned with the particular function or quality of the goods, i.e. alcohol content of spirits or engine capacity of cars, and it has no connection with those goods crossing a frontier, Article 95 will be the correct provision to apply rather than Article 12. In such circumstances the important element to determine the legality or otherwise of the measure will be based on whether there is discrimination against the product on the grounds of national origin or, alternatively, whether a protective effect has been afforded to some national product which might be in competition with it.

In *Dansk Denkavit*[72] the ECJ considered the compatibility with Community law of certain provisions of Danish law on the trade in, and importation of, compound animal feeding stuffs containing antibiotics and other additives. One of the questions raised was whether a Member State could collect an annual levy from undertakings where the levy was collected in the same amount from domestic producers and importers and where the total amount of the levy corresponded to the expenditure occasioned by the checks by random sampling carried out in accordance with a Community Directive.[73]

The ECJ noted that it had:

> consistently held that the prohibition . . . of any customs duty and charge having an equivalent effect in relations between Member States covers any charge levied on the occasion or by reason of importation specifically affecting an imported product to the exclusion of a similar domestic product. Such a charge however does not fall within that classification if, as in the present case, it relates to a general system of internal dues applied systemically and in accordance with the same criteria to domestic products and imported products alike, in which case it does not come within the scope of Article 9 but within that of Article 95 of the Treaty.

Thus, Articles 9 and 12 EC were not relevant in that the charge was not related to the crossing of a frontier. However, despite Denkavit's arguments that there was discrimination against the importers the ECJ held that this was not the case where the burden of the charge in question was borne by all traders, irrespective of the quantity of products imported or manufactured. Thus:

> Article 95 is complied with where an internal tax applies in accordance with the same criteria, objectively justified by the purpose for which the tax was introduced, to domestic

---

[71] Case 10/65, *Deutschmann* v *FRG, op. cit.*, note 35.
[72] Case 29/87, *Dansk Denkavit* v *Landbrugsministeriet* [1988] ECR 2965.
[73] Directive 70/524/EEC, OJ (Special edition) 1970 840, as amended by Directive 73/183/EEC OJ 1973 L124/17.

products and imported products so that it does not result in the imported product's bearing a heavier charge than that borne by the similar domestic product.

Thus, as Articles 9 and 12 EC were not applicable and the levy did not breach the provisions of Article 95 of the Treaty, the national measure was compatible with Community law and could be allowed to stand.

Application of Article 95 to exports

On its face, Article 95 has no relevance to exports. Indeed, while Article 96 is designed to ensure that an exporter of goods from a Member State is not 'repaid' internal taxation at a level higher than was originally charged, or in other words paid an export subsidy,[74] there would appear to be no reason based on the Treaty why exports could not be taxed at a level higher than that applied to production for the national market. However, in *Staten Kontrol* v *Larsen*[75] the ECJ extended the scope of Article 95 to cover just that situation. It appears, therefore, that the ECJ has been willing to develop the concept of tax neutrality to prevent both imports and exports being taxed more heavily than products for sale on the domestic market. This is consistent with the ECJ's general stance, in that to ensure the free movement of goods *all* barriers to trade must be removed and, in such a scenario, an export tax could be as effective a block to that free movement as an import tax.

The Common Customs Tariff and Common Customs Code

The aim of the Common Customs Tariff (CCT)[76] is to ensure that in their dealing with third countries Member States operate a system of customs duties and measures having equivalent effect[77] which treats goods from those third party countries in an identical manner, no matter which Member State they enter the Community by.[78] However, in practice, due to a lack of a provision similar in effect to either Article 12 or Article 95 with relation to the CCT, it appears that Member States may, in certain circumstances, adopt measures which do discriminate against third country products, for instance with respect to health inspections,[79] as the ECJ appears willing to accept rather wider derogations in the case of third country goods than it does with respect to goods produced within the Community.[80]

In October 1992, as part of the abolition of internal market borders, the Council adopted Regulation 2913/92/EEC which lays down the Community Customs Code.[81] The aim of the Community Customs Code is to codify the provisions of all relevant directives and regulations on customs procedures applicable to goods traded between the Community and non-Community countries. The Regulation thus simplifies and makes more coherent the basic

---

[74] Case 45/64, *Commission* v *Italy* [1965] ECR 857.

[75] Case 142/77, [1978] ECR 1543.

[76] Provided for by Articles 18–29 EC and enacted by Regulation 950/68/EEC, OJ (Special edition) 1968 275, revised in terms of nomenclature by Regulation 2658/87, OJ 1987 L256/1. Consolidated versions of the CCT are published annually.

[77] Measures having equivalent effect are not actually mentioned in the Treaty but in Joined Cases 37 and 38/73, *Sociaal Fonds voor de Dimantarbeiders* v *India-mex* [1973] ECR 1609 the ECJ extended the provisions for the CCT to cover such measures.

[78] Case 135/79, *Gedelfi Grosseinkauf GmbH & Co KG* v *Hauptzollamt Hamburg-Jonas* [1980] ECR 1713.

[79] Case 30/79, *Land Berlin* v *Wigei* [1980] ECR 151; Case 1/83, *IFG Intercontinentale Fleischhandelsgesellschaft* v *Freistaat Bayern* [1984] ECR 349.

[80] See further, Usher, 'The Single Market and Goods Imported from Third Countries' (1986) YEL 159.

[81] OJ 1992 L302.

rules and attempts to close all the remaining loopholes in the Community law in this area. In doing so it replaces and supplements over 30 legislative Acts which were passed between the years of 1968 and 1990.[82]

In Title I, Chapter 1 the Regulation both defines its scope[83] and provides some basic definitions.[84] In Title I, Chapter 2 it then sets out general provisions on people's rights and obligations with regard to customs legislation.[85]

Under Title II, the Regulation states the factors on the basis of which import duties or export duties and other measures prescribed in respect of trade in goods are applied. These are: the Customs tariffs of the EC and tariffs classification of goods;[86] the preferential origin of goods;[87] the non-preferential origin of goods;[88] the value of goods for customs purposes.[89]

Under Title III the Regulation lists the provisions applicable to goods brought into the customs territory of the Community until they are designated a customs-approved treatment or use. It describes the rules for temporary storage of goods and the provisions applicable to non-Community goods which have moved under a transit procedure.

Title IV sets out the rules for customs-approved treatment or use. It lays down rules for placing goods under a customs procedure, release of goods for free circulation, conditional exemption procedures, customs procedures with economic impact and export and internal transit. Special provisions cover the position of free zones and free warehouses and the re-exportation, destruction and abandonment of non-Community goods.

[82] Including the repeal of the following provisions and amendments to them: Regulation 802/68/EEC on the common definition of the concept of the origin of goods; Regulation 754/76/EEC on the customs treatment applicable to goods returned to the customs territory of the Community; Regulation 2779/78/EEC on the procedure for applying the European unit of account (EUA) to legal acts adopted in the customs sphere; Regulation 1430/79/EEC on the repayment or remission of import or export duties; Regulation 1697/79/EEC on the post-clearance recovery of import duties or export duties which have not been required of the person liable for payment on goods entered for a customs procedure involving the obligation to pay such duties; Directive 79/695/EEC on the harmonization of procedures for the release of goods for free circulation; Regulation 1224/80/EEC on the valuation of goods for customs purposes; Directive 81/177/EEC on the harmonization of procedures for the export of Community goods; Regulation 3599/82/EEC on temporary importation arrangements; Regulation 2763/83/EEC on arrangements permitting goods to be processed under customs control before being put into free circulation; Regulation 2151/84/EEC on the customs territory of the Community; Regulation 1999/85/EEC on inward processing relief arrangements; Regulation 3632/85/EEC defining the conditions under which a person may be permitted to make a customs declaration; Regulation 2473/86/EEC on outward processing relief arrangements and the standard exchange system; Regulation 2144/87/EEC on customs debt; Regulation 1031/88/EEC determining the persons liable for payment of a customs debt; Regulation 1970/88/EEC concerning triangular traffic under the out-ward processing relief arrangements and the standard exchange system; Regulation 2503/88/EEC on customs warehouses; Regulation 2504/88/EEC on freezones and free warehouses; Regulation 4151/88/EEC laying down the provisions applicable to goods brought into the customs territory of the Community; Regulation 1854/89/EEC on the entry in the accounts and terms of payment of the amounts of the import duties or export duties resulting from a customs debt; Regulation 1855/89/EEC on the temporary importation of means of transport; Regulation 3312/89/EEC on the temporary importation of containers; Regulation 4046/89/EEC on the security to be given to ensure payment of a customs debt; Regulation 1715/90/EEC on the information provided by the customs authorities of the Member States concerning the classification of goods in the customs nomenclature; Regulation 2726/90/EEC on Community transit, except for Article 3(3) (b); Regulation 717/91/EEC concerning the Single Administrative Document; Regulation 719/91/EEC on the use in the Community of TIR carnets and ATA carnets as transit documents.
[83] Articles 1–3.
[84] Article 4.
[85] These include a right of representation (Article 5), the control of decision-making relating to the application of customs rules (Articles 6–10) and the provision of binding tariff information (Articles 11 and 12).
[86] Title II, Chapter 1, Articles 20 and 21.
[87] Title II, Chapter 2, Article 27.
[88] Title II, Chapter 2, Articles 22–26.
[89] Title II, Chapter 3, Article 28.

Title VI deals with privileged operations and sets out the rules concerning relief from customs duty,[90] returned goods[91] and products of sea-fishing and other products taken from the sea.[92]

Title VII on 'customs debt' lays down the rules for security to cover customs debt, incurrence of a customs debt and the recovery of the amount of the customs debt. This Title also covers extinction of customs debt, repayment and remission of duty.

Title VIII sets out the right of appeal against decisions taken by customs authorities and against failure of customs authorities to give a decision relating to the application of customs legislation at the earliest opportunity.[93] That right of appeal may be exercised:

(a) initially, before the customs authorities designated for that purpose by the Member States;
(b) subsequently, before an independent body which may be a judicial authority or an equivalent specialised body, according to the provisions in force in the Member States.[94]

The right of appeal does not, however, apply where the aim is to achieve the annulment or revision of a decision taken by the customs authorities on the basis of criminal law.[95]

The Regulation also lays down the basis for the establishment of a Customs Code Committee[96] which is responsible for examining any matter relating to customs regulations raised by its chairman or by a Member State.[97] The Commission must consult with this Committee concerning measures to be taken under the Code.[98] Where the Committee accepts them, the Commission may proceed to adopt them.[99] Where the Committee does not accept them the Commission must submit them to the Council to be decided by a qualified majority.[100] If the Council fails to act within three months the Commission may proceed with the adoption of the measures.[101]

PHYSICAL AND TECHNICAL BARRIERS TO THE FREE MOVEMENT OF GOODS

Fiscal measures are an effective way of limiting the competitiveness of imported goods against domestically produced goods, although where the imported goods are of a higher quality or standard than the domestic products the consumer may be willing to pay a premium in order to obtain them. Therefore, customs duties and charges having an equivalent effect are not as effective an obstacle to the free movement of goods (and, thus, the protection of national markets and producers) as the imposition of restrictions upon the quantity or the value of goods that may be imported. Such quantitative restrictions have long been a well-known and often-used method of protectionism in international trade. A quantitative restriction may take the form of an upper limit to the amount of a product that

90 Title VI, Chapter 1, Article 184.
91 Title VI, Chapter 2, Articles 185–187.
92 Title VI, Chapter 3, Article 188.
93 Article 243(1).
94 Article 243(2).
95 Article 246.

96 Article 247.
97 Article 248.
98 Article 249(2).
99 Article 249(3)(a).
100 Article 249(3)(b).
101 Article 249(3)(c).

can be imported or, indeed, might be a total ban on imports of a certain good. Thus, in order to endure the effective functioning of the internal Community market, the drafters of the Treaty found it necessary to ensure that the ability to impose both actual quantitative restrictions and measures having a similar effect to quantitative restrictions was removed from the Member States in all but certain very limited circumstances.

Quantitative restrictions and measures having equivalent effect – Articles 30 and 34

Article 30 EC states that:

> Quantitative restrictions on imports and all measures having equivalent effect shall, without prejudice to the following provisions, be prohibited between Member States.

Article 34 (1) EC further states that:

> Quantitative restrictions on exports, and all measures having equivalent effect, shall be prohibited between the Member States.

Thus, unlike the issue of internal taxation under Article 95 EC, when dealing with issues of technical and physical barriers to trade the Treaty explicitly covers both imports and exports. The Articles, while addressed to the Member States, have been widely interpreted by the ECJ as applying to any institution that in some way can be seen to derive powers from public law.[102] They also apply even where there may be no legally binding measures.[103] The Community institutions, however, may act in what would otherwise technically be a breach of Articles 30 and 34 where they are expressly empowered to do so by some other provisions of the Treaty.[104] As with the Articles concerned with customs duties and charges having equivalent effect, Articles 30 and 34 apply to third country goods in free circulation within the Community under Article 9(2) EC.[105] It is clear that Community law interprets the term 'quantitative restriction' to mean both the imposition of quotas upon a product[106] and an outright ban.[107] Of the two prohibitions contained in the Articles it is the one against 'measures having equivalent effect' that has seen most use by the ECJ, which has had to develop a large and varied line of case law in order to tackle the increasingly ingenious attempts of the Member States to erect trade barriers to products from other Member States.

Quantitative restrictions on imports

True quantitative restrictions are an easy concept to understand. In *Geddo v Ente Nazionale Risi* [108] the ECJ held that they were 'measures which amount to a total or partial restraint of . . . imports, exports, or goods in transit'. This rule clearly covers both a situation where a

102 Case 222/82, *Apple and Pear Development Council* [1983] ECR 4083; Joined Cases 266 and 267/87, *R v Royal Pharmaceutical Society of Great Britain, ex parte API* [1989] ECR 1295.
103 Case 249/81, *Commission v Ireland* [1982] ECR 4005.
104 For example implementing measures under the CAP (Article 38(2) EC).
105 Case 41/76, *Donckerwolcke v Procureur de la République de Lille* [1976] ECR 1921; Case 212/88, *Re Felix, Levy and Another* [1989] ECR 3511.
106 Case 2/73, *Geddo v Ente Nazionale Risi* [1973] ECR 865.
107 Case 34/79, *R v Henn and Darby* [1979] ECR 3795.
108 Case 2/73, *op. cit.* note 106.

Member State bans all imports of a good from other Member States[109] and a situation where a quota system, either obvious[110] or hidden, is used to block free movement.

Measures having equivalent effect

A useful starting point for consideration of the meaning of measures having equivalent effect is Directive 70/50/EEC adopted under the powers given to the Commission by Article 33(7) EC, which allowed it to issue directives establishing the procedure and timetable for the abolition of measures equivalent to quotas. Article 2(1) of the Directive laid out the prohibited measures which it was deemed would ' . . . hinder imports which could otherwise take place, including measures which make importation more difficult or costly than the disposal of domestic production'. Those measures included measures which subjected imported goods to a condition, other than a formality[111] not required by domestic goods, which subjected imported goods to a different condition to that imposed on domestic goods, or which had the effect of giving aid, favour or preferred treatment to domestic goods.[112] Article 3 of the Directive provided a number of examples of measures which would be prohibited, a list which some Member States at times appear to have interpreted in a manner diametrically opposed to the aim of the Directive.[113] Article 2(1) of the Directive

---

[109] Case 7/61, *Commission v Italy* [1961] ECR 317.

[110] Case 13/68, *Salgoil v Italian Ministry for Foreign Trade* [1968] ECR 453.

[111] But note that in Joined Cases 51–54/71, *International Fruit Co NV v Produktschap voor Groenten en Fruit* [1971] ECR 1107 the ECJ held that a licensing system, even where the granting of a licence was a pure formality, would amount to a breach of Article 30 EC.

[112] Article 2(2) of the Directive.

[113] Prohibited measures included those designed to:

(a) lay down, for imported products only, minimum or maximum prices below or above which imports are prohibited, reduced or made subject to conditions liable to hinder importation;

(b) lay down less favourable prices for imported products than for domestic products;

(c) fix profit margins or any other price components for imported products only or fix these differently for domestic products and for imported products, to the detriment of the latter;

(d) preclude any increase in the price of the imported product corresponding to the supplementary costs and charges inherent in importation;

(e) fix the prices of products solely on the basis of the cost price or the quality of domestic products at such a level as to create a hindrance to importation;

(f) lower the value of an imported product, in particular by causing a reduction in its intrinsic value, or increase its costs;

(g) make access of imported products to the domestic market conditional upon having an agent or representative in the territory of the importing Member State;

(h) lay down conditions of payment in respect of imported products only, or subject imported products

to conditions which are different from those laid down for domestic products and more difficult to satisfy;

(i) require, for imports only, the giving of guarantees or making of payments on account;

(j) subject imported products only to conditions, in respect, in particular of shape, size, weight, composition, presentation, identification or putting up, or subject imported products to conditions which are different from those for domestic products and more difficult to satisfy;

(k) hinder the purchase by private individuals of imported products only, or encourage, require or give preference to the purchase of domestic products only;

(l) totally or partially preclude the use of national facilities or equipment in respect of imported products only, or totally or partially confine the use of such facilities or equipment to domestic products only;

(m) prohibit or limit publicity in respect of imported products only, or totally or partially confine publicity to domestic products only;

(n) prohibit, limit or require stocking in respect of imported products only; totally or partially confine the use of stocking facilities to domestic products only, or make the stocking of imported products subject to conditions which are different from those required for domestic products and more difficult to satisfy;

(o) make importation subject to the granting of reciprocity by one or more Member States;

(p) prescribe that imported products are to conform, totally or partially, to rules other than those of the importing country;

continued overleaf

provided the ECJ with the legislative grounding for its judgment in *Ianelli & Volpi* v *Paolo Meroni*[114] and the Directive has received sporadic mention in the jurisprudence of the ECJ since then. However, the ECJ has been increasingly inclined to concern itself rather more with its task of maintaining the principle of the free movement of goods than on searching for a legislative justification for its judgments. This has been viewed with some misgivings on the part of some legal commentators and, of course, the UK courts, to whom judicially created law is an anathema.

The ECJ has thus developed its own definition of measures having equivalent effect to quantitative restrictions, starting the process in *Procureur du Roi* v *Dassonville*[115] where it stated that:

> All trading rules enacted by Member States which are capable of hindering, directly or indirectly, actually or potentially, intraCommunity trade are to be considered as measures having an effect equivalent to quantitative restrictions.[116]

The *Dassonville* case concerned a requirement by the Belgian authorities that importers of Scotch whisky should possess a British certificate of authentication. This had the effect of discriminating between direct importers and those importing the goods from other Member States where they were already in free circulation, because of the difficulty that the latter faced in obtaining the certificate. The ECJ held that this 'channelling' of imports was capable of hindering intraCommunity trade and was thus contrary to Article 30 EC. The ruling in *Dassonville* was broader in scope than that suggested by Directive 70/50/EEC, concentrating on the effect of the national action and effectively ignoring its form, and seemed to indicate a determination on the part of the ECJ to use Article 30 to pursue all restrictive national laws that have the effect of hindering Community trade. The effect of this ruling was, however, tempered by the acceptance on the part of the ECJ in the same judgment that where an area is not regulated by the Community Member States could still take action to prevent unfair practices in a manner which conformed with Community law, if the measures used were reasonable.[117]

While it is not necessary for a national measure to have a marked or serious effect in the way of hindering intraCommunity trade, the ECJ has ruled on a number of occasions that measures must be actually capable of hindering intraCommunity trade. In the *Van de Haar* case[118] the ECJ considered the compatibility of the Dutch law on the excise duty on tobacco products[119] with Article 30, in particular the sentence which stated 'It shall be an offence to sell, offer for sale or supply tobacco products to persons other than re-sellers at a price lower than that appearing on the excise label'.

---

113 *Continued*
(q) specify time limits for imported products which are insufficient or excessive in relation to the normal course of the various transactions to which these time limits apply;
(r) subject imported products to controls or, other than those inherent in the customs clearance procedure, to which domestic products are not subject or which are stricter in respect of imported products than they are in respect of domestic products, without this being necessary in order to ensure equivalent protection;

(s) confine names which are not indicative of origin or source to domestic products only.
114 Case 74/76, [1977] ECR 557.
115 Case 8/74, [1974] ECR 837.
116 See also Case C-69/88, *H Krantz GmbH* v *Ontrager der Directe Belastingen* [1990] ECR I-583.
117 Sometimes known as the 'rule of reason' concept.
118 Joined Cases 177 and 178/82, *Jan van de Haar* [1984] ECR 1797.
119 *Wet op de Accijns van Tabaksfabrikaten* 1964.

Van de Haar and others were charged with having infringed that provision by offering for sale tobacco products to persons other than re-sellers at prices lower than those appearing on the excise labels. One of their arguments was that the fact that the excise duty was subject to an absolute minimum led to the formation of an absolute minimum selling price, which was contrary to Article 30 of the Treaty. The national court wanted to know whether the law could be considered a measure having equivalent effect as it only restricted imports to a very small degree, and other possibilities remained for the marketing of imported products.

The ECJ restated the *Dassonville* rule and then noted that:

> Article 30 of the Treaty does not distinguish between measures having an effect equivalent to quantitative restrictions according to the degree to which trade between Member States is affected. If a national measure is capable of hindering imports it must be regarded as a measure having an effect equivalent to a quantitative restriction, even though the hindrance is slight and even though it is possible for imported products to be marketed in other ways.

The ECJ went on to say that, while national price control rules applicable without distinction to domestic products and imported products did not, in general, produce an effect equivalent to quantitative restrictions, they might do so in certain specific cases.[120] At that time the Community had not sought to regulate tobacco and it was up to each Member State to choose its own system of fiscal control over tobacco products on sale in its territory.[121] Where no distinction was made between domestic products and imported products, such a system would generally have exclusively internal effects.

In *Oebel*[122] a Belgian law designed to protect workers in bakeries by forbidding the night-time production and delivery to customers and shops of bakery products was held not to breach Article 30 because it had no effect on overall Community trade. In *Quietlynn Ltd.* v *Southend Borough Council*[123] a UK law which required sex shops to obtain a licence to sell sex appliances was held not to breach Article 30 because there would be no effect on the intraCommunity trade in the goods caused by the national legislation, although the ECJ also noted that such goods could equally well be sold via other trading processes, such as mail order. This, on its face, would appear to be somewhat at odds with the ruling in *Van de Haar*, but is explicable to the extent that there is no discrimination between national and imported goods, merely a regulation of the way that both were to be sold.

The effect of the *Dassonville* judgment was further moderated in *Rewe-Zentral* v *Bundesmonopolverwaltung fur Branntwein* ('*Cassis de Dijon* case').[124] Here the ECJ considered a German law which prohibited the sale of certain liqueurs if their alcoholic strength was less than 25 per cent; French cassis, a blackcurrant liqueur, had an alcoholic strength of 15–20 per cent and a number of importers wished to import it, but were prevented from doing so. The ECJ in its judgment reiterated the *Dassonville* rule, but then added a new element:

> Obstacles to movement within the Community resulting from disparities between the national laws relating to the marketing of the product in question must be accepted in so far as those provisions may be recognised as being necessary in order to satisfy mandatory requirement relating in particular to the effectiveness of fiscal supervision, the protection of public health, the fairness of commercial transactions and the defence of the consumer.

120 Case 82/77, *Openbaar Ministerie* v *van Tiggele* [1978] ECR 25.
121 Case 13/77, *INNO* v *ATAB* [1977] ECR 2115.
122 Case 155/80, [1981] ECR 1993.
123 Case C-23/89, [1990] ECR I-3059.
124 Case 120/78, [1979] ECR 649.

However, if the national laws did not protect such a mandatory requirement then they merely served to act as a barrier to the free movement of goods. In the *Casis de Dijon* case the German government sought to claim both protection of public health and consumer protection as justifications for its law; the protection of public health because lower alcohol drinks might encourage consumers to drink more and consumer protection because purchasers might buy the lower strength drink mistaking it for the stronger version. The ECJ was unimpressed, stating that in the first case there was no obvious health risk that was not posed by the consumer diluting stronger spirits and in the second case that the consumers' interests could be adequately protected by proper labelling.

The role and purpose of mandatory requirements in the area of free movement of goods is a complex one. Directive 70/50/EEC in Articles 2 and 3 appeared to distinguish between rules which only applied to and explicitly discriminated against imports and those which applied to both national and imported goods, which had the effect of discriminating against the latter. The decision in *Dassonville*, however, did not appear to follow this reasoning. The *Cassis de Dijon* case on the other hand appeared to reinforce the impression that there was a distinction between the two. Thus, a situation arose where it might be necessary to have reference to the concept of a distinction between 'distinctly applicable' and 'indistinctly applicable' rules. Distinctly applicable rules are defined as those which make a distinction between domestic produce and imported produce; indistinctly applicable rules are defined as those which do not make such a distinction, but may nevertheless hinder trade. It has been suggested that where distinctly applicable rules are challenged the only defence is via one of the derogations provided for in Article 36 EC, whereas when an indistinctly applicable rule is challenged the 'rule of reason' concept will apply and the Member State may claim justification of its measures by reference to the mandatory requirements.[125] However, the relevance of this distinction would appear to be lessened by the fact that the ECJ itself does not always seem to take such distinctions into account when assessing national rules.[126]

What is clear from the *Cassis de Dijon* case is that where goods are lawfully produced and sold in one Member State, there must be clearly justifiable reasons why they cannot be sold in another, and national rules which purport to prevent this from happening will be very carefully scrutinised by the ECJ to ensure that, first, they are suitable measures to achieve the aim which the Member State concerned has declared and, secondly, that they contain no protective effect for national products. Thus, in *Gilli and Andres*,[127] which concerned the prohibition by the Italian authorities of the importation of apple vinegar from Germany because Italian law stated that vinegar could only be produced from wine, the ECJ stated that the rule was contrary to Article 30 because:

> In practice, the principal effect of provisions of this nature is to protect domestic production by prohibiting the putting on to the market of products from other Member States which do not answer the descriptions laid down by national rules.

If the Italian authorities argued that their aim was to ensure that Italian consumers' interests were protected this could be adequately ensured by proper labelling of products as 'wine' and

---

125 See Steiner, *EEC Law*, 3rd edn, at 86; and Weatherill and Beaumont, *EC Law*, at 428.

126 And other commentators do not seem particularly moved by the claims for the distinction between distinctly applicable rules and indistinctly applicable rules, see

Wyatt and Dashwood, *European Community Law*, 3rd edn and Green, Hartley and Usher, *The Legal Foundations of the Single European Market*.

127 Case 788/79, [1980] ECR 2071.

'apple' vinegar. A ban was therefore not an appropriate measure. Also by defining 'vinegar' in such narrow terms it was clear that the Italian authorities' sole purpose was to prevent the import of cheaper goods of the same type which could damage its own wine vinegar industry. Thus, the Italian law failed both legs of the test imposed by the ECJ.

This line of reasoning has been applied by the ECJ in a long list of cases primarily involving food products. For example, national rules were found to breach Article 30 in *Fietje*[128] where they required a particular form of labelling to be used; *Eyssen*[129] where the use of the antibiotic substance nisin in cheese was banned; *Rau*[130] where they stated that margarine could only be sold in cubes; *Oosthoeck's*[131] where the type of advertising used for a product was restricted or banned; *Commission* v *Germany*[132] where the term 'bier' could only be used for products brewed in accordance with Germany's *Biersteurgesetz*; and *GB-INNO-BM* v *CCL*[133] where they prevented temporary sales offers from stating the length of the offer or what the price of the goods on sale were prior to the offer.

The blurring of the distinction between discriminatory measures and those which afford some measure of protective effect to national products can be seen cases like *Prantl*[134] but it remains the case that the ECJ is willing to extend the *Cassis* ruling beyond those measures which are seen to be, or could be, discriminatory. This opinion was made clear in the *Cinéthèque*[135] case where it was noted by Advocate General Slynn that 'discrimination . . . although it may be sufficient, even conclusive, to bring a measure within Article 30, is not a necessary precondition for Article 30 to apply', a conclusion that was clearly reflected in the judgment.

Recent developments in the use of Article 30

Since the coming into force of the Single Market at the end of 1992 the ECJ has clearly considered that it is time to re-evaluate the case law concerning the free movement of goods. Article 30 EC has increasingly been invoked to challenge any national rules which limit traders' commercial freedom, even where those rules are not aimed at imports from other Member States;[136] for instance, the cases concerning the legality of Sunday trading in the UK which was largely banned by the Shops Act 1950.[137]

The first major move in that re-evaluation appears to have been taken in the case of *Keck*,[138] where the ECJ ruled that:

128 Case 27/80, [1980] ECR 3839.
129 Case 53/80, *Officier van Justitie* v *Koninklijke Kaasfabriek Eyssen BV* [1981] ECR 409.
130 Case 261/81, *Walter Rau Lebensmittelwerke* v *de Smedt pvbA* [1982] ECR 3961.
131 Case 286/81, *Oosthoeck Vitgeversmaatschapij BV* [1982] ECR 4575.
132 Case 178/84, [1987] ECR 1227.
133 Case C-362/88, [1990] ECR I-667.
134 Case 16/83, *Criminal proceedings against Karl Prantl* [1984] ECR 1299.
135 Joined Cases 60 and 61/84, *Cinéthèque* v *Fédération Nationale de Cinemas Françaises* [1985] ECR 2605.
136 C-332/89, *Andre Marchandise* [1991] ECR I-1027; Case 312/89, *Union Departementale des Syndicats CAT*

de L'Aisne v *Societe Internationale de Distribution d'Equipements Familiaux and Others*, *The Times*, 6 March 1991.
137 See Case 145/88, *Torfaen BC* v *B & Q Plc* [1989] ECR 3851; Case C-169/91, *Stoke-on-Trent City Council and Norwich City Council* v *B & Q plc*; Case C-306/88, *Rochdale Borough Council* v *Anders*; Case C-304/90, *Reading Borough Council* v *Payless DIY Limited and Others* [1993] 1 CMLR 426. Also Arnull, 'What shall we do on Sunday?' (1991) 16 EL Rev 112 and Diamond, 'Dishonourable Defences: The Use of Injunctions and the EEC Treaty; Case Study of the Shops Act 1950' (1991) 54 MLR 72.
138 Joined Cases C-267/91 and C-268/91, judgment of 24 November 1993, OJ 1994 C1.

> . . . contrary to what has been previously decided, the application to products from other Member States of national provisions restricting or prohibiting certain selling arrangements is not such as to hinder directly or indirectly, actually or potentially, trade between Member States within the meaning of the 1974 *Dassonville* judgment, provided those provisions applied to all affected traders operating within the national territory and provided that they affected in the same manner, in law and in fact, the marketing of domestic products and those from other Member States.

This case shows a recognition on the part of the ECJ that national legislation which imposes a general prohibition on resale of goods at a loss may restrict the total volume of sales and, by doing so, restrict the volume of sales of products from the other Member States, but that this fact is not decisive for the purpose of determining its validity for the purposes of Article 30 EC.[139] The fact that it was not the purpose of the national legislation, in imposing a general prohibition on resale at a loss, to regulate trade in goods between Member States meant that there was no breach.

> . . . the application of such rules to the sale of products from another Member State meeting the requirements laid down by that State was not by nature such as to prevent their access to the market or to impede access any more that it impeded the access of domestic products. Such rules therefore fell outside the scope of Article 30 of the Treaty. Article 30 of the EEC Treaty as amended is to be interpreted as not applying to legislation of a Member State imposing a general prohibition on resale at a loss.

As this decision appears to deny traders the right to invoke Article 30 EC and thus the 'import' argument in order to denounce Member States' legislation on selling arrangements, it seems likely that the Court will have to define, in the near future, what are and what are not 'selling arrangements'.

Derogations from Articles 30–34

Article 36

Article 36 EC provides the primary grounds of derogation from Articles 30–34 that are open to the Member States. It states that:

> The provisions of Articles 30 to 34 shall not preclude prohibitions on imports, exports or goods in transit justified on the grounds of public morality, public policy or public security; the protection of health and life of humans, animals or plants; the protection of national treasures possessing artistic, historic or archaeological value; or the protection of industrial or commercial property. Such prohibitions shall not, however, constitute a means of arbitrary discrimination or a disguised restriction on trade between the Member States.

Where a Member State claims that the measures at issue have been adopted under one of these derogations they must prove two things; first, that there is in fact a need for any measure to be adopted and, secondly, that the measure that has actually been chosen was the least restrictive means of achieving the objective sought, and remains the least restrictive.[140]

---

139 See further Mortelmans, 'Article 30 of the EEC Treaty and Legislation Relating to Market Circumstances: Time to Consider a New Definition?' 28 CML Rev 115.

140 The doctrine of proportionality, see Chapter 6: General Principles of Law.

Even where these are proven the measure will fail to obtain protection under Article 36 if it appears to allow for arbitrary discrimination or provides a disguised restriction on trade.[141] Arbitrary discrimination will be found where the measure provides advantages to the marketing of domestic products or imports or exports from a particular Member State, or benefits one channel of trade at the expense of another.[142] Disguised restrictions may be defined as practices which are passed off as being justified under one of the headings of Article 36 but which have the effect of restricting the free movement of goods.

Where the Community has taken action to ensure the harmonisation of an area of law with regard to protecting an interest found in Article 36, Member States can no longer justify national rules by reference to Article 36. Thus, if the Community harmonises the laws of the Member States[143] with regard to industrial or commercial property, national measures purporting to protect those interests will no longer be justifiable if it is shown that they breach Article 30 in some way.

Public morality

The public morality heading appears to be concerned primarily with trade in pornographic or obscene articles. The case law in this area appears to be mainly related to UK restrictions on such material, with the cases of *Henn and Darby*[144] and *Conegate* v *Customs and Excise Commissioners*[145] providing the primary guidelines as to its availability to Member States. The ECJ ruled in *Henn and Darby* that as the UK operated an internal ban on the sale of the type of pornographic material imported by the appellants, its seizure by the authorities was justified under Article 36. In *Conegate*, by contrast, the material in question was available for sale in the UK, although subject to certain regulations about where and to whom it might be sold. The ECJ held that seizure of those materials could not be justified under Article 36 on the grounds that there would be a degree of discrimination against imported goods. Thus, it can be seen that where trade in goods within a Member State is not prohibited or subject to serious penal or other sanctions, a restriction on the importation of such goods is not justified under the heading of public morality even if the goods cause offence to individuals within the Member State concerned.

Public policy

Public policy, in theory, applies where a Member State can show that the imports or exports in question would constitute a genuine and sufficiently serious threat to one of the fundamental interests of its society. This heading has a certain degree of potential for abuse by the Member States, but the ECJ has been careful to ensure that the scope of the derogations under this heading remain very narrow. Weatherill and Beaumont comment that the ECJ has had rather more success at defining what does not come under the heading of public policy than defining what does.[146] It seems clear that national justifications based on economic grounds will not be sustained[147] and arguments based on the likelihood of civil

---

141 Case 40/82, *Commission* v *United Kingdom* [1984] ECR 2793.
142 Case 4/75, *Rewe-Zentralfinanz* v *Landwirtschaft-skammer* [1975] ECR 843.
143 Presumably using the powers granted under Article 100 or 100a EC to make harmonisation legislation.

144 Case 34/79, R v *Henn and Darby, op. cit.,* note 107.
145 Case 121/85, [1986] ECR 1007.
146 Weatherill and Beaumont, *op. cit.,* note 125, at 400.
147 Case 231/83, *Cullet* v *Centre Leclerc* [1985] ECR 306, a case involving a French law fixing a minimum price for petrol.

unrest in the event that national measures restricting imports are removed must show that the civil unrest would be more than the national authorities could be expected to cope with.[148] Also unacceptable are arguments based on consumer protection,[149] which the ECJ considers is better protected under the head of mandatory requirements, and the fact that the measure in question is backed by criminal sanctions, which the ECJ has stated is simply not relevant to the determination of the measure's legality.[150]

Public security

The heading of public security will apply in circumstances where imports or exports must be restricted in order to safeguard the existence of the institutions of a Member State, its essential public services and the survival of its inhabitants. This heading is rarely used, possibly because the subject matter is not something which is best mediated via the ECJ, but perhaps can be handled more effectively through negotiation in Council and with the Commission. The case of *Campus Oil* v *Minister for Industry and Energy*[151] demonstrates the wariness of the ECJ where such issues are concerned. In this case the Irish government sought to justify a law which forced petroleum importers to buy one-third of their requirements from the only refinery in Ireland by stating that without the revenue brought in by that forced purchase the refinery would be uneconomical to run. Its closure would mean that Ireland would have no independent source of petroleum to supply key national institutions and services. The ECJ held that this was an acceptable use of the public security heading.

Protection of health and life of humans, animals or plants

The heading concerned with the protection of health and life of humans, animals and plants can be used to justify measures which are part of a seriously considered health policy but may not be used to justify measures intended to deal with a risk which is so remote as to be unreal. It is clear that Member States have attempted to abuse this head on occasion, an example being *Commission* v *United Kingdom*[152] where the UK sought to justify a ban on poultry imports to the UK just before Christmas 1981. When this was challenged the UK government stated that it was to prevent the spread of a poultry disease known as Newcastle disease. However, the UK introduced the ban with some haste and without consulting either the Commission or other Member States. It is clear from the judgment that the ECJ was not convinced by that argument and rather more inclined to believe that the issue which the UK government had really been concerned with was protection of UK poultry producers. However, the result of that abuse, a payment of over £3 million to French turkey producers by way of compensation, may well have given any other Member States thinking of similar fast moves, second thoughts.

The issue of additives in food and drink for human consumption has frequently been raised under this head. In *Commission* v *Germany*[153] the German Beer Purity legislation[154] was in question. One of the grounds of complaint was a ban on all additives unless authorised by

---

148 *Ibid.* Although from past experience it appears that the French authorities have been unable to deal with such dangerous bodies of individuals as farmers and fishermen, so perhaps they had a point.
149 Case 177/83, *Kohl* v *Ringelhan* [1984] ECR 3651.
150 Case 16/83, *Criminal proceedings against Karl Prantl* [1984] ECR 1299.

151 Case 72/83, [1984] ECR 2727.
152 Case 40/82, *op. cit.,* note 141.
153 Case 178/84, [1987] ECR 1227.
154 *Bierstuergesetz*, Law of 14 March 1952, *Bundesgesetzblatt* I, p. 149.

Article 11 of the Law on foodstuffs, tobacco products, cosmetics and other consumer goods,[155] designed, the German government claimed, to protect public health. The Court, in ruling on the issue, stated that the Community position on additives was essentially that:

> in so far as there are uncertainties at the present state of scientific research it is for the Member States, in the absence of harmonisation, to decide what degree of protection of the health and life of humans they intend to assure, having regard however to the requirements of the free movement of goods within the Community[156]

and that following the cases of *Sandoz BV*,[157] *Motte*[158] and *Ministere Public* v *Claude Muller & Others*[159] it was clear that Community law allowed Member States to adopt legislation which would subject the use of additives to prior authorisation, as this legislation would genuinely be protecting human health by restricting the unlimited use of food additives. However, in those cases the Court had made it plain that any prohibition on the marketing of products containing additives which were authorised in the Member State of production, but which were banned in the Member State of importation, would be subject to the proportionality test as to its necessity and effectiveness in protecting public health. Also the use of a specific additive authorised in another Member State must be authorised in the case of a product imported from that Member State, if it appears that the findings of international scientific research and the study of eating habits of the population of the importing State suggest that the additive is no risk to public health and is also a necessary technical aid. Further, in the *Muller* case it was held that the principle of proportionality meant that traders had to be able to apply easily and relatively quickly for specific additives to be granted authorisation by a measure of general application and that the burden of proof in disputes over public health lay with the Member States authorities. The German legislation, it was held, in applying a blanket exclusion to additives, including those permitted in other Member States, did not take particular notice of the eating habits of the German population and, furthermore, there was no system whereby traders could obtain authorisation. Regarding the technical need for additives the Court rejected the argument that beer made only from the raw materials in Article 9 of the German Beer Purity legislation did not require them, stating that this did not preclude the fact that some additives might meet a technical need, and that the narrow interpretation given to the concept of technical need was a disguised means of restricting the free movement of goods.

A similar attitude on the part of the ECJ with regard to Member States determining public health issues may be seen in the case of *R* v *Pharmaceutical Society ex parte API*.[160] Here the issue concerned the laying down of a Code of Ethics and Guidance Notes by the Pharmaceutical Society of Great Britain, the pharmacists' professional body, breach of which laid pharmacists open to disciplinary action by a committee upon which national legislation had conferred disciplinary powers, including removal from the register of persons authorised to exercise the profession.

Part of the Guidance Notes prohibited a pharmacist from substituting, except in an emergency, any other product for a product specifically named in the prescription, even

[155] *Gestez über den Verkehr mit Lebensmitteln, Tabakerzeugnissen, kosmetischen Mitteln und sonstigen Bedarfsgegenständen*, Law of 15 August 1974, *Bundesgesetzblatt* I, p. 1945.
[156] Case 174/82, *Sandoz BV* [1983] ECR 2445; see also Case 53/80, *Officier van Justitie* v *Koninklijke Kaasfabriek Eyssen Bv* [1981] ECR 409; Case 94/83, *Criminal proceedings against Albert Heijn BV* [1984] ECR 3263.
[157] *Ibid.*
[158] Case 247/84, *State* v *Motte* [1985] ECR 3887.
[159] Case 304/84, [1986] ECR 1511.
[160] Joined Cases 266 and 267/87, [1989] ECR 1295.

where he believed that the therapeutic effect and quality of the other product were identical. It also stated that a pharmacist should not deviate from the doctor's instructions when dispensing a prescription, except where this was necessary in order to protect the health of the patient.

This raised a number of issues. First, did a measure adopted by a professional body such as the Pharmaceutical Society of Great Britain fall under Article 30 EC? Secondly, did the rule stating that only the named pharmaceutical product could be supplied breach Article 30? Thirdly, did the derogation for public health under Article 36 apply to the rule?

The ECJ held that measures adopted by a professional body on which national legislation has conferred powers of the nature in that case can, if they are capable of affecting trade between Member States, constitute 'measures' within the meaning of Article 30 of the Treaty. This meant that a rule prohibiting a pharmacist from substituting another product for the product prescribed by the doctor, even if the substitute was manufactured by or with the consent of the British manufacturer and therapeutically identical or equivalent (but bearing a different trade mark), could be said to hinder intraCommunity trade in breach of Article 30 as a restriction on the sale of parallel imported products.

However, the ECJ stated that in the absence of Community legislation, Member States may decide on the degree to which they wish to protect human health and life and how that degree of protection is to be achieved. Such a rule may be justified under the public health exception in Article 36 EC if it was objectively justified and was not an obvious attempt to discriminate against parallel imports. In this case the ECJ could find no discrimination and was persuaded by the arguments of the Pharmaceutical Society with regard to the justification for the rule. Thus, the rule, despite being a restriction on the sale of parallel imported products and capable of infringing Article 30, was justifiable on public health grounds under Article 36.

Protection of national treasures possessing artistic, historic or archaeological value

The heading concerned with the protection of national treasures possessing artistic, historic or archaeological value is of unclear scope but appears to be limited to those objects which are of value to a Member State by reason of their artistic, historic or archaeological content. As far as objects of historic or archaeological value are concerned, it seems that their classification as 'national treasures' must be connected in some way to the history or archaeology of the Member State concerned.[161]

Protection of industrial or commercial property

The heading concerning the protection of industrial and commercial property applies where restrictions on importation or marketing are necessary to protect a trade mark, patent, copyright or registered design. Consideration was given to this issue by the ECJ in *Thetford Corporation v Fiamma Spa & others*[162] which concerned the compatibility of certain rules of

---

[161] See Case 7/68, *Commission v Italy* [1968] ECR 423. The Community has recently addressed the problem of the conflict between the free movement of goods and the protection of national treasures. After a Commission Communication to the Council in November 1989, COM(89) 594, which expressed concern that the opening of the internal market might result in the increased exportation of Member States' national treasure, the following legislation was passed: Directive 93/7/EEC on the Return of Cultural Objects Unlawfully Removed from the Territory of a Member State, OJ 1993 L74; Regulation 3911/92/EEC on the Control of the Export of Cultural Goods, OJ 1992 L395.

[162] Case 35/87, [1988] ECR 3585.

national patent law, especially that relating to 'relative novelty', with Article 30. The Thetford Corporation owned a number of UK patents referring to portable toilets and had sued Fiamma in the UK Patents Court for breach of two of those patents concerning portable toilets which were made in Italy and imported to the UK by Fiamma. The ECJ was asked to establish the extent to which the derogation from Articles 30–34 under Article 36 applied to any patent granted under the legislation of a Member State. It held that a Member State's patent law is in principle covered by the derogations in Article 36 if, as in this case, they did not constitute a means of arbitrary discrimination or a disguised restriction on trade between Member States.[163]

Mandatory requirements

The concept of 'mandatory requirements', created in the Cassis de Dijon case, has seen significant use and expansion by the ECJ. It is clear from the case law that unlike the Article 36 list of derogations, the list of mandatory requirements is not exhaustive, with issues such as the environment being recent additions to the list. The ECJ, in creating both the concept and the power to expand its scope almost at will, has developed for itself a powerful tool to mould the trade measures of the Member States into line with current concerns, the environment, again, being a useful example. It is a tool, however, which the ECJ has been unwilling to use in the area of economic justifications for trade restrictions between the Member States. In this sense, the mandatory requirements and Article 36 derogations are clearly related. The use of mandatory requirements by the ECJ suggests that there is a gap between Community legislation and the perceived needs of society, and that the Community is not at present either inclined, or in a position, to attempt to further develop Community primary legislation to deal with that gap. Thus, the movement towards the total free movement of goods is to a large degree dependant presently upon the activism of the ECJ and the success of the harmonisation measures adopted under Article 100a EC.

It has been argued that the areas covered by the mandatory requirements could be easily subsumed within the scope of the Article 36 derogations. This is possibly the most influential evidence for assuming a clear distinction between directly and indirectly applicable measures. However, as noted above, the ECJ does not uniformly examine to see whether directly and indirectly applicable measures are at issue and it would over-simplify the nature of the ECJ's attitude to Member States' attempts to impose barriers to the free movement of goods to view matters in that way. Another equally plausible view, based more on the observation of the socio-political aspects of the legal interaction between the Community institutions and the Member States than on pure legal reasoning,[164] is that the ECJ, employing a much larger degree of judicial activism than would be tolerated in the UK, has deliberately kept the scope of the Treaty-based Article 36 derogations as narrow as possible, while reserving the power, via the judicially created mandatory requirements, to develop and refine a reasoned jurisprudential approach to new aspects of the free movement of goods on its own terms rather than those of the Member States.

163 See Chapter 14: Intellectual Property.
164 That is, one looks to the underlying motivations and aims of the parties involved and the balance between them (Commission, Council, ECJ and Member States), rather than assuming that because there appear to be two types of derogation available (Article 36 and mandatory requirements) there necessarily must be a clear link with two types of potential breach to which they apply (distinctly and indistinctly applicable measures).

The main existing mandatory requirements are consumer protection, unfair competition, and the environment.

Consumer protection

Consumer protection is probably the most popular justification, after public health, made by Member States for national legislation which appears to restrict free movement of goods. Indeed, in the light of some of the case law concerning consumer protection, an outsider might be forgiven for thinking that EC consumers are either singularly dim or else extremely easily led. Amongst the items against which Member States have thought it necessary to 'protect' their consumers are: margarine packaged in shapes other than cubes;[165] milk substitutes;[166] the use of generic appellations by imported goods;[167] and a more acid beer than a Member State's drinkers were used to.[168] Very few of the attempts to justify derogations from Article 30 on the ground of customer protection have been accepted by the ECJ. Two cases which did succeed were *Oosthoeck*[169] and *Buet* v *Ministerie Public*.[170] In *Oosthoeck* the issue was a Dutch law which forbade the offering of free goods to purchasers of encyclopaedias, the rationale being that consumers might be induced to buy without being fully aware of the terms of the agreement that they were involving themselves in. The ECJ said that the law was a barrier to trade but that it served both to protect the consumer from deception and the honest trader from unfair competition and as such was justified. In *Buet* the issue involved French laws which forbade the sale by canvassing in private dwellings of documents and educational material for learning foreign languages.[171] The defendant sold, by canvassing, educational material for learning English devised by Encyclopaedia Britannica and imported from Belgium, and was successfully prosecuted. On the case being appealed the French *Cour d'Appel* referred the question of whether the French laws were compatible with Article 30 to the ECJ. The Court felt that it was possible in the majority of cases of canvassing at private dwellings to afford the customer adequate protection from pressure purchasing by allowing purchasers the right to cancel a contract in their home, probably in the form of some kind of 'cooling off' period. However, the canvassing of educational material presented a greater risk to the potential purchaser, in that they were likely to be behind in their education and open to sales pitches about improved job prospects by use of such material. If the material then turned out to be inadequate or low quality purchasers might not only have wasted their money but also damaged their prospects of improved employment or training. Under such circumstances the Court felt that it was quite permissible for the national legislature of a Member State to ban such canvassing rather than allow for a right of cancellation.

Unfair competition

In some senses, unfair competition measures adopted by the Member States are not dissimilar to intellectual property rights, notably in that they may allow for the exclusion of a product

165 Case 261/81, *Walter Rau Lebensmittelwerke* v *de Smedt PvbA, op. cit.*, note 130.
166 Case 76/86, *Commission* v *Germany* [1989] ECR 1021.
167 Case 12/74, *Commission* v *Germany* [1975] ECR 181.
168 Case 94/82, *Criminal proceedings against De Kikvorsch* [1983] ECR 947.
169 Case 286/81, *Oosthoeck Vitgeversmaatschapij BV op. cit.*, note 131.
170 Case 382/87, [1989] ECR 1235.
171 Law No. 556 of 12 July 1971 and Law No. 1137 of 22 December 1972.

from a national market because it competes unfairly with an existing national product. This analogy cannot, however, be carried too far as unfair competition laws may not be used to grant exclusive rights to market a product to an individual within a national territory. Rather, as the name suggests, such laws may be used where an importer takes advantage of the goodwill of an existing national producer by imitating his product in some way. This is not dissimilar to the concept behind the UK law of 'passing off' but much broader in scope. Unfair competition may also occur where an importer takes advantage of the work of a national producer, a version of this concept appears to have found its way into Community law in the draft Database Directive. In *BV Industrie Diensten Groep* v *JA Beele Handelmaatschappij BV*[172] the ECJ held that national law which sought to prohibit the precise imitation of another product, the sale of which is likely to cause confusion may, in certain circumstances, protect consumers and promote fair trading, and as such may justify a restriction on the free movement of goods. The issue of whether such law may be a mandatory requirement was supported by the fact that it was linked with the principle underlying Article 10 of the Paris Convention for the Protection of Industrial Property, as revised in 1967, which prohibited all acts of such a nature as to create confusion with the goods of a competitor, and by the fact that that rule was recognised in one form or another in the case law of the majority of the Member States.

However, in *Prantl*[173] the ECJ stated that a general practice of preventing the importation and marketing of goods which resembled domestic goods could not be justified, and each case where unfair competition was claimed had to be justified on its facts.

The environment

In *Commission* v *Kingdom of Denmark*[174] the Court considered whether a law which was adopted by the Danish government to protect the environment, by restricting the quantity of beer and soft drinks which might be marketed by a single producer in non-approved containers to 3000 hectolitres per annum (and provided that a deposit and return system was established), in order to enable more efficient recycling, was legitimate. The Danish government had originally required that producers and importers should only use approved containers, but the producers complained that such a law would force them to manufacture or purchase containers approved by the Danish Government at a substantial extra cost. The Danish government was aware that either system involved 'trading rules which are capable of hindering, directly or indirectly, actually or potentially, intraCommunity trade' and could thus be considered as measures having an effect equivalent to quantitative restrictions[175] and that the Court in a number of cases had ruled that requirements as to the type of packaging for goods which may be used are national measures capable of affecting trade between Member States.[176] However, in *Procureur de la Republique* v *Association de defense des bruleurs d'huiles usagees*[177] the Court had held that the protection of the environment is 'one of the Community's essential objectives' and that it might, therefore, justify certain limitations upon the principle of the free movement of goods. Indeed, this view, appears to

172 Case 6/81, [1982] ECR 707.
173 Case 16/83, *op. cit.*, note 150.
174 Case 302/86, [1988] ECR 4607.
175 Case 8/74, *Procureur du Roi* v *Dassonville* [1974] ECR 837, at 852

176 Case 261/81, *Walter Rau Lebensmittelwerke* v *de Smedt PvbA, op. cit.*, note 130; Case 104/75, *Adrian de Peijer (Centrafarm BV)* [1976] ECR 613; and Case 16/83, *Prantl, op. cit.*, note 150.
177 Case 240/83, [1985] ECR 531.

have been confirmed by changes made to the EC Treaty by both the Single European Act[178] and TEU.[179] It appeared that national measures taken for the protection of the environment were capable of constituting the type of mandatory requirements which were recognised in the *Cassis de Dijon* case as limiting the application of Article 30 of the Treaty in the absence of Community rules. However, the Advocate General in the *Kingdom of Denmark* case stated that the judgment in the *Cassis de Dijon* case could not be taken to mean that the Member States had free rein in their choice of measures, as the level of protection required to fall within those mandatory requirements cannot be excessive or unreasonable and the measures taken to achieve a particular requirement must be necessary and proportional.[180] The Court held that protection of the environment was an important objective, but that the measures taken by the Danish government were disproportionate to the objective pursued as, given the small percentage of imported beverages sold in Denmark, the risk to the environment from their containers was limited and did not justify a quantitative restriction upon their import. The Danish government in applying such a system was failing to fulfil its obligations under Article 30 of the EEC Treaty.[181]

Article 37

Article 37(1) requires that State monopolies of a commercial character should be adjusted in order to avoid any discrimination regarding the conditions under which goods are procured and marketed between nationals of Member States. Article 37(2) contains the stand-still rule that prohibits Member States from introducing any new measures which are contrary to Article 37(1). State monopolies are clearly in a position to affect the free movement of goods as they can control imports and exports from the Member States and the conditions in which trading in those goods takes place. Article 37 only applies to the provision of goods and not of services[182] and only to activities which are tied to the precise business of the monopoly.[183] It is directly applicable.[184]

Article 115 EC

Article 115[185] allows Member States to take protective measures in certain circumstances where they are experiencing economic difficulties. However, this is subject to the Member State having received authorisation from the Commission before they adopt those measures, the conditions and details of which are decided by the Commission. Even where matters are urgent Member States must request authorisation to take the necessary measures themselves from the Commission, which must then take a decision as soon as possible When it comes to a choice of measures paragraph 3 states that priority will be given to those which cause the

178 Which inserted into Part Three of the EEC Treaty a new Title VII which by Article 130 R included the preservation, protection and improvement of the quality of the environment as one of the objectives of action to be taken by the Community.
179 Which expanded and refined the provisions inserted by the SEA. See below Chapter 19.
180 Per Advocate General Sir Gordon Slynn [1988] ECR 4607, at 4622.
181 See further Krämer, 'Environmental Protection and

Article 30 EEC Treaty' (1993) 30 CML Rev 111.
182 Case 271/81, *Société d'insemination Artificielle* [1983] ECR 2057.
183 Case 119/78 *SA des Grandes Distilleries Peureux v Directeur des Services Fiscaux de Haute-Saone et du Territoire de Belfort* [1979] ECR 975.
184 Paragraph 1 – Case *59/75 Pubblico Ministreo v Manghera* [1976] ECR 91; paragraph 2 – Case 6/64, *Costa v ENEL* [1964] ECR 585.
185 As amended by Article G (30) TEU.

least disturbance to the functioning of the Common Market. The Commission may amend or abolish those measures at any time. Because the derogations permitted under Article 115 are exceptions to both Article 30 and Article 9 they have to be very strictly applied and interpreted.[186]

Other barriers to the free movement of goods

As well as the fiscal and physical barriers to the free movement of goods as discussed above, there are a number of specific areas of national law which, until they are harmonised by the Community, will continue to be barriers to the free movement of goods. In particular these include State aids and subsidies, public procurement, intellectual property and the use of national standards.

State aids and subsidies

State aids and subsidies are a well-known part of many Member States' economies. They may be used to prop up a failing industry which a Member State feels is economically and strategically important or, equally, an industry whose collapse is likely to cause social problems for a particular region of a Member State. They may also be used to support development of new industries and new technologies. While the area of State aids and subsidies is regulated in the main by Articles 92–94 EC, State aid may also affect the free movement of goods and as such may fall to be reviewed by the ECJ with regard to breach of Article 30. Indeed, the ECJ has held that Articles 30 and 92 play complimentary roles in ensuring the free movement of goods.[187] Measures taken under Article 92 cannot be used in contravention of Articles 30–36. In *Commission v Ireland*[188] a State-supported campaign to 'Buy Irish' was held to breach Article 30, regardless of any claim in its support under Article 92.

Public procurement

The area of public procurement within the Community must inevitably play a large role in determining the extent of the free movement of both goods and services within the Community, as it concerns all contracts for the supply, works and services of State or State-governed bodies.[189] It has long been an area dominated by national biases, with major contracts receiving little publicity outside the Member State concerned and national contractors being favoured at the expense of other Member States' contractors. These attitudes and practices were thus a considerable barrier to the free movement of goods and services.[190]

---

[186] See Case 62/70, *Werner A Bock v Commission* [1971] ECR 908; Case 41/76, *Donckerwolche v Procureur de la République* [1976] ECR 1921; Case 52/77, *Cayrol v Rivoira* [1977] ECR 2261; Case 179/78, *Procureur de la République v Rivoira* [1970] ECR 1147.

[187] Case 103/84, *Commission v Italy* [1986] ECR 1759.

[188] Case 249/81, *Commission v Ireland* [1982] ECR 4005.

[189] In 1985 it was calculated that public purchases represented 15 per cent of Community GDP, two-thirds of which were purchasing contracts subject to official procedures. In 1990 these figures amounted to 706 billion ECU and 423 billion ECU respectively.

[190] See, for example, Case 45/87, *Commission v Ireland* [1988] ECR 4929 concerning the use of national standards as a method of discriminating against non-Irish products in a public authority scheme.

During the 1980s the Commission began to concentrate on the issue of public procurement within the Community.[191] However, the Directives initially used were rarely fully or correctly implemented by the Member States and did little to combat the long-standing domestic biases. There was also no attempt at that time to provide a uniform Community-wide procedure by which individuals could seek redress for abuse of public procurement policy.

However, in the early 1990s, the Commission, conscious of the negative effect of an unreformed public procurement market upon the free movement of goods, moved to establish a timetable and programme for reform. This has resulted in a number of new directives designed to force Member States to open all their major public procurement contracts to Community wide tender,[192] and to provide a Community wide system of redress for abuse of that public procurement system.[193]

This new legislation, combined with a new determination on the part of the Commission to ensure that the Member States comply with their obligations in this area[194] suggest that this barrier to the free movement of goods should become a much lesser problem.

Intellectual property

Intellectual property rights can, under certain circumstances, form a potential barrier to the free movement of goods, in particular where such intellectual property rights are not protected by Community wide legislation. In such cases the Member States may be allowed to impose restrictions on imports if they would infringe national industrial or commercial property rights. The Community therefore has two issues to reconcile, the first is the issue of protection of rights in products placed on both the internal market and in world trade, and the second is the harmonisation of nation l legislation on intellectual property rights so as to remove the remaining restrictions on the free movement of goods between Member States. This topic is dealt with in detail elsewhere in the text.[195]

National standards

As is discussed in the Technology Chapter,[196] a high degree of standardisation in the

191 For an overview of this, see Arrowsmith, 'An Overview of EC Policy on Public Procurement: Current Position and Future Prospects' (1992) 1 PPLR 28.
192 Directive 90/531/EEC on the Procurement Procedures of Entities Operating in the Water, Transport, Energy, and Telecommunications Sectors, OJ 1990 L297, extended EC procurement rules to the four public sectors of water, energy, transport and telecommunications. Directive 93/36/EEC Co-ordinating Procedures for the Award of Public Supply Contracts, OJ 1993 L199 consolidates all existing EC public supply contract legislation including Directive 88/295/EEC. Directive 93/37/EEC Concerning the Co-ordination of Procedures for the Award of Public Works Contracts, OJ 1993 L199 is a consolidated version of the public works Directive 89/440/EEC which amended Directive 71/305/EEC.
193 Directive 89/665/EEC on the Co-ordination of the

Laws, Regulations, and Administrative Provisions Relating to the Application of Community Rules on Procedures for the Award of Public Supply and Public Works Contracts, OJ 1989 L395. This called on all Member States to provide national procedures and remedies to ensure that contractors and suppliers could receive, at any stage in the awarding procedure, effective and rapid remedies against any contract decision that breached the EC public procurement rules.
194 See, for example, Case 71/92, *Commission v the Kingdom of Spain,* judgment of 17 November 1993, concerning Spain's failure to fulfil its obligations under Directive 71/305/EEC Concerning the Co-ordination of Procedures for the Award of Public Works Contracts, and Council Directive 77/62/EEC Co-ordinating Procedures for the Award of Public Supply Contracts.
195 See Chapter 14: Intellectual Property.
196 See Chapter 15: Technology.

Community is required to overcome barriers to the free movement of goods as the Community strives for economic integration.

There are three main barriers to this, the first two of which have been the subject of discussion earlier in this Chapter and will only be mentioned here in passing. These are differences in national regulations which have generally been enacted to protect some aspect of the national concern, such as the public interest, health, and the environment, and testing and certification procedures which ensure the conformity of a product to national regulations or industrial standards. Both of these areas have been scrutinised in some detail by the ECJ with reference to Articles 30–34.

The third and more insidious barrier is that of national industrial standards.[197] These are prescribed by private organisations and include standards for product form, functioning, quality and compatibility. These are not usually legally binding and their effect, while not readily apparent, may be very significant.[198] It is these technical barriers that the Community has yet to successfully remove.

In May 1985 the Council adopted its 'New Approach to Technical Harmonisation and Standards'.[199] The concept behind this 'New Approach' was that the Council, when dealing with Directives concerning standards, should not concern itself with their technical and executive aspects but rather should limit itself to defining the essential objectives and requirements. The technical and executive process is then left to bodies competent in industrial standardisation: CEN,[200] CENELEC[201] and ETSI[202] which represent the Member States, manufacturers and consumers. The technical specifications prepared by these bodies are not mandatory for Community producers, but the Member States have to accept products complying with them as meeting the necessary standards outlined in the directives.

While the 'New Approach' to standardisation has helped, the process still tends to be slow and thus still hinders the free movement of goods. In a further attempt to address the issue, in October 1990 the Commission adopted a Green Paper on European standardisation designed to create more interest in European standardisation and to suggest ways in which both standardisation bodies and Member States could facilitate the standards creation process. As a result of this a Commission Communication was adopted in April 1992[203] which concentrated on improving procedures adopted by the standardisation bodies.

CONCLUSION

The attainment of the Community wide free movement of goods has engaged a significant portion of the Community institutions' time since the signing of the EC Treaty. The matter has taxed both the patience of the Commission and ECJ in applying the principles laid down in the Treaty in a coherent and legally certain manner, and the ingenuity of the Member States' governments in their efforts to protect their own producers from the full effects of having to compete in a Single Community Market. At present, after a long period of time

---

197 For example, DIN in Germany and the BSI in the UK.

198 An insurance company may, for instance, make its cover for particular items conditional upon their complying with national standards.

199 OJ 1985 C136.

200 Which deals with general standardisation issues.

201 Which deals with electrotechnical standardisation issues.

202 Which deals with telecommunications standardisation.

203 OJ 1992 C96.

where it must have seemed that the aim of achieving that principle would founder upon ambitions of the Member States, it seems that the Community is now moving inexorably towards the point where total free movement of goods within the Community finally will be achieved. The harmonisation of the Member States' laws relating to indirect taxation, public procurement, intellectual property and national standards will have played no little part in that success, and the fact that this is being achieved is due to a realisation amongst the Member States that the Community is faced with increasingly harsh competition from other world nations and trading groups. This competition has already proved too strong for certain Member State industries, such as the microelectronics industry and with the decisions made at the conclusion of the Uruguay Round of the GATT negotiations further paring away the protection afforded to Community producers, other industries and producers may yet follow. A truly open Community Market in which goods produced in each Member State can move freely has the potential, however, to allow the development of producers economically strong enough to hold their own in the world Market. Increasing harmonisation should, therefore, reduce the need for actions based on Articles 30 and 34 as Community legislation removes the need for Member States to legislate to protect the national concerns listed under the headings provided by Article 36 or the mandatory requirements. It is also clear that where legislation being challenged does not affect the pattern of Community trade, being concerned rather with the minutiae of selling arrangements, the ECJ has adopted a much less interventionary stance as regards the use of Article 30 than has previously been the case.

Further reading

Arnull, A., 'What shall we do on Sunday?' (1991) 16 EL Rev 112.

Diamond, P., 'Dishonourable Defences: The Use of Injunctions and the EEC Treaty; Case Study of the Shops Act 1950' (1991) 54 MLR 72.

Gormley, L., *Prohibiting Restrictions on Trade within the EEC* (1985).

Gormley, L., 'Actually or Potentially, Directly or Indirectly? Obstacles to the Free Movement of Goods' (1989) 9 YEL 197.

Krämer, L., 'Environmental Protection and Article 30 EEC Treaty'(1993) 30 CML Rev 111.

Mortelmans, K., 'Article 30 of the EEC Treaty and Legislation Relating to Market Circumstances: Time to Consider a New Definition?' (1991) 28 CML Rev. 115.

Oliver, P., *Free Movement of Goods in the EEC* 2nd edn (1988).

Steiner, J., 'Drawing the Line: Uses and Abuses of Article 30 EEC' (1992) 29 CML Rev 749.

Usher, J., 'The Single Market and Goods Imported from Third Countries' (1986) YEL 159.

White, E., 'In Search of Limits to Article 30 of the EEC Treaty' (1989) 26 CML Rev 235.

CHAPTER 12

Free movement of persons

INTRODUCTION

As noted in Chapter 11, the principles of the free movement of persons, goods, services and capital within the Community are essential to the establishment of the Common Market and are the four essential 'freedoms' regulated by the Treaty. It is obvious that without free movement of 'workers' the internal Community labour market would remain inconsistent, with areas of high unemployment and low wages, areas of labour shortage and high wages, and no effective mechanism for ensuring that the Community work-force could migrate away from the former to fulfil the need in the latter. As Hartley notes,[1] however, in economic terms it is not necessary for every person in the Community to have the right to free movement, only those who might be termed 'economically active'. The Treaty largely remains silent on the issue of those who are not deemed to be 'economically active'. This, not unnaturally, begs questions with regard to the purpose of the Treaty, as it was first formulated and how the aims and objectives of the Member States have changed from that point, notably with regard to issues of social policy. It is clear that while many of the Treaty provisions deal with the free movement of 'workers', in recent years the distinction between 'economically active' and 'non-economically active' has become impossible to maintain, primarily due to the fact that workers will often have dependants who may also need to be provided for by the host State. In addition, a narrow head such as 'workers' does not comfortably cover such categories of individuals as students, retired persons and the unemployed, for whom there may be a need or desire to move between the Member States. The Community has moved increasingly to a position where social issues are given a much higher priority by both the Institutions and the Member States, and the ECJ has long been of the opinion that workers should not just be treated as an economic resource:

> The migrant worker is not regarded by Community law – nor is he by the internal legal system – as merely a source of labour, but is viewed as a human being . . .[2]

Both SEA and TEU add new dimensions to the free movements of persons and this trend has been reinforced by recent secondary legislation, which has been clearly aimed to benefit those who are not 'economically active'.[3]

However, the free movement of persons involves some hazards for the Member States, as the much-reduced capacity to prevent the access and egress of Community nationals will also tend to include those who may be regarded as 'undesirables'. The principle of free movement of persons has been the most difficult of the free movement principles to enforce with

---

1 Green, Hartley and Usher, *The Legal Foundations of the Single European Market* (1992), at 91.
2 Per Advocate General Trabucchi in Case 7/75, *Mr & Mrs F v Belgian State* [1975] ECR 679.
3 Directive 90/364/EEC on the Right of Residence; Di-

rective 90/365/EEC on the Right of Residence for Employees and Self-employed Persons who have Ceased their Occupational Activity; and Directive 90/366/EEC on the Right of Residence for Students.

regard to the Member States. For instance, in the worldwide recession of recent years the Member States have sought to limit the impact of the free movement of persons in order to protect the position of their own nationals on their internal job market by the use of national vocational qualifications. There has also been concern in the past amongst the Member States to prevent individuals engaging in 'benefit tourism', that is, migrating to Member States where there is greater social security provision from Member States where social security provision is limited.

This Chapter will examine the development of the concept of the free movement of persons, the ways and means by which the law has evolved and its present state. It will deal with the issue of immigration, the controls allowable, the status of migrants and their rights both to work and to social security benefits, and the freedom to provide services will also be considered.

The origins of the principle of free movement of persons are found in the EC Treaty, Article 3(c) and (d) which states that:

> . . . the activities of the Community shall include . . . ;
>
> (c) an internal market characterised by the abolition, as between Member States, of obstacles to the free movement of . . . persons, . . . ;
>
> (d) measures concerning the entry and movement of persons in the internal market as provided for in Article 100c;[4]

Those aims are further elaborated in Part Three, Title III, Chapter 1 'Workers' Articles 48–51; Chapter Two 'Right of Establishment' Articles 52–58; and Chapter Three 'Services' Articles 59–66. In broad terms, Article 48 gives workers the right of free movement between the Member States, Article 52 gives the same right to the self-employed, which provides for freedom of establishment, and Article 59 deals with the right to provide services across the internal borders of the Community. However, the ECJ has shown itself to be relatively unconcerned in establishing clear differences between these categories, noting that they were all:

> . . . based on the same principles in so far as they concern the entry into and the residence in the territory of Member States of persons covered by Community law and the prohibition of all discrimination between them on grounds of nationality.[5]

In addition to those Articles, Article 6[6] and Part Two 'Citizenship of the Union' – Articles 8 and 8e provide a useful background against which the ECJ may resolve ambiguities or lacunae within the Treaty provisions or secondary legislation.

Article 6, paragraph 1, states:

> Within the scope of application of this Treaty, and without prejudice to any special provisions contained therein, any discrimination on grounds of nationality shall be prohibited.

While the ECJ has interpreted this prohibition quite widely,[7] and has ruled that it is capable of direct effect,[8] the words 'Within the scope of application of this Treaty' have been

---

4 As amended by Article G(3) TEU.

5 Case 48/75, *The State* v *Jean Noel Royer* [1976] ECR 497.

6 Formerly Article 7 EC, amended by Article G(8) TEU.

7 See for example, Case 24/86, *Blaizot* v *University of Liege* [1988] ECR 379.

8 Case 1/78, *Kenny* v *Insurance Officer* [1978] ECR 1489.

interpreted strictly. In *Walrave and Koch* v *Association Union Cycliste Internationale*[9] the Court held that the prohibition of discrimination on the grounds of nationality must be concerned with some form of economic activity without which Article 6 cannot apply. This clearly will affect the ability of those who are not defined as workers, self-employed or the families of either to use Article 6, although there appears to be some doubt as to the ECJ's current approach to the matter.

Articles 8–8e of the Treaty provide that nationals of the Member States are citizens of the EU and are entitled to enjoy the rights conferred by the Treaty, while being subject to the duties imposed by it. Article 8a(1) provides that all citizens of the Union have the right to move and reside freely within the Member States of the Union, subject to such limitations and conditions as are laid down in the Treaty or in measures adopted to give effect to Treaty provisions. Article 8a(2) provides that the Council may adopt provisions to facilitate the exercise of the rights in paragraph (1). Article 8b provides that an individual can vote and stand in both municipal[10] and European Parliament[11] elections in the Member State in which he resides on the same terms as nationals of that State.

THE FREE MOVEMENT OF WORKERS – ARTICLE 48 AND RELATED LEGISLATION

Article 48 is concerned with the freedom of movement of 'workers' and states that:

1. Freedom of movement for workers shall be secured within the Community by the end of the transitional period at the latest.
2. Such freedom of movement shall entail the abolition of any discrimination based on nationality between workers of the Member States as regards employment, remuneration and other conditions of work and employment.
3. It shall entail the right, subject to limitations justified on grounds of public policy, public security or public health:
    (a) to accept offers of employment actually made;
    (b) to move freely within the territory of Member States for this purpose;
    (c) to stay in a Member State for the purpose of employment in accordance with the provisions governing the employment of nationals of that State laid down by law, regulation or administrative action;
    (d) to remain in the territory of a Member State after having been employed in that State, subject to conditions which shall be embodied in implementing Regulations to be drawn up by the Commission.
4. The provisions of this Article shall not apply to employment in the public service.

The main pieces of secondary legislation enacted under Article 48(3)(d) and 49 are as follows:

- Directive 68/360/EEC on Suppression of Restrictions on the Movement and Residence of Workers and their Families Within the Community;[12]

---

[9] Case 36/74, [1974] ECR 1405.
[10] Article 8b(1).

[11] Article 8b(2).
[12] OJ (Special edition) 1968 (II) 485.

- Regulation 1612/68/EEC on Free Movement of Workers Within the Community;[13]
- Regulation 1251/70/EEC on the Right of Workers to Remain in the Territory of a Member State After Having Been Employed in that State;[14]
- Directive 64/221/EEC on Derogations from Free Movement Provisions Available to Member States on the Grounds of Public Policy, Public Security or Public Health.[15]

Article 48 is directly effective,[16] but is not generally applicable to the way in which the Member States treat their own nationals where the situations at issue are entirely internal to the Member States.[17] It was uncertain for some time as to whether the protection under Article 48, as applied to those who have migrated to seek work, as opposed to those who have migrated to take up an existing job, was of a finite duration. Following *R v IAT ex parte Antonissen*,[18] it appears that this is the case. Here, the UK sought to deport Antonissen, a convicted drug dealer, who had been in the UK for more than six months, but claimed he was still looking for work. The ECJ stated that the deportation would be permissible where the individual concerned had been in the Member States for more than six months, unless they could produce evidence that they were still seeking work and had a genuine chance of being employed.

The definition of a 'worker'

Neither Article 48 nor Regulation 1612/68/EEC provides details as to what attributes may be used to define who is and who is not a 'worker',[19] other than that they must be nationals of a Member State.[20] Thus, it has been left to the ECJ to fill the legislative gap. In *Levin v Staatssecretaris van Justitie*[21] concerning a part-time worker, the ECJ held that:

> . . . the terms 'worker' and 'activity as an employed person' may not be defined by reference to the national laws of the Member States but have a Community meaning. . . . The meaning and scope of the terms . . . should thus be clarified in the light of the principles of the legal order of the Community. . . . these concepts define the field of application of one of the fundamental freedoms guaranteed by the Treaty, and as such may not be interpreted restrictively.

The term 'worker' has been given a wide interpretation by the ECJ. In *Hoekstra v BBDA*[22] it was held that the term applied not just to an individual who was working at the point when the issue became relevant, but also an individual who, although not working at that point,

---

13 OJ (Special edition) 1968 (II) 475, latest revision of Part II of the Regulation adopted in July 1992 and published in Regulation 2434/92/EEC, OJ 1992 L245.
14 OJ 1970 L142.
15 OJ (Special edition) 1963–4 117.
16 Case 167/73, *Commission v French Republic* [1974] ECR 359; Case 41/74, *Van Duyn v Home Office* [1974] ECR 1337.
17 Case 175/78, *R v Sanders* [1979] ECR 1129; Case 180/83, *Moser v Land Baden-Wurttemberg* [1984] ECR 2539; Case 298/84, *Paulo Iorio v Azienda Autonoma delle Ferrovie dello Stato* [1986] 3 CMLR 669; Case 20/87, *Ministre Public v Gauchard* [1989] 2 CMLR 489; Cases 35 and 36/82, *Morson v Netherlands* [1982] ECR 3723.

18 Case C-292/89, [1991] 2 CMLR 373.
19 Indeed, the only Community legislation which does so is Regulation 1408/71/EEC, Article 1(a) concerning social security.
20 Nationality is determined with reference to the law of the Member State involved. With regard to transitional arrangements concerning individuals from States which have recently acceded to the Community, see Case C-9/88, *Lopes da Veiga v Staatsecretaris van Justitie* [1989] ECR 2989.
21 Case 53/81, [1982] ECR 1035.
22 Case 75/63, [1964] ECR 177.

was capable of doing so. The ECJ also stated that a worker is an individual who performs a service of some economic value for and under the direction of another person, in return for which they receive payment.

In the cases of *Levin*[23] and *Kempf* v *Staatsecretaris van Justitie*[24] the ECJ considered the issue of how much work or income generated by work was required to prove that an individual was a worker. In *Levin* the ECJ held that part-time work, other than that which was nominal or minimal, was sufficient and that as long as the work met the economic activity criteria it did not matter whether or not the individual could support themselves on the money earnt or had to rely on some other means for a percentage of their income. This was plainly restated in Kempf where the ECJ went further in saying that it did not matter whether the money used to supplement the income was obtained from the individual's private means or by way of public funds.

In *Lawrie-Blum* v *Land Baden Wurttemberg*[25] Ms Lawrie Blum, a British national, was refused permission to engage in a period of probationary teaching which would have qualified her for appointment as a teacher. This refusal was based on the ground that she was not a German national as was required by the law of the Land Baden Wurttemberg. She claimed that this was an infringement of her rights under Article 48(2) EC, while the Land stated that a probationary teacher was not a worker for the purposes of Article 48. The ECJ noted that a probationary teacher is under the direction and supervision of the school to which she is assigned, that she provides a service of some economic value and receives remuneration for services provided. Therefore, all three criteria for the determination of 'worker' status were fulfilled.[26] However, in *Bettray* v *Staatssecretaris van Justitie*[27] the ECJ refused to accept that an individual who was engaged in an activity for pay in a drug rehabilitation scheme was in fact a worker, because it was of the opinion that there was no real and genuine economic activity taking place. This may be contrasted in turn with *Steymann* v *Staatssecretaris van Justitie*,[28] where the individual concerned was a member of a 'religious' commune. He carried out work as a plumber within the commune and participated in other work of a commercial nature which was undertaken by the commune. In return the commune provided him with board, lodgings and pocket money, but did not pay a formal wage. The ECJ held that this labour, being a necessary part of the commune's self-sufficiency for which the commune was prepared to provide services in return and consisting, as it did, of genuine and effective activity, was sufficient to justify 'worker' status.

While the ECJ has gone to some lengths to provide a satisfactory definition of a 'worker', it is clear that even where an economically active person does not fall within the current definition of a 'worker' and thus receive the protection of Article 48, they are likely to be self-employed and thus covered by Articles 52 or 59. However, it must still be noted that an individual who has always worked as a self-employed person within a Member State (other than his own) will not have obtained 'worker' status and cannot rely on Article 48 should this issue become relevant.[29]

23 Case 53/81, *op. cit.*, note 21.
24 Case 139/85, [1987] CMLR 764.
25 Case 66/85, [1987] CMLR 389.
26 See also Case C-357/89, *Raulin* v *Netherlands Minister of Education and Science* [1992] ECR 1027; examined in O'Keefe, (1992) 29 CML Rev 1215.

27 Case 344/87, [1991] 1 CMLR 459.
28 Case 196/87, [1988] ECR 6159.
29 Case C-15/90, *Middleburgh* v *Chief Adjudication Officer* [1991] I ECR 4655.

REGULATION 1612/68 EEC

Regulation 1612/68/EEC deals with the issues of eligibility for employment,[30] employment and equality of treatment,[31] and workers' families.[32] It was passed to implement the provisions of Articles 48(2) and 48(3)(a) and (b) EC.

Eligibility for employment

Regulation 1612/68/EEC, Part I, Title I, provides that any national of a Member State has the right to take up and pursue activity as an employed person under the same conditions as those imposed on nationals of the host State[33] and must be afforded the same priority in obtaining available employment as the host State's nationals.[34] No Member State may therefore operate via law, regulation, administrative practice or provision discriminatory employment policies[35] and, in particular, Member States cannot discriminate in methods of recruitment, advertising of vacancies or eligibility to apply for employment.[36] National quota systems which provide for a limit to the percentage of foreign nationals in particular jobs cannot apply to nationals of other Member States.[37] Where assistance in finding employment is granted to nationals of a Member State it must apply equally to nationals of the other Member States.[38]

Employment and equality of treatment

The rights granted by Article 7–9 in Title II of the Regulation are granted expressly to workers. However, it appears that the ECJ has been willing to extend some of those rights to the families of workers. Article 7(1) states that:

> A worker who is a national of a member State may not, in the territory of another member State, be treated differently from national workers by reason of his nationality in respect of any conditions of employment and work, in particular as regards remuneration, dismissal, and should he become unemployed, reinstatement or re-employment.

Thus, where a Member State provides a concession to its workers this must be similarly conferred on migrant workers.[39] It must be stressed that this does not interfere with the Member States' ability to confer advantages, but merely requires that those advantages should be available and effective, on an equal basis, to both nationals of the Member States and migrants workers, for instance, separation payments for time spent away from their families.[40]

---

[30] Part I, Title I, Articles 1–6.
[31] Part I, Title II, Articles 7–9.
[32] Part I, Title III, Articles 10–12.
[33] Article 1.
[34] Article 2.
[35] Article 3(1). Language considerations are, however, exempted from this. See Case 397/87, *Groener* v *Minister for Education* [1990] 1 CMLR 401. The language requirement must be proportionate and necessary to the aim to be achieved.

[36] Article 3(2).
[37] Article 4, See Case 167/73, *Commission* v *French Republic*, op. cit., note 16 where the French *Code du Travail Maritime* of 1926 purported to impose a 75/25 per cent ratio of French crewmen to non-French crewmen on French merchant navy ships.
[38] Article 5.
[39] Case 15/69, *Sudmilch* v *Ugolia* [1969] ECR 363.
[40] Case 152/73, *Sotgiu* v *Deutsches Bundespost* [1974] ECR 153.

Article 7(2) states that a migrant worker 'shall enjoy the same social and tax advantages as national workers'. This term has been interpreted very widely by the ECJ. In *Fiorini* v *SNCF*[41] the ECJ held that unlike some of the provisions under Article 7(1), the rights granted under Article 7(2) do not have to be related to some contract of employment and may remain even when the worker dies so that his family may benefit from them. This was followed in *Ministerie Public* v *Even*[42] where the ECJ stated that the social advantages which accrued under Article 7(2) could be taken to mean all advantages 'generally granted to national workers primarily because of their objective status as workers or by virtue of the mere fact of their residence on national territory'.[43] Based on this reasoning, migrant workers have been held to be entitled to, amongst other things: a special discretionary childbirth loan which was purported to be payable only to German nationals in Germany;[44] a payment made to all old people in Belgium;[45] a Belgian minimum income payment;[46] a tiding-over allowance paid to young job seekers;[47] and a scholarship to study abroad which was part of a reciprocal arrangement between Belgium and Germany.[48]

Article 7(3) provides that migrant workers may avail themselves of vocational training and retraining courses which are provided for national workers.[49] Article 8 is concerned with the ability of migrant workers to avail themselves of membership of trade unions and attendant rights without discrimination.[50] Article 9 aims to ensure that both public and private housing are made available to migrant workers on the same terms and conditions that are given to nationals of the host State.

Workers' families

Regulation 1612/68/EEC, Part III, Article 10(1) defines what is meant by members of a worker's family for the purposes of deciding which individuals will be entitled to migrate with the worker to the host State.

They are:

(a) his spouse and their descendants who are under the age of 21 years or are dependants;

(b) dependant relatives in the ascending line of the worker and his spouse.

Individuals who are members of a worker's family are entitled to migrate with the worker regardless of their own nationality.[51] Article 10(2) states that Member States should facilitate the admission of any other family member who does not fall within Article 10(1), but who is dependant upon the worker or lived under his roof in his State of origin. What this means is not clear, but Steiner[52] suggests that once such other family members have been admitted and

[41] Case 32/75, [1975] ECR 1985.

[42] Case 207/78, [1979] ECR 2019.

[43] See also Case 137/84, *Ministere Public* v *Mutsch* [1985] ECR 2681.

[44] Case 65/81, *Reina* v *Landeskreditbank Baden-Wurttemberg* [1982] ECR 33.

[45] Case 261/83, *Castelli* v *ONPTS* [1984] ECR 3199.

[46] Case 249/83, *Hoeckx* v *Openbar Centrum voor Maatschappelijk Welzijn Kalmhaut* [1985] ECR 973; Case 122/84, *Scrivner* v *Chief Adjudication Officer* [1985] ECR 1027.

[47] Case 157/84, *Frascogna* v *Caisse des depôts et con-signations* [1985] ECR 1739; Case 94/84, *Deak* v *Office Nationale de l'Emploie* [1985] ECR 1873.

[48] Case 235/87, *Matteucci*. v *Communaute Française de Belgique* [1988] ECR 5589.

[49] Case 316/85, *Centre Public de l'Aide Sociale de Courcelles* v *Lebon* [1987] ECR 2811.

[50] Case C-213/90, *Association de Soutien aux Travailleurs Immigres* v *Chambre des Employes Prives* [1991] ECR I-3507.

[51] Although the worker must, of course, be an EC national.

[52] Steiner, *EC Law* 3rd edn (1992), at 197.

are resident with the worker, they should be treated in the same way as those covered by Article 10(1). The question of what constitutes support was raised in *Lebon*[53] where the ECJ stated that the issue is one of fact rather than of objective issues. If the worker supports an individual they are a dependant, whether or not the support is in fact essential. On the other hand, once a child reaches 21, he is no longer to be considered as a 'member of the family' unless he is still dependant on the worker.

In order for the migrant worker to be able to bring his family he must be able to provide housing for them which is considered to be normal for national workers in the region where he is living.[54] However, this proviso only applies at the time when the worker begins working in the Member State; any attempt to make it applicable to the entire time that the worker resides in the Member State is in breach of Community law.[55]

With regard to the position of spouses, the ECJ has made clear that the term 'spouse' means an individual who is married to the worker, a cohabitee is not able to rely on this provision.[56] In the event of marital disharmony, until such point as the marriage finally comes to an end by way of a divorce, the spouse is entitled to remain in the host State, even though the spouse is separated from, and no longer cohabiting with, the worker.[57] It appears that the status of the divorced spouse has still to be determined by the ECJ.[58]

Article 11 states that:

> Where a national of a member State is pursuing an activity as an employed or self-employed person in the territory of another member State, his spouse and those of the children who are under the age of 21 years or dependent on him shall have the rights to take up any activity as an employed person throughout the territory of that same state, even if they are not nationals of any member State.

In the case of *Emir Gül v Regierungsprasident Düsseldorf* [59] a Turkish-Cypriot who was married to an English woman working in Germany wished to practise medicine there full time, but was turned down on the grounds of his nationality. He was a qualified doctor who had already practised part time in Germany, and the ECJ held that if he was adequately qualified for the occupation he wished to take up, then under Article 11, as the spouse of an EC national, he was entitled to do so. Article 11 does not, however, give an independent right of residence to spouses.[60]

With regard to children, Article 12 provides that they are entitled to non-discriminatory access to general educational, apprenticeship and vocational training courses. This entitlement includes entitlement both to admission to courses and also such funding as may be available to aid in attendance.[61] The case of *Echternach and Moritz*[62] concerned children

---

53 *Op. cit.*, note 49.

54 Article 10(3).

55 Case 249/86, *Commission v Germany* [1989] ECR 1263.

56 See Case 59/85, *Netherlands v Reed* [1986] ECR 1283 where the scope of the term 'spouse' was questioned by a Dutch court. Ms Reed was living in Holland with her English cohabitee.

57 Case 267/83, *Diatta v Berlin* [1985] ECR 567.

58 Though in *R v Secretary of State (ex parte Sandhu)* [1982] 2 CMLR 553 the House of Lords held that the divorce of an Indian man and a German woman removed him from the scope of those individuals considered spouses. See, however, the ruling in Case C-370/90, *R v Secretary of State for the Home Department v Immigration Appeal Tribunal and Surinder Singh*, 7 July 1992, and Cullen, 'Spouses' Rights to Free Movement – Community Rules Prevail' [1993] JSWFL 77.

59 Case 131/85, [1986] ECR 1573.

60 Case 267/83, *Diatta v Berlin, op. cit.*, note 57.

61 Case 9/74, *Casagrande v Landeshauptsdadt Munchen* [1974] ECR 773.

62 Case 389 and 390/87, *Echternach and Moritz v Minister van Onderwijs en Wetenschapper* [1989] ECR 723.

of German parents working in Holland who, when their parents moved back to Germany, wished to remain in Holland to complete their college study, as Dutch qualifications were not recognised in Germany. The ECJ held that the integration of the children of migrant workers into the education system and society of the host nation was of great importance, and the value of this would be lost if when the parents decided to leave the host nation their children were in some way disadvantaged as a result. In such cases the children would retain their status as 'children of a family', even where the workers had returned to their home nation, although it seems that this status would naturally cease upon the completion of the course of education.

REGULATION 1251/70/EEC – THE RIGHT TO REMAIN IN THE TERRITORY OF A MEMBER STATE AFTER HAVING BEEN EMPLOYED THERE

Regulation 1251/70/EEC provides that under certain circumstances nationals of a Member State who have worked as employed persons in the territory of other Member States, and their families as defined by Regulation 1612/68/EEC [63] may continue to reside in the host Member State after the end of their employment there.[64] The three conditions for such continued residence are: where the worker has worked in the host Member State for the last 12 months, resided there for the last 36 months and has now retired;[65] where the worker has resided in the host Member State for the last 24 months and has ceased employment due to a permanent incapacity preventing work;[66] and where the worker, after 36 months employment and residence in the host Member State, takes up employment in another Member State while continuing to reside in the first Member State.[67] The worker's family can continue to reside in the host Member State after the death of the worker, if at the time of his death he had acquired the right to reside by virtue of the provisions in Article 2.[68] Even where the worker had not acquired such status at the time of his death, his family will be able to remain in the host Member State if any of the following conditions are met: he had resided there continuously for 24 months prior to death; he died as a result of an occupational illness or accident; or his surviving spouse is, or was prior to marrying the worker, a national of the host Member State.[69]

Periods of absence from the host Member State of less than three months do not count against continuity of residence, nor do absences due to obligatory military service. Similarly, involuntary unemployment and absences due to illness or accident do not count against continuity of employment.[70]

---

[63] See above for details.
[64] Article 1.
[65] Article 2(1)(a).
[66] Article 2(1)(b). Note that where the injury or disability is work-related and, as a result, subject to a pension from the Member State, the residence requirement does not apply.

[67] Article 2(1)(c).
[68] Article 3(1).
[69] Article 3(2). See further Evans, 'Nationality Law and European Integration' (1991) 16 EL Rev 190.
[70] Article 4.

DIRECTIVE 68/360/EEC – THE RIGHTS OF ENTRY AND RESIDENCE

Directive 68/360/EEC is primarily concerned with the control of the Member States' administrative procedures under Article 48. While the Directive makes it clear that Member States must remove all national restrictions on the freedom of movement and establishment of Community workers,[71] it also provides that those taking advantage of privileged Community status must be in a position to prove that they are entitled to it. The implication is that Community workers must have relevant documentation to prove that they are who they claim to be and that they are Community nationals, but that this documentation merely provides proof of those issues and should not therefore be regarded by the Member States as the source of their rights, as those rights are conferred directly by Article 48 EC.[72] Failure to acquire such documentation may be subject to penalties, but these penalties should be proportionate to the offence and should not automatically involve deportation of the individual as this would amount to a denial of the rights claimed rather than a punishment for hindering verification of those rights.[73]

This means that Member States should grant to their nationals the right to leave their territory and go to work in the other Member States, and to facilitate this they should issue an identity card or passport stating the holder's nationality. No other documentation is needed or may be required for exit from the Member States' territories.[74] Member States must allow individuals from other Member States to enter their territory on production of a valid ID card or passport, no other material may be required except from family members of the worker who are not nationals of any of the Member States.[75] Where a worker can provide the relevant entry documentation and material confirming that employment has been obtained the Member State concerned must grant a residence permit. Members of the worker's family can gain such a permit by production of the relevant entry documentation and proof of the relationship with the worker or, in the case of those covered by Article 10 (1) and (2) of Regulation 1612/68/EEC, proof from the authorities of the State of origin that they are dependant upon the worker or that they lived under the same roof in the Member State of origin.[76] The formalities of the residence permit may not hinder the start of the employment which the worker is contracted for.[77] The residence permit must be valid across the entire territory of the Member State of issuance, and must be valid for at least five years and renewable automatically, although this requirement is varied for those workers who are temporarily employed or involuntarily unemployed.[78] No other permits or formalities may be requested by the Member States.[79] The Member States have adopted a number of administrative practices with regard to this issue which have been subjected to scrutiny by the ECJ. In *R v Pieck*[80] a requirement by the UK authorities that individuals from other Member States should obtain a written 'leave' to enter the UK was held by the ECJ to be contrary to Article 3(2) of the Directive 63/360/EEC. The requirement that migrant workers should register with the police was considered in *Watson & Belmann*[81] and *Messner*.[82] In the former

---

[71] Article 1.
[72] See, for example, the wording of Article 4(2).
[73] Case 48/75, *The State v Jean Noel Royer* [1976] ECR 497.
[74] Article 2.
[75] Article 3.
[76] Article 4.
[77] Article 5.

[78] Articles 6 and 7.
[79] Case 8/77, *Sagulo v the State* [1977] ECR 1495.
[80] Case 157/79, [1980] ECR 2171.
[81] Case 118/75, *The State v Watson and Belmann* [1976] ECR 1185.
[82] Case C-265/88, [1989] ECR 4209.

case, the ECJ held that an Italian law which required an immigrant worker to report to the police within three days, and those providing accommodation to immigrant workers to report their arrival within 24 hours, were compatible with Community law where the time limits were reasonable. However, in *Messner*, concerning the same law, the three-day time-limit was held to be too short and the national law was thus in breach of Community law.[83] Finally, in *Roux v The Belgian State*[84] Ms Roux, a French national working in Belgium as a 'self-employed' waitress, was refused a Belgian residence permit and ordered to leave the country on the ground that the Aliens Office considered she was not self-employed but an employee, and all employees were required by Belgian law to be registered with a State social security scheme for employees. The ECJ held that failure to have the correct social security registration could not constitute a ground for refusal to issue the residence permit to a qualifying Community national enjoying freedom of movement under any of Articles 48, 52 and 59 EEC, and that such registration could not be used as a test of whether a Community national qualified as enjoying such freedom of movement. Correct classification as an employee or as self-employed was thus irrelevant to entitlement to the residence permit.

EXCEPTIONS TO THE FREE MOVEMENT OF PERSONS

There are two sets of exceptions to the provisions set out in Article 48 EC. These are the limitations contained in Article 48(3) concerning public policy, public security and public health, and the exception in Article 48(4) concerning employment in the public service. As with the provisions in the Treaty which allow Member States to place restrictions on the free movement of goods, these provisions have been interpreted very narrowly by the ECJ.

Article 48 (3) and Directive 64/221/EEC

It appears that the exceptions listed in Article 48(3) EC are only applicable in circumstances where a Member State wishes to exclude an individual from its territories, they cannot be used, once the individual has gained lawful entry, to discriminate against him in terms of the nature, scope and conditions of the employment he pursues:

> . . . on the grounds of public policy or public security a foreigner may not be permitted to enter a country and take up employment there, but those considerations have no bearing on conditions of work once employment has been taken up in an authorised manner.[85]

The case of *Rutili v French Minister of the Interior*[86] suggests that this is equally true of residence. Rutili, an Italian national resident in France, had been involved in trade union and political activities in the years 1967 and 1968. Because of this the French authorities sought to restrict his movements within France and in particular to forbid him to live in certain *départements* or regions of the country arguing that this was justified on the ground of public

---

83 It appears that an extension of the time-limit would bring the measure back into conformity with Community law. For other systems considered, see Case 321/87, *Commission v Belgium* [1989] ECR 997; Case C-68/89, *Commission v Netherlands*, 30 May 1991.

84 Case C-363/89, [1993] 1 CMLR 3.
85 Per Advocate General Gand in Case 15/69, *Sudmilch v Ugolia, op. cit.*, note 39.
86 Case 36/75, [1975] ECR 1219.

policy. The ECJ, however, stated that where a Member State did not have the power to limit the area of residence of its own nationals under particular circumstances, it equally could not limit the area of residence of nationals of other Member States in the same circumstances.

The Treaty provision is fleshed out by Directive 64/221/EEC which applies equally to workers, the self-employed, those receiving services, and the families of those groups.[87] This elaborates as to the meaning to be given to each of the three headings in Article 48(3) EC, noting that they may not be invoked for economic purposes.[88] In the event that a Member State takes measures against an individual, this action must be based solely on the personal conduct of that individual.[89] For the purposes of determining personal conduct the fact that an individual has past criminal convictions should not be used as the sole criteria for exclusion.[90] The fact that an individual's ID card or passport has expired while he is present in a host Member State will also not justify expulsion.[91] With regard to the public health justification, the Directive limits those diseases and disabilities which would justify exclusion to those contained in an annex to the Directive.[92] In the event that an individual contracts a disease or suffers a disability while resident in the host Member States this cannot be used to justify non-renewal of a residence permit or expulsion from the Member State.[93]

The remainder of the Directive is concerned with the administrative procedures and safeguards which the Member States should provide with regard to the use of the powers of exclusion. These aim to protect the rights of the individual and provide effective legal remedies in the event that the individual wishes to challenge a decision to exclude him from a Member State. Thus, an individual should be informed of the reasons upon which the decision to bar him from entry was taken, unless this would threaten State security;[94] he should be given at least 15 days' notice of the refusal to issue or renew a residence permit or of a decision to expel him, unless the situation is urgent;[95] and the same legal remedies should be open to him in the event of the refusal to issue or renew a residence permit or following a decision to expel him, as would be open to a national of the Member State with regard to acts of the administration.[96] The Directive then goes further and lays down a minimum standard of protection which should be ensured by the Member States, even where the protections of Article 8 are not provided.[97]

The direct effect of both Article 48 EC and Article 3(1) of the Directive and the scope of the public policy proviso were considered in the case of *Van Duyn* v *Home Office*.[98] Ms Van Duyn, who was a Dutch national, was refused entry to the UK to work at the headquarters of the Church of Scientology as a secretary, on the grounds that the UK government felt that Scientology was socially harmful. The ECJ decided that both provisions were capable of direct effect, and then turned to examine the UK's reasons for exclusion. The UK sought to justify its action on the ground of public policy, although the Church of Scientology was not

---

87 Article 1.
88 Article 2(2).
89 Article 3(1).
90 Article 3(2).
91 Article 3(3).
92 Article 4(1). For instance highly infectious diseases such as tuberculosis and syphilis, and disabilities such as drug addition or profound mental disturbance. For a discussion of the potential use of Article 4(1) against those individuals diagnosed as being either HIV positive or having full blown AIDS, see Van Overbeek, 'AIDS/HIV

Infection and the Free Movement of Persons within the European Economic Community' (1990) 27 CML Rev 791.
93 Article 4(2).
94 Article 6. See *R* v *Secretary of State for the Home Department ex parte Dannenberg* [1984] 2 CMLR 456 for a successful use of this Article.
95 Article 7.
96 Article 8.
97 Article 9.
98 Case 41/74, [1974] ECR 1337.

banned in the UK, nor was it a criminal offence to be a member, and it would, therefore, be possible for a UK national to take up the job. The ECJ, however, ruled that the UK was within its rights to exclude Ms Van Duyn on the grounds that her current personal conduct was at issue and she was associated with an institution that a Member State considered socially harmful.[99] Later in the case of *R v Bouchereau*[100] the UK authorities sought to deport Bouchereau, a French national who had been convicted of the illegal possession of drugs, on public policy grounds. He argued that this would be contrary to Community law as expressed by Article 3(2) of Directive 64/221/EEC, as it would be based on the fact that he had a prior criminal conviction. The ECJ held, however, that while a previous criminal record can only be taken into account inasmuch as the circumstances in which that conviction came about might be evidence of future personal conduct which could justify public policy arguments:

> Although in general, a finding that such a threat exists implies the existence in the individual concerned of a propensity to act the same way in the future, it is possible that past conduct alone may constitute such a threat to the requirements of public policy.

It then noted that as the circumstances that might justify changes in the scope of public policy requirements varied from time to time and from Member State to Member State, the Member States had to have an area of discretion within the limits imposed by the Treaty as to what and whom constituted a threat to public policy. However, it is clear that Member States may not deport individuals for reasons of a general preventative nature, especially in circumstances where the individual concerned is unlikely to engage in any further activity contrary to public policy.[101]

The above case law may be considered in the light of two UK cases, *Proll v Entry Clearance Officer Düsseldorf*[102] and *R v Secretary of State for the Home Department ex parte Marchon*.[103] In *Proll*, Ms Proll, a German national, had been involved with the Baader-Meinhof terrorist group in the early 1970s. In 1979 she returned to Germany to face trial and was convicted of armed robbery of a bank and falsifying documents. However, the German court imposed a minimum sentence because she had reformed and was expected not to commit any more crimes. She tried three times during the 1980s to obtain leave to enter the UK, once as a visitor, once to take up employment, and finally to carry out work for her German employer. On all three occasions she was refused entry on grounds of activities pre-1974. On the third occasion she appealed to the Immigration Appeal Tribunal which held, in allowing her appeal, that she could not be excluded under paragraph 85(b) of the Aliens Rules[104] which permitted the exclusion of those deemed to be a danger to the public good in the light of their character, conduct or associations. Her appeal was allowed because the German court had held in 1979 that she was no longer a threat to society and there was

---

99 But contrast this with Cases 115 and 116/81 *Adoui and Cornuaille v Belgium State* [1982] ECR 1665, concerning the issue of prostitution, where the ECJ held that a Member State cannot seek to expel or exclude a national of another Member State on the ground of public policy where the activity which is being stated as the reason for the use of the public policy ground can be carried out by nationals of that Member State without fear of similar repressive measures and sanctions being imposed on them.

100 Case 30/77, [1977] ECR 1999.

101 Case 67/74, *Bonsignore v Oberstadt direktor Koln* [1975] ECR 297. Expressions of remorse by the individual for past actions and a reduced or negligible sentence on behalf of the convicting court will also serve to indicate that the individual is 'reformed' and unlikely to pose any further risk.

102 [1988] 2 CMLR 357.

103 [1993] 2 CMLR 132.

104 HC 169.

other convincing evidence to support this. She could also not be excluded under paragraph 83 for having been convicted anywhere of an extraditable offence, as this head clearly could not apply to a Community worker.

In the *Marchon* case, Marchon, an Indo-Portuguese dual national and therefore a Community national, established himself in Britain as a doctor and finally as consultant psychiatrist at a National Health Service hospital. In 1986 he was convicted of importing four-and-a-half kilograms of heroin and sentenced to 14 years' imprisonment, later reduced to 11 years. No recommendation for deportation was made at the time but in 1990 the Home Secretary gave him notice that a deportation order would be made. On his appeal against that decision the court held that the construction of Article 3 of Directive 64/221/EEC as determined by the ECJ in *Bouchereau* should be applied, in that a defendant's past conduct leading to the past conviction could meet the requirements of Article 3 if that conduct was sufficiently serious. In this case the court held that the conduct was very serious indeed, the fact that Marchon was not likely to repeat the offence was not enough to overcome this and the use of the public policy exception to override his right to remain was justified.

The administrative safeguards provided by Directive 64/221/EEC may be considered with reference to the case of *R* v *Secretary of State for Home Affairs ex parte Santillo*.[105] Santillo was convicted of buggery and rape on one prostitute, and indecent assault and assault occasioning actual bodily harm on another prostitute, and sentenced to eight years' imprisonment. At the time of his conviction in 1974 the national court recommended that he be deported under the Immigration Act 1971. In 1978 the Home Secretary made a deportation order against him, to take effect when he was released. In April 1979 Santillo, after remission of sentence for good behaviour, was due to be released, but was instead held in detention until he could be deported. At this point he applied to have the deportation order set aside, claiming that as the order had been made over four years after his initial sentence it infringed his rights by breaching Article 9(1) of Directive 68/221/EEC. The ECJ, in considering Article 9(1), was of the opinion that its provisions were capable of direct effect. It went on to consider the meaning of the requirement contained in Article 9(1) that any decision which orders the expulsion of an EC individual from a Member State must be preceded by the opinion of a 'competent authority'. It held that the requirement:

> can only constitute a real safeguard if all the factors to be taken into consideration by the administration are put before the competent authority, if the opinion of the competent authority is sufficiently proximate in time to the decision ordering expulsion to ensure that there are no new factors to be taken into consideration, and if both the administration and the person concerned are in a position to take cognisance of the reasons which led the 'competent authority' to give its opinion – save where grounds touching the security of the State referred to in Article 6 of the directive make this undesirable.

The ECJ's ruling was, however, vague enough to leave two possibilities to the national court. First, that the gap between sentence and deportation order could cause the court's recommendation at sentencing to lose its force as an opinion or, secondly, that this would in fact only occur if there had been a change in circumstances in the intervening period. In the event the national court chose the latter route, decided that there were no intervening facts of merit and upheld the deportation order.[106]

[105] Case 131/79, [1980] ECR 1585.   [106] Green, Hartley and Usher, *op. cit.*, note 1, at 138.

With regard to penalties for failure to comply with Member States' administrative procedures, it can be seen from cases such as *Roux*,[107] *Royer*[108] and *Watson and Belmann*[109] that the ECJ has held consistently that penalties may be placed on migrant workers but these must be proportionate to the breach and may be no more excessive than those which would be levied on nationals of the Member State involved. In *Roux* it was noted that where there was non-compliance with the Belgian social security law this could be penalised, but not by refusal of a residence permit or deportation. Further to this, non-compliance with the Belgian social security law was not within the scope of either the public policy exception in Articles 48(3) or 56(1) EC and this could not, therefore, justify refusal to issue the residence permit.

Article 48 (4) EC – the public service proviso

While Article 48(4) EC states that the provisions of Article 48 do not apply to employment in the public service, it is clear that the ECJ has not been inclined to interpret this widely, not least because the definition of 'the public service' varies quite widely between the Member States. The provision appears to have been included in the Treaty in order that certain key positions within the public service of the Member States could be protected. Article 48(4) certainly does not apply to all positions within the public service, and when a national of another Member State is employed within the host nation's public service he cannot then be discriminated against by virtue of his nationality. In *Sotgiu v Deutsches Bundespost*[110] in answer to a question from the German *Bundesarbeitsgericht* the ECJ stated that Article 48(4) did not apply to all public service posts, being restricted to 'certain activities' connected with the exercise of official authority, and then could only be used to exclude nationals of other Member States from those activities. The ECJ expanded on this concept in *Commission v Belgium State*[111] where the Belgian authorities were of the opinion that the term 'public service posts', which were restricted by Belgian law to Belgian nationals, covered a vast range of positions including nurses, plumbers, electricians and architects. The ECJ was unimpressed with this argument, holding that public service was a Community concept not a Member State concept, and Article 48(4) referred only to those positions which involved safeguarding the interests of the State:

> . . . it removes from the ambit of Article 48 (1)–(3) a series of posts which involve direct or indirect participation in the exercise of powers conferred by public law and duties designed to safeguard the general interests of the State or of other public authorities. Such posts in fact presume on the part of those occupying them the existence of a special relationship of allegiance to the State and reciprocity of rights and duties which form the bond of nationality.

In its opinion, plumbers, electricians and the like did not carry out such weighty tasks. To this end, the ECJ has held that regardless of their classification for the purposes of the Member State, nurses,[112] school teachers,[113] and University teachers[114] are not employees in the public service with regard to the aim of Article 48(4).

---

107 Case C-363/89, *op. cit.*, note 84.
108 Case 48/75, *op. cit.*, note 73.
109 Case 118/75, *op. cit.*, note 81.
110 Case 152/73, [1974] ECR 153.
111 Case 149/79, [1980] ECR 3881.

112 See also Case 307/84, *Commission v France* [1986] ECR 1725.
113 Case 66/85, *Lawrie-Blum v Land Baden Wurtemberg, op. cit.*, note 25.
114 Case 33/88, *Allue and Coonan* [1989] ECR 1591.

The protective behaviour of the Member States with regard to the use of the public service proviso led the Commission to publish a Notice in 1988[115] stating that it intended to examine certain types of employment which it felt the ECJ had demonstrated were sufficiently far away from the activities which Article 48(4) was supposed to protect to fall very rarely under that proviso. Those areas were:

- public health care services;
- teaching in State educational establishments;
- research for non-military purposes in public establishments;
- public bodies responsible for administering commercial services.

SOCIAL SECURITY

Social security provisions in the Member States vary quite widely. However, to forbid migrant workers any protection via social security provisions would form a major barrier to worker mobility. Thus, the Member States are faced with the problem of attempting to decrease the differences between the various systems in such a way that workers are provided with a similar level of protection throughout the Member States. As stated in the introduction, without such harmonisation the Community is likely to be faced with 'social tourism' as individuals move from their State of origin in order to take advantage of more generous social benefits elsewhere amongst the Member States. The EC Treaty deals with the issue of benefits in Article 51:

> The Council shall, acting unanimously on a proposal from the Commission, adopt such measures in the field of social security as are necessary to provide freedom of movement for workers; to this end, it shall make arrangements to secure for migrant workers and their dependants:
>
> (a) aggregation, for the purpose of acquiring and retaining the right to benefit and of calculating the amount of benefit, of all periods taken into account under the laws of the several countries;
> (b) payment of benefits to persons resident in the territories of Member States.

It has further developed this area by way of secondary legislation, notably Regulation 1408/71/EEC, as amended and supplemented by Regulation 574/72/EEC, Regulation 1390/81/EEC and Regulation 3795/81/EEC.

Harmonisation

It will clearly not be possible to harmonise the different systems of the Member States completely in the near future because some Member States provide a very high amount of social security protection to their nationals and others only a relatively small amount. Some degree of approximation is, however, vital.

Recommendation No. 92/441/EEC[116] notes that it is necessary to ensure a citizen's general

---

115 Commission Notice 88/C 72/02, OJ 1988 C72/2 on the interpretation of Article 48 (4).
116 On common criteria concerning sufficient resources and social assistance in the national social protection systems, see OJ 1992 L245.

right to guaranteed resources and provides general principles designed to guarantee those resources and rights. It proposes a number of ways of implementation which specify the means of calculating and revising aid, and provides guidelines to those Member States which have already recognised the right to resources on how to develop or improve their national provisions and conditions and access procedures. This aims to complement existing systems without changing their general design and takes account of the financial constraints on Member States. It seems that no attempt will be made at present to set up such things as European benefit standards or implementation procedures.

The aim of the Member States will be: to guarantee a decent minimum standard of living and medical care for all people residing legally within the EC territory; to contribute to the social integration of all people who are able to exercise a remunerated activity; and to ensure that the standard of living of workers is not significantly affected in the case of illness, accident, maternity leave, disability, unemployment or retirement.

Legislation

While the introduction of a right to guaranteed resources has been a key component of the Community's anti-poverty policy, social security schemes have remained the responsibility of the Member States. However, via primary and secondary legislation the Community has devised a system whereby benefits will be paid to persons residing in the territory of one of the Member States and to enable migrant workers, members of their families, survivors, stateless persons and refugees to calculate and maintain their rights to benefits.

The main piece of legislation in this area is Regulation 1408/71/EEC[117] which deals with the application of social security schemes to employed persons, self-employed persons and to members of their families moving within the Community. It applies to the following categories of individual:

- employed and self-employed persons, presently or previously subject to the legislation of one or more Member States, who are nationals of a Member State or who are stateless persons or refugees residing in the territory of one of the Member States, and their families and survivors;[118]
- survivors of employed and self-employed persons, who were subject to the legislation of one or more Member States, regardless as to the nationality of those employed and self-employed persons, where their survivors are nationals of one of the Member States, or stateless persons or refugees residing in the territory of one of the Member States;[119]
- civil servants and those treated by legislation as civil servants presently or previously subject to the legislation of one or more Member States.[120]

The system envisaged by the Regulation is essentially that the legislation of the State where the employed or self-employed worker engaged in their economic activity will be applicable, regardless of the State of residence. That having been said, however, this principle is mitigated by many exceptions and procedures.[121]

---

117 OJ 1971 L149.
118 Article 2(1).
119 Article 2(2).

120 Article 2(3).
121 It is not proposed to go into those exceptions and procedures in detail.

The following social security benefits, whether part of general or special contributory or non-contributory schemes, are covered: illness and maternity; invalidity; survivors' grants; old age and death; occupational accidents and diseases; unemployment; family benefits and allowances.[122] However, social and medical assistance, benefit schemes for war victims or special schemes for civil servants and persons treated as such are excluded.[123] Due to the changing nature and scope of social security benefits the Commission finds it necessary to revise Regulation 1408/71/EEC every year. At the time of writing, the latest amendment is Regulation 1945/93/EEC.[124]

The procedures for the implementation of Regulation 1408/71/EEC are to be found in Regulation 574/72/EEC which is concerned with the calculation of the average cost of benefits in cash or in kind, the payment procedure and the prevention of overlapping benefits.[125]

As Regulation 1408/71/EEC and Regulation 574/72/EEC have been amended a number of times since they were first published, to make the amended versions more comprehensible and to give the readers a complete overview of the texts, the Commission has submitted a proposed consolidated version of the texts.[126]

The Role of the ECJ

The ECJ has long been concerned with the development of Community policy on social security law starting from the early days of the Community onwards[127] that if the Community did not ensure social security benefits for migrant workers, the free movement of such workers would inevitably be restricted. Its development of that policy has at times perhaps been somewhat more radical than the Member States would have liked.[128] There are a number of principles that the ECJ has undertaken to protect in this area. These include:

- the prevention of discrimination by virtue of nationality;
- the requirement that a Member State which owes a benefit to a worker must pay it regardless of which Member State the recipient intends to reside in;
- the fact that benefits may not overlap, preventing double benefit to a worker who may have contributed to schemes in more than one different Member State;

122 Article 4(1).
123 Article 4(4).
124 OJ 1993 L181.
125 Recent amendments to Regulation 1408/71/EEC and Regulation 574/72/EEC are: Regulation 3427/89/EEC, OJ 1989 L331 on family benefits; Regulation 1248/92/EEC, OJ 1992 L136 on the calculation of pensions for workers who have worked in several Member States; Regulation 1249/92/EEC, OJ 1992 L136 amending both Regulation 1408/71/EEC and Regulation 574/72/EEC regarding changes made in the national legislation of the Member States, especially sickness insurance in Germany, and widows' and invalidity benefits in the UK. See also Decision 91/423/EEC which concerned the payment of arrears of family benefits due to self-employed persons under Articles 73 and 74; Decision 91/424/EEC concerning the interpretation of Article 94(9) regarding the provisions on family allowances received by employed persons in France while members of their families reside in another Member State; and Decision 91/425/EEC on the application of Article 76 concerning overlapping rights to family benefits within the Community, OJ 1991 L235.
126 OJ 1992 C325.
127 Case 100/63, *Kalsbeek* [1964] ECR 565; Case 186/90, *Durighello*, 28 November 1991.
128 Case 44/65, *Hessische Knappschaft* v *Maison Singer* [1965] ECR 965, where the ECJ held that rights arising under Article 51 were not limited to migrant workers, but could apply to holidaymakers; Case 139/82 *Piscitello* v *INdP* [1983] ECR 1427, where the ECJ expanded the meaning of the 'family' for the purposes of Community law.

- that where necessary Member State institutions shall aggregate periods of time, work, residence for the purpose of benefit calculation, that is they must take into account all time, work and residence periods relevant to a benefit claim, regardless of which Member State those periods occurred in;
- the single State principle which states that a worker shall be subject to the legislation of a single Member State only; and
- the no disadvantage rule, where an individual may not be allowed to suffer a disadvantage as a result of the application of Community law.[129]

FREEDOM OF ESTABLISHMENT AND FREEDOM TO PROVIDE SERVICES

The category of 'workers' for the purposes of Article 48 EC and related measures as defined does not include the self-employed. Indeed, as noted above, the self-employed appear to be excluded from the benefits of Article 48. However, the freedoms that are granted to 'workers' are similarly granted to the self-employed by way of the freedom to establishment and the freedom to provide services. Freedom of establishment is provided for in Part III, Title III, Chapter 2, Articles 52–58 EC, and the freedom to provide services in Part III, Title III, Chapter 3, Articles 59–66 EC. Of these provisions, Articles 52, 59 and 60(3) are the most important. As Wyatt and Dashwood state, '. . . what Article 48 provides for the employee, Articles 52 and 59 provide for the employer, the entrepreneur and the professional'.[130]

Article 52 states that:

> Within the framework of the provisions set out below, restrictions on the freedom of establishment of nationals of a Member State in the territory of another Member State shall be abolished by progressive stages in the course of the transitional period. Such progressive abolition shall also apply to restrictions on the setting up of agencies, branches or subsidiaries by nationals of any Member State established in the territory of any Member State.
>
> Freedom of establishment shall include the right to take up and pursue activities as self-employed persons and to set up and manage undertakings, in particular companies or firms within the meaning of the second paragraph of Article 58, under the conditions laid down for its own nationals by the law of the country where such establishment is effected, subject to the provisions of the Chapter relating to capital.

The terms 'companies' and 'firms' are defined in Article 58(2) as being bodies which have been formed under civil or commercial law, which includes co-operative societies, and other legal persons who are governed by public or private law. An exception is made for those bodies which are non-profit making. Where such bodies are created in accordance with the law of the Member States and have their registered office, central administration or main place of business within the Community they are to be treated as natural persons of Member State origin.[131]

---

129 For a comprehensive survey of both the ECJ's case law and an overview of the Community system, see Steiner, *EC Law* 3rd edn (1992), at 233.

130 Wyatt and Dashwood, *European Community Law* (1993), at 278.

131 Article 58(1).

262 European Community Law

Article 59 states that:

> Within the framework of the provisions set out below, restrictions on freedom to provide services within the Community shall be progressively abolished during the transitional period in respect of nationals of Member States who are established in a State of the Community other than that of the person for whom the services are intended.

Here, again, the rights are granted to companies and firms which have been formed in accordance with the law of a Member State.[132] Both Article 52 and Article 59 are directly effective, despite the fact that Article 52 provides for the implementation of specific directives, by virtue of Articles 54(2) and 57(1). This, the ECJ has held, is due to the fact that Article 52 is based on Article 6 EC[133] and specifically implements the rule of non-discrimination contained therein.[134]

> . . . since the end of the transitional period, Article 52 of the Treaty is a directly applicable provision, despite the absence in a particular sphere, of the Directives prescribed by Articles 54(2) and 57(2) of the Treaty.

Freedom of establishment differs from freedom to provide services, inasmuch as the first involves the providers of a service actually settling in a Member State and becoming part of that host State's economic infrastructure, and the second involves the provision of a service from a person based in one Member State to individuals in the one or more other Member States. By way of example, a UK lawyer may move to Germany to set up a law firm specialising in advising German firms on how to deal with UK law, would be the exercise of the freedom to establish. By contrast, a UK lawyer might offer the same services to German firms from his offices based in the UK, occasionally flying to Germany or the other Member States to offer on-the-spot advice and briefings, this would be the exercise of the freedom to provide services. Where the two areas become difficult to separate clearly is where the activity at issue involves temporary residence in the Member State where a service is being provided. To continue the existing example, if a UK lawyer has a year-long contract with a German firm to advise them on UK law, but suffers hindrance from German law in this task, which involves him working in Germany for the entire year, is the matter one of freedom of establishment or of freedom to provide services? In general the ECJ's solution to this issue has been to read the two Articles as operating in parallel, thus a Member State law that would be unlawful under Article 52 will generally be unlawful under Article 59, rendering the distinction nugatory. However, as the right to establish has more serious and longer-term implications for the status of the individual seeking to operate in a host Member State, the ECJ will sometimes allow this to be reflected in the ability of the Member States to impose stricter measures of control.

Further to the Treaty provisions, Directive 73/148/EEC[135] and Directive 75/34/EEC[136] provide rights of entry and residence to self-employed persons in roughly the same terms as these rights are granted to workers. As with the freedom granted to workers under Article 48, the rights granted under Article 52 and 59 are limited by derogations granted to the Member States on the grounds of public health, public policy and public security.[137] It should

132 Article 66 EC.
133 Formerly Article 7 EC.
134 Case 2/74, *Reyners* v *Belgian State* [1974] ECR 631 (Article 52); Cases 110 and 111/78, *Ministerie Public* v *Van Wesemael* [1979] ECR 35 (Article 59).

135 OJ (Special edition) 1970 L142/24 402.
136 OJ 1975 L14/10.
137 Articles 56 and 66 EC and Directive 64/221/EEC, see below.

be noted that there is no equivalent Directive for the self-employed to Directive 1612/68/EEC applying to workers, thus the use of Article 6 with regard to non-discrimination is particularly important in this area.

The primary aim of Articles 52 and 59 is to prevent discrimination in the freedom of establishment and provision of services on the ground of nationality. In *Reyners v Belgian State*,[138] the ECJ held that the refusal to admit a Dutch lawyer holding a Belgian diploma to the Belgian Bar because Belgian legislation required lawyers to be of Belgian nationality was contrary to Article 52 EC. Similarly, in *Van Binsbergen Bestuur van de Bedrijfsvereniging voor de Metaalnijverheid v the Netherlands*[139] the same principle was applied to Article 59. Van Binsbergen had asked a Dutch national, resident in Belgium, to defend him in a social security dispute before a Dutch court. This was challenged as a Dutch law stated that only persons established in The Netherlands could act as legal representatives before the court. The Court ruled that any discrimination against a person providing a service by reason of his nationality or the fact that he habitually resided in another Member State rather than the one in which the service was to be provided was contrary to the Treaty. However, where the persons providing the service are not established in the State in which the service is to be provided that Member State may, without infringing the Treaty, impose certain condition on that provision. This provided a distinction between those requirements which were obtained from professional rules, justified in the interest of the general public, objectively necessary and proportionate to their aim, and those which simply discriminated against the persons providing the services by reason of their nationality or place of residence.

Professional rules, therefore, provide a method of protecting the public, but equally a way in which Member States and professional organisations may seek to prevent nationals of other Member States from engaging in their chosen activity. In general, the ECJ has applied the test from *Van Binsbergen* to any such professional rules. Thus, they must be non-discriminatory, justified in the interest of the public and proportionate.[140] Adding to this test in *Webb*,[141] the ECJ stated that in applying its own national professional rules the host Member State had also to consider the effect of the national professional rules of the Member States of origin upon the conduct of the applicant. In the co-insurance cases,[142] the ECJ developed this concept further, and in doing so created a fundamental difference between the freedom to provide services and the freedom to establishment. Having distinguished between the two freedoms in those cases, the ECJ stated that with regard to services, national legislation applied to permanently established businesses could not necessarily also be applied to the provision of services by businesses established in other Member States, as such regulation could hinder free movement of services. It was important to subject national measures affecting the provision of services to scrutiny to determine whether or not they were objectively justified, whether the aim required was not already secured by measures in the State of origin of the supplier of the service and whether the

138 Case 2/74, *op. cit.*, note 134. See also Case 71/76, *Thieffry v Paris Bar Council* [1977] ECR 765.
139 Case 33/74, [1974] ECR 1299.
140 Case 39/75, *Coenen v Sociaal-Economische Raad* [1975] ECR 1547.
141 Case 279/80, *Criminal proceedings against Alfred John Webb* [1981] ECR 3305. See also Case 427/85, *Commission v Germany (Re Restrictions on the Legal Professions)* [1988] ECR 1123.

142 Case 205/84, *Commission v Germany* [1986] ECR 3755; Case 206/84, *Commission v Ireland* [1986] ECR 3817; Case 220/83, *Commission v France* [1986] ECR 3663; Case 252/83, *Commission v Denmark* [1986] ECR 3713. See further, Edward, 'Establishment and Services: An Analysis of the Insurances Cases (1987) 12 EL Rev 231.

measure was proportionate. If any of these heads were not satisfied the measure would be in breach of Articles 59 and 60. The ECJ established for provision of services a set of rules which are broadly similar to those which it devised for the free movement of goods in the *Cassis de Dijon* case. It appears that these rules may have a similar effect upon the amount of litigation on the validity of national rules as that seen after the *Cassis* judgment.[143]

The ECJ's jurisprudence suggests that where a profession's rules of conduct have been harmonised or mutual recognition has been achieved by way of a Directive, that Directive will, where appropriate, provide a conclusive answer as to the permissibility of a national rule. The job of the Member States and, inevitably in some cases, the ECJ, will be to decide whether or not particular Directives in fact cover certain rules. It is also clear that where businesses attempt to use Community law to circumvent legitimate measures taken by the Member States the ECJ will not look on their arguments with much favour. For example in *R v HM Treasury ex parte Daily Mail and General Trust plc*[144] the *Daily Mail* wanted to move residence from the UK to The Netherlands in order to take advantage of the differing tax situations. British tax law required that such a move could only be made with the consent of the Treasury, but the *Daily Mail* argued that this requirement of consent was contrary to Article 52. The ECJ, however, stated that while Article 52 was directly effective, and Article 58 applied equally to companies leaving a Member State as well as to those entering, the ability of companies, as legal creations of the individual Member States and not the Community, to move between the Member States remained governed by national law. A move of the type envisaged by the *Daily Mail* could still be covered by a national provision requiring formalities and conditions to be met in advance of the move as Article 52 is not designed to provide to:

> companies incorporated under the law of a Member State a right to transfer their central management and control and their central administration to another Member State while retaining their status as companies incorporated under the legislation of the first Member State.

The principle of non-discrimination with regard the freedoms to establish and provide services is not confined to preventing discrimination with regard to the ability to take up a particular activity. It will also apply to national rules which purport to prevent individuals from other Member States from taking advantage of national schemes,[145] or from renting or purchasing particular residences or properties.[146]

It is clear that for workers to enjoy the right to establishment within the Community there is a need for the various kinds of professional qualifications to receive recognition by the relevant authorities within the Member States. However, while this is clear in theory, in practice the concept of a broad concept of recognition of professional qualifications to allow professionals to move easily between the Member States has proved extremely difficult to achieve on a Community wide basis. The Member States and Institutions have, however, recognised that attempting to harmonise all the various professional training qualifications

---

143 See, for example, Case C-154/89, *Commission v French Republic* [1991] ECR I-659; Case C-180/89, *Commission v Italy* [1991] ECR I-709; Case C-198/90, *Commission v Greece* [1991] ECR I-727; Case C-353/89, *Commission v The Netherlands* [1991] ECR I-4069.
144 Case 81/87, [1988] ECR 5483.

145 Case 63/86, *Commission v Italy* [1988] ECR 129, concerning the provision of a cheap mortgage facility which under Italian law was reserved for Italian nationals.
146 Case 197/84, *Steinhauser v City of Biarritz* [1985] ECR 1819.

for professional workers would inevitably turn out to be an expensive, time-consuming and potentially impossible endeavour. Thus, such harmonisation has rarely been attempted, an exception to this is the medical profession.[147]

A much quicker solution to the problem is to require mutual recognition on the part of the Member States of qualifications granted in the other Member States. This recognition would require Member States to accept qualifications granted by institutions in other Member States as being equivalent to their own institutions' qualifications. This solution is easier to apply in that where the training required for a qualification in the host Member State is equal or lower than that required in the Member State of origin, the host Member State must grant unconditional recognition of that qualification as being equal to its own. As was held in *Colegio Oficial de Agentes de la Propiedad Inmobiliaria and Ministerio Fiscal v JL Aguirre Borrell and others*[148] concerning an estate agent, in the absence of a directive on mutual recognition of diplomas, certificates or other qualifications relating to the occupation in question, where the training leading to a qualification in the Member State of origin is shorter or the experience required is less than that of the host Member State, further requests for proof of professional experience, the imposing of a training or probationary period or a requirement that the migrant worker complete a proficiency test are permitted. However, the decision to refuse a national of another Member State the recognition or approval as equivalent of a diploma or professional qualification obtained in the Member State of which he is a national, must be open to judicial review regarding its legality in Community law, and to facilitate this the applicant must be given the reasons for the decision. Where a Member State follows these rules it is then permissible to impose criminal penalties on a national of another Member State for exercising a regulated occupation in breach of the conditions required by the law of the host Member State.

For professions where Directives on the mutual recognition of diplomas, certificates and other evidence of formal qualifications exist, the ECJ has generally been unsympathetic to the protectionist aims of both Member States and their professional organisations. For example, in *Conseil National de l'Ordre des Architectes v Ulrich Egle*[149] it held that for the purposes of assessing equivalency of qualifications the Belgian Council of the Order of Architects' decision to reject an application for membership made by an individual of another Member State, on the grounds that that he did not meet the necessary conditions for recognition of diplomas, was incorrect. This was because, contrary to their decision, a requirement of four years' full-time education could be fulfilled by three years of theoretical study and two periods of six months' duration of practical training.

Further in *Broekmuelen*[150] the Court held that where a Directive has been issued for mutual recognition or harmonisation of qualifications in a profession, a Member State professional body may not insist on requirements above and beyond those required in the Directive, even where the individual concerned has not completed the type of specialised training required of the Member States' own professionals. In *Auer*,[151] however, the ECJ stated that where a directive is issued pursuant to Article 57 persons may not claim rights

---

[147] Case 246/80, *Broekmeulen v Huisarts Registratie Commissie* [1981] ECR 2311.

[148] Case 104/91, 7 May 1992; see also Case 340/89, *Irene Vlassopoulou v Ministerium fur Justiz, Bundes – und Europaangelegenheiten Baden–Wurttemberg* [1991] ECR I-2357.

[149] Case 310/90, 21 January 1992; see also Case 166/91, *Gerhard Bauer v Conseil National de l'Ordre des Architectes*, 8 April 1992.

[150] Case 246/80, *op. cit.*, note 147.

[151] Case 136/78, *Ministère Public v Auer* [1979] ECR 437.

under Article 52 and 59 EC based on it until its transitional period has expired.

In *Commission* v *Belgium*[152] the ECJ ruled that a Belgian law requiring pharmacists employed in hospitals to obtain a hospital pharmacists' certificate provided by Belgian universities was incompatible with Article 1 of Directive 85/433/EEC[153] which provides that any Community pharmacist with a diploma awarded in another Member State is eligible to prepare, inspect, store or dispense medicines in hospitals.[154] The Belgian government claimed that in practice the directives were applied by the administration despite not been transposed officially. The ECJ stated that simple administrative practices can change at the will of the administration and could not therefore constitute a valid transposition of directives into national law.

At the time of writing, the following areas and professions have had directives adopted relating to the mutual recognition of diplomas, certificates and other evidence of formal qualifications: wholesale trade and activities of intermediaries in commerce, industry and small craft industries;[155] self-employed persons in manufacturing and processing industries;[156] self-employed persons in retail trade;[157] self-employed persons in the food manufacturing and beverage industries;[158] self-employed persons in the personal services sector (restaurants, cafes, taverns and other drinking and eating places, hotels, boarding houses, camping and other lodging places);[159] self-employed persons in film distribution;[160] self-employed persons in the wholesale coal trade and in respect of activities of intermediaries in the coal trade;[161] activities relating to trade in and distribution of toxic products and activities entailing the professional use of such products including activities of intermediaries;[162] insurance agents and brokers;[163] effective exercise by lawyers of freedom to provide services;[164] services incidental to the transport and travel agencies and warehousing;[165] hairdressers;[166] architects;[167] pharmacists;[168] carriers of goods by waterway in national and international transport;[169] goods haulage operations and road passenger transport operations;[170] doctors, nurses responsible for general care, practitioners of dentistry, veterinarians and midwives;[171] civil aviation licences;[172] doctors.[173]

In 1985 the Council adopted Decision 85/368/EEC[174] on a system for the comparability of vocational training qualifications between skilled workers in the Member States. The purpose of this Decision was not to lead to the legal recognition of certificates, diplomas and qualifications but rather to simplify the procedures for applying for mutual recognition.

The area was not considered again, however, until 1988 when Directive 89/48/EEC[175] on the establishment of a general system of mutual recognition of higher education diplomas

152 Case 167/90, 22 April 1991.
153 OJ 1985 L253.
154 The Court also held Belgium in breach of Community law for failure to transpose Directives 85/433/EEC and 85/584/EEC on the mutual recognition of pharmacists' diplomas.
155 Directive 64/222/EEC, OJ 1964 L56.
156 Directive 64/427/EEC, OJ 1964 L117.
157 Directive 68/364/EEC, OJ 1968 L260.
158 Directive 68/366/EEC, OJ 1968 L260.
159 Directive 68/368/EEC, OJ 1968 L260.
160 Directive 68/369/EEC. OJ 1968 L260.
161 Directive 70/523/EEC, OJ 1970 L267.
162 Directive 74/556/EEC, OJ 1974 L307.
163 Directive 77/92/EEC, OJ 1977 L26.
164 Directive 77/249/EEC, OJ 1977 L78.
165 Directive 82/470/EEC, OJ 1982 L213.
166 Directive 82/1489/EEC, OJ 1982 L218.
167 Directive 85/384/EEC, OJ 1985 223.
168 Directive 85/433/EEC, OJ 1985 L253.
169 Directive 87/540/EEC, OJ 1987 L322.
170 Directive 89/438/EEC, OJ 1989 L212.
171 Directive 89/595/EEC, OJ 1989 L341, amending Directive 77/452/EEC; also Directive 89/594/EEC amending Directives 75/362/EEC, 77/452/EEC, 78/686/EEC, 78/1026/EEC and 80/154/EEC.
172 Directive 91/670/EEC, OJ 1991 L373.
173 Directive 93/16/EEC, OJ 1993 L165.
174 OJ 1985 L199.
175 OJ 1989 L19.

was adopted. This Directive enabled workers who had completed at least three years of university training[176] to pursue their activities in all other Member States. This initiative was followed in June 1992 by Directive 92/51/EEC[177] which aimed to complete the general system of mutual recognition and covered diplomas awarded for higher or post-secondary education studies and vocational certificates granted in secondary, general or professional educational programmes taking less than three years to finalise. All qualifications falling under the categories listed above will be now be mutually recognised throughout the Community.

Following the adoption of the above Directives, a Community national's qualifications in the areas covered should now, when obtained in one Member State, be recognised automatically by all the other Member States. The recognition does not require that there be any prior co-ordination of training for the profession concerned, the Member States are expected to accept the qualifications on the principle of mutual trust.

The Community has also been concerned to ensure that non-Community qualifications held by Community nationals should be accepted by the Member States. As Directive 92/51/EEC is only concerned with diplomas, certificates and other evidence of formal qualifications awarded in Member States, a further Resolution was published by the Council in July 1992.[178] This concerned nationals of Member States who hold a diploma or certificate which was awarded in a third country. The measure is aimed to encourage the Member States to allow EC workers who were awarded qualifications in third countries to engage in professions which require the holding of qualifications of that nature, by granting their qualifications equivalency with those obtained in the Community.

In 1990 following an interim report submitted by the Commission on the implementation of Decision 85/368/EEC the Council of Ministers adopted a Resolution on the comparability of vocational training qualifications.[179] This noted the importance of adequate information on the comparability of qualifications to increase the mobility of persons within the Community and stated first that, Community descriptions of professional activities must reflect the practical job requirements required by the labour market and, secondly, that vocational training qualifications should be more effectively described. This was followed in 1992 by another Resolution aimed at achieving transparency of vocational qualifications and certification within the Community[180] which called on the Commission to draft proposals which would facilitate the free movement of workers within the EC.

The main problem being addressed here lies in the fact that the diversity in qualifications which can be acquired in the Member States makes it hard for employers to gauge accurately the degree of skill and knowledge of workers who hold qualifications and work experience gained in other Member States. Such difficulty and confusion will clearly have the effect of placing applicants from other Member States at a disadvantage to national workers when applications for jobs are assessed. Thus, increased transparency of qualifications can only improve the free movement of workers within the Community.

With regard to the issue of vocational training qualifications for employees, the Commission has so far issued Communications on the comparability of such qualifications for the following individuals and areas of industry: the hotel and catering industry; motor vehicle repair service personnel; architects; the construction sector; the electrical/electronics

---

176 With the exception of those covered by specific directives.
177 OJ 1992 L209.

178 OJ 1992 C187.
179 OJ 1991 C109.
180 OJ 1993 C49.

sector; the agriculture sector; the textile-clothing sector; the metalworking sector; the textile-industry sector; office/administration; banking and insurance; the chemical industry; tourism; transport; the food industry; public works; graphic arts and the media; woodworking; iron and steel production; and leatherworking.

EXCEPTIONS

As mentioned above, as with Article 48 EC, the provisions concerned with the freedom of establishment and the freedom to provide services contain certain derogations, notably on the grounds of public health, public policy and public security. These are found in Articles 56 and 66 EC and Directive 64/221/EEC. Again, economic grounds cannot be used to justify restrictions and any measures taken must be proportionate to the aim to be achieved.[181] Also the public service proviso is similarly construed in very narrow terms by the ECJ.[182] The activity at issue must have some commercial or economic purpose,[183] or be connected to the provider of the service.[184]

RIGHT TO RECEIVE SERVICES

The role of Community law with regard to the cross-border provision of services is not limited to those circumstances where the providers of the services come to their market, but applies equally where those requiring services available in another Member State go to that Member States in order to receive them. In *Luisi and Carbone v Ministero del Tesoro*[185] the ECJ recognised that, above and beyond migrant workers, 'tourists, persons receiving medical treatment and persons travelling for the purpose of education and business' are equally to be regarded as individuals capable of enjoying free movement under Article 59. With regard to this issue Directive 64/221/EEC and Directive 73/148/EEC refer explicitly to a right to receive services. Directive 64/221/EEC states that there should be 'freedom of movement for employed or self-employed persons or the recipients of services',[186] while Directive 73/148/EEC provides a right for Member States' nationals to go to another Member State to receive a service.[187] Problems arise, firstly, in the area of those services which are provided by public funds, such as health and education and, secondly, in the area of services which are

---

[181] Case 352/85, *Bond van Adverteerders* [1988] ECR 2085.

[182] See Case 2/74, *Reyners v Belgian State, op. cit.*, note 134.

[183] Case 36/74, *Walrave and Koch v Association Union Cyclist Internationale* [1974] ECR 1405; Case 13/76 *Dona v Mantero* [1976] ECR 133.

[184] C-159/90, *SUPC Ireland Ltd v Grogan* [1991] CMLR 849. The provision of an information service on availability of abortion by an Irish student's union was held not to be covered as the union did not provide the

service nor did they receive any funding from the service providers. If the action had been brought by an abortion clinic or the union had received money for their service from the providers of the service, the outcome might well have been different. See Spahn, 'Abortion, Speech and the European Community' [1992] JSWFL 17.

[185] Case 26/83, [1984] ECR 377, following the line adopted in Case 118/75, *Watson & Belmann, op. cit.*, note 81.

[186] Article 1(1).

[187] Article 1(1) (b).

provided in another Member State which are not provided on public policy grounds in the Member States of origin of the individual requiring them.[188]

In the area of education, the jurisprudence of the ECJ reflects two main concerns. The first is the availability of free vocational training in a Member State to nationals of other Member States and the second is the availability of scholarships and grants made available by a Member State to nationals of other Member States. In *Gravier* v *City of Liege*[189] Ms Gravier was a French national who had been accepted on a course at the Liege Academie des Beaux-Arts and was charged the '*minerval*' which was a fee payable by foreign students. This fee was not levied upon Belgian students, nor EC nationals working in Belgium and their families. Ms Gravier brought an action alleging the fee was in breach of Article 59 as it infringed her freedom of movement to receive services and, that as the course was vocational, it was discriminatory to charge her a higher fee than the other two groups. The ECJ carefully avoided dealing with the more contentious issues contained within this case, deciding it eventually on a very wide interpretation of the principle of equal access to vocational training. This was followed shortly thereafter by *Blaizot et al.* v *University of Liege*[190] where students who had paid the *minerval* were attempting to claim it back again. The ECJ restated the definition of vocational training which it had used in *Gravier*. The criteria used were essentially wide enough to cover most University level courses. The next case *Belgium* v *Humbel*[191] took the analysis of vocational training a step further with respect to payment of fees, by considering the issue of fees paid for secondary education. The ECJ held that any course of general education can be held to be vocational if it is part of an overall programme of vocational education.

The above cases did not consider the issue of grants and scholarships in relation to whether a host nation should pay them to foreign nationals in order to allow them to take up a vocational course, but these matters were addressed in the cases of *Brown* v *Secretary of State for Scotland*[192] and *Lair* v *Universitat Hannover*.[193] Both cases concerned grants for university education and both appear to have been brought in reliance on the arguments raised in Gravier largely because the individuals concerned would have had difficulties claiming the grants as either 'workers' or 'children of workers'. Both cases failed, with the EC holding that while both would be entitled to fees on a par with those of the host Member State's nationals, grants did not fall within the scope of the Treaty, a decision greeted with considerable relief on the part of the Member States.

In terms of other public services *Cowan* v *Tresor Public*[194] demonstrates the ECJ's general approach. In this case an English tourist was mugged and injured in an incident on the Paris Metro. As a result he claimed compensation for personal injuries. French law stated that such compensation was to be paid from the public purse and could only be paid to French citizens. The ECJ found no difficulty in holding that as a tourist he was a recipient of services and thus entitled to equal protection against and compensation for any injuries suffered by way of an assault.

---

[188] See C-159/90, *SPUC Ireland Ltd* v *Grogan, op. cit.*, note 184. In this case the ECJ neatly avoided dealing with this issue which had serious constitutional implications for Ireland by deciding the case on different grounds.

[189] Case 293/83, [1985] ECR 593.

[190] Case 24/86, [1988] ECR 379.

[191] Case 263/86, [1988] ECR 5365.

[192] Case 197/86, [1988] ECR 3205.

[193] Case 39/86, [1988] ECR 3161.

[194] Case 186/87, [1990] 2 CMLR 613.

FREE MOVEMENT OF NON-WORKERS

The measures mentioned above all relate to the free movement of those engaged in economically active pursuits and their families. However, as noted above in the introduction, the Community has increasingly moved away from purely economic justifications and begun to emphasise the role of social policies. In this area of Community law that movement has translated itself into a number of measures designed to aid the free movement of those who are not economically active for a variety of reasons, but who still wish to have the freedom to move between and to take up residence in any of the Member States. Three Directives to ensure this right for students, retired persons and those not economically active were adopted by the Council in June 1990 and came into force in June 1992. They are:

- Directive 90/364/EEC on the right of residence;[195]
- Directive 90/365/EEC on the right of residence for employees and self-employed persons who have ceased their occupational activity;[196]
- Directive 90/366/EEC on the right of residence for students.[197]

However, the Member States' reaction to these Directives has not been wholly favourable. Further, the legal basis of Directive 90/366/EEC was challenged by the European Parliament and the measure ruled invalid by the ECJ in *European Parliament* v *Council of the European Communities*,[198] although it ruled that the Directive was to be annulled but would continue to have force until another directive was adopted with the appropriate legal basis. A proposal for such a measure was duly submitted by the Commission in early 1993.[199] This measure, based on Article 7(2) EC, repeats the main elements of Directive 90/366/EEC. Thus, students, their spouses and dependent children would be granted a residence permit valid for the duration of their course or their studies. This would be renewed annually and be conditional on the recipient holding a valid place in a university or other third level educational establishment. It would also be covered by a sickness insurance scheme in either the host or home Member State. It seems that under the measure, students could be required to sign a statement confirming that they have sufficient resources for their period of study and as a result will not require aid from the host State's social security system. The families of students who are EC nationals, that is, the spouse and the dependant children, will be allowed to take up employed or self-employed activities in the Member State of residency, and this will be so even when they do not hold nationality of an EC Member State.

In the case of the other Directives, residence permits will be issued for a five-year period for retired and economically inactive people, and their spouses, dependent descendants or ascendants who wish to reside in a host State rather than their State of origin. For both retired and economically inactive persons, a permit will only be given only where the person can prove that they have sufficient resources to avoid having to rely on the social security system of the host State.[200] In addition, the recipients must be covered by sickness insurance, and retired people must be in receipt of an invalidity pension, an old age pension or a

---

195 OJ 1990 L180 26.
196 OJ 1990 L180 28.
197 OJ 1990 L180 30.
198 Case C-295/90, judgment of 7 July 1992.

199 OJ 1993 C166.
200 As in the case of Directive 90/364/EEC on the right of residence, prompting the nickname 'the playboy Directive'.

pension in respect of an industrial accident or disease. The idea is that their financial resources should be higher than the minimum level of social security payment in the host country. Where such a permit is granted, it must be both renewable and non-discriminatory.

CONCLUSION

Ensuring the free movement of persons within the Community has been vital to the establishment of the single market. However, it has been an uphill struggle against the priorities and prejudices of the Member States. The area has also seen a partial rerun of the developments in the area of the free movement of goods, with regard to the development by the ECJ of a strict test against which to measure Member States' legislation with regard to the freedom to provide services. The ECJ's case law in this area demonstrates a subtle blend of judicial activism and political wisdom and, at times, not a little uncertainty as to the most effective way to develop particular strands of jurisprudence. In the main, however, the ECJ has proven an effective and competent moderator in this area, balancing the demands of the market against the social and financial constraints required by the Member States and showing a fine awareness of the shifts in social policy that have marked the recent years of the Community's existence. It is clear that in the run up to the signing of the TEU the social dimension of the Community has increasingly been pushed to the fore, and that has tremendous implications for the further development of the free movement of persons. The clear shift away from a concentration upon ensuring the free movement of 'economically active' individuals and towards a concept of free movement for the 'citizens of the EU' was announced by the three 1990 Directives, and it seems certain that this trend will continue. It seems likely, for instance, that the wholly artificial divide between the concept of 'fees' and 'grants' for vocational training at institutions within the Community must soon give way to an acceptance that the Member States will have to engage in the type of harmonisation that has marked the area of social security. At present the differences in nature, scope and length of such vocational courses is such that harmonisation would be far from easy, but its onset is increasingly likely. Whether, however, we will see a Community organisation responsible for Community-wide organisation of either vocational training or the payment of social security benefits, in the near future, is an entirely different matter.

Further reading

Brown, M., 'The Single Market after 1992 – Free Movement for Criminals?' (1991) *Commonwealth Law Bulletin* 1438.

Cath, I.G.F., 'Freedom of Establishment of Companies: a New Step Towards Completion of the Internal Market' [1986] YEL 247.

Eidenmüller, H., 'Deregulating the Market for Legal Services in the European Community: Freedom of Establishment and Freedom to Provide Services for EC Lawyers in the Federal Republic of Germany' (1990) 53 MLR 604.

Foster, N., 'European Community Law and the Freedom of Lawyers in the United Kingdom and Germany' (1991) 40 ICLQ 608.

Guild, E., 'Falling through the net: family reunion rights in EC law' (1993) (Autumn) *Lawyers' Europe* 2.

Hondious, F.M., 'Movement of Persons in Europe: A Situation Report 1990' (1990) 15 *International Legal Practitioner* 115.

Petersen, J.H., 'Harmonization of Social Security in the EC Revisited' (1991) 29 JCMS 505.

Spalin, E., 'Abortion, Speech and the European Community' (1992) 1 *JSWFL* 17.

Steiner, J.M., 'Social Security for Migrants' (1992) 1 *JSWFL* 33.

van Overbeek, J., 'AIDS/HIV Infection and the Free Movement of Persons within the European Economic Community' (1990) 27 CML Rev 791.

Whelan, C. and Barnet, D., 'Lawyers in the Market: Delivering Legal Services in Europe' (1992) 19, *Journal of Law and Society* 49.

Wikeley, N.J., 'Migrant Workers and Unemployment Benefit in the European Community' (1988) 5 *JSWFL* 300.

CHAPTER 13

Competition policy

INTRODUCTION

Competition policy in the EC Treaty is part of the establishment of the Single Market. It would be of little use to remove all customs duties, non-tariff barriers and limitations of free movement of persons and capital if private companies could partition the Union into 12 separate markets through the use of distribution contracts or if States could give unfair advantage to their own industries by subsidising them.

Since Community competition policy has been orientated towards developing the Single Market, the measures applied to it are not harmonising measures. Competition policy, therefore has a federal element to it. It is necessary to find a Community dimension to a competition issue before Community competition law will apply. In all other cases, national competition rules will apply as they exist, no matter how much those rules may differ from Member State to Member State. This concurrent jurisdiction can produce awkward situations, such as when Lloyds Bank and the Hong Kong and Shanghai Bank both sought to take over the Midland Bank in 1992. Since both Lloyds and the Midland were purely UK companies, the proposed takeover was examined under UK law, whereas the Hong Kong and Shanghai Bank bid was considered to have a Community dimension and was scrutinised under the Merger Regulation by the Commission.[1]

The ECJ, in many of its decisions, compares the behaviour of companies which have been investigated under Community competition law with a model or idea of perfect competition. Except through reference to Article 3(g) EC,[2] the ECJ does not define its model of a perfectly competitive market. This is by no means a common sense question. The questions of what is a market and what is a market with perfect competition are extremely controversial. Even libertarian theorists of the market have acknowledged that some State regulation to prevent unfair competition is justifiable, and have further admitted that the line between regulation to ensure the proper functioning of a market and intervention in that market is a difficult line to draw.[3] The only step that the Treaty itself takes is making the Single Market a goal. Defining it and policing it are the functions of the institutions. The ECJ has never decided whether the purpose of competition policy, beyond the integration of Member State markets into the Single Market, is to maximise the range of goods and services available, to minimise the prices which consumers must pay, both of these or some other goal.[4] While it is fairly clear that minimising prices is not the only goal of competition policy, the emphasis of Community competition policy has always been on abuses of power within the market. Article 86 EC,

---

[1] Noted, in particular, by Sir Gordon Borrie in the Foreword to Whish, *Competition Law*, 3rd edn (1993), at v.
[2] 'The activities of the Community shall include . . . (g) the institution of a system ensuring that competition

in the common market is not distorted.'
[3] For example, Hayek, *Law, Legislation and Liberty* (1982), at Chapter 15.
[4] See Whish, *op. cit.*, note 1, at 1–2, 4–11, for a critical approach to theories of perfect competition.

which prohibits abuse of a dominant position, is clearly aimed at this type of anti-competitive behaviour. However, the language of abuse of power, public and private, may be found throughout the case law on Community competition policy.

Community competition policy is also directed to other goals. This is demonstrated by the conditions for exemption of an agreement, decision or concerted practice from the prohibition of Article 85(1) EC, which permits agreements which otherwise would be deemed anti-competitive, but which improve the production or distribution of goods or which promote technical or economic progress. Consumer benefit must be demonstrated for the exemption to be allowed. This complicates the approach to be taken by the ECJ, which therefore, must compare behaviour not only with an idea of what good competitive behaviour should be but also with other social and economic goals. The Commission is probably in a better position to do this, since it is able to draw on a wider range of expertise, and it has done so by developing block exemptions to Article 85(1), which provide guidance to companies on which behaviour pursues goals of which Community law approves.

Article 85 EC – agreements, decisions and concerted practices

Article 85 EC prevents action by undertakings acting together which interfere with competition in the Single Market. In the broadest sense it prohibits cartels or arrangements between undertakings to control the market in some way:

> 1. The following shall be prohibited as incompatible with the common market: all agreements between undertakings, decisions by associations of undertakings and concerted practices which may affect trade between Member States and which have as their object or effect the prevention, restriction or distortion of competition within the common market, and in particular those which:
>
> (a) directly or indirectly fix purchase or selling prices or any other trading conditions;
> (b) limit or control production, markets, technical development, or investment;
> (c) share markets or sources of supply;
> (d) apply dissimilar conditions to equivalent transactions with other trading parties, thereby placing them at a competitive disadvantage;
> (e) make the conclusion of contracts subject to acceptance by other parties of supplementary obligations which, by their nature or according to commercial usage, have no connection with the subject of such contracts.
>
> 2. Any agreements or decisions prohibited pursuant to this Article shall be automatically void.
>
> 3. The provisions of paragraph 1 may, however, be declared inapplicable in the case of:
>
> – any agreement or category of agreements between undertakings;
> – any decision or category of decisions by associations of undertakings;
> – any concerted practice or category of concerted practices;
>
> which contributes to improving the production or distribution of goods or to promoting technical or economic progress, while allowing consumers a fair share of the resulting benefit, and which does not:

(a) impose on the undertakings concerned restrictions which are not indispensable to the attainment of these objectives;

(b) afford such undertakings the possibility of eliminating competition in respect of a substantial part of the products in question.

Definition of undertakings

The definition of 'undertakings' as developed under Article 85 has been applied to all the Community competition rules. The Commission is not concerned with the legal personality or form of the undertaking, but rather on whether it exercises an economic activity. In the *Polypropylene*[5] decision the Commission decided that an undertaking could be 'any entity engaged in commercial activities and in the case of corporate bodies may refer to a parent or subsidiary or to the unit formed by the parent and the subsidiaries together'. The key factor is that the body in question is carrying out some form of economic activity.[6] Economic activity is not the same as economic purpose – non-profit bodies may also constitute undertakings.[7] An undertaking can include individuals.[8] It does not, however, apply to public bodies acting in their capacity as public authorities, such as when they are providing a public service.[9] Furthermore, Article 85(1) is not concerned with national legislation, although Article 85 in conjunction with Article 5 requires Member States not to introduce or maintain measures which would undermine competition policy.[10] Since the legal form of the undertaking is not important, the successor to an undertaking being investigated may be considered to be, for competition law purposes, the same undertaking.[11]

Article 85 does not apply to agreements operating within a single undertaking. In terms of agreements between a parent company and its subsidiary, these will not be covered by Article 85 if the subsidiary cannot be considered to be an independent undertaking. A subsidiary will not be a separate undertaking if 'the undertakings form a single economic unit within which the subsidiary has no real freedom to determine its course of action on the market'.[12] However, a parent company outside the Community can be held liable for behaviour of a non-independent subsidiary within the Community.[13]

Behaviour prohibited by Article 85 EC

The inclusive phrase 'all agreements between undertakings, decisions by associations of undertakings and concerted practices' demonstrates that Community competition policy looks to the substance of behaviour rather than its form. Each of these three categories of

5 OJ 1986 L230/1, [1988] CMLR 347, at paragraph 99.

6 *Distribution of Package Tours During the 1990 World Cup*, OJ 1992 L326/31, at paragraph 43.

7 Joined Cases 209–15 and 218/78, *van Landewyck v Commission* [1980] ECR 3125.

8 *RAI/Unitel*, OJ 1978 L157/39.

9 Case 30/87, *Bodson v Pompes Funèbres des Regions Libérées SA* [1985] ECR 2479.

10 Most recently affirmed in Case C-2/92, *Meng*; Case C-185/91, *Bundesanstalt für den Güterfernverkehr v Gebrüder Reiff GmbH*; Case C-245/91, *Ohra Schadeverzekeringen NV*, all 17 November 1993. All

cases involved State rules, which, it was alleged, restricted competition – prohibitions on insurance agents transferring their commission to clients, uniform road tariffs and prohibitions on insurance companies offering rebates or other financial advantages.

11 Joined Cases 29 and 30/83, *Compagnie Royale Asturienne des Mines SA v Commission* [1984] ECR 1679, at paragraph 9.

12 Case 22/71, *Beguelin Import v GL Import Export* [1971] ECR 949.

13 Case 15/74, *Centrafarm v Sterling Drug Inc* [1974] ECR 1147.

behaviour is defined broadly. As a result, the scope of Article 85(1) covers all forms of co-operative behaviour between undertakings.

Agreements

The Commission and the ECJ have chosen to define 'agreements' broadly rather than to include only legally enforceable contracts, and include almost everything else as a 'concerted practice'. Specifically, a 'gentlemen's agreement' supplementing a written agreement has been included where it 'amounted to the faithful expression of the joint intention of the parties to the agreement with regard to their conduct in the Common Market'.[14] There must be some binding element to the agreement for it to be caught by Article 85(1).[15] The Commission has extended the scope of 'agreement' within recent years. The *Polypropylene* decision is a good example of this practice. The Commission found that the arrangements between the parties constituted an agreement despite the fact that they were oral, not binding in law, attached to no specific sanctions and some members of the cartel had not fully observed the agreement.[16]

Decisions by associations of undertakings

The concept of a decision under Article 85 has not had much impact on the development of the law as applied by the Commission and the courts. The breadth of the concepts of agreement and concerted practice have left little interest in the concept of decision. Its main use has been to enable the Commission to hold an association liable for the anti-competitive behaviour of members.[17] Additionally, the constitution of an association may be a decision rather than an agreement.[18] The regulations of an association will often be considered a decision, as the Commission found in the *Net Book Agreement* case.[19] A somewhat confusing direction of the case law on decisions is that an agreement within an association of undertakings may be a decision for the purposes of Article 85, where those agreements actually influence conduct.[20]

Concerted practices

The main case on concerted practices is *ICI* v *Commission*, the *Dyestuffs* case.[21] Given the liberal definition of agreements, the first task of the ECJ in this case was to set out the distinction between an agreement and a concerted practice. A concerted practice 'does not have all the elements of a contract but may *inter alia* arise out of co-ordination which becomes apparent from the behaviour of the applicants'.[22] However, since agreements need not be legally binding contracts this is not a sufficient explanation of the difference between the two concepts. The more general statement made by the ECJ was that a concerted practice 'without going so far as to amount to an agreement properly so called, knowingly substitutes

---

14 Case 41/69, *ACF Chemiefarma NV* v *Commission* [1970] ECR 661, at paragraph 112.
15 *Ibid.*, at paragraph 113, where the ECJ noted that the 'gentlemen's agreement contained a clause that the breach of its provisions would be considered a breach of the written agreement'.
16 OJ 1986 L230/1, *op. cit.*, note 5, affirmed by the CFI in Case T-7/89, *SA Hercules* v *Commission* [1992] 4 CMLR 84.
17 *AROW* v *BNIC*, OJ 1982 L379/1, [1983] 2 CMLR 240.

18 *National Sulphuric Acid Association*, OJ 1980 L260/24, [1980] 3 CMLR 429.
19 *Publishers' Association – Net Book Agreements*, OJ 1989 L22/12, [1989] 4 CMLR 825, upheld on appeal, Case T-66/89, *Publishers' Association* v *Commission* [1992] 5 CMLR 120; appeal to ECJ as Case C-360/92P, *Publishers' Association* v *Commission*.
20 Joined Cases 96–102, 104, 105, 108 and 110/82, *IAZ International* v *Commission* [1983] ECR 3369.
21 Case 48/69 [1972] ECR 619.
22 *Ibid.*, at paragraph 65.

a practical co-operation for the risks of competition'.[23] The essence of a concerted practice is the parallel behaviour of the parties which leads to market conditions other than those which would have existed normally.[24] This determination is made by looking at the market as well as the behaviour of the parties. The determination of a concerted practice, therefore, will be closely linked to the substantive determination as to whether or not the practice is anti-competitive. The applicants argued that the market for dyestuffs was naturally oligopolistic,[25] but the ECJ agreed with the Commission that the market did not display the features of an oligopolistic market, such as a history of interdependence between traders and transparency of prices.[26] In a later case the ECJ defined the type of conduct which would amount to a concerted practice as non-independent economic conduct:

> The criteria of co-ordination and co-operation laid down by the case law of the Court, which in no way require the working out of an actual plan, must be understood in the light of the concept inherent in the provisions of the Treaty relating to competition that each economic operator must determine independently the policy which he intends to adopt on the Common Market.[27]

The breadth of conduct which could constitute a concerted practice includes any direct or indirect conduct which leads to anti-competitive behaviour. It is, nonetheless, unlikely that 'innocent' parallel action would be caught, since in *Compagnie Asturienne* the ECJ decided that conduct would not be considered to be a concerted practice if the applicants could provide any explanation for parallel behaviour other than an attempt to distort competition.[28]

Selective distribution systems have been investigated by the Commission as anti-competitive behaviour under Article 85 EC. The counter-argument made is that the selection of distributors is a unilateral act and therefore cannot infringe Article 85. In *AEG-Telefunken* v *Commission*[29] the ECJ rejected this view, stating that such systems were part of an undertaking's contractual relations and refusals to admit certain distributors must be seen in the context of the undertaking's contractual relations with its actual distributors.

'Object or effect'

In *Société Technique Minière* v *Maschinenbau Ulm*[30] the ECJ confirmed that the words 'object or effect' are to be read disjunctively. This means that the Commission or the courts look first to the purpose of an agreement. If its purpose is acceptable, it is then necessary to look at its effects. The object of an agreement refers to its aims, not the intention of the parties, which is irrelevant.[31]

23 *Ibid.*, at paragraph 64.
24 *Ibid.*, at paragraph 67.
25 A market whereby a few traders dominate and the natural process of the market is for the participants to be interdependent, whereby the automatic reaction of one trader is to follow the practices of the others. A concerted practice, on the contrary, is collusive activity between traders in order to control a market which would otherwise be much more diverse. The distinction is not always clear. See Green, Hartley and Usher, *The Legal Foundations of the Single European Market* (1991), at 210–11.
26 In *A Ahlström Oy* v *Commission* [1993] 4 CMLR 407 (the *Wood Pulp* case), on the substantive issues the

ECJ found that the oligopolistic nature of the market and the transparency of prices provided an alternate, innocent explanation for the co-ordination of prices and, therefore, annulled the Commission's decision in part.
27 Joined Cases 40–48, 50, 54–56, 111, 113 and 114/73, *Suiker Unie* v *Commission* [1975] ECR 1663.
28 Joined cases 29 and 30/83, *op. cit.*, note 11, at paragraph 16.
29 Case 107/82, [1983] ECR 3151.
30 Case 56/65, [1966] ECR 235.
31 Joined Cases 29 and 30/83, *Compagnie Royale Asturienne, op. cit*, note 11, at paragraph 26.

Theoretically, if the purpose of an agreement is anti-competitive the Commission need not prove effects on the market and, therefore, need not analyse the structure of the market. However, the CFI considered the definition of the market necessary in any event in *Società Italiano Vetro* v *Commission*.[32] In order to determine the effect of an agreement, it is necessary to examine this in its market context.[33] The Commission and the courts will examine the agreement as a whole. If the agreement's entire operation affects trade it is irrelevant that certain provisions do not.[34] An agreement affecting a single Member State may affect trade between Member States, for example because it reinforces compart- mentalisation on a national basis.[35]

Horizontal and vertical agreements

The application of Article 85 to vertical as well as horizontal agreements was established early, in *Consten and Grundig* v *Commission*.[36] Vertical agreements are agreements not between competitors in the same market (which are horizontal agreements), but between undertakings at different levels of an economic process, such as manufacturers and distributors. Most of these agreements will not have an anti-competitive object, although a deliberate agreement between a manufacturer and a distributor to eliminate a distribution competitor by refusing to supply goods to that competitor would have an anti-competitive object. While the extension of Article 85 EC to agreements between parties who are not competitors has been criticised for reducing economic freedom of action, cases like *Consten and Grundig* demonstrate that distribution systems can be used to maintain high prices to the detriment of consumers. The fact that there is a block exemption on the subject of distribution agreements shows that the Commission is aware that most distribution agreements do not cause problems for Community competition law.

Preventing, restricting or distorting competition

The use of the list prevention, restriction or distortion indicates that Article 85 EC is intended to catch all forms of anti-competitive behaviour. The Commission, the ECJ and the CFI use the phrase as expressing a single concept, rather than three separate categories. There is an illustrative list of prohibited behaviours in Article 85(1). While the list is not intended to be exhaustive, most anti-competitive behaviour will fit into one of the listed categories.

Examples

Price fixing: In the *Publishers' Association* case the resale price maintenance elements of the British Net Book Agreement was considered to distort competition. This is probably a classic type of competition case, with competitive undertakings agreeing a common price structure for their products.

---

[32] Joined Cases T-68, 77 and 78/89, [1992] 5 CMLR 302, at paragraph 159.

[33] Case 23/67, *Brasserie de Haecht* v *Wilkin* [1967] ECR 407. Whish, *op. cit.*, note 1, at 204, concludes that it is, therefore, necessary to determine relevant product and geographic markets.

[34] Case 193/83, *Windsurfing International* v *Commission* [1986] ECR 611.

[35] Case 8/72, *Vereeniging van Cementhandelaren* v *Commission* [1972] ECR 977.

[36] Joined Cases 56 and 58/64, [1966] ECR 299.

Exclusive distribution: *Consten and Grundig* was the first of the exclusive distribution cases. While exclusive distribution need not always be competitive, this agreement permitted the distributor to prevent parallel imports. Parallel importing occurs when a retailer purchases from a distributor in another Member State rather than from the distributor in its own Member State. The import is parallel to the distribution system within the retailer's Member State. Preventing parallel imports often prevents price competition within Member States and creates a market separated into national compartments.

Selective distribution: Selective distribution, like exclusive distributorships, can maintain high prices artificially by preventing competition between distributors (intra-brand competition) and, more likely, by restricting supply. It can also reduce competition by effectively putting some distributors out of business by refusing to supply them with goods which the consumer wants. *Metro v Commission*[37] is a demonstration of selective distribution as a *prima facie* anti-competitive behaviour. The practice was, however, considered to be justified under the criteria in Article 85(3) EC.

Franchising: In *Pronuptia v Schillgalis* the ECJ decided that franchising was not a method of distribution but rather 'a way for an undertaking to derive financial benefit from its expertise without investing its own capital' while allowing the franchisee 'to benefit from the reputation of the franchiser's business name'.[38] Franchising also differs from distribution in that there is a single business name and a uniformity of doing business. It involves elements of know-how as well as distribution, and often other intellectual property rights as well. However, franchising agreements may restrict competition through geographic limitations which partition territory in such a way that one franchisee is unlikely to compete with another, and through price-fixing. These types of terms in a franchising agreement will make it restrictive of competition.

The rule of reason
The concept of a rule of reason derives from American competition law, whereby agreements which are not automatically illegal under the relevant legislation are analysed within their market contexts to decide whether or not they are anti-competitive. Many commentators have argued for a rule of reason to be developed by the Commission and the ECJ since, in their view, pro-competitive agreements have been declared illegal under Article 85.[39] However, EC competition law does not make the distinction between automatically anti-competitive agreements and potentially justifiable ones. Article 85(3) sets out explicit grounds upon which an agreement may be exempted. While there may be procedural problems in obtaining an individual exemption, it would seem contrary to the explicit words of Article 85 EC to set up an alternative system of exemption operating under Article 85(1), and possibly not subject to the same strict requirements, particularly that of benefiting the consumer. Furthermore, many of the types of agreements which are held out as beneficial and, therefore, should be subject to such a rule of reason, are the subject of block exemptions, ie research and development agreements, intellectual property licences and exclusive distribution contracts.

37 Case 26/76, [1977] 1875.
38 Case 161/84, [1986] ECR 353, at paragraph 15.
39 Green, Hartley and Usher, *op. cit.*, note 25, at 225–6; Schechter, 'The Rule of Reason in European Competition Law' [1982] 2 LIEI 1; Whish and Sufrin, 'Article 85 and the Rule of Reason' (1987) YEL 1.

The ECJ has recognised that certain types of agreements do not count as anti-competitive, which has led to arguments that it is, in fact, adopting a rule of reason approach. However, these cases do not amount to an alternative system of exemptions and Whish[40] argues that they are developments based on three concepts, necessity, protection for risk-taking innovation and selective distribution as a *sui generis* situation, rather than a new framework of interpretation. The main cases are:

- *Société Technique Minière*:[41] Exclusive distributorships need not be anti-competitive if they are necessary in order to market the goods, and will not cause a great degree of interference with the Common Market, in particular that it will not partition the market;
- *Nungesser*:[42] In the field of research and development of new technology, where it may be difficult to encourage the development of this technology at all, it is permissible to protect the licensee from competition with an open exclusive licence, but not a closed one. Where the licensee is bearing this type of risk, it is entitled to a certain extent of protection from competition;
- *Remia BV* v *Commission*:[43] Non-competition undertakings contained in the sale of the assets of a business may not violate Article 85(1) if they are necessary in order to give full effect to the sale. By giving effect to the sale, the ECJ means that if the seller can essentially gain his business back through competition with the buyer then the sale will have been illusory. In such a case competition would be reduced by not restricting it in the agreement of sale. However, to be valid, non-competition clauses must be necessary and limited;
- *Pronuptia de Paris* v *Schillgalis*: In this case the ECJ found that many typical clauses in franchise agreements would not be anti-competitive because they are necessary in order to ensure that the franchiser's know-how is not passed on to competitors or to ensure the identity of the franchiser's network;
- *Metro* v *Commission*:[44] While this case was also decided on the basis of the exemption criteria under Article 85(3), the ECJ stated, in discussing the application of Article 85(1), that a selective distribution system would not be anti-competitive if distributors were selected on the basis of objective criteria such as ability to provide after-sales service, and that the criteria were applied in a non-discriminatory manner.
- *Delimitis* v *Henniger Bräu*:[45] Exclusive purchasing obligations under a public house tenancy with a brewery are not anti-competitive if they do not, within the entire context of the market, prevent access to the market by other brands. This does not seem to fall within any of Whish's categories, since the decision is not based on necessity or innovation, but rather on contextual analysis. In this way it may demonstrate an expansion of the rule of reason for the future.

[40] *Op. cit.*, note 1, at 209–10.
[41] Case 56/65, *op. cit.*, note 30.
[42] Case 258/78, [1982] ECR 2105. See also Case 27/87, *Erauw-jacquery* v *La Hesbignonne* [1988] ECR 1919.
[43] Case 42/84, [1985] ECR 2545.
[44] Case 26/76, *op. cit.*, note 37. In a second *Metro* case, Case 75/84, *Metro* v *Commission (No 2)* [1986] ECR 3021 the ECJ said that the existence of a proliferation of selective distribution systems could be anti-competitive if they allowed no room for other forms of distribution or resulted in a rigidity of price structure. However, it found that the Commission had not erred in renewing the exemption for selective distribution of consumer electronics goods in Germany.
[45] Case C-234/89, [1991] ECR I-935.

Effect on trade between Member States

The effect on trade between Member States is where the boundary between the jurisdiction of national competition law and Article 85 EC will be determined. It has, however, been interpreted very broadly, not just covering the partitioning of the Single Market into national markets.[46] The concept of trade itself has been interpreted broadly. It includes services[47] as well as goods and includes all forms of commercial activities.

One of the earliest competition law cases decided by the ECJ set out the broad view of this requirement, which is still followed and has been extended to free movement of goods case law under Article 30 EC. *Société Technique Minière* v *Maschinenbau Ulm*,[48] set out that it is necessary to demonstrate a foreseeable influence direct or indirect, actual or potential, on the pattern of trade between Member States. Later the same year in *Consten and Grundig* v *Commission*[49] the ECJ repeated this test and added that the effect included increases of trade as well as decreases. This requirement, although essential for liability under Article 85 EC, is primarily to distinguish competition cases with a Community law dimension from national competition law cases. Therefore, often the question is not whether the defendant is liable but rather where that liability is legally situated. *Windsurfing International* v *Commission*[50] has added a gloss to the general test under *Technique Minière* by requiring that the agreement be evaluated as a whole to see whether it affects intraCommunity trade. If the agreement, seen globally, affects trade between the Member States, then it is irrelevant that certain restrictions on competition within the agreement might themselves only affect national trade.

Under the *Technique Minière* test, even potential effect on intraCommunity trade will bring the agreement within Article 85. In *AEG-Telefunken* v *Commission* the ECJ confirmed the Commission finding that although there were certain technical obstacles to trade between Member States in colour televisions, this trade was not impossible and AEG's actions were eliminating the possibility of traders entering the German market which might become a more attractive proposition in the future.

Even agreements between parties in a single Member State can effect intraCommunity trade. The CFI judgment in *Publishers' Association*[51] found that there could be national and intraCommunity effects of an agreement. Because the books sold under the agreement and exported to Eire constituted a large proportion of the books sold in Eire, trade between Member States was affected. The ECJ, in *Vereeniging van Cementhandelaren* v *Commission*[52] found that national agreements can reinforce partitioning of the Single Market and thereby effect intraCommunity trade In *Pronuptia* v *Schillgalis*[53] franchising agreements, because they involve the sharing of markets between the franchiser and franchisees, can affect trade between Member States. Similarly, agreements concerning external trade can be caught by Article 85.[54]

---

[46] Whish, *op. cit.*, note 1, at 216 goes so far as to say that 'it would be reasonable to start with a presumption that agreements that restrict competition will fall within Article 85 unless a clear case can be made to the contrary'.

[47] For example, banking, see Case 172/80, *Zückner* v *Bayerische Vereinsbank AG* [1981] ECR 2021.

[48] Case 56/65, *op. cit.*, note 30.

[49] Joined Cases 56 and 58/64, *op. cit.*, note 36.

[50] Case 193/83 *op. cit.*, note 34.

[51] OJ 1989 L22/12, *op. cit.*, note 19.

[52] Case 8/72, *op. cit.*, note 35.

[53] Case 161/84, *op. cit.*, note 38.

[54] *Franco-Japanese Ball-Bearings Agreement*, OJ 1974 L343/19, [1975] 1 CMLR D8; *French-West African Ship-owners' Committees*, OJ 1992 L134/1.

Sometimes, particularly when a case is being argued under both Articles 85 and 86 EC, the ECJ has used reasoning similar to that under Article 86 in order to decide whether there is an effect on intraCommunity trade for the purposes of Article 85. In these cases the ECJ looks not at actual or potential effects, but rather at the impact of the agreement on the structure of competition within the Community.[55]

The Commission may take jurisdiction over agreements with effects outside the Member States. Such agreements may explicitly affect intraCommunity trade, such as by prohibiting re-export to a Member State. However, the Commission and the ECJ have recently gone further by taking jurisdiction over an agreement whose effects would be felt within the Community. In the *Wood Pulp* case[56] a concerted practice engaged in by undertakings all located outside the Community was held to be within the Commission's jurisdiction because its implementation was effected within the Community through a reduction in price competition in sales of wood pulp to Community undertakings. Despite the breadth of jurisdiction granted by the ECJ by virtue of this judgment, the Commission could experience many practical problems in investigating extra-territorial violations of competition law. It cannot oblige non-Member States to co-operate with its investigations, and some states may refuse to grant the Commission authority to conduct investigations on their territory. The effects doctrine, therefore, is likely only to have effects on Community competition where the information about the agreement in question is held within the territory of the Community.

The de minimis rule

While even potential effect on trade is included within the scope of Article 85 EC, the effect must be sufficiently significant to merit regulation by the Community.[57] The Commission assisted businesses considerably in this matter by adopting in 1968 the Notice on Agreements of Minor Importance,[58] which, while not binding, does provide reasonably reliable guidance on the issue, thereby avoiding the necessity of obtaining negative clearance for a large number of agreements. In Article 1 of the Notice, the Commission notes that the notice applies particularly to small and medium-sized businesses. In Article 7 the general rule on what constitutes an agreement of minor importance is set out:

> – the goods or services which are the subject of the agreement (hereinafter referred to as 'the contract products') together with the participating undertakings' other goods and services which are considered by users to be equivalent in view of their characteristics, price and intended use, do not represent more than 5% of the total market for such goods or services (hereinafter referred to as 'products') in the area of the common market affected by the agreement and
> – the aggregate turnover of the participating undertakings does not exceed 200 million ECU.

Article 8 allows for the exceeding of the turnover limit by up to 10 per cent for up to two successive years. Articles 9–15 of the Notice deal with defining the elements of the rule in

55 See, for example, Joined Cases 6 and 7/73, *Commercial Solvents v Commission* [1974] ECR 223.
56 Joined Cases 89, 104, 114, 116, 117 and 125–129/85, *Ahlström Oy v Commission* [1988] ECR 5193.
57 The first case to apply this was Case 5/69, *Volk v Vervaecke* [1969] ECR 295, which found that an exclusive distributorship agreement with protection against parallel imports was not prohibited by Article 85 because Volk's market share was too small to matter – less than one per cent of the German market for washing-machines.
58 The most recent version of this Notice adopted in 1986, may be found at OJ 1986 C231/2.

Article 7. Article 16 provides that the Notice will not apply where competition is distorted by the cumulative effect of networks of agreements set up by a number of manufacturers or dealers, as has been decided by the ECJ in, for example, *Brasserie de Haecht SA v Wilkin*.[59] The ECJ has disapproved of the notion of a purely quantitative approach to the importance of an agreement in *Distillers Co Ltd v Commission*.[60]

Exemptions

Article 85(3) EC sets out the principles which govern exemptions from the prohibition under Article 85(1). If an agreement is found to violate Article 85(1) EC it may, nonetheless, be exempt because it makes a positive contribution to the market in some way and is not too restrictive. The Commission or the courts may apply this. The Commission also follows a practice of providing informal individual notices of exemption, called 'comfort letters'.

Under Community law there has developed, in addition to the individual procedures, a system of binding and non-binding measures from the Commission which will deal with categories of agreements and provide guidance as to what terms in such agreements will not violate Article 85(1) EC. While not actually exemptions, the Commission issues Notices, in addition to the Notice on Agreements of Minor Importance, indicating which types of agreements it will not regard as anti-competitive for the purposes of Article 85(1). These are known as block negative clearances. These are to be distinguished from block exemptions, which take the form of Regulations and are, therefore, binding Community law.[61] Notices are no more than guidelines, expressing the Commission's general opinion on the issue, although the Commission does follow its own notices.

Article 85(3) EC

The exemption provision of Article 85 EC will become relevant where the Commission has established to its own satisfaction, or that of the CFI or ECJ, that a violation of Article 85(1) has been made out. Only the Commission can grant exemptions, either in the circumstances of an investigation or when parties subject to a possibly anti-competitive agreement may apply to the Commission for an individual exemption.

Of the four conditions set out in Article 85(3) EC, two relate to the benefit provided by the agreement (the positive conditions) and two to the limited restriction on competition caused by the agreement (the negative conditions).

The first positive condition is that the agreement must contribute to the production or distribution of goods or to promoting technical or economic progress. Therefore, it must provide a benefit to the Single Market as a whole.[62] The courts are not always clear as to which of the categories of benefit an agreement falls into, and the Commission will often list more than one category as having been satisfied.[63] The second positive condition is that consumers must receive a fair share of the resulting benefit. Consumers means anyone,

[59] Case 23/67, [1967] ECR 407. See, however, *Delimitis v Henniger Bräu, op. cit.*, note 45, which has led to the Commission adopting a Notice specifically on beer agreements, OJ 1992 C 121/2.

[60] Case 30/78, [1980] ECR 2229. See also *Irish Banks Standing Committee*, OJ 1986 L195/28, [1987] 2 CMLR 334, where the Commission used a qualitative approach to the *de minimis* rule.

[61] On the nature of a regulation see Chapter 5.

[62] *Consten and Grundig v Commission, op. cit.*, note 36.

[63] Furthermore in *Metro v Commission, op. cit.*, note 37, at paragraph 43, the ECJ referred to the stabilisation of employment as a permitted goal in the context of improving the general conditions of production.

including another business undertaking, who consumes the goods or services covered by the agreement.[64] In *Re VBBB and VBVB Agreement,*[65] lack of choice resulting from the publishers' agreement meant that the agreement did not meet this criterion. An agreement that benefits consumers now might not be considered to do so in the future.[66]

The two negative agreements both import elements of proportionality into the evaluation, but a very strict version of proportionality. This is particularly true for the first negative condition, that there must be no restrictions on competition that are not indispensable to producing the benefit. In the *Publishers' Association* case[67] this criterion was primarily in issue in the appeal to the CFI. The CFI agreed with the Commission that certain conditions might be convenient for the parties operating the agreement, but were not indispensable to the operation of the agreement. The Publishers' Association had not proved that abolishing the Net Book Agreement would result in an excessive administrative burden for booksellers. The second negative condition is that the agreement must not create the possibility for the undertakings involved to eliminate competition in respect of a substantial part of the products in question. An example of the application of this criterion is *Van Landewyck* v *Commission*[68] where through the agreement the undertakings involved controlled over 80 per cent of the cigarettes in Belgium and, therefore their attempt to justify the agreement under Article 85(3) failed. In order to decide this point it sometimes becomes necessary to define the relevant product and geographical markets in order to determine how much of that market was covered by the agreement and, therefore, how much competition might have been eliminated by the agreement if granted an exemption.[69]

Article 86 EC does not provide for any possibility of exemption. Some competition cases are argued on the basis of both Articles 85 and 86, so the possibility exists of an exemption being obtained under Article 85(3) when, if the case had been decided primarily on the basis of Article 86, the exemption would not have been possible. The CFI dealt with the question of the relationship between Article 85(3) and Article 86 EC in *Tetra-Pak Rausing SA* v *Commission*[70] where it upheld the Commission's view that the fact that a practice might be covered by a block exemption under Article 85 did not prevent the possibility of liability under Article 86.

Block exemptions

The utility of block exemptions is that an agreement which fulfils the terms of a block exemption need not be notified to the Commission for exemption. As long as the parties are correct that the agreement is covered by the block exemption the agreement is legally clear, because a Regulation is binding in Community law.[71] This is much more certain than a notice, which is not binding on the Commission or the courts. Certainty in practice is often achieved by agreements being drafted in similar terms to the relevant block exemption, even to the point of using the same language. Block exemptions essentially have two parts. There

[64] See *Re ACEC/Berliet Agreements*, OJ 1968 L201/7, [1968] CMLR D 35.
[65] OJ 1982 L54/36, [1982] 2 CMLR 344, upheld on appeal as Joined Cases 43 and 63/82, *VBBB and VBVB* v *Commission* [1984] ECR 19.
[66] *Screensport/EBU*, OJ 1991 L63/32, [1992] 5 CMLR 273.
[67] *Op. cit.*, note 19.

[68] Joined Cases 209–215 and 218/78, [1980] ECR 3125.
[69] See *Bayer/BP Chemicals*, OJ 1988 L150/35, [1989] 4 CMLR 24. On the definition of product and geographical markets generally, see discussion under Article 86.
[70] Case T-51/89, [1991] ECR II-309.
[71] However, this assumes that the Regulation is itself valid under Community law.

will be a list of permitted clauses, or a 'white' list, and a list of clauses that will not be considered consistent with competition policy, or a 'black' list. A 'grey' list of permitted clauses which may or may not be consistent with Article 85(1) may also be included. Block exemption regulations always contain a saving provision which allows the Commission to withdraw the benefit of the exemption from agreements which it considers do not meet the requirements of Article 85(3) EC. The duration of the block exemption will also be specified.

An agreement may be refused the protection of a block exemption because it does not fit within the subject-matter of the relevant regulation. An agreement may have been drafted to conform with one block exemption which should have been been drafted to conform with another.[72] The agreement, in order to claim benefit of the block exemption, must satisfy any conditions set out in the regulation. However, it is not compulsory to comply with a block exemption – an individual exemption may be sought.[73]

While the block exemption regulations are passed by the Commission, it requires a delegation of power from the Council in order to do so. This delegation arises by virtue of Regulation 19/65/EEC (on exclusive dealing agreements and intellectual property licences), Regulation 2821/71/EEC (on standardisation agreements, research and development agreements and specialisation agreements), Regulation 1534/91/EEC (on the insurance sector) and Regulation 3976/87/EEC[74] (on transport). The Commission has passed several block exemption regulations as a consequence of these empowering Regulations. The most important of the block exemptions are:

- Regulation 1983/83/EEC on exclusive distribution agreements;
- Regulation 1984/83/EEC on exclusive purchasing agreements;
- Regulation 2349/84/EEC on patent licences;
- Regulation 417/85/EEC on specialisation agreements;
- Regulation 418/85/EEC on research and development agreements;
- Regulation 4087/88/EEC on franchise agreements;
- Regulation 556/89/EEC on know-how licensing.

Some regulations[75] contain an opposition procedure which provides a halfway house between block and individual exemption. Agreements within the general area of a block exemption regulation which do not satisfy the terms of the regulation may, if the regulation so provides, take an accelerated procedure to an individual exemption. However, because it is not specifically provided for in the EC Treaty or in the Council Regulations empowering the Commission to pass block exemptions, it is subject to a certain amount of legal certainty, and is not much used.[76]

---

72 *Delta Chemie/DDD*, OJ 1989 L309/34, [1989] 4 CMLR 535, where the agreement was drafted under the exclusive distribution regulation but should have been under the know-how agreements regulation.
73 Case 10/86, *VAG France SA* v *Établissements Magne SA* [1988] 4 CMLR 98.
74 Most recently amended by Regulation 3411/92/EEC.

75 The regulations on patent and know-how licensing, specialisation and research and development, and franchising.
76 See the Commission's annual reports on Competition Policy.

Effect of a declaration of violation under Article 85(1) EC

By virtue of Article 85(2) EC any agreement, decision or concerted practice which violates Article 85(1) is automatically void. The ECJ has generally applied a notion of severability, nullifying only the clauses or portions of an agreement, decision or concerted practice which are in violation, not necessarily the entire act.[77]

Article 86 EC – abuse of a dominant position

Article 86 provides that:

> Any abuse by one or more undertakings of a dominant position within the common market or in a substantial part of it shall be prohibited as incompatible with the common market in so far as it may affect trade between Member States.
>
> Such abuse may, in particular, consist in:
>
> (a) directly or indirectly imposing unfair purchase or selling prices or other unfair trading conditions;
> (b) limiting production, markets or technical development to the prejudice of consumers;
> (c) applying dissimilar conditions to equivalent transactions with other trading parties, thereby placing them at a competitive disadvantage;
> (d) making the conclusion of contracts subject to acceptance by the other parties of supplementary obligations which, by their nature or according to commercial usage, have no connection with the subject of such contracts.

This provision has generated more controversy than Article 85, since it requires the Commission and, more questionably, the courts, to engage in a significant amount of economic analysis in order to determine whether an undertaking is dominant and to decide whether the behaviour complained of is in fact abusive, or anti-competitive. Arguments have been made that the ECJ has contradicted itself in its judgments.[78] However, the ECJ, and now the CFI, appear to be aware of the dangers of undertaking economic analysis in a judicial setting and generally will not overturn Commission decisions on such a basis. The judicial idea of the model of competition which it is trying to protect is vague and undefined as a consequence, despite clear statements that the ECJ is attempting to compare behaviour against a model of perfect competition.

Existence of a dominant position

Article 86 penalises abusive behaviour on the part of dominant undertakings only. It is not a general fair trading provision. It only seeks to prevent powerful undertakings from controlling trade within the Single Market. However, it goes beyond monopolies. Dominance can exist, depending on the market, at market shares far below monopoly status. Generally,

---

[77] For example, see *Consten and Grundig, op. cit.,* note 36.
[78] In Case 27/76, *United Brands* v *Commission* [1978] ECR 207 the ECJ found that bananas formed a distinct market from other soft fruits. In Case 193/85, *Coopera-* *tive Co-Frutta* v *Amministrazione delle finanze dello stato* [1987] ECR 2085, as noted by Green, Hartley and Usher, *op. cit.,* note 25, at 40, for the purpose of the free movement of goods rules, bananas were found to occupy one product market of all fruits.

the ECJ has understood dominance to mean a certain freedom from market forces and a certain amount of control over the market unrelated to the usual principles of supply and demand:

> The dominant position thus referred to relates to a position of economic strength enjoyed by an undertaking which enables it to prevent effective competition being maintained on the relevant market by affording it the power to behave to an appreciable extent independently of its competitors, its customers and ultimately of the consumers.[79]

As Korah explains, only a dominant undertaking can change marketing strategy, such as raising or lowering prices or advertising its products in a different way, without undergoing risk of eroding its current market position.[80]

Relevant product market

Dominance does not exist in the abstract, it must be in relation to a particular market. The three elements which the Commission and the courts examine in order to determine the relevant market are the product market, the geographical market and the temporal market. Of these, the definition of the product market tends to generate the greatest amount of case law, as it is the most fluid of the three elements to define. For example, should all automobiles be considered part of the same market or should the market be divided into economy or family cars, luxury cars and performance cars? Are beer and wine part of the same market?[81]

The centrality of this issue was emphasised by the ECJ in *Europemballage and Continental Can Co. v Commission*,[82] where the Commission's failure to identify the relevant product market was the ground on which the applicants succeeded in their appeal against the Commission decision that they had violated Article 86. The ECJ appears to define the relevant product market in terms of interchangeability, which mirrors its approach of substitutability under Article 95 EC on non-discriminatory internal taxation. Thus, in the *Continental Can* case[83] it said that the Commission must look to 'characteristics of the products in question by virtue of which they are particularly apt to satisfy an inelastic need and are only to a limited extent interchangeable with other products'. In *United Brands v Commission* the ECJ applied the notion of interchangeability to the market for fruit. It found that bananas formed a distinct market because other soft fruits were not adequate substitutes because '[t]he banana has certain characteristics, appearance, taste, softness, seedlessness, easy handling, a constant level of production which enable it to satisfy the constant needs of an important section of the population consisting of the very young, the old and the sick'.[84]

For the most part, the Commission and the courts look to demand side substitutability, meaning the question of whether a purchaser of the product would regard another product as meeting the same purpose. This can be determined in part by considering cross-elasticity of demand, which means that if the price of one product goes up, purchasers will switch to

[79] Case 85/76, *Hoffman-LaRoche* v *Commission* [1979] ECR 461, at paragraph 38.
[80] Korah, 'Concept of a Dominant Position within the Meaning of Article 86' (1980) 17 CML Rev 395.
[81] For a discussion of this question in the context of Article 95 EC (requirement of non-discriminatory internal taxation), see Chapter 11.

[82] Case 6/72, [1973] ECR 215, at paragraphs 32–7. See also the introductory statement of the ECJ in *United Brands* v *Commission*, *op. cit.*, note 78, at paragraph 11.
[83] Case 6/72, *op. cit.*, note 82, at paragraph 32.
[84] Case 27/76, *op. cit.*, note 78, at paragraph 31.

another product rather than pay the higher price. Often this will require the production of empirical studies in order to prove allegations.[85] Other relevant factors will be physical characteristics, price and intended use. The intended use criterion has justified the narrow definition of the relevant market for spare parts, because the requirement of fit often means that only the supplier of the original product can supply the parts for it.[86] The ECJ will also look at the circumstances in which a product is purchased, which means that apparently similar products could be considered to exist in separate markets. For example in *Nederlandsche Banden-Industrie Michelin NV v Commission* the ECJ found that replacement tyres could be considered on this basis to be a separate market from that for tyres to be supplied with a new vehicle.[87] Finally, statutory markets may exist. In two cases concerning automobile manufacturers, the fact that the manufacturer was given a certain monopoly over the supply of approval certificates, required by law, for its own cars, made cars of that type a separate market for the purpose of the certificates.[88] The fact that a product has two uses will not usually justify the definition of separate markets for each.[89]

Occasionally, supply side interchangeability will be relevant. This refers to whether or not another supplier can switch over from its current output to producing a product in order to compete with an allegedly dominant undertaking. The best example of this is in *Tetra-Pak Rausing SA v Commission*[90] where the CFI confirmed the Commission's decision that producers of milk-packaging machines could not easily switch over to producing aseptic packaging machines and cartons, which justified a finding that the aseptic packaging formed a separate market.

Relevant geographic market

The definition of the geographic market is necessary in order to decide which undertakings may be considered to be in competition with the alleged dominant undertaking. Theoretically, the European Union itself should define the relevant geographical market for most products and services, since in a Single Market there should be no barriers to trade anywhere in the Union. However, there may be legal barriers to trade which have not yet been removed or which are permitted under Community law.[91] There may be practical reasons why a market is limited, for example with perishable foodstuffs. An example of practical limitations occurred in the *Magill TV Guide* cases, where the market for TV listings for RTE, BBC and ITV was considered to be Eire and Northern Ireland, since it was in this

---

85 For example, in *United Brands v Commission, op. cit.*, note 82, the ECJ noted data from the Food and Agriculture Organisation, a specialised agency of the United Nations.

86 Case 238/87, *Volvo v Veng* [1988] ECR 6211, and Case 53/87, *CICRA v Renault* [1988] ECR 6039. In these cases the existence of intellectual property rights over the products also affected the nature and scope of the market.

87 Case 322/81, [1983] ECR 3461.

88 Case 226/84, *British Leyland v Commission* [1986] ECR 3263, and Case 26/75, *General Motors v Commission* [1975] ECR 1367.

89 In *Hoffman-LaRoche v Commission, op. cit*, note 79, the fact that certain vitamins could be used as antioxi-

dants as well as for nutritional purposes did not justify creating two separate markets – one for vitamins in nutritional use and another for vitamins in industrial use. Similarly, in *AKZO*, OJ 1985 L374/1, appealed to ECJ as Case 62/86, [1991] ECR I-3359, AKZO produced peroxides for two purposes: for flour milling and for plastics. The Commission decided that there was only one product market involved. The two uses could not justify the definition of two markets. The ECJ agreed that the markets were not separate, since the behaviour of AKZO in the flour milling market was intended to protect itself against competition in the plastics market.

90 Case T-51/89, *op. cit.*, note 70.

91 See Chapter 11.

area that the companies broadcasted.[92] Similarly, if transportation costs make a wide geographic market unfeasible, then the market will be defined narrowly.[93] Finally, there may be traditional reasons why patterns of trade may be limited. For example, the geographical market in *United Brands* v *Commission*[94] excluded the UK and France because these two countries had trading arrangements with former colonies which meant that the patterns of trade in bananas was different in these two countries. In *Michelin* the ECJ agreed with the Commission that due to the purchasing practices of consumers, a single Member State could be the relevant geographical market for tyres.[95] In some transportation cases a single route has been defined as the relevant market.[96]

Relevant temporal market

The relevant temporal market will only rarely be in issue. It will become relevant for seasonal products, as in *United Brands* v *Commission* where the market for bananas changed in the summer months when other fresh fruit was widely available. The Commission nonetheless decided that there was only one banana market and the ECJ did not deal directly with the question, although it noted that the fresh fruit season did not affect the market for bananas significantly.[97] A temporal market may also be created by particular circumstances existing for a relatively short period of time, especially in a crisis situation, whereby a dominant undertaking may be able to take unfair advantage of a situation where its much weaker competitors are unable to react so quickly or effectively to sudden market changes, or where consumers are unable to exercise much choice in their sources of supply, as in *ABG*[98] where the early period of the energy crisis constituted a distinct temporal market for oil companies.

Factors demonstrating dominance

Once the market has been defined it is then possible to assess the position of the allegedly dominant undertaking within it. In *United Brands* v *Commission* the ECJ set out the following definition of dominance:

> The dominant position . . . relates to a position of economic strength enjoyed by an undertaking which enables it to prevent competition being maintained on the relevant market by affording it the power to behave to an appreciable extent independently of its competitors, customers and ultimately of consumers.[99]

Thus, while most undertakings must function within the context of market supply and demand, the dominant undertaking is able to ignore the market and set its own rules, without suffering a significant loss of its position in the market. This, to a certain extent,

---

92 Case T-69/89, *RTE* v *Commission* [1991] 4 CMLR 586; Case T-70/89, *BBC* v *Commission* [1991] 4 CMLR 669; Case T-76/89, *ITP Publications* v *Commission* [1991] 4 CMLR 745.
93 *Napier Brown-British Sugar*, OJ 1988 L284/41, [1990] 4 CMLR 196.
94 Case 27/76, *op. cit.*, note 78.
95 Case 322/81, *op. cit.*, note 87, paragraphs 26–8.
96 *British Midland* v *Aer Lingus*, OJ 1992 L96/34, [1993] 4 CMLR 596 (Heathrow-Dublin).
97 Case 27/76, *op. cit.*, note 78. At paragraph 34 the ECJ noted that 'a very large number of consumers hav-

ing a constant need for bananas are not noticeably or even appreciably enticed away from the consumption of this product by the arrival of other fresh fruit on the market and that even the personal peak periods only affect it for a very limited period of time and to a very limited extent from the point of view of substitutability'.
98 OJ 1977 L117/1, [1977] 2 CMLR D1, overturned on other grounds as Case 77/77, *BP* v *Commission* [1978] ECR 1513.
99 Case 27/76, *op. cit.*, note 78, at paragraph 38.

creates a circular argument with the issue of abuse. Can the presence of an abuse be used to demonstrate that the undertaking must be dominant? The structure of Article 86 would seem to preclude this, but the way that the Commission and the courts have analysed Article 86 cases seems to demonstrate a certain convergence. Capacity for market-independent action is the essence of dominance, but most evidence of market- independent behaviour will be of abusive behaviour. In *United Brands* v *Commission* the ECJ opened up the possibility of this type of argument by allowing evidence of conduct to be admitted on this issue of dominance. In *Michelin* the applicant argued that this sort of circular reasoning should not be allowed, but the ECJ upheld the Commission's reasoning that Michelin's pricing practices constituted evidence of dominance.[100] In *AKZO* the ECJ upheld the Commission's argument that AKZO's ability to eliminate or weaken its competitors was evidence of dominance.[101]

The primary measure of dominance is market share. This will include monopolies created by national laws, although such companies may be justified under Article 90(2).[102] However, a large market share is evidence of dominance, not a definition of it:

> The existence of a dominant position may derive from several factors which, taken separately, are not necessarily determinative but among these factors a highly important one is the existence of very large market shares . . .
>
> Furthermore, although the importance of the market shares may vary from one market to another the view may legitimately be taken that very large market shares are in themselves, and save in exceptional circumstances, evidence of the existence of a dominant position.
>
> An undertaking which has a very large market share and holds it for some time by means of the volume of production and the scale of the supply which it stands for – without those having much smaller market shares being able to meet rapidly the demand from those who would like to break away from the undertaking which has the largest market share – is by virtue of that share in a position of strength which makes it an unavoidable trading partner and which, already because of this secures for it, at the very least during relatively long periods, that freedom of action which is the special feature of a dominant position.[103]

The ECJ insists that other factors are examined as well. While there is no strict determination of what will be a very large market share, in *AKZO* the ECJ indicated that even 50 per cent could be considered very large.[104] In fact, undertakings with less than 50 per cent of the market have been found to be dominant, as in *United Brands* v *Commission*.[105] However, in *Hoffman-LaRoche* v *Commission* the ECJ overturned the Commission's finding of dominance in respect of one vitamin where Hoffman-LaRoche only had, in terms of quantity, at most 41 per cent of the market.[106] In the 10th report on Competition Policy the Commission stated that dominance exists at 40–45 per cent and that it could potentially exist even with a market share as low as 20 per cent. A smaller market share is likely to sustain dominance if competitors' market shares are very small in themselves, as in *Michelin* where the nearest competitor had eight per cent of the market, although Michelin's share had never exceeded 65 per cent.[107]

---

100 Case 322/81, *op. cit.*, note 87.
101 Case 62/86, *op. cit.*, note 89.
102 Case 41/83, *Italy* v *Commission* [1985] ECR 873.
103 *Hoffman-La-Roche* v *Commission, op. cit.*, note 79, at paragraphs 39 and 41.

104 Case 62/86, *op. cit.*, note 89, at paragraph 60.
105 Case 27/76, *op. cit.*, note 78.
106 Case 85/76, *op. cit.*, note 79, at paragraphs 57–8.
107 Case 322/81, *op. cit.*, note 87, at paragraph 33.

Of the other factors indicating dominance, the Commission and the courts will look primarily at barriers to entry of other competitors. If it is unlikely that any potential competitor could challenge any abusive behaviour by an undertaking by offering consumers better terms, then it is likely that the undertaking is dominant. Intellectual property rights can provide a form of monopoly over a product which will preclude, at least temporarily, new entrants into a market:[108] Superior technology, such as a significant amount of unused production capacity, is another barrier to entry,[109] as is access to capital which would facilitate rapid expansion[110] or effective distribution networks which mean that the undertaking is considerably integrated into the market.[111]

An undertaking must be dominant over a substantial part of the Single Market in order to be caught by Article 86. This issue cannot be answered simply by reference to the definition of the relevant geographical market, although in *Michelin* the two issues were converged by the ECJ.[112] Substantiality will, therefore, be evaluated on grounds other than territorial scope, including:

> the pattern and volume of the production and consumption of the said product as well as the habits and economic opportunities of vendors and purchasers.[113]

However, there has been no particular guidance on percentages which will be considered substantial within the Single Market. This question is rarely in issue in Article 86 cases.

Collective dominance

Article 86 EC clearly allows for the possibility of collective dominance by referring to abuses by 'one or more' undertakings. In some cases, therefore, collective action by two or more undertakings may be investigated under both Articles 85 and 86. Until recently the position has not been clear as to what types of collective action would be more appropriately considered under Article 86 rather than Article 85. Some cases dealt with issues of dominance where more than one undertaking is involved, but it could be argued that these legally separate undertakings were, in fact, single economic units.[114] In *Hoffman-LaRoche* v *Commission*[115] it was stated that Article 86 is not applicable to natural oligopolies. This position has been, at least to some extent, reversed by the Commission decision in *Italian Flat Glass*[116] where the conduct was found to infringe both Article 85 and 86. The Commission recognised the three undertakings as an oligopoly, but found that they were occupying collectively a dominant position on the market because they presented themselves on the market as a single economic unit. Collective dominance, it would therefore seem, would exist not simply as an alternative to Article 85 but, where the undertakings are so closely linked that they are for the purposes of competition, one undertaking. It is more than the 'parallel courses of conduct' which *Hoffman-LaRoche* v *Commission* identified with

[108] Case 22/78, *Hugin* v *Commission* [1979] ECR 1869. See also the *Volvo* v *Veng* and *CICRA* v *Renault* cases, *op. cit.*, note 86.
[109] *Hoffman-LaRoche* v *Commission, op. cit.*, note 79, at paragraph 48.
[110] *United Brands* v *Commission, op. cit.*, note 78, at paragraphs 121–2.
[111] *Ibid.*, at paragraphs 78–81.
[112] Case 322/81, *op. cit.*, note 87, at paragraphs 23–8.
[113] *Suiker Unie* v *Commission, op. cit.*, note 27, at paragraph 371.
[114] For example, *Commercial Solvents* v *Commission*,

op. cit., note 55.
[115] Case 85/76, *op. cit.*, note 79, at paragraph 39:
A dominant position must also be distinguished from parallel course of conduct which are peculiar to oligopolies in that in an oligopoly the courses of conduct interact, while in the case of an undertaking occupying a dominant position the conduct of the undertaking which derives profits from that position is to a great extent determined unilaterally.
[116] OJ 1989 L33/44, [1990] 4 CMLR 535.

oligopolistic behaviour. This interpretation would avoid substantial overlap with Article 85. The CFI[117] overturned the decision on the grounds that the Article 86 violation had not been properly analysed, particularly with respect to the relevant market, but confirmed the possibility of collective dominance falling under Article 86:

> There is nothing, in principle, to prevent two or more independent entities from being, on a specific market, united by such economic links that, by virtue of that fact, together they hold a dominant position *vis-à-vis* the other operators on the same market. This could be the case, for example, where two or more independent undertakings jointly have, through agreements or licences, a technological lead affording them the power to behave to an appreciable extent independently of their competitors, their customers and ultimately their consumers.[118]

This approach, while accepting that the joint dominance may arise, at least in part, from an agreement, stays within the principles of Article 86 by emphasising that the important element is that the undertakings must be able to act independently of the market. The Commission has also applied the concept of collective dominance in *French-West African Shipowners' Committees*.[119]

Concept of abuse

Like Article 85, Article 86 provides an illustrative list of behaviours which will constitute a violation. While it is a non-exhaustive list, most forms of abuse will be caught by one or more of the listed examples. It is, nonetheless, essential to define the abuse. Merely being dominant is not an offence. In fact, a fairly operated dominant undertaking may act as the most efficient and effective way of running a market. While there are no exemptions in Article 86 as there are in Article 85, the process of determining whether or not there has been abusive behaviour serves the same function, in allowing the consideration of whether the activities of the dominant undertaking may actually be good for consumers and the market in general. The courts have occasionally, as in *Tetra Pak Rausing SA* v *Commission*,[120] considered whether there is an objective justification for seemingly abusive behaviour, but this has not proved a profitable line of argument.

Abuse as a general concept was explained by the ECJ in *Hoffman-LaRoche* v *Commission*:

> The concept of abuse is an objective concept relating to the behaviour of an undertaking in a dominant position which is such as to influence the structure of a market where, as a result of the very presence of the undertaking in question, the degree of competition is weakened and which, through recourse to methods different from those which condition normal competition in products or services on the basis of the transactions of commercial operators, has the effect of hindering the maintenance of the degree of competitions still existing in the market or the growth of that competition.[121]

---

117 Case T-68/89, *Società Italiano Vetro* v *Commission* [1992] 5 CMLR 302.
118 *Ibid.*, at paragraph 358.
119 *Op. cit.*, note 54.
120 Case T-51/89, *op. cit.*, note 70. In Case T-65/89, *BPB Industries* v *Commission*, [1993] 5 CMLR 32 the

CFI stated that the fact that the applicants were retaliating against unfair commercial practices was irrelevant to the determination of whether or not there had been abuse.
121 Case 85/76, *op. cit.*, note 79, at paragraph 91.

Abuse of a dominant position, therefore, appears to be conduct which would tend to eliminate or prevent the emergence of other competition within the relevant market. In *Michelin*[122] the ECJ admonished dominant undertakings that they have a 'special responsibility not to allow [their] conduct to impair undistorted competition on the common market'.

Often, abuses are sorted into two categories: exploitative abuses and anti-competitive abuses.[123] The former relates to imposing unfair conditions on consumers and the latter to preventing or weakening the possibility of other undertakings competing against the dominant undertaking. However, while some abuses may be clearly one or another (for example, undercutting competitors' prices in order to eliminate them from the market may, at least initially, be of benefit to consumers), many abuses affect both consumers and competitors negatively, such as discriminatory pricing.

Exploitative abuses tend to fall within paragraphs (a) and (b) of the illustrative list in Article 86, whereas anti-competitive or mixed abuses fall into paragraphs (c) and (d), since these involve unfair terms in contracts with other traders. Anti-competitive abuses will include activities which affect the structure of the market as well as actions directed against a particular competitor:[124]

> By prohibiting the abuse of a dominant position within the market in so far as it may affect trade between Member States, Article 86 therefore covers not only abuse which may directly prejudice consumers but also abuse which indirectly prejudices them by impairing the effective competitive structure as envisaged by Article 3(f) of the Treaty.

The statement by the ECJ in *Hoffman-LaRoche* v *Commission* at the beginning of this section makes clear the fact that abusive conduct is *unusual* conduct because it is conduct outside the limits of normal competition. However, neither the Commission nor the courts have ever provided a reasonably complete definition of what is to be considered normal competition.

Anti-competitive behaviour can include discriminatory pricing, as was found by the Commission in *British Telecom*,[125] where message-forwarding was charged at a higher rate if the message came from elsewhere in the Union. Tied selling to distributors or retailers can be abusive, as was the case in *Hoffman-LaRoche* v *Commission*. Behaviour which restricts imports would obviously apply as anti-competitive because such behaviour would have a partitioning effect within the Common Market. However, the ECJ has gone further and determined that conduct which tends to reduce exports will also be considered anti-competitive.[126] Refusal by a dominant undertaking to supply distributors with goods can have the effect of putting a trader out of business and is, therefore, anti-competitive.[127] However, it is only arbitrary and unjustified refusal which is caught by Article 86 EC. It would be unlikely, in the absence of other factors, that it could be considered abusive to refuse to supply a distributor who is seriously in arrears with payment. Similarly, denial of essential facilities can be abusive. The Commission found in *Sealink/ B and I – Holyhead: Interim*

122 Case 322/81, *op. cit.*, note 87, at paragraph 57.
123 For example, in Whish, *op. cit.*, note 1.
124 *Hoffman-LaRoche* v *Commission*, *op. cit.*, note 79, at paragraph 125. See below under merger control for the application of Article 86 EC to mergers which might affect the competitive structure of the market.

125 OJ 1982 L360/36, [1983]1 CMLR 457.
126 *Suiker Unie* v *Commission*, *op. cit.*, note 78, at paragraphs 168, 182–3.
127 *United Brands* v *Commission*, *op. cit.*, note 27.

Measures[128] that the organisation of ferry schedules at the Holyhead port to favour Sealink's own ships would undermine others' ability to compete and was therefore abusive.

Effect on trade between Member States

The meaning of this concept under Article 86 is similar to that under Article 85, particularly in those cases where the effect has been analysed in terms of effect on the structure of competition rather than the free flow of goods and services.[129] However, the two ideas of effect are related. In a market where competition is rigid, that structure of competition could contribute to the partitioning of the market along national lines and therefore constitute an obstacle to the establishment of a Single Market.[130]

Commission procedure on Article 85 and 86 investigations

Under the EC Treaty, the Commission is foreseen as the main body enforcing the competition policy under Community law. However, there are far more cases arising than the Commission is able to deal with. The Member States are given the competence to initiate proceedings under Article 85 or 86 EC as long as the Commission has not done so.[131] However, the Member States tend to apply their national competition rules rather than Community law in this area. It is also possible to raise Article 85 or 86 in proceedings between private parties. This will often depend on the knowledge of the parties' legal representatives concerning Community competition law and the willingness of the national court to apply it.

In enforcing competition law the Commission's powers are set out primarily in Regulation 17/62/EEC.[132] This Regulation specifies both the investigative and punitive powers of the Commission, as well as empowering it to grant individual exemptions and negative clearances. The ECJ has held that granting investigative and punitive powers to the same institution does not violate general principles of Community law.[133] The ECJ has also confirmed the scope of Commission powers of search in *National Panasonic (UK)* v *Commission*,[134] rejecting an argument that these powers could violate human rights as general principles of Community law. However, the ECJ has been concerned to ensure that undertakings being investigated have a right to be heard in any proceedings taken against them.[135]

Articles 11 and 14 of Regulation 17/62/EEC set out the main powers of the Commission in investigating possible violations. Article 11 deals with requests for information. The Commission may request information from 'Governments and competent authorities of the Member States and from undertakings and associations of undertakings'. If requesting information from an undertaking or association of undertakings, a copy must be forwarded

---

128 [1992] 5 CMLR 255.

129 For example, in *Commercial Solvents* v *Commission*, *op. cit.*, note 55.

130 *French-West African Shipowners' Committees*, *op. cit.*, note 54.

131 Article 9(3) of Regulation 17/62/EEC.

132 Competition in the transport sectors is governed by a series of specialised regulations.

133 Joined Cases 100–103/80, *Musique Diffusion Française* v *Commission* [1983] ECR 1825.

134 Case 136/79, [1980] ECR 2033.

135 See Chapter 7.

to the national authorities. The request must include its legal basis and purpose, as well as a warning of the penalties for supplying incorrect information. Where information is not supplied the Commission may order it by decision, which is reviewable by the CFI. Article 14 deals with the Commission's investigatory powers. These powers are very broad and include, specifically, the powers:

- to examine the books and other business records;
- to take copies of or extracts from the books and records;
- to ask for oral explanations on the spot;
- to enter any premises, land and means of transport of undertakings.

The Commission is not obliged to obtain the consent of the undertaking, if acting by virtue of a decision, or even to notify it in advance. It must, however, inform the national competition authorities, who may be asked to assist with the investigation, and who are obliged to assist where the undertaking obstructs the Commission investigation. In *Hoechst v Commission*, the ECJ held that the national authorities, when requested to assist an investigation which is being obstructed by the undertaking, have no right to second-guess the Commission's evaluation of the necessity of the investigation.[136] Fines may be imposed if the undertaking refuses to submit to the investigation or if it does not produce complete records, as requested during the course of the investigation. It may, however, withhold documents containing business secrets[137] or legally privileged documents.[138]

In certain circumstances the Commission may issue an interim decision granting temporary conservatory measures.[139] It may only do so on the basis of urgency, to protect the party requesting them or the public interest generally, from 'serious and irreparable harm'.[140] It appears that the potential damage will only be serious and irreparable if the Commission could not remedy any damage suffered in its decision on the merits.[141] However, the party requesting the interim measures need only prove a *prima facie* case.[142] As a decision, it must meet all the Treaty requirements, including a statement of reasons, which would enable the CFI to review the decision if necessary.[143]

The Commission may issue a provisional decision in proceedings relating to the notification of an agreement for individual exemption under Article 85(3). Normally, an undertaking may not be liable for fines under Article 15 of Regulation 17/62/EEC between the time of notification and the issuing of a decision. However, Article 15(6) removes the benefit of this provision if the Commission issues a provisional decision that the agreement does not qualify for an exemption. If the Commission is of the opinion that an agreement

136 Joined Cases 46/87 and 227/88, [1989] ECR 2859.
137 *AKZO, op. cit.*, note 89.
138 Case 155/79, *AM & S v Commission* [1982] ECR 1575, discussed in detail in Chapter 6.
139 The ECJ confirmed that the Commission does have the power to make interim decisions in Case 792/79R, *Camera Care v Commission* [1980] ECR 119, at paragraphs 14–18. Notably, at paragraph 17, the ECJ stated that: 'To this end the possibility cannot be excluded that the exercise of the right to take decisions conferred upon the Commission should comprise successive stages so that a decision finding that there is an infringement may

be preceded by any preliminary measures which may appear necessary at any given moment'.
140 *Ibid*, at paragraph 19. The serious and irreparable harm may be to a party or to the public interest generally. Furthermore, the procedural safeguards of Regulation 17/62/EEC must be observed.
141 Case T-44/90, *La Cinq v Commission* [1992] 4 CMLR 449.
142 *Ibid*.
143 *Camera Care v Commission, op. cit.*, note 139, at paragraph 19.

notified to it falls outside Article 85 and 86 altogether, it may issue a 'negative clearance' under Article 2 of Regulation 17/62/EEC, which is a certification 'that, on the basis of the facts in its possession, there are no grounds under Article 85(1) or Article 86 of the Treaty'. The Commission may alter its position at a later date due to a change of circumstances or new facts which have come to light. For an individual exemption under Article 85(3) EC, a Commission decision must be issued and published. The exemption may be for a limited period of time. For both negative clearances and individual exemptions the Commission must hear all interested parties, as required by Article 19 of Regulation 17/62/EEC.

The Commission's highest profile work in competition policy is infringement proceedings. Here it investigates practices which possibly infringe Article 85 or 86. Infringement proceedings are initiated by the Commission, but may be the result of an application by a Member State or an interested undertaking. In infringement proceedings, as opposed to the investigation which may lead up to such proceedings, a statement of objections must be served on the undertakings concerned if the Commission contemplates imposing fines. Otherwise, a notice in the *Official Journal* is sufficient. The statement of objections forms the limits of the proceedings and must contain the alleged infringements and the facts sustaining such allegations.[144] After the hearing[145] the Commission consults the Advisory Committee on Restrictive Practices and Monopolies and then adopts its decision. The decision may require the termination of any practices which infringe Article 85 or 86, and may impose fines on the undertakings.[146] The amount of the fine may be reviewable as are the other elements of the decision.[147]

Commission action in enforcement of Community competition policy may be reviewed by the CFI, and from there appealed to the ECJ.[148] A complainant whose complaint has not been acted upon may take an action for failure to act under Article 175 EC.[149] However, the Commission is not obliged to proceed with an investigation if it considers that the matter does not raise sufficient Community interest.[150] The position of the subject of infringement proceedings is clearer. It may seek the judicial review of any decision[151] addressed to it under Article 173 EC. An undertaking subject to a Commission decision that it has infringed Community competition law, and which is seeking judicial review, may apply for the suspension of the decision under Articles 185 and 186 EC. Occasionally, a complainant who is dissatisfied with the decision of the Commission may also seek review of the decision, if it can demonstrate *locus standi*.[152]

Control of public undertakings

Public monopolies are prohibited under Article 90(1) of the EC Treaty only insofar as they are incompatible with competition policy in general:

---

144 Joined Cases 89, 104, 114, 116, 117 and 125–9/85, *Ahlström Oy* v *Commission*, *op. cit.*, note 56, at paragraphs 152–4.

145 On the procedural rights in infringement actions, see the discussion of right to a hearing in Chapter 6.

146 The limits of the fines which can be imposed are set out in Articles 15 and 16 of Regulation 17/62/EEC.

147 Article 172 EC.

148 For the scope of jurisdiction for judicial review, see Chapter 7.

149 See, for example, Case 210/81, *Demo-Studio Schmidt* v *Commission* [1983] ECR 3045, and Case T-28/90, *Asia Motor France* v *Commission* [1992] 5 CMLR 431; Case T-24/90, *Automec* v *Commission (No 2)* [1992] 5 CMLR 431.

150 *Asia Motor France* v *Commission, ibid.*

151 This includes any binding act of the Commission: see Case 60/81, *IBM* v *Commission* [1981] ECR 2639.

152 Case 26/76, *Metro* v *Commission* [1977] ECR 1875.

> In the case of public undertakings and undertakings to which Member States grant special or exclusive rights, Member States shall neither enact nor maintain in force any measure contrary to the rules contained in this Treaty, in particular to those rules provided for in Article 6 and Articles 85 through 94.

Public undertakings, in a definition approved by the ECJ, include 'any undertaking over which the public authorities may exercise directly or indirectly dominant influence by virtue of their ownership of it, their financial participation therein, or the rules which govern it'.[153] 'Special or exclusive rights' suggests some kind of quasi-monopoly situation: where other bodies are not precluded by law from performing the same functions the requirement will not have been met.[154] It has not yet been established whether 'special' and 'exclusive' are separate concepts or whether 'special or exclusive rights' denotes a single concept.[155]

Although Article 90(1) contains a prohibition, it is a dependent one. It can only be invoked in association with another Article of the Treaty. Article 90 itself specifically mentions two areas: discrimination on the basis of nationality (Article 6 EC)[156] and competition policy (Articles 85–94 EC). Recently, the ECJ has dealt with the Article 90 prohibition in relation to Article 86 EC. In *Höfner* v *Elser and Macrotron*[157] it decided that the legal monopoly given to the German Federal Employment Office was an infringement of Article 90 because the exercise of such exclusive rights would involve an abuse of a dominant position under Article 86, although the granting of the monopoly was not itself a breach. This is consistent with the general approach to Article 86 that dominance is not itself a breach of Community law, only the abuse of dominance. The Federal Employment Office was unable to satisfy all of the demand for its services and tolerated the presence of competitors, despite the fact that these would have been acting illegally. Nonetheless, the fact that if the Office had tried to prevent the operation of its competitors it would have contravened Article 86 was sufficient.[158] A somewhat different issue arose in *RTT* v *GB-INNO-BM*[159] where the monopoly for telephone services was considered acceptable, but its extension to a monopoly over the equipment was ruled abusive in terms of Article 86.

In addition to Article 177 EC proceedings raised in a dispute between two parties before a national court, the Commission may take an enforcement action against a Member State under either Article 169 EC[160] or Article 90(3) EC:

> The Commission shall ensure the application of the provisions of this Article and shall, where necessary, address appropriate directives or decisions to Member States.

Article 90(3) would appear the preferable option, since it gives the Commission alone the power to adopt measures in order to deal with violations, and still leaves the option of using an enforcement action under Article 169 if the Member State does not remedy the violation

---

153 Joined Cases 188-190/80, *France* v *Commission* [1982] ECR 2545. Compare with the definition of 'emanation of the State' for the purpose of delimiting the scope of vertical direct effect of directives, see Case C-188/89 *Foster* v *British Gas* [1990] ECR 3313, discussed in Chapter 4.
154 *GEMA*, OJ 1971 L134/15, [1971] CMLR D35.
155 Whish, *op. cit.*, note 1 is of the opinion that Case C-202/88, *Commission* v *France* [1992] 5 CMLR 552 indicates that the phrase does contain two separate concepts.

156 Before the TEU Article 7.
157 Case C-41/90, [1991] ECR I-1979.
158 See also Case C-179/90, *Merci Convenzionale Porto di Genova* v *Siderurgica Gabrielli* [1991] ECR I-5889 and Case C-260/89, *ERT* v *Dimotiki* [1991] ECR I-2925.
159 Case C-18/88, 13 December 1991.
160 See Chapter 8.

as required by the decision or directive.[161] It is, therefore, somewhat surprising that this power was not much used until the mid-1980s. Since then, however, a number of sectors have been affected by measures adopted under Article 90.[162] Measures adopted under Article 90(3) may, of course, be subject to judicial review for annulment.[163] The use of directives under this provision has been particularly controversial. Three directives have been challenged, all unsuccessfully.[164] In one of these cases the ECJ pointed out that Articles 90(3) and 169 have different purposes. Article 90(3) enables the Commission to provide greater precision on the obligations under Article 90(1), and Article 169 is for specific infringements.[165] This indicated that the ECJ does see limits to the Commission's powers under Article 90(3), and that the Commission does not have a free choice whether to use one means or the other to enforce Treaty obligations with respect to public undertakings.

Exceptions

Article 90(2) provides for the exception to the Article 90 prohibition:

> Undertakings entrusted with the operation of services of general economic interest or having the character of a revenue-producing monopoly shall be subject to the rules contained in this Treaty, in particular to the rules on competition, in so far as the application of such rules does not obstruct the performance, in law or in fact, of the particular tasks assigned to them. The development of trade must not be affected to such an extent as would be contrary to the interests of the Community.

As with most exceptions and derogations, this provision is to be construed strictly.[166] The concept of necessity underlies this exception – only if a Treaty rule would jeopardise the functioning of a public economic undertaking will the Commission or the ECJ be willing to allow a defence under Article 90(2). In particular, the undertaking will have to demonstrate that there is no feasible alternative to the practice which violates the Treaty.[167]

State aids

State aids are dealt with by Articles 92–94 EC. The basic prohibition is set out in Article 92(1):

> Save as otherwise provided in this Treaty, any aid granted by a Member State or through State resources in any form whatsoever which distorts or threatens to distort competition

---

[161] See, for example, Case 226/87, *Commission v Greece* [1988] ECR 3611, where the ECJ emphasised that, like all decisions, decisions adopted under Article 90(3) EC were binding in their entirety on the addressee by virtue of Article 189 EC.

[162] For a discussion of the directives on telecommunications equipment and services, see Chapter 15.

[163] A successful challenge to an Article 90(3) decision was made in Joined Cases C-48 and 66/90, *Netherlands PTT v Commission*, 12 February 1992, on the ground of infringement of the right to a hearing. More recently, in Case C-325/91, *France v Commission*, 16 June 1993, the ECJ annulled a Commission Communication on 'Appli-

cation of Articles 92 and 93 of the Treaty and of Article 5 of Commission Directive 80/723/EEC to public undertakings in the manufacturing sector' which should have been adopted under Article 90(3) EC, rather than being adopted as a non-binding Communication.

[164] Case 188/80, *Commission v France* [1982] ECR 2545; Case C-202/88, *Commission v France, op. cit.*, note 155; Joined Cases C-271/90 etc., *Spain, Belgium and Italy v Commission*, 17 November 1992.

[165] Case C-202/88, *Commission v France, ibid.*

[166] Case 127/73, *BRT v SABAM* [1974] ECR 313.

[167] *ANSEAU-NAVEWA*, OJ 1982 L167/39, amended at OJ 1982 L325/20.

by favouring certain undertakings or the production of certain goods shall, in so far as it affects trade between Member States, be incompatible with the common market.

State aid is defined as any practice by which Member States:

in pursuit of their own economic and social objectives give, by unilateral and autonomous decisions, undertakings or other person resources or procure for them advantages intended to encourage the attainment of the economic or social objectives sought.[168]

As with other aspects of the Treaty intended to establish the Single Market, Article 92 prevents Member States from pursuing policies which could partition the market, in this case by giving an advantage to national industries.[169] While this does limit the capacity of Member States to pursue policies which they may consider important and which may be widely supported by their populations, it is intended to prevent anti-competitive behaviour in the same way that Articles 85 and 86 do. The exceptions, particularly the discretionary exceptions, do allow Member States to pursue legitimate goals such as creating or maintaining jobs in areas of high unemployment or developing new industries. Since the TEU came into force Member States may even be permitted to aid cultural industries. Ultimately, therefore, Article 92 is intended to ensure free and fair competition, not to prevent the pursuit of important socio-economic policies. Aid will be evaluated, however, in terms of its effects rather than its goals or its form, which means that some forms of social policy may be considered to act as a disguised subsidy.[170]

An aid must have a gratuitous character. What is given by the State must be in excess of what the undertaking receiving the aid provides in return. A State authority purchasing goods or services from a company at an economic price would not be granting an aid, no matter how sought-after such a contract might be amongst undertakings.

Aids incompatible with the Common Market: automatic exceptions

Article 92(2) sets out the scope of aid which will not be incompatible with the Treaty.

The following shall be compatible with the common market:
(a) aid having a social character, granted to individual consumers, provided that such aid is granted without discrimination related to the origin of the products concerned;
(b) aid to make good the damage caused by natural disasters or other exceptional occurrences;
(c) aid granted to the economy of certain areas of the Federal Republic of Germany affected by the division of Germany, in so far as such aid is required in order to compensate for the economic disadvantages caused by that division.

Interestingly, the final paragraph was not repealed by the TEU despite the unification of East Germany into the Federal Republic in 1990. These categories of aid have caused little dispute within the Community and no decisions. They are all quite narrow exceptions, and most are

---

168 Case 61/79, *Amministrazione delle finanze dello stato v Denkavit* [1980] ECR 1205, at 1228.
169 Case 730/79, *Philip Morris Holland* v *Commission* [1980] ECR 2671: providing such an advantage 'affects trade between Member States'.

170 Case 173/73, *Italy* v *Commission* [1974] ECR 709; see also Case 323/82, *Intermills* v *Commission* [1984] ECR 3809 (State purchase of shares of a company constitutes an aid).

clear from their language. The reference to 'exceptional occurrences' aid in subparagraph (b) is somewhat cryptic. Logically, it would appear to exclude 'serious disturbance in the economy of a Member State' which is mentioned in Article 92(3)(b). If exceptions are to be construed strictly, then it would seem right that a matter which potentially could fall under one of two provisions should fall under the one which requires supervision by the Commission.

Aids incompatible with the Common Market: discretionary exceptions

Article 92(3) sets out the forms of aid which, if approved by the Commission, will be considered to be compatible with the Treaty.

> The following may be considered to be compatible with the common market:
> (a) aid to promote the economic development of areas where the standard of living is abnormally low or where there is serious underemployment;
> (b) aid to promote the execution of an important project of common European interest or to remedy a serious disturbance in the economy of a Member State;
> (c) aid to facilitate the development of certain economic activities or of certain economic areas, where such aid does not adversely affect trading conditions to an extent contrary to the common interest. However, the aids granted to shipbuilding as of 1 January 1957 shall, in so far as they serve only to compensate for the absence of customs protection, be progressively reduced under the same conditions as apply to the elimination of customs duties, subject to the provisions of this Treaty concerning common commercial policy towards third countries;
> (d) aid to promote culture and heritage conservation where such aid does not affect trading conditions and competition in the Community to an extent that is contrary to the common interest;[171]
> (e) such other categories of aid as may be specified by decision of the Council acting by a qualified majority on a proposal from the Commission.[172]

While the Commission is given discretion to decide which aids are compatible with the Common Market in terms of the above exceptions, it takes the view that not only must the goal be legitimate, but the aid must be necessary in order to achieve the goal.[173] This is consistent with justifications and exceptions to Community law rules in several areas.[174] The Commission examines the aid in light of Community objectives, particularly the achievement and maintenance of the Single Market.

Subparagraph (a) must be understood in distinction to the two subparagraphs which follow. It is not intended to deal with economic emergencies, as is subparagraph (b), and is not intended to deal with general regional development, as is subparagraph (c). The abnormality of the economic situation in the region is evaluated against the general standard within the entire European Union, not just against the situation in the Member State.[175]

Aid has been approved for both categories covered by subparagraph (b). Aid was allowed in order to relieve serious economic disturbance during the recession of the mid-1970s.[176]

---

171 Added by the TEU.
172 Before the TEU this was subparagraph (d).
173 *Philip Morris Holland* v *Commission, op. cit.*, note 169.

174 For example, Article 36 EC, as discussed in Chapter 11.
175 *Philip Morris Holland* v *Commission, op. cit*, note 169.
176 Fifth Report on Competition Policy (1975).

More frequently, aid has been allowed in order to pursue European projects. *Executif Regional Wallon and Glaverbel* v *Commission*[177] set out the criteria for a valid project under this category: it must form part of a transnational European programme and must be supported by several Member States or arise from concerted action by Member States to combat a common threat. This type of aid has, therefore, been possible for developing new technology, completing infrastructure projects and dealing with environmental problems.

Subparagraph (c) represents most of the requests for approval of aids under Article 92. It allows aid to regions or to industries and, because of its breadth, the Commission must make some very difficult determinations as the guardian of the collective Community interest. Often, the proposed aid will be directed at both issues. Regions may become economically disadvantaged because of 'sunset industries', industries which are in decline and are, therefore, shedding jobs at a high rate. Aid may be necessary in order to attract new industries to these regions and to reskill the work-force in order to enable them to obtain jobs in these new industries. In this category, like all the categories of potentially permissible aid under Article 92(3), the means as well as the goal must be examined. As a result, the Commission rejected a proposed aid to the French textile industry because it was being financed by a charge on domestic and imported textile products. The protectionist nature of the means of financing the aid counterbalanced the legitimate objective pursued.[178] An example of an acceptable means of financing the restructuring of an industry was set out in *Intermills* v *Commission*, where the ECJ, overturning the Commission's decision, found that payment of a company's debts would not necessarily cause an adverse affect on the common interest of the Community.[179]

It is too early to say how the new subparagraph (d) will be applied and interpreted. One possible field where it may be applied is to Member State support of national film industries, which France, in particular, fought to protect during the recent GATT negotiations. Under subparagraph (e), formerly subparagraph (d), the Community institutions have taken the view that 'decision' is not being used in its technical sense, as in Article 189 EC, and have acted under these powers by means of directives. These directives have been directed at permitting aid to the shipbuilding industry within the Community.[180]

Procedures

The procedures by which State aid is supervised is contained in Articles 93 and 94:

> (93) 1. The Commission shall, in co-operation with Member States, keep under constant review all systems of aid existing in those States. It shall propose to the latter any appropriate measures required by the progressive development or by the functioning of the common market.
> 2. If, after having given notice to the parties concerned to submit their comments, the Commission finds that aid granted by a State or through State resources is not compatible with the common market having regard to Article 92, or that such aid is being misused, it shall decide that the State concerned shall abolish or alter such aid within a period of time to be determined by the Commission.

---

[177] Joined Cases 62 and 72/87, [1988] ECR 1573.
[178] Case 47/69, *France* v *Commission* [1970] ECR 487.
[179] Case 323/82, *op. cit.* note 170.

[180] The most recent being Directive 93/115/EC of 16 December 1993.

If the State concerned does not comply with this decision within the prescribed time, the Commission or any other interested State may, in derogation from the provisions of Articles 169 and 170, refer the matter to the Court of Justice direct.

On application by a Member State, the Council may, acting unanimously, decide that aid which that State is granting or intends to grant shall be considered to be compatible with the common market, in derogation from the provisions of Article 92 or from the regulations provided for in Article 94, if such a decision is justified by exceptional circumstances. If, as regards the aid in question, the Commission has already initiated the procedure provided for in the first subparagraph of this paragraph, the fact that the State concerned has made its application to the Council shall have the effect of suspending that procedure until the Council has made its attitude known.

If, however, the Council has not made its attitude known within three months of the said application being made, the Commission shall give its decision on the case.

3. The Commission shall be informed, in sufficient time to enable it to submit its comments, of any plans to grant or alter aid. If it considers that any plan is not compatible with the common market having regard to Article 92, it shall without delay initiate the procedure provided for in paragraph 2. The Member State concerned shall not put its proposed measures into effect until this procedure has resulted in a final decision.

(94) The Council, acting by a qualified majority on a proposal from the Commission, and after consulting the European Parliament,[181] may make any appropriate regulations for the application of Articles 92 and 93 and may in particular determine the conditions under which Article 93(3) shall apply and the categories of aid exempted from this procedure.[182]

There are two procedures under Articles 93 and 94: review of existing aid[183] and clearance for new aid. The distinction between the two categories is sometimes unclear and may be an issue in a judicial review of a Commission decision that a new aid was incompatible with the Common Market.[184] For Member States it is preferable to categorise the aid as existing, since the review process is less strict. If, upon review, the Commission decides that an aid is incompatible with the Common Market or is being misused, it may take enforcement proceedings under paragraph (2) of Article 93.[185]

For the clearance procedure, Member States must notify any proposed aid to the Commission. Until recently, the Commission took the view that failure to notify aid prior to its implementation was fatal to its compatibility with the Common Market. In other words, even if an aid was substantively acceptable, if it had been granted without the clearance procedure under Article 93(3) having been passed the aid would always be incompatible with the Common Market. The ECJ rejected this approach in *France* v *Commission (Boussac)*[186] where the Court refused to accept that breach of procedures can make an otherwise legal aid regime illegal. A decision that an aid which has already been granted is compatible with the Common Market can only be prospective, however. The compromise between Commission and Member State interests set out in the judgment is that the Commission should be able to issue an interim order suspending the aid pending the review that should have taken place

---

181 This requirement was added by the TEU.
182 The powers granted by this Article have never been exercised.
183 'Existing' aid refers to aid in place at the time of the adoption of the EC Treaty or accession to membership.
184 The ECJ is of the opinion that the issue of whether

an aid is new or existing is within its sole jurisdiction: Case C-312/90, *Spain* v *Commission*; and Case C-47/91, *Italy* v *Commission*, both 30 June 1992.
185 This procedure is discussed in Chapter 8.
186 Case 301/87, [1990] ECR I-307.

before the aid was granted. This power to make interim orders is new and strengthens the Commission's position under Article 93.[187]

In authorising an aid under the preliminary clearance procedure, the Commission may impose conditions which the Member State must respect in granting the aid. In a recent judicial review case taken by Italy[188] the ECJ supported the Commission's view that a decision to allow aid subject to conditions could form the basis of a subsequent decision that the aid was incompatible with the Common Market because the Member State had not observed the conditions. The Court rejected the Italian government's arguments that the Commission's decision on incompatibility could only be based on Article 93 itself and not on an earlier decision by the Commission. However, the Commission cannot use a later decision in order to *enforce* a previous decision[189] – it may only take into account the conditions imposed by the previous decision as factors in its evaluation under Article 93(3) EC.

A decision that an aid is incompatible with the Common Market or has been misused will often be accompanied by an order to the recipient of the aid to repay it to the Member State authorities.[190] Such a remedy has been confirmed by the ECJ as proportionate to the aims of the State aids policy in the Treaty.[191] Only where it is objectively impossible to recover the aid will the ECJ not enforce this remedy.[192]

The merger control Regulation

Before the adoption of the merger control Regulation, mergers and takeovers could only be reviewed by the Commission if they constituted potential breaches of Article 85 or 86 EC. As noted above, Article 86 does not penalise the existence of dominance and, therefore, a merger could generally only be reviewed after it had taken place and had produced anti-competitive results.[193] There has been no case law dealing directly with mergers under Article 85[194] but the issue has been raised under Article 86 by the Commission and dealt with by the ECJ. It was confirmed in the *Continental Can* case[195] that Article 86 could be applied to mergers, even without explicitly abusive actions having been done by any of the undertakings participating in the merger. Where an already dominant undertaking merges with a competitor, the mere fact of the merger increases the level of dominance in that market and thereby creates automatically an adverse impact on competition. This is consistent with the general approach to Article 86 EC that conduct which affects the competitive structure of the Single Market may be reviewed. The *Continental Can* judgment, however, provides only a limited power to declare mergers *per se* anti-competitive because it

---

187 Winter, 'Supervision of State Aid: Article 93 in the Court of Justice' (1993) 30 CML Rev 311, at 314.
188 Case C-261/89, *Italy* v *Commission*, 3 October 1991.
189 Case C-294/90, *British Aerospace and Rover* v *Commission*, 4 February 1992. In such cases, according to the ECJ, the Commission must proceed by way of Article 93(2) EC.
190 This power is not directly granted by the Treaty, but was first accepted as valid in Case 70/72, *Commission* v *Germany* [1973] ECR 813.
191 Case C-142/87, *Belgium* v *Commission* [1991] ECR I-959.
192 Case 52/84, *Commission* v *Belgium* [1986] ECR 89.

193 Article 66 ECSC does provide for the review of mergers of undertakings falling within the ambit of that Treaty.
194 The only case which came close to applying Article 85 to mergers was Joined Cases 142 and 156/84, *BAT Ltd and R.J. Reynolds Inc* v *Commission and Philip Morris* [1987] ECR 4487, which dealt with the acquisition of a minority shareholding in another company.
195 *Europemballage and Continental Can* v *Commission*, *op. cit.*, note 82. The Court annulled the Commission's decision on other grounds, namely that the relevant market had not been properly analysed.

only applies to mergers and takeovers involving undertakings who are dominant at the time of the merger. For the most part the Commission was still required to wait until a merged undertaking abused the dominance it acquired as a result of the merger.

Proposals for legislation dealing specifically with mergers have been made since the early 1970s, but only recently have the Member States been able to agree on an approach.[196] Regulation 4064/89/EEC, specifically dealing with mergers, was passed in 1989. Its legal basis is stated as Articles 87 and 235 EC. The merger control Regulation is organised in a peculiar way. It does not deal with the definition of 'concentration', which is crucial to the Regulation and is mentioned in Articles 1 and 2, until Article 3.[197]

Scope of the Regulation

The scope of the Regulation is defined by two Articles. Article 3 defines 'concentration' and Article 1 defines the notion of a concentration with a 'Community dimension'. Both are necessary in order to invoke the Commission's jurisdiction under the Regulation.[198] 'Concentrations' covers both mergers and takeovers:

> (3)1. A concentration shall be deemed to arise where:
>   (a) two or more previously independent undertakings merge, or
>   (b) – one or more persons already controlling at least one undertaking, or
>   – one or more undertakings
>
> acquire, whether by purchase of securities or assets, by contract or by any other means, direct or indirect control of the whole of parts of one or more other undertakings.

The Regulation displays a cautious attitude towards joint ventures. Those which, although involving the co-ordination of competitive behaviour, allow the several undertakings to remain independent, are not concentrations (co-operative joint ventures). However, if they involve a more permanent integration of economic functions, which could be seen as a *de facto* merger, they will constitute concentrations (concentrative joint ventures).[199] In particular, the Commission will examine whether the joint venture is acting independently of the sponsoring undertakings. The autonomy must be 'on a lasting basis', which means that temporary transfers of rights will not meet the autonomy test.[200]

The means by which, under Article 3, control may be acquired over another undertaking, are broadly defined to include both ownership (of shares or assets) and contract. The Commission has itself interpreted the concept of control broadly, including a case where it accepted that the acquisition of a minority shareholding, plus contractual guarantees of influence over management decisions, was sufficient for the new minority shareholder to be in control.[201]

---

[196] See Halvorsen, 'EC Merger Control: Competition Policy or Industrial Policy? Views of a US Practitioner' [1992] 2 LIEI 49, at 61.

[197] However, almost every academic discussion of the Regulation begins with the definition of 'concentration'!

[198] Goyder, in *EC Competition Law*, 2nd edn (1993), at 394–5, identifies both these definitional points as going to jurisdiction.

[199] On the distinction between co-operative and concentrative joint ventures, see the *Commission Notice regarding Concentrative and Co-operative Operations Under Council Regulation 4064/89*, OJ 1990 C203/10.

[200] *Baxter/Nestlé/Salvia*, (IV/M58) OJ 1990 C37/11, [1991] 4 CMLR 245.

[201] *Lyonnaise des Eaux Dumez/Brochier*, (IV/M76) OJ 1991 C188/20.

Only concentrations which have a 'Community dimension' are covered by the Regulation. It had been hoped that Community legislation on mergers would allow for 'one-stop shopping' and remove the anomalies and uncertainties arising from the co-existence of national and Community competition policies. To a certain extent this has been achieved, since mergers within the definition of the Regulation, by virtue of Article 21, need only be approved by the Commission[202] and otherwise need only be approved under national law. However, if two rivals are bidding to take over a company, one from within the same Member State as the target company and one from another Member State, the rival bids will likely be reviewed by different bodies.[203] A Community dimension to a concentration will exist in terms of Article 1(2) of the Regulation under the following circumstances:

(a) the combined aggregate worldwide turnover of all the undertakings concerned is more than ECU 5000 million; and

(b) the aggregate Community-wide turnover of each of at least two of the undertakings is more than ECU 250 million, unless each of the undertakings concerned achieves more than two-thirds of its aggregate Community-wide turnover within one and the same Member State.[204]

The inclusion of a threshold relating to worldwide turnover allows for the review of concentrations involving non-Community undertakings. Some concentrations taking place outside the European Union, but which may affect the Community, will be covered by the Regulation in this way.[205] This is consistent with the extent of extra-territorial application of other competition rules.

Criteria for review

Article 2 of the Regulation defines which concentrations shall be considered incompatible with the Common Market:

1. Concentrations within the scope of this Regulation shall be appraised in accordance with the following provisions with a view to establishing whether or not they are compatible with the common market.

In making this appraisal, the Commission shall take into account:
(a) the need to preserve and develop effective competition from undertakings located either within or without the Community;
(b) the market position of the undertakings concerned and their economic and financial power, the opportunities available to suppliers and users, their access to supplies or markets, any legal or other barriers to entry, supply and demand trends for the intermediate and ultimate consumers, and the development of technical and economic progress provided that it is to consumers' advantage and does not form an obstacle to competition.

---

202 However, Article 21(3) allows Member States to protect legitimate interests other than those dealt with by the Regulation, although these must be consistent with Community law as a whole. The examples given in Article 21(3) are public security, plurality of ownership of media and prudential rules.

203 See the discussion of the Midland Bank takeover in the Introduction to this Chapter.

204 Paragraph 3 of this Article provides that these thresholds will be reviewed after four years.

205 Whish, *op. cit.*, note 1, at 715, questions the appropriateness of this.

2. A concentration which does not create or strengthen a dominant position as a result of which effective competition would be significantly impeded in the common market or in substantial part of it shall be declared compatible with the common market.

3. A concentration which creates or strengthens a dominant position as a result of which effective competition would be significantly impeded in the common market or in a substantial part of it shall be declared incompatible with the common market.

Article 2 uses many phrases and concepts from Articles 85 and 86 EC, with particular emphasis on the concept of dominant position. Unlike Article 86 the merger control Regulation allows the Commission to declare the fact of dominance itself to be anti-competitive. Interestingly, the Commission is obliged, in this context, to take into account the kind of factors which lead to exemptions under Article 85(3). For some Member States the inclusion of these considerations has not gone far enough. The best example of this is the refusal of the Commission to allow the takeover of DeHavilland by Aerospatiale and Alenia.[206] If the takeover had been allowed the resulting entity would have controlled 67 per cent of the Community market in small 'commuter' aircraft. Due to this and other factors, including the practical difficulties for customers to switch suppliers in this field, the Commission decided that the takeover would create a dominant position. As a result of this decision both the French government and the Community Industry Commissioner advocated changes to the merger control procedure which would allow greater weight to industrial policy.[207]

Generally, the analysis undertaken by the Commission under Article 2 most resembles that for Article 86 EC. It must identify the relevant market and then whether dominance is likely to be created or strengthened. One of the preambular recitals of the Regulation indicates that there may be a *de minimis* level of 25 per cent of the Common Market or a substantial share of it before dominance can be declared to exist. The result of the dominance must be the 'impeding' of competition, but it is not yet clear whether this is part of the definition of dominance or a second condition which must be met in order for a concentration to be incompatible with the Common Market.

As with Article 86, the merger control Regulation raises the question of whether collective dominance is within the scope of its prohibition. In the *Nestlé/Perrier* case[208] the Commission decided that the drafting of Article 2(3) did not exclude the possibility of collective dominance being prohibited. The Commission decided that the relevant product market was bottled water. Nestlé owned two major brands and, by acquiring Perrier through a hostile takeover in which Nestlé was supported by the French food company BSN, would control four other brands. BSN owned several brands of bottled water and, after the takeover, Nestlé was to sell Perrier's fifth brand to BSN. The three companies involved controlled a total of 82.3 per cent of the market in France. The Commission decided, on the basis of these facts, that the takeover would lead to a duopolistic dominance in the bottled water market in France, a specific finding of collective dominance.[209] It issued a statement of objections and

206 (IV/M53) OJ 1991 L334/42.
207 See Halvorsen, *op. cit.*, note 196, at 64–5. He notes that the list of factors that the Commission must consider does not appear to be exhaustive, which means that it could decide to take industrial policy into account.
208 (IV/M190) OJ 1992 L356/1.

209 Winckler and Hansen, 'Collective Dominance Under the EC Merger Control Regulation' (1993) 30 CML Rev 787, at 812–13, list the factors which the Commission relied on in its finding. In this article they also analyse the significance of these factors and their likely implications.

decided to allow the takeover after Nestlé agreed to divest itself of some of its holdings in this field, including some of the bottled water brands it then owned. Nestlé also agreed, at the Commission's insistence, to undertake not to disseminate its market information.[210] The implication by the Commission that collective dominance was established if collusion would be made more likely or easier by the concentration suggests a less strict test than established in the *Italian Flat Glass* case under Article 86 EC.[211]

Relation to other Community competition rules

Article 22(2) of the Regulation excludes the application of Regulation 17/62/EEC, which means that the Commission cannot undertake a review under the merger control Regulation and an investigation under Article 85 or 86 EC as well. However, these provisions could be raised, to the extent that they create direct effects in national law, in any proceedings concerning merger control under national law. The Commission could possibly use Articles 85 and 86 indirectly through its general power to investigate anti-competitive behaviour in Article 89 EC, which is not affected by the Regulation. This would be relevant where a proposed concentration did not meet the thresholds for a Community dimension.

Procedures

The remainder of the Regulation deals with procedural issues. The Commission is given wide investigative powers, similar to those granted under Regulation 17/62/EEC. Like State aids, proposed Community-dimension mergers are to be notified to the Commission.[212] Parties which fail to notify within the specified period, one week after an agreement or bid is made, can be fined under Article 14. A Member State may request that the Commission act, or allow its national authorities to act, where a proposed concentration having a Community dimension creates serious competition problems for a national market.[213] A Member State may also request a Commission investigation where the proposed concentration does not have a Community dimension if the concentration would significantly impede competition within the Member State.[214] The Commission publishes a list of notifications which it considers are covered by the Regulation in the *Official Journal*. Between the triggering event and notification, and for three weeks afterwards, the parties must suspend all activity directed towards the completion or implementation of the transaction, but this can be suspended by the Commission if the suspension would cause serious damage to a party to the transaction or to a third party.[215] As is apparent from the short period of suspension, the Commission must examine the notification immediately and come to a decision within a month of the day following notification. The Commission may, at this stage, declare a proposed concentration compatible or incompatible with the Common Market. If, however, the Commission considers that the concentration raises serious doubts as to its compatibility with the Common Market, then it will commence proceedings for a full investigation by sending the parties a statement of objections. This is done in a small number of cases. Most

---

210 Winckler and Hansen, *ibid.*, at 815, consider that this measure was intended to prevent collusion.
211 *Ibid.*, at 816–17 and 828.
212 Article 4(1).

213 Article 9. The Commission has generally not acceded to such requests.
214 Article 22(3).
215 Article 7.

are dealt with, if they raise doubts, by undertakings given to the Commission by the parties at the initial stage of examination.

After sending the parties a statement of objections, the Commission will come to its final decision within four months. Article 8 of the Regulation sets out the possible decisions which the Commission may reach at this second stage:

- that, following modifications, the concentration will be compatible with the common market; this decision can be revoked if the undertakings given by the parties are not observed, or if the Commission discovers facts which shed new light on the matter;
- that the concentration is incompatible with the common market;
- that, in order to ensure fair competition, a concentration which has already been implemented must be reversed.

In the second possible type of decision the Commission 'shall also cover restrictions directly related and necessary to the implementation of the concentration'.[216] This requires the Commission to identify those terms which, although restrictive of competition, are necessary for the implementation of a concentration which is generally not anti-competitive. For guidance the Commission has issued a *Notice on Ancillary Restraints*.[217]

The ECJ has the power to review any challenged decisions made under the Regulation.[218]

CONCLUSION

Competition policy is one of the most developed areas of Community law. It has generated a large amount of case law and a significant amount of secondary legislation. Ironically, it is the policy area in which the courts have been least clear on the policy issues which they are pursuing. A number of goals have been cited: the assurance of a model of 'normal' or perfect competition, the use of competition policy to ensure the completion of the Single Market and the protection of consumers and the protection of legitimate industrial policy.[219] The first two goals arise primarily out of the Commission and court findings of violation of competition rules and the latter primarily, although not exclusively, from the findings of exception or justification. However, on a theoretical basis it would appear difficult to reconcile the first two goals with the last two, at least within free market competition theories. The free market libertarian argument for competition policy is that it is as wrong for private actors to distort the market as it is for States to do so. The Commission and the courts, by the use of similar language in competition cases and free movement of goods cases, seem to have adopted this type of underlying theory. However, the ECJ has also used consumer protection language in justifying the rules against abuse of a dominant position, which would seem to draw from a more social market-based theory. Furthermore, the Treaty itself, as well as the interpretations of it, have brought in non-free market considerations such as innovation and protection of employment to justify *prima facie* violations of Articles 85 and 92.

The Commission and the courts have developed a strong body of case law under the competition rules and judgments are largely consistent with each other. However, there seems

---

216 Article 8(2).
217 OJ 1990 C203/5.
218 Articles 16 and 21.

219 On the uneasy relationship of competition policy to industrial policy, see Halvorsen, *op. cit.*, note 196.

to be no single underlying theory of competition in this case law, and the relationship of competition policy to other areas of economic policy, such as regional development, has not yet been clearly defined. Probably the Commission is better situated than the courts to develop this theoretical base, but in the past there seems to have been no great pressure to do so. As regional development policy and job creation[220] become concerns of Community policy-makers, the need to understand this relationship may become more pressing.

Further reading

Goyder, D., *EC Competition Law*, 2nd edn (Oxford: OUP, 1993).

Green, N., Hartley T.C. and Usher J., *The Legal Foundations of the Single European Market* (Oxford: OUP, 1991), at Chapters 14–21.

Halvorsen, J.T., 'EC Merger Control: Competition Policy or Industrial Policy? Views of a US Practitioner' [1992] 2 LIEI 49.

Korah, V., 'Concept of a Dominant Position within the Meaning of Article 86' (1980) 17 CML Rev 395.

Schechter, M.C., 'The Rule of Reason in European Competition Law' [1982] 2 LIEI 1.

Whish, R., *Competition Law*, 3rd edn (London: Butterworths, 1993).

Whish R., and Sufrin, B., 'Article 85 and the Rule of Reason' (1987) YEL 1.

Winckler A., and Hansen, M., 'Collective Dominance Under the EC Merger Control Regulation' (1993) 30 CML Rev 787.

Winter, J.A., 'Supervision of State Aid: Article 93 in the Court of Justice' (1993) 30 CML Rev 311.

---

220 See Conclusion to Chapter 17.

CHAPTER 14

Intellectual property

INTRODUCTION

This Chapter will examine the development of Community rules relating to intellectual property, especially the draft directives on copyright, and look at how Community rules fit into the framework of national and international intellectual property protection. It will also note the problems, currently faced by all jurisdictions, in placing modern technology, especially computer software, within current modes of intellectual property protection and evaluate how effectively the EC has managed to tackle this problem.

Intellectual property rights are an essential tool of business, giving rights over inventions, works of art, music or literature and even the name and logo of a business. These rights, however, are always a form of monopoly which potentially creates problems for the creation of a Single Market. The main forms of intellectual property rights which the ECJ has dealt with, and which the Community has legislated on, are the following:[1]

Patent: an exclusive right to exploit an invention for a product or a process. This right allows the owner to prevent the production of any invention which copies the principles of the invention, not only exact copies. Registration is required.

Copyright: an exclusive right to make copies of a literary, dramatic, artistic or musical work, or any derivative work (such as sound recordings or films). This right allows the owner to prevent any substantial copy of the *expression* of the copyright work. Registration is not required; the right arises as soon as the work is fixed to a medium such as paper, recording tape or film.

Trade mark: any mark, whether a word or symbol, which designates products or services coming from a single source. The owner may prevent the use of any mark which is sufficiently similar so as to cause confusion between the owner's mark and the competitor's mark. Registration is required.

Design rights: an exclusive right to make articles to a particular functional design or to affix a particular decorative design to an article. Some designs must be registered, some arise from the fixation of the design to an article.

Plant breeders' rights: a right, analogous to patent, over new species of plants. Registration is required.

There are several international Treaties which have harmonised the basic features of many intellectual property rights and provide for reciprocal recognition of some rights such as copyright. Some aspects of the rights are not internationally harmonised, however, and some Member States are not party to every convention.

---

1 For a more complete discussion of intellectual property rights, see Bainbridge, *Intellectual Property,* 2nd edn. (1994) or Phillips and Firth, *Introduction to Intellectual Property Law*, 2nd edn (1990).

It would appear, from an initial reading of the EC Treaty, that intellectual property rights, sometimes also called industrial property, are not within the scope of Community law. Article 222 EC specifically states that 'This Treaty shall in no way prejudice the rules in the Member States governing the system of property ownership'. A further indication that intellectual property rights are left intact by Community law lies in Article 36 EC, which lists industrial property rights amongst the grounds for exclusion or restriction of goods which will not violate the prohibition on quantitative restrictions or measures having equivalent effect. However, this has not turned out to be the case. The ECJ has developed a more subtle and complex system of rules on when intellectual property rights will infringe not only the rules on free movement of goods but also the competition rules. The primary basis on which these rules have been developed is a distinction between the *existence* of intellectual property rights, and their *exercise*. Community law, according to the case law of the ECJ, may not interfere with the existence of intellectual property rights but may prohibit certain forms of exercise of these rights where they are used to circumvent Single Market freedoms. This distinction was first developed in competition law cases, where no guarantee of intellectual property rights equivalent to Article 36 EC exists. It has, nonetheless, been extended to free movement of goods cases in defining the extent of the protection for intellectual property rights in Article 36 EC. Applying the existence/exercise dichotomy has not always been easy for the ECJ and has resulted in the only case to date where the ECJ has explicitly overruled one of its previous decisions. The perceived uncertainties in the ECJ's handling of intellectual property cases caused the UK courts to avoid referring cases to the ECJ where it seemed possible that the application of Community competition rules might restrict national intellectual property rights.[2]

However, this partial judicial harmonisation of intellectual property rights has left intact many differences between intellectual property rights between the Member States. In addition, the fact that certain rights, such as trade marks, must be registered in each Member State leads to extra costs of doing business throughout the Single Market, as opposed to in a single Member State. As a result, the Community has adopted several measures directed at harmonising intellectual property rights and, where possible, to the creation of a single registration giving rights throughout the Community.

The effect of Community law on national intellectual property rights

The efforts of the ECJ to prevent the use or abuse of intellectual property rights in order to defeat the purposes of the Single Market could be said to have resulted in a partial harmonisation of these rights. Intellectual property rights, such as copyright, fall within the scope of application of the EC Treaty, which means that national intellectual property laws must provide equal treatment for all Community nationals, even where no international intellectual property Treaty requires reciprocal recognition of rights.[3] The ECJ has decided that certain elements of the rights which could undermine free movement of goods or free competition must be declared invalid. The law of the Member States has been harmonised insofar as these elements have been eliminated. The basic rule that results from the case law is that a business has the right to use intellectual property rights to control how its products

---

2 Arnull, 'Article 177 and the Retreat from *Van Duyn*' (1983) 8 EL Rev 365.

3 Joined Cases C-92 and C-326/92, *Collins* v *Imtrat Handelsgesellschaft mbH*, 20 October 1993.

are put onto the market, for example by prohibiting unauthorised copying of its products. However, the business may not use intellectual property rights to control its goods once they have been put on the market, for example to prevent resale.

Intellectual property rights and Community competition policy

Most of the cases on the conformity of intellectual property rights with Community competition policy deal with Article 85 rather than Article 86 EC. Licencing of intellectual property has been seen as a potential distortion of competition, because it can be used to reinforce distributorship agreements which could partition the market. Some writers have questioned whether the Commission's emphasis on intellectual property licences has been wise, given that such licences are often between non-competitors and are often the easiest way of developing an invention.[4] This may be a legitimate question concerning patents and plant breeders' rights and, possibly copyright, but in the case of trade marks the Commission's concern may be justified. Trade marks can be used in order to prevent competition between distributors in different Member States and thereby to prevent parallel imports. There is, furthermore, evidence that the Commission and the ECJ are sensitive to the needs of businesses developing new inventions. The Community has passed block exemptions on patent and know-how agreements,[5] and the ECJ has developed a more lenient approach to new technology.[6]

The dichotomy between the existence of intellectual property rights and their exercise was first developed in competition law cases. This is not surprising since the EC Treaty contains no provisions relating to intellectual property rights as they relate to fair competition. This emerges from one of the first major cases on competition law, *Consten and Grundig* v *Commission*.[7] In addition to the sole distributorship element of the challenged contract, the contract provided that Consten would register the 'GRUNDIG' trade mark in France, which would allow it to oppose the use of the trade mark by anyone else within France. The applicants tried to rely on Articles 36 and 222 EC, but the ECJ confirmed that Article 36 could not be applied to competition law. Using trade mark rights in order to prevent parallel imports was a violation of Article 85 EC and went to the exercise of intellectual property rights rather than their existence. The ECJ was concerned to prevent the use of intellectual property rights as a means of fragmenting the Single Market into several national markets. The distinction between existence and exercise was explained in greater detail in *Parke, Davis* v *Centrafarm*:[8]

1. The existence of rights granted by a Member State to a holder of a patent is not affected by the prohibitions contained in Articles 85(1) and 86 of the Treaty.
2. The exercise of such rights cannot of itself fall either under Article 85(1), in the

4 Green, Hartley and Usher, *The Legal Foundations of the Single European Market* (Oxford: OUP, 1991), at 247–8.
5 Regulation 2349/84/EEC (patent licences) and Regulation 556/89/EEC (know-how licences). The latter is discussed in Odle and Zeyen, 'The EC Block Exemption Regulation 556/89 on Know-how: Practical Difficulties and Legal Uncertainties' (1991) ECLR 231. The pre-

regulation situation on know-how licences is discussed in Corones, 'The European Commission's Approach to Know-how Licencing: A Critical Commentary' (1984) 33 ICLQ 181.
6 See Case 258/78, *Nungesser* v *Commision* [1982] ECR 2015 discussed below.
7 Joined Cases 56 and 58/64, [1966] ECR 299.
8 Case 24/67, [1968] ECR 55.

absence of any agreement, decision or concerted practice prohibited by this provision, or under Article 86, in the absence of any abuse of a dominant position.

3. A higher sale price for the patented product as compared with that of the unpatented product coming from another Member State does not necessarily constitute an abuse.

The ECJ has, in more recent cases, developed a more nuanced approach to the existence of intellectual property rights. In matters other than trade mark, the ownership of intellectual property is not a single right but a collection of related rights. This is particularly true of copyright. In *Coditel* v *Ciné-Vog (No 2)*,[9] the copyright owner in a film granted to one company the right to show the film in Belgian cinemas and to another the right to broadcast the film on German television. When the film was broadcast on German television, Coditel picked up the broadcast and relayed it to its cable television subscribers in Belgium, without the permission of the copyright owner. Coditel argued unsuccessfully that the right had been exhausted by the broadcast in Germany[10] and then argued that the licensing scheme which granted exclusive licences in each of the Member States infringed Article 85(1) EC. The ECJ agreed that it was possible for such a system of licences to be anti-competitive, but that it was necessary to look at the specific characteristics of an industry and its markets. In the situation of the exploitation of films the copyright owner must be allowed to exploit all the elements of copyright and anyone alleging otherwise must establish that the licensing system distorts or prevents competition. The Commission has also refined its approach to intellectual property rights. In a 1990 decision the Commission reviewed a clause obliging the licensee not to challenge the licensor's trade marks.[11] The Commission decided that prohibiting challenge of the ownership of the mark was a legitimate matter for regulation by agreement between the parties, but that an agreement not to challenge the validity of the trade mark could be anti-competitive because an invalid trade mark would fall into the public domain and, therefore, the preservation of an invalid mark could constitute a barrier to trade.

The ECJ has also recognised the necessity of strong intellectual property rights in research and development of new products. In *Nungesser* v *Commission*[12] it developed the 'new technology doctrine' which requires a more lenient approach than the Commission takes normally. The agreement being scrutinised under Article 85 involved the testing of a new breed of maize. The contractor was granted an exclusive licence to use and market the maize in Germany. The licence, by virtue of a grant of plant breeder's rights, excluded even the developer of the maize, as well as its assignees and licensees, from competing with the company which agreed to test and market the maize. The ECJ agreed with the Commission that absolute territorial protection of the marketer's territory was anti-competitive and could not be justified as promotion of technical progress under Article 85(3) EC. However, it did overturn the Commission's decision that the fact of granting an exclusive licence through the assignment of plant breeder's rights was itself anti-competitive in the circumstances. An open exclusive licence, one which does not attempt to prohibit parallel imports but only promises that no other licences will be granted for the territory and that the licensor will not directly compete with the licensee, is acceptable in circumstances where new technology is being

9 Case 262/81, [1982] ECR 338.

10 Case 62/79, *Coditel* v *Ciné-Vog (No 1)* [1980] ECR 881, argument based on freedom to provide services throughout the Single Market as set out in Article 59 EC.

11 Decision 90/186, OJ 1990 L100/32.

12 Case 258/78, [1982] ECR 2015.

developed. Otherwise, the ECJ accepted, businesses would be unwilling to take the risks associated with the development of new technology:

> The exclusive licence which forms the subject-matter of the contested decision concerns the cultivation and marketing of hybrid maize seeds which were developed by INRA after years of research and experimentation and were unknown to German farmers at the time when the co-operation between INRA and the applicants was taking shape. For that reason the concern shown by the interveners as regards the protection of new technology is justified.
>
> In fact, in the case of a licence of breeders' rights over hybrid maize seeds newly developed in one Member State, an undertaking established in another Member State which was not certain that it would not encounter competition from other licensees for the territory granted to it, or from the owner of the right himself, might be deterred from accepting the risk of cultivating and marketing that product; such a result would be damaging to the dissemination of a new technology and would prejudice competition in the Community between the new product and similar existing products.[13]

Issues of intellectual property in relation to abuse of a dominant position have a shorter history in ECJ case law. This is, perhaps surprising, given that Article 86 EC is intended to prohibit anti-competitive monopolies, and all intellectual property rights give the owner a form of monopoly. However, probably because a monopoly over a single work of copyright or patent, or even a single trade mark, is unlikely to create dominance over a substantial part of the Single Market, the issue arises more frequently from the manipulation of intellectual property licences rather than from the simple use of an intellectual property right. The ECJ has itself put forward this view: the ordinary use of intellectual property rights is not itself an abuse. Some additional factor, such as refusal to supply or price fixing, must be present.[14] An abuse of intellectual property rights, therefore, is more likely to occur where the undertaking exploits many rights. The best example of this situation is a performing rights organisation. Such organisations are given the authority, under national statute, to take assignments of rights in copyright works, usually musical works, and to exploit and enforce the copyrights. These organisations then pay royalties to the musicians who assign rights to them. A performing rights organisation is better able to police infringements of musical copyright than individual musicians, so they are seen as providing a benefit to the original copyright owners. However, they do control a large number of copyrights and are often given certain policing powers under national statute. As a result, the potential for abuse of a dominant position arises. In *Re GEMA*[15] the Commission objected to the practice of the German performing rights organisation of requiring musicians to assign all rights in all present and future works, although the assignment of present and future works for a particular category of exploitation was seen as less problematic if it was necessary for the efficient exploitation of those rights.

Recently, the Court of First Instance has clarified the basis upon which the use of intellectual property rights could constitute an abuse of dominant position. In *BBC v Commission*[16] the BBC (as well as ITV and RTE, in separate cases) were accused of using their copyrights in television and radio listings in order to prevent competition to their own publications of those listings. The Court found, at least in this case, that copyright represented control over information and that information could be a product over which dominance could be exercised. The copyright over the listings information meant that any

---

13 *Ibid.,* at paragraphs 56–7.
14 Case 53/87, *CICRA v Renault* [1988] ECR 6039.

15 [1971] CMLR D35.
16 Case T-70/89, [1991] 4 CMLR 669.

potential competitors were dependent on the BBC in order to engage in competition, indicating that it was dominant over this information. Therefore, the refusal to supply this information constituted an abuse within the meaning of Article 86 EC.

Intellectual property rights and free movement of goods

The ECJ recognised at an early stage of the development of the case law on free movement of goods that unharmonised intellectual property rights could create barriers to intra-Community trade.[17] However, most cases dealing with the issue of whether intellectual property rights are being used in conformity with the rules on free movement of goods focus on Article 36 EC, which allows for the protection of intellectual property rights as an exception to the prohibition on quantitative restrictions and measures having equivalent effect. Rarely has the ECJ explained why use of intellectual property rights can interfere with free movement of goods in the first place.[18] In *Musik-Vertrieb Membran GmbH v GEMA*,[19] however, the ECJ did set out how intellectual property rights could operate as measures having an equivalent effect to quantitative restrictions:

> no provision of national legislation may permit an undertaking which is responsible for the management of copyrights and has a monopoly on the territory of a member-State by virtue of that management to charge a levy on products imported from another member-State where they were put into circulation by or with the consent of the copyright owner and thereby cause the Common Market to be partitioned. Such a practice would amount to allowing a private undertaking to impose a charge on the importation of sound recordings which are already in free circulation in the Common Market on account of their crossing a frontier; it would therefore have the effect of entrenching the isolation of national markets which the Treaty seeks to abolish.[20]

The intellectual property owner, therefore, has the right to produce and market goods subject to the right, but cannot use the right to prevent those goods from circulating throughout the Community. The right is considered to be exhausted once goods subject to the intellectual property right are put on the market.

This distinction between the existence of an intellectual property right, and its exercise, was first applied to Article 36 EC in *Deutsche Grammophon GmbH v Metro-SB-Grossmarkte GmbH*.[21] Deutsche Grammophon supplied its musical recordings directly to retailers in Germany, as well as to two wholesalers. All recordings marked with the 'POLYDOR' trade mark were subject to resale price maintenance and retailers signed agreements agreeing to the pricing scheme, even for recordings supplied by the wholesalers rather than Deutsche Grammophon itself. Metro purchased 'POLYDOR' recordings from Deutsche Grammophon but did not observe the pricing scheme. Deutsche Grammophon broke off business relations with Metro, which then obtained 'POLYDOR' recordings from a wholesaler. These recordings had been supplied to Deutsche Grammophon's French subsidiary and returned to the German wholesaler via Strasbourg, which raised the Community dimension. Deutsche Grammophon then tried to stop Metro from selling the

---

17 *Parke, Davis* v *Centrafarm, op. cit.,* note 8.
18 Marenco and Banks, 'Intellectual Property and the Community Rules on Free Movement: Discrimination Unearthed' (1990) 15 EL Rev 224.

19 Joined Cases 55 and 57/80, [1981] ECR 147.
20 *Ibid.,* at paragraph 18.
21 Case 78/70, [1971] ECR 487.

recordings by alleging copyright infringement.[22] Deutsche Grammophon argued that the exception for industrial property rights in Article 36 EC allowed it to use the copyright in its recordings to regulate the movement of its recordings. The ECJ applied the existence/exercise distinction to Article 36 EC and added that the exception in that Article applied to the 'specific subject-matter of the right' or that which makes copyright works different from other goods. This concept is applied only to Article 36 intellectual property cases to explain how certain uses of intellectual property violate free movement of goods principles, yet the exception protecting intellectual property rights is preserved. The 'specific subject-matter of the right' will be defined with reference to national intellectual property rights, in the absence of Community harmonisation.[23] The notion of 'specific subject-matter' will prevent someone from making an unauthorised copy but not from dealing with copies already on the market.[24] For example, in patent law the 'specific subject-matter' consists of the exclusive right to use an invention with a view to manufacturing industrial products and putting them into circulation for the first time, either directly or through licensees, as well as the right to prevent infringement.[25]

This basic rule does not, however, deal with all the potential issues arising out of the use of intellectual property rights. The idea that goods subject to the intellectual property right must be marketed with the owner's consent raises problems with rights which may be subject to compulsory licence.[26] The right owner has not consented to the marketing of the goods but has been paid a royalty by the licensee. It is not analogous to an infringement, where the right owner is receiving no economic benefit from the marketing of the copied goods. Community law has not been consistent on this point, reflecting, perhaps, the difficulties which this issue raises. In *GEMA* the Commission found that the right was exhausted despite the fact that the recordings were made under compulsory licence without the consent of the copyright owner.[27] However, in *Pharmon BV v Hoechst AG* the ECJ found that a compulsory licence does not exhaust the existence of the intellectual property right as protected by Article 36 EC, at least for the purposes of allowing the patent owner in one Member State to prevent the importation of products produced under a compulsory licence in another Member State.[28] The patent owner, according to the ECJ, could not be seen as having put the goods voluntarily on the market, whether personally or through a licensee chosen by it. Of the two cases, *Pharmon* probably represents the better view in that the issue of compulsory licence was not explicitly dealt with in the Commission's decision in *GEMA*, whereas it constituted the main justification of the decision in *Pharmon*. In recent cases on

---

22 Until this case, under most copyright laws dealing in copies of a copyright work without the permission of the owner amounted to a secondary infringement. Most copyright statutes have been amended in conformity with Community law, for example s 18 of the Copyright, Designs and Patents Act 1988 (UK).
23 Case 144/81, *Keurkoop* v *Nancy Kean Gifts* [1983] ECR 2853. Marenco and Banks, *op. cit.,* note 18, at 237 see the issue of 'specific subject-matter' as a way for the ECJ to question whether national law allows the intellectual property right owner to discriminate against other Community-produced goods, contrary to Article 30 EC. They conclude that the ECJ is only willing to limit rights granted by national law where they will affect imports.
24 *Ibid.* See also *CICRA* v *Renault, op. cit.,* note 14

where the ECJ agreed that Renault could use its design rights in automobile body parts in order to prevent CICRA from manufacturing them in Italy and marketing them in other Member States without Renault's consent.
25 Case 434/85, *Allen & Hanbury's Ltd* v *Generics (UK) Ltd* [1988] ECR 1245.
26 A compulsory licence allows someone other than the owner of a patent to exploit the patent if they can establish that the owner is not properly exploiting the invention. This regime is intended to prevent patent owners from suppressing inventions which are in the public interest. In some countries, other types of intellectual property right may also be subject to compulsory licence.
27 *Op. cit.,* note 16.
28 Case 19/84, [1985] 3 CMLR 266.

compulsory licencing the ECJ has decided that the rules concerning compulsory licenses go to the existence rather than the exercise of the right, but that the Member State may not apply those rules in such a way as to constitute discrimination prohibited by the rules on free movement of goods.[29]

A further question is to what extent the rights arising from intellectual property ownership are exhausted by the marketing of goods subject to the right. For example, copyright in films may be exploited by performance, sale or rental. A copyright owner selling copies of a film may only be deemed to be granting a licence for one purpose. In *Warner Brothers* v *Christiansen*[30] the applicants had sold videotapes of films in the UK over which they held copyright. Christiansen purchased a Warner Brothers videotape in the UK and then rented it from his shop in Denmark. The ECJ agreed with Warner Brothers that selling a videotape of a film did not exhaust the rental right in that film, which Warner Brothers was entitled to reserve. Each separate aspect of the 'specific subject-matter' of an intellectual property right may be exhausted separately.

Particular problems arise in the case of trade marked goods. The purpose of trade marking is to protect business goodwill by ensuring that a word or symbol designates one source of goods only. However, it would be very easy for businesses to partition the Single Market by using different trade marks in each country. This circumstance could arise even in the absence of intention to circumvent Community law – the different languages used in Member States may require the use of different names for a product, depending on the country in which it is to be sold. A different trade mark may be added by a distributor in another Member State. The ECJ has allowed the repackaging of trade marked goods in circumstances whereby the original trade mark was still visible and the packaging indicated the names both of the manufacturer and the distributor.[31]

The opposite problem arises where businesses in different Member States are using the same trade mark. If the trade marks have independent origins, meaning that the two businesses have been using the trade marks in their own Member States and there is no reason to believe that one is trying to take advantage of the other's name and reputation, then each may rely on their national law to prevent the other from using the trade mark in each other's Member State.[32] The ECJ sees this as a matter of protecting the existence of the trade mark, since it is the nature of this right that a trade mark should designate goods from a single source. This is the type of situation which the exception in Article 36 EC was intended to address. However, the matter is less clear where the two trade marks, although independently used, are from a common source. The ECJ required two attempts at the same case in order to sort out this issue.

The cases involved the trade mark 'HAG' for decaffeinated coffee. The trade mark was originally registered by HAG GF AG in Germany in 1907, and in Belgium and Luxembourg in 1908. In 1927 HAG AG set up a subsidiary in Belgium and in 1935 transferred the Belgian and Luxembourg trade mark rights to the subsidiary. In 1944 the subsidiary was sequestered as enemy property and sold to a Belgian company. In 1971 the Belgian and Luxembourg trade marks were assigned to Van Zuylen Frères. In 1972 HAG AG began

---

[29] Joined Cases C-235/89 and C-30/90, *Commission* v *Italy; Commission* v *UK* [1992] 2 CMLR 709, and Case C-191/90, *Generics (UK) Limited* v *Smith, Kline and French Laboratories Limited* [1993] 1 CMLR 89.

[30] Case 158/86, [1988] ECR 2605.

[31] Case 1/81, *Pfizer Inc* v *Eurim-Pharm* [1981] ECR 2913.

[32] Case 119/75, *Terrapin* v *Terranova* [1976] ECR 1039.

exporting coffee to Luxembourg and Van Zuylen sued HAG AG, where a reference was sought from the ECJ.[33] The ECJ found in favour of HAG AG, stating that to prohibit free movement goods marked with a trade mark from the same origin would be incompatible with the Single Market. This meant that neither company could prevent the other from marketing in its territory, which potentially could undermine their trade mark rights, if two companies were using the same trade mark. This distinction between the approach to trade marks with a common origin and independent origins remained until 1990. However, in the intervening years the ECJ dealt with a case of common origin of trade marks where one of the parties was a non-EC company and decided that the trade mark owner, since it owned the trade mark throughout the EC, could oppose the use of the trade mark by the non-EC owner.[34] The so-called 'common origin doctrine' was therefore limited to trade marks with a common origin where the owners of the separate marks were both or all in the Community. The rule was widely criticised,[35] but the ECJ did not reconsider its position until the 'HAG' trade mark was once again brought before it. In 1979 Van Zuylen was purchased by a Swiss company which set up SA CNL-Sucal NV to market the coffee in Belgium. Sucal began to market the coffee in Germany and HAG AG sued Sucal. Once again the case was referred to the ECJ, which explicitly overruled its previous decision (the only instance where it has done so).[36] In this case the ECJ considered the nature of trade mark rights more carefully than in the first HAG case. The purpose of trade marks is to designate a single origin of goods and thereby to avoid confusion in the minds of consumers, for whom it functions as a guarantee of origin. Furthermore, the system of trade marks is designed to prevent unfair competition, in that a business may not take advantage of the goodwill built up by another business. The existence of trade mark rights means the right to use the mark for the first marketing of the trade marked goods. Whether or not the origin of two similar trade marks is common or independent:

> the decisive fact is the absence of any element of consent, on the part of the owner of the trade mark right protected by national legislation, to the marketing in another member-State, under a mark which is identical or may cause confusion, of similar product manufactured and marketed by an enterprise which has no tie of legal or economic dependence with that owner.[37]

As a result, the owner must be able to prevent the use of a mark which is likely to cause confusion amongst consumers and potentially undermine the trade mark.

Since the ECJ has been concerned to guarantee the existence of intellectual property rights, and since the possibility exists of inadvertent partitioning of the Single Market due to good faith use of similar trade marks in different Member States, the Commission began to concern itself with the possibility of harmonising various intellectual property rights. Such harmonisation would not prevent situations such as that of the 'HAG' trade mark for existing rights but could prevent future conflicts over independent concurrent use.

33 Case 192/73, *Van Zuylen Frères v HAG AG* [1974] ECR 731.
34 Case 51/75, *EMI Records Limited v CBS United Kingdom Limited* [1976] ECR 811.
35 Oliver, 'Of Split Trade Marks and Common Markets' (1991) 54 MLR 587. In the second HAG case Advocate General Jacobs criticised the common origin doctrine as being based on fallacious logic.
36 Case C-10/89, *SA CNL-Sucal NV v HAG GF AG* [1990] ECR 3711.
37 *Ibid.*, at paragraph 15.

The Community Patent Convention

At present, there is no patent right which is automatically valid throughout the Community. An applicant for a patent may, at his or her option, decide to obtain a patent from the European Patent Office rather than the UK Patent Office, but the European Patent Convention system is a Treaty regime which has nothing to do with the Community. All Member States of the Community, except Ireland and Portugal, are States Parties to the Convention on the Grant of European Patents of 1973, which began operating in 1978.[38] The applicant for a patent at the European Patent Office may designate any or all of the States Parties to the European Patent Convention as States in which the patent is to apply.[39] A Convention for a Community Patent[40] opened for signature in 1975 but has never come into force. In 1989 the Convention was amended and procedural aspects were added.[41] However, it appears that the amended convention is no more likely to come into operation than the original one. At an intergovernmental conference in 1992 a compromise solution was put forward by Portugal, then holder of the EC Presidency, which gained the support of all the EC governments except Spain. However, since this point no further progress has been made and Spain continues to make ratification of the Convention subject to the basing of the Community Trade Mark Office in Madrid. If the Community Patent system is finally created it would not end immediately the European Patent Convention system because there are several non-Community European States who are parties to the European Patent Convention. Perhaps, with the enlargement of the Community, the pressure for the unification of patent law will become more acute, the Community Patent will finally come into existence and the European Patent, and possibly national patents, will be replaced.

HARMONISATION OF INTELLECTUAL PROPERTY RIGHTS

In recent years there has been a clear intent on the part of the Commission to speed up the harmonisation of intellectual property rights within the Community. In the light of the case law mentioned above it is fairly obvious why this policy has come about. The issues raised by the variations between the Member States' intellectual property laws have serious implications for the development and interpretation of both Community competition law and the principle of free movement of goods.[42] Variations from the Community legal order caused by national differences in the various intellectual property rights may lead to confusion amongst traders and discrepancies in the Common Market. The Commission has, thus, embarked on a number of measures designed to harmonise the major intellectual property rights and, in doing so, has created some new or *sui generis* rights to deal with issues previously not easily dealt with under the existing rights. The Commission is also, in areas such as software protection, database protection and the regulation of intellectual property rights in relation to satellite broadcasting, attempting to address issues of modern technology

---

[38] Groves et al., *Intellectual Property and the Internal Market of the European Community* (1993), at 16.
[39] *Ibid.*, at 20.
[40] OJ 1976 L17/1. For the history, see Groves et al., *ibid.*, at 36. Ireland and Denmark have not ratified this convention.

[41] OJ 1990 L401/1.
[42] See, for example, the Preamble to Directive 92/100/EEC on rental rights and lending rights and on certain rights related to copyright in the field of intellectual property, OJ 1992 346.

in a manner which suggests that it intends to try to lead the way in the development of any international intellectual property regulation in these areas.

The Trademarks Directive

The First Council Directive 89/109/EEC to Approximate the Laws of the Member States Relating to Trademarks[43] has as its main purpose the harmonisation of national laws which appear most likely to hamper the free movement of goods. As such, it does not attempt a complete harmonisation of national laws and, therefore, national trade marks laws, with their attendant problems for Community trade, remain in place. It has been proposed to create a Community-based system of trade marks, but the Regulation to put that system in place has yet to be agreed.[44] The disagreements over the Regulation[45] have, in turn, led to delays in the implementation of the Directive.[46]

The Directive applies to all registered marks of the Member States concerning products and services including individual, collective and guarantee marks, and lists the reasons that may be given by Member States for refusal. Some of these reasons are optional, those which are not include where the trade mark consists solely of signs, is devoid of any distinctive character, consists solely of the shape of goods determined by the 'nature of the goods themselves', or is a shape 'necessary to obtain a technical result' or 'which gives substantial value to the goods', includes signs liable to mislead the public, is contrary to public order or to accepted principles of morality, or is granted when the goods to which they apply have already been marketed in another Member State under other trade marks by the proprietor or with his consent.[47]

The Directive states that a trade mark can take the form of 'any sign capable of being represented graphically, particularly words including personal names, designs, letters, numerals, the shape of goods or of their packaging, provided that such signs are capable of distinguishing the goods or services of one undertaking from those of other undertakings'.[48]

It also lists the rights of the proprietor of a trade mark, who has an exclusive right to prevent others from using, without his permission, a sign which, due to its similarity to his, might cause confusion on the part of the public.[49] A trade mark may be licensed in part or whole of the Member State concerned, and the licence may be exclusive or non-exclusive.[50] The trade mark owner must make use of his trade mark as failure to do this may result in the trade mark being revoked if it is not used over a continuous period of five years in the Member State concerned.[51]

43 OJ 1989 L40.
44 Proposed Community Trade Mark Regulation, OJ 1980 C351, amended by OJ 1984 C230, re-amended by COM(92) 443.
45 Concerned with the siting of the proposed Community Trade Mark Office.
46 Other regulations in this area are Regulation 3842/86/EEC Laying Down Measures to Discourage the Release for Free Circulation of Counterfeit Goods, OJ 1986 L357 and Regulation 3077/87/EEC Laying Down

Provisions for the Implementation of Regulation 3842/86/EEC Laying Down Measures to Prohibit the Release for Free Circulation of Counterfeit Goods OJ 1987 L291.
47 Article 3.
48 Article 2.
49 Article 5(1).
50 Article 8.
51 Article 12.

The Trademarks Regulation

The purpose of the proposed Regulation is to produce a trade mark system which would permit trade marks to be valid in the whole of the EC by submitting an application to the Community Trade Mark Office, thus creating one unified legal procedure. This is seen by the Commission as the only means of ending the problems caused by differing national laws. However, the Commission was forced to accept a system in which Community trade marks would coexist with existing national trade marks.

The proposed Regulation provides a definition of the Community trade mark which may consist of 'words (including surnames), designs, letters, numerals, combinations of colours, the shape of goods or of their packaging, or of any other signs which are capable of distinguishing the goods or services of one undertaking from those of other undertakings'. The proposal contains all details necessary for the registration and continued existence of a Community trade mark. Registration would initially be for 10 years but could be renewed for further periods of 10 years. It does not, however, seem likely that the ongoing disputes over the site of the Community Trade Mark Office and related issues will be resolved in the near future.

The Copyright Directives

In 1988 the Commission published its Green Paper on copyright: The challenge of technology – copyright issues requiring immediate action.[52] This paper was designed as a discussion document and, rather than proposing a Community-wide copyright system, instead listed a number of areas where the Commission felt that action could more usefully be taken at Community level than at national level. It contained seven chapters concerning the following issues:

- copyright and the European Community;
- piracy of copyright material;
- audio-visual home copying;
- distribution right, exhaustion and rental right;
- computer programs;
- databases;
- the role of the Community in bilateral and multilateral external relations.

This was succeeded in 1991 by a document entitled 'Following up to the Green Paper'[53] in which the Commission examined the progress made in the area of copyright law and put forward further concrete proposals for action in the sphere of copyright law. This paper contained eight chapters concerning:

1. A Global Approach – in this chapter the Community was concerned to involve itself in intellectual property protection at an international level, in particular via the Trade Related Intellectual Property Rights (TRIPS) negotiations which formed part of the Uruguay Round of GATT negotiations. The intention was to institute a two-level process of developing copyright protection, the first level being harmonisation of the Member States, laws and the

[52] COM (88) 172 final.   [53] COM (90) 584.

second level being to encourage the accession of Member States to international conventions and agreements such as the Berne Convention.[54]

2. Piracy – here the Community identified a need for harmonisation of protection for performing artists, producers of phonograms and videograms and broadcasting organisations. The result of this was the proposed Directive on Rental and Lending Rights submitted in 1990 and proposals to extend the scope of Regulation 3842/86/EEC which lays down measures to prohibit the release for free circulation of counterfeit goods[55] and Regulation 3077/87/EEC which lays down measures for the implementation of Regulation 3842/86/EEC to cover pirated goods.[56]

3. Home Copying of Sound and Audiovisual Recordings – while there were proposals to impose a levy on blank audio and video cassettes for distribution to performers and authors, these met with opposition in Council and, despite Commission optimism, no proposal for legislation has yet appeared.

4. Distribution Rights, Exhaustion and Rental Rights – this was seen as a particular priority, and Directive 92/100/EEC on Rental Right, Lending Right, and on Certain Rights Related to Copyright[57] was adopted in January 1991.

5. The Legal Protection of Computer Programs – by the time of the follow-up paper the draft Directive, which became Directive 91/250/EEC on the Legal Protection of Computer Programs[58] was already in progress.

6. Databases – the interest in this area resulted in a formal proposal for a draft directive, Proposal for a Council Directive on the legal protection of databases.[59]

7. The Role of the Community in Multilateral and Bilateral External Relations – this examined the Community's relations with other international organisations such as GATT, WIPO and the EFTA countries and noted that Community industries were still experiencing great difficulties in the area of intellectual property when dealing with countries outside the EC.

8. Other Community Initiatives – these included a recognition that the different durations of copyright in the Member States was likely to cause problems and that this was a prime candidate for harmonisation.

Software Copyright Directive

One area in which legislation has already been adopted is software copyright, where Directive 91/250/EEC on the Legal Protection of Computer Programs[60] has been implemented to harmonise the varied legislation of the Member States. The extent of this variation can be seen in the difference between the standards of originality required for software to be copyrightable. In the UK originality means that the program is an original product of the author and some relatively limited degree of skill, judgment and labour must be shown. By contrast, in Germany the German Federal Court held in the *Inkassoprogram* Case[61] that a computer program would only be capable of being protected by copyright if it showed an originality over and above that which could be expected of a reasonably competent programmer. In consequence, as little as 15 per cent of software in Germany was protected

---

[54] See for instance the Resolution on Increased Protection for Copyright and Neighbouring Rights, OJ 1992 C138.
[55] OJ 1986 L357.
[56] OJ 1987 L291.
[57] OJ 1992 L346.
[58] OJ 1991 L122/42.
[59] OJ 1992 C156/4.
[60] OJ 1991 L122/42.
[61] German Federal Court (1986) IIC 681.

and German computer-users were purchasing half as much software as their UK equivalents. The duration of copyright was similarly varied. In France it ran for 25 years from the time of creation, in the UK for 50 years from the death of the copyright holder and in Germany for 70 years from the death of the copyright holder.

The Directive requires that the Member States must protect software within a copyright framework based on the Berne Convention for the Protection of Literary and Artistic Works and, as such, it treats computer programs as if they were literary works.[62] While this is identical to the UK model, it was a form alien to other Member States, even those who had adopted copyright protection for software. It is regrettable, if understandable in terms of compatibility with existing international Treaties, that the EC did not take the opportunity to create a *sui generis* method of software protection. While the possibility of a *sui generis* right was discussed, it was not put forward as a serious proposal and even the draft Directive made no mention of why the Commission decided against it. Such a *sui generis* right might have enabled the Member States to avoid a number of problems currently troubling those systems which deal with the protection of computer programs by copyright, such as the fact that the traditional protection afforded by copyright will only protect expression of an idea, and courts in a number of jurisdictions have struggled to apply this concept with any clarity to software.[63] Indeed, in the Directive, ideas and those principles underlying elements of a computer program are expressly excluded from protection.[64] It is noticeable that programs are protected if they are individual creations of software authors and that the test is similar to that of the UK rather than that of Germany,[65] suggesting a fairly low requirement of originality.[66] Wehlau suggests that as the requirements for the test of copyrightability are to be found in the preamble of the Directive, rather than in the main text, full harmonisation on this point may prove difficult if not impossible to achieve without the aid of the ECJ, as the preamble is not legally binding on Member States or national courts.[67] Groves, however, appears to be of the opinion that this will pose no problems.[68]

The question of authorship is provided for in the Directive, but the issue of who may acquire that title as author, in terms of legal personalities, is left to the Member States' legislation.[69] Thus, where that legislation states that only natural persons can hold copyrights, entities such as firms will be excluded. Where a program is written by an individual in the normal course of his work, or on instruction from his employer, the employer will hold 'all economic rights' in that work unless otherwise varied by contract.[70] This is similar to the situation already existing in the UK. There are a number of ways that this could be achieved, for instance by granting the employer both authorship and copyright directly. It was suggested in the draft Directive that copyright in commissioned software should rest with the person who commissioned it rather than the programmer, which would have been a significant break with UK law, but was not incorporated in the final Directive.[71]

There are certain acts relating to the use of software which may only be authorised by the

---

62 Article 1(1).

63 See, for instance, the problems faced by the American courts in the cases of *Whelan Associates Inc v Jaslow Dental Laboratory Inc* [1987] FSR 1 and *Computer Associates International Inc v Altai Inc* (1992) 982 F 2d 693.

64 Article 1(2).

65 See the *Inkassoprogram* Case, *op. cit.* note 61.

66 Article 1(3).

67 Wehlau, 'Software protection under European Community law' (1993) 2 *Law Computers and Artificial Intelligence* 3, at 8.

68 Groves et al., *op. cit.*, note 38, at 83.

69 Article 2(1).

70 Article 2(3).

71 Groves et al., *op. cit.*, note 38, at 84.

rightholder[72] which include the reproduction,[73] translation, adaptation or arrangements[74] and the distribution of programs. More importantly, the Directive provides that the sale of a copy of a program leads to the exhaustion of the rightholder's control over further commercial acts pertaining to that copy.[75] Again, this concept is not a new one to the UK, but it was not previously used in the other Member States.

There are, however, significant exceptions to the requirement that lawful holders of a program must gain authorisation from the rightholder when wishing to carry out restricted acts.[76] Thus, use of the program for its intended purpose including the correction of errors in the program to render it viable for that purpose[77] and the making of back-up copies[78] are acts which do not require prior authorisation, even where, in other circumstances, they would be restricted by Article 4. When a lawful user performs any of the acts he is entitled to do, such as loading, running or storing the program, he may also observe and test the program in order to discover its underlying ideas and principles.

The 'decompilation' or 'reverse translation' of a program from object code to source code also does not require authorisation by the rightholder where this decompilation is necessary to obtain information about software interfaces. Such interfaces are necessary to allow for the interoperability of a new program with the translated program.[79] In theory such information should only be used to achieve interoperability, but it would seem impossible to enforce in practice. Software suppliers may be able to avoid the use of the decompilation right by publicising the fact that decompilation is not necessary as, when requested, they will provide to legitimate users the necessary code for interoperability purposes,[80] although it would seem that in such cases they would have to make the relevant code available at little or no cost.

In order to ensure that the Directive is effective at protecting software, Member States are required to provide remedies against the following acts; knowingly putting into circulation an infringing copy of a computer program;[81] knowingly possessing an infringing copy of a computer program;[82] and putting into circulation or possessing devices or software which are especially designed to circumvent the copy protection of programs.[83] Member States must provide legislation for the seizure of items in the first two categories[84] and have the option to do so in the third.[85] Despite this, there is no compulsion on the Member States to provide for criminal penalties and the Community cannot legislate in criminal law. Thus, enforcement is left largely to the discretion of the Member States.

The duration of the copyright was originally a minimum period of 50 years, beginning with the death of the author,[86] but it became clear from the negotiations concerning the draft EC general copyright term harmonising measure[87] that this was considered too short by some Member States, notably Germany. It was unsurprising to find, therefore, that the resulting

---

[72] Article 4.
[73] Article 4(a).
[74] Article 4(b).
[75] Article 4(c).
[76] Article 5.
[77] Article 5(1).
[78] Article 5(2).
[79] Article 6.
[80] Article 6(1)(b).
[81] Article 7(1)(a).
[82] Article 7(1)(b).

[83] Article 7(1)(c).
[84] Article 7(2).
[85] Article 7(3).
[86] Article 8, Article 8(2) allowed Member States with longer terms of protection to maintain them until a more general harmonisation provision is produced.
[87] Proposal to harmonise the term of protection for copyright and neighbouring rights, OJ 1992 C92/6, amended. OJ 1993 C27.

Directive[88] repealed Article 8 of the software Directive and replaced the 50-year term with a 70-year term.[89] In fact, it is unlikely, given the speed of development of software, that protection of such a duration will in fact ever be necessary and that a term of copyright for software in line with the French duration would be equally as viable.[90] The Directive does not prejudice other legal provisions which might be used to protect software such as patent rights, trade marks etc. It is interesting to note that the list contains 'unfair competition'. This is a remedy currently unavailable in the UK, but used in the civil law countries, and it may help to explain their attitude to the creativity rule, inasmuch as if a program is not considered to be creative enough for copyright protection and is copied, the creator could claim breach of the rule of unfair competition instead.

Issues such as the moral rights of authors, including the right to be named as the creator of a program, have also been left to the proposed EC general copyright harmonising measure.

The software Directive leaves a number of unresolved questions in the area of software protection, such as the status of shrink wrap contracts,[91] the ability to protect the 'look and feel' of a program[92] and the degree of protection afforded to computer-generated works. It is likely that these issues will only be resolved by the national courts and the ECJ.

Directive 92/100/EEC on Rental Right, Lending Right and on Certain Rights Related to Copyright

Directive 92/100/EEC[93] was designed primarily to harmonise rental and lending rights, in particular to provide a high standard of protection for films and phonograms, products where piracy has long been a problem. It requires that the Member States introduce a right to authorise or prohibit the rental and lending of originals and copies of copyright works. 'Rental' for this purpose means making available for use for a limited period of time for profit and would be the type of activity carried out, for instance, by video rental shops.[94] 'Lending' also involves a limited loan for use but in circumstances where the loan is not for profit-making purposes, an example of this can be seen in the case of public libraries.[95]

This exclusive right is granted to:

- the author in the case of the original and copies of his work;
- the performing artist in the case of fixations of his performance;
- the phonogram producer in respect of phonograms;
- and, finally, the producer of the first fixation of a film in respect of the original and copies of his film. A 'film' is defined as a cinematographic or audiovisual work or moving images, whether or not accompanied by sound.[96]

---

88 Directive 93/98/EEC Harmonising the Term of Protection of Copyright and Certain Related Rights, OJ 1993 L290, with which Member States are obliged to comply by July 1995.
89 Articles 1 and 8 of Directive 93/98/EEC.
90 Note that in the database Directive the term of protection afforded under the *sui generis* right is only 15 years.
91 The contracts found on packages containing software media such as floppy disks, which state that the user is bound by the terms and conditions of the manufacturer, contained thereon, in the event that the user opens the package. Such contracts have an uncertain legal status.
92 See *Whelan Associates Inc v Jaslow Dental Laboratories Inc* [1987] FSR 1.
93 OJ 1992 L346.
94 Article 1(2).
95 Article 1(3).
96 Article 2.

However, when a performer signs a film production contract with a producer this creates a presumption, which may be rebutted, that he has assigned those rental rights, granted by the provisions above, to the producer.[97] However, this is only so where the individual is in a position to benefit from the money raised by the performance. This equitable right to remuneration is unwaivable, a device designed to protect the performer.[98] It applies equally to authors. The Commission appears inclined to support the development of collecting societies such as the Performing Rights Society (PRS), which collect money for performers, but the Directive allows Member States to regulate their work.[99]

It is also noticeable that the Directive contains a derogation which allows the Member States to abrogate the exclusive lending right conferred by copyright, where it is considered necessary for cultural reasons. This would appear mainly to apply to the ability to lend copies of an author's works via public libraries, although the types of works to which this would apply are left to the discretion of the Member States.[100]

The other rights related to copyright, for which the Member States are obliged to provide protection, are concerned with the protection of rights in the various aspects of performace and broadcasting. These four stages are fixation,[101] reproduction,[102] broadcasting and communication to the public,[103] and distribution.[104] The effect is, in theory at least, to provide a comprehensive framework for protection of rights in performances, phonograms and films throughout their lifetime. These related rights are, however, subject to limitation by the Member States under certain circumstances, such as the use of short excerpts of broadcasts for reporting current events or for teaching and scientific research.[105] The provisions in this Directive with regard to the duration of protection to be afforded[106] were repealed and replaced by Directive 93/98/EEC.[107]

Directive 93/83/EEC on the Co-ordination of Certain Rules Concerning Copyright and Neighbouring Rights Applicable to Satellite Broadcasting and Cable Retransmission

Directive 93/83/EEC[108] appears to have as its aim resolving the issue of copyright in relation to cross-border transmission of programmes within the Community and the rebroadcasting of such programmes by cable retransmission. In a Community where no harmonisation of copyright and neighbouring rights was to exist, such transmissions could cause immense problems, in that it would quickly become difficult to untangle the web of intellectual property rights that would come about.

An example of this would be where a programme made in Germany is transmitted by satellite to an area including France, Germany and Spain. From those countries cable

---

97 Article 2(5), (6), (7).
98 Article 4.
99 Which, given the recent alleged losses attributed to the PRS in relation to a failed attempt to develop a computer system to handle the collection of money for performers, and the subsequent threats of litigation, seems a reasonable safeguard.
100 Article 5.
101 Article 6. Fixation refers to the taking down or recording, in any form, of a performance or broadcast.
102 Article 7. Reproduction refers to the copying of fixations.

103 Article 8.
104 Article 9. Distribution refers to the sale, rent or otherwise of a fixation.
105 Article 10.
106 Article 11 concerning authors' rights and Article 12 concerning the rights of performers, phonogram producers and broadcasting organisations.
107 See op. cit., note 88, Articles 2, 3, and 11.
108 OJ 1993 L248.

providers retransmit the broadcasts to Denmark, Belgium and the Netherlands. If the copyright and neighbouring rights provisions of the Member States were all different it would be difficult for the service providers to know whether they had a legitimate right to broadcast the material in certain Member States, and equally difficult for those whose programmes are being shown to ensure even and adequate protection of their intellectual property rights throughout the Community.

Such difficulties might then lead to service providers deciding not to broadcast all or some of their programmes to certain Member States or programme producers refusing to allow multinational satellite broadcasts of their work. In both cases there would be interference in what the Commission considers the necessary free circulation of programmes within the Community.

The Directive takes its lead from Directive 92/100/EEC and applies, to satellite communications to the public, those rights found in Articles 6, 7, 8 and 10 of that Directive. It also continues the development of a legal framework designed to ensure a single audiovisual area within the Community as envisaged by Directive 89/552/EEC.[109]

It includes, however, a much more powerful role for collecting societies than was provided for in Directive 92/100/EEC. Indeed, with regard to cable retransmission the collecting societies appear to be the only bodies which can exercise the right to grant or refuse authorisation to a cable operator for a cable retransmission[110] and right-holders have no choice about whether to transfer the management of their rights to a collecting society, merely the choice, where there are options, of which of the collecting societies will manage their rights.[111] Where there is disagreement between the collecting society and the cable companies regarding authorisation of retransmission the Directive provides for a mediated settlement procedure.[112] There is a clear logic to this apparent interference in the rights of the individual, inasmuch as it is obvious that cable companies will be able to deal much more efficiently with an individual organisation than they would with a large number of individual rightholders. However, it will be important for both the Member States and the Commission to ensure that the collecting societies do not abuse their powers in relation to either cable companies or right-holders.

It is, of course, debateable as to the efficacy of any national or, indeed, supranational rules relating to satellite broadcasting.[113] It is possible that with the fall in price of the necessary technology we may see similar developments in satellite broadcasting as occurred in radio broadcasting in the 1960s, with transmissions being beamed in to the Member States via satellite from uplink stations based outside the Community in order to avoid Community regulation. If such satellite broadcasters can obtain their finance from advertising alone, rather than via the kinds of rental system run by existing companies, it is difficult to see any way in which the Member States or the Community could prevent breaches of intellectual property rights occurring.

---

109 OJ 1989 L298.
110 Article 9(10).
111 Article 9(2).
112 Article 11.

113 And in this respect rules to protect intellectual property rights may prove no less difficult to enforce than rules regulating the content of what is broadcast.

The draft database Directive

The draft database Directive[114] has two main aims. The first is the harmonisation of national laws concerning the copyright protection of databases and the second is the creation of a *sui generis* right, now lasting 15 years, designed to prevent the unauthorised[115] extraction of a database's contents.[116]

The draft Directive as amended[117] defines a database as ' . . . a collection of data, works or other materials arranged, stored and accessed by electronic means, and the materials necessary for the operation of the database. . . '. The definition limits the scope of the draft Directive to electronic databases and does not include within its protection the database software itself.[118] Copyright may already subside in works held in a database, in the selection and arrangement of those works and in the database itself under Article 2(5) of the Berne Convention.[119] These methods of protection are left unaffected by the draft Directive.[120]

The major point requiring harmonisation is the degree of originality required for a database to be allowed the protection of the Directive. As with the software Directive the test is satisfied if the selection or arrangement of materials contained within the database is the author's own intellectual creation.[121] The materials contained within the database themselves derive no extra protection from the Directive, whether they are already protected or not.[122] With regard to the issue of authorship and ownership of copyright in a database, the draft Directive again mirrors the software Directive.[123] As far as the material which is incorporated into the database is concerned, if it is protected by copyright the creator of the database must obtain permission to incorporate it.[124] However, if it takes the form of 'brief abstracts, quotations or summaries which do not substitute for the original works themselves' no such permission is required. In this context 'substitution' means that the incorporated material describes the original work but cannot replace it in terms of utility.[125]

Those acts which are restricted under the terms of the copyright granted by the draft Directive are basically the same as for any other copyright work.[126] However, there are exceptions to these restricted acts, in that where a lawful user of the database needs to carry out any of the restricted acts listed in Article 6 in order to use the database in accordance with a contractual arrangement with the right-holder[127] or where there are no contractual arrangements and a lawful user carries out any restricted act in order to access and use the database, there is no need for permission to be granted by the right-holder.[128] However, those exceptions cover only the structure of the database and not the contents, so right-holders in

---

114 Proposal for a Council Directive of the Legal Protective of Database, COM (92) 24 final – SYN 393, OJ 1992 C156/4, as amended COM (93) 464 final – SYN 393, OJ 1993 C308.

115 In the original draft Directive this was termed less precisely as 'unfair' extraction.

116 This draws upon *sui generis* laws already found in Scandinavian countries and also upon elements of unfair competition law found in those Member States which operate a civil law.

117 See Anon, 'Amended Proposal for a Database Directive' (1993) 1 (10) *IT Law Today*, at 1.

118 Article 1(1).

119 Article 2(5) of the Berne Convention states:
   Collections of literary or artistic works such as encyclopaedias and anthologies which, by reason of the

selection and arrangement of their contents, constitute intellectual creations shall be protected as such, without prejudice to the copyright in each of the works forming part of such collections.

120 Article 2.
121 Article 2(3).
122 Article 2(4).
123 Article 3.
124 Article 5(1).
125 Article 5(2).
126 Article 6.
127 Article 7(1).
128 Article 7(2).

the actual materials may have their copyright infringed in such circumstances if permission is not granted.[129]

The unauthorised extraction right is provided for in Articles 10(2) and 11. Unauthorised extraction refers to the extraction and reuse of all or a substantial part of the contents of a database, whether or not it is eligible for copyright, for commercial purposes, although the term 'commercial purposes' is not defined.[130] Where the database's contents are already covered by copyright, Article 10(2) does not apply.

Article 11 provides for compulsory licensing, on fair and non-discriminatory terms, of a database where either:

- the information on a publically available database cannot be independently created, collected or obtained from any other source;
- the database has been made publicly available by a public body established to assemble or disclose information under statute or regulation or has a general duty to do so; or
- the database has been made publically available by firms or entities which enjoy a monoploy status because of an exclusive concession by a public body.

It also provides that lawful users may extract and use insubstantial amounts of the database for both private and commercial use without first obtaining permission. The remedies for unauthorised extraction are left up to the Member States.

The copyright protection of the database is that afforded to literary works[131] and the right to prevent unauthorised extraction ends either 15 years after the date at which the database is first made available to the public or 15 years after the last substantial change.[132] It is here that an important change in the amended draft Directive has been made with the redefining of the term 'substantial change'. In the original draft it would have been extremely difficult for databases to have met the conditions for 'substantial change' because changes necessary for a database to continue to function in the way in which it was intended by its maker to function, for instance the addition of new and up-to-date data to a database, were classed merely as 'insubstantial change' which had no effect on the status of the database.[133] Article 12(2) of the amended draft Directive backs off from this stance by stating that 'substantial change' may come about by the 'successive accumulation of insubstantial additions, deletions or alterations . . . resulting in substantial modification to all or part of a database'. Thus, any database which is carefully maintained by its owner will be likely to be able to gain successive terms of protection.

The original draft database Directive was criticised on a number of grounds, but primarily because of the *sui generis* right and the 10-year term of protection afforded by the unfair extraction right. Criticism of the *sui generis* right is likely to have been subdued by the amendments in that it centres on the fact that, as the *sui generis* right is not a neighbouring right, it does not fit within the framework of the Berne Convention, and the use of such a non-standard right weakens the international framework of copyright protection.

The 15-year duration of the unauthorised extraction right, while an improvement on the 10 years suggested in the original draft Directive, may still be felt to be too short, because

---

129 Article 7(3).

130 Articles 10(1) and 10(2). What constitutes 'commercial purposes' is defined in Article 11(7).

131 Article 9(1).

132 Article 12(1).

133 Article 1(4) in the unamended Directive.

modern databases are often huge and take a long period of time to establish, build and run. Due to the high start-up costs of building a database, a new database might just be starting to show a profit when its protection is removed and it has been argued that this would be a major disincentive to potential database providers. The relaxing of the meaning of substantial change would, however, appear to ameliorate this problem to a large degree.

It should be noted that in the amended Directive the Commission has accepted that the technology in this area is advancing so rapidly that the rules governing it require frequent review. To this end Article 16(3) provides that the Commision will review the operation of the Directive after the first five years following implemenation and every two years after that.

CONCLUSION

The Community has found the area of intellectual property to be a difficult one to deal with, not least because the Member States have been inclined to assert their own models of rights, and the wide variations between Member States laws have made it difficult for Commission and Council to reach compromise positions on harmonisation.[134] It would be fair to say that the ECJ has endured similar difficulties in attempting to ensure that a proper balance is struck between intellectual property rights and Community competition law, with the 'HAG' case being a prime example of the type of judicial backtracking that has occasionally been necessary. As with the other areas in which individual rights have come into conflict with the prime objectives of the Community, the need for a coherent strategy of harmonisation to prevent total chaos and widespread abuse of the differences between the Member States' legal systems has long been apparent. The Community measures so far implemented have been the subject of a great deal of criticism but, taken as a whole, they show that the Commission and Council are striving to form a clear pattern of rights which can then be incorporated into successive measures. This can be seen in the fact that parts of the software Directive are mirrored in the draft database Directive and, similarly, that the satellite and cable rights Directive further extends the scope of the copyright-related rights to be found in the rental rights Directive.

If blame is to be allotted for the failure of the Community to move rapidly to a coherent and harmonised position on intellectual property rights, it must rest firmly with the Member States. They have refused to compromise on certain issues which often appear to be trivial[135] and, perhaps more importantly, they have set their face against the use of *sui generis* rights in areas such as software protection, where such *sui generis* rights could end, once and for all, the problems implicit in the use of the established intellectual property rights.

Further reading

Anon, 'Software licensing in the light of the current EC competition law considerations (Dir 91/250)' (1992) 13 ECLR 5.

---

134 Grove et al., *op. cit.*, note 38, at 82 point out that the draft Directive on computer software was only accepted after 'the most protracted passage of any piece of Community legislation'.
135 For example, as note above, there was much wrang-ling and delay over the issue of whether the duration of copyright of software should be 50 years or 70 years when, in practice, 20 years would almost certainly be sufficient.

Anon, 'The distinction between existence and exhaustion in EEC intellectual property rights revisited' (1989) 26 CMLR 193.

Dreier, T., 'The Council Directive on the Legal Protection of Computer Programs' [1991] 9 EIPR 319.

Marenco, G. and Banks, K., 'Intellectual property and the Community rules on free movement: discrimination unearthed' (1990) 15 EL Rev 224.

Robertson, A., 'Compulsory copyright licensing under EC Law' (1992) 108 LQR 39.

Vajda, C., 'The application of Community competition law to the distribution of computer parts and products' (1992) 13 ECLR 110.

Wehlau, A., 'Software protection under European Community Law' (1993) 2 *Law Computers and Artificial Intelligence* 3.

CHAPTER 15

Technology

INTRODUCTION

As soon becomes apparent from a study of the history of technological development in the Community,[1] the governments of the Member States realised what was required of them rather late in the day than the governments of Japan or the US. In order for significant technological developments to be achieved and then exploited in a sensible fashion, they realised that they would have to play a major role in the encouragement and regulation of the research, development and marketing processes. That realisation, combined with the likelihood that national producers in the EC were unlikely to be strong enough by themselves to compete successfully on the world stage, made it inevitable that the Community institutions, and in particular the Commission, would have to intervene in the development and regulation of a broad spectrum of technological processes.

This chapter will examine the two areas of development and regulation, beginning with a brief description of the way in which the Community has attempted to fund the development of various forms of technology and a short analysis of the success of this funding. It will then consider the developmental and regulatory aspects of the EC telecommunications market. Finally we will turn to the Community's attempts to regulate the development of high-volume information processing which advances in technology have afforded. We shall examine the provisions of the draft Directive on data protection, which appears to be strongly guided by the principle of personal privacy, and those aspects of the Schengen Convention which appear to make the aim of protection of personal privacy rather less certain.

COMMUNITY INVOLVEMENT IN TECHNOLOGICAL DEVELOPMENT

As noted above, the Community was a late starter on the technology front; indeed, until the SEA in 1987, all technology policies for research and development (R&D) not covered by the Euratom Treaty had to be based upon the catch-all provision in Article 235 EC.[2] This allowed Community action, in areas where no specific powers had been granted, where there was a unanimous decision by the Council following consultation with the Parliament.

The SEA added a new Title to the Treaty which stated that;

> The Community's aim shall be to strengthen the scientific and technological base of European industry and to encourage it to become more competitive at an international level. In order to achieve this it shall encourage undertakings, including small and medium-sized undertakings, research centres and universities in their research and

---

[1] See for instance Sharp, 'The Community and New Technologies' in Lodge (ed.), *The European Community* *and the Challenge of the Future* (1993). [2] See Chapter 3 at p 44.

technological development activities; it shall support their efforts to co-operation with one another, aiming, in particular, at enabling undertakings to exploit the Community's internal market to the full, in particular through the opening up of national public contracts, the definition of common standards and the removal of legal and fiscal barriers to that co-operation.[3]

The SEA also provided that there should be a two-stage mechanism for implementing that policy. This comprises the Member States adopting by unanimity a Framework Programme to run for a set number of years.[4] This Framework Programme sets out the scientific and technological objectives to be achieved, including some degree of prioritisation of those objectives. The objectives are then implemented by a number of smaller programmes adopted by the Council by qualified majority voting, after consultation with Parliament and the Economic and Social Committee.

The development programmes

As noted above, the fact that the Community institutions were not automatically provided with the necessary powers to engage in the assistance of R&D meant that early attempts to achieve these aims on a Community level had to use the general power granted in Article 235. This inevitably meant that they were going to face difficulties due firstly to a lack of consensus between the Member States as to how such aims were to be achieved, and secondly to conflicts with national interests and priorities. Also, throughout the 1970s, the Community and the Member States were less concerned with the development of new industries than with dealing with the consequences of the decline of older industries such as steel, shipbuilding and textiles. This included combating national protectionism and the formation of 'crisis cartels'.

An example of the problems of the time is amply provided by the failure of Community intervention in the European computing sector. It was clear as early as the 1960s that this sector was going to be a rapid growth area, and it was equally clear that US firms, notably IBM, were in a position to dominate the market, unless some form of joint action was taken by the major European computing firms. However, it proved impossible to create the kind of cross-Community consortium that would be required to give an effective and competitive strategy in this sector. National governments simply refused to co-operate, preferring to act to support and protect their own national producers rather than to work towards any concept of Europe-wide co-operation and consolidation. Thus the high point of the Community's activities in this area during this period was reached in 1974 with a Council resolution which backed a medium-term programme on the application, development and production of data processing systems. This, however, came to nothing, being undermined by Member States' manoeuvring in order to benefit what they perceived as their national interest. The result of this lack of unanimity in the computing sector during that period is clearly visible in the 1990s. Many of the former major European players, such as Siemens, ICL and Bull, have simply failed to compete successfully with US and Japanese firms, such as IBM, Digital and Fujitsu, and as a result are either being propped up by heavy subsidies from

3 Article 130 EC.
4 After the TEU, Parliament must also approve this Framework Programme. The Third Framework Pro-

gramme, currently in progress, will end in 1994, and the Commission is drawing up specific proposals for the Fourth Framework proposal.

their national government, or are now wholly or partially owned by the successful world producers.[5] Thus many of the advantages of innovative R&D work carried out in Europe over the last 30 years have been lost to non-Community competitors, and it is difficult to see Community producers being able to reconquer this area of the technology market.

An area where a modicum of success was achieved during this period was aerospace.[6] Here with projects such as Concorde, the European Airbus and the European Space Agency, a high degree of co-operation was demonstrated between the Member States. Part of the success appears to have been in convincing Member States that national issues should not be allowed to dominate, and that market forces rather than government policy should determine the nature and scope of projects. However, in recent recessionary years, the problems and Member State infighting that have occurred on high-profile projects such as the European Fighter Aircraft (EFA) suggest that some of the old difficulties have re-emerged.[7]

As Sharp notes,[8] there are a number of lessons to be learnt from the period from the late 1960s to the end of the 1970s, notably that successful industrial R&D programmes could not be based on a pattern which demanded the co-operation and participation of all the Member States, needing rather to be designed with the project rather than the potential partners in mind. Programmes required a clear aim that the Member States could readily perceive as capable of being obtained, and the co-operation, if not participation, of the major economic players of the time, France and Germany, was almost always vital to a project's viability. Finally, projects needed to be seen to be of value to European industry rather than being perceived as flag-waving events for the Member States' governments, in order that the necessary levels of industry support and funding were forthcoming.

Thus, by the early 1980s, it was clear that the European technology sector was in serious trouble, with the EC importing the majority of its needs in IT goods and services. There were still further threats on the horizon as both US and Japanese governments were supporting successful collaborative research programmes in a number of areas of high technology, thus creating a potential innovation gap between their producers and those of Europe. These developments were combined with a further threat, the relaxation of anti-trust regulation of both AT & T and IBM by the US authorities. This move allowed both firms to seek new markets, notably in telecommunications, outside the US. The effect of these developments was to force a joint move by both Commission and European producers to pressurise the Member States into some form of united and long-term action.

The end result of this pressure was the creation of the ESPRIT programme[9] which was designed to facilitate collaborative R&D between major Community companies, small and medium enterprises (SMEs), and the various research institutions, such as universities.

The pilot phase of the ESPRIT programme was launched in December 1982, and was sufficiently successful for the Commission to feel able to move ahead with the main programme. This consisted of a ten-year plan running from 1984 to 1993, divided into two

---

5 Fujitsu, for instance, is now to all intents and purposes owner of ICL, formerly the UK's leading computer manufacturer.

6 See Sharp, *op. cit.* note 1, at 204.

7 Although in the case of the EFA, the reunification of Germany and the suspension of the Cold War have muddied the issue. It is clear, however, that there is little consensus between the Member States on the nature and scope of the project in the 'New World Order' with a number of nations indicating a desire to modify, or even scrap, the project. Similarly, as with most military-oriented projects, market forces are not the driving force behind their implementation.

8 Sharp, *op. cit.*, note 1, at 204.

9 European Strategic Programme for Research and Development in Information Technology.

five-year parts. The first part of the project (ESPRIT I) dealt with pre-competitive R&D in microelectronics, advanced information processing, and software technology. The second phase (ESPRIT II) was concerned with similar areas, but whilst this too was theoretically concerned with the pre-competitive aspects of research in these areas, the distinction between pre-competitive and competitive R&D had become increasingly blurred and difficult to enforce.

The Community, however, appears to have considered the benefits of such a programme to be worth the cost,[10] as the model provided by the ESPRIT programme has since been used for a variety of other Community initiatives, a number of which are noted in the telecommunications section of this chapter.

The effect of the development programmes[11]

What then have been the effects of ESPRIT and subsequent research programmes? Certainly, in permitting the creation of the original ESPRIT programme, the Member States appear to have acknowledged that there were difficulties in the technology sector that could only be addressed by Community action. However, the effect of the Community's involvement in the sector requires careful evaluation. It has to be said, at the start, that at times the Community bias of the programmes may actually have delayed and hindered progress in certain fields, because the involvement of relevant US and Japanese firms has not been permitted. The move away from national producers to Community producers has also meant that the number of those producers has been significantly reduced, as the Community market was defragmented. It is also arguable that all the Community has achieved is to create a body of 'Community-dependant producers' which it has sought to protect from competition by subsidies and trade protection devices such as tariffs on goods from non-Community producers. If the increasing pressure on the EC to withdraw its trade barriers, in a forum such as the GATT negotiations, leads to the removal of those advantages, the 'Community-dependant producers' may then struggle to compete on the world market.

To add to this, many of the programmes have shown little in the way of visible success, and the trade deficit in IT, which sparked the original ESPRIT project, has grown still further, from $5 billion in 1980 to $21 billion in 1991. The issue of the refusal to fund research beyond the pre-competitive stage has also been criticised as unrealistic, with firms calling for issues such as product development and marketability to be taken into account in the various Community programmes. The support of pre-competitive research, it is argued, is beneficial to a point, but the area in which EC producers have all too often fallen short is not the ability to innovate, but rather the ability to develop and package their end-product so as to attract the consumer away from competitor's goods.

On the other hand, the EC has gained a major role, via its various programmes, in the area of standard setting. Standard setting is increasingly seen as an important weapon in competitive trading. A standard used uniformly across a market the size of the Community

---

10 The cost to the Community of ESPRIT I was about 750 million ECU; ESPRIT II about 1600 million ECU; and ESPRIT III, the current phase, about 1350 million ECU. Thus the program has so far cost the Community around 3700 million ECU. The overall cost of the pro- ject including industrial financial input will be approximately double this figure.

11 A special Court of Auditors' report evaluating the ESPRIT programme was published in early 1994, OJ 1994 C45.

market will inevitably have a highly-influential effect on the determination of worldwide standards as other producers seek to enter that market.

The major point of interest which arises, both from the collaborative aspects of the programmes and the fact that they have a tendency to reduce the number of producers in a given field, is that the philosophy behind them appears to fly directly in the face of the movement towards liberalisation and deregulation presently championed by the Commission, a movement which is particularly evident in the telecommunications sector. Those twin aims, of competition and collaboration, are clearly uncomfortable bedfellows. On the other hand, as Sharp argues, whether this twin-track approach was designed or reached by accident, it seems that it may at the end of the day turn out to be potentially useful. This is because the tension between the two aims may help to prevent the problem of the formation of 'Community dependant producers' from former 'national producers' in that the competitive element of a free market will help to balance out the protective effect of the programmes.[12]

The future

It is seems from current activities that the Community's strategy for industrial development and competition will continue to focus upon the use of R&D programmes as outlined above and further discussed in the telecommunications section. What is less certain is the degree to which such programmes can remain fixed solely at supporting the pre-competitive stage of such R&D, and the extent to which they can be allowed to continue to exclude relevant non-EC producers.

With regard to supporting technological innovation, the Community institutions now have the legal framework within which to work, but while the acquisition of this framework was a valuable step, much still depends on the willingness of the Member States to co-operate and put aside national concerns. The tensions and sentiments raised during the process of ratification of the TEU show that there are vocal forces in the Member States who are opposed to co-operation of the type proposed by the Commission, especially where such co-operation will be at the expense of national interests.

TELECOMMUNICATIONS

The area of telecommunications is an ideal one to examine because, from the early 1990s, it has been developing into one of Europe's fastest-growing markets. Indeed, it has been said that telecommunications companies will become a larger equity sector than banks before the turn of the century.[13] The development of the 'information highway' concept exemplified by the US NREN and NII[14] projects is likely to revolutionise the role of telecommunications companies as service providers, with US firms already offering services such as low-cost Internet access[15] and audio-visual services. On a worldwide scale, there has been a move away from state-owned telecommunication monopolies towards privatised telecommunications

12 Sharp, *op. cit.*, note 1, at 220.
13 Coopers and Lybrand, *EC Commentaries: Telecommunications*, 24 February 1994.
14 National Research and Education Network and National Information Infrastructure.

15 The Internet is a network of networks which links some 2 million computers and 20 million individual users in over 60 countries based around the US National Science Foundation network.

organisations (TOs), and this trend seems set to accelerate. The Community has been actively engaged in attempting to maximise the potential of the EC telecommunications sector since the early 1980s, being mindful of the failure of European companies to compete with any major success in other areas of high technology such as electronics and IT.

Community concern with telecommunications

The Commission has been particularly concerned to achieve the following aims:

- the break-up, partial or total, of national monopolies;
- increasing the level of competition within the Community;
- achieving a high degree of telecommunications standardisation within the Community;
- achieving a consistent level of internal Community pricing and service.

The break-up of state monopolies is essential for the stimulation of competition within the Community for, if Member States maintain protected telecommunications monopolies, the Community market will remain effectively partitioned. The Commission is also aware that many of the problems it faced in the electronics and IT spheres were caused by Member States championing national producers at the expense of any coherent support for Community producers. By forcing Public TOs into the competitive market-place and away from reliance on state monopolies, it appears that the Commission hopes to homogenise the internal Community market to the point where TOs largely lose their identity as national producers. The success of the first of the privatised European TOs, British Telecom, in forming international alliances[16] and achieving network ownership and management outside the UK,[17] is likely to encourage other Member States to follow the UK's example in total or partial privatisation. Indeed, by 1998 most of the main European public TOs are expected to be privatised to some degree.

Increased competition within the Community is considered desirable to promote the level of research and development, which will be required to ensure that Community producers remain competitive on the world market. This competition, it is hoped, will in turn ensure the provision of modern equipment and infrastructure throughout the Community. As modern telecommunications provision will be increasingly essential to all levels of business and industry in the coming years, so the fate not just of the telecommunications industry within the Community but also of the service industries, such as banking, rests on ensuring that both infrastructure and services are adequate to meet the likely demands.

While the concern with infrastructure and Community-wide compatibility is one reason for the drive for standardisation, the other is the ambition on the part of the Commission to create a large enough market within Europe to place Community producers in a position of strength when international standards are being determined. The theory is that if the Community market remains fragmented, with varied standards of equipment and service provision, Community producers will run the risk of being marginalised on the world market. If, however, the Community market is largely or entirely standardised, it will be such a large uniform sector of the world market that its sales potential will be impossible to

---

16 Notably the MCI, the second largest US long-distance carrier.

17 Coopers and Lybrand, *EC Commentaries: Telecommunications,* 24 February 1994.

ignore, and its standards will be more attractive to producers outside the Community who will be seeking to win orders within it.

However, despite its considerable concern with the ability of Community producers to compete effectively on the world market, the Commission is also concerned to ensure that service standards are both maintained and improved across all sections of the telecommunications market, and not just in the lucrative business markets. The risk it faces is that, with widespread privatisation of the Community TOs, the temptation for those privatised bodies will be to all but abandon those areas of the Community where telecommunications provision is unlikely to show a clear short-term profit. Thus the Commission has to consider both its role in ensuring that there is genuine competition between producers, and its role in ensuring that the provision of essential services is maintained.

Development

As already described, both the ability of Community TOs to compete on the world market and the future development of the telecommunications sector within the Community are dependant upon the ability of the industry to finance and support the necessary research and development processes. In order to ensure that this finance and support occurs, the Commission has begun a number of research and development programmes. These aim to achieve the objectives of the 1987 Green Paper on Telecommunications[18] and thus to strengthen the general competitiveness of the industry. Such programmes usually provide up to 50 per cent of the total costs of projects supported.

The Community's Third Framework Programme for Research and Development serves as a basis for most of the current EC funding for telecommunications projects. It was originally projected to end in 1993, but was extended into 1994.[19] A Fourth Framework Programme for Research and Development has been proposed by the Commission. This would run for five years from 1994 to 1998.[20] Further to this, the Commission has published a working document concerning the nature of the specific programmes which would be used in implementing the Fourth Framework Programme.[21] Both the European Regional Development Fund (ERDF) and the European Investment Bank (EIB) also provide funding opportunities for telecommunications-related projects.

The Community has a number of ongoing R&D programmes which are targeted at the telecommunications sector, such as: STAR, RACE, TEDIS, SPRINT, IMPACT II, COST, EUREKA and ESPRIT III, and these are briefly outlined below. A number of these programmes have a specific legal element with regard to overcoming technical and procedural barriers in the Member States.[22]

Special Telecommunications Action for Regional Development (STAR)

The objective of the STAR programme, which is financed through the ERDF, is to integrate the poorer Community regions into the advanced telecommunications networks set up across the Community.[23] It provides financial assistance to peripheral regions in Greece, Italy, Spain,

18 See below at p 341.
19 OJ 1993 C225.
20 OJ 1993 C230.
21 October 1993, COM (93) 459.
22 See, for example, the TEDIS programme.
23 Regulation 3300/86/EEC, OJ 1986 L305.

Portugal, Ireland, the United Kingdom (Northern Ireland) and France, and encourages improved access to advanced telecommunication services. It thus aims to speed up the ongoing process of digitalisation and promote links with those advanced networks which already operate within the Community. The main purpose of STAR is to support both feasibility studies and measures to stimulate the demand for, and also to encourage the use of, advanced services. This is particularly aimed at SMEs as these tend to be a vital part of the peripheral region's economies.

Research and Development in Advanced Communication Technologies for Europe (RACE)

The RACE programme is the R&D part of the Community's telecommunications policy. There was a pilot phase in 1985, followed by the first phase of projects (RACE I) in 1988.[24] In 1991 RACE II was implemented. This is a specific research and technological development programme in the field of communication technologies.[25] The major aim of the RACE programme has been to develop an integrated broadband communications network (IBC) by the turn of the century. This will then take over from the current Integrated Services Digital Network (ISDN), which has proven unsuitable for the transmission of data flows on the scale that are expected to be reached by the year 2000, due to bandwidth limitations. More generally, RACE is designed to provide a boost for the Community's telecommunications industry, giving the European network operators optimal conditions in which to develop their services provision. Thus, RACE by its very nature will cover a broad spectrum of interests. At present it covers the entire area of telecommunications, including satellite communications, line-linked terrestrial networks and mobile telecommunications. It also has a role to play in the development and oversight of service provision, and in the assessment of the larger socio-economic picture which is developing with regard to telecommunications.

Trade Electronic Data Interchange Systems (TEDIS)

This is a Community programme set up to co-ordinate the development of electronic data interchange (EDI) systems for trade and industry, an area of increasing interest worldwide and within the Community. It is hoped that the programme will aid in the creation and development of trans-European EDI networks. At the time of writing, TEDIS is entering its second phase (TEDIS II)[26] which will run for three years. The implementation of the programme is co-ordinated with existing Community policies in telecommunications, particularly Open Network Provision. TEDIS II deals with a sub-category of EDI, the electronic transmission of commercial or administrative 'forms' between computers. As such, it involves projects concluded with a wide range of bodies within the EC and also in other, third countries, especially EFTA members.

Strategic Programme for Innovation and Technology Transfer (SPRINT)

The aims of SPRINT[27] are to strengthen the innovative capacity of European suppliers of goods and services, in view of the 1992 Single Market. SPRINT promotes the use of new

24 OJ 1988 L16.
25 Decision 91/352/EEC, OJ 1991 L192.
26 Decision 91/385/EEC, OJ 1991 L208. See Commission Activity Report on the TEDIS programme 1988–89, COM (90) 361 final, for an overview of the

developments within the TEDIS project up to that point.
27 Decision 89/286/EEC, OJ 1989 L112. The lifespan of this programme was extended to the end of 1994 by Decision 94/5/EC, OJ 1994 L6.

technologies throughout the Community economy, particularly in those regions and industrial sectors where they are not yet fully integrated. The main areas of support concern training in innovation management, networks of experts and associated promotional activities such as conferences and publications.

Programme for the Establishment of an Information Services Market (IMPACT II)

IMPACT II constitutes the main phase of the IMPACT programme.[28] The aims of IMPACT were broadly: to set up an internal information services market; to reinforce the competitive capability of European suppliers of information services; to promote the use of advanced information services in the Community; and to encourage joint efforts to achieve the internal and external cohesion of the Community with respect to information services.[29] IMPACT II takes these aims further by concentrating on developing an Information Market Observatory to provide market intelligence data with which to analyse the Community's strengths and weaknesses in this area, measures to overcome legal and administrative barriers, initiatives to increase the user-friendliness of services and to improve information literacy, and support for strategic information initiatives.

European Co-operation in the Field of Scientific and Technical Research (COST)

The COST Programme is based on European co-operation in the field of scientific and technical research involving 19 countries including the EC Member States, Norway, Sweden, Finland, Switzerland, Austria, former Yugoslavia and Turkey. The programme was established in 1971 by a General Resolution of the Ministerial Conference for European Co-operation in the field of R&D.[30]

Projects undertaken under the auspices of COST are designed to improve co-ordination of research programmes and promote both basic and applied scientific and technical research. They are thus aimed mainly at the area of pre-competitive research and complement European Community activities designed to aid in the creation of scientific networks. COST projects have so far covered a wide range of subject areas, including informatics, telecommunications, transport, environmental protection, medical research, and public health and social sciences.

Technical Co-operation between European Industries in the Field of Innovation (EUREKA)

This provides a framework for technological co-operation in Europe between firms and research institutions and encompasses 17 countries and the Commission. Its purpose is to increase productivity and to strengthen the competitiveness of Europe's industries and national economies by aiding the development of new products or services that can compete in world markets. Any high-tech product, service or process may be developed. All participants finance their research endeavours from their own funds, from external private financial sources and any public funds made available by their governments.

28 Decision 91/691/EEC, OJ 1991 L377.
29 See Commission report of 19 April 1993 on the main events and developments in the electronic information services market in 1991, COM (93) 156.
30 OJ 1979 C100.

Specific Programme of Research and Technological Development in the Field of Information Technologies (ESPRIT III)

As described above, the ESPRIT programme was first set up in 1982. It has since been renewed and the latest programme is ESPRIT III.[31] The current phase of the programme has run from 1990 to 1994 and will, apart from the research carried out under ESPRIT II, support ongoing programmes.[32] Areas of new activity that will receive priority funding under ESPRIT III include: microelectronics; information processing systems and software; computerised systems and peripherals in the office and home; and computer integrated production and engineering.

Specific Programme of Research and Technological Development in the Field of Telematic Systems [33]

This programme has run from 1990 to 1994 and during this period has in particular supported research in the areas of: the development of trans-European networks between administrations; the development of integrated trans-European services, using advanced IT in communications, to improve the performance of passenger and goods transport services (DRIVE II); the provision of telematic health services (AIM II); distance learning (DELTA II); the provision of computerised bibliographies, international interconnection of systems, new library services and telematic products and services for libraries; linguistic research and engineering; and the development of effective and modern telematic systems for rural areas.

Regulation

Regulation of the telecommunications industry became an issue of Community concern as early as 1984, with the conception by the Council of a strategy regarding the development of a European telecommunications network. This strategy envisaged that such a network would enable freer and fairer competition with regard to public telecommunications procurement contracts. It would also allow for the development of telecommunications and common infrastructural projects on a Community-wide basis.[34] Further, the creation of a Community-wide market for terminals and equipment would benefit Community producers and would aid the pressure for Community-wide open standards. In addition, the Council wanted to ensure the even spread of advanced services and networks throughout the Community to prevent the poorer areas of the Community from falling behind. The strategy also made allowance for the creation of the RACE programme to aid R&D in the Telecommunications sector,[35] and attempted to prepare the way for the introduction of digital mobile communications.

The Council's initiative was followed by a Green Paper from the Commission in 1987 which analysed the future development of telecommunications in the Community and proposed a framework programme of regulatory changes.[36] Its overall aim was to initiate liberalisation and reform of the telecommunications sector in the Member States. In addition

---

31 Decision 91/394/EEC, OJ 1991 L218.
32 See the Court of Auditors report of February 1994 evaluating the ESPRIT programme, OJ 1994 C45.
33 Decision 91/353/EEC, OJ 1991 L192.
34 Notably the creation of the Integrated Services Digital Network (ISDN) which was widely regarded as the state

of the art at the time. As noted above, this is now to be phased out over the next 5–10 years in favour of Integrated Broadband Communications (IBC).
35 See above at 339.
36 COM (87) 290.

to the measures suggested in the Council strategy, the Green Paper also suggested a number of other aims. These included measures designed to forward the cause of standardisation within the Community, such as the creation of a body specifically to deal with telecommunications standards;[37] and agreement on common definition of a set of conditions for Open Network Provision (ONP). Another measure was a common Community position with regard to its dealings with third countries and international organisations containing non-Member States, such as CEPT or CEN/CENELEC.[38] Also noted by the Commission as areas worthy of further consideration were the issue of the development of interconnecting service networks, the lack of a coherent Community position on satellite communications, and the need for an analysis of the social impact of new telecommunications developments.

At the same time as it published its Green Paper, the Commission introduced a large-scale consultation procedure in order to discover the state of institutional and regulatory conditions in the telecommunications sector of the Member States, with a view to formulating further policy for improvement at Community level. The Green Paper provided the basis for that period of consultation between the various interest groups involved in the telecommunications area. This consultation then led to an action programme to implement the Green Paper being submitted to the Council in February 1988.[39]

Competition

As part of the action programme, the Commission adopted guidelines, in a Communication in July 1991 on the application of competition rules in the telecommunications sector.[40] This Communication describes the application of EC competition rules to both private and public telecommunication services. Its aim is to ensure the development of networks and services at the lowest cost and of the highest quality within the Community. Thus, telecommunications operators must ensure full interconnectivity between public networks in order that the aims of technological innovation, economic progress and better service provision to the end-user can be achieved. Those aims must, however, be obtained in conformity with the Community's competition rules, which are designed to remove trade barriers and restrictive practices created or maintained by both state monopolies and private companies.

The guidelines contained in the Communication are not, of course, capable of creating enforceable rights nor will they affect the application of competition rules by the ECJ or by Member States' authorities. Their purpose is:

- to clarify the application of Articles 85, 86 and 90 EC to the telecommunications sector;
- to explain the relationship between these rules and other Community legislation to deregulate the industry; and
- to create new standards.

For example, the guidelines provide examples of situations where abuses of dominant position by public operators might take place, such as the refusal to provide access to the

---

[37] The European Telecommunications Standards Institute (ETSI), tasked with improving the speed and scope of standardisation procedures in this area, had been dominated by the European Conference of Postal and Telecommunication Administrations (CEPT) which had proved slow and inefficient.

[38] CEN – European Committee for Standardisation
CENELEC – European Committee for Electrotechnical Standardisation.
[39] COM (88) 48.
[40] OJ 1991 C233.

network and cross-subsidisation of non-reserved activities. Similarly, in the case of private businesses, examples are given of abuses such as the refusal to supply necessary interfaces.

The Commission's first legislative step concerning the application of competition rules to the services area of the telecommunications sector came when it adopted Directive 90/388/EEC. This was designed to open up access to the telecommunications market by abolishing all special or exclusive rights relating to the supply of telecommunications services other than voice telephony.[41] The Commission justified its action in taking this step by reference to Article 90(3) EC which concerns public undertakings and the Commission's right to take appropriate measures, including adoption of secondary legislation, to ensure Community competition law is not breached. In brief, Directive 90/388/EEC requires the deregulation of services, including leased lines connected to the public switched network. This should mean that any service provider could offer voice or data communication to a company or a group of companies. The result of this is to provide an effective mechanism to break up both state and private monopolies in telecommunications services.

The use of Article 90(3) in that instance followed its use in the equipment area of the telecommunications sector where the Commission had adopted Directive 88/301/EEC,[42] which required that the Member States:

- publish the technical specifications which their equipment must meet so that equipment from other Member States can be adapted to the national network;
- ensure the separation of the regulatory and commercial functions of telecommunications authorities as network operators, which had enabled these authorities to keep competitive products away from the market;
- release subscribers from contracts to accept the terminal equipment supplied by the telecommunications authorities, allowing users to obtain their equipment from an alternative source.

However, the use of Article 90 to break up the various forms of telecommunication monopoly has not been greeted favourably by the Member States, not least because it enables the Commission to adopt a Directive without first consulting the Council of Ministers. Both telecommunications Directives created on the basis of Article 90 have been contested by the Member States before the ECJ. In both cases, however, the ECJ's rulings were broadly in favour of the Commission's actions.

The first case was brought by France against the Commission in connection with the adoption of Directive 88/301/EEC.[43] Here, France, supported by four other Member States,[44] applied for the annulment of Directive 88/301/EEC, firstly, on the grounds that the Commission could not adopt such legislation under Article 90(3) EC, and secondly because it obliged the Member States to:

- ensure the withdrawal of special or exclusive rights which they had granted to undertakings dealing in telecommunications terminal equipment;[45]

---

[41] OJ 1990 L192.
[42] OJ 1988 L131.
[43] Case C-202/88 *Re Telecommunications Terminal Equipment: France* v *Commission* [1992] 5 CMLR 552.

[44] Italy, Belgium, Germany and Greece.
[45] Article 2.

- ensure that independent standards authorities were established;[46]
- make it possible for consumers to terminate long-term leasing or maintenance contracts for terminal equipment concluded when special or exclusive rights existed;[47] and
- report to the Commission annually on compliance with those obligations.[48]

The ECJ held that the Commission had not misused its powers under Article 90(3) since the Directive did not make specific findings that particular Member States failed to fulfil their obligations under the Treaty and that the Commission was entitled to adopt the Directive as part of its supervisory function under Article 90(3). Further, the ECJ stated that the existence of exclusive rights with respect to the importation, marketing, connection and bringing into service of telecommunications terminal equipment was incompatible with Article 30 EC and that therefore the Commission was justified in requiring their withdrawal. However, the obligation to withdraw special rights was invalid since the Commission had failed to specify in the Directive the type of rights involved or in what way they were contrary to the Treaty. The obligation to establish independent standards authorities was justified to protect competition, but the obligation to provide for termination of long-term contracts was invalid since there was no State involvement in concluding those contracts. In general, therefore, the ECJ held that the Directive was sufficiently reasoned with respect to its valid provisions. Thus the Directive was allowed to stand, although those parts of Article 2 of the Directive related to special rights, Article 7 in its entirety, and those parts of Article 9 related to the former provisions, were annulled.

The second case was *Spain, Belgium and Italy* v *Commission*.[49] The Member States in this case applied for the annulment of Directive 90/388/EEC.[50] In its ruling the ECJ restated the fact that Article 90 did not restrict the Commission's activities to merely ensuring that Community rules were correctly applied in the Member States. It could also be used to end exclusive rights, particularly where these rights were in contravention of Article 86 EC.[51] The Court therefore supported the measures taken by the Commission in Directive 90/388/EEC to abolish the exclusive rights of establishment and exploitation of telecommunications services given to telecommunications organisations by the Member States.

However, the ECJ went on to state that Article 90 does not give the Commission the right to cancel special rights where those rights are not clearly defined in the Directive, and Article 1 of the Directive did not specify exactly what kinds of rights were being targeted, or indeed the ground on which those rights could be said to breach Treaty provisions. In addition, other provisions from the EC Treaty should have been used by the Directive to enable users, bound by long-term service supply contracts, to terminate them as of 1 January 1993. The Commission is expected to propose an amendment to Directive 90/388/EEC as a result of this ruling which will specify the nature of the special rights that are being targeted in the 1990 Directive.[52]

[46] Article 6.
[47] Article 7.
[48] Article 9.
[49] Joined Cases C-271/90, C-281/90 and C-289/90, published in OJ 1992 C326. Decision of October 1990.
[50] *Op. cit.* at note 41.

[51] By allowing, or creating, an abuse of a dominant position. See Chapter 13: Competition policy.
[52] Coopers and Lybrand, *EC Commentaries: Telecommunications*, 24 February 1994.

Standardisation

One of the Community's main aims in the area of technology has been the achievement of Community-wide standards, and in the area of telecommunications this is particularly important to ensure the open and competitive market required to support Community businesses. In order for the Commission to oversee this process properly, it must have all relevant information before it adopts any technical provisions. To this end a number of legislative measures have been adopted to provide a gradual harmonisation of telecommunications standards within the Community.

A procedure for the provision of information in the field of technical standards and regulations is laid down in Directive 83/189/EEC.[53] This states that the Commission, the Member States and their standards institutions are to be informed of plans by any of the standards institutions to draw up or to amend a national standard. This is primarily designed to ensure that Member States' standards institutions do not introduce standards in a field in which a European standard is being prepared. The Commission may also request information on national standardisation programmes in order to review the development of standardisation activity in the telecommunications sector.

Further consultation is required by Recommendation 84/549/EEC[54] on a common approach in the field of telecommunications. This aims to ensure that the Member States' telecommunications administrations engage in consultation with each other before introducing any new service, and that all new services are introduced on the basis of a common approach to recognised EC standards.

The issue of standardisation in the field of information technologies and telecommunications is dealt with in Decision 87/95/EEC.[55] It lists measures required to be adopted so as to achieve the required level of standardisation. These measures cover IT standards and specifications for services concerning electronic data and information interchange offered over public telecommunications networks. It further provides a schedule for the standardisation of information and telecommunications technology, noting that public buyers are obliged to refer to the EC standards in any procurement tender calls.

Following these measures the Commission published a Green Paper on the Development of European Standardisation Action for Faster Technological Integration in Europe,[56] designed to stress the importance of the harmonisation approach to the completion of the internal market and accelerate the formation of EC standards.

The adoption of Directive 89/336/EEC[57] on the approximation of the laws of the Member States relating to electromagnetic compatibility was designed to protect public telecommunication networks and equipment connected to them from electromagnetic disturbances. This seeks to harmonise the national legislation in this field and to guarantee the free movement of electrical and electronic apparatus without lowering the existing levels of protection. While national standards will be enforceable during the transitional period, they will have to undergo a Community inspection procedure to ensure they satisfy the protection objectives set out in the Directive. In early 1994 the Commission published a

---

[53] OJ 1983 L109, as amended by OJ 1992 L221.
[54] OJ 1984 L298.
[55] OJ 1987 L36.
[56] OJ 1991 C20.
[57] OJ 1989 L139, amended by Directive 92/31/EEC, OJ

1992 L126 – extension of transition period; and Directive 93/68/EEC, OJ 1993 L220 – amends Article 12 in line with legislation on the affixing and use of the CE mark of conformity on industrial products.

Communication setting out the titles and references of harmonised standards under the Directive.[58]

In accordance with a proposal contained in the Green Paper on Telecommunications, the European Telecommunications Standards Institute (ETSI) was established in March 1988. ETSI plays an important role on the European telecommunications standards scene. Its main role so far has been to prepare a common standard for the establishment of a Community-wide ISDN system.

Further to this a Resolution was adopted in 1989 on standardisation in the field of information technology and telecommunications[59] which required all Member States to participate in the ETSI standard adoption procedure. It also requested that ETSI and CEN/CENELEC began negotiations with regard to the creation of a single European standardisation body, and that ETSI's members ensured that any pre-standardisation and standardisation work was carried from a common position as early as possible.

Pricing and service

An issue of concern to the Commission has been the pricing of telephone calls within the Community and, in particular, the high prices charged to the EC consumer when combined with a general lack of real competition between the TOs. Thus, in 1990, it began an investigation of international telephone charges. The purpose of this investigation was two-fold, first to establish pricing levels, and second to ensure that Community competition law was not being breached. This action was based upon a Council Resolution in 1988[60] which had called for lower tariffs in order that the customer would be charged a sum closer to the actual costs incurred by the TOs. It was followed in 1991 by a formal inquiry which focused upon international charges to customers and the level of costs and accounting rates which are decided by the Community's fifteen telecommunications groups.

In 1992 the Commission submitted to the Council a Communication entitled *Towards Cost Orientation and the Adjustment of Pricing Structures – Telecommunications Tariffs in the Community*.[61] This noted that there were large disparities in telephone charges in the different Member States and that a continuing lack of trans-European structures was preventing effective development of EC-wide telecommunications.[62] However, the Commission, in attempting to combat such disparities, faces the difficult task of balancing the need of the Community TOs to raise sufficient revenue to develop their telecommunication networks and compete effectively against their rivals against the Community aim of reducing or eliminating existing tariff barriers.

In the Communication, the Commission suggested that TOs should publish and make available to customers all tariffs and subsequent changes, as this would allow consumers to make an informed choice as to the nature, and provider, of their services. TOs should also reduce, or remove entirely, those tariffs which discriminated by virtue of a transborder element, and be more flexible in their use of tariff zones within the Community. The aim of these measures was to benefit residential users in less developed areas and also develop national and cross-border integration of services. The Commission also requested that, where

---

58 OJ 1994 C49.
59 OJ 1989 C117.
60 OJ 1988 C257.
61 SEC(92) 1050.

62 A call made from one Member State to another may cost up to three times more than an internal call in that Member State, over the same distance. Equally rates between Member States vary considerably.

the TOs' costs were reduced by large-scale service provision, they pass on a significant element of this reduction to the consumer. Other consumer benefits proposed were wider use of off-peak reductions on telecommunications tariffs, and special pricing schemes for pensioners and the handicapped.

In response to that Communication, the Council adopted a Resolution[63] concerned with cost orientation and the adjustment of pricing structures and telecommunications tariffs in the Community. This called upon the telecommunications organisations to reduce the price of services closer to the costs of their provision, especially for intraCommunity telecommunications services. Similarly it required a general lowering of accounting rates for intraCommunity telecommunications traffic. The Commission was urged both to undertake studies and consult with interested parties, in order to determine the type of measures required to bring about a uniform service throughout the Community. The aim of this was that, following the consultation and study period, the Commission would provide a clear framework and timetable for the regulation of the Community's telecommunications market.

Such regulation and harmonisation of services, however, has proved difficult to achieve. Some idea of the problems that surround the issue of providing uniform public telecommunications services within the Community can be gained from an examination of the seeming inability of the Member States and TOs to provide for even basic services.

The Council, in Decision 91/396/EEC,[64] required the introduction of a single European emergency call number. The intention was that the number chosen, '112', would be introduced in public telephone networks, parallel to any other existing national emergency numbers, by 31 December 1992. It then adopted Decision 92/264/EEC[65] to harmonise the international telephone access codes in the Community, which aimed to introduce the prefix '00' in all Member States for access to the international telephone network in the EC from 1 January 1993. Finally it adopted a Resolution[66] on the promotion of European-wide co-operation on numbering of telecommunications services. The objective of this Resolution was to adopt a unified European access code to be used when dialling from outside the EC.

None of these measures seems particularly radical, yet so far the response to them has been poor. With regard to the single European emergency call number, an extended deadline of 31 December 1996 was provided for special cases, but it appears that some Member States may not achieve even that target. As for the introduction of the harmonised international access code, by early 1994 only Greece, of those countries not already using the '00' prefix, was able to show compliance with its provisions. Thus the requirement that the harmonised prefix must be operational throughout the Community by 1 January 1998 and available in all Member States by 1 January 1996 seems increasingly unlikely. In the light of these difficulties, blamed upon technical problems within the Member States, a unified European access code seems similarly far off. Seemingly undeterred, however, the Commission is currently proposing the harmonisation of the use of magnetic public telephone cards. At present each Member State has its own type of card and, unsurprisingly, none are compatible with those of other Member States. Another concept that is also being promoted by the Commission is that of 'universal services' and to this end it has adopted a Communication

63 OJ 1993 C2.
64 OJ 1991 L217.
65 OJ 1992 L137.
66 OJ 1992 C318. The Resolution also provides for the creation of a 'European Numbers Office' (ENO) which would be responsible for setting up a forum to carry out analyses of the long-term market and technology implications of numbering recommendations.

'Developing Universal Services for Telecommunications in a Competitive Environment'. This defines the term 'universal services'[67] and contains a Council Resolution on universal services.[68] The Communication states that such universal services should be the right of all consumers, including the disabled and other disadvantaged users, and should be provided at a reasonable cost. These universal services should be paid for by direct contribution from TO revenues; by access charges on new operators and service providers; and by the Community itself, notably in disadvantaged regions. Such an ideal would appear to be somewhat at odds with the competitive aspect of the telecommunications sector, and again reveals the often schizophrenic attitude of the Community towards competition and regulation.

The future

At present the European TOs appear to be in a strong position, with the prospect of an increasingly unified and standardised Community market in which to operate. However, as with the information technology market of 20 years ago, there is already strong foreign competition, notably from US TOs, such as the varied 'Baby Bells'.[69] If the Community cannot manage the balancing act between deregulation for the purposes of competition at a national level and regulation to ensure a consistent level of services at the Community level, the Member States may well relapse into the type of protectionist tactics that surrounded the demise of both the old-style industries, such as steel and shipbuilding, and the information technology sector.

THE CONTROL OF DATA AND PROTECTION OF PUBLIC PRIVACY IN THE COMMUNITY

Increasingly, technology has begun to pose wider problems for the Community institutions and Member States than merely to ensure that Community producers can hold their own in the world markets. Amongst the new problems is the fact that technological advance has vastly increased the ability of individuals and businesses to process information. With even basic desktop personal computers it is now possible to process data at speeds and levels of complexity that would previously have been impossible to achieve with even the best manual methods of data processing. It is clear that the ability to process data in this manner not only has implications for trade, but may equally affect individual rights, and it is in this area that the Community institutions have developed a regulatory role for themselves which clearly moves considerably beyond consideration of purely economic factors.

In the modern state, it has to be accepted that there will be a conflict between the individual's right to privacy and the need for a free flow of information. The aim of regulation in this sphere is thus to achieve a balance between the two. Privacy cannot be an absolute right, as it is essential for society to have certain information about the individual, but on the other hand questions have to be asked about the type of information that society

---

[67] The right to have a phone, to have a good quality of service and maintenance, to have clear and fair procedures governing relations between customer and TO, and to be offered new services as they are developed.

[68] OJ 1994 C48.

[69] The US Regional Bell Operating Companies (RBOCs) formed when the US federal courts forced the break-up of American Telephone & Telegraph (AT & T) in 1983.

needs, how to ensure that the information held is only used for legitimate needs, and how the individual can ensure that the information concerning him or her is accurate and complete, and not subject to misuse. With regard to these questions it is important to distinguish between the information that an individual has to give, for example information given to the authorities for the purpose of assessing social benefits, and information which the individual has given voluntarily, such as information on a consumer survey questionnaire. That distinction is however blurred by the fact that individuals may have to provide information in order to obtain services they cannot do without, such as the utilities. Even where information is given voluntarily, there will still be a need to ensure some degree of data protection. The amount of information that is available in a given society will depend on a number of different factors including social and political traditions. However, in all cases the advantages provided by computerisation will inevitably lead to increasing amounts of personal data being stored, processed and manipulated.

The use of computerised data in the trading environment is increasingly a key part of the modern economy, and it is therefore essential that the Member States and their producers are in a position to make use of the information thus provided. Given the nature of the Community, it is obvious that, because data protection rules will determine the extent to which businesses can use this data technology, where there are inequalities in the strength of protection provided this will play a part in determining the competitiveness of national firms. As the Commission is attempting to create a level playing field for businesses within the internal market, some degree of harmonisation of national data protection legislation would appear desirable. However, it is also the case that the Community and its institutions have begun to develop a social dimension in addition to the original economic theme, and this social dimension is couched in terms of protecting the rights of Community citizens to the highest possible level. It is also presently the case that some Member States, for instance Germany, have indicated their unwillingness to allow data to be transferred from their territory, where a high protection is given to personal data, to territories where there is lesser or indeed no protection afforded to such data, such as Spain. This too militates for a Community-wide solution to the question of data protection. The question is, how can this be achieved?

There appear to be two main approaches. The first would entail the adoption of general principles based on a widespread consent between the Member States, and the second, harmonisation by way of exact Community legislation. The former approach was taken by the Convention of the Council of Europe on the computerised processing of personal data,[70] which is presently the only international Convention that exists on the issue, but this leaves open a large number of options for the implementation of the framework principles and has only been ratified by seven Member States.[71] The latter approach, harmonisation by legislation, has been adopted by the Commission in the draft Directive on data protection. In the light of the vast differences between the protection afforded by Member States, such as Germany and Spain, it appears that achieving widespread consent will be at best difficult and at worst impossible. Thus the Commission's approach appears to offer the best chance of success.

In 1990 the Commission submitted a Communication[72] to the Council on the protection of

[70] 108/81, 28 January 1981.
[71] As of early 1994. Those states are the UK, Germany, Denmark, France, Ireland, Luxembourg and Spain.
[72] COM (90) 314.

personal data and information security which introduced six proposals designed to provide an overall framework ensuring Community nationals a high level of protection with regard to data processing and transfer. The first of these led to the draft Directive on the protection of individuals with regard to the processing of personal data and the free movement of such data, presented by the Commission in July 1990.[73]

The draft framework Directive concerning the protection of individuals in relation to the processing of personal data

The original draft Directive of 1990 was amended by the Commission in October 1992, partly as a result of its first reading by the European Parliament, where no less than 158 amendments were proposed,[74] and also because of industry pressure based on the fact that the proposal was seen to be excessively rigid. The amendments have resulted in an overall simplification of the text, but specific changes from the first draft include that:

- press exemptions will be left up to the Member States;
- the draft Directive will cover data processed by associations and foundations, subject to special derogations;
- the principle of protection of individuals will be identical for both the public and private sector;
- the criteria relating to the notification of data processing to the supervisory authorities have been improved;
- the issue of transfer of data to third countries has been clarified.

The draft Directive seeks to remove the barriers to the free movement of personal data between Member States while ensuring a high level of protection for individuals. It is necessary because Greece, Belgium, Italy, Spain and Portugal had no specific data protection legislation to protect private 'data subjects'. It applies the principle of subsidiarity and lays down the main guidelines for legislation, leaving it up to the Member States to implement the common principles of the Directive and to select the methods and procedures for ensuring that those principles are effectively applied.

The draft data protection Directive applies to both data held on computerised systems and to data held in manual files.[75] The Directive is designed to protect the rights and freedoms of individuals with respect to the processing of personal data within the Member States, especially their privacy, but may not be used by a Member State to restrict or prohibit the flow of data between the Member States.[76] Personal data is defined as data which can be related to an identified or identifiable natural person or 'data subject'. Data which falls outside this definition is not subject to the Directive.[77] Also not subject to the Directive is data processed in the course of an activity which falls outside the scope of Community law or which is processed by a natural person in the course of a purely private and personal activity.[78] In terms of territorial application, the Directive will apply to data processed by a

[73] OJ 1990 C227/3 last amended in OJ 1992 C311/30.
[74] See OJ 1992 C311.
[75] Article 3(1). Unlike, for instance, the UK's Data Protection Act 1984 which applies only to computerised data.

[76] Article 1.
[77] Article 2.
[78] Article 3(2).

controller within a Member State's territory or within its jurisdiction, and to data processed by a controller outside the Community who uses a means within the Community.[79] Where the controller is located outside the Community he must name an individual within the Member States who will be responsible for the oversight of his rights and obligations.[80]

Data processing will only be lawful if it is carried out in accordance with the principles contained in Chapter II of the draft Directive.[81] In Section I this provides that data must be collected and processed fairly and lawfully,[82] for specified, explicit and legitimate purposes, and that its use must be compatible with those purposes.[83] The data must also be adequate, relevant and not excessive for the purpose for which it is to be used.[84] It should also be accurate and up to date, and provision should be made for deletion of inaccurate or out-of-date material.[85] Its storage should be in a form which allows for the identification of individual data subjects only for the purpose for which it was collected.[86] All of the above tasks are the responsibility of the controller of the data.[87]

Further, Section II states that personal data may only be processed if the data subject has consented; where the processing is necessary for the preparation or performing of a contract with the data subject; where the processing is required by a provision of national or Community law; or to protect the vital interests of the data subject; or the performance of a task in the public interest; or where it is necessary to the legitimate interests of the controller or a third party to whom the data is disclosed, except where these are overridden by the rights of the data subject.

Section III relates to special categories of data which are subject to particularly stringent checks on their use. This includes data which reveals the racial or ethnic origin of the data subject, their political persuasions, religion, philosophical or ethical persuasion, membership or otherwise of trade unions and data concerning health and sex life.[88] General processing of this data is forbidden, but exceptions may be made where the data subject authorises the processing;[89] where it is carried out by a foundation or non-profit making association of a political, philosophical, religious or trade union character as part of its legitimate business and only when the processing concerns data on its own members or those who have regular contact with it, and that the data may not be passed on to third parties;[90] or in circumstances where there is no infringement of privacy or the data subject's fundamental freedoms.[91] A derogation is also left to the Member States on public interest grounds to provide exemptions from the above rule, but exercise of this derogation must be by national legislative provision and: state the nature of the data to be processed, determine those to whom the data may be disclosed, designate a controller or controllers, and provide suitable safeguards.[92] A similar provision relates to data concerning criminal convictions.[93] The Directive leaves the issues of national ID numbers or similar identifiers[94] and exemptions for the media[95] subject to the control of the relevant Member States.

[79] Article 4(1).
[80] Article 4(2).
[81] Article 5.
[82] Article 6(1)(a).
[83] Article 6(1)(b).
[84] Article 6(1)(c).
[85] Article 6(1)(d).
[86] Article 6(1)(e).
[87] Article 6(2).
[88] Article 8(1).

[89] Unless the Member State concerned prevents the data subject from waiving the prohibition of processing.
[90] Article 8(2)(b).
[91] Article 8(2)(c).
[92] Article 8(3).
[93] Article 8(4).
[94] Article 8(5).
[95] Article 9.

Sections IV and V of the Directive deal with the issue of the information which should either be given, or be made accessible, to the data subject. This includes the right to know that a processing operation exists, its purpose, the type of data used, those to whom the data will be passed and the name and address of the controller or his representative.[96] Member States may provide exemptions from such disclosure where issues of national security, defence, criminal proceedings and public safety are involved, as well as situations where a paramount economic and financial interest of either the Member State or the Community is affected, or a public authority monitoring or inspection function is at issue, or an equivalent right of another individual will be affected.[97] Similarly when the data is disclosed to a third party the controller should ensure that the data subject is informed of this fact and of his rights to relevant information.[98] However, if the data subject has been informed in advance that it is likely that third parties will be given the data, or disclosure is for a legal reason which lays down an exemption from the need to disclose, or the disclosure is for the reasons listed in Article 14(1), such notification is not necessary.[99] When the data is collected, the controller should ensure that the data subject knows why it is being collected, whether or not the answers the subject is asked to give are voluntary or compulsory, the consequences of failure to answer, who will receive the data, the fact that the data subject may access the data and have it corrected if necessary, and the name and address of the controller or his representative.[100] This is subject to exception where such information would make the verification and supervision functions of a public authority more difficult, or threaten public order.[101]

Data subjects must also be granted the right to obtain, both quickly and cheaply, confirmation that data is being held on them, what that data is, where it was obtained and what it will be used for. Also the data subjects must be able to refuse access to their data for the benefit of a third party, unless that third party request is based on national or Community law. In the event that incorrect, incomplete, or illegally-held data is found, the data subject will be given the right to rectification, erasure or blocking of the data, including in relation to the transmission of data to third parties.[102] Data subjects are also permitted to object on legitimate grounds to any data processing involving data concerning themselves,[103] and may not, subject to certain exceptions, be subjected to an administrative or private decision which is based solely on an automatically-processed personality profile.[104]

The data controller is obliged to ensure the security of the processing, transmission and storage of the data,[105] and must notify the national supervisory agency before carrying out any processing activity.[106] Where the data processor or his representative cause damage to a data subject by unlawful processing, they will be liable in damages,[107] and Member States are required to provide for dissuasive penalties for those processors who do not comply with national regulations made in conformity with the Directive.[108]

With regard to third countries, Member States are required to ensure that personal data

96 Article 10(1).
97 Article 14(1).
98 Article 12(1).
99 Article 12(2) and (3).
100 Article 11(1).
101 Article 11(2).
102 Article 13.
103 Article 15.

104 Article 16.
105 Article 17.
106 Article 18. See below for details of the national supervisory agencies.
107 Article 23.
108 Article 25, misprinted in the *Official Journal* as a second Article 24.

may only be transferred to such countries if they provide an adequate degree of protection. However, exceptions are made where the data subject has consented to the transfer, or the transfer is necessary for performance of a contract between data subject and controller, or the transfer is in the public interest or the best interests of the data subject.[109] Member States may inform the Commission if they think that a third country does not reach the required level of protection,[110] and the Commission may then enter into negotiations with the country to remedy this.[111] It remains to be seen how well third countries will take, firstly, to being told that their data protection rules are inadequate and, secondly, to having the Commission try to pressure them into change.[112]

The draft Directive provides for the creation of national supervisory agencies.[113] These will be independent and responsible for monitoring the application of the national rules under the Directive. The authorities will carry out prior checks on processing operations that pose specific risks, conduct investigations, bring infringement actions in front of national courts, co-operate with one another and publish annual reports. A member of each of these national bodies will then sit on a Community working party which will assess the application of the national rules, and the level of protection provided in the Community and third countries, and provide advice to the Commission on further measures to protect the privacy of individuals.[114]

The overall result of the draft Directive would be to place relatively severe limits upon the ability of businesses within the Community to categorise people for purposes such as targeting them for direct mail services. As matters stand, it will allow Member States' governments to provide broad exemptions, but even with this apparent concession the draft Directive is regarded unfavourably by institutions such as the financial-services and mail-order businesses, as these rely to a large extent upon 'profiling' personal data to market their services to certain target groups. It has been suggested by the British Direct Marketing Association, that far from reducing the amount of junk mail which individuals receive, the main effect of the Directive will be to create more junk mail as the ban on 'profiling' would oblige firms to send more letters out to get an equivalent response to the one they would have got if they had targeted their mailings.[115] At present the draft Directive is being opposed by a broad spectrum of businesses, including the broadcasting industry, direct-mail firms, advertisers, banks and insurance companies, on the grounds that it would effectively prevent them using databases and lists either to target customers or judge potential clients. It should be noted, however, that the Member States' ability to simplify the Directive's scope, or even exempt those operations which are 'not liable to infringe data subjects' rights' when creating the relevant national legislation, could in fact mean that up to 80 per cent of all current processing operations would not be affected.

At present the compliance date for Member States to implement the provisions of the draft Directive is 1 July 1994, with processing operations begun before that date to be brought

---

109 Article 26. Given the vagueness of the Directive with regard to what constitutes an adequate level of protection, it is difficult to say how much of a problem this might be for those involved in trade or data processing agreements with third countries' nationals.
110 Article 26(3).
111 Article 26(4).
112 The US has on occasion used economic pressures on third countries to enforce issues which as recognition of

intellectual property rights, but this has been highly controversial.
113 Chapter VI, Article 30.
114 Chapter VI, Articles 31–32.
115 By way of example, the BDMA states that, in Germany, where the 'opt-in' system operates, private households receive on average 63 pieces of unsolicited commercial mail per year, while in the UK, where the 'opt-out' system exists, the average is 43 pieces.

into compliance with it by 1 July 1997. However, such are the differences between the Member States that, should it finally be accepted, application of the proposal is not likely to occur until at least 1995 or 1996.

Other Community proposals

With regard to the other five proposals set out in the 1990 Commission Communication to the Council on the protection of personal data and information security,[116] these were as follows:

- a proposal for a Council Resolution to extend protection to any kind of personal data in public sector files which do not fall within the scope of Community law;
- a proposal for a Commission Declaration for protection principles to cover data held by Community institutions and bodies;
- a proposal for a Council Directive concerning the protection of personal data and privacy in the context of public digital telecommunications networks, in particular the integrated services digital network (ISDN) and public digital mobile networks.[117] These services require a high level of personal data protection in line with the new digital telecommunications environment discussed above.
- a proposal for a Recommendation to initiate negotiations for the Community's adhesion to the Council of Europe Convention already ratified by seven Member States. This will allow the Community to establish official contacts with non-Community countries party to the Convention, including Eastern European countries.
- a proposal for a Council Decision in the field of information security.

Only the last of these proposals has so far resulted in any legislation being adopted.[118] With the rapid increase in the amount of electronically-processed and transferred information, the degree of security of that information and, in particular, measures to further increase that security, have become of worldwide importance. The aim of the Decision is to set about the creation of an effective and practical system of security for electronic information for general users, administrations and the business community, but to attempt to do so without compromising the rights of the general public. The plan, carried out over a 24-month period, constitutes the first comprehensive information security plan worldwide and includes work to be carried out to improve the development of standard specifications and for the harmonisation of existing information security provisions. As a result of this, a Senior Officials Group has been created to advise the Commission on the adoption of further measures designed to protect the security of information systems.

The Schengen Convention – developing a Community policing database?

The removal of internal checks at Member States' borders may have improved the ability of goods and persons to achieve free movement within the Community, but it has created

---

116 *Op. cit.*, note 72.
117 OJ 1990 C277/4.

118 OJ 1992 L123.

serious problems for those involved in the area of law enforcement. This is because the ability to control, to some degree, access and egress from one Member State to another has long played an important part in European law enforcement agencies' strategies for prevention of international crime, such as drug smuggling and terrorism. The loss of that ability means that those law enforcement agencies have now been forced to consider other methods of dealing with these problems. A major initiative designed to tackle some of these problems was agreed at Schengen in 1990 with the signing of the Schengen Convention.[119] Whilst this is not strictly a Community measure, only Denmark, the UK[120] and Ireland are presently not members, so it has generated much discussion amongst Member States and Community commentators.[121] The Convention deals with a large number of issues, such as cross-border observation and the cross-border pursuit of criminals,[122] but the majority of these are outside the scope of this chapter, which will concentrate primarily on the computer system to be set up for the exchange of data between Member States' law enforcement agencies, the Schengen Information System (SIS),[123] and the proposed regulation of the exchange of data other than that contained in the SIS.[124]

One of the major aims of the Convention is to ensure the efficient exchange of information between the signatories, in particular concerning asylum seekers, individuals wanted for arrest and missing persons. The main channel for that information will be the Schengen Information System, a joint computerised information system, the idea for which was mooted during the initial Schengen Accord discussions in 1985. By 1988 actual negotiations were underway, and at this time four of the five original members of the Schengen group already had some sort of computerised system to process police data.[125] The actual design of the system was problematic, with four possible alternatives:

- a direct link between the national police information systems of the Schengen countries;
- a dedicated Schengen computer in each participating country linked via a network;
- a central database on a central Schengen computer in one country;
- identical national information systems in each country kept up to date by a central information system.

In the event, the last of these options was chosen. This system operates on the principle that only the national authority responsible for placing particular information on the central database can change or delete that data. The central system is theoretically designed to ensure data integrity and make sure that all the national systems remain identical with all changes having to pass through the central system.[126]

---

119 Following the 1985 Schengen Accord concerning the gradual abolition of the checks at the common borders. *European Yearbook*, Vol. XXXII 1986 at 17–25. At this stage Germany, Belgium, France, Luxembourg and The Netherlands were involved.

120 The UK's position is that the links between the police forces of the 12 Member States used to discuss co-operation, made under the TREVI (Terrorism, Radicalism, Extremism, Violence International) arrangements, are the correct forum for the types of issue currently being considered under the Schengen agreement.

121 See for instance, O'Keeffe, 'The Schengen Conven-

tion: A Suitable Model for European Integration' (1991) 11 YEL 185; Schutte, 'Schengen: Its meaning for the Free Movement of Persons in Europe' [1991] 28 CMLR 549; Dumortier, 'Data Protection in the Schengen Convention' in Proceedings of the International Conference on Computers and Law held in Montreal, 30 September–3 October 1992, Section B4.4.

122 The so-called 'hot pursuit' proposal.

123 Title IV of the Convention.

124 Title VI of the Convention.

125 Germany, Belgium, France and The Netherlands.

126 For further details see Dumortier, *op. cit.* note 121.

What may be contained in the SIS is defined in Article 94 of the Convention which limits the data to that required for the purposes of achieving the objectives noted in Articles 95 to 100. Before submitting a report to the SIS, the State concerned must be sure that the seriousness of the case merits its inclusion. This includes data about individuals, vehicles and other objects, such as firearms, banknotes and ID documents. A report on an individual may contain up to 10 pieces of information, including forename and surname, first letter of second forename, visible and permanent physical features, date and place of birth, sex, nationality, a note stating 'armed' or 'violent', the reason for the report and the action which the reporting nation requires to be taken, such as 'arrest'. There are five categories of individual who may be the subject of an SIS report: those required to be arrested for extradition;[127] those aliens already refused entry to the Schengen States;[128] individuals listed as missing persons or required in protective custody;[129] witnesses and others required to appear before the courts in criminal proceedings;[130] and those under covert surveillance or direct checking.[131]

Access to the data contained in the SIS is restricted;[132] only those authorities responsible for border checks and other internal police and customs checks have the right to search all the data, while authorities responsible for issuing visa or residence permits have a lesser access to reports of aliens for the purpose of refusing entry. Data from the SIS may only be used for the purpose for which the report was made,[133] unless prior consent is obtained from the reporting State and the data is needed to prevent a serious and imminent threat to public order, a serious breach of State security, or the commission of a serious offence.[134] Personal data recorded in the SIS can only be kept for the time necessary to achieve the purpose for which it was supplied. After three years on the SIS, the need to retain a piece of data must be reviewed by the State which reported it, as the CSIS will otherwise automatically delete it. If necessary the reporting State may ask for an extension to the three-year period. Only the reporting State may amend, supplement, correct or delete data which it has introduced into the SIS.[135]

In theory, any individual may have access to information held on him in the SIS,[136] although this may be refused on a variety of grounds.[137] This access can be exercised in the State of the individual's choice and, as the degree of access will depend on the law of that State, there appears to be nothing to stop an individual from 'shopping around' in order to find the national rules which provide best access. If an individual discovers factually-inaccurate information held on him in the SIS, he is entitled to have it corrected; if it is legally incorrect, it must be deleted.[138] This can be achieved before the courts or the relevant authority under domestic law and such decisions, including decisions to award compensation, will be binding.[139] Each State is responsible under its national laws for any injury caused to an individual via its use of the national data file of the SIS.[140] Each State has

---

[127] Article 95(1).
[128] Article 96.
[129] Article 97.
[130] Article 98.
[131] Article 99.
[132] Article 101.
[133] Article 102(1).
[134] Article 102(3).

[135] Article 106(1).
[136] Article 109.
[137] Article 109(2). An example is where releasing the information would hinder the ability to carry out the legal task specified in the report.
[138] Article 110.
[139] Article 111.
[140] Article 116.

to provide an independent supervisory authority to monitor its national data file,[141] and a central independent supervisory body will be set up to monitor the CSIS.[142]

The problem with these provisions is that they are, as currently stated at least, lacking in the degree of precision that one would hope for in a system of such potential importance. In the absence of formal Community harmonisation, which would be provided by the adoption of the present draft Directive on data protection, there is only a very low level of personal data protection across the Schengen States, and some States such as Italy provide no protection at all. As the Convention relies heavily on the use of the States' own laws to protect individual rights, this means that there will be a very unequal spread of rights across the contracting States. Certain of the Articles are also open to potential abuse due to their having been drafted in vague terms. For instance Article 99(2)(b) provides that a report can be made 'where an overall evaluation of the person concerned, in particular on the basis of offences committed hitherto, gives reason to suppose that he will also commit extremely serious offences in the future'. This would, first, seem to run counter to the ECJ's line of reasoning on the free movement of persons and, second, allow a very wide amount of discretion to the reporting body. The derogations provided to the States are also couched in very wide terms with no indication of what 'public order and public safety' entail. As it appears that this will be left to the States' own courts to decide there is a risk that a number of different formulations will arise.

It is with respect to aliens that the potential problems are clearest. An alien reported on the SIS by a State as not to be admitted entry to any of the Schengen States will be barred even though the reason for the report may not be considered to be a reason for reporting in all of the States. Indeed it has been suggested that aliens can be reported on the SIS on the grounds of unimportant convictions, unproven suspicions and non-compliance with domestic immigration regulations, as none of these things are prevented by the existing rules. Any legal remedy for such a disproportionate report will depend on the protection afforded by the national courts, and thus will vary from State to State. It should also be noted that there is no duty to inform an alien that data is being held on him in the SIS, thus rendering the issue of access to remedies irrelevant, as the individual will have no knowledge on which to base an appeal.

It is clear that there is considerable scope for conflict between Community law and the provisions of the Convention, both in the area of data protection and the free movement of persons. However, it should be noted that the draft Convention between the EC Member States on the crossing of their external borders (External Borders Convention) would provide for a common computer system containing a list of undesirable third country nationals who have been banned by one Member State and would thus be barred from entering all the other Member States to prevent them circumventing that ban. It is clear therefore that the Schengen Convention provides a clear indication of both the trend in the storage and use of computerised data to monitor the movement of individuals both when entering and when moving within the Member States, and the problems that are likely to arise as a result, if proper and precise controls are not applied to the holding and use of that data.

---

141 Article 114.   142 Article 115.

CONCLUSION

This chapter has taken a broad look at the impact of Community law upon a number of areas of technology. However, even given the diversity of topics covered, there are general points which can be drawn from this survey. Probably the most important concerns the changing role of the Community, as it moves away from the goal of purely economic regulation towards developing a more social dimension. As a consequence of this shift, the aim of increased competitiveness amongst European producers has been tempered by a desire to ensure that individuals or regions do not suffer as a consequence. These two aims may often seem incompatible. For example, in the field of telecommunications, the Community, while promoting deregulation and competition on the one hand, on the other risks burdening Community producers with social obligations. This can only be to the advantage of less heavily socially-regulated, non-Community competitors who will be able to avoid the cost involved in maintaining non-profitable regions of the Community. By contrast, in the area of data protection, the degree to which the Commission has sought to protect individual rights has been considerably diluted as a result of the vociferous opposition of the Member States and those industries which rely on intensive personal data processing.

As has been noted above, there is a similar strange dichotomy between the Commission's desire to encourage competition between European producers and its provision of programmes for their collaboration on technology projects. The idea that collaboration in such technical research can be restricted to some vaguely defined pre-competitive phase or, indeed, that in such matters there is a pre-competitive phase, has proven to be a contentious one. With the Commission increasingly inclined to use its powers under Community competition law where it perceives a breach, it is likely that the issue of pre-competitive research will have to be more exhaustively defined, if necessary by the ECJ, lest producers find themselves accused of forming cartels or engaging in concerted practices.

Finally, the developments surrounding the Schengen Convention suggest that the Community itself will increasingly come to rely upon technological solutions to the policing of its external frontiers and, indeed, of its own population. However, as yet it appears to have neither adequate legal measures to prevent the abuses of individual rights made possible by such solutions, nor the ability to prevent the migration of information to unregulated data havens outside the Community.

The draft Database Directive, even in its attenuated form, appears to provide limited protection to the individual, at the expense of considerable inconvenience for data processors within the Community. It is thus arguable that the Community, in its current form, is potentially risking both the rights of its citizens and its economic future.

The area of technology is therefore one full of policy contradictions, influenced heavily by the diverse social and political aims of both the Community institutions and the Member States. As a result, it is likely to see increasing friction, and resulting resort to the law, between the Institutions, the Member States, and the Community's producers and citizens.

Further reading

Hoeren, T., 'Electronic Data Interchange: the perspectives of Private international law and data protection' [1992] 1 *Law, Computers and Artificial Intelligence* 329.

O'Keeffe, D., 'The Schengen Convention: A Suitable Model for European Integration' (1991) 11 YEL 185.

Prins, C., 'Legal Aspects of Electronic Data Interchange Standardisation: the boundaries and effects of standardisation and network use' [1992] 1 *Law, Computers and Artificial Intelligence* 311.

Schutte, J. J. E., 'Schengen: Its meaning for the Free Movement of Persons in Europe' [1991] 28 CMLR 549.

Tapper, C., 'New European Directions in Data Protection' (1992) 3 JLIS 9.

CHAPTER 16

Sex discrimination law

INTRODUCTION

Community policies on sex discrimination are, perhaps, more properly considered as part of the development of the idea of 'Social Europe' and, therefore, simply as an aspect of social policy, which is considered in Chapter 17. Certainly, the ideas underlying the development of sex equality legislation are similar. However, sex discrimination law in the Community has a somewhat separate history from other aspects of social policy. Sex discrimination law draws on the general principle of equality, which gives it a more solid legal foundation within the Community than many other aspects of social policy, most of which arise out of the Community's general harmonisation powers.[1]

Both economic and social considerations led to the inclusion of the first sex equality rule, Article 119 EC in the 1957 Treaty. Article 119 provides that:

> Each Member State shall . . . ensure and . . . maintain the application of the principle that men and women should receive equal pay for equal work.
>
> For the purpose of this Article 'pay' means the ordinary basic or minimum wage or salary and any other consideration, whether in cash or in kind, which the worker receives, directly or indirectly, in respect of his employment from his employer.
>
> Equal pay without discrimination based on sex means:
> (a) that pay for the same work at piece rates shall be calculated on the basis of the same unit of measurement;
> (b) that pay for work at time rates shall be the same for the same job.

This provision reflected economic considerations more than social ones. France, having national equal pay legislation, wanted to ensure that all Member States would be subject to the same obligations, so that labour costs in all Member States would be subject to the same factors. Perhaps because sex discrimination law in the Community was not initially thought of as social protection for vulnerable workers, Member States were by no means diligent in implementing its principles into their law. Nor was the Commission as vigorous in its pursuit of Member States in early years as it was later to become, as will be seen in the discussion of the temporal effect of equal pay judgments by the ECJ.

The attitude of the Commission has changed drastically from its initial reluctance, which produced few initiatives. Since 1980, the Commission has initiated three action programmes on equality between men and women, with the support of the European Parliament. The third action programme covers the period of 1991–95, with an emphasis on subsidiarity[2] and

---

[1] See Docksey, 'The Principle of Equality between Men and Women: a Fundamental Right Under Community Law' (1991) 20 ILJ 258; Arnull, *The General Principles* *of EEC Law and the Individual* (1991).

[2] See Chapter 3.

co-operation between levels of government. These action programmes combine research, monitoring of existing rights and efforts to improve the legal protection of women under Community law. However, most of the important legislation on equality of women and men comes from the 1970s, such as the Equal Pay Directive 75/117/EEC and the Equal Treatment Directive 76/207/EEC. Since 1980 the Council has been unable to agree to pass most of the proposed legislation put forward by the Commission, and most of the legislation which was passed could be termed fine-tuning rather than the introduction of new principles. A notable recent exception is the pregnancy and maternity Directive, passed during the British presidency in late 1992, which will be discussed at the end of this chapter. Also, there has been an increasing use of so-called soft law, such as recommendations and resolutions. These types of legislation do not produce binding obligations on Member States, as set out in Article 189 EC, but have proved useful as standard-setting mechanisms in difficult and controversial areas, such as sexual harassment.

Article 16 of the Community Charter of the Fundamental Social Rights of Workers provides for equal treatment between women and men. Chapter 8 of the Commission's Action Programme for the Charter is directed to the implementation of this principle[3] and focuses on some of the agenda of the Equal Treatment Action programmes, such as parental leave, burden of proof in discrimination cases and retirement age. Pregnancy is also dealt with as a health and safety issue.

Equal pay in the Treaty: Article 119 EC

The original economic motive for Article 119, avoiding competitive disadvantage or 'social dumping', has changed to a more social approach, seeing gender equality as a fundamental right.[4] However, Member States did not adhere to their obligations to reduce pay differentials within the transitional period, which ended on 1 January 1962. The Commission monitored the failure to implement but failed to take any enforcement actions under Article 169.[5] It was only as a result of the Article 177 reference in *Defrenne* v *SABENA*, over a decade later, that the ECJ had the opportunity to declare the infringement of Article 119 by a Member State.

Gabrielle Defrenne was an air hostess with the Belgian airline SABENA. Her contract required her to retire at the age of 40, whereas male cabin attendants were not required to retire at that age. Further, she found that although she was principal cabin attendant, women were paid less than men. Women also received a smaller State pension than men did. The last of these grounds of complaint was the first to be brought before the ECJ, which ruled that State pensions were not covered by the EC Treaty.[6] After this unsuccessful action against the Belgian state, Gabrielle Defrenne took two actions against her employer, SABENA, one concerning equal pay and one concerning the consequences of the differential retirement ages. The last of these two cases also failed on the ground that the applicant's complaints related to working conditions rather than pay.[7]

---

3 COM (89) 568 final Brussels.
4 On the political history of Article 119, see Nielsen and Szyszczak, *The Social Dimension of the European Community* (1991), at 81–2.
5 *Ibid*, at 82.
6 Case 80/70, *Defrenne* v *Belgian State* [1971] ECR

445. Issues relating to State pensions are now dealt with in the State Social Security Directive 79/7/EEC, discussed below.
7 Case 147/77, *Defrenne* v *SABENA* [1978] ECR 1365. Issues of working conditions are now dealt with in the Equal Treatment Directive 76/207/EEC, discussed below.

Gabrielle Defrenne was, however, successful in her equal pay claim.[8] Advocate General Trabucchi reminded the Court that Article 119 enabled Member States to fulfil their obligations under International Labour Organisation Convention No 100 on equal pay for work of equal value. The Court responded that Member States were obliged to have implemented the principle of equal pay arising out of Article 119 by the end of the transitional period and that individuals could rely on the direct effects of the Article against both public and private sector employers despite the failure to implement in good time.[9]

The meaning of 'pay'

As is apparent from the drafting of Article 119, the scope of the concept of pay is much wider than merely salary or wages. Pensions have posed a particular problem for the ECJ in its interpretation of 'equal pay', and will be dealt with separately below. In general, the Court has taken the language of Article 119 as far as possible in bringing reward-based conditions of employment under its scope. This is understandable for two reasons. Primarily, there appears to be a desire to put as much as possible within the ambit of Article 119, which, being a Treaty Article, has horizontal direct effects and can, therefore, be invoked against private sector employers. Secondly, the Court has tried, in its judgments, to eliminate methods by which employers could undermine the spirit of the equal pay guarantee. If equal pay only covered basic salary then it would be impossible to challenge an employer whose male employees had greater access to perks such as company cars or entertainment allowances.

The key to this wide interpretation is the use of language such as *'en raison de l'emploi'* or *'in ragione dell'impiego'* which translates as 'by reason of the employment'. This form of words would imply a less strict connection between the reward and the contract of employment than does the actual English version 'in respect of his employment'. Advocate General Ver Loren Van Themaat argued in *Burton v British Railways Board* that the broader wording in the non-English language versions should be followed, and that the English version itself should be seen to express the same spirit.[10] In terms of monetary rewards the Court began an inclusive interpretation of pay even before the *Defrenne* case. In *Sabbatini v European Parliament*, a case decided on the grounds of the general principle of equality, the Court decided that expatriation allowances should be subject to this principle of equal pay.[11]

Any employer contributions which influence the level of entitlement of a worker to a State benefit will count as pay, not just payments by the employer to the employee. In *Worringham v Lloyds Bank*[12] employees receiving employer contributions towards their pensions in the form of a higher salary never even held the money. The payment was purely notional and was removed immediately to the employee's pension plan. However, the employer contribution was pay for two reasons: (1) employees under the contributory scheme received a reimbursement of those sums if they left before entitlement to the pension and, more

---

8 Case 43/75, *Defrenne v SABENA* [1976] ECR 455.
9 For further details on the direct effect issue, see Chapter 5, and for a discussion of the difficulties arising out of this delayed clarification of the law, see 'Temporal effect problems' below.
10 Case 19/81, [1982] ECR 555, at 588–9.

11 Case 32/71, [1972] ECR 345. Similarly, in Case 58/81, *Commission v Luxembourg* [1982] ECR 2175 head-of-household allowances were considered to be pay for the purposes of Article 119.
12 Case 69/80, [1982] ECR 767.

importantly, (2) the contribution was included in gross salary for the purposes of calculating other entitlements such as redundancy payments. As will be explained in greater detail below, state social security schemes are not pay, but any employer contribution to such schemes, if it affects gross salary for the purpose of calculation of a benefit linked to salary, will be pay and covered by Article 119.[13]

The concept of pay has been taken even further, to totally non-monetary forms of reward. *Garland* v *British Rail* [14] was the first case to discuss the issue of non-pay benefits or 'perks', in that case entitlement to reduced rail fares for the employee and his or her family. Not surprisingly the ECJ decided that the material form of pay was irrelevant and that it did not have to arise from the contract of employment itself, thus confirming that the phrase 'in respect of' employment did indeed have the same scope as 'by reason of' employment. The formula used by the ECJ, most recently in *Arbeiterwohlfahrt der Stadt Berlin* v *Botel* [15] is that pay includes 'all consideration, whether in cash or in kind, whether immediate or future, provided that the worker receives it, albeit indirectly, in respect of his employment from his employer, whether under a contract of employment, by virtue of legislation or on a voluntary basis'. This last factor is very important. If employers' discretionary payments, such as bonuses, were not covered by the Article, it would be a simple matter for employers to avoid their obligations under the equal pay principle. In *Barber* the Court found that 'Although it is true that many advantages granted by an employer also reflect considerations of social policy, the fact that a benefit is in the nature of pay cannot be called in question where the worker is entitled to receive the benefit in question from his employer by reason of the existence of the employment relationship'.[16] Even payments to which an employer contributes pursuant to a statutory regime, such as sick pay, count as pay under Article 119 because they amount to a replacement for wages.[17]

The problem of pensions[18]

Pensions have created conceptual problems for the ECJ. State pensions are specifically covered by Directive 79/7/EEC. In *Burton* v *British Railways Board* the Court considered that conditions governing the eligibility for early retirement pensions under a voluntary redundancy scheme were an issue of working conditions rather than of pay. In *Defrenne (No 1)* the Court clearly found that State pensions could not be covered by Article 119, even before Directive 79/7/EEC was enacted. The Court said that this applied even when the employer contributed to such pensions. However, this left open the question of the status of private pensions, whether supplementary to or in replacement of, the State pension. In the first case in which the Court dealt with non-State pensions, *Bilka-Kaufhaus GmbH* v *Weber von Hartz*,[19] it did so cautiously. Advocate General Darmon presented the view that each individual scheme must be examined to determine whether or not it constituted pay. In that

13 Case 23/83, *Liefting* v *Directie van het Academisch Ziekenhuis bij Universiteit van Amsterdam* [1984] ECR 3225, at 3239. See also Case 192/85, *Newstead* v *Department of Transport* [1987] ECR 4753.
14 Case 12/81, [1982] ECR 359.
15 Case C-360/90, [1992] 3 CMLR 446.
16 Case C-262/88, *Barber* v *Guardian Royal Exchange Assurance Group* [1990] ECR I-1889, at 1950. See also

Case 33/89, *Kowalska* v *Freie und Hansestadt Hamburg* [1990] IRLR 447.
17 Case 171/88, *Rinner-Kuhn* v *FWW Spezial-Gebaudereinigung GmbH* [1989] IRLR 493. See also *Botel*, op. cit., note 15, where compensation for attendance at training courses was included as pay.
18 See Curtin, 'Occupational Pension Schemes and Article 119: Beyond the Fringe?' (1987) 24 CML Rev 215.
19 Case 170/84, [1986] ECR 1607.

case, involving a 'top-up' pension scheme, he argued that it was covered by Article 119 because 'it applies only in so far as it is incorporated in the employment relationship, after negotiations with employers and employees'.[20] The Court agreed, on the basis that the scheme was grounded at least partly in contract rather than statute and that it was funded at least partly by the employer. This decision set up the essential distinction which the Court has made between pensions as pay and pensions as social security: as pay, pensions arise from contract, and as social security, from legislation. Nonetheless, because the Court had only decided on the issue of *supplementary* pensions, many argued that contracted-out pensions, which replace the State pension rather than supplement it, would not be regulated by Article 119 but only by the State Social Security Directive 79/7/EEC. In *Worringham*, the issue of contracted-out pensions was raised, but the court did not deal with the issue. Advocate General Warner did, however, submit that they were outside Article 119 if they were intended not to supplement State pensions, but in whole or in part to replace them. The Court finally clarified the issue, rejecting the proposed reasoning of Advocate General Warner, in *Barber* v *Guardian Royal Exchange Assurance Group*:[21]

> this concept, as defined in Article 119, cannot encompass social security schemes or benefits, in particular retirement pensions, directly governed by legislation without any element of agreement within the undertaking or the occupational branch concerned, which are compulsorily applicable to general categories of workers.[22]

The Court then proceeded to define the distinguishing characteristics of a pension scheme which qualifies as pay rather than social security:[23]

> . . . it must be pointed out first of all that the schemes in question are the result either of an agreement between workers and employers or of a unilateral decision taken by the employer. They are wholly financed by the employer or by both the employer and the workers without any contribution being made by the public authorities in any circumstances. Accordingly, such schemes form part of the consideration offered to workers by the employer.
>
> Secondly, such schemes are not compulsorily applicable to general categories of workers . . . affiliation to those schemes derives of necessity from the employment relationship with a given employer. Furthermore, even if the schemes in question are established in conformity with national legislation and consequently satisfy conditions laid down by it for recognition as contracted-out schemes, they are governed by their own rules.
>
> Thirdly, . . . even if the contributions paid to those schemes and the benefits which they provide are in part a substitute for those of the general statutory scheme, that fact cannot preclude the application of Article 119 . . . occupational schemes such as that referred to in this case may grant to their members benefits greater than those which would be paid by the statutory scheme, with the result that their economic function is similar to that of the supplementary schemes which exist in certain Member States [such as in the *Bilka-Kaufhaus* case].[24]

---

20 Case 170/84, *op. cit.*, note 19, at 1614.

21 Case C-262/88, *op. cit.*, note 16.

22 *Ibid.*, at 1951. Note that in a more recent case, Joined Cases C-110/91 and C-200/91, *Coloroll Pension Trustees Ltd* v *Russell*, Opinion delivered 28 April 1993, Advocate General Van Gerven was of the opinion that Article 119 applies not only to contracted-out pension schemes, but to all other forms of occupational pensions, and that it is immaterial whether or not the pension scheme was funded exclusively from employers' contributions or also from employees' contributions, whether voluntary or compulsory. The Court has yet to decide this case.

23 See Fitzpatrick, 'Equality in Occupational Pensions: The New Frontiers after *Barber*' 54 MLR (1991) 271.

24 Case 170/84, *op. cit.*, note 19, at 1951–2.

It should be noted that *Barber* requires that each element of pay be non-discriminatory.

As a result of the implications of the breadth of this judgment, Article 119 partially overtakes the Occupational Social Security Directive 86/378/EEC. In fact, insofar as this Directive provides for less generous rights to equal treatment in occupational pensions, it may even breach Article 119 and be partially illegal.[25]

The meaning of 'equal work'

Defrenne dealt with the situation where a man and a woman are doing the same job for the same employer in the same establishment, which is a straightforward discrimination issue. However, what happens if a man and a woman do the same job during different time periods? What if they do similar but not identical work? What if they do very different jobs, one of which requires more skill or qualification but is compensated by a lesser salary? What happens when you have only women working in an undertaking who are paid less than the industry standard?

Macarthys Ltd v Smith[26] considered the first of these problems. The applicant discovered that she was being paid less than the man she replaced. The Court decided that the scope of equal work is concerned exclusively with the nature of the services in question. Advocate General Capotorti was of the opinion that same work included jobs which are highly similar although not identical. The Court has not specifically pronounced on the issue of comparison with persons working for different establishments, which was raised but not answered in *Commission v Denmark*.[27] The Court in *Macarthys*, however, insisted on the existence of some form of actual, not hypothetical, male comparator.[28] Where the jobs themselves are segregated by sex, this may only constitute indirect discrimination, requiring extensive evidence as to reasons for pay patterns.[29] However, the existence of a comparator is not always crucial, as was decided in *Dekker v Stichting Vormingscentrum Voor Jonge Volwassen Plus*, which involved discrimination based on pregnancy.[30]

Equal value claims

Murphy v Bord Eireann Telecom[31] dealt with women doing work which involved services of greater value. The Court found that a woman could claim for equal pay, but not greater pay, than a man doing a lesser job. Article 119 does not require a precise proportionality between services and pay, only that women are not undervalued with respect to any available male comparator.

In *Defrenne* the Court said that equal value claims could only be remedied via Community secondary legislation. It appears, however, that since *Jenkins v Kingsgate (Clothing Productions) Ltd*[32] the Court accepts work of equal value, not only identical work, as a basis for a claim under Article 119. It found that Equal Pay Directive 75/117/EC did not create new rights or alter the scope of Article 119 but facilitated its implementation. More explicitly

---

25 See Curtin, *op. cit.*, note 18.
26 Case 129/79, [1980] ECR 1275.
27 Case 143/83, [1985] ECR 427.
28 Advocate General Van Gerven reaffirmed this view in his recent opinion in Case C-200/91, *Coloroll Pension Trustees Ltd v Russell*.

29 *Macarthys Ltd v Smith, op. cit.*, note 26, at 1289.
30 Case 177/88, [1991] IRLR 27.
31 Case 157/86, [1988] ECR 673.
32 Case 96/80, [1981] ECR 911.

in *Worringham* the Court said:[33] 'Article 1 of the Directive explains that the concept of "same work" contained in the first paragraph of Article 119 of the Treaty includes cases of "work to which equal value is attributed" '.[34] In *Murphy* this concept was extended to mean 'work of *at least* equal value'. The applicants were telephone maintenance workers in a factory who were paid less than a man who was a stores labourer. The Irish Equality Officer found that the applicants' work was of higher value and, therefore, not 'like work' (work of equal value) under Irish legislation. The applicants' case, therefore, failed, until reference to the ECJ from the Irish High Court, where the Court, on an *a fortiori* principle of interpretation, found that Article 119 should apply. If it applied to equal pay for work of equal value it must apply even more forcefully where an applicant was paid less for work of greater value than the male comparator. The Court also based its decision on the principle of effectiveness, saying that if such cases were not covered by Article 119 employers could evade the effect of the equal pay principle easily by giving one sex heavier responsibilities than the other, which would therefore allow the employer to pay them lower wages with impunity. Under the Equal Pay Directive, the Court, in *Commission* v *UK*[35] said that someone should 'be entitled to claim before an appropriate authority that his work has the same value as other work'.

Direct and indirect discrimination

Direct discrimination occurs when one sex is treated differently from another to its detriment. Indirect discrimination involves practices which make distinctions on other grounds but, in effect, act as discrimination based on sex. Even in *Defrenne*, the Court recognised that Article 119 must cover both direct and indirect discrimination. However, it confused the matter somewhat by distinguishing between the two types on the basis of overt, as opposed to disguised, conduct. This distinction is not particularly helpful in understanding the distinction between direct and indirect discrimination. Indirect discrimination involves practices which are often quite open, exactly because they do not purport to discriminate.[36] Such discrimination may even be unintentional, being simply the maintenance of traditional working practices. The overt/disguised distinction has been dropped in later cases and was explicitly rejected by Advocate General Ver Loren Van Themaat in *Burton*, although the Court had repeated the distinction in *Macarthys*.

It was in *Jenkins* v *Kingsgate (Clothing Productions) Ltd* [37], the first case where indirect discrimination was truly in issue, where the overt/disguised distinction was dropped and the notion of 'adverse impact' introduced. The applicant was a part-time worker who received 10 per cent less salary than male co-workers doing the same job full time. The question to the ECJ was whether Article 119 prohibits paying part-time workers less than full-time workers when the former category is composed exclusively or predominantly of women. The Court ruled that: 'the fact that part-time work is paid at an hourly rate lower than pay for full-time work does not amount *per se* to discrimination prohibited by Article 119 provided that the hourly rates are applied to workers belonging to either category without distinction based on sex'. The Court also ruled that:

[33] Case 69/80, *op. cit.*, note 12, at 790–1.
[34] *Jenkins, op. cit.*, note 32.
[35] Case 61/81, [1982] ECR 2601.

[36] Ellis, *European Community Sex Equality Law* (1991), at 69–70.
[37] Case 96/80, *op. cit.*, note 32.

. . . if it is established that a considerably smaller percentage of women than of men perform the minimum number of weekly working hours required in order to be able to claim the full-time hourly rate of pay, the inequality in pay will be contrary to Article 119 of the Treaty, where regard being had to the difficulties encountered by women in arranging to work that minimum number of hours per week, the pay policy of the undertaking in question cannot be explained by factors other than discrimination based on sex.[38]

Although the Court did not specifically resolve the issue of whether unintentional indirect discrimination was covered, the Employment Appeal Tribunal interpreted the relevant UK legislation as covering unintentional acts when the case returned to it after the reference.[39]

In *Bilka-Kaufhaus GmbH* v *Weber von Hartz*[40] the Court appeared to endorse the idea of Article 119 covering unintentional acts, with respect to differential treatment between part-time and full-time workers. The situation in this case was that part-time workers could only claim rights under a pension scheme if employed for 15 years out of 20, whereas no such requirement was placed on full-time workers. The Court found discrimination in favour of full-time workers and said that if full-time workers were predominantly men exclusion of part-time workers would violate Article 119 'where, taking into account the difficulties encountered by women workers in working full time, that measure could not be explained by factors which exclude any discrimination on the grounds of sex'.[41] The only defence would be 'objectively justified factors unrelated to any discrimination on grounds of sex'.[42] The prohibition, therefore, would appear to cover unintentional acts of indirect discrimination. The presence or absence of an intention to discriminate based on sex is, therefore, irrelevant. Even if the employer is acting only with the intention of discriminating in favour of full-time workers he or she may still be said to have committed indirect sex discrimination. In *Rinner-Kuhn* the Court reiterated the requirement of objective justification in the context of legislative regimes which constituted indirect discrimination. Recently, Advocate General Van Gerven argued that the use of actuarial tables to justify differing pension contributions or benefits to women and men could not be accepted, and such use constituted discrimination.[43]

Discrimination is also prohibited where the distinction is not women/men, but certain classes of women as against the rest of women and men. In *Liefting* v *Directie van het Academisch Zienkenthuis*[44] discrimination was found where a system of employer-contributions to certain types of pension scheme discriminated against female civil servants married to civil servants, and in *Worringham*, the discrimination was against female employees under 25. In *Dekker*, pregnancy, although only affecting some female employees, was held to be direct sex discrimination.

The draft Directive on Burden of Proof in Indirect Discrimination[45] used an adverse impact test, covered any 'provision, criterion or practice' and explicitly ruled out defences based on intention. A later version of the draft Directive dropped mention of intention, and the proposal was ultimately vetoed by the UK.

38 *Ibid.*, at 925.
39 Ellis, *op. cit.*, note 36, at 71–2.
40 Case 170/84, [1986] ECR 1607.
41 *Ibid*, at 1627.
42 *Ibid*, at 1626–7. See also Case 33/89, *Kowalska, op. cit.*, note 16.

43 Case C-200/91, *Coloroll, op. cit.*, note 28.
44 Case 23/83, [1984] ECR 3225.
45 OJ 1988 C/176/5, COM(88) 269 final.

Defences and justifications

Defences to direct discrimination were considered in *Macarthys*:[46] '. . . it cannot be ruled out that a difference in pay between two workers occupying the same post but at different periods in time may be explained by the operation of factors which are unconnected with any discrimination on grounds of sex'. It may well be that this is not so much a defence but an argument that there is no discrimination in the first place. In cases of indirect discrimination *Bilka-Kaufhaus* developed the idea of objectively justified factors which are unrelated to any discrimination based on sex:

> If the national court finds that the measures chosen by Bilka correspond to a real need on the part of the undertaking, are appropriate with a view to achieving the objectives pursued, and are necessary to that end, the fact that the measures affect a far greater number of women than men is not sufficient to show that they constitute an infringement of Article 119.[47]

The elements of this test are threefold: the real need of the enterprise, appropriateness and necessity. The latter two elements can be seen as aspects of a proportionality requirement.

The test developed in *Bilka-Kaufhaus* was applied in *Handels-OG Kontorfunktionaerernes Forbund i Danmark v Dansk Arbejdsgiverforening (acting for Danfoss)*[48] where the court said that if the employer's criterion of 'flexibility' meant quality of work, it justified differential pay because it was neutral, unless, systematically, female employees were never so rewarded. If it meant adaptability to variable work schedules and places then it could operate to the detriment of female workers with greater familial responsibilities. With flexibility and vocational training, differential rewards could be justified if they were of importance for the performance of the specific duties entrusted to the worker. Seniority, however, the Court held, did not have to be so justified, even though it recognised that this could have adverse impact on women who often leave the workplace for several years when they have children, or only enter it after the children are of school age. However, in *Nimz v Freie und Hansestadt Hamburg*[49] the Court recognised that the use of seniority as a criterion could amount to indirect discrimination and its objectivity would depend on the circumstances of the pay scheme as a whole.

In *Rinner-Kuhn*, on the question of State legislation which could constitute indirect discrimination, the Court laid down a strict interpretation of the *Bilka-Kaufhaus* test, as applied to State action:[50]

> If . . . the Member State is in a position to establish that the means selected correspond to an objective necessary for its social policy and are appropriate and necessary to the attainment of that objective, the mere fact that the legislative provision affects a considerably greater number of female than of male workers cannot be regarded as an infringement of Article 119.

[46] Case 129/79, *op. cit.*, note 26, at 1289.
[47] Case 170/84, *op. cit.*, note 40, at 1628. This idea was most recently applied in Case C-127/92, *Enderby v Frenchay Health Authority and Secretary of State for Health*, judgment of 27 October 1993, where the ECJ decided that where statistics demonstrate a significant difference in pay for jobs of equal value, one which is carried out almost exclusively by women and the other mostly by men, the employer must show that the difference is based on objectively justified factors unrelated to sex.
[48] Case 109/88, [1989] ECR 3199.
[49] Case C-184/89, [1992] 3 CMLR 699.
[50] Case 171/88, *op. cit.*, note 17, at 496.

The burden of proof is on the State.[51] This would require the intervention of the State in cases between individuals and their employers, the latter relying on the national legislation. In *Kowalska* v *Freie und Hansestadt Hamburg*[52] the Court found that where the pay discrimination arises out of a collective agreement the operation of Article 119 confers automatically on the disadvantaged group the same rights as those of the favoured group. This means that the Article does not merely annul the infringing measure but also remedies it without need for further action by the applicant.

Temporal effect problems

Since neither the Member States nor the Commission had taken seriously the obligations to equalise pay under Article 119, Member States and employers claimed that the judgment in *Defrenne* took them by surprise. This argument was made despite the fact that the Equal Pay Directive had been passed prior to the judgment. Member State interventions in the case led to a consideration by the Court of whether the judgment should apply to all cases going back to the deadline for implementation, or whether it should apply only to the future. The Court accepted the arguments of Member States that the Commission had essentially induced them to think that the full obligations under Article 119 were not in force, particularly since the Commission had never taken enforcement proceedings under Article 169 against any Member State. This inaction, according to the Court, raised an issue of legal certainty, which the Court found compelling. Criticisms of this ruling have been numerous.[53] Ultimately, the most compelling argument against the Court's decision is its incoherence. The rule in Article 119 is not for the benefit of the Commission but for that of individual workers, mostly women. Therefore, it is not for the Commission to waive the rule or to create what is, in effect, an estoppel.

The problems of the prospective ruling in *Defrenne* were largely questions of fairness. However, a similar ruling in the *Barber* case has created numerous practical problems as well. Here the problem was, as discussed above, the uncertainty over the status of contracted-out pensions. As with pay, Member States simply maintained their existing law rather than seeking clarification on the issue. The result was that when *Barber* was decided the potential consequence was a breakdown of the entire pensions system in the Community if employers had to compensate pensioners retrospectively. Once again the ECJ accepted these consequentialist arguments and restricted the effect of the ruling to the date of judgment, 17 May 1990.[54] As in *Defrenne*, there was an exception made for persons who had pending proceedings on the issue. The essential problem is what event is caught by the effective date? Does it require a change for existing pensioners or only for those whose pensions begin to be paid to them after the date? Or for those who leave employment after the date or for benefits accruing after the date? Or, most restrictively, only for those joining pension schemes after the date? This is the reason for the protocol on Article 119 EC, which

51 See Szyszczak, 'European Court Rulings on Discrimination and Part-time Work and the Burden of Proof in Equal Pay Claims' (1990) 19 ILJ 114.
52 Case 33/89, *op. cit.*, note 16.
53 Re prospective effect, see Wyatt, 'Prospective Effect of a Holding of Direct Applicability' (1975–76) 1 EL Rev 399; Neville Brown, 'Agromonetary Byzantinism and Prospective Overruling' (1981) 18 CML Rev 509; Ellis,

op. cit., note 36, at 85.
54 Since the Court was doing this for a second time it set down criteria for the use of a prospective ruling: 'A restriction of that kind may be permitted only by the Court in the actual judgment which gives the ruling on the interpretation requested', Case C-262/88, *op. cit.*, note 21, at 1956.

states that the *Barber* judgment does not apply to 'benefits . . . attributable to periods of employment prior to 17 May 1990'.

The protocol did not entirely remove doubt and, consequently, there has been new litigation demanding clarification on the issue of the temporal effect of the *Barber* judgment. Several cases from different Community jurisdictions were brought in 1991, and in April 1993 Advocate General Van Gerven issued his opinion. On the temporal effect of *Barber* he proposed that the ECJ rule that:

> The direct effect of Article 119 of the Treaty may not be relied upon in order to claim entitlement to an occupational pension which was acquired in connection with periods of employment served prior to the date of the judgment of 17 May 1990 in Case C-262/88 *Barber*, except in the case of workers or those claiming under them who have before that date initiated legal proceedings or raised an equivalent claim under the applicable national law.

The key factor has, therefore, been re-affirmed as the period of employment for which the pension is claimed. Consequently, anyone who retired before the judgment date is excluded from claiming, and those who retired afterwards can only claim in respect of the part of their employed life which occurred after the judgment. While this proposed ruling would prevent the upheaval which the pensions industry feared, it does lead to a very long transitional period. For example, a person who started work at the age of 16 in 1989 would probably not retire until 2038, but his or her pension would only partly be governed by the *Barber* rule.

Remedies

The *Defrenne* judgment requires levelling-up of pay, not levelling-down. In other words, the lower-paid workers must be raised to the level of the higher-paid workers. Similarly, in *Kowalska*[55] the principle was applied to collective agreements, and to pensions in the Advocate General's opinion in *Coloroll*[56], although he indicated that it might be possible to introduce new schemes with lower pension benefits for all.

The Equal Pay Directive 75/117/EEC

The original purpose of Directive 75/117/EEC was to harmonise national law on equal pay. However, before its implementation period had expired the *Defrenne* decision had been issued, making Article 119 directly effective horizontally. This Directive is, therefore, seen as providing implementation mechanisms for equal value claims, rather than creating new rights. Originally, in *Defrenne*, when it seemed that Article 119 only covered 'equal work', the respective roles of the Treaty and the Directive seemed clear. It appeared that the purpose of the Directive was to go beyond the provisions of the Treaty, which had, as its legal basis, Article 100 rather than Article 119. However, once 'equal value' claims could be made by means of Article 119 the Directive was more 'to facilitate the practical application of the principle of equal pay outlined in Article 119 of the Treaty'.[57] The Directive can, therefore, be seen as having an explanatory or elucidatory purpose, although it has been argued that

[55] *Op. cit.*, note 16.
[56] *Op. cit.*, note 22.

[57] *Jenkins, op. cit.*, note 32, at 927.

the Directive was always intended as an expansion of the principle of equal pay from the Treaty.[58]

It should be noted that the possible direct effect of the Directive has been put before the Court several times, but has never been resolved.[59]

'Equal value' in Article 1 of the Directive

Unlike Article 119, the Equal Pay Directive has been the subject of several enforcement actions by the Commission. *Commission* v *UK* [60] dealt with UK law which provided for equal pay where people doing 'like work' or jobs were rated as equivalent in a job evaluation study, which could only be ordered with the consent of the employer. The UK argued that Community law did not give a right to the evaluation of one's job, only to equal pay once the job was considered of equal value. The Court responded that job classification was only one of several methods of determining equal value, which was the essence of the right:

> The UK's interpretation amounts to a denial of the very existence of a right to equal pay for work of equal value where no classification has been made . . . Such a position is not consonant with the general scheme and provisions of the Equal Pay Directive 75/117.[61]

Further, the Court ruled that where there is disagreement as to the application of the equal value concept, it must be possible for a worker to bring a claim for the determination of equal value and, if successful, to receive a binding decision acknowledging his or her equal pay rights. The UK had failed to live up to its obligations under the Directive by failing to provide measures which could be used by any employee who felt that he or she had an equal value claim. In *Commission* v *Denmark*[62] the Danish government had failed to implement the Directive properly by only providing for equal work and not equal value claims, and by failing to provide machinery by which workers could seek redress. The Danish government could not rely on the fact that most workers were covered by collective agreements which implemented the equal pay principle – the State was obliged to see that all workers were covered by the principle, when not covered by a collective agreement or where such agreement did not sufficiently guarantee the principle. This is particularly the case, according to the Court, because non-unionised workers are generally the most vulnerable to abuse. In both of the above cases the Court rejected arguments based on declarations made by the States upon the passing of the Directive – unilateral declarations cannot interpret or change State obligations.

It could be questioned whether 'all aspects and conditions of remuneration' in Article 1(1) of the Directive goes further than 'pay' in Article 119 even as interpreted by the Court. However, this is unlikely. Note that in *Barber*, on Article 119, discriminatory *access* to pay was considered to be prohibited discrimination.

Job classification systems

The proper application of job classification systems can be crucial to the successful implementation of the Equal Pay Directive. *Rummler* v *Dato-Druck GmbH*[63] gave the Court the opportunity to analyse a job classification scheme used by an employer. The applicant

---

58 Nielsen and Szyszczak, *op. cit.*, note 4, at 86–7.
59 See Ellis, *op. cit.*, note 36.
60 Case 61/81, [1982] ECR 2601.
61 *Ibid.*, at 2615.
62 Case 143/83, [1985] ECR 427.
63 Case 237/85, [1986] ECR 2101.

challenged the evaluation criteria, saying that she should have been put in a higher-paid category because, for her, packing parcels of 20 kg was heavy physical work. Her employer argued that the job in itself only made light physical demands. The Court dealt with the question as an issue of indirect discrimination, which allowed for objective justification by the employer. The Court's judgment is somewhat equivocal on the question of criteria such as strength, which may appear to be objective but create an adverse impact on women. The Court asserted that criteria must be used which do not differ according to whether the work is done by a man or a woman. This rejected the applicant's argument concerning her subjective experience of the level of physical effort required. On the other hand, the Court ruled that if the effect of the criteria was to discriminate against one sex or another then the job classification scheme would be in breach of the Directive. Physical effort was considered to be a valid criterion but it would be prohibited discrimination to use the average performance of one sex as a scale on which to classify everyone. The Court ultimately said that it was the scheme as a whole which must be examined to see whether it amounted to discrimination. Apparently, from this judgment, suspect job classification criteria will be viewed within the context of the whole system of job classification under the criteria for justifying indirect discrimination, as developed in *Bilka-Kaufhaus*. The ruling in *Rummler* puts to rest a fear arising out of the *Commission* v *UK* case, that if an employer provided a job evaluation as required by the Directive, a worker could no longer complain that he or she was not receiving equal pay for work of equal value, even if the job classification system was clearly designed to entrench discriminatory pay practices.

Burden of proof

In order to make the guarantee of equal pay for work of equal value effective, it is necessary that a worker should be able to determine with ease where he or she should fit into the pay scale and job classification system. This requirement has been termed 'transparency'.[64] In *Danfoss* the Court said that where the pay system lacked transparency the burden of proof would be on the employer to establish that the pay system was not discriminatory. The job classification scheme had basic pay rates which were supplemented by the employer under the criteria of flexibility, vocational training and seniority, as discussed above under Article 119 EC.

The Equal Treatment Directive 76/207/EEC

The legal basis of this Directive is Article 235, which provides that:

> If action by the Community should prove necessary to attain, in the course of the operation of the common market, one of the objectives of the Community and this Treaty has not provided the necessary powers, the Council shall, acting unanimously on a proposal from the Commission and after consulting the Assembly, take the appropriate measures.

The powers under Article 100 EC for the harmonisation of laws for the establishment and functioning of the Common Market were thought inadequate to justify a Directive on sex discrimination other than pay, since only pay is explicitly mentioned in the EC Treaty. Equal

[64] The Commission recently adopted an Opinion on equal pay, OJ 1993 C248, which stresses the principle of transparency of salaries and wage structures.

treatment is defined and explained in Article 2 of the Directive and covers both direct and indirect discrimination. The Court has yet to decide whether Article 119 EC and this Directive are mutually exclusive. However, given the greater utility of Article 119 against private sector employers, it seems likely that any areas of potential overlap would be resolved in favour of the Treaty Article.

Article 2(1) of the Directive also covers discrimination based on marital or family status, which clarifies a potential area of dispute. Since the *Dekker* case, which is discussed in full below, it is clear that the Directive's prohibition on sex discrimination covers discrimination based on pregnancy.

Article 3: access to employment

Article 3 of the Directive covers all issues relating to hiring and promotion. In *Dekker* v *Stichting Vormingscentrum Voor Jonge Volwassen Plus*[65] the Court decided that, as a matter of direct discrimination, refusal to employ a woman because she was pregnant was a breach of Article 3. Elizabeth Dekker applied for a job at a youth training centre. The selection committee recommended her as the most suitable candidate, but the centre refused to hire her when she revealed that she was pregnant because its insurer would not reimburse sickness benefits if the employer knew that she was pregnant when it hired her. The insurer was permitted under Dutch law to do so. The Dutch courts considered that this constituted sufficient justification, but on reference to the ECJ the possibility of such an economic justification was rejected because the Court saw discrimination based on pregnancy as direct rather than indirect discrimination. The Court further decided that it was not necessary to find a comparable situation for a man, which the UK courts and tribunals have required. Refusal to employ someone based on pregnancy is a motive which attaches uniquely to the female sex. Therefore, the motive for refusal is inherently discriminatory. A distinction has been drawn, nonetheless, between pregnancy itself and illness caused by pregnancy. The *Hertz*[66] case made illness arising from pregnancy a matter of indirect sex discrimination and, therefore, subject to the objective justification criteria. This would only apply beyond the normal maternity leave period, however.

The issue of discrimination based on pregnancy is due to be refined further when the ECJ decides the case of *Webb* v *Emo Air Cargo (UK) Limited*.[67] This case involves a woman who was hired in order to replace another employee who was about to take maternity leave. She then revealed to her employer that she was also pregnant, which resulted in her dismissal. The question is whether she can claim that she has been discriminated against on the grounds of sex. The judgment of the ECJ in *Dekker* would indicate that she should succeed in her action, since discrimination on the ground of pregnancy is direct discrimination. However, the position of the employer, who must now find a replacement for the replacement, is somewhat more sympathetic than that of the employer in *Dekker*. It would appear, however, that the only way in which the employer can succeed is if the ECJ dilutes or abandons its ruling in *Dekker*.

In the enforcement action against the United Kingdom,[68] paragraph 2 of Article 3 was in

---

[65] Case 177/88, *op. cit.*, note 30.

[66] Case 179/88, *Handels-OG Kontorfunktionaerer-nes Forbund I Danmark (acting for Hertz) v Dansk Arbejds-giverforening (acting for Aldi Marked K/S)* [1991] IRLR 31.

[67] The House of Lords decision can be found at [1993] 1 CMLR 259.

[68] Case 165/82, [1983] ECR 3431.

374 European Community Law

issue. The Commission argued that the UK had failed to implement its obligations under the Directive because no law in the UK prohibited discrimination in collective agreements or internal company or professional rules. The Court held that the Directive applied to collective agreements or employers' rules, whether or not they were intended to produce legal effect, as long as they in fact governed the employment relationship. This is consistent with the view taken by the Court in the *Kowalska* case,[69] discussing Article 119, where it said that discrimination in collective agreements was covered by Community law and should be remedied by the disadvantaged group having the same provisions applying to them as the favoured group, in proportion to their situation, such as in ratio to the number of hours worked.

Article 4: vocational training

Article 4 takes a broad view of training and includes vocational guidance and retraining. It was raised in *Johnston* v *Chief Constable RUC*[70] to argue that the applicant should be able to receive the same firearms training as male officers.

Article 5: conditions of work/dismissal

The definition of dismissal given in the *Burton* case was that the concept should be 'widely construed so as to include termination of the employment relationship between a worker and his employer, even as part of a voluntary redundancy scheme'.[71] The applicant failed here, however, because the scheme in question was linked to the statutory pensions and, under the State Social Security Directive 79/7, discrimination in pension ages has been specifically allowed. Retirement and related issues continued to be problematic because of the close relationship to entitlement to State pensions. It was originally unclear whether dismissal would cover compulsory retirement. Traditionally in the UK, compulsory retirement ages have been linked to eligibility for State pension and, therefore, usually occurred at age 60 for women and 65 for men. In *Marshall* v *Southampton and Southwest Hampshire Area Health Authority (Teaching)*,[72] this issue was finally clarified in a challenge to the UK practice. In *Marshall* the Court made a clear distinction between entitlement to State pension and the decision by an employer to set compulsory retirement ages. In other words, retirement age and pension age are two separate concepts. This result is largely a reflection of emerging practices, particularly in managerial and professional areas, where retirement ages are usually the same regardless of sex. In fact, compulsory retirement itself has come to be viewed as controversial in some fields and, even when compulsory retirement has been abolished, a standard pension age is still set by the State. Retirement age and State pension age are increasingly separate areas of regulation, particularly when an increasing number of workers participate in contracted-out pensions, which are usually more flexible as to the age at which workers can retire and claim their pension. The Court in *Marshall* attempted to distinguish the *Burton* case on the ground that the retirement regime in *Marshall* was not *tied* to pension ages as was the regime in *Burton*. In the cases on pay and pensions, *Bilka-Kaufhaus* and *Barber*, the Court has clearly read the exemption in the Social Security Directive as strictly

[69] Case 33/89, *op. cit.*, note 16.
[70] Case 222/84, [1986] ECR 1651.
[71] Case 19/81, *op. cit.*, note 10, at 575.
[72] Case 152/84, [1986] ECR 723.

limited and has not, therefore, allowed it to permeate other legislation. In *Roberts* v *Tate and Lyle Ltd*[73] the Court added that even where a redundancy scheme involves receiving an early retirement pension it is covered by Directive 76/207/EEC rather than the State Social Security Directive 79/7/EEC and that the fixing of different ages for the offer of early pension was a violation of Article 5 of the Equal Treatment Directive:

> However, in view of the fundamental importance of the principle of equality of treatment, which the Court has reaffirmed on numerous occasions, Article 1(2) of Council Directive 76/207, which excludes social security matters from the scope of that Directive, must be interpreted strictly. Consequently, the exception to the prohibition of discrimination on the grounds of sex provided for in Article 7(1)(a) of Council Directive 79/7 applies only to the determination of pensionable age for the purposes of granting old-age pensions and to the consequences thereof for other social security benefits.[74]

This discussion, of course, also raises questions about the relative spheres of application of the Equal Treatment Directive and Article 119 EC – when is the issue one of dismissal/retirement as opposed to one of pay/pension? Advocate General Van Gerven, in his opinion in *Barber*, said that the two legal provisions were not mutually exclusive, but then made the distinction between a condition governing the grant of a payment and a condition governing the continuation of the employment relationship.[75] The former would be governed by Article 119 and the latter by the Equal Treatment Directive.

The ECJ recently allowed a restriction of the scope of application of Article 5 in *Kirsammer-Hack* v *Sidal*[76] where it decided that it was permissible for national legislation to exclude workers from the protection of unfair dismissal legislation on the basis of number of hours worked, where there was no evidence that a considerably greater number of women than of men were affected by this exclusion.

Article 6: obligation to provide remedies

Article 6 of the Directive has been interpreted in light of the principle of effectiveness, which requires that Member States do everything necessary to ensure the full effect of Community law in their national systems. In terms of remedies the ECJ has applied the principle of effectiveness to ensure not only that the victims receive adequate compensation, but that the threat of sanction on employers who do not respect the principle of equal treatment is sufficient to deter them from attempting to avoid their obligations.

This principle of effectiveness in remedies is sometimes known as the *Von Colson*[77] principle. The decision of the Court in that case, where a violation of the principle of equal treatment was found, was that the applicant does not have the right to insist that she be hired, but remedies must be sufficient to fulfil the objectives of the legislation, in this case including a deterrent effect on the employer. Therefore, compensation must be sufficient, where it is awarded, to achieve this aim of deterring future misdeeds. The discretionary element of the implementation of a directive is maintained, in that Member States have the

73 Case 151/84, [1986] ECR 703.
74 *Ibid.*, at 704.
75 Case C-262/88, *op. cit.*, note 16, at 1929.
76 Case C-189/91, judgment of 30 November 1993.
77 Case 14/83, *Von Colson and Kamann* v *Land Nord-* *rhein Westfalen* [1984] ECR 1891. See Arnull, 'Sanctioning Discrimination' (1984) 9 EL Rev 267; Curtin, 'Effective Sanctions and the Equal Treatment Directive: The *Von Colson* and *Hartz* Cases' (1985) 22 CML Rev 505.

discretion whether or not to use damages as a remedy, but whatever remedy is chosen it must be sufficient to achieve the goals of the directive.[78] In *Dekker* the Court added that if a State uses 'a civil law sanction, a contravention of the prohibition of discrimination in itself should be sufficient in order for *full* liability of the discriminator to arise. No grounds for justification in national law can be accepted'.[79] This seems to require that States make sex discrimination a strict liability offence, at least for cases of direct discrimination. A second *Marshall* case also dealt with the issue of effectiveness of a damages remedy, specifically the existence of statutory limits on damages.[80] Advocate General Van Gerven issued an opinion in this case arguing that Article 6 is directly effective and, further, that an upper limit on compensation is incompatible with Article 6, although he did not think that the imposition of an upper limit was an automatic failure to implement the Directive. His conclusion was based both on the principle of effectiveness and the notion of adequacy of compensation to the victim of discrimination. The ECJ agreed that Article 6 of the Directive was directly effective and decided that both the upper limit on compensation and the denial of interest on the compensation were inconsistent with the requirements of Article 6.

The *Von Colson* case also decided that Article 6, unlike the substantive Articles of the Directive, was not capable of producing direct effects because it was not sufficiently clear and unconditional, but that national courts were obliged to interpret national law in light of the provisions in Article 6 (see Chapter 5). However, in *Johnston* the Court found that Article 6 was directly effective insofar as it guaranteed access to some sort of judicial remedy.[81]

In *Danfoss* the Court put the burden of proof on the employer when it operated a non-transparent pay system, where the average pay of female workers is less than that of male workers. While this applied only to equal pay, it has been argued that this can be seen as a general reversal of the burden when a *prima facie* case is made by the applicant, partly because the general policy considerations of both Directives are the same and partly because, in *Danfoss*, the Court relied on a Community staff case dealing with the general principle of equality, *France v Commission*, where the issue was a non-transparent recruitment policy, rather than pay policy.[82]

Article 2: exceptions

In matters of direct discrimination, no justification based on economic considerations is accepted. In *Dekker*, for example, such arguments on the part of the employer were rejected. However, there are explicit exceptions contained in Article 2 of the Directive. It appears that the Court considers these exceptions to be exhaustive, as it has rejected an argument for exception on the basis of public safety put forward by the UK.[83] In the same case the Court laid great emphasis on the principle of proportionality as a guideline for acceptable limitations, which must be appropriate and necessary. In the enforcement action against Germany[84] the Court stated that Member States must compile a verifiable list of excluded

---

[78] For a discussion of the issue of remedies, see Shaw, 'European Community Judicial Method: its Application to Sex Discrimination Law' (1990) 19 ILJ 228.

[79] Case 177/88, *op. cit.*, note 30.

[80] Case C-271/91, *Marshall v Southampton and Southwest Hampshire Area Health Authority (No 2)*, judgment of 2 August 1993.

[81] Case 222/84, *op. cit.*, note 70.

[82] Case 318/86 [1988] ECR 3559; see Ellis, *op. cit.*, note 36, and also discussion of transparency, below.

[83] *Johnston, op. cit.*, note 70 at 1652–3.

[84] Case 248/83, *Commission v Germany* [1985] ECR 1459.

occupations and notify this to the Commission so that the Commission may fulfil its supervisory function.[85]

Article 2(2): sex of the worker a determining factor

In *Commission* v *UK* three exceptions in the Sex Discrimination Act were challenged: (1) employment for the purposes of a private household; (2) employment in an undertaking where the number of persons employed did not exceed five; and (3) the profession of midwife. The arguments of the UK concerning the sensitivities and personal relationships involved in the first two examples were not accepted by the Court, partly because of the blanket nature of the exemptions. Only in the final instance was the exception maintained because of the 'personal sensitivities' involved, although it indicated that it may take a different view in the future, as social conditions change. In fact, the UK government had intended this exception to be transitional only and has now included midwives in the Act, from an amendment in 1983. Arguments based on the context of the work performed were accepted by the Court in *Johnston*[86] concerning the restriction on the use of firearms by female police officers:

> However, it must be recognised that the context in which the occupational activity of members of an armed police force are carried out is determined by the environment in which that activity is carried out. In this regard, the possibility cannot be excluded that in a situation characterised by serious internal disturbances the carrying of firearms by policewomen might create additional risks of their being assassinated and might therefore be contrary to the requirements of public safety. In such circumstances, the context of certain policing activities may be such that the sex of police officers constitutes a determining factor for carrying them out.[87]

The Court does not explain why the risk of assassination only applies to women, or why it is more acute for women. It did, however, alert the national court to the necessity of ensuring that the principle of proportionality is respected. The Court also insisted, as the Directive requires, that such exemptions be reviewed periodically. In *Commission* v *France*, also concerning police activities, the Court set out certain criteria for the application of Article 2(2): 'the exceptions provided for in Article 2(2) may relate only to specific activities, that is, they must be sufficiently transparent as to permit effective supervision by the Commission, and that in principle they must be capable of being adapted to social developments'.[88]

Article 2(3): protection of women

In *Commission* v *Italy*[89] the Court accepted the extension of maternity leave rights to women but not men who had adopted children, as justified protection of maternity. This approach was also used in *Hofmann* v *Barmer Ersatzkasse*[90] where extra leave was granted to mothers, but not fathers, between the expiry of regular maternity leave and the child reaching the age of six months, rejecting the applicant's argument that the leave was for the benefit of the baby, not the mother alone. Protection of maternity does not only concern the biological condition of giving birth, but also the relationship between mother and child.

[85] See Docksey, *op. cit.*, note 1, at 268 on the differing approaches of Member States to the determination of excluded occupations.
[86] See Ellis, 'Can Public Safety Provide an Excuse for Sex Discrimination?' (1986) 102 LQR 496.
[87] *Johnston, op. cit.*, note 70, at 1686–7.
[88] Case 318/86, [1988] ECR 3559.
[89] Case 163/82, [1983] ECR 3273.
[90] Case 184/83, [1984] ECR 3047.

Beyond the protection of pregnancy and maternity the Court has been reluctant to accept arguments relating to the protection of women, on the ground that many such exemptions belong to a more paternalistic period, when male and female occupations were more distinct.[91] In terms of physical protection of workers, it is difficult to think of a danger posed to women, which does not also face men at least to some extent, including that of sexual assault. In *Johnston*, where this exemption was also argued as a basis for excluding female police officers from firearms training, the Court said:

> . . . it is clear from the express reference to pregnancy and maternity that the Directive is intended to protect a woman's biological condition and the special relationship that exists between a woman and her child. That provision of the Directive does not therefore allow women to be excluded from a certain type of employment on the ground that public opinion demands that women be given greater protection than men against risks that affect women and men in the same way and which are distinct from women's special needs of protection, such as those expressly mentioned.[92]

Other attempts to justify exemptions from the principle of equal treatment on the basis of protection of women have failed, such as *Ministere Public* v *Stoeckel* [93] which concerned German legislation instituting a general ban on night work for women.

Article 2(4): affirmative action

The justification of affirmative action has been argued once, without success, to attempt to justify special protection for women, rather than special opportunities for hiring, training or promotion.[94]

State Social Security Directive 79/7/EEC[95]

Directive 79/7/EEC is also based on Article 235. Commentators have argued that the Directive is not well designed to meet the current needs of workers in the Community since it is intended to deal with the situation of one-income families and, therefore, the possibility of discrimination is always present.[96] In addition, it is narrower than its title might suggest in that it only deals with social security related to the status of worker and does not protect against discrimination in matters of welfare. Matters such as income support and housing benefit have been ruled to be outside the scope of the Directive.

Scope

The scope of Directive 79/7/EEC emerges from a reading of the description of persons to whom the Directive applies, in Article 2, and the list of risks to which it applies, in Article 3. Article 2 states that the Directive applies to the 'working population', which is defined as 'including self-employed persons, workers and self-employed persons whose activity is interrupted by illness, accident or involuntary unemployment and persons seeking

91 See Case 312/86, *Commission* v *France* [1988] ECR 6315.

92 Case 222/84, *op. cit.*, note 70, at 1688.

93 Case C-245/89, not yet reported.

94 *Commission* v *France, op. cit.*, note 91.

95 See Hoskyns and Luckhaus, 'The European Community Directive on Equal Treatment in Social Security' (1989) 17 *Policy and Politics* 321.

96 See, for example, Ellis, *op. cit.*, note 36.

employment' and 'retired or invalided workers and self-employed persons'. The list of risks in Article 3(1)(a) consists of:

- sickness
- invalidity
- old age
- accidents at work and occupational diseases
- unemployment

and to:

- social assistance, in so far as it is intended to supplement or to replace the schemes referred to in (a).

Jackson and Cresswell v *Chief Adjudication Officer*[97] confirmed that the Directive only deals with those types of social security which act as replacement for a worker's wage, not those which act as a safety net against poverty. It was in *Drake* v *Chief Adjudication Officer*[98] that the Court first established that social security which is not related to loss of employment income is not covered. Nonetheless, in that case invalid care benefit was covered because the applicant had left her job in order to care for her disabled mother. If she had not been able to establish that she had given up work in order to act as a carer she would not have succeeded. However, giving up work to look after a family where illness is not a factor is outside the Directive, as was decided in *Acterberg-te Riele* v *Sociale Versekeringsbank*[99] where it was held that the applicants were outside the scope of the Directive because they had ceased to work for a reason other than the Article 3 risks. The ECJ emphasised that Community equality law was only concerned with equality in the status of 'worker'. The Directive can, therefore, be considered as ancillary to the equal pay and treatment Directives in a strict sense, because it only protects social security benefits which are received by the same people protected by the earlier legislation, namely workers.

Drake allowed a certain liberality in the interpretation of the risks clause in Article 3, including another's illness or invalidity as covered by the list of risks.[100] However, in *Jackson and Cresswell* it became clear that the Court regards the list as exhaustive and will not interpret it to include social security which does not have a sufficient nexus with the world of work. Advocate General Van Gerven attempted to develop a test of the 'practical result', which looked to whether the benefit *in fact* protected against one of the risks in Article 3, but this approach was not taken up by the Court. In general, the Advocates General appear to have taken a much more liberal approach to this Directive than the Court. For example, in *R v Secretary of State for Social Security, ex parte Smithson*[101] the Court found that housing benefit was not covered by the Directive, despite a link to invalidity pension, which was itself covered by the Directive. Despite recommendation to the contrary by Advocate General Tesauro, the Court decided that the benefit was not 'directly and effectively' linked to one of the risks listed in Article 3. It should be noted, however, that transitional measures which

[97] Joined Cases C-63 and 64/91, [1992] CMLR 389.
[98] Case 150/85, [1986] ECR 1995.
[99] Joined Cases 48, 106 and 107/88, [1989] ECR 1963.

[100] Luckhaus, 'Payment for Caring: A European Solution?' (1986) *Public Law* 526.
[101] Case C-243/90, [1992] 1 CMLR 1061.

bridge pre-Directive and post-Directive law must comply with the principles laid down in the Directive.[102]

Article 4 actually outlaws discrimination in State social security, as defined by Articles 2 and 3. It specifically requires equality of treatment with respect to scope of schemes, access, contributions and calculation of benefits. Like the Equal Treatment Directive, there is a specific obligation on Member States to abolish laws, regulations and administrative provisions contrary to the principle of equal treatment, contained in Article 5 of the Directive.

Teuling v *Bedrijfsvereniging voor de Chemische Industrie*[103] applied the Directive to cases of indirect discrimination, specifically the factor of having a dependent family, and therefore such a factor could be seen as justified, except where adverse impact was proved. The applicant failed because the benefit was intended to provide subsistence, not to replace wages and was, therefore, justified. This result, however, would seem to have more to do with the absence of a sufficient 'direct and effective' link with an Article 3 risk, rather than a *Bilka-Kaufhaus/Rinner-Kuhn* type of economic or social policy justification. However, when the discrimination has been between full-time and part-time workers the Court has required objective justification within the meaning in *Bilka-Kaufhaus*. The ECJ in *Ruzius-Wilbrink*[104] found that the State was not permitted to justify differential invalidity benefits on the basis that the benefit was greater than part-time workers' actual wages, since this occurred sometimes with full-time workers as well. Where invalidity benefits for part-time workers were related to previous income, whereas for full-time workers it was a minimum subsistence income, this was held to be indirect discrimination against women. The Court also said that Article 4 could be directly effective.

The requirement of a close relationship between Directive 79/7/EEC and employment leads to the question of possible overlap between this Directive and the Equal Treatment Directive. This issue was dealt with in *Jackson and Cresswell*, where the Court looked to the exclusion of social security from Article 1(2) of the Equal Treatment Directive. However, remarking that in *Marshall* it had asserted that this exclusion should be interpreted strictly, the Court decided that a social security scheme could fall within the Equal Treatment Directive if its subject-matter was access to employment, training or working conditions.

Exceptions

Survivors' benefits and family benefits, other than increases to benefits actually covered by the Directive, are excluded under Article 3(2). Article 4(2) exempts measures for the protection of maternity. Article 7(1) lists the main exemptions from the scope of the Directive:

• paragraph (a), determination of pensionable ages;[105]

---

[102] See Case 80/87, *Dik* v *College van Burgemeester en Wethouders der Gemeente Arnheim/College van Burgemeester en Wethouders der Gemeente Winterswijk* [1988] ECR 1601; and Case 384/85, *Borrie-Clark* v *Chief Adjudication Officer* [1987] ECR 2865.

[103] Case 30/85, [1987] ECR 2497.

[104] Case 102/88, *ML Ruzius-Wilbrink* v *Bestuur van de Bedrijfsvereniging voor Overheidsdiensten* [1989] ECR 4311.

[105] See earlier discussion of Case 152/84, *Marshall, op. cit.*, note 72, on the distinction between pensionable ages and retirement ages. In Case C-9/91 *R* v *Secretary of State for Social Security, ex parte The Equal Opportunities Commission* [1992] 3 CMLR 233 the Court stated that this exemption includes differential concluding dates for contributions to pension schemes.

- paragraph (b), benefits relating to persons who have brought up children;
- paragraph (c), old age or invalidity benefits acquired by virtue of status as wife;
- paragraph (d), increases in benefits for a dependent wife;
- paragraph (e), exercise of option before adoption of Directive, not to acquire rights or obligations under a statutory scheme.

Remedies

Article 6 of the Directive obliges Member States to provide adequate remedies, in exactly the same language as Article 6 of the Equal Treatment Directive. As a result the decisions discussed above concerning remedies under the Equal Treatment Directive should be applicable in interpreting the obligation to provide remedies under Directive 79/7/EEC. In terms of effectiveness of remedies, *Emmott* v *Minister for Social Welfare*[106] held that time limits on actions in enforcing rights under the Directive could not begin to run until the Directive had been properly transposed into national law, and that such time limits may not be more onerous than time limits for similar actions.

The usual remedy is levelling up. In *Netherlands* v *Federatie Nederlandse Vakbeweging*[107] where the Court decided that, until a new system properly implementing the Directive was in place, women were entitled to rely on the rules currently applied to men. In a rejection of the single-income family model which informs most European welfare systems, *McDermott and Cotter* v *Minister for Social Welfare and Attorney-General*[108] said that the contested benefit must be paid equally, even if it resulted in double payment to a family (this case dealt with a situation where married women received less benefit than men or single women).

Occupational Social Security Directive 86/378/EEC

The Occupational Social Security Directive 86/378/EEC has only become fully effective as of 1 January 1993. Its legal bases are Articles 100 and 235. It was intended to deal with a perceived gap in sex discrimination law in that pensions were not thought to be covered by Article 119 EC at the time of its drafting and only State pensions are covered by Directive 79/7/EEC. As all pensions except those covered by Directive 79/7/EEC appear to be included in the scope of Article 119 it is questionable whether Directive 86/378/EEC has any use. As discussed above, some provisions of the Directive may be illegal since they are less generous than Article 119 has turned out to be.

Equal Treatment for the Self-employed Directive 86/613/EEC

Directive 86/613/EEC deals with same issues as Directive 76/207/EEC, but obliges Member States to remove all discriminatory measures with respect to self-employed persons, including farmers and professionals. New provisions include an obligation not to make it more difficult for spouses than for other persons to set up a company together, and an obligation to allow spouses of self-employed persons who are involved in the business to join a contributory

---

[106] Case C-208/90, [1991] IRLR 387.

[107] Case 71/85, [1987] CMLR 767, confirmed recently in Case C-154/92, *Van Cant* v *Rijksdienst voor Pensioenen*, judgment of 1 July 1993.

[108] Case 286/85, [1987] ECR 1453. This case also decided that Article 4 of Directive 79/7/EEC was capable of having direct effects.

social security scheme voluntarily, where a contributory social security scheme exists for self-employed workers and where the spouse is not already a participant in that scheme.

NEW DEVELOPMENTS

Pregnancy

The first sex discrimination Directive adopted since the enactment of the Social Charter is the Pregnancy and Maternity Directive 92/85/EEC of 19 October 1992, which is an expansion of the pregnancy exception in the Equal Treatment Directive 76/207/EEC, Article 2.[109] The legal basis of the Directive is the Framework Directive on Health and Safety 89/391/EEC.

The Directive does not deal with refusal to engage a pregnant woman, which will continue to be covered by Article 3 of the Equal Treatment Directive, and the *Dekker* and *Hertz* judgments. However, Article 10 of the Pregnancy and Maternity Directive does prohibit dismissal for reason of pregnancy, from the beginning of pregnancy to the end of maternity leave. This is a wide-ranging prohibition, covering all workers, full-time and part-time. An employer is obliged to suspend a pregnant worker who cannot continue to perform her normal duties, or where to do so would constitute a health risk, but the employer cannot dismiss the pregnant employee for that reason. Furthermore, there is a right to return to the job.

Article 9 of the Directive provides for the right to time off for ante-natal care, without loss of pay. Article 8 gives the pregnant worker the right to 14 weeks of leave as a minimum entitlement, regardless of length of service, although there is no right to maternity pay guaranteed by the Directive.

The Directive must be implemented by 19 October 1994 and will be subject to a review in 1999.

Sexual harassment

It is likely that sexual harassment would be prohibited under Article 5 of Directive 76/207/EEC, to the extent that such harassment would amount to discriminatory working conditions.[110] 'The Dignity of Women at Work: A Report on the Problem of Sexual Harassment in the Member States of the European Communities'[111] recognised sexual harassment as direct discrimination against workers on the grounds of sex. This led to the adoption of Council Resolution of 29 May 1990 on the protection of the dignity of women and men at work[112] which includes a definition of sexual harassment as:

> conduct of a sexual nature, or other conduct based on sex affecting the dignity of women and men at work, including the conduct of superiors and colleagues [which] constitutes an intolerable violation of the dignity of workers or trainees and is unacceptable if:
> (a) such conduct is unwanted, unreasonable and offensive to the recipient;
> (b) a person's rejection of or submission to such conduct on the part of employers or

109 For a discussion of the background to the Directive and its implementation within the UK, see Cromack, 'The EC Pregnancy Directive – Principle or Pragmatism?' (1993) JSWFL 261.

110 Ellis, *op. cit.*, note 36, at 149–50.
111 Rubenstein, V/412/1/187–EN def (1987).
112 OJ C157/3, 27 June 1990.

workers (including superiors and colleagues) is used explicitly or implicitly as a basis for a decision which affects that person's access to vocational training, access to employment, continued employment, promotion, salary or any other employment decisions; and/or

(c) such conduct creates a hostile or humiliating work environment for the recipient.

The Resolution relates sexual harassment to the Equal Treatment Directive, seeing such conduct as a possible violation of the substantive articles of the Directive. The other legislation on sexual harassment is Commission Recommendation 92/131 of 27 November 1991[113] on the Protection of the Dignity of Women and Men at Work, which sets a code of good practice, including formal and informal complaint procedures, information and employer declarations of opposition to sexual harassment.[114]

Childcare

Recently, the Council has adopted a Childcare Recommendation,[115] committing Member States to the development of childcare measures for working parents, the generalisation of parental leave, working conditions to enable working mothers to care for their children and measures to ensure the equitable distribution of parental responsibilities between men and women.

CONCLUSION

Sex equality law has been one of the success stories of Community law. The Community has taken a relatively narrow Treaty provision and, through judicial interpretation and further legislation, has created a detailed legal regime which has enabled a large number of individual litigants to enforce their rights, and has had a significant impact on national legal systems.

One of the most significant developments contributed by the ECJ is the concept of indirect discrimination.[116] This concept takes into account the social conditions of women's work, particularly the combination of work and family responsibilities which most often falls to women. By enforcing sex discrimination law in circumstances where the discrimination focuses on part-time work or qualities such as flexibility or seniority, many of the practices which have prevented women from achieving pay and employment equity have fallen. However, the restrictive interpretations by the ECJ of the State Social Security Directive have failed to address another problem which women workers face: access to the job market from a position of welfare.

Historically, it has been easier for the Member States to reach a consensus on matters of sex discrimination than on other areas of social policy, although this consensus often takes years to achieve. The initiative of the Commission on equal pay[117] indicates that this will continue to be a growing area. Perhaps the era of major Directives, such as those on equal

---

113 92/C 27/04, OJ C27, 4 February 1992.

114 See Rubenstein, 'Note: Sexual harassment: European Commission Recommendation and Code of Practice' (1992) 21 ILJ 70.

115 92/241/EEC, OJ 1992 L123.

116 Prechal, 'Combating Indirect Discrimination in Community Law Context' [1993] 1 LIEI 81.

117 Op. cit., note 64.

pay and equal treatment, is over, but developments in important areas such as the pregnancy and maternity Directive will continue to advance legal equality of women within the Single Market.

Further reading

Arnull, A., *The General Principles of EEC Law and the Individual* (Leicester: University of Leicester Press, 1991).

Cromack, V., 'The EC Pregnancy Directive – Principle or Pragmatism?' (1993) JSWFL 261.

Curtin, D., 'Occupational Pension Schemes and Article 119: Beyond the Fringe?' (1987) 24 CML Rev 215.

Curtin, D., 'Effective Sanctions and the Equal Treatment Directive: The *Von Colson* and *Hartz* Cases' (1985) 22 CML Rev 505.

Docksey, C., 'The Principle of Equality between Men and Women: a Fundamental Right Under Community Law' (1991) 20 ILJ 258.

Ellis, E., *European Community Sex Discrimination Law* (Oxford: OUP, 1991).

Luckhaus, L., 'Payment for Caring: A European Solution?' (1986) *Public Law* 526.

Nielsen R., and Szyszczak, E., *The Social Dimension of the European Community* (Copenhagen: Handelshojskolens Forlag, 1991).

Prechal, S., 'Combating Indirect Discrimination in Community Law Context' [1993] 1 LIEI 81.

Rubenstein, M., 'Note: Sexual harassment: European Commission Recommendation and Code of Practice' (1992) 21 ILJ 70.

Szyszczak, E., 'European Court Rulings on Discrimination and Part-time Work and the Burden of Proof in Equal Pay Claims' (1990) 19 ILJ.

Wyatt, D., 'Prospective Effect of a Holding of Direct Applicability' (1975–76) 1 EL Rev 399.

CHAPTER 17

Social policy

INTRODUCTION

Provisions of a social nature have been part of Community law since the EEC Treaty (now the EC Treaty), but it is only since the mid-1970s that the Community has sought to legislate extensively in this area. In the preamble to the EC Treaty the second and third recitals demonstrate a concern with the social aspects of integration:

> *Resolved* to ensure the economic and social progress of their countries by common action to eliminate the barriers which divide Europe;
> *Affirming* as the essential objective of their efforts the constant improvement of the living and working conditions of their peoples.

In the body of the EC Treaty, social policy is covered by only a few articles (Articles 117–122 EC), of which only Article 119 EC, on equal pay between men and women, grants directly effective rights to individuals. Of the remaining articles, only Article 118a, added by the Single European Act, provides a legislative power. All other social measures have been adopted under the harmonisation and residuary powers articles, Articles 100 and 235 EC. The social policy articles of the Treaty are largely directed to the promotion of dialogue between management and labour, often termed the 'social partners'[1] in Community law and policy.

The first legislation dealing with social policy was Regulation 1408/71/EEC, prohibiting discrimination between Community national workers on social security matters.[2] The scope of this legislation was narrow in that it did not require any minimum guarantees for all Community nationals, but only that the benefit of national social security law was extended to workers and self-employed persons from all Member States. In recent years, social policy has become far more controversial. When the Community began to be concerned with the harmonisation of labour standards, the divergent approaches of the Member States to industrial relations, labour standards and social security emerged, and a consensus has been difficult to find and almost impossible to maintain. In 1989 the Community Charter of the Fundamental Social Rights of Workers was adopted, with an Action Programme for the development of new legislation in the social field. However, few of the intended measures have been adopted. The Treaty on European Union (TEU) was intended to contain an expanded social policy Chapter, which would form the basis of future Community action, but the opposition of the UK to the expansion of Community competence in this area prevented the further development of social policy within the Treaty. Instead, social policy is

---

1 Social dialogue is conducted at the Community level by UNICE, the Union of Industries of the European Community; ETUC, the European Trade Union Con- federation; and CEEP, the European Centre for Public Enterprises.
2 See Chapter 12.

relegated to an intergovernmental Protocol which provides for co-operation between the other 11 Member States on the development of Community social policy.

The important areas of expansion in Community social policy since the mid-1970s have been in the preservation of basic employment rights and health and safety. Worker information and consultation has been a continuing issue, but with no concrete results aside from ancillary rights given in measures on other matters. These areas, which will be discussed in detail below, have been important developments, particularly in the face of the deregulation of employment relationships in the UK during the 1980s. It is this conflict, between the UK's national policy orientation and the social partnership model favoured by the Commission and most other Member States, which has shaped the social policy debate in the Community's recent history.

The role of the UK in slowing the pace of development of Community social policy is comparable to France's 'empty chair' strategy in the 1960s, which led to the adoption of the Luxembourg Compromise and the prevalence of unanimous voting in the Council of Ministers. The strategy of the Commission has, therefore, been to take an expansive view of the scope of the few provisions of the Treaties which allow for social policy legislation, particularly those which permit qualified majority voting, rather than unanimity. In this way, and through partial exemptions and other concessions, the UK's objection to the involvement of the Community in social policy legislation has been managed. As a result of these factors, Community social policy lacks a coherent approach, in that the measures which are adopted do not necessarily relate to each other, but share only a characteristic of being relatively uncontroversial or susceptible of passage by qualified majority vote. Community law, therefore, has not been as influential in social policy as it has been in other areas such as competition policy.

The development of Community social policy

The important question to ask in the matter of Community social policy is why so few concrete measures have been produced. The Commission, the Parliament and many Member States have placed great emphasis on social policy. A great deal of time that has been spent on the discussion of social policy issues. Despite all this, the history of Community social policy is one of frustrated attempts and diluted measures.

Early Community approaches to social policy

There was no secondary legislation on social policy, as such, until the 1970s. Although regulations and directives were passed elaborating on the Treaty rules on free movement of persons,[3] conceptually this was considered to be part of the establishment of the Common Market rather than the development of what was later termed the 'social dimension'. The four freedoms were intended to establish a Common and, later, a Single Market in all the factors of production including labour. The fact that ensuring non-discrimination on the basis of nationality and, therefore, guaranteeing equal access to welfare benefits, may improve the situation of some workers, was incidental. During the early years of the Community some

---

3 Including Regulation 1408/71/EEC, which provides
only for non-discrimination in social security matters
between Community nationals.

measures of soft law[4] or of an information-gathering character were also passed.[5] Concern with social policy in isolation from the four freedoms began with the Paris Summit of 1972. This led to the first Action Programme on Social Policy in 1974.[6] The objectives of the programme were ambitious even by the optimistic standards of the early 1970s – full and better employment, improvement of living and working conditions and worker participation. The achievements of the Community under the Social Action Programme, however, were distinctly limited. *Full and better employment* only yielded directives protecting against the loss of employment rights in the event of transfers of undertakings, insolvencies and collective redundancies, as well as the sex equality directives discussed in the previous chapter. *Improvement of living and working conditions* led to a few specific health and safety directives arising from an Action Programme specifically on that topic, but the real impetus for development in this area only came with the Single European Act. *Worker participation* has never yielded any specific measures except for some incidental rights to information and consultation as set out in the employment rights, and some health and safety directives.

A recession in the mid-1970s and then another in the early 1980s dampened whatever little enthusiasm there had been amongst the Member States for achieving a consensus on social policy. In addition, the movement of the UK and, to a lesser extent, other Member States in the 1980s towards more deregulated labour markets made such a consensus less likely to be achieved.[7] In particular, at this time the Council and the Commission were in frequent conflict, as Member States advocated 'flexibility' in labour relations and the Commission persisted in proposing measures for the protection of vulnerable workers or workers in vulnerable circumstances.[8]

From the Single Market to the Social Charter

This impasse was, to some extent, broken by the efforts towards the achievement of the Single Market. Jacques Delors, then President of the Commission, advocated a link between the finalising of the Single Market and the development of social policy. Some Member States agreed, but no political consensus was reached.[9] The Single European Act (SEA) provided new possibilities for social policy development in several ways. First, there were new explicit articles on social policy. The most important of these is Article 118a EC, which grants explicit powers to the Community to legislate on health and safety issues. Articles 130a through 130e set out the goal of economic and social cohesion throughout the Community, with the permission to use the structural funds[10] for the purpose of achieving that goal. Secondly there is the increased use of majority voting, especially in the context of Article 118a EC, which prevents single Member States from having an effective veto over Community measures. Thirdly, the Community is empowered to take measures necessary for the achievement of the Single Market under Article 8a EC, with Article 8b obliging the Commission to ensure in its proposals the balanced progress of all sectors. Article 100a EC sets out the procedure to be followed in adopting the harmonisation measures necessary for

4 Non-binding measures such as recommendations and opinions.
5 Nielsen and Szyszczak, *The Social Dimension of the European Community* (1991), at 24–8.
6 OJ 1974 C12.
7 Nielsen and Szyszczak, *op. cit.*, note 5, at 30–1.

8 *Ibid.*
9 Vogel-Polsky, 'What Future is There For a Social Europe Following the Strasbourg Summit?' (1990) 19 ILJ 65, at 75.
10 European Agricultural Guidance and Guarantee Fund, European Social Fund, European Regional Development Fund.

the achievement of the Single Market. Although qualified majority voting is the rule under Article 100a, an exception is made for measures concerning 'the rights and interests of employed persons' where unanimity is still required. The definition of 'the rights and interests of employed persons' is, therefore, controversial, in that some Member States want to see greater harmonisation of social policy than others.[11] The differences arise out of disagreements as to whether the setting of labour standards is a matter of creating what is called a 'level playing field' and preventing social dumping[12] and is, therefore, part of the Single Market, or whether it is a separate matter which should be dealt with according to the traditions of the Member States.[13]

In the same year as the signing of the SEA, the Community produced a new Action Programme in the social policy field. The Action Programme for Employment Growth,[14] while endorsing the move to flexible patterns of employment, also put priority on helping the long-term unemployed. However, it was very much a Council-inspired document and the Commission responded with a report emphasising the need for social protection. The Commission and the European Parliament both advocated the need for a framework of social rights.[15] In 1988 there appeared to be a convergence of views when the European Council also acknowledged the importance of the social dimension.[16] This led to the Commission working paper entitled 'The Social Dimension of the Internal Market', which, in turn, led to the request from the Commission to the Economic and Social Committee that the elements of a draft Community Charter of Social Rights be suggested.[17]

In this way the current period of social policy development began. While the attitude of Member States towards the regulation of labour relations and labour standards had not changed, the Commission and other Community bodies were determined to set out a comprehensive floor of basic social rights to which all Community citizens would be entitled. The Economic and Social Committee recommended a Charter of social rights similar to the Council of Europe's European Social Charter.[18] The first draft was presented to the Council in May 1989, and the final version of the Community Charter on the Fundamental Social Rights of Workers (the Social Charter) was adopted on 9 December of that year. Between the first and final versions, several fundamental changes were made. The scope of the Social Charter was narrowed significantly. The Social Charter was originally to apply to 'citizens', or all persons under Community jurisdiction, but was amended to apply only to 'workers'. The European Parliament had advocated a Social Charter which would be a binding legal instrument but, ultimately, it became only a solemn declaration, not a binding act such as a regulation, directive or decision.[19] This is unique in Community law since there is no

---

11 On the possible interpretations of this phrase, see Vogel-Polsky, *op. cit.*, note 9 at 70–3.

12 The practice of employers 'dumping' production into countries with low wages and minimal labour standards, see Nielsen and Szyszczak, *op. cit.*, note 5 at 31–2; see also Wedderburn, 'The Social Charter in Britain – Labour Law and Labour Courts?' (1991) 54 MLR 1 at 16: 'Whether regulation is seen – to take the three main views – as a natural part of a "social market", or as an undesirable "burden on business", or as the pre-condition for a labour market to operate effectively, all schools agree that regulation is not neutral.'

13 See Spicker, 'The Principle of Subsidiarity and the Social Policy of the European Community' (1991) 1 JESP 3.

14 1986 OJ C340.

15 Nielsen and Szyszczak, *op. cit.*, note 5 at 33.

16 Watson, 'The Community Social Charter' (1991) 28 CML Rev 37 at 44.

17 *Ibid.*

18 For an introduction to the European Social Charter, see Robertson and Merrills, *Human Rights in the World*, 3rd edn (1989), at 245–55.

19 Hepple, 'The Implementation of the Community Charter of Fundamental Social Rights' (1990) 53 MLR 643, at 644. On the nature of binding Community acts, see Chapter 5.

particular status attributed to declarations or charters in Article 189 EC.[20] Neither is it a Treaty nor an amending protocol to the existing Community treaties.[21] It might be possible to use it as an interpretative guideline[22] but it has been used exclusively as a framework for the development of Community action in the social policy field.

Since the Social Charter is directed towards declaring the rights of workers, rather than universal social rights, certain rights which might otherwise be included are not present, such as the right to education.[23] In addition, some rights which are included are restricted in comparison with other human rights documents – the right to health, for example, becomes a right to health and safety in the work place. This dilution has led to criticisms that the Social Charter is ordinary employment law masquerading as fundamental rights.[24] There are 12 rights, or, perhaps more appropriately, categories of rights (since each heading contains several articles), in the Social Charter:

- freedom of movement;
- employment and remuneration;
- improvement of living and working conditions;
- social protection;
- freedom of association and collective bargaining;
- vocational training;
- equal treatment for men and women;
- information, consultation and participation for workers;
- health protection and safety at the work place;
- protection of children and adolescents;
- elderly persons;
- disabled persons.

In each area the Commission proposed measures of implementation in the Action Programme which accompanied the final version of the Social Charter.[25]

Article 27 of the Social Charter provides that primary responsibility for implementation lies with Member States rather than the Community itself. The Commission, however, is empowered under Article 28 to submit proposals for the adoption of implementing measures in areas which fall within the Community's competence, which is the basis of the Action Programme. Since some of these rights are already the subject of Treaty articles, such as health and safety or free movement of workers, the legal basis for action in these areas is unproblematic. For other areas, the harmonising powers under Articles 100, 100a and 235 EC would be necessary – the Charter, as a non-binding instrument, does not give the Community any new competencies in social policy.[26] The situation is, therefore, no different under the Social Charter than under the Treaties as amended by the SEA. It is in the areas where there is no explicit grant of Community power in the Treaties that Article 28's restriction of

20 Watson, *op. cit.*, note 16, at 45.

21 Hepple, *op. cit.*, note 19, at 644.

22 Or possibly as a source of general principles of Community law, see Hepple, *ibid.*, at 644–5.

23 Compare with the Council of Europe's European Social Charter, or the International Covenant on Economic, Social and Cultural Rights, to which Member States of the European Union are party.

24 Hepple, *op. cit.*, note 19, at 649–50.

25 COM (89) 568 final. The contents of these provisions and the proposed measures under the Commission's Action Programme are summarised by Watson, *op. cit.*, note 16, at 50–63.

26 Vogel-Polsky, *op. cit.*, note 9, at 67, comments that any proposals for action under the Charter will therefore 'have to follow the conventional route of the Community assault course'.

Commission initiative to areas in which the Community has competence becomes relevant. This raises the issue of subsidiarity, since the scope of Community competence in many areas is not clear and is often concurrent with that of Member States.[27] The Action Programme claims to be limited, in accordance with the principle of subsidiarity, to those measures whose objectives are better achieved at the Community level, but this approach to the application of subsidiarity to social policy has been controversial.[28] Member States have frequently opposed Community action in social areas where there is no explicit competence under the Treaties, and in harmonising measures unanimity is usually required.

As a result, it is not surprising that most of the areas in which implementation of the Social Charter has taken place at the Community level are those which are familiar areas of Community activity, such as the Pregnancy and Maternity Directive 92/85/EEC and further developments in free movement of persons. In other respects, the outcome of the Social Charter Action Programme has been disappointing.[29] The Action Programme contains proposals for 47 legislative acts, approximately half of which would be binding and half non-binding acts, such as recommendations. The only measure adopted to date which can be seen as breaking new ground is Directive 91/533/EEC on an employer's obligation to inform employees of the conditions applicable to the contract or employment relationship.[30] Only one measure, of three proposed measures, on atypical (part-time, temporary and casual) workers, has been passed despite the concern of the Commission with this issue.[31]

The implementation of the Social Charter is a combination of the Community approach of adopting binding measures at Community level and the international human rights law approach of Member State implementation supervised by a reporting system. Article 29 obliges the Commission to prepare an annual report on implementation of the Charter by the Member States and the Community.[32] However, reporting systems are relatively weak methods of implementation of rights and will rarely have the impact that results from the possibility of enforcing rights before national courts.[33]

Social policy in the TEU – 12 Member States or 11?

Another attempt was made to move social policy forward in the drafting of the TEU. The original intention was to develop the existing social policy Chapter within the EC treaty, to provide policy-making with a firmer foundation than the Social Charter, and a more detailed foundation than the harmonisation provisions of the EC Treaty, in particular by instituting greater recourse to majority voting.[34] The end result, however, was no substantive change to the social policy provisions of the Treaty, and a Social Policy Protocol of questionable status. The Protocol notes an agreement between 11 Member States to build on the *acquis communautaire* in social policy, and authorises them to use the Community institutions for

---

27 Subsidiarity, now recognised in Article 3b EC, added by the TEU, is discussed in detail in Chapter 3.
28 See Watson, *op. cit.*, note 16, at 46–7 and Hepple, *op. cit.*, note 19, at 646–7.
29 Watson, 'Social Policy after Maastricht' (1993) 30 CML Rev 481, at 484.
30 This Directive is discussed in full below.
31 Three draft Directives have been passed on to the Council – see COM (90) 228, OJ 1990 C224/90, as amended by COM (90) 533, OJ C305/90. Directive 91/383/EEC,

OJ 1991 L206, guaranteeing atypical workers equal treatment with salaried workers in matters of health and safety protection was the only proposal passed.
32 The first three annual reports on the implementation of the Social Charter can be found at COM (91) 511, COM (92) 562 and COM (93) 668.
33 On alternative methods of implementing EC social law, see Hepple, *op. cit.*, note 19, at 653–4.
34 Watson, *op. cit.*, note 29, at 486.

the purpose of adopting relevant measures for that purpose.[35] Appended to the Protocol is the agreement between the Member States, excluding the UK, to 'implement the 1989 Social Charter on the basis of the *acquis communautaire*'. The decision to expand social policy provisions in a Protocol rather than the Treaty itself is largely due to the opposition of the UK to the 'social market' approach advocated by the Commission and other Member States and, therefore, to any expansion of Community competence over social policy, particularly on the basis of majority voting.[36] The effect is that social policy measures may still be adopted under the EC Treaty, but the Member States other than the UK can adopt measures under the Protocol as well. Measures adopted by virtue of the Protocol will only be applicable in the 11 Member States who have subscribed to it.

The Agreement annexed to the Protocol, instead of creating workers' rights, establishes a series of objectives, contained in Article 1 of the Agreement, for the contracting States to achieve:

- the promotion of employment;
- improved living and working conditions;
- proper social protection;
- dialogue between management and labour;
- the development of human resources with a view to lasting high employment;
- the combating of social exclusion.

These objectives are more ambitious than the rights of the Social Charter but are more general. Article 2 of the Agreement is the main provision dealing with implementation and, like the Social Charter, provides for achievement of the Agreement's objectives both by Member State and collective action. Paragraph 1 of Article 2 states that 'the Community shall support and complement the activities of the Member States in fields of health and safety, working conditions, worker information and consultation, equality between men and women and combating social exclusion'. Paragraphs 2 and 3 enable the participating Member States to pass directives in Council in order to further the objectives of the Agreement. The implementation of such directives may be entrusted to management and labour in any participating Member State, at their joint request.

It is in this context that the status of the Agreement becomes an issue. The Agreement has status only as between 11 of the Member States. There is no amendment to the Treaties on the legislative procedure, except for the statement in the Protocol that the UK will take no part in the Council when adopting or deliberating on any measures under the Agreement, with a consequential redefinition of qualified majority voting for this purpose. The co-operation procedure is required for some types of measures and the consultation procedure for others, largely in conformity with the requirements for each policy area under the EC Treaty. For example, health and safety measures are to be adopted under the co-operation procedure, as is required if such measures were adopted by all the Member States under Article 118a EC. If the Agreement is actually part of the European Union Treaty

35 *Ibid.*, at 489–94; see also Curtin, 'The Constitutional Structure of the Union: A Europe of Bits and Pieces' (1993) 30 CML Rev 17. It is disputed whether the Protocol is part of the TEU or whether it is a separate intergovernmental agreement between the 11 participating Member States.

36 See Watson, *op. cit.*, note 29, at 486–8.

structure, then there is no problem. However, if the Agreement is separate from the Treaties, and governed only by the normal rules of public international law, then there is not sufficient incorporation of the legislative structures of the Treaties for the 11 States, parties to the Agreement, to use the Community institutions in the way foreseen. The Agreement embodies a truth about the institutions of the Community which is acknowledged in fact, though not law – that the Council is of a different nature to the Commission and the European Parliament. The Protocol provides that the UK will not participate in Council deliberations or voting on any measures adopted under the Agreement. However, the UK-nominated Commissioner is not precluded from participating in Commission adoption of proposals under the Agreement. This is understandable since Commissioners are required to be totally independent from the Member State which nominates them. Nor are UK MEPs prevented from debating proposed measures in the European Parliament which, by virtue of Article 2(3) of the Agreement, must be consulted. This is more problematic, since UK MEPs are the directly elected representatives of the British people, who will receive no direct benefit or burden from any measures adopted under the Protocol. The UK is, therefore, only excluded from participation *as a Member State*, which is its role within the Council. Its nominees and the representatives of its people continue to act under the Agreement.[37]

Articles 3 and 4 of the Agreement also present problems. Article 3 empowers the Commission to consult with management and labour with a view to promoting social dialogue. If it thinks Community action is necessary it will consult with management and labour concerning the content of any proposals which, presumably, would then go forward to the Council-minus-the-UK. Article 4 provides for management–labour agreements at the Community level, which will then be implemented either by the States or by a Council decision. The problem with these provisions is with the use of the term 'Community'. It does not seem possible for such acts to be at Community level when one of the Community Member States is specifically foreseen as not participating and any such acts would not apply in that Member State. Either the Agreement authorises a 'two-speed Europe' or it is incoherent. The 'two-speed Europe' interpretation is reinforced by the preamble which declares the desire to implement the Social Charter on the basis of the *acquis communautaire,* which raises the question of whether measures adopted under the Agreement form part of the *acquis.* If they do, again there is incoherence because that part of the *acquis* does not apply to the UK. The only way of understanding the Agreement is as a separate Treaty between the 11 Member States, which may have been incorporated by reference into the TEU, through the social policy Protocol.[38]

Articles 5 and 7 of the Agreement foresee further Commission activity under it. Article 5 requires the Commission to facilitate co-operation between Member States and the co-ordination of their social policies. Article 7 obliges the Commission to prepare an annual report on the achievement of the Article 1 objectives, and empowers the European Parliament to request reports from the Commission on social issues.

Article 6 is the only provision to deal with a particular social policy area, rather than the Article 1 objectives in general. Its first two paragraphs reiterate the provisions of Article 119 EC. The third paragraph authorises the Member States to maintain or adopt 'measures . . . in order to make it easier for women to pursue a vocational activity or to prevent or

[37] Watson, *op. cit.,* note 29, at 504–5.

[38] Fitzpatrick, 'Community Social Law after Maastricht' (1992) 21 ILJ 199, at 202.

compensate for disadvantages in their professional careers'. This provision permits the adoption of positive discrimination or affirmative action measures in order to promote employment equity between the sexes.[39]

The utility of the Protocol and the Agreement remains to be seen. Since there is a general reluctance on the part of Member States and the Community institutions to create a 'two-speed Europe' it is likely that the Commission will attempt to proceed under the pre-TEU law in furthering social policy where possible.[40] If the action is taken under the Agreement, particularly with respect to minimum labour standards, there is a danger that social dumping may take place, since employers would be able to relocate in the UK with all the benefits of the internal market and lower-cost labour.[41] For the UK the opposite danger presents itself, that the most skilled and best-educated workers will choose to work outside the UK where greater employment protection is provided.

Health and safety/the working environment

One specific area of social law in which the Community has been active is the regulation of health and safety in the work place, or the 'working environment'. The use of two different descriptions for this area of regulation is significant. Article 118a EC uses both phrases:

> Member States shall pay particular attention to encouraging improvements, especially in the *working environment*, as regards the *health and safety* of workers and shall set as their objective the harmonisation of conditions in this area, while maintaining the improvements made. [emphasis added]

The use of 'working environment' raises a wider view of the permissible regulation under Article 118a EC because of the significance of the phrase in Nordic law. Denmark, along with other Nordic states, has used this term in national employment law for over two decades. It has a much broader scope than the physical safety of the work place, and includes all elements of the work surroundings, including social aspects, such as isolation, and psychological aspects, such as monotony.[42] This approach could potentially include all aspects of employment standards legislation, possibly even management–labour relations.[43] The UK opposes this approach to Article 118a EC, and has argued against its use for matters relating to the organisation of work rather than physical hazards.[44] This opposition has crystallised around the directive on the organisation of working time, which is supported by all Member States except the UK. Since Article 118a requires only a qualified majority in order to pass such a directive, except if the Council wishes to overrule an amendment made by the European Parliament, the opposition of the UK to the use of Article 118a EC is part of a general strategy. Article 118a EC, of all possible bases for social legislation, presents the greatest likelihood of success, due to its less stringent voting requirements.[45] If Article 118a

[39] Watson, *op. cit.*, note 29, at 499 gives examples of measures which might be covered by this provision.

[40] Fitzpatrick, *op. cit.*, note 38, at 204.

[41] *Ibid.*, Fitzpatrick, at 512–13.

[42] Nielsen and Szyszczak, *op. cit.*, note 5, at 183.

[43] *Ibid.* Nielsen and Szyszczak note that the European Parliament has supported this interpretation (EP Doc A2-0226/88). Possibly this is due to the fact that Article 118a requires the use of the co-operation procedure,

whereas harmonisation in relation to 'the rights and interests of employed persons' only requires that the Parliament be consulted.

[44] Wedderburn, *op. cit.*, note 12, at 5–6, notes that support for regulation against hazards at work is considered by many libertarian theorists to be consistent with opposition to other forms of regulation of the labour market.

[45] Szyszczak, '1992 and the Working Environment' (1992) JSWFL 3, at 4.

EC is not a sufficient legal basis for the adoption of this directive, then Article 100 EC would be required. Unanimity would be necessary in order to pass a directive under Article 100 EC, giving the UK an effective veto over the directive if opposition to its substance was maintained. If a consensus was reached between the Commission, the European Parliament and the majority of Member States to use Article 118a EC to proceed with further harmonisation of employment law, there could be development of protection in the working environment equivalent to the developments on sex equality in the work place.[46] Regulation of many aspects of working conditions could be brought in through a broad interpretation of the scope of Article 118a EC and, without a requirement of unanimity, the legislative process could be quite efficient in introducing new labour standards.

Health and safety was an early concern of the Commission, which established a Health and Safety Division in 1962.[47] Until the inclusion of a specific provision on health and safety in the SEA, most measures adopted by the Community were non-binding soft law, such as recommendations.[48] Two Action Programmes on health and safety produced only a few directives, aimed at specific physical hazards in certain types of work, rather than general policy on health and safety in all work places.[49] An Advisory Committee on Health and Safety was established in 1974.[50]

In addition, some issues such as health and safety are considered more generally as Single Market issues, in that conditions such as shop opening hours have been challenged as obstacles to free movement of goods.[51] Technical and other standards may be discussed as matters coming under Article 100a EC concerning the removal of barriers to the Single Market. Article 36 EC and the *Cassis de Dijon* line of authority allow Member States to maintain differing standards where they can be justified on, among other grounds, public health.[52]

The significant point in the development of health and safety regulation within Community law was the addition of Article 118a EC by the SEA. This Article specifically empowers the Community to regulate work place health and safety. With new specific powers to legislate over health and safety, the progress on regulating this area was significantly greater than during the period 1970–85. This led to the Action Programme of 1987, which gave a wide interpretation to the scope of regulation under Article 118a EC.[53] The measures adopted under Article 118a EC are intended to improve, to the greatest extent possible, the environment at the work place. Many recent directives include 'non-regression' clauses, which prohibit Member States with high levels of protection from using a harmonising directive as an excuse for eroding workers' rights to health and safety.[54]

---

[46] Szyszczak, *ibid.*, at 5.

[47] Nielsen and Szyszczak, *op. cit.*, note 5, at 27.

[48] However, recently an early Recommendation on health and safety was found to have interpretative significance: Case C-322/88, *Grimaldi v Fonds de Maladies Professionnelles* [1989] ECR 4407.

[49] Nielsen and Szyszczak, *op. cit.*, note 5, at 184–5.

[50] Szyszczak, *op. cit.*, note 45, at 6.

[51] Case 145/88, *Torfaen Borough Council v B & Q* [1989] ECR 3851 and Case C-169/91, *Stoke-on-Trent City Council v B & Q* [1993] 1 CMLR 426.

[52] Nielsen and Szyszczak, *op. cit.*, note 5, at 194–207 on health and safety and technical standardisation within the context of the Single Market. Article 36 EC and the *Cassis de Dijon* case are discussed in detail in Chapter 11.

[53] COM (87) 520 Final. See Szyszczak, *op. cit.*, note 45, and Eberlie, 'The New Health and Safety Legislation of the European Community' (1990) 19 ILJ 81, at 90–1.

[54] For example, Article 1(3) of Directive 89/391/EEC.

The Health and Safety Framework Directive 89/391/EEC

The current momentum in health and safety law came with the Framework Directive 89/391/EEC.[55] This Directive provided for several so-called 'daughter' directives dealing with specific risks.

Article 1(2) sets out the principles underlying the Directive: 'the prevention of occupational risks, the protection of safety and health, the elimination of risk and accident factors, the informing, consultation, balanced participation in accordance with national laws and/or practices and training of workers and their representatives'. The obligations of employers are found in Articles 5–12. Article 5 contains the general obligation of employers, which is to ensure health and safety of workers in all aspects of work-related activity. The specific duties include the elimination of avoidable risks and reduction of dangers of unavoidable risks, duty of awareness, duty to identify and evaluate risks, duty of awareness of capabilities of workers and duty of strategic planning to avoid risks.[56] Throughout the Directive there is a duty to replace the dangerous with the non- or less-dangerous. This approach is called the substitution principle in Nordic working environment legislation, and disallows economic justifications for not following the principle;[57] nor must the costs be transferred to the worker.[58]

Fundamental to the scheme within the Directive is the training of workers to avoid or minimise work place hazards. Article 12 imposes a general duty to ensure that workers are adequately trained to deal with risks to health and safety on the job. Articles 6(2)(i) and (3)(d) oblige the employer to provide adequate instructions to workers so that they can avoid risks and only to allow access to dangerous areas to those workers who have been properly instructed.

Article 16 enables the Council, on a proposal from the Commission, to adopt directives based on the Framework Directive, particularly, but not exclusively, concerning the areas listed in the Annex to the Directive: work place, work equipment, personal protective equipment, work with visual display units, handling of heavy loads involving risk of back injury, temporary or mobile work sites, and fisheries and agriculture. Twelve daughter directives have been passed under the Framework Directive. The earlier daughter directives tended to deal with areas listed in the Annex. Later directives have dealt with specific hazards or specific categories of worker, some of which, such as pregnant workers, are not listed in the Annex:[59]

(1) Directive 89/654/EEC concerning the minimum safety and health requirements for the work place;
(2) Directive 89/655/EEC concerning the minimum safety and health requirements for the use of work equipment;
(3) Directive 89/656/EEC concerning minimum safety and health requirements for the use of personal protective equipment by workers;

[55] Pre-framework directive measures on health and safety are listed in Nielsen and Szyszczak, *op. cit.*, note 5, at 184–5.
[56] Articles 6 and 7.
[57] Szyszczak, *op. cit.*, note 45, at 10, and Nielsen and Szyszczak, *op. cit.*, note 5, at 190–1. Eberlie, *op. cit.*, note 53, at 95–6 compares the level of the employer's duties under the Framework Directive with then current UK health and safety law.
[58] Article 6(5).
[59] However, Article 15 of the Framework Directive does specify that particular risk groups must be protected against the dangers which specifically affect them.

(4) Directive 90/269/EEC concerning safety and health requirements for the manual handling of heavy loads involving a risk of muscoloskeletal injury to workers;

(5) Directive 90/270/EEC concerning the safety and health requirements for work with visual display units;

(6) Directive 90/394/EEC on the protection of workers from the risks related to exposure to carcinogens at work;

(7) Directive 90/679/EEC on the protection of workers from the risks related to exposure to biological agents a work;

(8) Directive 92/57/EEC on the implementation of minimum safety and health requirements at temporary or mobile construction sites;

(9) Directive 92/58/EEC on the minimum requirements for the provision of safety and/or health signs at work;

(10) Directive 92/85 concerning measures to encourage improvements in the safety and health of pregnant workers and workers who have recently given birth or are breastfeeding;[60]

(11) Directive 92/91/EEC on the minimum requirements for improving the safety and health protection of workers in the mineral-extracting industries through drilling;

(12) Directive 92/104/EEC on the minimum requirements for improving the safety and health protection of workers in surface and underground mineral-extracting industries.

Other health and safety legislation

Health and safety provisions under the Social Charter Action Programme focus on measures for the protection of particular risk groups and particular situations:

- Directive 92/29/EEC concerning the safety and health requirements for work on board vessels and Directive 93/103/EEC concerning the minimum health and safety requirements for work on board fishing vessels;[61]
- Directive 91/383/EEC on atypical work contracts guarantees treatment of atypical workers similar to that of full-time workers in health and safety matters.

Machine safety has been extensively regulated, starting from the earliest measures on health and safety passed under Community law:

- Directive 79/196/EEC, as amended by Directive 90/487/EEC (ATEX Directive), harmonising technical standardisation of electrical equipment, in order to reduce the risk of explosion;
- Directive 84/532/EEC on construction plants and equipment (framework Directive);
- Directive 86/188/EEC on the safety and health of workers on the job regarding exposure to risks arising from noise and vibrations or other physical agents;
- Directive 89/392/EEC on safety of machinery, as amended by Directive 91/368/EEC;
- Directive 89/686/EEC on the approximation of the laws of the Member States relating to personal protective equipment, as amended by Directive 93/68/EEC.

---

[60] Discussed in detail in Chapter 16.

[61] See also Directives 92/48/EEC and 91/493/EEC, relating to health and safety issues in the fishing industry.

The Working Time Directive and the future of Community health and safety law

The controversial Working Time Directive 93/104/EC was finally adopted by the Council on 22 November 1993. It was first proposed in August 1990, but the Council's common position was only reached in June 1993, without the agreement of the UK.[62] There were some attempts in June 1993 to encourage the UK to agree to the Directive by offering the possibility of delaying its implementation, but these were ultimately unsuccessful.[63] The Directive is to come into effect on 24 November 1996, but the Social Affairs Council agreed to allow six- or 10-year delays for implementation, in its attempt to secure the support of the UK. The Directive is based on Article 118a EC, which means that the measure can be adopted by qualified majority and, therefore, without the consent of the UK. The Directive, since it is adopted under the EC Treaty, will apply within the UK, unlike any measures which may be adopted under the TEU Social Policy Protocol. Therefore, the UK has stated its intention to challenge the legal basis of this Directive before the ECJ, arguing that this measure is not essentially a health and safety measure but rather one which harmonises conditions of employment.[64] On this view it could only be justified by Articles 100 and 235 EC, which require unanimity, thereby creating the possibility of a UK veto. The ECJ will have to decide whether Article 118a EC is about the working environment in the sense in which that term is used in Nordic employment law, or whether it concerns only matters which are purely risks to the physical health and safety of workers. While working long hours arguably increases the risk of industrial accident, it appears that the Directive deals also with the perceived unfairness of requiring workers to work long hours without rest.

Many of these rest periods or maximum periods of work are decided by averaging against a reference period, so that an employer is allowed a certain amount of flexibility in assigning work timetables.

- Maximum 48-hour work week, including overtime; the average week is to be calculated over a period of four months (Article 6); this may be extended to six months by law or agreement with the social partners, or to 12 months with the agreement of the social partners. Employers may ask workers to exceed the maximum work week through voluntary agreement, and workers who refuse to do so must receive the full protection of law. Member States may delay implementation until up to the year 2004.
- Workers should have 11 consecutive hours off each day (24-hour period) (Article 3). This is to be calculated over 14 days.
- Where the working day is longer than six hours, there must be a minimum daily rest period, to be decided by collective agreement or national legislation (Article 4).

[62] 'Social Affairs Council: EC Ministers Reach Common Position on Working Hours' *European Social Policy*, European Information Service, 15 June 1993, Section No 31.

[63] *Ibid.* The exemptions nominally apply to all Member States, despite the fact that they were intended to meet the UK's objections to the Directive. Italy has declared that it will not take advantage of the additional delays beyond the basic three-year implementation period.

[64] 'Social Affairs Council: UK Accused of Holding Up European Social Policy' *European Social Policy*, European Information Service, 16 December 1993, Section No 36. It is interesting to note that Coopers and Lybrand in *EC Commentaries*, Social Affairs, 3 February 1994, discuss this Directive under the category of 'Legislation to Harmonise Employment Contracts' rather than with the other health and safety directives.

- Minimum 24 hours rest every seven days, in principle on Sunday, in addition to the 11 daily hours of the preceding or following day[65] (Article 5).
- At least four weeks' paid holidays for each 12 months worked; this entitlement cannot be exchanged for additional remuneration (Article 7). Member States may delay implementation until 2000, and then may implement over a transitional period of up to three years, where annual leave is to be at least three weeks (Article 18).
- Night workers[66] may not be required to work more than eight hours each day (24-hour period) (Article 8).

Article 17 of the Directive permits a number of derogations from the above provisions.

- Executives and others with autonomous decision-making power, family workers or workers in religious communities are excluded from the protection of the Directive: this derogation excludes the provision relating to holidays.
- For the following categories of worker, the provisions relating to rest periods may be derogated from where compensatory rest periods are offered or other appropriate protection under law or collective agreement exists:

workers at sea or in 'sea exploitation';
workers carrying out security and surveillance activities;
workers in fields where continuity of service or production is required, such as hospitals.

Any worker may be temporarily excluded, where there is an increase in activity beyond the employer's control.

Considering the delays in the implementation period and the scope of the derogations, this Directive may not be very effective in reducing the hours worked within the EU. Particularly in the case of vulnerable workers, a guarantee that no legal consequences can arise from his or her refusal to work beyond the 48-hour limit may be illusory. Furthermore, the reference periods could allow for extremes of timetabling – long hours for some weeks and long breaks in others. Finally, the issue of who is considered to be sufficiently autonomous to be equivalent to an executive could have implications for professionals such as lawyers, who are nominally independent in their work but may, nonetheless, be employees.[67]

The next controversial area will be the protection of young workers.[68] Once again, the proposed Directive made a difficult passage to the reaching of a common position, which was finally adopted in November 1993. The basic aim of the Directive is to prohibit work by children under 15 and to regulate strictly the work of young persons between the ages of 15 and 18. Exceptions are provided for cultural, artistic, sports or advertising activities, and for those who are at least 14, and in work-training or work-experience or light work (children of 13 may perform light work for a limited number of hours per week). Since this Directive is

---

[65] This would prevent shops which will be permitted, under the amended Shops Act (UK) 1950, to open on Sundays, from requiring workers as a condition of employment to work seven days a week.
[66] Defined as those whose normal workday includes at least three hours of work between midnight and 5 am.
[67] The same question could be posed concerning lecturers!
[68] Draft Directive to Protect Young People at Work, OJ 1992 C84, amended by OJ 1993 C77.

also being adopted under Article 118a EC, the UK is again questioning not only the Directive but its basis. A derogation period has been offered, but this has led to opposition from Member States supporting the Directive.[69] So far, there has been no statement of intent to challenge the Directive if it is passed in its present form. The issue of a legal challenge before the ECJ may depend largely on the outcome on the challenge to the Working Time Directive 93/104/EEC.

In November 1993 the Commission adopted the Health and Safety Framework Programme for the years 1994–2000.[70] This framework programme emphasises both the correct implementation of existing Community law in this area and the further development of the law. In addition, the Commission aims to promote Community health and safety norms in non-EU Member countries.

Preservation of employment rights

Three directives, arising out of the 1974–76 Action Programme, provide protection for workers in the event of fundamental changes in the structure of their employment. In particular, these directives prevent employers from using the restructuring of an undertaking in order to undermine established rights of the work-force. As directives which aim to harmonise the laws of the Member States, these directives are based on Article 100 EC.

In each of these directives, Member States are allowed opportunities of reducing the protection provided. The provisions allow limitations of liability or ceilings on compensation and allow Member States to designate certain occupations as excluded from the application of the directive. Perhaps, most significantly, the directives allow Member States to define who is an employee for the purposes of the directive. While these exclusions and opt-outs may have been necessary in order to obtain the consensus in favour of their adoption, it is easy to question whether a delay in achieving that consensus would have been preferable to the diluted rights in the directives as they exist. The Collective Redundancies Directive 75/129/EEC has recently been amended in order to improve the protection of workers provided in that Directive. The other directives remain as they were enacted.

Collective Redundancies Directive 75/129/EEC

The Collective Redundancies Directive 75/129/EEC has recently undergone a significant amendment under Directive 92/56/EEC, which must be implemented by 24 June 1994. The amendments provide more detailed rights of consultation and the Directive now includes redundancies arising out of business closure resulting from a judicial decision. In enforcement proceedings against Belgium under the earlier version of the Directive it had been argued unsuccessfully that Belgian law only covered collective redundancies arising out of the closure of a business resulting from a judicial decision because, historically, it was extremely unlikely that closure leading to redundancies could come about except from a judicial decision.[71] The ECJ insisted that even the rare event of a closure which was not the result of judicial decision must be dealt with by proper implementing legislation. The amended version of the Directive now ensures that the usual situation under Belgian law will also be covered.

---

69 'Social Affairs Council: EC Ministers Agree on Young Workers' Directive', *European Social Policy*, European Information Service, 14 October 1993, Section No 34.

70 COM(93) 560.

71 Case 215/83, *Commission v Belgium* [1985] ECR 1039.

Article 1(1) of the Directive provides alternative definitions of collective redundancies by virtue of the numbers of workers dismissed in a period of 30 or 90 days:

(a) 'Collective redundancies' means dismissals effected by an employer for one or more reasons not related to the individual workers concerned where, according to the choice of the Member States, the number of redundancies is:
–either, over a period of 30 days:
(1) at least 10 in establishments normally employing more than 20 and less than 100 workers;
(2) at least 10 per cent of the number of workers in establishments normally employing at least 100 but less than 300 workers;
(3) at least 30 in establishments normally employing 300 workers or more;
–or, over a period of 90 days, at least 20, whatever the number of workers normally employed in the establishments in question.

. . .

For the purpose of calculating the number of redundancies provided for the first subparagraph of point (a), terminations of an employment contract which occur on the employer's initiative for one or more reasons not related to the individual workers concerned shall be assimilated to redundancies, provided that there are at least five redundancies.[72]

Article 1(2) excludes workers on short-term contracts except where the redundancy takes place before the expiry of the contract, public sector workers and the crews of sea-going vessels.[73] Dismissal is in the discretion of the employer, however, and the Directive does not appear to include forms of constructive dismissal, such as a statement by the employer that it can no longer guarantee the payment of wages.[74]

Article 2 sets out the obligations of consultation with workers' representatives, defined in Article 1(1)(b) as 'the workers' representatives provided for by the laws or practices of the Member States'. Under the original version of this Article, the information to be provided to workers was at least 'the reasons for the redundancies, the number of workers to be made redundant, the number of workers normally employed and the period over which the redundancies are to be effected'.[75] Under the amended Directive the employer must 'in good time':

(a)   supply them with all relevant information; and
(b)   in any event notify them in writing of:
      (i)   the reasons for the projected redundancies;
      (ii) the number and categories of workers to be made redundant;
      (iii) the number and categories of workers normally employed;
      (iv) the period over which the projected redundancies are to be effected;
      (v)   the criteria proposed for the selection of the workers to be made redundant in so far as national legislation and/or practice confers the power therefor upon the employer;

---

[72] This final paragraph was added by Directive 92/56/EEC.

[73] Directive 92/56/EEC repealed Article 1(2)(d), which read, 'workers affected by the termination of an establishment's activities where that is the result of a judicial decision'. The list of exclusions is exhaustive, see *Com-*

mission v *Belgium, op. cit.,* note 71.

[74] Case 284/83, *Dansk Metalarbejderfobund and Specialarbejderfobundet i Danmark* v *H Nielsen & Son, Maskinfabrik A/S* [1985] ECR 553.

[75] Article 2(3) of the original version of the Directive.

(vi) the method for calculating any redundancy payments other than those arising out of national legislation and/or practice.[76]

The purpose of the consultation and information process, under Article 2(2), is to discuss possible ways of avoiding or reducing redundancies and ways of mitigating the effects of any redundancies, such as through redeployment or retraining. This amended provision does not change the scope of the consultation procedure from the original Directive, but does set out in detail the expected ways of mitigating the effect of the redundancies where possible. The consultation and information process is the main purpose of the Directive.[77]

Articles 3 and 4 of the Directive set out the procedure to be followed by the employer when planning collective redundancies. First, under Article 3, the employer must inform the public authorities, with a copy of the notification forwarded to the workers' representatives.[78] Notification shall contain all relevant information concerning the projected redundancies and the consultations required under Article 2. In particular, the reasons for the redundancies, the number of workers affected, the number of workers normally employed and the period over which the redundancies are to take effect must be included in the notification. A delay of at least 30 days must then follow, although Member States may allow the public authority the discretion to reduce this period.[79] During this time the public authority must 'seek solutions in the problems raised by the projected collective redundancies'. However, Member States are not required to apply this mediation procedure where the collective redundancies arise out of closure resulting from a judicial decision.

The Directive operates without prejudice to more favourable provisions under law, administrative procedure or, under the amended Directive, collective agreement.[80] However, Member States must ensure that workers not governed by collective agreement have the benefit of the guarantees under the Directive by virtue of legislation.[81]

Transfers of Undertakings Directive 77/187/EEC

The Transfers of Undertakings Directive 77/187/EEC applies to circumstances where a business is transferred, specifically, according to Article 1 'to the transfer of an undertaking, business or part of a business to another employer as a result of a legal transfer or merger'. It applies insofar as the business which is transferred is located within the Community, but not to sea-going vessels.[82] Employees, for the purpose of the Directive, are those who are protected as employees by national law.[83] The purpose of the Directive is to protect the

---

76 Article 2(3) of the amended Directive. A copy of this information must be forwarded to the competent public authority.

77 *Dansk Metalarbejderforbund and Specialarbejderforbundet i Danmark v H Nielsen & Son Maskinfabrik A/S, op. cit.*, note 74.

78 Under the amended Directive, in the event of redundancies arising out of closure resulting from judicial decision Member States may provide that the obligation to inform the public authorities need only arise on the request of the authority.

79 Article 4(1). Under Article 4(3) if the period is less than 60 days Member States may grant the public authority the power to extend the period to 60 days 'where

the problems raised by the projected collective redundancies are not likely to be solved within the initial period'. Wider powers of extension may also be granted. The employer must be notified of any extension before the expiry of the initial period.

80 Article 5.

81 Case 91/81, *Commission v Italy* [1985] ECR 3531.

82 Article 1(2) and (3).

83 Case 105/84, *Foreningen af Arbejdsledere i Danmark. v A/S Danmols Inventar* [1985] ECR 2639. The potential for this discretion to undermine the rights of employees under British law is highlighted by Hepple and Byre, 'EEC Labour Law in the United Kingdom – A New Approach, (1989) 18 ILJ 129, at 137.

continuity of the worker's employment and conditions of employment,[84] unlike the purely procedural rights granted under the collective redundancies Directive. It prevents the use of a business transfer as a justification for redundancies. Article 3 explicitly provides that the original employer's rights and obligations under existing employment contracts or relationships are to be automatically transferred to the transferee. Member States may provide that the original employer shall continue to be liable to the employee along with the transferee. The transferee is obliged to respect the terms of any collective agreement until its expiry, although Member States may limit the period during which such agreements must be observed, as long as the period is at least one year. The only rights which may be excluded are supplementary pension schemes operated by the original employer.[85]

Article 4 guarantees that the transfer may not be used as an excuse for dismissal. This includes forms of constructive dismissal:

> If the contract of employment or the employment relationship is terminated because the transfer within the meaning of Article 1(1) involves a substantial change in working conditions to the detriment of the employee, the employer shall be regarded as having been responsible for termination of the contract of employment or the employment relationship.

Furthermore, the ECJ has decided that termination *with effect from the date of the transfer* constitutes a dismissal prohibited by Article 4.[86] Such employees must be considered still to be employed when the transfer takes place. However, this guarantee is significantly undermined by the exclusion of 'dismissal that may take place for economic, technical or organisational reasons entailing changes in the work force', and the possibility for Member States to exclude categories of employees 'who are not covered by the laws or practice of the Member States in respect of protection against dismissal'. In circumstances other than merger the representation of workers in its existing form must be preserved, unless the national rules applying to reappointment of representatives are fulfilled.[87] If, however, under national law the representation expires with the transfer, then only the legal protection of the representatives must continue, such as prohibitions on dismissal by reason of trade union activity.

Worker consultation and information is provided for in Article 6. The workers' representatives must be informed in good time of the following: the reasons for the transfer, the legal, economic and social implications of the transfer for the employees and any measures envisaged in relation to the employees. The transferee must provide the same information to its employees, before those employees are directly affected. If any measures in relation to employees are planned, then a consultation procedure must be implemented in order to seek agreement on the application of such measures. The information and consultation procedure under the Directive may be replaced by national guarantees to a right to arbitration where such a right exists in national law. Member States may limit the information and consultation obligations where the number of employees is sufficient to

---

[84] Case 19/83, *Knud Wendelboe m fl* v *L J Music* [1985] ECR 457. In Case 237/84, *Commission* v *Belgium* [1986] ECR 1247 this was held to include minimum notice periods.

[85] Article 3(3). Member States must, nonetheless, protect the interests of existing pensioners of the original employer.

[86] Case 101/87, *P Bork International A/S* v *Foreningen af Arbejdsledere i Danmark* [1988] ECR 3057. Collins, in 'Transfer of Undertakings and Insolvency' (1989) 18 ILJ 144, at 149 argues that this interpretation goes beyond the apparent provisions of Article 4, although it is probably consistent with the purpose of the Directive.

[87] Article 5.

permit the election of a body representing the employees and may provide that where there are no worker representatives the employees themselves must be informed in advance of any transfer.

Defining the scope of application of the Directive has proved difficult. The ECJ has decided that the Directive does not apply to transfers of ownership due to insolvencies, although Member States may extend it to these circumstances.[88] The Directive does apply to transfers, in the course of bankruptcy or winding up, to another undertaking – the question, therefore, is the stage of proceedings.[89] The Directive does apply where the transferor has suspended the payments of his debts[90] or where the transfer results from the repudiation of a contract.[91] However, since the legal identity of the employer must be preserved[92] it does not apply to sales of assets of a business.[93] The business must be seen to be continued by the transferee. Since the Directive covers transfers of parts of businesses, the subcontracting of one facet of the transferor's business will be covered by the Directive.[94] The ECJ has said, however, that it is for national courts to decide whether the complainant employees were actually transferred with the part of the business which was transferred.

In *Foreningen af Arbejdsledere i Danmark v A/S Danmols Inventar*[95] the ECJ explained the limitations of the Directive. It only aims to achieve partial harmonisation by ensuring that transfers do not undermine any existing rights. It does not establish a minimum standard which is to be applied throughout the Community. The rights which are preserved upon transfer will depend on the rights granted under national law. This, coupled with the fact that the definition of an employee will depend on national law, weakens the Directive significantly. However, as the ECJ affirmed in *Foreningen af Arbejdsledere i Danmark v Daddy's Dance Hall A/S*[96] the provisions of the Directive are mandatory, and improved rights on one point cannot justify denying rights on another.

Insolvencies Directive 80/987/EEC

The aim of the Insolvencies Directive 80/987/EEC is not to preserve the employment itself, but rather to protect certain rights under the contract of employment, such as wages. The Directive obliges Member States to establish a competent national guarantee institution and to provide for the payment by the institution of the outstanding claims by workers.[97] Specifically, under Article 1 the Directive 'shall apply to employees' claims arising from contracts of employment or employment relationship and existing against employers who are

88 Case 135/83, *HBM Abels v The Administrative Board of the Bedrijfsvereniging voor de Metaalindustries en de Electrotechnische Industrie* [1985] ECR 469.
89 See, for example, *A/S Danmols, op. cit.,* note 83.
90 *Ibid.*
91 Joined Cases 144 and 145/87, *Berg v Besselsen* [1988] ECR 2559.
92 Most recently affirmed in Case C-29/91, *Dr Sophie Redmond Stichting v Bartol,* judgment of 19 May 1992.
93 Case 24/85, *Spijkers v Gebroeders Benedik Abattoir CV and Alfred Benedik en Zonen BV* [1986] ECR 1119. Nielsen and Szyszczak, *op. cit.,* note 5, at 145 state that the Directive would also not apply to the sale of the majority of shares of a company.

94 Case C-209/91, *Rask v ISS Kantineservice A/S,* judgment of 12 November 1992.
95 Case 19/83, *op. cit.,* note 83.
96 Case 324/86, [1988] ECR 739. This interpretation of the Directive was applied in British law in *Litster v Forth Dry Dock and Engineering Co Ltd* [1989] 2 WLR 634.
97 In Joined Cases C-6 and 9/90, *Francovich v Italy* [1993] 2 CMLR 66 the ECJ decided that this Directive does not create direct effects, but failure to implement the Directive properly may attract State liability as a matter of Community law.

in a state of insolvency within the meaning of Article 2(1)'.[98] The definition of insolvency for the purposes of the Directive is as follows:

(a) where a request has been made for the opening of proceedings involving the employer's assets, as provided for under the laws, regulations and administrative provisions of the Member State concerned, to satisfy collectively the claims of creditors and which make it possible to take into consideration the claims referred to in Article 1(1), and
(b) where the authority which is competent pursuant to the said laws, regulations and administrative provisions has:

– either decided to open the proceedings,
– or established that the employer's undertaking or business has been definitively closed down and that the available assets are insufficient to warrant the opening of the proceedings.

The Directive explicitly reserves the right of Member States to determine the definitions of employee, employer, pay, 'right conferring immediate entitlement' and 'right conferring prospective entitlement' under national law. This area of discretion has the potential to reduce the scope of protection under the Directive markedly.

Under Article 3 Member States must ensure that guarantee institutions guarantee the payment of workers' claims prior to, at the option of the Member State, any of the dates set out below, with the liability of the guarantee institution limited, optionally, under Article 4, as follows:

- the onset of the employer's insolvency, in which case the entitlement must be at least payment for the last three months of employment during the six months preceding the insolvency;
- the notice of dismissal issued because of the insolvency, in which case the entitlement must be at least payment for the last three months of the employment preceding the notice of dismissal; or
- either the onset of insolvency or the date on which employment was terminated because of the insolvency, in which case the entitlement must be at least payment for the last 18 months of employment preceding the onset of insolvency or the termination of the employment. Member States may, in this option, limit the liability to pay corresponding to a period of eight weeks or to several shorter periods totalling eight weeks.[99]

These guarantees are strict. It is not open to Member States to argue that they have provided equivalent protection, except where they have excluded certain categories of worker on this ground under Article 1(2).[100]

Member States may set ceilings on payments, under Article 4, but must inform the Commission of the criteria for the ceiling. Member States may, under Article 6, exclude from the regime set out by the Directive employers' contributions to national or supplementary

[98] Article 1(2) provides that certain categories of employee may be excluded from the application of the Directive, as listed in the Annex to the Directive. This may only be done where there is an employment contract or relationship 'of a special nature' or where equivalent guarantees are provided. The ECJ will scrutinise the adequacy of these alternative guarantees: Case C-53/88, *Commission* v *Greece* [1990] I-ECR 3917.
[99] Articles 3 and 4.
[100] Case 22/87, *Commission* v *Italy* [1989] ECR 143.

social security schemes. However, Articles 7 and 8 require Member States to ensure that employees and former employees (such as pensioners) continue to benefit from national social security, as long as their contributions were deducted at source from their pay in the case of current employees.

Article 5 provides for the structure and organisation of the guarantee institutions, in particular that employers shall contribute to its financing,[101] and that its assets shall be inaccessible in insolvency proceedings. Furthermore, failure of employers to contribute shall not affect the institution's liability.

There is a gap between this Directive and the Transfer of Undertakings Directive 77/187/EEC, however. The Insolvencies Directive does not address the issue of transfer of the business as the consequence of insolvency, and the Transfer of Undertakings Directive has been held not to apply to such transfers.[102]

Worker consultation and information

Worker consultation and information has been a constant concern of the Commission in its plans for the development of Community social policy.[103] These rights are recognised in the Social Charter and the Social Policy Protocol. This area has, nonetheless, seen little success. Some rights of information and consultation have been included in directives regulating other social policy matters,[104] but a general system of worker consultation has yet to be established.

The debate over worker consultation and information has taken place not only in the context of social policy itself, but also in the development of Community company law. Part of the reason for this failure may arise from the fact that harmonisation of collective aspects of employment law is more difficult than harmonising individual employment rights, such as equal pay. Collective aspects of employment law, such as collective bargaining, result from historical processes and vary greatly from one Member State to another in the range of application and the degree of trust and co-operation presumed to exist between management and labour.[105] Providing a legislative framework to the social dialogue and creating general obligations of consultation could result in fundamental changes in the industrial relations of some Member States. This is unlikely to be accepted, except, perhaps, during a period of economic stability within Member States and consensus between them.

The failure of the draft Vredeling Directive

The first efforts towards establishing workers' rights of information and consultation in Community law began in the 1970s, as such rights were increasingly recognised in the national laws of the Member States.[106]

---

101 Unless the institution is fully funded by the State.

102 Collins, *op. cit.*, note 86, at 158.

103 Nielsen and Szyszczak, *op. cit.*, note 5, at 160–2; Docksey, 'Information and Consultation of Employees: The United Kingdom and the Vredeling Directive' (1986) 49 MLR 281.

104 See the section on the Employment Rights Directives, *op. cit.*, and Articles 10 and 11 of Health and Safety Framework Directive 89/391/EEC.

105 Fitzpatrick, *op. cit.*, note 38, 209–12. Nielsen and Szyszczak, *op. cit.*, note 5, at 157 argue that collective labour law is a matter for national governments in accordance with subsidiarity.

106 Däubler, 'The Employee Participation Directive – A Realistic Utopia?' (1977) 14 CML Rev 457, at 457–9.

A draft Directive, called the 'Vredeling' Directive after its proposer, on procedures for informing and consulting the employees of undertakings with complex structures, in particular transnational undertakings, was submitted to the Council in 1980.[107] An amended version was submitted in 1983.[108] Under the category of information the two obligations imposed by the draft Directive on companies were to provide information on a periodic basis and before the taking of major decisions. It would have applied to any undertaking or group of undertakings with at least one place of business in the European Union, and having at least 1000 employees in the Union. The draft Directive did not set out to harmonise the worker consultation procedures in the Member States, but rather required regular consultation between parent companies and establishments in the Union through national representation structures. It is possible, nonetheless, that the ECJ, on a reference or Commission enforcement proceeding, would have found a Member State in violation of the Directive if its national structures were inadequate to ensure a proper level of consultation. The draft Directive, which would have required unanimity, was never passed. In 1984 a further draft was drawn up, but not adopted by the Commission for submission to the Council.[109] In 1986 the Council issued a Resolution acknowledging the importance of convergence in this area and called on the Commission to prepare another proposal.[110] The approach of the Vredeling Directive has, however, been dropped and the efforts of the Commission have been focused on consultation rights under the European Company and the European Works Council.

The European company

Worker participation has been part of proposals for the harmonisation of company law since 1972.[111] While the idea of protecting employee rights through company law may seem unusual in the common law tradition, the law of other Member States imposes greater duties on companies.[112] In particular, companies are seen as having a constituency which includes their employees, rather than just their shareholders.

The proposed fifth company Directive[113] would, in harmonising the structure of public limited companies within the European Union, also require companies to elect a type of worker participation model for their supervisory boards. This supervisory board was originally intended to be one of two boards of directors of the company, the other being the executive board. The amended proposal now requires a single board exercising both supervisory and executive functions. A further change in the amended Directive is the choice of models of employee participation, whereas under the 1972 draft, employee appointment to the board was the only possibility. Now, the choice is between:

- workers elect at least one-third and at most one half of the members of the supervisory board;

107 OJ 1980 C297. See Pipkorn, 'The draft Directive on procedures for informing and consulting employees' (1983) 20 CML Rev 725.
108 OJ 1983 C217.
109 Docksey, *op. cit.*, note 103; Adinolfi, 'The Implementation of Social Policy Directives through Collective Agreements?' (1988) 25 CML Rev 291, at 308.
110 OJ 1986 C203.

111 Daübler, *op. cit.*, note 106 at 459–61.
112 Wedderburn, 'Companies and Employees: Common Law or Social Dimension?' (1993) 109 LQR 220, at 233–5.
113 Proposed Fifth Directive on the Structure and Administration of Public Limited Companies, OJ 1972 C131, as amended by OJ 1983 C240 and OJ 1991 C7.

- a body representing the workers, but separate from the organs of the company;
- a collectively agreed system concluded within the company.

Currently, a proposal is before the Council for a Directive which would complement the Regulation on the Statute for a European Company (*Societas Europaea*) by providing for worker representation on the management board of such companies.[114] Only corporations formed as European companies would be affected by the Directive. Three models of worker participation are contained in the draft Directive.[115] These models are the same as under the proposed fifth company law Directive. Member States would be able to choose one or more, and the management and employee representatives would then be able to choose from those approved models. All the models guarantee the right of workers to be consulted before major decisions are taken. The agreements on worker participation would be concluded for each establishment of a company. It would not be possible for a company located in the UK to dictate the form of participation to be followed at its Italian branch office.

The European works council

The efforts to develop Community legislation on a harmonised works council began in late 1990 and appear, at the time of writing, to have the greatest chance of success in creating Union-wide rights of information and consultation. The Draft Directive on the Information and Consultation of Workers Within European-scale Undertakings[116] was developed as part of the Social Charter Action Programme.

The Directive would apply to all companies with over 1000 employees, in two or more Member States, each location having at least 100 employees, including companies based outside the EU. The setting up of a works council would be a matter of negotiation between management and the representatives of the workers, but management would be obliged to create the conditions and means necessary for the institution of works councils. Member States have the discretion to provide whether and how members of any group negotiating a European works council should be appointed or elected, but there must be a minimum of one member per Member State where the company operates. All the aspects of the works council would be determined by the agreement reached by the negotiating group, but Article 6 of the draft Directive provides that it must cover at least:

- the nature and composition of the European works council;
- its functions and powers;
- procedures for information and consultation;
- place, frequency and duration of meetings;
- financial and material resources.

However, the works council must only deal with matters affecting the company as a whole, or at least two of its operations. If the negotiating group agrees not to set up a European

114 OJ 1970 C124, as amended by OJ 1989 C263 and OJ 1991 C138.
115 These models correspond roughly with existing Ger-
man, French and Scandinavian models: see Nielsen and Szyszczak, *op. cit.,* note 5, at 179.
116 OJ 1991 C39, as amended by OJ 1991 C336.

works council or cannot agree, minimum national requirements for information and consultation must be met.[117]

The works council would have jurisdiction to discuss both the company's current situation and future development. Information must be made available to the works council unless it is confidential information likely to damage the interests of the company if disclosed. Confidentiality must be determined on an objective basis. Possibly, on the principle of effectiveness of Community law, national courts would, therefore, be required to review any contested decision to withhold information. Member States must ensure, through the relevant national bodies, that companies fulfil their obligations under the Directive.

The draft Directive is supported by 11 Member States, the UK dissenting. There is disagreement whether to proceed on the basis of the 11 agreed Member States, in other words under the TEU Social Policy Protocol, or to continue to negotiate and to attempt to formulate a version which would be acceptable to all the Member States, which could then be adopted under Article 100 EC.[118]

Proof of Employment Contract Directive 91/533/EEC

Directive 91/533/EEC, in force since 31 July 1993, obliges Member States to adopt legislation requiring employers to provide all workers with an employment contract or with a declaration stating the main terms of employment. While this measure does not create rights for workers directly, it does give them the means to enforce their existing rights. This is particularly important for workers on short-term, part-time or other atypical modes of employment.

Employers must provide a work contract, a reference to a collective agreement or written document stating the main terms of the employment. Article 1(2) provides that, at the option of the Member State, it may not apply to those working less than eight hours a week or to those employed by a company for less than one month, or to employment contracts or relationships 'of a casual and/or specific nature provided, in these cases, that its non-application is justified by objective considerations'.

The essential elements of the contract which must be supplied are set out in Article 2. These are:

- identities of the parties;
- place of work, or the statement that the employee is employed at various places and the registered place of business or the domicile of the employer;
- title, grade, nature or category of the work, and a brief specification or description of the work;
- date of commencement;
- for temporary contracts, its expected duration;
- entitlement to paid leave;
- periods of notice for termination, or the means of determining this;

---

117 Nielsen and Szyszczak, *op. cit.*, note 5, at 175 suggest that an agreement which purported to be an agreement to set up a European works council, but which was a disguised attempt to avoid the requirements of the Di- rective, would probably be considered as an agreement not to set up a European works council.

118 Coopers and Lybrand, *EC Commentaries, op. cit.*, note 64, section 10.2.

- basic pay, other remuneration and frequency of payment;
- length of normal working day or week;
- where appropriate, reference to relevant collective agreements.

Article 3 provides that this information must be supplied within two months of the commencement of the employment, by means of either a contract, a letter of engagement and/or other written documents. If these are not supplied within the delay the employer must supply the employee with a written declaration as to the information required by Article 2. If the employee is not still working for the employer at the end of two months the information must, nonetheless, be supplied within that period. Any change in employment terms must also be notified, except as results from a change in law or a collective agreement.

Article 4 provides that when an employee is posted abroad, the necessary documents must be supplied before the employee leaves his or her home country and must contain the following additional information:

- duration of employment abroad;
- currency to be used for payment;
- benefits in cash or in kind associated with the posting;
- where appropriate, conditions governing repatriation.

This does not apply if the posting will last one month or less.

Article 9 enables Member States to implement this Directive by means of collective agreements, but they must ensure that the rights under the Directive are applied in all cases. Further, under Article 8, Member States must ensure that there are effective legal remedies for breach of the Directive.

CONCLUSION: THE FUTURE OF COMMUNITY SOCIAL POLICY

In November 1993 the Commission produced a Green Paper on social policy.[119] This Green Paper is intended to stimulate debate over the future direction of Community social policy, as a follow-up to the Social Charter Action Programme. It initiates a consultation procedure which ends on 31 March 1994, which will lead to a White Paper, a more focused policy document, being produced in autumn 1994. However, it seems that the future of social policy will include a greater emphasis on job-creation. The Communication on a Community-wide Framework Programme for Employment was published by the Social Affairs Commissioner Padraig Flynn on 26 May 1993.[120] The divergence between the Commission approach to employment and that promoted by the UK government is again prominent. The Framework Communication emphasises new forms of work organisation, including working time structures, and training. Where the costs of employment are mentioned, it is in the context of altering taxation systems rather than lowering wages. The Framework Communication also suggests co-ordinated action in developing new industries in environment, the arts and household services. Its version of subsidiarity is to promote the idea of local initiatives and support for small to medium-sized businesses.

[119] COM (93) 551.   [120] COM (93) 238.

If Community social policy is a 'sickly infant'[121] it is currently in mortal danger. The social dimension must face up to the challenges of a radically changed employment market at a time when the possibility for consensus and harmonisation has been weakened by the non-participation of the UK in the Social Policy Protocol. The other Member States may attempt to pass as much legislation as possible under Article 118a EC, arguing the Nordic 'working environment' interpretation. Far-reaching new programmes, such as those which are likely to result from the 1993 initiatives, will require the unanimous consent of the Member States, or at least a clear acknowledgement of two-speed Europe.

Further reading

Collins, H., 'Transfer of Undertakings and Insolvency' (1989) 18 ILJ 144.

Docksey, C., 'Information and Consultation of Employees: The United Kingdom and the Vredeling Directive' (1986) 49 MLR 281.

Eberlie, R.F., 'The New Health and Safety Legislation of the European Community' (1990) 19 ILJ 81.

Fitzpatrick, B., 'Community Social Law after Maastricht' (1992) 21 ILJ 199.

Hepple, B., 'The Implementation of the Community Charter of Fundamental Social Rights' 53 MLR (1990) 643.

Hepple, B. and Byre, A., 'EEC Labour Law in the United Kingdom – A New Approach (1989) 18 ILJ 129.

Nielsen, R. and Szyszczak, E., *The Social Dimension of the European Community* (Copenhagen: Handelshojskolens Forlag, 1991).

Spicker, P., 'The Principle of Subsidiarity and the Social Policy of the European Community' (1991) 1 JESP 3.

Szyszczak, E., '1992 and the Working Environment' (1992) JSWFL 3.

Vogel-Polsky, E., 'What Future is There For a Social Europe Following the Strasbourg Summit?' (1990) 19 ILJ 65, at 75.

Watson, P., 'The Community Social Charter' 28 CML Rev (1991) 37, at 44.

Watson, P., 'Social Policy after Maastricht' 30 CML Rev (1993) 481.

Wedderburn, 'The Social Charter in Britain – Labour Law and Labour Courts?' (1991) 54 MLR 1.

Wedderburn, 'Companies and Employees: Common Law or Social Dimension?' (1993) 109 LQR 220.

---

[121] Wedderburn, *op. cit.*, note 112, at 262.

CHAPTER 18

The Common Agricultural Policy

INTRODUCTION

The Common Agricultural Policy (CAP) has, over the last 10 years, become increasingly marginalised in academic writings, both legal and political. This is perhaps due to a perception of it as an area of interest only to farmers and statisticians and is also due to the substantial growth in size and importance of other areas of Community activity. Yet the CAP retains a notoriety, particularly in the UK and France, unparalleled by any other Community activity, not least because it is clearly an area where the Community has significantly expanded its exclusive competence at the expense of the Member States.[1]

It is true that recent statistics show that the CAP has begun to diminish slightly in financial importance. For instance, in 1992 it accounted for 2.9 per cent of EC gross national product,[2] whereas in 1983 the figure had been 3.9 per cent.[3] In the period 1979 to 1983 the cost of the CAP was between 63 per cent and 76 per cent of the Community budget,[4] while in 1992 it was down to 58.2 per cent.[5] However, when one looks behind the percentages the monetary amounts are still staggering. In 1983 the CAP cost the Community 14.194 billion ECU,[6] in 1992 it cost 33.539 billion ECU,[7] and despite the recent reforms designed, amongst other aims, to cut the cost of the CAP, it is estimated that the CAP will cost over 39 billion ECU by 1997.[8]

In terms of international trade the CAP has been a major obstacle to the EC's ability to reach trading agreements with other nations, a notable example being the disputes with the US and the Cairns Group[9] in the Uruguay Round of the General Agreement on Tariffs and Trade (GATT). The CAP, therefore, cannot be ignored as a primary influence on Community

1 Blumental, 'Implementing the Common Agricultural Policy: Aspects of the Limitations on the Powers of the Member States' (1984), 35 NILQ 28, at 32. See comments by the ECJ with reference to this in Case 48/74, *Charmasson* v *Minister for Economic Affairs and Finance* [1974] ECR 1383; Case 68/76, *Commission* v *French Republic* [1977] ECR 515.
2 Commission of the European Communities, *The Agricultural Situation in the Communities: 1992 Report* (1993), at T/20.
3 Commission of the European Communities, *The Agricultural Situation in the Communities: 1983 Report* (1984), at 187.
4 *Ibid.*, at 155.
5 Commission of the European Communities, *Our Farming Future* (1993), at 23.
6 Commission of the European Communities, *The Agricultural Situation in the Communities: 1983 Report* (1984), at 154.
7 Commission of the European Communities, *The Agri-*

cultural Situation in the Communities: 1992 Report (1993), at T/84. Although the figure seems to vary depending upon the Community publication, EC Commission, *Our Farming Future* (1993), at 23 puts the cost at 36.417 billion ECU. At time of writing this would amount to approximately £28.4 billion.
8 EC Commission, *Our Farming Future, ibid.*, at 25.
9 The Cairns Group was formed in 1986 by a group of developed and developing agricultural exporters comprising of Argentina, Australia, Brazil, Canada, Chile, Colombia, Hungary, Indonesia, Malaysia, New Zealand, Thailand and Uruguay, who wanted to have some influence on the agenda of the Uruguay Round. Its third meeting at Ministerial level was at an Australian beach resort, hence its name. The group, led by Australia, was active throughout the Uruguay Round, but its influence was greatly diminished after the Brussels Ministerial. Its major contribution to the final bargaining was to ensure that agriculture could not be left out of the package.

policy-making, whether that policy-making is concerned with internal issues, such as the environment or external issues, such as trade agreements.

The CAP still accounts for a large percentage of Community legislation and 42 per cent of cases before the ECJ.[10] It is worth remembering too, that many of the general principles presently used by the ECJ were first used, and then adapted and refined, in cases concerning the CAP, in particular, proportionality and non-discrimination.

This Chapter will give a brief overview of administrative workings of the CAP and discuss the major case law arising from it,[11] as well as its impact on Community relations with other world agricultural producers. It will also examine the issue of fraud against the Community, as the CAP is by far the sector of Community activity most prone to fraudulent activity.

ORIGINS, AIMS AND METHODS

The basic framework of the CAP is to be found in the EC Treaty, Articles 38–47. Article 38 defines agricultural products[12] and declares that, unless otherwise exempted, the provisions of the Common Market apply to agricultural products.[13] It states that all products that fall under Articles 39–46 will be listed in Annex II of the Treaty[14] and provides for the establishment of a Common Agricultural policy.[15]

The principal aims are contained in Article 39. These aims are:

(a) to increase agricultural productivity by promoting technical progress and by ensuring the rational development of agricultural production and the optimum utilisation of the factors of production, in particular labour;

(b) thus to ensure a fair standard of living for the agricultural community, in particular by increasing the individual earnings of persons engaged in agriculture;

---

10 Commission of the European Communities, *XXVIth General Report on the activities of the European Comminities 1992* (1993), at 506 (184 cases out of a total of 438 brought in 1992).

11 For more detailed, if somewhat dated, studies, see Snyder, *Law of the Common Agricultural Policy* (1985) and Fennel, *The Common Agricultural Policy of the European Community* (1987). A brief but more recent study can be found in Butler, 'The EC's Common Agricultural Policy' in Lodge, J. (ed.) *The European Community and the Challenge of the Future*, 2nd edn (1993).

12 Article 38(1) 'the products of the soil, of stockfarming and of fisheries and products of first stage processing directly related to these products'. It should be noted that the ECJ has interpreted 'products of first stage processing directly related to those products' fairly widely, stating that the test to be satisfied was that there was 'a clear economic interdependence between basic products and products resulting from a productive process', and that where this was proven, the product was a product of first stage processing 'irrespective of the number of operations involved therein'. Case 185/73, *Hauptzollamt Bielefeld* v *Offene handelsgesellschaft in Firma CC König* [1974] ECR 607.

13 Article 38(2), ie Article 42 which provides for the suspension of the rules on competition where the Council feels it is necessary.

14 Article 38(3) as extended by Regulation 7a/59/EEC, OJ 1961 7. If a product is not contained within Annex II of that Regulation it is not an agricultural product and this not covered by the CAP. The ECJ has interpreted this strictly, see Case 2–3/62, *Commission* v *Luxembourg and Belgium* [1962] ECR 445, which appears to be due to the ECJ wishing to limit the number of products potentially able to claim the exemptions from provisions of the Common Market which can be granted to agricultural products under Article 38(2).

15 Article 38(4). It has been suggested that this Article does not restrict CAP-related provisions to the same limits imposed by the Common Market. This was certainly the view expressed by Advocate General Mayras in his opinion in Case 180/73, *Officer van Justitie* v *Van Haaster* [1974] ECR 1123, at 1138. This concerned Article 10 of Regulation No 234/68/EEC which went further than Articles 30 and 34 of the EC Treaty inasmuch as it prohibited restrictions on trade within Member States as well as between Member States.

(c) to stabilise markets;

(d) to assure the availability of supplies;

(e) to ensure that supplies reach consumers at reasonable prices.[16]

In July 1958, the Stresa Conference, involving the six original Member States and representatives of their farming organisations, set out further details of the Community's policy, notably that Community agriculture had to be more competitive, but without damaging existing farm structure based on the family unit. Prices were to be made uniform over a period of time, at a higher price than world market level as Community production costs were higher, but not so high as to encourage overproduction. The Community need not be self-sufficient, but its role in world trade should be balanced to avoid distortions in the internal market.

Following this, the Commission submitted proposals to the Council which adopted the principles creating the CAP in 1960. Those guiding principles were the creation of the Single Market, Community preference and financial solidarity.

The Single Market requires that there should be free movement of agricultural products between Member States. The achievement of this means that there can be no customs duties or other trade barriers between Member States, and Member States are not permitted to grant subsidies to their own producers. The Community attempts to enforce common pricing and competition rules, stabilise agro-exchange rates and approximate administrative, public health and veterinary rules and regulations.

Community preference requires that Community produce be given a higher sale priority than imports. This is difficult to achieve because, in general, Community prices are higher than those on the world market. Thus, the levels of imports and exports of agricultural produce must be regulated to protect the Community market. The Community will also pay subsidies to Community producers of products which cannot adequately be protected by regulation of imports and exports.

Financial solidarity underpins the other two principles. Creating a Single Market and ensuring Community preference requires Member State finance. The CAP can only work if that financial burden is shared by all Member States, without prejudice as to the product or Member State being supported.

It is probably fair to say that the aims of the Stresa Conference, influenced as it was by the dominance of the French and German farmers, have never been met satisfactorily, in that the number of farmers and farm workers in the original six members of the Community has more than halved in the last 30 years;[17] there has been considerable overproduction in a number of areas, notably butter and wine; and the Community's role in world trade has sometimes verged on the catastrophic. On the other hand, it would also be fair to state that, with the exception of the final point, the principles contained in Article 39(1) of the Treaty have, to a large extent, been achieved, but at considerable financial cost.

The role of the ECJ

The ECJ has played a pivotal role in the development of the CAP, not least in helping to

---

[16] Article 39(1).

[17] From 10 402 000 in 1960 to 4 802 000 in 1990. EC Commission, *Our Farming Future, op. cit.,* note 7, at 16.

determine that the Treaty articles concerning the CAP have largely been interpreted in favour of the producers of agricultural products rather than the consumers. The five fundamental objectives of the CAP laid down in Article 39(1) have, in effect, been given differing degrees of priority by the ECJ. This has been justified by the argument that it is often impossible to protect both the interests of the farmers and the consumers and that the principle of Community preference as expressed in Article 44(2) permits the Council to take action to protect Community producers even where that action restricts availability of supplies and forces up the cost of products to the consumer.[18] The ECJ has also held that as far as Article 39(1)(e) is concerned, the term 'reasonable prices' should not be taken to mean that the consumer is entitled to the lowest available prices.[19] Indeed, the consumer seems to have lost out to the producer at every turn,[20] even where prioritising the producer's interests has clearly been contrary to the interests of the consumer.[21] The ECJ has not, however, decided upon a rigid list of priorities within Article 39(1). Indeed, it has held that it may be possible to temporarily prioritise one of the objectives[22] and, while the situation *vis-à-vis* producers and consumers shows clearly the interests of the producers to be almost always favoured, in theory at least no one objective may be prioritised in such a manner as to make any of the others impossible to achieve.[23]

With regard to the exercise by the Council of its legislative powers, Article 40(3) provides that 'The common organisation shall be limited to pursuit of the objectives set out in Article 39'. The ECJ has noted in several cases that legislation must not exceed the Article 39 objectives or it will be held invalid.[24] The Council is also constrained in the exercise of its powers by the principles of non-discrimination and proportionality, which are expressly mentioned in Article 40(3),[25] and the other general principles of Community law as developed by the ECJ.

For Community legislation to be held to be discriminatory it must be shown to treat comparable situations in different ways. The applicant must demonstrate that there is discrimination in substance[26] and that the differences in treatment alleged are arbitrary in nature.[27] Despite its wording, Article 40(3) is not concerned with discrimination between producers and consumers in the sense that legislation treats producers favourably at the

---

18 Case *5/67, Beus v Hauptzollampt Munchen* [1968] ECR 83, at 98.

19 Case *34/62, Germany v Commission* [1963] ECR 131.

20 With, for instance, Article 39(1)(c) concerning the stabilisation of markets apparently being construed as an objective aimed at supporting the producers rather than protecting the consumer. in early case law, see for example Joined Cases 106–7/63, *Alfred Toepfer v Commission* [1965] ECR 405.

21 Case *5/73, Balkan-Import-Export v Hauptzollampt Berlin Packhof* [1973] ECR 1091, at 1112; Case 113/75, *Giordano Frecassetti v Amministrazione delle Finanze dello Stato* [1976] ECR 983.

22 Case *5/67, Beus v Hauptzollampt Munchen, op. cit.,* note 18; Case *5/73, Balkan-Import-Export v Hauptzollampt Berlin Packhof, op. cit.,* note 21, Joined Cases 54–60/76, *Compagnie Industrielle et Agricole du Comte de Loheac v Council and Commission* [1977] ECR 645; Case C-311/90, *Josef Hierl v Hauptzollamt Regensberg* [1992] 2 CMLR 445.

23 Case *9/73, Firma Carl Schluter v Hauptzollamt Lorrach* [1973] ECR 1135; Joined Cases 197–200, 243, 245 and 247/80, *Ludwigshafener Walzmuhle Erling KG v Council and Commission* [1981] ECR 3211.

24 Case 11/70, *Internationale Handelsgesellschaft GmbH v EVST* [1970] ECR 1125; Case *5/73, Balkan-Import-Export GbmH v Hauptzollamt Berlin-Packhof* [1973] ECR 1091; Case 138/78, *Hans-Markus Stölting v Hauptzollamt Hamburg-Jonas* [1979] ECR 713.

25 Non-discrimination – Article 40(3) '. . . shall exclude any discrimination between producers and consumers within the Community'.
Proportionality – Article 40(3) 'The common organisation . . . may include all measures required to attain the objectives set out in Article 39 . . .'

26 Case 6/71, *Rheinmuhlen Dusseldorf v EVST* [1971] ECR 823.

27 Case 11/74, *Union des Minotiers de la Champagne, Reims v Minister for Agriculture* [1974] ECR 877; Case 167/88, *AGPB v ONIC* [1989] ECR 1653.

expense of consumers, as this is held to fall within Article 39. Instead, it is concerned with discrimination between groups of producers or groups of consumers, for instance, if sugar producers in the various Member States are treated differently without good reason or, indeed, if producers of other sweetener products are treated differently from sugar producers without good reason.[28] The non-discrimination rule in Article 40(3) applies equally to the Member States as well as the Community institutions[29] and applies irrespective of nationality.[30] It is clear that the ECJ is of the opinion that not every difference of treatment will amount to discrimination, not least because this would make the market organisations unworkable.[31]

Proportionality requires that while the market organisations may include all measures required to attain the objectives set out in Article 39, they should attempt to ensure that the measures that they adopt are the least restrictive to achieve the aim required and the measures do not have larger effects than necessary on producers.[32]

With regard to the Commission, when it acts under the discretionary powers granted by a Council Regulation the ECJ permits it a wide discretion in the evaluation of economic factors, even in those cases where the ECJ clearly reaches a different conclusion regarding the economic situation.[33]

As noted in the introduction, as well as proportionality and non-discrimination, the CAP has been an area which has seen extensive use and development of the other general principles of law by the ECJ. These principles include protection of human rights,[34] *force majeure*,[35] legal certainty,[36] legitimate expectation,[37] non-retroactivity,[38] legal clarity,[39]

[28] Case 5/73, *Balkan-Import-Export GmbH v Hauptzollamt Berlin-Packhof*, op. cit., note 24; Cases 103, 145/77, *Royal Scholten-Honing (Holding) Limited v The Intervention Board for Agricultural Produce, Tunnel Refineries Limited v The Intervention Board for Agricultural Produce* [1978] ECR 2037.
[29] Case 31/74, *Filippo Galli* [1975] ECR 47; Case 223/78, *Adriano Grosoli* [1979] ECR 2621.
[30] Case 43/72, *Merkur v Commission* [1973] ECR 1055.
[31] Cases 9 and 11/71, *Compagnie d'approvisionnement v Commission* [1972] ECR 391; Case 43/72, *Merkur v Commission*, op. cit., note 30; Joined Cases 63 and 69/72, *Firma Wilhelm Werhahn Hansamuhle and Others v Council and Commission* [1973] ECR 1229; Case 139/77, *Denkavit Futtermittel GmbH v Finanzamt Warendorf* [1978] ECR 1317; Case 166/78, *Italy v Council* [1979] ECR 2575; Cases 138 and 139/79, *Maizena Gesellschaft mbH and SA Roquette Frères v Council* [1980] ECR 3333.
[32] Case 25/70, *EVST Getreide v Koster* [1970] ECR 1161; Case 5/73, *Balkan-Import-Export GmbH v Hauptzollamt Berlin-Packhof*, op. cit., note 24; Cases 63–69/72, *Firma Wilhelm Werhahn Hansamuhle and Others v Council and Commission*, op. cit., note 31; Case 95/75, *Firma Effem v Hauptzollamt Luneburg* [1976] ECR 361; Case 114/76, *Bela-Muhle Josef Ber-*

mann KG v Grows-Farm GmbH & Co KG [1977] ECR 1211; Case 116/76, *Granaria BV v Hoofdproduktschap voor Akkerbouwprodukten and Other* [1977] ECR 1247; Cases 119 and 120/76, *Olmuhle Hamburg AG v Hauptzollamt Hamburg Waltershof* [1977] 1269; Case 122/78, *Buitoni SA v Fonds d'Orientation et de Regularisation des Marches Agricoles* [1975] ECR 677; Case 808/79, *Fratelli Pardini* [1980] ECR 2103; Cases 138 and 139/79, *Maizena Gesellschaft mbH and SA Roquette Frères v Council*, op. cit., note 31.
[33] Case 78/74, *Firma Deuka Deutsche Kraftfutter GmbH B J Stolp v EVST* [1975] ECR 421.
[34] Case 44/79, *Liselotte Hauer v Land Rheinland-Pfalz* [1979] ECR 3727.
[35] Case 68/77, *IFG-Intercontinentale Fleischhandelsgesellschaft mbH & Co KG v Commission* [1978] ECR 353.
[36] Case 1/73, *Westzucker GmbH v Ein fuhr- und Vorratsstelle fur Zucker* [1973] ECR 723.
[37] Case 74/74, *Comptoir National Technique Agricole (CNTA) SA v Commission* [1975] ECR 533.
[38] Case 98/78, *Firma A Racke v Hauptzollamt Mainz* [1979] ECR 69.
[39] Case 32/79, *Commission v UK* [1980] ECR 2403; Case 169/80, *Administration des Douanes v Gondrand Frères SA and Garancini SA* [1981] ECR 1931.

fairness and natural justice,[40] unjust enrichment,[41] abuse of law or good faith[42] and continuity.[43]

Market organisations

Article 40, which governs the implementation of the CAP provides *inter alia* that, in order to attain the objectives set out in Article 39, a common organisation of agricultural markets is to be established and that that organisation may include all measures required to attain those objectives.[44] The creation of the market organisations for the various agricultural products were provided for in Article 40(2) and (3) and their development began in 1961. When the CAP came into force in 1962, market organisations had been agreed for six products. By 1970 87 per cent of agricultural production was covered by a market organisation and this reached 91 per cent by 1986.[45] At present only agricultural alcohol and potatoes[46] have no market organisation.[47] While the term 'common organisation of the market' is used to describe each of the individual basic regulations which govern agricultural products, the form that these market organisations take differs from product to product. Not only are different

[40] Case 5/73, *Balkan-Import-Export GmbH v Hauptzollamt Berlin-Packhof, op. cit.*, note 28; Case 78/77, *Firma Johann Luhrs v Hauptzollamt Hamburg-Jonas* [1978] ECR 169; Case 87/78, *Firma Welding & Co v Hauptzollamt Hamburg-Waltershof* [1978] ECR 2457.

[41] Cases 66, 127 and 128/79, *Amministrazione delle Finanze dello Stato v Srl Meridionale Industria Salumi* [1980] ECR 1237; Case 66/80, *SpA International Chemcial Corporation v Amministrazione delle Finanze dello Stato* [1981] ECR 1191.

[42] Case 125/76, *Firm Peter Cremer v Bundesanstalt fur landwirtschaftliche Marktordnung* [1977] ECR 1593.

[43] Case 124/80, *Officier van Justitie v Vennootschaponder firma Fa J van Dam & Zone* [1981] ECR 1447; Case 84/81, *Staple Dairy Products Ltd v Intervention Board for Agricultural Produce* [1982] ECR 1763.

[44] Case 138/78, *Stolting v Hauptzollamt Hamburg-Jonas* [1979] ECR 713.

[45] The following are the legislative basis for those products for which there is currently a common organisation of the market.
Vegetable oils and fats – Regulation 136/66/EEC, OJ 1966 172, last amended by Regulation 356/92/EEC, OJ 1992 L39; live trees, plants, flowers, bulbs etc – Regulation 234/68/EEC, OJ 1968 L55, last amended by Regulation 3991/87/EEC, OJ 1987 L377; milk and milk products – Regulation 804/68/EEC, OJ 1968 L148, last amended by Regulation 2071/92/EEC, OJ 1992 L215; beef and veal – Regulation 805/68/EEC, OJ 1968 L148, last amended by Regulation 125/93/EEC, OJ 1993 L18; other agricultural products (Annex II EC Treaty) – Regulation 827/68/EEC, OJ 1968 L151, last amended by Regulation 789/89/EEC, OJ 1989 L85; raw tobacco – Regulation 727/70/EEC, OJ 1970 L94, last amended by Regulation 2075/92/EEC, OJ 1992 L215; flax and hemp – Regulation 1308/70/EEC, OJ 1970 L146, last amended by Regulation 1557/93/EEC, OJ 1993 L154; hops – Regulation 1696/71/EEC, OJ 1971 L175, last amended by Regulation 3124/92/EEC, OJ 1992 313; seeds – Regulation 2358/71/EEC, OJ 1971 L246, last amended by Regulation 1740/91/EEC, OJ 1991, L 163; fresh fruit and vegetables – Regulation 1035/72/EEC, OJ 1972 L118, last amended by Regulation 638/93/EEC, OJ 1993 L69; cereals – Regulation 2727/75/EEC, OJ 1975 L281, last amended by Regulation 2193/93/EEC, OJ 1993 L19; pig meat – Regulation 2759/75/EEC, OJ 1975 L282, last amended by Regulation 1249/89/EEC, OJ 1989 L129; eggs – Regulation 2771/75/EEC, OJ 1975 L282, last amended by Regulation 1235/89/EEC, OJ 1989 L128; poultry meat – Regulation 2777/75/EEC, OJ 1975 L282, last amended by Regulation 3714/92/EEC, OJ 1992 L378; rice – Regulation 1418/76/EEC, OJ 1976 L166, last amended by Regulation 1544/93/EEC, OJ 1993 L154; dried fodder – Regulation 1117/78/EEC, OJ 1978 L142, last amended by Regulation 2275/89/EEC, OJ 1989 L218; sheepmeat and goatmeat – Regulation 3013/89/EEC, OJ 1989 L289, last amended by Regulation 363/93/EEC, OJ 1993 L42; sugar – Regulation 1785/81/EEC, OJ 1981 L177, last amended by Regulation 1548/93/EEC, OJ 1993 L154; products processed from fruit and vegetables – Regulation 426/86/EEC, OJ 1986 L49, last amended by Regulation 1568/92/EEC, OJ 1992 L166; wine – Regulation 822/87/EEC, OJ 1987 L84, last amended by Regulation 1566/93/EEC, OJ 1993 L154, Corrigendum in OJ 1993 L185; bananas – Regulation 404/93/EEC, OJ 1993 L47; addition of certain products to Annex II to the Treaty – Council Regulation 827/68/EEC, amended by Regulation 638/93/EEC, OJ 1993 L69.

[46] Except those used to make starch, which fall under the market organisation for cereals.

[47] Although proposals have been made for both potatoes are currently the subject of a Commission proposal OJ 1992 C333. However, the re-amended Commission proposal concerning ethyl alcohol, OJ 1979 C193, was withdrawn in August 1993, OH 1993 C288.

mechanisms used, but identical mechanisms may be employed in different manners.[48]

The primary type of market organisation which covers over 70 per cent of agricultural protection is based on two elements, internal intervention and external protection. The market organisation for cereals will be used to demonstrate this mechanism. The process of internal intervention in this market organisation relies on the relationship between three prices. These are the target price, the intervention price and the threshold price. [49] (*See* p 418.)

- The target price[50] is the price that the Community decides will give a fair return to farmers.
- The intervention price[51] (lower than, and derived from, the target price) is the price at which the Community will buy in produce when supply exceeds demand and the market price falls.
- The threshold price[52] is the price fixed by the Community as being the minimum for products imported from third countries.

Intervention purchasing is run by national agencies, who must buy all Community produce offered to them at the intervention price. In some sectors, due to continuing surpluses, intervention has been restricted in scope, by limiting it to certain quantities and quality, as in the case of sugar; or to certain times of year, as in the case of sheepmeat.

The second largest type of market organisation, which covers about 25 per cent of production, is external protection without intervention. Here the protection takes the form of levies or customs duties or both. Again, the method of protection varies from sector to sector.

The other market organisations are based on aid to complement prices or 'flat rate aids'. In the case of products for which the EC has agreed under GATT to maintain import duties at either a constant low level or at nil, it is not possible to use external protection methods to support the market organisations. The Community thus pays deficiency payments to the producers to supplement the market price or subsidies to the processing industries of such products to allow them to use Community products in the face of cheap imports. This is termed 'aid to complement prices'. Products so supported include tobacco, oilseeds and sheepmeat.

Flat rate aid is used only for very specialised products which form a tiny percentage of Community production and is paid per hectare or by quantity produced. Examples of these products are flax, hemp, silkworms and hops.

REFORMS OF THE CAP

Early reforms

The operation of the market organisations has lead to persistent surpluses in a number of

[48] The ECJ has been prepared to interpret Article 40 in fairly broad terms, see Case 17/67, *Neumann v Hauptzollampt Hof/Saale* [1967] ECR 441.
[49] It should be noted that these terms are not uniformly used by the various market organisations which fall within this category.

[50] Also known as the 'guide price' (veal and beef) or 'basic price' (pigmeat).
[51] Also known as the 'buying in price' (pigmeat and wine) or 'withdrawal price' (fruit and vegetables).
[52] Also known as the 'reference price' (fruit and vegetables) or 'sluicegate price' (eggs and poultry meat).

Target price

Threshold
price

Unloading and
Transport costs

Levy
(Variable)

Intervention
price

Market prices

Refund
(Variable)

free on quay
Community port

Import Price
(cif)
(Variable)

World price
(Variable)

Import

Export

Agricultural expenditure
EAGGF protion of EEC budget
Own resources of the EEC budget

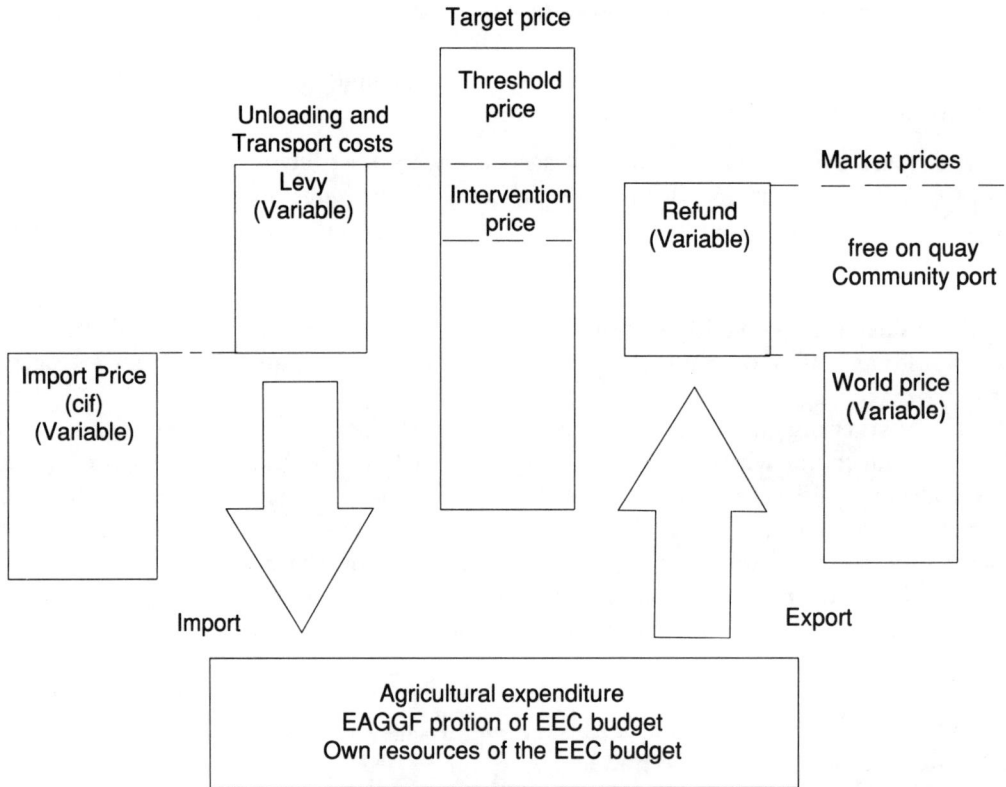

Diagram from 'A Common Agricultural Policy for the 1990s' (5/1993) European Documentation, p 18

sectors. This problem was foreseen as early as 1968 when a Commission memorandum, usually known as the Mansholt Plan, proposed a restructuring of European agriculture to avoid just such surpluses. However, this plan was only partially implemented and in its attenuated form failed to have a significant impact on the agricultural structure. The general political and economic crises of the early and mid-1970s effectively prevented further attempts at reform during that time. By the late 1970s it was clear that such surpluses could not be dealt with by the existing mechanisms. The Commission put forward proposals to stabilise those sectors, notably milk, sugar and cereals. In the milk sector, co-responsibility levies were introduced in 1979. These, however, proved inadequate to cut the milk surplus and in 1984 production quotas were introduced.

The 1988 reforms[53]

In 1988 the Council, alarmed at burgeoning EC spending on agriculture, imposed a ceiling on farm spending of 74 per cent of Community GNP growth. They also introduced guarantee limits for all major EC products, apart from milk and sugar which were already regulated.[54] The limits, known as stabilisers, were intended to control spending on a sector-by-sector basis. If production in a particular sector surpassed its maximum guaranteed quantity (MCQ), support payments to all farmers in that sector were reduced. By way of example, in the cereal sector the MCQ was set at 160 million tonnes per annum. The aim was that if production rose above this, a price cut of three per cent would be implemented the year after that harvest. If the sector overproduced for a second year a further three per cent cut, on top of the first, would be made.[55] Set aside schemes whereby farmers were paid not to farm specified land for a five-year period were introduced for the first time. Further to these measures, co-responsibility levies were introduced in some sectors. The effect of these reforms and, in particular, stabilisers has been mixed, outside pressures such as the relative weakness of the dollar against European currencies have reduced their effectiveness at cutting costs. A Commission report in June 1989 stated that the stabilisers were effective over their first two years of use, but recent Community documents suggest that this optimism was probably misplaced.[56] Certainly the situation was such that by 1991 it was clear that further and more radical reforms were required.

The 1992 reforms[57]

The aim of the 1992 reform of the CAP is to cut costs and alleviate the surpluses problem. This is to be achieved by turning from price support policy towards more specifically directed aid for producers. By directing finance to those areas of agriculture that are most vulnerable

[53] Often known as the Delors package. See OJ 1988 L110 for the schemes which make up the 1988 reform package.
[54] Stabilising mechanisms have been implemented for the following products; cereals, sugar, oilseeds and protein plants, olive oil, wine, tobacco, cotton, fruit and vegetables (fresh and processed), milk, beef/veal, sheepmeat and goatmeat.
[55] In the 1992/93 marketing year there was an automatic price support cut of 11 per cent in the cereals sector due to an overproduction of 8.9 million tonnes in 1991.
[56] Commission of the European Communities, *Our Farming Future* (1993), *op. cit.*, note 7, at 18.
[57] See Butler, 'The EC's Common Agricultural Policy' *op. cit.*, at 115–18 for the background to these reforms.

rather than offering support across the board the Community is attempting to address the problem that while it has significant over-capacity in some sectors, with resulting long-term storage and disposal costs, it remains the largest importer of agricultural goods in the world.[58] The reforms also seek to take into account the Community's concern with the state of the environment and also the social and economic problems faced by rural areas. The reforms are to be phased in over a three-year period from 1993.

More specifically, the reforms are aimed at obtaining a better balance of the agricultural markets, making EC products more competitive by cutting their cost, de-intensifying production methods to protect the environment, redistributing financial support and ensuring employment for farmers and farm workers.

The major measures in the reform package are:

- the reduction of the price of cereals by about 30 per cent. The basic regulations governing this sector are Regulation 2727/75/EEC,[59] Regulation 1765/92/EEC[60] and Regulation 1766/92/EEC.[61] The latter two Regulations will apply from the 1993/94 marketing year. It is planned that the target price for this sector will be reduced from 130 ECU per tonne in 1993 to 110 ECU per tonne in 1996. Proposed intervention prices will also fall from 117 ECU per tonne in 1993 to 100 ECU per tonne in 1996. The threshold price will be set at 45 ECU higher than the target price. It is hoped that this price cut will have a knock-on effect on production costs for other products such as pigmeat and poultrymeat. Beef prices will also be reduced by 15 per cent over the three years;
- payment of permanent compensatory payments in order to counter the decline in farmers' wages caused by the reduction in cereals prices;
- a compulsory annual set-aside scheme for farmers wishing to claim permanent compensatory payments, where they will be paid not to farm a certain percentage of their land;[62]
- an agri-environmental action programme to provide aid for farmers to adopt less intensive and less polluting methods of production. It will also provide aid for the preservation of the countryside and for natural resource conservation;
- financial incentives for farmers who agree to partial or total afforestation of their land;
- a voluntary early retirement scheme for farmers and farmworkers designed to promote structural adjustment of production, notably in those Member States with less viable production structures.

These reforms appeared to mark a significant change in policy for the Community, with a clear acceptance of some of the financial absurdities of the existing system. The reforms also went some way to meeting the demands of other world producers that the Community be

[58] In 1990 the Community imported agricultural products worth 55.889 million ECU and exported agricultural products worth 35.186 million ECU. *Ibid.*

[59] OJ 1975 L281, as amended by Regulation 1738/92/EEC, OJ 1992 L180 and Regulation 1715/93/EEC, OJ 1993 L159.

[60] OJ 1992 L181, as amended by Regulation 1738/92/EEC, OJ 1992 L180.

[61] OJ 1992 L181, as amended by Regulation 1709/93/EC, OJ 1993 L159 and Regulation 2193/93/EEC, OJ 1993 L196.

[62] That percentage will be determined by Council, for 1993/94 it was set at 15 per cent for rotational set-aside, non-rotational set-aside is likely to be set higher. However, for farmers producing less than 92 tonnes of cereal, set-aside will not be compulsory.

less protectionist about its agricultural sector.[63] It is still difficult, however, to come to terms with farmers being paid not to farm, or to devise ways to be less efficient in their farming methods. Also at odds are the Commission's avowed intention to encourage farmers to remain on the land, and the afforestation and early retirement proposals, especially in the light of the fact that the number of farmers has approximately halved in the original six Member States in the last 30 years.[64] It remains to be seen if the recent reforms will have the effects that the Commission and Council hope, but they will almost certainly not reduce the controversy surrounding the aims, methods and financing of the CAP.

EUROPEAN AGRICULTURAL GUIDANCE AND GUARANTEE FUND (EAGGF)

In 1962, in accordance with Article 40(4) EC, the Member States implemented Regulation 25/62/EEC[65] to set up the European Agricultural Guidance and Guarantee Fund (EAGGF)[66] to administer the finance of the CAP. It was designed to achieve the aim of financial solidarity by ensuring that the financial consequences of the market organisations in agriculture devolved upon the Community rather than the Member States. Under the Regulation the Fund would finance refunds on exports to third countries, intervention aimed at stabilising markets and 'common measures adopted in order to attain the objectives set out in Article 39(1)(a)'.[67] However, the rules concerning the structure and activities of the EAGGF were not put in place until 1964 when Regulation 17/64/EEC[68] divided the work of the EAGGF between two sections, the Guarantee Section and the Guidance Section. The current basis for the financing of the CAP, although much amended, remains Regulation 729/70/EEC.[69] This stated that the EAGGF would become part of the Community budget in line with the provisions of Article 201 EC.[70] The EAGGF is administered by the Commission and an EAGGF Committee.

Thus, the EAGGF forms part of the Community budget and its appropriations are fixed according to budgetary procedures as with other Community expenditure. However, the CAP also generates income by way of revenues collected via the market organisations. These revenues form part of the Community's own resources and take the form of levies on agricultural imports from third countries and payments collected under the common organisation of the market in sugar.[71] Other agricultural income is considered to be as a

---

63 Somewhat eccentrically, the Commission seemed to have taken the public position that the reforms were purely to deal with Community problems. 'The Community has its own reasons for reforming the CAP and these have nothing to do with the Uruguay Round' (EC Commission, *Our Farming Future, op. cit.*, note 7, at 26). It is clear from the nature of the concessions that the Community had to make during the early stages of the Uruguay Round negotiations that such statements should be taken with a degree of scepticism.
64 EC Commission, *Our Farming Future, op. cit.*, note 7, at 16.
65 Sp OJ 1959–62 as amended by Regulation 130/66/EEC, OJ 1966 165/1965, following the Luxembourg compromise.
66 Often known by its French acronym FEOGA (*Fonds europeen d'orientation et de garantie agricole*).
67 Article 2(2), paragraph 1.
68 Sp OJ 1963–64.
69 Sp OJ 1970.
70 Concerning the replacement of Member State financing by the Community's own resources.
71 A production levy on sugar and isoglucose production, storage levy for sugar and additional elimination levy. These levies are designed to reduce the Community surplus of sugar, as the Community currently over produces the needs of domestic consumption significantly.

result of measures to stabilise the agricultural markets and is directly deducted from the agricultural expenditure of that year in the sector concerned.[72] Such income does not, therefore, form part of the Community's own resources.

EAGGF Guarantee Section

The EAGGF Guarantee Section's role has primarily been the responsibility for the financing of the common organisation of the agricultural markets by way of refunds on exports to third countries and measures to stabilise agricultural markets. The latter measures can be by way of production aids or premiums, price compensatory measures, compensation for the withdrawal of products from the market or storage aid. However, in recent years its tasks have expanded beyond that relatively limited role to include the financing of measures against fraud and to promote quality, the collection of information on rural development and the set-aside of arable land. It is also involved in the financing of many of the measures taken under the recent reform of the CAP. The largest part of EAGGF expenditure is taken by the Guarantee Section which took 97 per cent of funds in 1987. Of this money some 60 per cent was taken by intervention devices and 40 per cent by export refunds. Expenditure on markets and prices is initially supported by the Member States via their intervention agencies which make export refund and storage cost payments and this money is then refunded to them by the EAGGF. The process of clearing of Guarantee Section accounts involves the Commission in verification procedures and on-the-spot checks of files. Disagreements between Member States and the Commission over clearance of accounts are frequent and often appear before the ECJ. The Guarantee Section is also subject to an early warning procedure for spending. This is based on monthly expenditure profiles for each area of guarantee activity compiled by the Commission for the previous three years. The Commission then presents both Council and Parliament with monthly reports comparing ongoing expenditure for the current year with the previous profiles for that period. If it appears that expenditure is too high, the Commission will use the various mechanisms provided by the market organisations to attempt to bring it back within acceptable bounds. If this is not enough the Commission has to bring proposals to the Council to strengthen stabiliser effectiveness upon which the Council has to act within two months.

EAGGF Guidance Section

The EAGGF Guidance section is one of three Community structural funds.[73] Its role is to provide the resources for the common policy on agricultural structures, that is, changing or improving the way in which farming is carried out in given areas. This role was enhanced considerably by the reform of the Community structural funds, which came into force in 1989,[74] in which the Council recognised the need for a coherent strategy of

---

[72] For example, the 'co-responsibility levy' found in the market organisation for milk and milk products. This is paid by producers when milk production quotas for a given period are exceeded. The money raised is used to finance the disposal of surpluses or to finance other specific measures.

[73] The others being the European Social Fund and the European Regional Development Fund.

[74] As required by the SEA, which included a call for amendments to the structure and operational rules of the structural funds. See the resulting Regulation 2052/88/EEC, OJ 1988 L185 on the tasks of the structural funds; and Regulation 4256/88/EEC, OJ 1988 L374, specifically on the EAGGF.

semi-Community-funded agricultural structural reform. Following those reforms, the Guidance section's main tasks have been to finance the development and structural adjustment of the less-developed regions of the Community, and to speed up the adjustment of agricultural structures with a view to reform of the CAP. The main thrust of the reform has been to increase the amount of part-financing of Community-implemented operational programmes, although Community aid schemes, where the Member States are responsible for implementation, still take a large share of funding.

INSTITUTIONAL FRAMEWORK

While some reasons for the seeming decline in interest in the CAP were suggested in the introduction above, a list of that nature would be incomplete without a mention of the institutional framework of the CAP. The epithet 'Kafkaesque' may have been much over-used in recent times, but in that institutional framework, we have a collection of committees and procedures truly deserving of its bestowal. Space does not allow for a detailed examination of the minutiae of this arrangement and, in general, this section will concentrate on those areas which have generated a degree of controversy.

On a simple analysis, Article 43(2) EC provides the basic procedure for the adoption of regulations and directives by the Council to regulate the CAP.[75] The actual division of implementation powers is then spread wider by delegation. The Council tends to retain for itself those powers which are of primary importance to the CAP, either because they involve dealing with the primary rules of the CAP or because they are otherwise of some political significance. An example of this would be the decisions on annual price-fixing. The Commission in turn is given implementing power over areas of secondary importance, generally those areas requiring some level of technical expertise. Member States' national authorities are then responsible for implementation at the national level on a day-to-day basis. The machinery by which this apparently simple process is governed has, however, since the amendment of Article 145 EC by the SEA[76] and the 'Comitology' Decision[77] become rather more complex and controversial.[78]

The Council of the European Union

At the Council of the European Union, discussions of CAP issues are dealt with by the Agricultural Council, which comprises the agriculture ministers of the Member States.

---

[75] Article 43(2)iii.
   The Council shall, on a proposal from the Commission and after consulting the European Parliament, acting unanimously during the first two stages and by a qualified majority thereafter, make regulations, issue directives, or take decisions, without prejudice to any recommendations it may also make.
   Article 43(2) thus provides the legal basis for the regulations or directives establishing the COM, the Agricultural Guidance and Guarantee Funds, the application of the competition rules to production of, or trade in, agri-

cultural products and all measures designed to implement the objectives of Article 39.
[76] To allow the Council to confer powers of implementation, of rules which the Council has laid down, upon the Commission.
[77] OJ 1987 L197.
[78] See Pearce, 'The Common Agricultural Policy: The Accumulation of Special Interests' in Wallace, Wallace, and Webb, *Policy Making in the European Community* (1983), at 153–7 and Annex 1 of the Agriculture section of the Coopers and Lybrand *EC Commentaries* 1993.

However, the functions usually carried out by COREPER[79] are dealt with, instead, by the Special Committee on Agriculture (SCA) which is staffed by agricultural officials,[80] but the role of which is otherwise broadly similar to that of COREPER, in terms of discussing proposals and, where necessary, delegating matters to technical and sectoral committees. If a proposal is agreed upon by the SCA, it may be confirmed by the next Council of the European Union, whether or not that Council is the Agricultural Council.[81] If there is an objection at the SCA by a representative of either the Member States or the Commission the matter will be referred to the Agricultural Council.[82]

It has been said that the role of the SCA in facilitating the quick processing of agricultural proposals has been considerably undermined due to the tactic adopted by Member States of turning even the most uncontroversial proposals into bargaining counters.[83] It is also possible to argue that, with the Community often accused of over-administration and over-staffing, there is no justification for a separate specialist body of administrators for the CAP alone, given that COREPER has shown itself capable of dealing with the wide range of other Community activities.

Measures adopted by the Council are made under Article 43 EC and only require a qualified majority vote. The votes of each Member State are weighted so that 54 out of the possible 76 votes will satisfy the requirement of qualified majority voting in Article 43(2) third indent.[84]

Prior to the SEA, the Luxembourg Compromise was used to prevent the adoption of agricultural legislation in the absence of unanimity, particularly where one or more Member States opposed a measure to protect a 'vital national interest'. The situation at present, after both the SEA and TEU, is that issues falling within the sphere of the CAP are covered by Article 43(2), which allows for adoption by qualified majority. Despite this, it seems likely that where a Member State can show prejudice to a 'vital national interest' the remaining States will attempt to reach a compromise acceptable to all, rather than forcing legislation through by majority vote.

In *Re Agricultural Hormones: United Kingdom v Council*[85] some indication of the scope of Article 43 can be seen. The case concerned an action brought by the UK against the Council, contesting the validity of a directive prohibiting the administration to farm animals of certain hormonal substances,[86] which was adopted by qualified majority[87] on the basis of Article 43 alone and not Article 43 and Article 100[88] as had been the Council's previous practice for such legislation. The UK government argued that the directive should have been adopted on a dual legal basis as, in addition to having agricultural policy objectives, it was to harmonise national laws with a view to the protection of consumers and public health, the aim of which comes under Article 100.

The Court, however, held that the measure was in essence an agricultural measure, and Article 43 was sufficient basis for any legislation concerning the production and marketing of

[79] See Chapter 2.
[80] Except public health and veterinary matters, which are dealt with by COREPER.
[81] These are known as 'A' points.
[82] These are known as 'B' points.
[83] Annex 1 of the Agriculture section of the Coopers and Lybrand *EC Commentaries* 1993.
[84] In accordance with Article 148(2), as amended by Article 14 of the Act of Accession of Spain and Portugal.
[85] Case 68/86 [1988] ECR 855. Denmark intervened in support of the UK and the Commission intervened in support of the Council.
[86] Directive 85/649/EEC, OJ 1985 L382/228.
[87] United Kingdom and Denmark voting against.
[88] Which requires adoption by unanimity.

agricultural products listed in Annex II to the Treaty, which contributed to the achievement of one or more of the objectives of the Common Agricultural Policy set out in Article 39 EC. This would be so even though consumer protection may have been one of the motives of the legislation. There was, thus, no need to have recourse to Article 100 EC where such legislation involved the harmonisation of provisions of national law in that field.[89] The Council's previous practice of using a dual legal basis (Articles 43 and 100) did not estop it from reverting to what could be considered the more correct use of the single Article.[90]

The ECJ went on to state that in *Pigs Marketing Board (Northern Ireland)* v *Raymond Redmond*[91] and *Pigs and Bacon Commission* v *McCarren and Company Limited*[92] it had been held that Article 38(2) of the Treaty gives precedence to specific provisions in the agricultural field over general provisions relating to the establishment of the Common Market. As a result, even where the legislation in question is directed both to objectives of agricultural policy and to other objectives which, in the absence of specific provisions, are pursued on the basis of Article 100 EC, that Article, a general one under which directives may be adopted for the approximation of the laws of the Member States, cannot be relied on as a ground for restricting the field of application of Article 43 EC.

It seems that the Commission will continue to base its proposals for agricultural legislation on Article 43 rather than on Article 100A.[93] This is because although both require a decision by qualified majority, use of the latter would mean recourse to the co-operation procedure in Article 189b. As noted above, this procedure involves two readings of a proposal, by both the EP and the Council, instead of the single reading required by the consultation procedure. The significance of this lies in the power given to the EP to reject the common position of the Council under the second reading, a step which obliges the Council to reach unanimity instead of qualified majority in order to adopt the contested measure.

An area of some controversy has been the extent to which the Council can delegate powers to the Member States. Blumental suggested in 1984[94] that it was clear from the *Societe des Usines de Beauport and others* v *Council*[95] proceedings the Council did delegate a certain measure of discretion to the Member States, but that the validity of such delegation had not been fully considered by the ECJ and thus remained uncertain. He went on to suggest that while that discretion was fettered by guidelines laid down by the Council by way of derogation from the COM, that such delegation 'must still present a potential threat to the common Community structure'.[96]

Following the ECJ's ruling in *Spronk* v *Minister van Landbouw en Visserij*[97] in 1990, concerning milk quotas, it would seem that the perceived uncertainty has now been removed:

---

89 The directive was, however, held to be invalid for breach of an essential procedural requirement under Article 6(1) of the Council's Rules of Procedure (OJ 1979 L268/1) as recourse was had to written procedure without the required agreement of all parties (UK disagreed). It was replaced by Directive 88/146/EEC, unsuccessfully challenged in Case C-331/88, *Regina* v *Minister of Agriculture, Fisheries and Food and Another, ex parte Federation Europeenne de la Sante Animale (Fedesa) and Others* [1991] 1 CMLR 507.

90 As the Court had previously held in the Case 45/86, *Commission* v *Council* [1988] 2 CMLR 131, in the organisation of the powers of the Community the choice of the legal basis for a measure must be based on objective factors and these are amenable to judicial review. A mere practice on the part of the Council cannot derogate from the rules laid down in the Treaty and cannot, therefore, create a precedent binding on Community institutions with regard to the correct legal basis.

91 Case 83/78, [1978] ECR 2347.

92 Case 177/78, [1979] ECR 2161.

93 As amended by Article G (22) TEU.

94 Blumental, *op. cit.*, note 1.

95 Joined Cases 103–109/78, [1979] ECR 17.

96 *Ibid.*, at 36.

97 Case C-16/89, [1990] ECR I-3185.

It follows from all the foregoing considerations that the answer to the first and second questions must be that the second indent of the first subparagraph of Article 3(1) of Council Regulation 857/84 must be interpreted as conferring a discretionary power on the Member States for the purpose of determining the allocation of special reference quantities to the producers covered by that provision.

The ECJ would also appear to have been aware of the threat to the common Community structure, for it has made it clear that the exercise of such delegated discretion would be held strictly subject to the doctrines of proportionality and non-discrimination.[98]

The Commission

At the Commission agricultural matters are dealt with by the Directorate General for Agriculture (DG VI). The Commission has considerable power in the agricultural sphere in that much of Community agricultural legislation takes the form of implementing measures adopted by the Commission using the management and executive powers conferred by Article 155. It has been delegated a wide discretion over a number of important areas of agricultural policy, not least in its relations with the COMs. Commission implementation normally takes place under the 'management committee' procedure, discussed in the next section. Unlike the position of the Council this wide discretion does not, however, allow the Commission to sub-delegate management powers to a Member State.[99]

The COM management committees

Every COM has its own management committee. These committees are created by the regulations setting up the COMs and are composed of representatives of the Member States' agriculture ministries with a Commission official as chair.[100] Their major tasks are to decide matters such as export tenders. Management committees meet when asked to do so by Member States or by the Commission. COM regulations provide for a management committee procedure which requires the Commission to submit any proposals for a given COM to that COM's management committee.[101] However, the COM management committee has no actual decision-making power and their opinion on any given proposal, whether in favour, against or undecided, may essentially be ignored by the Commission,[102] although a negative opinion (which is very rare in practice) may result in the Commission delaying adopting the proposal for a month, during which time the Council may override the Commission proposal.[103] Failure by the management committee to issue an opinion does not affect the validity of the measures adopted by the Commission as 'it is only if the Commission adopts measures which are not in accordance with the opinion of the committee

---

[98] *Ibid.*

[99] Case 23/75, *Rey Soda* v *Cassa Conguaglio Zucchero* [1975] ECR 1279.

[100] For example, Article 25 of Regulation 2727/75/EEC states that 'a Management Committee for Cereals shall be established consisting of the representatives of the Member States and presided over by a representative of the Commission'.

[101] See Annex 1 of the Agriculture section of the

Coopers and Lybrand *EC Commentaries* 1993 for the voting procedure.

[102] Case 25/70, *Einfur- und Vorratsstelle fur Getreide und Futtermittel* v *Koster, Berodt & Co* [1970] ECR 1161; Case 57/72, *Westzucker GmbH* v *EVst fur Zucker* [1973] ECR 321; Case 256/85, *Italian Republic* v *Commission* (Transcript), 4 February 1988.

[103] Case 256/85, *Italian Republic* v *Commission, ibid.*

that those measures must be communicated to the Council'.[104] In certain cases, such as matters of urgency, or routine matters, such as the calculation of levies the Commission may enact legislation without consulting the management committees at all.

It should be noted that the original EC Treaty made no mention of the management committee procedure, that it appeared to have no direct legal basis in Community law. Indeed, in *Koster*[105] the legality of the management committee procedure introduced by Articles 25 and 26 of Regulation 19/62/EEC[106] was challenged as contrary to and, thus, incompatible with, various articles of the EEC Treaty.[107] It was also claimed that the management committee procedure constituted an interference in the Commission's right of decision, such that it put in issue the independence of that institution; and the interposition between the Council and the Commission of a body which was not provided for by the Treaty was alleged to have the effect of distorting the relationship between the institutions and the exercise of the right of decision. However, the Court of Justice held that the procedure was legitimate on the grounds that:

> . . . if the Council could confer implementing powers on the Commission under Article 155 of the Treaty it could also make the exercise of those powers subject to a management committee procedure which enabled the Council to take the decision itself if it saw fit, and that the legality of the management committee procedure could not be disputed in relation to the institutional structure of the Community.[108]

The ECJ further elaborated on the role of the Management Committee procedure in *Westzucker*[109] where it was alleged by the applicants that the Commission had, during the Management Committee procedure, yielded to improper pressures from the French and Italian Governments to promote certain interests of those States. The ECJ held that:

> One of the aims of the management Committee procedure is to enable the Commission to prepare its intervention measures in close co-operation with the national authorities charged with the management of the market sectors concerned. It is consonant with the very idea of the Community that, within the framework of the mechanics of collective discussion set up with a view to the implementation of the common agricultural policy, the Member States should emphasize their interests, whilst it falls to the Commission to arbitrate, through the measures taken by it, between possible conflicts of interest from the point of view of the general interest.[110]

It appears that as a result of the changes to Articles 145 and 155 of the EC Treaty made by the SEA, the management committee procedure has, to an extent, been legally formalised: 'It has gone from being a procedure repeatedly used in practice to being a standard procedural model defined in general and abstract terms'.[111] This conclusion is drawn from an examination of the three 'Procedures' laid out in Article 2 of Council Decision 87/373/EEC (the Comitology Decision)[112] which, in turn, was based on the amended Article 145 of the EC Treaty.

104 Case 95/78, *Dulciora SpA* v *Amministrazione delle Finanze dello Stato* [1979] ECR 1549, at 1568.

105 Case 25/70, *op. cit.*, note 102.

106 On the progressive establishment of a common organisation of the market in cereals, OJ 1962, at 933.

107 Articles 43(2), 155, 173 and 177 and the first paragraph of Article 189.

108 Case 25/70, *op. cit.*, at paras 9 and 10; see also the opinion of Advocate General Lenz in Case 264/86, *Re Tuna Producers: France (Spain intervening)* v *Commission* [1988] ECR 973.

109 Case 57/72, *op. cit.*, note 102.

110 *Ibid.*

111 See the reasoning of Advocate General Darmon and the ECJ's judgment in Case 16/88, *Commission* v *Council* (Transcript), 24 October 1989.

112 OJ 1987 L197, at 33. See Chapter 2.

Other committees

There are a number of other committees similar in composition to the COM management committees to which proposed legislation must be referred, should it fall within their remit. These fall roughly into three groups. The first group follows the same procedures as the COM management committees and consists of:

- the Standing Committee on Agricultural Structure;
- the Community Committee on the Farm Accountancy Data Network;
- the Standing Committee on Seeds and Propagating Material;
- the European Agricultural Guidance and Guarantee Fund (EAGGF) Committee;
- the Standing Committee on Agricultural Research.

The second group follow a different procedure. These committees are:

- the Standing Veterinary Committee;
- the Standing Committee on Feeding Stuffs;
- the Standing Committee on Plant Health;
- the Standing Committee on Zootechnics.

Where committees in this group disagree with, or fail to reach a decision on, the Commission's proposal, the Commission has no option but to present a further proposal to the Council with regard to the proposal in dispute. The precise procedure which follows that submission by the Commission to the Council varies depending on which of the committees is involved, but the end result is that the Council is in the position to be able to block Commission proposals. This is unpopular with both the Commission and the European Parliament, and the European Parliament has called for the procedure to be made consistent with that of the first group.

The third group of committees have procedures which are essentially a hybrid of the other two groups and consist of:

- the Standing Committee on Agricultural Statistics;
- the Standing Committee for Agricultural and Forestry Tractors.

European Parliament

Article 43(2) EC requires the Council to consult with the European Parliament. In the *Isoglucose* cases,[113] the Court held that failure to engage in that consultation was a breach of an essential procedural requirement and, as such, could found an action for annulment under Article 173.[114] However, the European Parliament has no such legal right to consultation in the management committee procedure and can have only a very minor part to play in day-to-day management and expenditure. The Commission has, however, bowed to pressure from the Parliament and now makes a practice of explaining its management strategy to

---

[113] Case 138/79, *Roquette Frères* v *Council* [1980] ECR 3333 and Case 139/79, *Maizena* v *Council* [1980] ECR 3393.   [114] See Chapter 7.

Parliamentary Committees. The expanded role played by the Parliament in the budgetary procedure has also increased its ability to scrutinise and criticise Commission policy.

FRAUD

In 1989 the British House of Lords Select Committee on the European Communities noted that:

> The huge sums which are being lost due to fraud and irregularity against the Community are losses borne by all the taxpayers and traders of Europe. This strikes at the roots of democratic societies, based as they are on the rule of law and its enforcement, and is a public scandal.[115]

Certainly, the scope for financial irregularities, mismanagement and fraud under the CAP is immense, and it is clear that this has increased significantly over the last 10–12 years. In the period 1 July 1980 to 30 June 1981 it was reported that there were 306 irregularities amounting to just over 18 million ECU reported by the Member States. Of these the majority (257) concerned the Guarantee Fund and only 1 806 367 ECU had been recovered.[116] By 1992 the Commission's annual report on fraud connected with the EC budget noted a total of 1030 cases of irregularities amounting to 117.8 million ECU.[117] Again, the majority of cases involved the Guarantee Fund and only about eight per cent of money obtained illegally from the Community budget was recovered. The report notes that these figures are, in effect, the tip of the iceberg, and estimates elsewhere have put the figure for losses to the Community at between £2 billion and £6 billion per annum.[118]

An example of an area which appears to be particularly prone to fraud is tobacco production. The majority of production is based in Spain, Italy and Greece and costs the EC around 1.3 billion ECU in subsidies per annum. A report in 1993 by the Court of Auditors[119] stated that one result of the EC subsidy schemes was that huge quantities of low-priced and commercially worthless tobacco were exported from those countries, to countries such as Hungary, Russia and Albania, solely for the purpose of claiming export subsidies. Further, a high percentage of exports which were supposed to have been made from Greece and Italy to Albania, and on which export subsidies were paid, never in fact arrived. It was estimated that in 1990 this cost the Community about 34 million ECU. The EC also spent over 800 million ECU, over a five-year period, subsidising the production of varieties of tobacco for which there was simply no demand or market.[120]

The Commission has been spending increasing amounts of money on fighting fraud against the Community. In 1992 it spent 76.5 million ECU, and in 1993 133.2 million ECU, an

115 House of Lords Select Committee on the European Communities, *Fraud against the Community*, HL 27 February, 21 1989, at para 205.

116 Commission of the Euorpean Communities, *Fifteenth General Report on the Activities of the European Communities in 1981* (1982) 174.

117 Commission of the European Communities, Annual Report from the Commission on the fight against fraud, at 9. Of these, 366 cases involved Italian olive oil and accounted for some 79.5 million ECU.

118 House of Lords Select Committee on the European Communities *Fraud against the Community, op. cit.,* note 115, at paras 10 and 11.

119 See *The Independent*, 2 February 1994, at p 10.

120 The report also noted that the subsidy level for tobacco was 23 times that for cereals, and that the Community could have halved the cost of tobacco production by giving farmers the equivalent of their income in cash rather than attempting to manage the market.

increase largely due to the implementation of new systems under the CAP reform. However, the Commission is highly dependent on Member States playing their part in the anti-fraud process and it appears that some Member States are unwilling to address the problem for financial or political reasons. Member States and their agencies may fail to report relevant information to the Commission, or may simply not bother to collect such information. Even where irregularities are discovered, Member States may be reluctant to begin criminal or administrative proceedings against the perpetrators.[121]

Another problem is that there appears to be no clear idea or definition of what does, or should, constitute fraud for the purposes of preventing abuses of the CAP. It has been noted that while many practices fall quite clearly within the definition of fraud within the Member States' criminal law, a number are more what might be termed 'sharp practice' and, while reprehensible, are not subject to criminal sanction – thus, the adoption of the vague term 'irregularities' to cover these practices. The Community has reacted to this problem in three ways. First it has begun studies on ways in which to simplify existing legislation, thus removing the ambiguities and other infelicities which allow irregularities to take place. Secondly, it has introduced a system to assess the susceptibility of proposed legislation to fraud or irregularities. Thirdly, it has engaged in studies of the laws, regulations and administrative provisions of the Member States on fraudulent practices with a view to ensuring that where fraud is discovered it can be adequately defined and penalised.

Another reaction to the increase in irregularities has been the introduction of legislation,[122] including Regulation 4045/89/EEC[123] under which the Member States are obliged to scrutinise all transactions forming part of the system of financing by the Guarantee Section of the EAGGF. This Regulation replaced Directive 77/435/EEC[124] which was designed to achieve the same aim, after it became clear that there was a significant divergence in standards of observance of the Directive between Member States and tightened up the general standard of post-payment reporting undertaken by the Member States.

More recently there has been an ambitious legislative attempt to create a sophisticated system to ensure better administration and control over a number of aid schemes, applying primarily to selected premiums and compensatory allowances in the crop and livestock sectors. The primary legislation is Regulation 3508/92/EEC[125] which is reinforced by Regulation 3887/92/EEC[126] which lays down detailed rules for applying the administration

---

121 See Case 68/88, *Commission* v *Greece* [1989] ECR 2965. Here Greece was held to have failed to fulfil its obligations under Article 5 EC due to its failure to take criminal or other disciplinary action against those involved in fraud against the Community. The case is also notable for the number of Greek ex-government ministers implicated in the fraud in question.

122 See also Regulation 354/90/EEC, OJ 1990 L38, amending Regulation 3665/87/EEC as regards proof of arrival at destination in third countries of agricultural products qualifying for a variable refund; Regulation 386/90/EEC, OJ 1990 L42 concerning the monitoring carried out at the time of export of exports of agricultural products receiving refunds or other amounts; Regulation 1863/90/EEC, OJ 1991 L170 laying down detailed rules for the application of Regulation 4045/89/EEC on scrutiny by Member States of transactions forming part of the system of financing by the EAGGF guarantee sec-

tion and repealing Directive 77/435/EEC; Regulation 307/91/EEC, OJ 1991 L37 on reinforcing the monitoring of certain expenditure chargeable to the EAGGF Guarantee Section; Regulation 967/91/EEC, OJ 1991 L100 laying down detailed rules for the application of Regulation 307/91/EEC on reinforcing the monitoring of certain expenditure chargeable to the EAGGF Guarantee Section; Regulation 595/91/EEC, OJ 1991 L67 concerning irregularities and the recovery of sums wrongly paid in connection with the financing of the CAP and the organisation of an information system in this field and repealing Regulation 283/72/EEC.

123 OJ 1989 L388.

124 OJ 1977 L172.

125 OJ 1992 L355.

126 OJ 1992 L391.

and control system and Directive 92/102/EEC[127] on the identification and registration of animals. The system will be made up of a computerised database, a numerical identification system for agricultural parcels and for the identification and recording of animals, annual statements and a harmonised control system. It will also involve administrative and on-the-spot checks on all aid applications submitted and the use of aircraft or satellite surveillance for verification.[128]

The Community has also responded to the fraud problem by moving towards increased use of computers to check and verify expenditure, with database systems such as IRENE (IRegularities, ENquiries, Exploitation) operational since December 1991, covering agriculture, own resources, mutual assistance and the Structural Funds and DAF (Documentation antifraude). Also computer-based research programmes such as SCENT (transmission of messages relating to irregularities detected or suspected, questioning of databases and statistical research) have been employed. A number of agreements have also been concluded with non-Member States with the aim of detecting and preventing fraud within the Community. Such agreements include interim agreements with Poland, Hungary and the Czech and Slovak Republics which entered into force in March 1992 and an agreement with Albania in May 1992 containing provision for anti-fraud co-operation.

A possible solution to some of the problems surrounding fraud in the Community would be to allow the Community institutions to play a role in the criminal law of the Member States, indeed Regulation 2891/77/EEC, in theory, allows the Commission to do just that. However, such 'outside interference' is viewed unfavourably by both the Member States and their criminal investigation bodies and it would be difficult, if not impossible, to use this method alone.[129] Other partial solutions, such as a 'Community Crimes Treaty'[130] or a harmonised definition of 'fraud against the Community'[131] have run into similar problems. The 'Community Crimes Treaty' fell by the wayside due to the inability of the Council of Ministers to reach agreement over it. A harmonised definition of 'fraud against the Community' falls foul of the differing ways in which such fraud is dealt with by the different Member States, that is, in some Member States it would be a criminal offence and in others an administrative offence.

THE CAP AND GATT[132]

The General Agreement on Tariffs and Trade (GATT) came into being in 1948 and today regulates over 85 per cent of world trade between 122 countries. In the words of Petersmann:[133]

> It is the first and only multilateral international treaty applied so far in the history of international relations that provides general rules and procedures for world-wide trade

---

127 OJ 1992 L355.
128 'EC roots out sly farmers' *Computing*, 11 February 1993, at 1; see also Commission of the European Communities, Annual Report from the Commission on the fight against fraud, at 32 and 34.
129 See Case 267/78, *Commission v Italy* [1980] ECR 31 for an illustration of potential problems.
130 OJ 1976 C222.

131 As suggested by the Court of Auditors in their Annual Report for 1986, OJ 1987 C336.
132 White, 'GATT Law and Community Law: Some comparisons illustrated by recent trade disputes', in White and Smythe (eds.) *Current Issues in European and International Law* (1990).
133 Hilf, Jacobs and Petersmann, *The European Communities and GATT*, vol 4 *Studies in Transnational Economic Law* (1986), at 24.

liberalization and for the co-ordination of trade policies of States and customs unions such as the EEC.

All the Member States were GATT contracting parties at the time of their conclusion of, or accession to, the Community and have retained their legal status as individual GATT contracting parties. The EEC itself has never formally acceded to GATT, but the EC Commission takes part in the activities of all GATT bodies other than the Budgetary Committee[134] and has assumed the exercise of the vast majority of the rights and obligations of the Member States, in the name of the EEC.

However, the EC's relationship with GATT has rarely been other than a tempestuous one. As early as 1960 in the 'Dillon Round' and 1964–67 in the 'Kennedy Round' there was discussion and negotiation concerning the compatibility of both the Common Customs Policy and the CAP with GATT and a number of countries, such as Australia and the US, have repeatedly complained about activities of the EC which, they contend, are contrary to GATT. Of those complaints, the majority have related to agricultural products. Areas complained of include:

- minimum import prices, licences and surety deposits – eg by the US in 1976 concerning processed fruits and vegetables which resulted in a GATT Council ruling that the system for tomato concentrates violated Articles XI and II;[135]
- refunds on exports – eg by Australia and Brazil in 1978 concerning exports of sugar resulting in Council rulings that the EEC system of export refunds for sugar had caused serious prejudice to the interests of Australia[136] and Brazil[137] under Article XVI:1. This was followed by a further complaint in 1982 by Argentina, Australia, Brazil, Colombia, Cuba, Dominican Republic, India, Nicaragua, Peru, and the Philippines, subsequently dropped;
- preferential agreements – eg by the US in 1982 concerning EEC tariff treatment on imports of citrus products from certain Mediterranean countries, which the US claimed was seriously depressing their own citrus industry. A GATT panel was set up and found in favour of the US under Article I:1, but the EC prevented the adoption of the report by the GATT Council. A brief trade skirmish ensued in 1985, with the US imposing high customs duties on EC pasta products, and the EC retaliating with similar increases on US imports of walnuts and lemons. The issue was eventually resolved in 1986 with the US accepting concessions from the EC on citrus fruits and almonds in return for refraining from further complaints;
- enlargement of the Community – there was some degree of hostility voiced towards the Community regime on the accession of Greece in 1983. This was followed by requests for compensation from the US and Argentina in 1986 on the accession of Spain and Portugal. The US claimed that its exports of maize, sorghum and soya to Spain and Portugal were affected. The EC was not sympathetic to this claim, and there was another trade skirmish, at the conclusion of which, in 1987, the EC agreed to make some trade concessions. Agreement was also reached with Argentina in 1987.

---

134 Member States continue to pay their own budgetary contributions to GATT.
135 BISD 25 S/68, 103, 107.
136 BISD 26 S/290, 319.
137 BISD 27 S/69, 97.

More current disputes concern the subsidies granted by the Community to oilseeds and other animal feed proteins, and the EC's ban on marketing and importation of meat treated with growth promoting hormones.[138] At the time of writing, neither of these disputes have finally been settled, although agreements have been reached in principle.

The Uruguay Round

The Uruguay Round of multilateral negotiations began in September 1986 and, while they were concerned with a number of trading issues, the consequence of the Punta del Este Declaration of 1986 was that they would concentrate upon world agricultural trade. At Punta del Este, the EC agreed that the CAP would be subjected to review during this process. The Uruguay Round negotiations were supposed to conclude in 1990 but, due to fundamental differences of opinion between the contracting parties, notably the EC and the US, they had to be re-scheduled to end in December 1993. While it appears that agriculture was not the only trade issue preventing agreement at that time, it was widely seen as the main obstacle.

The position agreed within the Community on reform of the CAP in 1992[139] appears to have been that adopted as the starting point for US–EC talks. These ended with an agreement between the Commission and the outgoing Bush Administration in the form of the Blair House Accord, in December 1992. This agreement was supposed to represent a compromise position between the US and the EC which would allow a successful end to the GATT negotiations. However, it appeared that the Blair House Accord would have involved larger cuts in the CAP than those to be found in the 1992 reforms. This was unacceptable to the French government who, throughout the GATT negotiations, had been steadfastly opposed to the type of major alterations to the CAP demanded by the US. This opposition, combined with a degree of dissatisfaction with the Blair House Accord on the part of the new Clinton Administration in the US, was to play a large part in the failure of a number of compromise positions put forward by both sides, throughout 1993. The strength of French government opposition was certainly influenced by an extremely vocal French agricultural lobby which now, as in the past, has an influence on French and EC agricultural policy out of proportion to the input which agriculture has into the French economy. That opposition, including the assertion that the EC Commissioner involved in negotiating the Accord had overstepped his negotiating authority, resulted in the EC failing to reach agreement on the acceptance of the Accord. This, in turn, resulted in a series of increasingly tense discussions between the Community and the US in the weeks leading up to the end of December 1993. A face-saving agreement was finally reached in which the basic Blair House Accord was maintained, but the agreed subsidy reductions within the CAP were changed from the original model. This model called for a 'front loaded' reform of EC subsidies consisting of large subsidy reductions early in the reform process and was replaced by a model which will begin with smaller percentage subsidy cuts in the early years leading up to larger cuts in the later years, thus leading to a more evenly distributed reduction in subsidies over the proposed time frame.

---

138 Directive 88/146/EEC, OJ 1988 L70. See Peterson, 'Hormones, Heifers and High Politics – Biotechnology   and the Common Agricultural Policy' [1989] 67 PA 455.
139 See above at 419.

The new GATT Accord

As a result of the conclusion of the Uruguay Round, and following ratification by a majority of GATT members, the new GATT Accord will take effect from 1 January 1995. Under the Accord, farm policies will be restricted by three sets of GATT disciplines relating to domestic support, import access, and export commitments.[140]

To conform with the domestic or internal support provisions, those countries involved in the Accord were obliged to calculate an Aggregate Measure of Support (AMS), as an annual average for a three-year base period consisting of the years 1986–88. Over the six years of the new Accord this AMS must be reduced by 20 per cent. It has been noted that while this seems a harsh cut in support, in practice, due to the effect of other economic factors, it is likely to have a very limited effect as far as the EC is concerned.[141]

With regard to import access, it consists of the following elements:

- 'tariffication': all existing border measures such as the various import levies on products such as wheat and sugar are to be converted into tariffs;
- all tariffs are to be reduced by a minimum of 15 per cent and on average by 36 per cent, over the lifetime of the agreement;
- a minimum access clause: countries are to make arrangements to allow imports to capture a minimum of three per cent of the home market in the first year, rising to five per cent in year six.[142]

The head of export commitments appears to have been the most controversial of the three, in that it was under this head that the 'front loading' of cuts in export subsidies which the French found so objectionable were to be found. As noted above, it was the shift from that model of subsidy cuts to a more evenly spread model which paved the way for the US–EC agreement necessary to allow for the conclusion of the GATT negotiations.

CONCLUSION

Despite the recent apparent lack of interest in the CAP on the part of legal and political commentators, it is clear from the above examples that it is still a significant factor in determining general EC policy, and that the Member States have yet to reach a consensus as to its future development. With regard to the concluded GATT negotiations, it could be argued that in the short term the protectionist stance of the French government has been successful, in that the GATT Accord does not appear to require extensive revision of the CAP reforms of 1992, nor require significantly heavier cuts in subsidies. Whether the resulting package will be as successful for the Community as a whole remains in doubt, as it is has been estimated that the cost to the EC of the reforms is likely to be an increase in EAGGF Guarantee section costs of up to 10 billion ECU over five years.[143] What is certain is

---

140 The following explanation is fairly simplistic as space does not allow for a more complex analysis. For a clear and detailed account, see Swinbank, 'GATT, CAP and the Manager's Dilemma' in Errington (ed.) *Farm Business Data* (1993), University of Reading, at 46.

141 *Ibid.*

142 *Ibid*, at 48.

143 See the Agriculture section of the Coopers and Lybrand *EC Commentaries*, 1993.

that while world trading conditions remain depressed, the level of subsidies under the CAP will remain an object of contention between the EC and the other members of GATT, and that the conclusion of the Uruguay Round will not end calls for more radical cuts than those already conceded. Failure on the part of the Community to deal with the current distortion of world produce markets caused by the CAP will lead inevitably to other States and trading alliances taking tariff-based measures to protect their own producers.[144]

The current restructuring of the CAP, while welcome, has been met with a number of significant legal challenges, creating problems for the Commission and slowing the pace of reform. It is certainly possible to argue that the ECJ, in its attempts to ensure that individuals in the agricultural sphere are treated fairly, has unwisely ignored the wider policy imperatives faced by the Commission and Council, with resulting cost to the Community.[145]

It is also obvious that the EC is struggling with the fraud problem, both in terms of developing effective guidelines for its prevention and in mustering the will to enforce those guidelines. The technological aids proposed for fraud prevention may make detection more likely, but if Member States are unwilling to fund them or follow up discovery of fraudulent activity with legal action, it is unlikely that any significant decrease in fraud will result.[146]

Further reading

Blumental, M., 'Implementing the Common Agricultural Policy: Aspects of the Limitations on the Powers of the Member States' (1984) 35 NILQ 28.

Butler, F., 'The EC's Common Agricultural Policy' in Lodge, J. (ed.) *The European Community and the Challenge of the Future*, 2nd edn (Pinter, 1993).

Demekas, D.G., Bartholdy, K, et al., 'The effects of the Common Agricultural Policy of the European Community: a survey of the literature' (1988) 27 JCMS 113.

Fennel, R., *The Common Agricultural Policy of the European Community* (BSP Professional Books, 1987).

Hilf, M., Jacobs, F.G. and Petersmann E-U., *The European Communities and GATT*, vol. 4, *Studies in Transnational Economic Law* (Kluwer, 1986).

House of Lords Select Committee on the European Communities, *Fraud against the Community* HL 27, 21 February 1989.

Pearce, J., 'The Common Agricultural Policy: The Accumulation of Special Interests' in Wallace, H., Wallace, W. and Webb, C., *Policy Making in the European Community* (Wiley, 1983).

Peterson, J., 'Hormones, Heifers and High Politics – Biotechnology and the Common Agricultural Policy' [1989] 67 PA 455.

Sherlock, A. and Harding, C., 'Controlling Fraud within the European Community', (1991) 16 EL Rev 20.

Snyder, F.G., *Law of the Common Agricultural Policy* (Sweet & Maxwell, 1985).

Snyder, F.G., *New Directions In European Community Law*, (Weidenfeld & Nicholson, 1990).

White, G., 'GATT Law and Community Law: Some comparisons illustrated by recent trade disputes' in White R. and Smythe B. (eds.) *Current Issues in European And International Law* (London, 1990).

144 For example, the GATT agreement of late 1993 seems to have averted, in the short term at least, the near certainty of a serious US–EC trade war.

145 See, for instance, Case 120/86, *J Mulder v Minister Van Landbouw en Visseri* and Case 170/86, *Georg Von Deetzen v Hauptzollampt Hamburg-Jonas*, the details of which are to be found in Chapter 6 at 123.

146 The newspaper of the European Parliament, *EP News*, reported in its edition of 13–17 September 1993 that one of the major casualties of the 1994 draft budget would be the anti-fraud unit which would lose 25 million ECU of funding.

CHAPTER 19

Environmental policy

INTRODUCTION

Community environmental policy has developed to the point that it now has a significant impact upon virtually all other areas of Community policy. It is also an area of law that is growing apace, so much so that it would be impossible to deal in detail with every aspect in a book of this nature.[1] This chapter attempts, therefore, to chart the growth of that policy, consider the particular sectors that most concern the Community and examine the methods used to monitor and implement Community-wide environmental protection. In particular it examines the role of the Community institutions, the widespread use of directives to achieve the Communities' aims and the reactions of the Member States to the increasing regulation of environmental issues. There is also a brief consideration of the role of the Community in the field of international environmental protection, for the significant developments in this sphere have been responsible for much recent legislation.

The origins of Community environmental policy

When the Community was established in 1958, environmental policy did not feature as highly on the political agendas of the Member States as it does today. Issues such as global warming and the depletion of the ozone layer were either unknown or relatively unpublicised. It is, perhaps, unsurprising, therefore, that those drafting the Treaty, in concentrating upon economic issues, do not appear to have considered making any provision within it for developing a Community environmental protection strategy. Thus, the Treaty made no clear reference to environmental issues. In the late 1960s and early 1970s, some directives dealing with environmental issues were issued,[2] but these were of limited scope and could not be said to form part of a coherent Community policy. It was not until 1972, following the high profile, UN-lead Stockholm Conference[3] that the Community, at the Paris Summit of the Heads of States and Governments, held in October 1972, came to an agreement on the development of such a policy.[4] The Summit Communiqué stated:

> Economic expansion is not an end in itself . . . It should result in an improvement in the
> quality of life as well as in standards of living . . . particular attention will be given to

---

1 For wider coverage see Johnson and Corcell, *The Environmental Policy of the European Communities* (1989); Krämer, *EEC Treaty and Environmental Protection* (1990); Krämer, *Focus on European Environmental Law* (1992).

2 For example Directive 67/548/EEC (classification, packaging and labelling of dangerous substances); Directive 70/220/EEC (pollutant emissions of motor vehicles). See Krämer, *EEC Treaty and Environmental Protection*, *op. cit.* note 1, at 1; Krämer, at *Focus on European Environmental Law, op. cit.*, note 1, at 7.

3 United Nations Conference on the Human Environment (UNCHE), UN Doc.A/CONF.48/14/REV.1.

4 The issue had been raised by the Commission via both memorandum (1970) and formal communication (1971) to Council, stating the need of a formal Community Action Programme on the Environment. Krämer, *EEC Treaty and Environmental Protection, op. cit.*, note 1, at 1.

intangible values and to protecting the environment, so that progress may really be put at the service of mankind.[5]

This expression of intent was based on the Preamble to the EEC Treaty, rather than the Treaty itself, where it was stated that one of the aims of the Community was:

> Affirming as the essential objective of their efforts the constant improvement of the living and working conditions of their peoples.

With a certain amount of licence on the part of both those at the Summit, and the Commission, apparently based on interpreting 'improvement of living and working conditions' to mean 'quality of life' and then moving to include a clean environment to be an essential part of 'quality of life', this sentence from the Preamble was interpreted as being sufficient to ground a Community policy for the protection of the environment.[6]

The Summit also called on the Community institutions to draw up a Community environmental policy and towards the end of 1973 a four-year Community Action Programme on the Environment was approved by the Community and representatives of the Member States.[7] This programme has been followed by four successive action programmes,[8] the latest of which will cover the period from 1993–2000.[9] The action programmes themselves are not necessary for the legal implementation of Community environmental policy. However, they set out, prioritise and explain the measures planned for the period in question.

THE TREATY FRAMEWORK

The EEC Treaty

The main problem for the Communities was that the lack of a clear constitutional basis for an environmental policy meant that the procedural machinery for such a policy was not readily apparent in the Treaty. This was overcome to a large extent by the use of Articles 100 and 235 of the Treaty.

Article 100 states that:

> The Council shall, acting unanimously on a proposal from the Commission, issue directives for the approximation of such provisions laid down by law, regulation or administrative action in member States as directly affect the establishment or functioning of the common market.

This article, designed with economic policies in mind, proved problematical to use in the environmental protection sphere. While it was possible to argue that differences between the national legislation of the Member States relating to environmental protection could cause problems in inter-State trade by virtue of such differences being used to hinder competition and the free movement of goods,[10] the ECJ had held in *Commission* v *Italy* that:

5 EC Commission, 6th General Report, at 8.
6 Freestone, 'European Community Environmental Policy and Law' (1991) 18 JLS 135, at 136.
7 OJ 1973 C112/1.
8 Second Action Programme (1977–1981), OJ 13.6.77 C139; Third Action Programme (1982–1986), OJ 17.2.83 C46; Fourth Action Programme (1987–1992), OJ 7.12.87 C328.
9 Fifth Action Programme, OJ 1993 C138. See below.
10 See Rehbinder and Stewart, *Environmental Protection Policy*, vol. 2 *Integration Through Law* (1985), at 15.

It is by no means ruled out that provisions on the environment may be based on Article 100 of the Treaty. Provisions which are necessary by considerations relating to the environment and health may be a burden upon the undertakings to which they apply and if there is no harmonisation of national provisions on the matter, competition may be appreciably distorted.[11]

This argument, being linked to the attainment of a unified market, was limited in scope to certain areas of environmental protection such as water quality or noise emission,[12] as it was almost impossible to demonstrate in other areas such as the protection of fauna and flora.[13]

Thus, in situations where Article 100 could not easily be used the Commission and Council had to have recourse to Article 235 which states:

If action by the Community should prove necessary to attain, in the course of the operation of the common market, one of the objectives of the Community and this Treaty has not provided the necessary powers, the Council shall, acting unanimously on a proposal from the commission and after consulting the European Parliament, take the appropriate measures.

In these situations, the necessary link with the objectives of the Treaty was provided by the sentence from the Preamble mentioned above. Freestone[14] notes that this led to some odd results, for instance:

the claim that the conservation of species of wild bird is necessary for 'the harmonious development of economic activities through the community and a continuous and balanced expansion'.[15]

It was often the case that the Community would base its actions on both Article 100 and Article 235.[16]

The pressing problem with the use of Article 100 and Article 235 was that by their nature the Community found itself only in a position to react to environmental problems rather than act to prevent them occurring in the first place. Thus, the development of environmental protection forward policy was subordinated to matters such as control of existing industrial pollution.[17] That having been said, the Community managed to produce over 170 pieces of environmental legislation during this period, and by 1983 the ECJ was of the opinion that the protection of the environment was 'one of the Community's essential objectives' and that it might, therefore, justify certain limitations upon even the major Community legal principles, such as the principle of the free movement of goods.[18]

11 Case 91/79, [1980] ECR 1099, at 1106.
12 Freestone, *op. cit.*, note 6, at 136.
13 Vandermeersch, 'The Single European Act and the Environmental Policy of the European Economic Community' (1987) 12 EL Rev 407, at 410.
14 Freestone, *op. cit.*, note 6, at 137.
15 10th paragraph of the Preamble to Directive 79/409/EEC.
16 For example Directive 78/659/EEC 18 July 1978. See Vandermeersch, *op. cit.*, note 13, at 412.

17 Primarily as a result of the limited focus of the First Community Action Programme.
18 Case 240/83, *Procureur de la Republique* v *Association de defense des bruleurs d'huiles usagees* [1983] ECR 531, at 549. See also Krämer, 'Environmental Protection and Article 30 EEC Treaty' (1993) 30 CMLR 111.

The Single European Act

The problems inherent in the use of Article 100 and Article 235 of the Treaty to provide legislation for the protection of the environment were addressed in 1987 by the Single European Act (SEA), which inserted into the Treaty Article 130, paragraphs r, t, and s.[19] These new provisions can be said to have put Community environmental policy on a clear 'constitutional' footing.

Article 130r[20] sets out the objectives of the Community's environmental policy, determines how the Community should exercise its powers in order to achieve those aims and the factors it should take into account, reserves some areas of action to the Member States[21] and provides for international co-operation on the part of both the Community and the Member States with other nations and international organisations. Article 130s[22] deals with the legislative process of creating Community environmental law, and Article 130t[23] provides that Member States can, if they so wish, impose more stringent measures in national legislation than those provided by Community law.

Two important principles can be seen in Article 130r(2); the 'preventive' principle and the 'polluter pays' principle. The preventive principle requires that activities which cause damage to the environment must be eliminated and where possible this should take place at the source of the pollution. Environmental policy is no longer a matter of clearing up damage after the fact. The polluter pays principle would appear to be similarly straightforward, in requiring that the individual causing the pollution must pay the cost of preventing and eliminating that pollution. Indeed, this principle has been a part of Community environmental policy since the first Action Programme. It would seem logical, therefore, that no State aid would be possible as, if it were, the taxpayer rather than the polluter would be paying. However, in practice this is not always feasible and the principle as outlined in the first four Action Programmes allowed for 'certain exceptions and special arrangements,

---

[19] Title VII consisting of Articles 130r, 130s and 130t, was added to Part Three of the Treaty by Article 25 of the SEA.

[20] Article 130r:
  1. Action by the Community relating to the environment shall have the following objectives:
  (i) to preserve, protect and improve the quality of the environment;
  (ii) to contribute towards protecting human health;
  (iii) to ensure a prudent and rational utilisation of natural resources.
  2. Action by the Community relating to the environment shall be based on the principles that preventive action should be taken, that environmental damage should as priority be rectified at source, and that the polluter should pay. Environmental protection requirements shall be a component of the Community's other policies.
  3. In preparing its action relating to the environment, the Community shall take account of:
  (i) available scientific and technical data;
  (ii) environmental conditions in the various regions of the Community;
  (iii) the potential benefits and costs of action or lack of action;
  (iv) the economic and social development of the Community as a whole and the balanced development of its regions.
  4. The Community shall take action relating to the environment to the extent to which the objectives referred to in paragraph 1 can be attained better at Community level than at the level of the individual Member States. Without prejudice to certain measures of a Community nature, the Member States shall finance and implement the other measures.
  5. Within their respective spheres of competence, the Community and the Member States shall co-operate with third countries and with the relevant international organisations. The arrangements for Community co-operation may be the subject of agreements between the Community and the third parties concerned, which shall be negotiated and concluded in accordance with Article 228.
  The previous paragraph shall be without prejudice to Member States' competence to negotiate in international bodies and to conclude international agreements.

[21] Thus, Article 130 action is subject to the principle of subsidiarity.

[22] Article 130s:
  The Council, acting unanimously on a proposal from the Commission and after consulting the European Parliament and the Economic and Social Committee, shall decide what action is to be taken by the Community.
  The Council shall, under the conditions laid down in the preceding subparagraph, define those matters on which decisions are to be taken by a qualified majority.

[23] Article 130t:
  The protective measures adopted in common pursuant to Article 130s shall not prevent any Member State from maintaining or introducing more stringent protective measures compatible with this Treaty.

provided that they cause no significant distortion to international trade and investment.' The situation under Article 130r(2) which does not provide explicitly for exceptions, would appear to be similar, in that State aid for subsidising environmental investment is acceptable under certain conditions.[24] The principle that the polluter pays is not applied uniformly across the Community and must, therefore, be seen more as a political guideline than a concrete legal measure, as legal consequences can rarely, if ever, be drawn from it.[25]

Alongside the changes to Article 130 concerning environmental policy the SEA also made changes of some consequence to Article 100, concerning the harmonisation of Member States' laws, by adding Article 100a. Amongst other headings, Article 100a explicitly makes reference to environmental legislation. Under Article 100a(1), the Council may, after necessary consultation, adopt measures by majority vote. Under Article 100a(3) the Commission, in making environmental policy proposals to the Council, is obliged to 'take as its basis a high level of protection', probably to prevent environmental issues being placed second to other issues of Single Market integration. Where a qualified majority vote occurs a Member State may adopt stricter measures than those taken by the Community, but such measures must be notified to the Commission, which will check to ensure that they are not 'a means of arbitrary discrimination or a disguised restriction on trade between Member States' (Article 100a (4)).

While the SEA has made the creation of environmental legislation procedurally less complex, it has resulted in disagreements between the Commission and Council as to which article certain legislation should be based upon. A number of these disagreements have now reached the ECJ.[26]

The Treaty on European Union

The Treaty on European Union (TEU) has gone still further in prioritising the Community's policy of environmental protection. Title XVI of the TEU amends Article 130 EC again, by recasting paragraphs r, s, and t.

Article 130r contains both important additions and a significant subtraction. To the list of policy objectives in Article 130r(1) is added the promotion of measures at an international level in order to deal with regional or worldwide problems. In Article 130r(2) the reference to a 'high level of protection' previously found in Article 100a is extended from Commission proposals to Community policy, and the sentence 'Environment protection requirements shall be a component of the Community's other polices' has been strengthened into 'Environment protection requirements must be integrated into the definition and implementation of other Community policies'.

---

[24] I.e. where it does not exceed 15 per cent net grant equivalent of the value of the investment, and where it is granted to companies which have installations in operation for at least two years before the entry into force of the new standards. There are other exemptions under Article 92(3)(b) EC.

[25] For an assessment of the polluter pays principle, see Meli, 'The polluter pays: some conceptual problems' (1992) 3(3) *Water Law* 79.

[26] For example, Case 300/89, *Commission v Council,*

The Times, 21 August 1991, concerning Directive 89/428/EEC on titanium dioxide waste, where the Court ruled the Directive void; Case 155/91, *Commission v Council*, concerning the framework Directive 91/156/EEC on waste disposal, where the Directive was held valid, see below at note 113; Case 86/92, *Commission v Council*, concerning Directive 91/689/EEC on hazardous wastes, presently before the Court.

A major addition is the precautionary principle, contained in Article 130r(2). This principle goes a step further than the preventative principle found in the SEA, in that it requires that action should be taken to ensure that potentially damaging impacts on the environment are eliminated, even where there is no clear link between the activity in question and the damage to the environment. Thus, someone wishing to engage in an activity that might potentially harm the environment could be asked to prove in advance that the activity was not in fact damaging, rather than being required to prevent further damage at a point when harm is proven by actual damage to the environment. This is obviously a potentially stricter principle which may, in turn, lead to stricter environmental regulations.[27]

The paragraph noticeably absent from the revised Article is the previous Article 130r(4) concerning the issue of subsidiarity. However, this is due to the insertion of a general clause in Article 3b which transforms subsidiarity from a relatively minor principle concerning the environment into a fundamental principle of Community law.[28] As Brinkhorst notes,[29] however, the change is more complex than that. Where Article 130r(4) talks in terms of Community action being justified if it would be more *effective* than action at Member State level, Article 3b is couched in terms of assessing the *necessity* of action at Community rather than Member State level. This change could make Community environmental action more difficult to justify in the face of recalcitrant Member States, and also, potentially, make the job of deciding the level at which responsibility should have been taken more difficult for the ECJ. In practice, however, it is suggested that changes in the role and nature of the principle of subsidiarity will have relatively little effect in the environmental sphere given the highly co-operative nature of the relationship between Commission and Council in this area, and the ability of Member States to take more stringent measures than those proposed by the Community under Article 130t.

Article 130s is also considerably changed. The result of these changes is that the majority of environmental legislation will be adopted by qualified majority voting, with the exception of the following five areas: provisions of a fiscal nature; measures concerning town and country planning and land use, with the exception of waste management, measures of a general nature and management of water resources; Member State choice of energy sources and structure of energy supply. It has been noted that the result of the changes in voting will increase the influence of the European Parliament in environmental policy, as measures that are subject to majority voting will fall within the co-operation procedure. Parliament will be able to veto action programmes, but will not have the right of veto on second readings of general legislation.[30] Article 130r(5) provides that if the Council adopts a measure under Article 130r(1) which will result in the public authorities of a Member State being faced with a disproportionate cost, the Council may provide for temporary derogations and/or financial support from the new Community Cohesion Fund.[31] Article 130t is amended to require Member States wishing to adopt stricter measures than those proposed by the Council under Article 130s to ensure that they are compatible with the Treaty and to notify the Commission.

---

[27] Freestone, 'The 1992 Maastricht Treaty – Implications for European Environmental Law' (1992) EELR 1 (1) 23, at 24.

[28] As noted in Chapter 3.

[29] Brinkhorst, 'Subsidiarity and European Community Environment Policy: A Panacea or a Pandora's Box?' (1993) 2 (1) EELR 8, at 18.

[30] Freestone, *op. cit.*, note 27.

[31] See Article 130d TEU, 'The Council . . . shall before 31 December 1993 set up a Cohesion Fund to provide a financial contribution to projects in the fields of environment and trans-European networks in the area of transport infrastructure'.

ROLE OF THE INSTITUTIONS

European Council

The European Council has on more than one occasion shown an interest in environmental protection both within and by the Community although, as Freestone somewhat acerbically notes,[32] much of this interest has tended to come either in the wake of major environmental disasters (such as the programme on sea pollution agreed in 1978 following the well-publicised wreck of the *Amoco Cadiz*), in response to the growth of popular support within the Community for environmental issues, or following high-profile international expressions of concern over potential ecological catastrophe. It may be suggested, therefore, that the European Council has generally approached environmental issues with an attitude of being seen to be doing something about immediate issues rather than being concerned with playing a major part in developing a coherent long-term strategy.

The Council of the European Union

The Council of the European Union in the form of the Environmental Council wields the most influence over the direction of Community environmental policy. Unfortunately, due to the widely differing attitudes taken by the Member States as to the type, level and cost of environmental protection required in any given circumstance, this area has seen some long-running and bitterly fought battles at Council level. The UK, in recent years, has been possibly more prominent than most in its opposition to a number of proposals, including uniform emission standards in water quality control, the use of catalytic converters and the dumping of sewage sludge in the sea, and its attitude in these matters has frequently been perceived as profoundly self-serving. It appears, however, that despite disagreements of this sort the Council has managed, on balance, to achieve a broad level of consensus on environmental policy at Community level, and is actively engaged in promoting environmental strategy at an international level.

The Commission

The Commission has the joint tasks of implementing Community environmental policy and ensuring, through monitoring and enforcement proceedings, that the Member States comply with it.[33] Macrory notes, however, that it was not until the early 1980s that the Commission began to involve itself actively in the environmental sphere, even though by that time the Community had had a clear environmental policy for over a decade.[34] As outlined below, much of the pressure for the Commission to carry out adequate monitoring and enforcement came from the European Parliament, reflecting the more radical stance on the environment taken by that body. The attitude of some of the Member States towards implementation of Community environmental legislation clearly requires that the Commission take a stern line. In the most recent report by the Commission to the European Parliament on the enforcement

---

[32] Freestone, *op. cit.*, note 27, at 138.
[33] In line with the role given to it by Article 155 EC.
[34] Macrory, 'The Enforcement of Community Environ-

mental Laws: Some Critical Issues' (1992) 29 CMLR 347, at 349.

of Community law[35] none of the Member States had completed full notification of measures to the Commission concerning the relevant 110 Directives, with Greece and Portugal lagging furthest behind. As Kramer notes, Community environmental law, unlike, for instance, competition law, has no vested interests willing to secure its enforcement.[36]

The Commission does have a complaints procedure which allows members of the public to complain of infringements direct to the Commission. Complaints need not take a particular form,[37] contain full evidence or quote provisions or Directives, but must be specific enough for the Commission to take action. Each complaint is entered into a special complaints register, and the complainant informed of this fact. At the same time the Commission requests legal and factual data from the Member State in question. If the Commission cannot find a breach of Community law it will end the procedure and inform the complainant. There is no appeal from this decision to discontinue the procedure, but a complainant may forward further evidence in the light of which the Commission will reconsider its decision not to proceed.

The general public has made use of this facility to such an extent that about 50 per cent of the complaints which the Commission receives each year are concerned with the environment, although there are major differences in the numbers of complaints received from each Member State. A major criticism made of this approach to tackling infringements concerns its reactive, rather than pro-active, nature.[38] However, the Commission, like the European Parliament, is aware of the power of negative publicity, and in 1990 published details of the numbers of Article 169 letters sent on a country-by-country basis, something that caused no little disquiet on the part of some Member States.

The European Parliament

The European Parliament has played an increasingly important role in both the creation of environmental legislation and in the provision of information necessary for the public in the Community to play a part in promoting and supporting environmental protection. That role has come about not least because of an awareness that ecological issues have, since the mid-1980s, been a significant concern of the Parliament's electorate.[39] Indeed, the Environment, Public Health, and Consumer Protection Committee of the Parliament has gained itself a very high profile and influential role in environmental matters. As Freestone points out, it is the technical and detailed work carried out by this Committee which has allowed the Parliament to have considerable input into the debate on a variety of environmental legislation proposals.[40]

In the course of its campaign to increase its power and position within the Community institutions, and especially in the decision-making process, Parliament has also been prepared to put pressure on both Commission and Council to provide better environmental information. As a result of this pressure, the Commission now presents a general annual

---

35 OJ 1993 C138. The report, which contains a State-by-State breakdown of infractions, also notes an increase in unsatisfactory transposition and incorrect application, and a resulting rise in complaints.

36 Krämer, *EEC Treaty and Environmental Protection*, *op. cit.*, note 1, at 26.

37 Although the Commission has published a model form for this purpose, OJ 1989 C26/6.

38 *Ibid.*, Macrory, *op. cit.*, note 34, at 363.

39 Note, for instance, the 15 per cent share of the vote captured by the Green Party in the UK in the 1989 European Elections (although this was not rewarded with any seats).

40 Freestone, *op. cit.*, note 27, at 141.

report to Parliament on the Commission's monitoring of the application of Community law, which includes much information on Member States' application of environmental law.[41] In early 1993 Parliament, irritated both by the three-year delay in establishing the European Environmental Agency[42] over an argument about its seat[43] and by the Council's dilution of the Agency's powers[44] first issued a Resolution[45] calling for the deadlock to be resolved, and then threatened to use its budgetary powers to force the Council to proceed with the creation of the Agency.

POLICY IMPLEMENTATION

Legislation

The Community has a number of methods of implementing its policy in this area. The primary method is by legislation, and this legislation has generally taken the form of directives. The reason for this can be found in the historical development of Community environmental law.

Prior to the SEA, when the Commission was using Articles 100 and 235 EC upon which to base its legislation, the use of directives was essentially the only way to proceed. Article 100 only authorises action by directive and, while Article 235 does not contain such a restriction, commentators have suggested that the Commission generally refrained from the use of regulations under this head for fear of facing widespread challenge for acting beyond its powers as granted by the Treaty.[46]

Since the SEA, under Article 130s, regulations have still been used only sparingly, primarily to provide Community-wide rules in line with obligations stemming from international agreements,[47] although some proposals for environmental regulations have been made with a view to achievement of the internal market.[48] It has also been pointed out that there are a number of problems with present environmental regulations.[49] First, they frequently contain elements which are not directly applicable, due to the inability of the Commission to carry out certain tasks, such as monitoring, for itself. Thus, Member States must implement certain procedures. Secondly, the failure of the Community to fix sanctions in the regulations for non-compliance, leaving this to the Member States, may result in some Member States fixing inappropriate sanctions to achieve the Community aim. Finally, where Article 130s is used as a basis for regulations which affect trade, rather than Article 100a, Member States may invoke Article 130t and restrict trade, leading to potential legal complications.[50]

---

[41] See, for example, the *Tenth Annual Report to Parliament on Commission monitoring of the application of Community law – 1992*, OJ 1993 C233, at 40.
[42] See below for further discussion of this entity.
[43] Since resolved in favour of Copenhagen.
[44] The Parliament wanted the European Environmental Agency to have both inspection and enforcement powers, both of which were withheld.
[45] Resolution A3-0317/92, OJ 1992 C337.
[46] Rehbinder and Stewart, *op. cit.*, note 10, at 36.
[47] For example, Regulation 348/81/EEC, concerning the import of whales and certain other cetacean products, OJ 1981 L39/1; Regulation 3625/82/EEC, concerning

trade in endangered species, OJ 1982 L384/1. Krämer, 'Community Environmental Law – Towards a Systematic Approach' (1991) 11 YEL 151, at 157.
[48] For example, Proposal on transport of waste, OJ 1990 C289/1; and see Krämer, *ibid.*
[49] Krämer, *ibid.*
[50] For example, Regulation 594/91/EEC which applied restrictions upon the import, export, production and use of all fully halogenated CFCs, halons carbon tetrachloride and methyl chloroform. Denmark and Germany have used Article 130t to restrict trade in CFCs with the intent of phasing out their use by 1995.

The way in which directives are used to achieve environment aims, however, also tends to differ from what might generally be considered the norm. Rather than simply taking the traditional form of the directive, as defined in Article 189 EC,[51] environmental directives, according to Rehbinder and Stewart,[52] appear also to come in two other categories, the 'regulation type' directive and the 'framework' directive. The 'regulation type' directive tends to impose on Member States rigid standards, such as the level of pollution by a particular compound which may not be exceeded, and details of how testing procedures are to be implemented. The effect of these obligations is to remove all discretion from the Member States as to the way in which the directive is to be implemented. 'Framework' directives are designed to lay down the general aims of the Community for a particular environmental sector, and the detail required to achieve those aims then tends to be filled in by the use of regulation type directives. Thus, Directive 76/464/EEC[53] outlines the Community aims with regard to discharge of dangerous substances into water, and Directives such as 83/513/EEC[54] and 84/491/EEC[55] are used to fill in that framework. This use of framework and regulation type directives has, to a certain degree, blurred the distinction between regulations and directives in this area but, as yet, no successful challenge has been brought against such directives.[56]

Given the regulatory style of many environmental directives it would seem inevitable that the ECJ will hold some of them to be sufficiently clear, precise and unconditional as to fulfil the requirements of the doctrine of direct effect.[57] Thus, while Freestone[58] suggested in 1991 that the doctrine of direct effect had not had much noticeable effect on this area, Jans[59] in 1993 suggested that despite national cases such as *Twyford Parish Council and others* v *Secretary of State for the Environment and others*[60] the trend set by the ECJ in cases such as *Commission* v *Germany*[61] and *Commission* v *Netherlands*[62] show that there is increasing movement towards the idea that environmental directives must bestow rights upon individuals in order to ensure adequate protection in the event of Member State breaches.

Co-ordination and monitoring

The Community has also taken on the task of co-ordinating and monitoring the implementation of Community environmental law by the Member States. This role is

---

[51] That is that directives are binding as to the result to be achieved, but the methods used to gain that result are left to the Member States.

[52] *Op. cit.*, note 10, at 33–6 and 137ff.

[53] OJ 1976 L129, amended by Directive 91/692/EEC, OJ 1991 L377.

[54] Concerning cadmium discharges, OJ 1983 L291, amended by Directive 91/692/EEC, OJ 1991 L377.

[55] Concerning hexachlorocyclohexane discharges, OJ 1984 L274, amended by Directive 91/692/EEC, OJ 1991 L377.

[56] Freestone, *op. cit.*, note 27, at 146 notes that a challenge has been brought against a directive for being inconsistent with Article 189, but that it was eventually dropped after a political settlement. See Case 78/79, *BTP Tioxide* v *Commission* and Case 79/79, *Laporte Industries* v *Commission* OJ 1979 C153/5.

[57] See Krämer, 'The Implementation of Community Environmental Directives within Member States: some Implications of the Direct Effect Doctrine' (1991) *Journal of Environmental Law* 39.

[58] Freestone, *op. cit.*, note 27, at 146.

[59] Jans, 'Legal Protection in European Environmental Law' (1993) EELR 151.

[60] [1992] CMLR 276. In that case the High Court held that, if applicants seeking to rely on the direct effect of provisions of a directive could not show that they had suffered in some way as a result of the Member States' failure to implement the directive within the prescribed time, they could not enforce the directive against the defaulting Member State.

[61] Case C-59/89, [1991] ECR I-2607.

[62] Case C-190/90, not yet reported.

primarily taken by the Commission, although other Community bodies are involved, such as the Court of Auditors[63] and the European Environmental Agency.

The European Environmental Agency and the European Environment Monitoring and Information Network were established by Regulation 1210/90/EEC[64] to provide a permanent monitoring and information collection system. To achieve this the European Environmental Agency is supposed to create links between national, regional, public and private information sources. The eventual aim is to provide the Community in general and the Commission in particular, with a Community-wide technical and scientific body capable of offering assessments and forecasts as to the state of the Community ecosystem. It would also provide the necessary research and technical know-how to allow the drafting of more effective environmental policy. The European Environmental Agency has no role beyond the provision of information, ie no policing function.[65] Its primary areas of interest are air quality and atmospheric emissions, water quality, pollutants and water resources, the state of the soil and of vegetation and land use and resource management.

The concept of the European Environmental Agency is based upon a previous project, the CORINE programme, which aimed to set up a Community-wide environmental information system. The CORINE programme will continue in those areas not covered by the European Environmental Agency.[66]

The major problem that had faced the European Environmental Agency and, indeed, had effectively prevented its establishment, was an ongoing argument between the Member States as to where it would be sited. This argument became, somewhat unfortunately, embroiled with the long-running battle over the seat of the European Parliament and other Community institutions. As a result, no decision had been made by early 1993 and, as mentioned above, the European Parliament then threatened to block the Community budget in the event that this state of affairs continued.[67] Whether that threat, by itself, had the necessary effect is debatable, but shortly afterwards Copenhagen was chosen as the site for the Agency.

Legislation for the purpose of providing information to the Community and the general public has resulted in two important directives. With regard to facilitating monitoring, Directive 85/337/EEC on the assessment of the effects of certain public and private projects on the environment[68] provides that an environmental impact assessment should be made for public and private projects listed in its two Annexes which are likely to have an impact on the local environment because of their size, nature or location. Annex 1 contains projects that should always be assessed, such as oil refineries, power stations and major road projects, while Annex 2 contains a long list of smaller projects which may be assessed if the Member

63 See, for instance, the Special Report No 3/92 on the environment made by the Court of Auditors following its audit of the Commission and six of the Member States, OJ 1992 C245, which was critical of the lack of systematic monitoring of the Community environmental action programmes and environmental projects. It also felt that on structural fund programmes the lack of consultation with national institutions with responsibility for the environment combined with the lack of environmental planning in structural development was at best handicapping attempts at environmental protection and at worst causing further environmental damage. In general the Court appears to feel that EC environmental policy

was not being developed quickly or completely and the use of directives alone to achieve this end was questioned. See (1993) 4 (1) *Water Law* 9.
64 OJ 1990 L120.
65 However, Article 20 of the Regulation setting up the European Environmental Agency provides that two years after that set up the Council will examine whether some of the tasks concerning implementation of environmental legislation can be transferred to it.
66 Decision 85/338/EEC, OJ 1985 L176, OJ 1990 L81.
67 Coopers and Lybrand *EC Commentaries*, July 1993.
68 OJ 1985 L175.

States consider it necessary. Projects concerned with national defence are exempt automatically, and other projects may be exempted, providing that the Member State notifies both the public and the Commission of the reason.

The assessment process involves two stages: first, the provision of information by those running the project, the extent of which is largely determined by the Member State involved, although certain information must be disclosed; and secondly, a consultation stage involving the competent authorities, the public and other Member States potentially affected. Information elucidated by this process must be taken into account by the competent authorities when deciding whether or not to allow the project to go ahead.

Directive 90/313/EEC[69] on public access to environmental information seeks to harmonise national provisions on public access to government files and provides that individuals will have equal access rights to Member States records, regardless of nationality. The public are entitled to access to information on the condition of air, soil and water, animal and plant life, and natural habitats. The information covered is that in official documents or on electronic databases held by public bodies.

Enforcement

The Commission bears the burden of ensuring that Community law is implemented by the Member States, but at present does not have the manpower or information to carry this out effectively in the area of environmental law. To highlight this problem the discrepancy between competition law and environmental law can be considered, in that where the Commission suspects that a company has breached Community competition law it may send inspectors to raid the company's offices, but if it believes that the company is in breach of environmental law it only has the option of writing to the company.[70]

Enforcement procedure against Member States is via an Article 169 EC action where, if found to be in breach, Member States are supposed to take the necessary steps to comply with the ECJ's decision.[71] It has been the case that in environmental matters the ECJ has sometimes been forced to make a second ruling due to non-compliance by a Member State with the first ruling.[72]

In defining implementation the Commission has developed three headings:

* non-communication of domestic laws and other measures implementing Community legislation;
* non-conformity of domestic law with Community law due to incorrect or incomplete transposition; and
* poor application of Community law in practice.

With regard to the first heading, Member States are supposed to notify the Commission of the texts of implementing national legislation. If no notification is received the Commission will begin Article 169 proceedings. It appears that informal measures are not utilised before an Article 169 action begins, probably because Member States are generally reminded twice before the deadline set out in the directive that such texts are required.

[69] OJ 1990 L158.
[70] Krämer, *op. cit.*, note 47, at 169.
[71] Article 171 EC.

[72] For example, Cases 227–230/85, *Commission v Belgium* [1988] ECR 1 which concerned failure to transpose waste directives into national law.

Incomplete or incorrect transposition occurs where the first heading is complied with, but it is determined by the Commission that the national legislation does not meet the aims of the directive. This determination can be a very difficult task, especially where Member States have not drawn up new legislation but are claiming that pre-existing legislation is sufficient.[73] The Commission, backed by the ECJ, has also increasingly insisted that transposition should be by legislation and not by mere administrative means such as circulars.[74]

The decision that Community law has been poorly applied is difficult to determine and very often controversial. It has been pointed out that frequently the reason given for non-implementation or poor implementation of directives is the unwillingness of Member States to face the cost of compliance with their provisions.[75] The drinking water cases[76] following Directive 80/778/EEC[77] provide good examples of both the latter heads.

SCOPE OF COMMUNITY ENVIRONMENTAL POLICY

Community environmental policy covers a wide range of activities, which are probably best examined under the heads established by the Commission in its Community Environmental Policy 1967–87. These were general policy and nature protection, air and noise, chemicals and waste, and water.

General policy and nature protection

This area of Community environmental policy has probably attracted the most public attention and this, in turn, has resulted in Community action such as the ban on import of skins of baby seals,[78] the ban on importation of certain whale products for commercial purposes[79] and a ban on the importation of raw and worked ivory from the African elephant.[80] These and other specific wildlife protection measures are, however, just a small part of the area covered by this heading. The more important multi-directive policies are probably those which deal with the protection of habitats,[81] the promotion of large-scale environmental programmes[82] and the conservation of fishery resources.[83] In implementing

---

73 This claim was made in Case 360/87, *Commission v Italy* (not yet reported) and Case 131/88, *Commission v Germany* (not yet reported) concerning Directive 80/68/EEC on the protection of ground water against pollution by dangerous substances. In both cases the Member State's submission failed.

74 Case 361/88, *Commission v Germany* [1991] ECR I-2567 and Case C-59/89, *Commission v Germany*, *op. cit.*, note 61, concerning failure to properly implement Directive 80/779/EEC and Directive 82/884/EEC on limit values for sulphur dioxide and lead in the air.

75 McCrory, *op. cit.*, note 34, at 358.

76 Case C-42/89, *Commission v Belgium* [1990] ECR I-2821; Case 337/89, *Commission v United Kingdom*, 25 November 1992, not yet reported; Case C-237/90, *Commission v Germany*, not yet reported.

77 OJ 1980 1229/11.

78 Directive 83/129/EEC, OJ 1983 L91, last amended OJ 1989 L163.

79 Regulation 348/81/EEC, OJ 1981 L39.

80 Regulation 2496/89/EEC, OJ 1989 L240.

81 For example, Directive 92/43/EEC Protection of Natural and Semi-Natural Habitats and of Wild Fauna and Flora, OJ 1992 L206.

82 For example, Regulation 563/91/EEC Action by the Community for the Protection of the Environment in the Mediterranean Regions, OJ 1991 L63; Regulation 3908/91/EEC Community Action to Protect the Coastal Zones and Coastal Waters in the Irish Sea, North Sea, English Channel, Baltic Sea and North East Atlantic Ocean, OJ 1991 L370.

83 Regulation 170/83/EEC Community System for the Conservation and Management of Fishery Resources, OJ 1983 L24.

these policies, the Community has had to overcome a considerable degree of resistance from the Member States who, especially pre-SEA, were inclined to argue that such measures were best left to their exclusive jurisdiction.

That the Commission takes wildlife protection seriously can be seen from its willingness to enforce the aims of the Directive on the Conservation of Wild Birds.[84] This Directive, which aims to balance exploitation and conservation, places strict obligations on the Member States to maintain populations of wild birds, preserve, maintain or re-establish a diverse and sufficient habitat for birds covered by the Directive, regulate the transport and possession of birds and regulate hunting, trapping and killing of wild birds. While it has been noted that changing the habits of some Member States has been difficult[85] the Commission has not shied from commencing proceedings against Member States for failing to fulfil their obligations. Germany,[86] Italy[87] and Spain[88] have been the subject of Article 169 actions, and a project in the UK which would have used an important habitat in Islay for a whisky distillery was halted after a visit by a member of the Commission.[89]

However, it is probably fair to say that the majority of Community action in this area will continue to be driven by public pressure, as there is no sign at present of an EC-wide nature protection policy.

Air and noise

Air pollution has long been a concern of the Community and some of the first Community environmental legislation were measures designed to cut air pollution.[90] Community policy has rarely been concerned with human health issues in the strict sense, rather with the large-scale environmental issues such as acid rain and other habitat destroyers, ozone depletion and global warming.[91] Air pollution control has not attempted to identify and cut all pollutants, concentrating, instead, on those identifiable as causing the above large-scale problems. There are directives to control sulphur dioxide[92] and nitrogen dioxide emissions,[93] major contributors to acid rain; directives for the control of levels of lead[94] and asbestos,[95] harmful to the general environment; directives for the control of emission from industry[96] and

---

[84] Directive 79/409/EEC, OJ 1979 L103.

[85] Freestone, *op. cit.*, note 27, at 142.

[86] Case 57/89, *Commission v Germany (Leybucht Dikes Case)* (not yet reported) where the Court held there was no breach of the Directive as no significant damage was done to the habitat in question. See Freestone, 'The *Leybucht Dikes* Case' (1991) 2 *Water Law* 153.

[87] Case 334/89 and Case 157/89, *Commission v Italy* where the Court held that Italy was in breach of the Directive in permitting the hunting of various species of birds during their rearing season and various stages of reproduction, and in permitting the hunting of migratory birds while they were returning to their rearing grounds.

[88] Case C-335/90, *Commission v Kingdom of Spain* (not yet reported) where the Court held that in both failing to classify Marismas de Santona (an endangered habitat) as a special protection area or take appropriate measures to avoid pollution or deterioration of the habitats in that area, Spain had failed to fulfil its obligations.

[89] Letter from a member of the Nature Conservancy Council in (1990) 1 *Water Law* at 105.

[90] For example, Directive 70/220/EEC concerned with reducing the pollutant emissions of motor vehicles, OJ 1970 L76.

[91] See Macrory, 'Air Pollution Legislation in the United States and the Community' (1990) 15 EL Rev 298 for a comparative examination of the aims, methods and achievements of the EC and US air pollution legislation.

[92] Directive 80/779/EEC, OJ 1980 L229, amended by Directive 89/427/EEC, OJ 1989 L201.

[93] Directive 85/203/EEC, OJ 1985 L87.

[94] Directive 82/884/EEC, OJ 1982 L378.

[95] Directive 87/217/EEC, OJ 1987 L85.

[96] For example, Directive 88/609/EEC, OJ 1988 L336, proposed amendment in OJ 1993 C17 on air pollution from large combustion plants.

motor vehicle emissions,[97] culprits in both the global warming process and acid rain; and directives to control CFCs and HCFCs, implicated in the damage to the ozone layer.[98] Such measures are often very costly to implement and Article 169 actions are quite frequent.[99]

The Community is heavily engaged in programmes of monitoring[100] and scientific research[101] in this area and is actively involved at an international level (see the discussion of the (UNCED) Earth Summit Conventions, the Vienna Convention on the protection of the ozone layer and the Montreal Protocol on substances which deplete the ozone layer under international agreements, below). It is, therefore, expected that a further wave of legislation will result from these existing programmes within the next three years.

There is at present no general Community legislation on noise, although the Commission is reported to be working on one.[102] The Commission has concentrated on directives to harmonise both methods of measuring noise levels[103] and maximum noise levels for particular products.[104]

Chemicals and waste

As chemical pollution can be devastating to the environment[105] the Community has been concerned to ensure that it is minimised. The primary methods of controlling chemical pollution have been by controlling the marketing, production, import and transportation of dangerous products. This area, having been regulated to some degree from the late 1960s when purely environmental issues were much less influential, still shows its trade consideration background. There are two major framework Directives to consider which are Directive 67/548/EEC on classification, packaging and labelling[106] and Directive 76/769/EEC[107] on the use and marketing of dangerous substances. Both have been considerably amended or adapted over time, primarily due to advances in science.[108] In addition, Regulation 2455/92/EEC concerns the development of a common notification system for the export and import of certain hazardous chemicals. Annex 1 of this Directive lists 24 chemicals that are banned or the use of which is severely restricted within the

---

97 For example, Directive 70/220/EEC, OJ 1970 L76. This Directive has been extended twice and amended no less than eight times – see, for instance, Directive 91/441/EEC for small, light and medium-sized motor vehicles, OJ 1991 L242, proposed amendment in OJ 1993 C56.

98 See below.

99 For example, Case C-361/88, *Commission v Germany* [1993] 2 CMLR 821, failure to comply completely within the allotted period with Directive 80/779/EEC concerning sulphur dioxide levels; Case C-59/89, *op. cit.*, note 61, failure to comply completely within the allotted period with Directive 82/884/EEC concerning lead levels.

100 For example, Decision 93/389/EEC for a monitoring mechanism for Community CO2 and other greenhouse gas emissions.

101 For example, the Council Resolution adopted in 1989 (OJ 1989 C183) on global warming.

102 Cooper and Lybrand *EC Commentaries*, July 1993.

103 For example, Directive 77/311/EEC, OJ 1977 L105,

amended by Directive 82/890/EEC, OJ 1982 L378 concerning driver-perceived noise level of tractors.

104 For example, Directive 78/1015/EEC, OJ 1978 L349, last amended by Directive 89/235/EEC, OJ 1989 L98 concerning motorbikes; Directive 84/537/EEC, OJ 1984 L300, amended by Directive 85/409/EEC, OJ 1985 L233 concerning pneumatic concrete-breakers and picks; Directive 84/538/EEC, OJ 1984 L300, adapted by Directive 87/252/EEC, OJ 1987 L117, amended by Directive 88/181/EEC, OJ 1988 L81 concerning lawnmowers.

105 Witness the massive fish kills in the Rhine in 1986.

106 OJ 1967 L196.

107 OJ 1976 L262.

108 Directive 67/548/EEC has been amended seven times, the last amendment being Directive 92/32/EEC, OJ 1992 L154 – and adapted 18 times, the latest in OJ 1993 L110. Directive 76/769/EEC has been amended 11 times and amendments 12 (OJ 1991 C46), 13 (OJ 1992 C157) and 14 (OJ 1993 C116) are currently in progress.

Community and obliges Member States to impose strict sanctions upon those who import or export them.

The 'Seveso' Directive,[109] so called because it was adopted following the Seveso incident,[110] creates Community policy for the prevention of major industrial accidents and measures to limit the damage to humans and the environment in the event of such an accident. It has been twice amended,[111] the second amendment significantly increasing the scope and strength of the original Directive. A third amendment is under consideration by the Commission which will simplify the Directive and to extend the degree of information required to be made public by manufacturers in line with the 1990 Directive on the public right of access to environmental information.[112]

Waste is quantitatively the largest environmental problem facing the Community, with the Member States producing over two billion tonnes per annum. Of this total up to 30 million tonnes is industrial chemical waste, which poses severe problems for the environment due to the attendant risks such as toxicity, degradation of water quality, and the threat to health. There is, therefore, extensive Community legislation on waste, especially waste that is considered to be toxic or dangerous.

A major concern of the Community in recent years has been 'waste tourism', that is, with the removal of internal frontiers, that waste can move freely within the Community. This may lead to two major problems: first, that large quantities of waste are on the move within the Community with all the attendant risks that transporting waste entail; and, secondly, that some Member States may, in effect, end up as dumping grounds for the waste of the others, with all the risks to their environment that this entails.[113]

The Community's policy with regard to waste is to be found in a Commission Communication of 1989.[114] It contains five Action Programmes, waste prevention, reuse or recycling, collection and transportation, disposal and decontamination. In general, under these heads the Community aims to cut down on the amount of waste produced by use of new technology, increase reuse and recycling, ensure that waste is dealt with as close to its source of origin as possible, tighten regulations on incineration and landfill use and clean up existing waste blackspots within the Community.

In terms of legislation, Directive 75/442/EEC[115] was the first Directive to lay down guidelines for the collection, disposal, recycling and processing of waste and, in 1991, it was turned into Framework Directive 91/156/EEC.[116] This does not cover a number of types of waste, including hazardous waste which is dealt with in Directive 78/319/EEC on Toxic and Dangerous Wastes[117] or radioactive waste, dealt with under a separate Community

---

109 Directive 82/501/EEC, OJ 1982 L230.
110 A factory disaster involving large-scale contamination of an area around the Seveso plant by dioxins, which are highly carcinogenic. A further twist was added to this affair when a number of drums of contaminated matter from this accident were transported from Italy to France and then disappeared, resulting in the renewal of debate in the Community as to liability for damage caused by such accidents and their aftermath.
111 Directive 87/216/EEC, OJ 1987 L85 – correction of technical errors; Directive 88/610/EEC, OJ 1988 L336.
112 Directive 90/313/EEC, OJ 1990 L158.
113 Given the present governmental support for nuclear waste processing in the UK, notably at Sellafield, UK en-

vironmental campaigners are particularly worried about the implications of 'waste tourism'.
114 SEC (89) 934.
115 OJ 1975 L194.
116 OJ 1991 L78. This process was delayed by Case 155/91, *Commission* v *Council* (not yet reported) where the Commission argued that contrary to the decision by Council, the Directive should be based on Article 100a and not on Article 130s and should, thus, be declared void. The Court rejected this argument, stating that the Directive was only incidentally related to trade and competition and Article 130s was the correct legal basis.
117 OJ 1978 L84, replaced on 12 December 1993 by Directive 91/689/EEC, OJ 1991 L377.

Programme. Other specific directives have been adopted on the recycling of liquid containers[118] and urban waste water treatment[119] and directives are planned for dumping and burning of waste at sea[120] and dumping at landfill sites.[121]

Waste legislation has been, like water legislation, contentious. This has been mainly because of the cost of compliance, either in providing necessary facilities or in changing previous practices, which has led Member States to drag their feet over implementation.

A more recent problem has been that while waste is not exactly a product in the normal Community sense, it is possible to trade in it. This has resulted, first, in the conflict, noted above, between Council and Commission over whether some directives concerning waste should be based on Article 100a with regard to the harmonisation of the Single Market or on Article 130s as an environmental issue and, secondly, to a number of cases being brought before the ECJ concerning whether bans by Member States on the import and export of waste for disposal are contrary to the principle of free movement of goods.[122]

In cases involving export bans the ECJ has emphasised that such a ban must be shown to benefit the environment. In order for this criteria to be fulfilled the ban must lead to a reduction in the level of pollution within the Community. A ban which merely causes the pollution resulting from disposal to be restricted to one Member State rather than being relocated within the Community does not reduce the overall level of pollution and is, therefore, unlawful.

In the case of import bans the issue is less clear. The judgment in the *Walloon Import Ban Case*[123] raised more questions on this issue than it answered, in that the ECJ failed to present a clear and coherent argument to justify its decision that Belgium could legitimately bar imports of foreign waste on the ground of environmental protection. It may be that a case currently before the ECJ, brought by three French waste treatment companies,[124] will help to answer some of those questions. The waste treatment companies are requesting the annulment of Article 4(3)(a)(i) of Regulation 259/93/EEC[125] on the supervision and control of shipments of waste within, into and out of the European Community, and the award of damages for Community non-contractual liability.[126] They allege that the Council misused its powers in adopting the Regulation because it did so in the interest of France who was seeking to prevent the import of waste from other Member States.

Water

The reduction of water pollution has been allotted the highest priority in the Community's environmental policy since the First Environmental Action Plan, and policy in this area is the best developed.[127] Community policy is essentially divided into two parts; first, the

118 Directive 85/339/EEC, OJ 1985 L176.
119 Directive 91/271/EEC, OJ 1991 L135.
120 A proposal for a Directive, OJ 1985 C245, as amended by OJ 1988 C72. This Directive, which would end dumping at sea, has been held up for a number of years by the UK.
121 OJ 1991 C190, as amended in COM(93) 275.
122 For example, Case 172/82, *Syndicat national des fabricants raffineurs d'huile de graissage* v *GIE Inter-Huiles* [1983] ECR 555 and Case 118/86, *Openbaar Ministerie* v *Nertsvoederfabriek Nederland* [1987] ECR 3883.
123 Case C-2/90, *Commission* v *Belgium*, not yet re-

ported. See Hancher and Sevenster, [1993] 30 CML Rev 351 and von Wilmowsky, 'Waste Disposal in the Internal Market: The State of Play after the ECJ's Ruling on the Walloon Import Ban' [1993] 30 CML Rev 541.
124 Case 145/93, *Buralux SA and others* v *Council*, not yet reported.
125 OJ 1993 L30.
126 Under Article 215(2) EC.
127 Johnson and Corecells, *op. cit.*, note 1, at 25 call it 'the oldest and most complete sector of Community Environmental Policy'.

establishment of water quality standards; and, secondly, the control of emissions into the aquatic environment.

The first part of the policy has been achieved by a number of directives setting physical, microbiological and chemical standards which various types of waters must meet. These directives leave the designation of the waters to which a directive may apply to the Member State, and rely upon the relevant authorities of the Member State to carry out the testing and monitoring. There are presently directives for drinking and surface water,[128] bathing water,[129] fresh water supporting fish-life[130] and water used for rearing shellfish.[131]

Directive 80/778/EEC,[132] while effectively part of this grouping of directives, differs in that it establishes mandatory standards for water intended for human consumption. As noted above, there have been considerable problems with obtaining Member State implementation of these standards, resulting in both a significant number of complaints to the Commission and a number of Article 169 actions.[133]

The primary legislation for the second part of the policy is Framework Directive 76/464/EEC[134] which sets out two lists of substances which are hazardous to the aquatic environment, decided by reference to their toxicity, persistence and bioaccumulation. The first list or 'blacklist' contains highly harmful substances, the pollution from which the Member States must take measures to eliminate.[135] The second list or 'grey list' contains those substances which are less hazardous or are only hazardous under certain circumstances and the pollution of which the Member States must take measures to reduce. In order to eliminate 'blacklist' substances Member States have to enforce limit values which determine either the maximum permissible concentrations of those substances in discharges (uniform emission standards (UES)) or in the receiving waters (environmental quality objectives (EQO)). With 'grey list' substances the EQO approach is used.[136]

The Council is empowered to decide whether the lists should be extended and whether substances should be moved between the categories, subject to unanimity.[137]

Both the nature of the Framework Directive and the relatively slow speed at which measures have been taken under it have been attributed, to some degree, to the attitude of

---

128 Directive 75/440/EEC, OJ 1975 L194; Directive 79/869/EEC, OJ 1979 L271. These Directives were amended by Directive 91/692/EEC, OJ 1991 L377. See also Directive 79/869/EEC which fixes measurement procedures and sampling frequency guidelines for surface water intended for use as drinking water, OJ 1979 L271, last amended in OJ 1981 L319 and OJ 1991 L377.
129 Directive 76/160/EEC, OJ 1976 L31.
130 Directive 78/659/EEC, OJ 1978 L222.
131 Directive 79/923/EEC, OJ 1979 L281.
132 OJ 1980 L229, as amended by Directive 91/692/EEC.
133 See Somsen, 'EC Water Directives' (1990) 1 *Water Law* 96, who notes that 'more individuals have approached the Commission about non-compliance with the drinking water directive than any other piece of EC environmental law'.
134 OJ 1976 L129, last amended by Directive 91/692/EEC. See also Directive 80/68/EEC on the Protection of Groundwater against Pollution caused by Certain

Dangerous Substances, OJ 1980 L20, amended by Directive 91/692/EEC, enacted within this framework.
135 Currently blacklisted are 129 substances including mercury (Directive 82/176/EEC, OJ 1982 L81, amended by Directive 91/692/EEC) and cadmium (Directive 83/513/EEC, OJ 1983 L291, amended by Directive 91/692/EEC).
136 Freestone, *op. cit.*, note 27, at 144.
137 Amendments designed to expedite the decision-making process, which had been painfully slow, were made by Directive 86/280/EEC, OJ 1986 L181, modified by Directive 88/347/EEC, OJ 1988 L158 and updated by Directive 90/415/EEC, OJ 1990 L219. A further amendment, OJ 1990 C55, as currently proposed, would make decisions on value limits, quality objectives and their means of application, subject to a qualified majority, but would leave inclusion on, or removal from, the two lists subject to unanimity.

the UK, which disagreed with the methods and standards to be used, primarily, it seems, for political reasons.[138]

The 13 major Directives spanning both areas were recently amended by Directive 91/692/EEC[139] which is designed to improve the information available to the Commission on Member States' implementation of environmental legislation by way of sectoral questionnaires,[140] and three-yearly reports on the implementation of the water Directives. The first of these reports is due in September 1996.

THE FIFTH ENVIRONMENTAL ACTION PROGRAMME[141]

The Fifth Environmental Action Programme (EAP), which will run until 2000, was adopted by the Council in February 1993 and takes over from the Fourth Environmental Action Programme. Its main objective is to provide guidelines for environmental policy for all sections of the Community, governments, regional and local authorities, commercial concerns, pressure groups and individuals. It is concerned to increase awareness of a shared responsibility for the environment and aims to effect this by providing for greater co-operation in the drafting process of environmental legislation, particularly in the early stages. This heavy emphasis on co-operation is an interesting development in Community policy, but it remains to be seen how such proposed co-operation will work in practice.[142]

The Programme seeks to develop an awareness of environmental issues amongst individuals within the Community and, to this end, intends to develop information and educational schemes, promote land and sector specific planning, strengthen research and development projects, improve public information on the environment and extend the use of economic and fiscal instruments. All these areas are given long-terms objectives and a timetable by which they are supposed to be achieved. It will be remembered, however, that the EAPs are guidelines only and have no legal force. Therefore, failure to achieve such aims in the times set will attract no sanction.

The Fifth EAP also targets five sectors for particular attention in this time period. These are, industry, energy, transport, agriculture and tourism.

In the industrial sector the emphasis will be on developing the environmental elements of strategic planning, improving management and control of production processes, increasing product standards so that at all stages of use products have minimal impact on the environment, encouraging self-regulation, developing effective waste management and improving the information links between industry and the public. The Fifth EAP recognises that small and medium enterprises (SME) must be involved in all the measures outlined, with the proviso that such involvement should not be disproportionately burdensome.

In the energy sector the primary interest is reducing emissions of Sulphur dioxide (SO_2), Nitrogen-oxygen compounds (NO_x) and Carbon dioxide (CO_2). There are also the aims of improving energy efficiency and the development of renewable energy sources.

---

138 See Freestone, *op cit.*, note 27, at 143, also Boehmer-Christiansen 'Environmental Quality Objectives versus Uniform Emission Standards' in Freestone and Ijlstra (eds) *The North Sea: Perspectives on Regional Environmental Co-operation*, (1990), at 139.
139 OJ 1991 L377.

140 Also applicable to air, waste and nature legislation.
141 OJ 1993 C138. See also (1992) 1 (1) EELR 16.
142 In the UK, for instance, there is a feeling that present governmental policy of consultation and co-operation, especially in the environmental sphere, does little more than pay lip-service to the concept as first envisaged.

In the transport sector there is emphasis on the improvement and better management of infrastructure, notably public transport, reduction of emissions by technical improvement of vehicles and fuels, and the promotion of changes in driving habits by methods such as speed limits.

In the agriculture sector progress centres on changes based on the reform of the Common Agricultural Policy, with reductions in the use of nitrate fertilisers and pesticides, action to prevent overgrazing and the continuing reduction of surpluses. The promotion of a better forestry programme, including protection of existing forests, afforestation of farm land and better forest management is aimed at cutting Community imports of timber and reducing damage by acid rain and fires.

In the tourism sector it is proposed that tourism be better managed, from the staggering of holidays to spread the tourist load and prevent stress on the environment, to prevention of harmful activities such as illegal housing and destruction of sensitive areas, such as wetlands, by tourist resorts.

A review and revision of the Programme is planned for 1995. This may, however, be brought forward, if changes in strategy are required, following discussion with Council, Parliament and the sectoral groups.

INTERNATIONAL AGREEMENTS

Article 130r(5) of the EC Treaty[143] provides that the Community[144] and the Member States may co-operate and make agreements with international organisations in environmental matters, and the Community has been taking an increasingly active role in the international environmental forum, although this has sometimes been with mixed results. The following two sets of international environmental agreements are used to illustrate the type of role which the Community has adopted for itself, those agreements being the largest that the Community has been involved with. They are by no means the only ones, but space precludes a discussion of all such agreements.[145] The Community has also incorporated environmental chapters into other non-environmental specific conventions such as the LOMÉ IV Convention. This now contains an environmental chapter which includes a prohibition on exporting dangerous waste from the Community to the LOMÉ signatories.[146]

The Vienna Convention on protection of the ozone layer and the Montreal Protocol on substances that deplete the ozone layer

Both the Community and individual Member States are party to the Vienna Convention on the protection of the ozone layer and the Montreal Protocol on substances that deplete the

143 Inserted by Article 25 SEA.
144 Pursuant to Article 228 EC.
145 For example, the Paris Convention for the prevention of Marine Pollution from Land Based Sources, OJ 1975 L194/5; the Berne Convention on the Conservation of European Wildlife and Natural Habitats; OJ 1982 L210/10; and the Geneva Convention on Long Range Transboundary Air Pollution, OJ 1981 1171/11. See also the water and marine Treaties to which the Community is a party, listed in Vousden 'EC Environmental Law Digest' (1992) 3 *Water Law*, at 189–90.
146 Fourth Convention ACP-EEC, 15 December 1989, Part 2, Title 1, Articles 33–44.

ozone layer.[147] The former provides that parties to it endeavour to prevent harm to both the environment and human life by means of measures to minimise damage to the ozone layer by human activities; the latter is a supplementary convention concerning the reduction of the use of chlorofluorocarbons (CFCs) and halons by those party to it.[148]

A number of pieces of Community legislation have stemmed directly from these Protocols, including Regulation 594/91/EEC[149] which replaced Regulation 3322/88/EEC[150] and applies restrictions on the import, export, production and use of all fully halogenated CFCs, halons, carbon tetrachloride and methyl chloroform. It also states that production of CFCs should cease by June 1997, some three years earlier than the international deadline. This has since been brought forward further by Regulation 3952/92/EEC[151] which requires production of CFCs to cease by the end of 1995. The Commission has also presented a draft Regulation concerning the reduction of the use of hydrochlorofluorocarbons (HCFCs).[152] The Commission has based it on Article 130s EC, which means that it must be passed by unanimous vote of the Council. Voluntary agreements have been made between the Commission and aerosol manufacturers, foam and plastic industries and the refrigeration industry to cut the use of CFCs following recommendations addressed to each industry.[153] There has been Community activity in other related areas, such as control of volatile organic compound (VOC) emissions, the monitoring of CO_2 and other greenhouse gases and the setting up of a Pollution Emission Register.

The United Nations Conference on Environment and Development (UNCED) Earth Summit Conventions

This environmental conference, which attracted worldwide attention, was held in June 1992 in Rio de Janeiro with 178 UN Member States attending. The Community played an active role in pushing for action rather than mere discussion, despite disagreements based on the perceived lack of commitment on the part of the US, although not as active a role as the European Parliament's Environment Committee would have liked.[154] The conference resulted in the following Conventions, Declarations and other texts being adopted or approved.[155]

- Rio Declaration on Environment and Development, a non-legally binding declaration consisting of 27 essential principles of global environmental management, such as the polluter pays.
- Agenda 21, the Summit Agenda and a 40-chapter political commitment to develop policies to deal with matters such as protection of the atmosphere, deforestation, protection of the oceans etc.

---

147 Following Decision 88/540/EEC, OJ 1988 L297.

148 The Montreal Protocol has proven to be inadequate to the task of controlling damage to the ozone layer and has been amended, with far stricter provisions, no less than four times. See Decision 91/690/EEC on the amendment to the Montreal Protocol after a meeting in London in 1990 (OJ 1991 L377); and the draft proposal for a Decision proposed by the Commission following the amendment to the Montreal Protocol after a meeting in Copenhagen in 1992 (OJ 1993 C103).

149 OJ 1991 L67.

150 OJ 1988 L297.

151 OJ 1992 L405.

152 COM(93) 202.

153 See, for example, Recommendation 89/349/EEC OJ 1989 L144 – CFCs in aerosols.

154 Not least because EC Environment Commissioner Carlo Ripa di Meana refused to attend on the grounds that his doing so would achieve nothing. This, it was claimed, allowed the US to dominate the proceedings to their detriment. See Bramwell, 'Earth Summit at Rio' (1992) 1 (2) EELR 52, at 53 and Johnson, 'Did we really save the earth at Rio?' (1992) 1 (3) EELR 81, at 84.

155 Bramwell, op. cit., note 154, at 52.

- Framework Convention on Climate Change, essentially a world agenda for monitoring and control of greenhouse gases.
- Convention on Biological Diversity, concerning, amongst other matters, international protection of genes, species and environments, and intellectual property issues.
- Statement of Principles on Forests, which was made as no agreement on a Convention could be reached.
- Principles of drawing up a Convention on Desertification.

Whether the conference was a success or not remains to be seen.[156] The Community and Member States are in the process of ratifying the Framework Convention on Climate Change[157] and the Convention on Biological Diversity[158] and it was intended that both should be ratified before the end of 1993, but disagreements between the Member States look set to delay matters well into 1994.[159]

FUTURE DEVELOPMENTS

To gain some idea of the Community's aims for the future and, indeed, some of the problems it will face, it is useful to examine some of the developments proposed or just implemented by the Commission. The three examined here are the Eco-Management and Audit Scheme Regulation,[160] the Eco-Label Regulation 880/92/EEC[161] and a possible pollution tax in the form of a proposal for a directive on a CO_2 tax.[162]

The Eco-Management and Audit Scheme Regulation, which will enter into force in April 1995, is designed to encourage both the voluntary assessment of environmental performance of industrial sites and to use those assessments to determine feasible targets for improvement in that performance. The Regulation covers all manufacturing companies, plus those involved in the production of electricity, gas, steam and hot water, and waste management and permits Member States to expand it on an experimental basis to other sectors, such as transport.

Under the Regulation a company will set up an environmental policy programme for all activities on a given site. After a rigorous verification process, including the preparation of an environmental statement for the site and use of external accredited verifiers to check the company's procedures,[163] the company, upon making its validated environmental statement public, may apply for registration by the relevant national authority. The maintenance of this registration is dependent upon a constant report and audit system on a three-year cycle, which is stricter for larger companies. Companies so registered will be able to use a special logo on corporate brochures, headed paper, reports and in corporate advertisements. They will not be able to use in it product advertisements.

---

156 Johnson, *op. cit.,* note 153, at 85, suggests that while it was not really a success, nether was it a disaster and that the Community will probably have an increasing role to play in future environmental debate of this type.
157 OJ 1993 C44.
158 COM(92) 509.
159 The UK's objections to the carbon tax plan, which has been enthusiastically endorsed by other Member States, look set to delay ratification of the Climate Convention well beyond that point. At the time of writing it appears that only about 31 nations have ratified the Climate Convention, which requires 50 countries to ratify it before it goes into effect.
160 OJ 1992 C76, amended in OJ 1993 C120, final text not yet published.
161 OJ 1992 L99.
162 OJ 1992 C196.
163 A list of who must be established by each Member State and sent to the Commission.

The Eco-label Regulation for products, with a Community eco-label for qualifying 'green' products, is already in force. It is designed along similar voluntary lines, including assessment of each product put forward for the label by an independent body, and full publication of all information relating to a product's acceptance, or rejection, as being eco-label worthy. It is also geared to the size of the company involved, with the fee for using the label being related to the volume of sales within the EC of the product.

These schemes play upon the increased awareness among the general public of environmental issues and it is clearly hoped to persuade companies that gaining registration will give them some kind of competitive edge. The fact that the rules of the eco-management and audit scheme are relaxed for smaller companies and the eco-label fee takes into account volume of sales, also suggests a realisation on the part of the Council that smaller companies are less likely to consider the scheme to be cost effective than the larger firms.

These schemes appear to mark a significant shift in Community policy from reactive to pro-active policy, even if at present 'enforcement' is left up to market forces. It will be interesting to see if the population of the Community, when the majority of Member States are still deep in recession, are as willing to pay extra for the environment as the Community institutions appear to hope.

The proposal for a tax on CO_2 emission, levied by way of taxing energy sources, is not, unsurprisingly, considerably more contentious as it would involve a mandatory scheme and considerable cost to Community producers. Member States are also concerned that taxes of that nature might represent an erosion of their sovereignty in fiscal matters. However, it is doubtful that the proposal will lead to Community legislation in the near future, as it was designed more as a challenge, prior to the UNCED summit at Rio, to the other major emittors of CO_2, notably the US. Until action is taken by other major emittors comparable to that proposed in the Community, which presently seems highly unlikely, no such tax will be implemented, as it seems obvious that a unilateral tax would unduly burden Community producers, making them uncompetitive on the world markets. What is encouraging about the proposal is that the Community felt the need to make it, reflecting both its increasing concern about global warming and its determination to lead the way in suggesting strategies to help combat the problem. This may mark a trend in world environment policy away from the faltering leadership of the US, heavily criticised over its attitude in Rio, towards a more dynamic, European-led strategy.

CONCLUSION

Developments in EC environmental policy, following the SEA and TEU amendments to the EC Treaty, would seem to be working towards a central role for environmental policy in Community decision-making. However, it seems that for all the potentially positive developments in primary Community legislation there are some who still doubt the will of the Community and the Member States to promote environmental policy where it clashes with economic objectives. As Somsen put it after the adoption of the measures in the SEA (but before the TEU):

> The inclusion of environmental provisions in the Treaty cannot be said to have led to an
> increased importance in environmental objectives. Action in the field of the environment

will continue to be weighted against trade objectives and when a conflict arises there is little in Title VII of the Treaty which will contribute to tipping the balance towards environmental considerations. On the contrary the principles listed in Article 130R(3) . . . when rigidly adhered to, will often prove to be an insurmountable obstacle.[164]

While the gloomy message of that thesis has not been entirely borne out in practice, it can be argued convincingly that solution to the present problems with environmental policy, at both Community and Member State levels, does not lie in the current Treaty and will not be found in the ratification of the TEU. Indeed, as has been mooted, the subsidiarity issue that arises out of the TEU may make conflict between Community institutions and Member States more, rather than less, likely. Given the current, weak Community position with regard to monitoring and enforcement, it is more probable that the proposed changes in those areas will bring about the main improvements in design and implementation of environmental legislation in the near future, although international developments may play an increasingly larger part. However, it is clear that without the necessary will at the Member State level, both amongst the public and in government, environmental policy will never achieve its full potential within the Community.

Further reading

Bramwell, E., 'Earth Summit at Rio' (1992) 1 (2) EELR 52.

Brinkhorst, L.J., 'Subsidiarity and European Community Environment Policy: A Panacea or a Pandora's Box?' (1993) 2 (1) EELR 8.

Davidson, J.S., 'The Single European Act and the Environment' (1987) 2 *International Journal of Estuarine and Coastal Law* 259.

Freestone, D., 'European Community Environmental Policy and Law' (1991) 18 JLS 135.

Freestone, D., 'The 1992 Maastricht Treaty – Implications for European Environmental Law' (1992) EELR 1 (1) 23.

Jans, J.H., 'Legal Protection in European Environmental Law' [1993] EELR 151.

Johnson, S.P., 'Did we really save the earth at Rio?' (1992) 1 (3) EELR 81.

Johnson, S.P. and Corcelle, G., *The Environmental Policy of the European Communities* (1989).

Krämer, L., 'Community Environmental Law – Towards a Systematic Approach' (1991) 11 YEL 151.

Krämer, L., *EEC Treaty and Environmental Protection* (London: Sweet & Maxwell, 1992).

Krämer, L., 'Environmental Protection and Article 30 EEC Treaty' (1993) 30 CMLR 111.

Krämer, L., *Focus on European Environmental Law* (London: Sweet & Maxwell, 1992).

Krämer, L., 'The Implementation of Community Environmental Directives within Member States: some Implications of the Direct Effect Doctrine' (1991) *Journal of Environmental Law* 39.

Krämer, L., 'The Single European Act and Environmental Protection; Reflections on Several New Provisions in Community Law' (1987) CML Rev 659.

Macrory, R., 'Air Pollution Legislation in the United States and the Community' (1990) 15 EL Rev 298.

Macrory, R., 'The Enforcement of Community Environmental Laws: Some Critical Issues' (1992) 29 CMLR 347.

164 Somsen, 'EC Water Directives' (1990) *Water Law* 93.

Meli, M., 'The pollutor pays: some conceptual problems' (1992) 3(3) *Water Law* 79.

Rehbinder, E. and Stewart, R., *Environmental Protection Policy*, vol. 2 *Integration Through Law* (1985).

Sands, P., 'European Community Environmental Law: Legislation, the European Court of Justice and Common-Interest Groups' (1990) 53 MLR 685.

Vandermeersch, D., 'The Single European Act and the Environmental Policy of the European Economic Community' (1987) 12 EL Rev 407.

von Wilmowsky, P., 'Waste Disposal in the Internal Market: The State of Play after the ECJ's Ruling on the Walloon Import Ban' (1993) 30 CML Rev 541.

CHAPTER 20
Conclusion

A FEDERAL FUTURE FOR THE EUROPEAN UNION?

At least in the UK, the debate continues over whether or not the European Union should become more federal. In 1996, this debate will be in the forefront of the Intergovernmental Conferences. The Member States will have to decide whether more legislative authority will be given to the European Parliament and, thereby, shift the balance of legislative power from the statist side of the institutions to the supranational side. This would alter the institutional balance within the Union.

A more federal Union would require a clearer understanding of the division of powers between the Member States on one side, and the Union on the other. This would involve a significant change from the existing nature of the Union. The non-Community pillars of the Union are strictly intergovernmental in nature, with the European Council and the Council of Ministers as the dominant institutions. A federal Union would have more explicit legislative powers outside the European Community Treaty, and would have to give greater influence, or even power, over the content of legislation to the Commission and the European Parliament.

A more federal Union might also be a more regional union. During the negotiations over the TEU, the regions, the German Länder in particular, were concerned to have a greater role in policy-making. In orthodox international law terms, Member States in the Council of Ministers have the authority to agree to legislation, which is then binding on all bodies within the Member State, including local and regional authorities. The TEU established the Committee of the Regions, but this is merely a consultative body. If the regions of the European Union still feel that inappropriate Community (and Union) legislation is being imposed on them there may be renewed pressure to give the regions an explicit role in the structure of the Union. The endorsement of subsidiarity in the TEU will lend support to such demands, since the understanding of subsidiarity in most parts of the Union goes beyond Community–Member State relations to include the relations between all governmental institutions and, sometimes, even non-governmental institutions. However, in general it seems unlikely that subsidiarity will have much effect on policy-making – certainly not the effect contemplated by the UK in the negotiations leading up to the TEU.

Whether or not the European Union becomes fully federal is very much an open question. With enlargement, attaining a consensus on the future direction may be extremely difficult. After the prolonged and obstacle-ridden process of ratification of the TEU, some Member States may not readily be willing to engage in a similar process over a new Treaty. However, the Community has become federalised to a large extent, because of the amount of Community regulation which affects people in the Member States directly. Federalism may not be inevitable within the European Union, but federalisation is. The distinction is important – federalism describes a state of organisation, federalisation describes a process.

THE PROSPECTS FOR ENLARGEMENT

While the prospects for reforms of the institutions and structures of the Union seem mixed, the prospects for enlargement seem very good. The broadening of the Union is a goal which is widely shared by Member States, although Spain is said to be reluctant about increasing the number of Member States because of the likelihood that any individual Member State's power will be restricted as a result.

The first stage of post-TEU enlargement has already begun. Austria, Finland, Norway and Sweden are already in negotiations for membership, with the goal of entry on 1 January 1995. Currently, these States are part of the EEA and are, therefore, already subject to a great deal of Community law. This next enlargement will create, with Denmark, a Scandinavian bloc within the Council of Ministers. These new Members all have stable economies and democratic systems and are expected to be net contributors to the Community Budget.

In the longer term, at least, some Eastern European States are expected to be seriously considered for membership early in the next century. These States are still restructuring both their economic and political systems. It is unlikely that they would be net contributors to the Community budget for a number of years and would be likely to receive a great deal of regional aid. Like Spain and Portugal, these States regard European Union membership as an anchor to their newly-established democracy.

The consequences for the institutions

In a European Union of 16 and possibly 20 Member States, the institutions will undergo a certain amount of change. For the Commission the main question is whether the large States (France, Germany, Italy, Spain, UK) will continue to be allotted two Commissioners. In general, the five large States are likely to see a dilution of their power (if not their influence) in a larger Union. A redefinition of qualified majority voting will be necessary. The UK and Spain have indicated that they favour retaining the current blocking minority of 23 votes (usually three states) and, therefore, increasing the proportion of votes necessary to pass legislation by qualified majority vote. The other Member States, as well as the current applicants for membership, favour the retention of the proportion of votes necessary to pass a measure by qualified majority and, therefore, increasing the number of votes in the blocking minority to 27, which generally would require an additional Member State to oppose the proposed measure. Moving to the system favoured by the UK and Spain would constitute a fundamental change in the Community legislative process, almost equivalent to the Luxembourg Accords.

The European Parliament faces its own numbers game. Currently, there are 518 MEPs. On enlargement, the question must be whether to keep the same number of MEPs and distribute them amongst a larger number of Member States or to increase the overall number of MEPs at each enlargement. The argument in favour of increasing the overall number is that the constituencies of MEPs are currently large and people do not seem to attach anywhere near the same value to their European representative as they do to their local, regional and national representatives. Making larger constituencies, which must occur if the same number of MEPs is spread out over a larger geographic area and population, would create further difficulties for MEPs trying to serve their constituencies. The next enlargement will be likely to increase the number of Social Democrat and Green MEPs, which could have an impact on the European Parliament's actions, particularly under the co-operation and co-decision procedures, where it has the greatest opportunity for influencing the content of Community legislation.

The institutional uncertainties raised by the prospect of enlargement has led Leo Tindemans, now European Parliament leader of the European Peoples' Party, to state that this type of uncertainty demonstrates the correctness of the European Parliament's view on institutional reform. During the Intergovernmental Conferences leading up to the adoption of the TEU the European Parliament argued that institutional reform must be a precursor to enlargement, so that the Union had a concept of how the institutions were to operate, rather than making *ad hoc* decisions with each enlargement over issues like the redefinition of qualified majority voting.

THE FUTURE OF COMMUNITY POLICY-MAKING

For Community lawyers the question of the future of Community policy-making is probably of greatest interest. Will health and safety directives replace sex equality directives as the site of judicial and legislative innovation? This is very likely to occur. In addition to the new working time directive and the draft young workers directive, which have already expanded the notion of regulation under the ambit of Article 118a EC, the increased influence of Nordic law within the Union after the expected accessions of Finland, Norway and Sweden is likely to gain greater acceptance for the 'working environment' interpretation of health and safety regulation.[1]

There will probably be even more marked changes to the policy direction of Community law. A first order question is the extent to which the other pillars of the TEU will result in legal regulation of the matters under their ambit. The subsidiary question to this is what form any legal rules under those pillars will take. The Union may adopt measures similar to regulations, directives or decisions, but they may also decide to work by means of intergovernmental agreements or Treaties which, like the Schengen Agreement, exist outside the Community legal framework.

Multi-speed Europe

The issue of a two (or more)-speed Europe can no longer be ignored. Due to the opt-outs allowed under TEU, two-speed policies exist in two areas: social policy and monetary policy. This may have less significance than appears at first. Social policy continues to be developed under the EC Treaty and there appears to be no pressure as yet to move to the Social Policy Protocol and achieve a higher level of protection except to exclude the UK from the obligations of implementing that policy. In monetary policy, a number of Member States, not only the UK and Denmark, appear to have reservations about proceeding with monetary union, in light of the economic difficulties being experienced within Europe as a whole. The necessary convergence of economic policy and economic performance has not yet occurred

---

1 On this approach to the permissible scope of health and safety regulation, see Chapter 17.

and seems unlikely to do so in the future. Furthermore, the budget deficit reduction foreseen in the lead-up to full economic and monetary union would not be attractive to Member States or their populations if it involved the reduction of social welfare programmes or job creation. The result is that although the TEU sets the stage for two-speed Europe, the Union continues, at present, on a single set of policies.

The more difficult question is whether the expanded Union could continue to progress at one rate, particularly once the Eastern European States begin to join. The result could be core Europe, probably North-western continental Europe, and periphery Europe, probably the former Eastern bloc countries, with possibly a middle ground for the UK, Eire, the Scandinavian countries and the Mediterranean countries. If there is no longer a need to keep everyone moving at the same pace, States like Germany may refuse to continue to fund items like regional development, which have been crucial to the economic development of a number of Member States. Such a move would simply reinforce the different rates of progress towards full economic integration. A question more relevant to the UK, with its opposition to the expansion of social rights, is the potential result of opting out of Community social policy. If some States have lower social protection, will the Member States who have taken on the obligation of greater social rights provision begin to put up barriers to prevent social dumping? Again, this development would reinforce divisions within the Union.

Emerging policy areas

A change in government in the UK might change the direction of social policy regulation in Community law and lead to new areas of regulation, such as minimum wage policies. The Commission has already moved to new issues of social policy with the recent Communication by Social Affairs Commissioner Flynn.[2] Its emphasis on job creation would require the co-operation of all the Member States and the development of a more detailed and wider-ranging policy than directives currently provide, which tend to deal with a narrow, specific subject-matter. However, the issue of unemployment, its costs and its causes, is one that exercises the minds of all European governments at present, so the political will for such intensive policy-making at the Community level may not be impossible to attain.

Two other areas in which Community regulation is likely to increase are technology and the environment. On the environment, the presence of the other Scandinavian States, which have a history of strict environmental regulation, will either encourage or suppress regulation. On one side is their advocacy of environmental protection. On the other side is a fear of harmonising measures which would require them to reduce the level of protection from their high level to an agreed Community standard. The result could be directives which set minimum levels of protection, but allow Member States to maintain higher levels. The Commission's intention is to use framework directives which would allow for the application of subsidiarity in their implementation. Furthermore, environmental policy is beginning to infiltrate other policy areas within the Community.[3] In technology, Community regulation is necessary because of the internationalised nature of the subject-matter. National regulation is probably insufficient to meet the problems raised by new technologies, such as electronic data interchange, or by new uses of existing technologies, such as telecommunications.

---

2 See Chapter 17.

3 See Freestone, 'EC Environmental Law after Maastricht', forthcoming NILQ.

STUDYING COMMUNITY LAW IN THE YEAR 2000

The European Union is at a crucial turning point. This statement has probably been made by some commentator or other at every stage of the development of the Community/Union. However, it seems likely that at least some areas of Community law will have changed radically within the next decade. The balance between intergovernmental and supranational or federal elements within the structure of the Union has probably not been so much in question since the Luxembourg Accords. While the TEU and the introduction of multi-speed policies reinforces intergovernmentalism, the reaction of the Commission to subsidiarity[4] and the European Parliament's new powers to approve enlargement[5] prove that supranational elements in the structure of the Union are difficult, if not impossible, to stifle. The ECJ has, in the past, proved to be a motor of integration when all else was stalled – this may be equally true in the future, where judicial extension of Community competence under, for example, Article 118a EC, may provide the greatest opportunity for new policies in controversial areas.

With the growth of regional trading blocs such as ASEAN (Association of South-East Asian Nations) and NAFTA (North American Free Trade Agreement), it seems highly unlikely that the European Union will dissolve altogether. But a Union of 20 economically diverse States in the early years of the next millennium is fundamentally different from a Community of six continental States with similar economic systems and a clear memory of European war. The loss of the memory of war may ultimately be the greatest threat to a group of States founded on the goal of peace through integration.

---

4 See Chapter 3.   5 Article O TEU.

INDEX